ROUTLEDGE HANDBOOK ON MEN, MASCULINITIES AND ORGANIZATIONS

This Handbook provides new theoretical and empirical insights into men, men's practices and masculinities across many kinds of organizations and forms of organizing. Most mainstream studies of organizations, leadership and management do not seem to notice they are often talking a lot about men and masculinities. The Handbook challenges this general tendency to avoid gendering men by bringing together a range of theoretical and methodological approaches that:

- engage with not only formal organizations, such as businesses and state organizations, but also processes of organizing within and beyond organizations;
- address emergent and future issues on men, masculinities and organizations, such as tech masculinities, men's emotions, sexualities and violences, animal advocacy and environmental issues, and men and masculinities in pandemics

Targeted at scholars, policymakers, practitioners and students interested in links between men, masculinities, organizations and organizing, this landmark Handbook is an invaluable resource for those working in and beyond such fields as gender studies, organization, leadership and management studies, political science, sociology, social and public policy, and social movement studies.

Jeff Hearn is Professor Emeritus of Management and Organization at Hanken School of Economics, Finland; Senior Professor of Human Geography at Örebro University, Sweden; and Professor of Sociology at the University of Huddersfield, UK.

Kadri Aavik is Associate Professor of Gender Studies at Tallinn University, Estonia.

David L. Collinson is Distinguished Professor of Leadership and Organization at Lancaster University Management School.

Anika Thym is completing her PhD in Gender Studies at the University of Basel, Switzerland.

ROUTLEDGE INTERNATIONAL HANDBOOKS

ROUTLEDGE INTERNATIONAL HANDBOOK OF MULTIDISCIPLINARY PERSPECTIVES ON DESCENDANTS OF HOLOCAUST SURVIVORS
Edited by Judith Tydor Baumel-Schwartz and Amit Shrira

ROUTLEDGE INTERNATIONAL HANDBOOK OF VISUAL-MOTOR SKILLS, HANDWRITING, AND SPELLING
Edited by Yanyan Ye, Tomohiro Inoue, Urs Maurer, and Catherine McBride

ROUTLEDGE HANDBOOK OF ENVIRONMENTAL POLICY
Edited by Helge Jörgens, Christoph Knill and Yves Steinebach

THE ROUTLEDGE HANDBOOK OF SOFT POWER (2ND EDITION)
Edited by Naren Chitty, Lilian Ji, Gary D Rawnsley

THE ROUTLEDGE HANDBOOK OF URBAN LOGISTICS
Edited by Jason Monios, Lucy Budd and Stephen Ison

THE ROUTLEDGE HANDBOOK OF COMPARATIVE GLOBAL URBAN STUDIES
Edited by Patrick LeGalès and Jennifer Robinson

THE ROUTLEDGE HANDBOOK OF TRANSATLANTIC RELATIONS
Edited by Elaine Fahey

THE ROUTLEDGE INTERNATIONAL HANDBOOK OF DISABILITY HUMAN RIGHTS HIERARCHIES
Edited by Stephen J. Meyers, Megan McCloskey and Gabor Petri

THE ROUTLEDGE HANDBOOK OF PUBLIC SECTOR ACCOUNTING
Edited by Tarek Rana and Lee Parker

ROUTLEDGE HANDBOOK ON MEN, MASCULINITIES AND ORGANIZATIONS
Edited by Jeff Hearn, Kadri Aavik, David L. Collinson and Anika Thym

ROUTLEDGE HANDBOOK ON MEN, MASCULINITIES AND ORGANIZATIONS

Theories, Practices and Futures of Organizing

Edited by Jeff Hearn, Kadri Aavik, David L. Collinson and Anika Thym

Routledge
Taylor & Francis Group
LONDON AND NEW YORK

Designed cover image: © Shutterstock Inc.

First published 2024
by Routledge
4 Park Square, Milton Park, Abingdon, Oxon OX14 4RN

and by Routledge
605 Third Avenue, New York, NY 10158

Routledge is an imprint of the Taylor & Francis Group, an informa business

British Library Cataloguing-in-Publication Data
A catalogue record for this book is available from the British Library

Library of Congress Cataloging-in-Publication Data
Names: Hearn, Jeff, 1947– editor.
Title: Routledge handbook on men, masculinities and organizations : theories, practices and futures of organizing / edited by Jeff Hearn, Kadri Aavik, David L. Collinson, Anika Thym.
Description: Abingdon, Oxon ; New York, NY : Routledge, 2024. | Series: Routledge international handbooks | Includes bibliographical references and index.
Identifiers: LCCN 2023022038 (print) | LCCN 2023022039 (ebook) | ISBN 9781032045153 (hbk) | ISBN 9781032045160 (pbk) | ISBN 9781003193579 (ebk)
Subjects: LCSH: Organizational change. | Masculinity. | Men.
Classification: LCC HD58.8 .R69363 2024 (print) | LCC HD58.8 (ebook) | DDC 658.4/06—dc23/eng/20230718
LC record available at https://lccn.loc.gov/2023022038
LC ebook record available at https://lccn.loc.gov/2023022039

ISBN: 978-1-032-04515-3 (hbk)
ISBN: 978-1-032-04516-0 (pbk)
ISBN: 978-1-003-19357-9 (ebk)

DOI: 10.4324/9781003193579

Typeset in Galliard
by Apex CoVantage, LLC

CONTENTS

FIGURES

CONTRIBUTORS

Kadri Aavik is Associate Professor of Gender Studies at Tallinn University, Estonia. She works in gender studies (with a focus on critical studies on men and masculinities), critical animal studies, vegan studies and their intersections. Her recent books are *Contesting Anthropocentric Masculinities Through Veganism: Lived Experiences of Vegan Men*, 2023 and *Feminist Animal and Multispecies Studies: Critical Perspectives on Food and Eating* (co-edited with Kuura Irni and Milla-Maria Joki, 2023).

Sofia Aboim is a researcher and associate professor at the Institute of Social Sciences of the University of Lisbon. Her research interests include gender, feminisms, masculinity studies as well as social theory, justice, inequality and postcolonial studies. She is currently working on a book project about gender, power and the spaces of socio-political struggle. She has been enrolled in numerous research projects, including a Consolidator Grant awarded by the European Research Council in 2014. Currently, she leads a research project on race and race inequality funded by the Portuguese Science Foundation, where she explores gender intersections with migration and race/ethnicity in Portugal, Europe and the postcolonial world.

F. Oya Aktaş has a PhD in Political Science and International Relations from Istanbul University, Turkey. Her research interests lie primarily in the fields of Critical Studies on Men and Masculinities and modernization in Turkey. She is currently Assistant Professor at Kirklareli University, Turkey.

Daniel Alsarve is a researcher in sport science at Örebro University, Sweden and Jyväskylä University, Finland. He recently finished a four-year project, "Ice hockey in change: Masculinity ideals and violence norms in Swedish hockey ca. 1965 until the present", funded by the Swedish Research Council for Sport Science. His research interests include sports, gender, violence, democracy and historical change. He is currently involved in research projects about managing social sustainability in high-performance sports organizations in Finland, how the Corona pandemic affected Swedish sports and how the Swedish Sports Confederation organized this crisis. In 2021, he was awarded the "Little Prize for Sports Science" by the Swedish Central Association for the Promotion of Athletics.

Dag Balkmar is Docent and Senior Lecturer in Gender Studies at Örebro University, Sweden. His research focuses on men and masculinities, gender and entrepreneurship, gender equality and inclusion in organizations, and gendered mobilities. He has published within the areas of masculinity studies, gender and technology, gender and mobility, and risk and violence. He is PI for the Swedish part of *Overcoming the Entrepreneurial Ecosystem Gender Divide: A Cross-Cultural Perspective* (GENRE, GENDER-NET Plus) and is currently working in the project AdvanCing behavioural Change Through an INclusive Green deal (ACCTING, EU Horizon 2020). His research encompasses several interactive research projects on gender and innovation, including projects in collaboration with the Swedish Innovation Agency and global corporations such as the Volvo Group.

Gabriela Bard Wigdor is a professor at the National University of Cordoba (UNC), Argentina, where she studied Social Work and pursued her doctoral degree in Gender Studies. She also has a Diploma in "Community and Popular Feminisms in Abya Yala" from the National University of Jujuy, Argentina. She is an adjunct researcher at the National Commission of Science and Technology in Argentina in Feminist Studies and Decolonial Studies, focusing on Feminist Studies of Masculinity. She leads research projects and works with various graduates and postgraduate students. She actively is involved in participatory action-research networks and diverse social spaces of social commitment.

Jennifer L. Berdahl (PhD, Social & Organizational Psychology, University of Illinois) is Professor of Sociology at the University of British Columbia. Berdahl has studied harassment as a means of social control in organizations to police gender, race and power in the workplace. Berdahl's recent work has focused on the role of organizational culture in fostering work environments that tolerate sexual harassment. She co-edited the *Journal of Social Issues*' volumes on the flexibility stigma (2013) and work in a masculinity contest (2018), and regularly presents her research to professional, media and academic audiences. Berdahl serves as an expert witness for individual and class action discrimination cases in both the United States and Canada.

Ingrid Biese has a PhD in Sociology from the University of South Australia and works as University Lecturer at the School of Business and Economics at Åbo Akademi University in Turku, Finland. Her primary areas of research are "opting out", sustainable working cultures and career models, and alternative solutions for work. Her books, *Opting Out and In: On Women's Careers and New Lifestyles*, 2017, and *Men Do It Too: Opting Out and In*, 2021, have been well received internationally. Her areas of interest include gender, masculinities, diversity, identity, globalization and individualization. She blogs about her research on theoptingoutblog.com.

Stephen Burrell is Leverhulme Early Career Fellow in the Department of Sociology at Durham University, where he is also a deputy director of the Centre for Research into Violence and Abuse (CRiVA). His research focuses on men, masculinities and violence, and he is currently studying how to engage with men and boys about the climate crisis, environmental violence and caring for the planet. He also co-hosts a podcast with Sandy Ruxton called "Now and Men: Current conversations about men's lives" and is a trustee for White Ribbon UK and co-chair of the steering group for Changing Relations CIC.

Anne-Charlott Callerstig is a senior researcher of Gender Studies at Örebro University, Centre for Feminist Social Studies (CFS), School of Humanities, Education and Social Sciences. Her research interests include gender and organization, equality policy and organization, gender and entrepreneurship, gender and innovation, equality policy implementation and evaluation, and interactive research approaches. She has long experience in both research and working practically with gender-equality policy issues and gender mainstreaming in Sweden and on a European level. She has published several articles and book chapters on gender-equality policy implementation and evaluation.

Marta Choroszewicz (DSocSci, Docent in sociology) is a university researcher in the Department of Social Sciences at the University of Eastern Finland. Her work as a sociologist concentrates on the intersection between research on professional work, feminist theories, and science and technology studies. In her research, she has broadly investigated social inequalities in professions and in relation to the development and deployment of data technologies in public organizations. More broadly, she has also engaged with the issue of building a digital welfare state via the use of new data technologies. Her work has appeared in various international and national peer-reviewed journals, including Information, Communication & Society, and Human Relations. She has also co-edited, with Tracey L. Adams, the book *Gender, Age and Inequality in the Professions*, 2019.

Richard Collier, FAcSS, FRSA, is Professor of Law and Newcastle University, UK. He has published widely in the area of law and gender with a particular focus on men and masculinities in relation to families and family law, fatherhood, the legal profession and legal education. He is presently researching and publishing in the field of well-being and mental health in the legal community and, drawing on recent projects, is completing a book on the topic. He was Member of Research Team Coordinating "Life in the Law" a 2021 National study of well-being in the UK Legal Professions. His previous books include *Men, Law and Gender: Essays on the Man of Law*; *Fragmenting Fatherhood*, with Sally Sheldon; *Fathers' Rights and Law Reform in Comparative Perspective*; and *Masculinities, Crime and Criminology*. He was recently awarded the Socio-legal Studies Association 2022 Prize for Contributions to the Socio-Legal Community.

David L. Collinson is Distinguished Professor of Leadership and Organization at Lancaster University Management School. Previously at the Universities of Manchester, Warwick, St Andrews and South Florida, he is Founding Co-Editor of the journal *Leadership*, and Founding Co-Organizer of the International Studying Leadership Conference, both with Keith Grint. David's publications focus on critical approaches to leadership, gender, management and organization. His primary research interests explore leadership and followership dialectics; power, identities and insecurities; gender, men and masculinities; resistance, dramaturgy and conformity; and humour, positivity and Prozac leadership. His work has been published in leading journals including *Organization Studies*, *Human Relations*, *Journal of Management Studies*, *Work, Employment & Society*, *Organization*, *Gender, Work & Organization* and *Leadership Quarterly*.

Raewyn Connell is Professor Emerita, University of Sydney, and Life Member of the National Tertiary Education Union. She has taught in several countries and is a widely cited sociological researcher, the author of *Gender & Power*, *Masculinities*, *The Men and the Boys*,

Southern Theory, and many journal articles. Her recent books include *The Good University* and *Gender: In World Perspective* (currently in its fourth edition). Her work has been translated into 24 languages, and she is the current holder of the International Sociological Association's quadrennial Award for Excellence in Research and Practice. She has been active in the labour movement, and in work for education, gender equality and peace. Details are at www.raewynconnell.net.

Marianne Cooper is a senior research scholar at Stanford University's VMware Women's Leadership Innovation Lab and an affiliate at the Stanford Center on Poverty and Inequality. Cooper conducts research on gender, women's leadership, DEI and the future of work. A LinkedIn Top Voice for gender equity, she has written for *The Atlantic*, *The New York Times* and *Harvard Business Review*, among others. Cooper is an author of the Women in the Workplace reports by LeanIn.org and McKinsey, an impact leader for Politico's Women Rule, a senior advisor to McKinsey and an affiliated educator for the Center for Institutional Courage.

Josephine Cornell is a lecturer in psychology at Birmingham City University in the United Kingdom. Josephine completed her PhD in social psychology at the University of Cape Town in 2021. Josephine's work has largely been situated within critical social and community psychology. Her research interests include identities, inequalities, social change and resistance.

Sam de Boise is a senior lecturer in musicology at the School of Music, Theatre and Art at Örebro University, Sweden, with a doctorate in sociology. His research has focused on questions of emotions in relation to masculinity, how gender shapes musical engagement and, recently, how masculinist, extremist movements use music. He is the author of *Men, Masculinity, Music and Emotions*, 2015, and co-editor of *NORMA: International Journal for Masculinity Studies*.

Alex Demirović, born in 1952 in Darmstadt, Germany, has a PhD in Philosophy, 1979, and Habilitation in Political Science and Sociology, 1992. He is a research fellow at the Institute of Social Research in Frankfurt-am-Main. He has taught at several universities: Frankfurt-am-Main, Wuppertal, Vienna, Berlin, Basel and Paris.

Laura Eigenmann is a postdoctoral research associate at Freie Universität Berlin, Institute for Sociology, Research Unit Gender Studies. She holds a PhD in Gender Studies from the University of Basel, Switzerland. Before joining the FU, she was a lecturer and coordinator for the Gender Studies programme in Basel, a visiting researcher at King's College London, the School for Advanced Legal Studies in London and Temple University in Philadelphia. Her research interests include critical policy analysis, national and EU identity discourses, LGBTI activism, homonationalism and queer history. In her PhD project, she investigated the EU's LGBTI policy development, asking why and how LGBTI rights came to be seen as a symbol and "core value" of the EU.

Peter Glick is Henry Merritt Wriston Professor at Lawrence University. He co-developed ambivalent sexism theory, with Susan Fiske, which posits that sexist ideologies combine paternalism (benevolent sexism) with antagonism (hostile sexism) to reinforce lower status for women. Glick and Fiske's foundational empirical article on ambivalent sexism received the Allport Prize for best paper on intergroup relations. He also co-developed the stereotype content model, with Fiske and Amy Cuddy, defining a taxonomy of prejudices that depend on structural relations between groups, and winning the 2022 Scientific Impact Award from the Society for Experimental Social Psychology. In addition to more than 80 articles, he has co-edited or co-authored three books, including the *Sage Handbook of Prejudice*. He has also testified in federal court as an expert witness on sex discrimination. Website: *https://faculty.lawrence.edu/glickp/*

Michele Rene Gregory is Professor and Program Coordinator of Sociology at York College of the City University of New York. She is the author of *The Face of the Firm: Corporate Hegemonic Masculinity at Work* (2016), as well as numerous articles on the intersection of organizational and managerial masculine embodiment, gender, race, power and sports. Gregory has been interviewed by media outlets such as the BBC and appeared on public television shows, recently discussing the politics of WNBA basketball star Brittney Griner's release from a Russian prison. Prior to becoming an academic, Gregory worked in asset and wealth management for various multinational financial services corporations.

Jeff Hearn is Professor Emeritus of Management and Organization, Hanken School of Economics, Finland; Senior Professor of Human Geography, Örebro University, Sweden; and Professor of Sociology, University of Huddersfield, UK. He is co-managing editor, *Routledge Advances in Feminist Studies and Intersectionality* book series, and was (co-)chair of RINGS, the International Research Association of Institutions of Advanced Gender Studies 2014–2020. He has researched long term on gender, sexuality, violence, age, work, organizations, policy, ICTs and transnational processes, with a special interest in critical studies on men and masculinities. Recent books include *Age at Work*, with Wendy Parkin (2021); *Knowledge, Power and Young Sexualities*, with Tamara Shefer; and *Digital Gender-Sexual Violations*, with Matthew Hall and Ruth Lewis (both 2022).

Richard Howson is Associate Professor in Sociology at the University of Wollongong. His research is in critical studies of masculinities, social theory and political sociology. He is the sole author of the monographs *Sociology of Postmarxism* (2017) and *Challenging Hegemonic Masculinity* (2006), as well as co-editor of the volumes *Hegemony* (2008), *Migrant Men* (2009) and *Engaging Men in Gender Equality* (2015).

Majda Hrženjak is a sociologist and researcher at the Peace Institute in Ljubljana, Slovenia. Her research topics are gender studies and social politics with a focus on the concept of care in relation to intersectional inequalities, labour, citizenship, migration and feminist ethic of care. Her recent publications include monographs *Dimensions of Care Work*, 2018, and *Changing Fatherhood: Men between Work and Parenthood* (ed.), 2016. She co-edited thematic issue "Paid Domestic Work in Post-socialist Contexts", of the journal *Laboratorium*, 2016, and was a guest editor of the thematic issue "First Gender: Critical Studies of Men and Masculinities" of the *Journal for the Critique of Science, Imagination, and New Anthropology*, 2017.

Chieh Hsu is Assistant Professor of Intercultural Competence at the St. Gallen Institute of Management in Asia, the Asian hub of the University of St. Gallen. She received her doctorate in Sociology from Heidelberg University and published her monograph, *Family*

Migration and the Path to an Occupation: The (Early) Experiences of Skilled Taiwanese and Chinese 'Wives', with Routledge in 2020. She was a postdoctoral researcher at the Global Asia Research Center and the Department of Sociology at National Taiwan University and had engaged in several cross-national or interdisciplinary research projects. Her work focuses on migration regimes, intercultural intimacy and dynamics, gender and the welfare state, and family and employment.

Tigist Shewarega Hussen is a postdoctoral researcher at the Hub for Decolonial Feminist Psychologies in Africa, Department of Psychology, at the University of Cape Town. Her research interest focuses on the exploration of a digital Pan-African constellation of feminist activism for social justice across the continent. She also works in the Women's Right Program (WRP) at Association for Progressive Communication (APC). She is Feminist Research Lead in Feminist Internet Research Network (FIRN) project.

Liisa Husu is a sociologist and senior professor in Gender Studies at Örebro University, Sweden and affiliated scholar at Hanken School of Economics Department of Management and Organization. Her research and publications focus on gender dynamics and inequalities in academia, research funding organizations and research policy. She has been engaged in gender issues in academia in research, policy and civil society since the early 1980s in Nordic countries, Europe and beyond. She is an internationally recognized gender expert, advising ministries, national and international agencies, funding organizations and universities.

Henri Hyvönen is a postdoctoral researcher at the Department of Social Sciences at the University of Eastern Finland. He currently works in the Formations of Hybrid Manhood in the Experience Economy (EXMEN) project funded by the Kone Foundation. His research interests encompass theoretical and empirical examinations of men and masculinities as well as men's bodies, embodiment, bodywork and health behaviours in the contexts of work and organizations.

Liela A. Jamjoom is Research Fellow at Dar Al-Hekma University, Saudi Arabia. Her research interests lie at the intersection of leadership, gender and postcolonial feminism. She is also interested in reflexive research, including autoethnography and narrative inquiry. She holds a PhD in Management from Saint Mary's University, Canada, where her study focused on amplifying the voices of Saudi women in leadership. Her work appears in outlets such as *Human Relations*; *Gender, Work & Organization*; *Qualitative Research in Organizations and Management*; and a book with the Routledge Leadership series, *Women Business Leaders: Identity, Resistance, and Alternative Forms of Knowledge in Saudi Arabia*. She is Associate Editor at *Qualitative Research in Organization and Management* and an executive member at the Critical Management Studies Division, Academy of Management.

Robert W. Livingston has served on the faculty of Harvard University's John F. Kennedy School of Government since 2015. Prior to his appointment at Harvard, he held full-time professorships at the University of Wisconsin-Madison, the Kellogg School of Management at Northwestern University, and the University of Sussex where he was also Director of the Centre for Leadership, Ethics and Diversity (LEAD). His research on the challenges facing women and minority leaders (e.g. the "Teddy Bear Effect") has been published in multiple top-tier journals and has appeared in prominent media outlets. He also serves as a diversity consultant for a wide array of local, state, and federal agencies, non-profit organizations and Fortune 500 corporations.

Helen Longlands is a lecturer in Education and International Development at University College London, and Programme Leader for the MA Education, Gender and International Development. Her research interests are interdisciplinary, and centre on issues relating to gender, inequality and social justice. She has a particular interest in masculinities and transnational relationships of power, and the ways these are experienced, embedded and challenged in international and local contexts, as well as an interest in international development policy, measurement processes and discourse on education and gender equality.

Mabel Machado is a lecturer in Cultural Entrepreneurship at the Department for Culture, Media and Creative Industries, King's College London. She is interested in interdisciplinary research and teaching focusing on cultural and social change processes. She is a contributing researcher to a Trans-Atlantic Platform-funded project on social innovation in and around multinationals. She worked previously as an academic at Loughborough University London and the University of Havana, and as a journalist and editor in Cuban media organizations.

Andrea Maihofer is Professor Emerita of Gender Studies and former Director of the Centre for Gender Studies at the University of Basel. Main research areas are critical social theory, gender studies, change and persistence in gender relations, norms and normalization, and, currently, collective memory and changing consciousness of injustice, masculinity and right-wing populism.

Nick Malherbe is a researcher at the Institute for Social and Health Sciences, University of South Africa, and the South African Medical Research Council-University of South Africa Masculinity and Health Research Unit. He researches community psychology, violence, visual methods and discourse, and works with social movements, cultural workers and young people. He lives in South Africa.

Lauren McCarthy is Senior Lecturer in Corporate Social Responsibility at Bayes Business School at City, University of London. Her research explores the relationship between business, gender and responsibility, particularly in global supply chains. She has researched cocoa in Ghana, cotton in India, gold in Tanzania, and is currently investigating the impacts of COVID-19 on women garment workers in Cambodia. Her work has been published in *Business Ethics Quarterly*, *Human Relations*, *Organization Studies*, and *Gender, Work & Organization*, among others.

Ulf Mellström is an anthropologist and professor of Gender Studies at Karlstad University, Sweden. He has published extensively within the areas of masculinity studies, transport- and mobility studies, gender and technology, gender, risk and crisis management, engineering studies, globalization and higher education, and Southeast Asian Studies. He is the founder and editor-in-chief of *NORMA: the International Journal for Masculinity Studies.* Recent publications include *Posthumanism and the Man Question: Beyond Anthropocentric Masculinities*, co-edited with Bob Pease, 2023, and Routledge International Handbook of Masculinity Studies, co-edited with Lucas Gottzén and Tamara Shefer, 2020.

Albert J. Mills is Professor of Management, Saint Mary's University, Canada, and Professor of Innovation Management, University of Eastern Finland. He is the former Co-Chair of the Academy of Management's Critical Management Studies Division; President of the Administrative Sciences Association of Canada; and President of the Atlantic Schools of Business. He is currently Co-Chair of the Board for International Critical Management Studies and the Co-editor of the journal *Qualitative Research in Organizations and Management*. The author of 50 books and edited collections, his latest books include *History and Business Storytelling*, 2023; *Management and Organization History: A Research Overview*, 2020; and *Insights and Research on the Study of Gender and Intersectionality in International Airline Cultures*, 2017.

Jean Helms Mills is Professor Emerita, Department of Management, Saint Mary's University, Canada, Docent at The Swedish School of Social Science, University of Helsinki, Jyväskylä University and University of Eastern Finland. Jean's research focuses on critical sensemaking, gender, intersectionality and historiography. Jean is Co- Editor of *Qualitative Research in Organizations and Management* and past Co-Division Chair of The Academy of Management, Critical Management Studies Division.

Ana Luisa Muñoz-García is Doctor in Educational Culture, Policy and Society from the State University of New York at Buffalo. She is Assistant Professor in the Faculty of Education at the Pontifical Catholic University of Chile. Her focus has been educational research and the construction of knowledge in academia, internationalisation and gender in higher education. Today, she is leading a research project on gender and knowledge within academia, funded by the National Agency of Research and Development (ANID). She also has been an associated researcher at the Millennium Project on "Trajectories of students in higher education" funded by the Minister of Economy since 2018.

Julia Nentwich is Associate Professor in Psychology at the University of St. Gallen, Switzerland, where she teaches psychology and critical thinking. In her research, she is interested in social and discursive practices of (un)doing gender, organizational change, change agency and resistance. With her research on men working in nurseries, as well as male allies fostering equal opportunities in leadership positions, she has contributed rich empirical insights into men's struggles with hegemonic and alternative masculinities. She has published widely on these topics, in both English and German. She holds a PhD in psychology from the University of Tübingen, Germany.

Banu Ozkazanc-Pan is Professor of Practice at the School of Engineering and Academic Director of the IE Brown EMBA programme. She is also Founder and Director of the Venture Capital Inclusion Lab at the Nelson Center for Entrepreneurship. Her research interests are mainly in the areas of diversity and inclusion in organizations and entrepreneurial ecosystems. She is currently Joint Editor-in-Chief of *Gender, Work & Organization*. Recent publications include *Transnational Migration and The New Subjects of Work: Transmigrants, Hybrids and Cosmopolitans*, 2019, and *Entrepreneurial Ecosystems: A Critical Gender Perspective*, 2021. She is currently working on *A Transnational Approach to Entrepreneurial Ecosystems*, 2023.

Bob Pease is Honorary Professor in the School of Humanities and Social Sciences at Deakin University and Adjunct Professor in the School of Social Sciences at the University of Tasmania. He has published extensively on masculinity politics and critical social work practice. His most recent books include *Facing Patriarchy: From a Violent Gender Order to a Culture of Peace*, 2019; *Post-Anthropocentric Social Work: Critical Posthuman and New Materialist Perspectives*, co-editor, 2021; *Undoing Privilege: Unearned Advantage and Systemic Injustice in an Unequal World*, 2022; and *Posthumanism and the Man Question: Beyond Anthropocentric Masculinities*, co-editor, 2023.

Ann Phoenix is Professor of Psychosocial studies at the Thomas Coram Research Unit, Social Research Institute, UCL Institute of Education. Her research focuses on the ways in which psychological experiences and social processes are linked and intersectional. It includes racialized and gendered identities, mixed-parentage, masculinities, consumption, motherhood, families, migration and transnational families. Recent books include *Environment in the Lives of Children and Families: Perspectives from India and the UK*, with Janet Boddy, Catherine Walker and Uma Vennan, 2017; and *Nuancing Young Masculinities: Helsinki Boys' Intersectional Relationships in New Times*, with Marja Peltola, 2022.

Kopano Ratele is Head of the African Centre for Critical and Creative Thought and Professor of Psychology at Stellenbosch University, South Africa. He is the former director of the South African Medical Research Council-University of South Africa's Masculinity and Health Research Unit and former research professor at the University of South Africa. He has been a member of the second Ministerial Committee on Transformation of South African Universities, former chairperson of Sonke Gender Justice, and former president of the Psychological Society of South Africa. Currently, he is on the management committee of the joint Department of Science and Innovation-National Research Foundation (DSI-NRF) Centre of Excellence in Human Development, and a national advisory board member for the Future Professors Programme.

Sandy Ruxton is independent Policy Advisor and Researcher and an expert in gender and masculinities. He is Honorary Fellow in the Department of Sociology at Durham University, UK, and works with colleagues in the Centre for Research into Violence and Abuse (www.mmasc.org.uk). He is a founder member of the MenEngage Europe network and co-hosts the podcast "Now and Men: Current conversations about men's lives", with Stephen Burrell. A trained teacher, he has worked with boys and young men in schools, the community and prisons. He has volunteered for grassroots mutual aid organizations, delivering food support and essential supplies to at-risk households.

Birgit Sauer is Professor of Political Science, Department of Political Science, University of Vienna. Her research fields include feminist state and democratic theory, right-wing populism and gender, politics, affects and emotions. She has been a member of several international research co-operations and projects on these issues. Recently she conducted two research projects on state transformation and affective governmentality. She was a director of the graduate school "Gender, Violence and Agency in the Era of Globalisation" (GIK), the University of Vienna. Recent publications include *Governing Affects. Neoliberalism, Neo-Bureaucracies, and Service Work*, with Otto Penz, 2020; *Populism and the Web: Communicative Practices of Parties and Movements in Europe*, co-edited with Mojca Pajnik, 2020; "Worldwide Anti-Gender Mobilization: Right-wing Contestations of Women's and Gender Rights" with Julia Roth, in *Global Contestations of Gender Rights*, 2022.

Tamara Shefer is Professor of Women's and Gender Studies in the Faculty of Arts and Humanities at the University of the Western Cape, Cape Town. Her scholarship has foregrounded the study of gender and sexualities within postcolonial, transnational feminist and critical masculinities thinking. She is also engaged in reconceptualizing higher education and working with feminist and decolonial pedagogies and research praxis. Recent books include *Knowledge, Power and Young Sexualities: A Transnational Feminist Engagement*, co-authored with Jeff Hearn, 2022; and *Routledge International Handbook of Masculinity Studies*, co-edited with Lucas Gottzén and Ulf Mellström, 2020.

Mara Silva Hope holds a BVA from the Universidad de Chile and a BEd and MEd from the Pontificia Universidad Católica de Chile. She is currently working at the Cape Horn International Center, the Latin American Network of Deans of Education, and the Center for Policy and Practice in Education at the Pontificia Universidad Católica de Chile. She has participated as a coordinator and research assistant in different research projects associated with policies on higher education, gender and knowledge.

Vivek Soundararajan is Associate Professor of International Management at the School of Management, University of Bath. He is also United Kingdom Research and Innovation Future Leader Fellow and leads a research initiative called Embed-Dignity. He conducts research on the governance of labour rights in supply chains and inequalities in and around organizations. His research has been published in journals such as *Business Ethics Quarterly*, *Journal of Operations Management*, *Journal of World Business* and *Human Relations*. His research has received awards and nominations from top academic associations, journals and media.

Shahnaaz Suffla is Associate Professor at the Institute for Social and Health Sciences, University of South Africa, Senior Researcher affiliated with the Medical Research Council-University of South Africa Masculinity and Health Research Unit, and current Past President of the Psychological Society of South Africa. Shahnaaz's research interests draw from the intersections of decolonial, African, community and peace psychologies, and public health, and are located within liberatory philosophies and epistemologies.

Nurseli Yeşim Sünbüloğlu is a visiting faculty in the Core Program at Kadir Has University in Turkey. Sünbüloğlu completed her MA in Gender Studies at Central European University and her PhD in Sociology at the University of Sussex, UK, with her thesis titled *Politics of the Rehabilitation of Disabled Veterans: Masculinity, the Body and Militarism in Turkey*. She has published articles and chapters focusing on masculinities, disability, militarism and nationalism. She edited a volume in Turkish (*Erkek Millet, Asker Millet*) on militarism, nationalism and men/masculinities in Turkey, in 2013. She is a member of the Initiative for Critical Studies of Masculinities (ICSM), and on the editorial board of a peer-reviewed bilingual journal, *Masculinities: A Journal of Culture and Society*. She has coordinated two gender projects, "Non-Violent Masculinities Workshops Manual" (2020–2021) and "e-Gen (Equality Generation) Module for Young Men at High Schools" (2022–2022), and has been a researcher in others focusing on GBV, gender backlash and institutionalization of gender equality.

Scott Taylor is Professor of Leadership and Organization Studies at Birmingham Business School, University of Birmingham, UK. His research contributes to our understanding of human experiences of work through interpretive analysis of qualitative data. He has collaborated on projects exploring religion at work, men's responses to positive discrimination initiatives and contemporary craftwork.

Anika Thym is completing her PhD in Gender Studies at the University of Basel, Switzerland. Her dissertation investigates how some men from leadership positions in finance think critically about their entanglement in hierarchical gender and class relations. Main research interests are social and gender theory, critical studies on men and masculinities, care and reproduction, and equality and diversity. She is founding member of the research network "transformation of masculinities" in Switzerland and co-editor of the book *Contemporary Analysis of Masculinities in Switzerland* (original in German).

Nicole Westmarland is Professor of Criminology at Durham University where she is also the Director of the Durham Centre for Research into Violence and Abuse (CRiVA). She has conducted many research and consultancy projects in the field of domestic and sexual violence. Her books include *Violence against Women*, 2015, and *Researching Gender, Violence and Abuse: Theory, Methods, Action, with Hannah Bows*, 2018. Her most recent book is Men's Activism to End Violence against Women', with various co-authors (2021) and is free to download as an e-book.

Joan C. Williams is an expert in the field of social inequality, and Sullivan Professor of Law and Founding Director of the Center for WorkLife Law at the University of California Law San Francisco. Her team has done eight studies on how gender and racial bias play out in organizations. She holds an honorary PhD from Utrecht University in the Netherlands for her research on workplace bias and received the Distinguished Publication Award from the Association for Women in Psychology (2005). She is one of the few people to receive both the American Bar Foundation's Outstanding Scholar Award (2012) and the ABA's Margaret Brent Women Award for Lawyers of Achievement (2006). Her contributions to work–family studies began with her prize-winning *Unbending Gender* (2000); she received the Work Life Legacy Award from the Families and Work Institute in 2014. Her team has written over 30 articles in *Harvard Business Review*.

Ling Eleanor Zhang is Associate Professor in Management at ESCP Business School, London Campus, UK. Her expertise covers a wide range of topics in cross-cultural management, such as global mobility, geopolitics, multiculturalism and multilingualism in international business, and workplace diversity and inclusion. She has published her research widely in academic journals such as *Gender, Work & Organization*, *The Journal of World Business* and *International Business Review*. She also disseminates her research findings in both academic and commercial book formats.

ACKNOWLEDGEMENTS

We first thank the authors of the chapters that comprise this Handbook, for their conscientiousness, easy cooperation, responsiveness and promptness in producing great work.

We would like to thank our Commissioning Editor Emily Briggs, Senior Editorial Assistant Lakshita Joshi, and all at Routledge for their support and collaboration in the editing process and the production of the Handbook. We also thank Venkatesh Sundaram at Apex CoVantage for dealing with many matters in the final production, and the Indexer Katie Landmark for their thorough work.

Anika: I would like to thank Kadri, Jeff and David for the mutually supporting, enriching and fun collaboration, in which I learned a lot personally and intellectually. In addition, I would like to appreciate my family and friends, for this context particularly, Brigitte Röder, Constantine Panga, Laura Eigenmann, Matthias Luterbach and Sophie Bürgi, for their wonderful caring support.

David: Thanks to Anika, Kadri and Jeff. It's been great working on the Handbook together. Over the past three years or so, we've enjoyed some really interesting international Zoom sessions. I would also like to thank Pam Pantiru for all her thoughtful encouragement during this process, as well as family and friends for their care and support.

Jeff: I would like to first thank Anika, David and Kadri for such supportive collaboration, and for so much fun that, in our monthly meetings, we often had to call a premature halt to the laughing in order to get to the business of editing! I also thank Liisa Husu, Charlotta Niemistö, Sofia Strid and Eleonóra Tógyer, among many others, for all their continuing support.

Kadri: I very much appreciated the opportunity to work with Jeff, Anika and David. It has been very inspiring and fun to co-edit this book with you! I am grateful to my family members for the love and support (notably, childcare!) they have given me throughout the process of editing this book and beyond.

We also thank the many colleagues and students in the universities of Basel, Hanken School of Economics, Huddersfield, Lancaster, Tallinn and Örebro for many debates and discussions, agreements and disagreements.

***

Chapter 2 is a slightly edited version of the article, Raewyn Connell (2019). New maps of struggle for gender justice: Rethinking feminist research on organizations and work. *Gender, Work & Organization*, *26*(1), 54–63. https://onlinelibrary.wiley.com/doi/epdf/10.1111/gwao.12332. Permission to reprint this article was granted by the author and John Wiley & Sons, and with thanks to *Gender, Work & Organization*.

Chapter 10 is adapted and edited from the open-access article, Work as a masculinity context, by Jennifer L. Berdahl, Marianne Cooper, Peter Glick, Robert W. Livingston, and Joan C. Williams, in the *Journal of Social Issues*, *28*(3), 2018, 422–448: https://spssi.onlinelibrary.wiley.com/doi/10.1111/josi.12289. The article introduced the Special Issue edited by Jennifer L. Berdahl, Marianne Cooper, and Peter Glick (Special Issue Editors). For a full listing of the Special Issue papers, see http://onlinelibrary.wiley.com/doi/10.1111/josi.2018.74.issue-3/issuetoc. Permission to adapt and reprint extracts of this article was granted by the authors. Thanks to John Wiley & Sons, the *Journal of Social Issues*, and the Society for the Psychological Study of Social Issues.

Chapter 25 is edited and adapted from the open-access article: Lauren McCarthy, Vivek Soundararajan and Scott Taylor (2021). The hegemony of men in global value chains: Why it matters for labour governance. *Human Relations*, 74(12), 2051–2074. https://journals.sagepub.com/doi/10.1177/0018726720950816. Permission to adapt and reprint extracts of this article was granted by the authors, with thanks to *Human Relations*, and Sage Publications.

Chapter 26 is edited, adapted and translated from Alex Demirović and Andrea Maihofer (2013). Vielfachkrise und die Krise der Geschlechterverhältnisse. In H. M. Nickel & A. Heilmann (Eds.), *Krise, Kritik, Allianzen: Arbeits- und geschlechtersoziologische Perspektiven* [*Crisis, Critique, Alliances: Work and Gender Sociological Perspectives*] (pp. 30–48). Weinheim: Beltz Juventa. Permission to adapt and reprint extracts of this article was granted by the authors. With thanks to Quinn Allison for the translation from German.

ABBREVIATIONS

CLS – Critical leadership studies
CMNI – Conformity to Masculine Norms Inventory
CSMM – Critical studies on men and masculinities
ICTs – Information and communication technologies
MNRI – Masculine Role Norms Inventory
MNRS – Masculine Role Norms Scale

1

STUDYING MEN, MASCULINITIES, ORGANIZATIONS AND ORGANIZING

Introducing the Handbook

Jeff Hearn, Kadri Aavik, David L. Collinson and Anika Thym

A topic that is always topical

The links between men, masculinities, organizations and organizing are many and various. Studying these connections is particularly important because of the ubiquity, influence and power of organizations and organizing as pervasive human endeavours. Many contemporary societies are highly organized and organizational in character, so that from even before birth to even after death, lives are structured, shaped and mediated by organizations and organizing. While organizations and organizing can have transnational and global impacts, they can also reach into areas often considered to be the most personal and private.

Men continue to dominate many organizations, in particular, in their positions of power, authority and leadership, and effectively direct several forms of organizing, whether on the local and immediate, the national or the global scale. Men's contribution in bringing on and exacerbating some of the current crises of global dimensions is significant. For instance, men's practices and masculinities are central to understanding war, as in the Russian Federation's invasion of Ukraine,[1] the ecological crises (Pulé & Hultman, 2021),[2] the concentrations and inequalities of the global economic system,[3] and the rise of populism, nationalism, the manosphere (Sugiura, 2021) and viral masculinity (Ashcraft, 2022).

Moreover, often such political and organizational issues are presented in strangely gender-neutral terms. To take just one item in the news, reported as we completed this Handbook, namely, that "1,000 super-emitting methane leaks risk triggering climate tipping points", mostly from oil and gas facilities in various locations across the globe, but especially Russia, Turkmenistan and the United States. One leak alone is equivalent to 67 million running cars. While there is no mention of gender in the report, these leaks are very much the business of certain men and masculinities, in terms of the ownership and economic interests of the sector, neglect and lack of care, and the actions of individuals and groups (Kűhne et al., 2022; Carrington, 2023).

The connections between men, masculinities, organizations and organizing recur across multiple social realms – from global political economy and transnational flows to societal

DOI: 10.4324/9781003193579-1

gender orders and regimes, the organization of society and societies, gendered labour markets, social movements, vertical and horizontal gender divisions in and around organizations, to leadership, management and organizational cultures – all frequently reflecting and reinforcing men and masculinities. More conceptually, they are also central to questions of practice(s), discourses, communicative practices, identities, embodiments, stereotypes and symbols, social processes, and social structures – of different scales and scopes.

It is important to draw attention to men and masculinities in relation to not only (social) organization and organizations but also various forms of organizing. The concept of organizing can itself refer to several different aspects and phenomena. These include internal processes within formal organizations; organizing as action/agency, both individual and collective; organizing outside formal organizations, for example, social movement organizing; various kinds of distributed, dispersed and network organizations; online/digital/cyberorganizing; as well as what has come to be known as "organizationality". All of these meanings extend beyond what is sometimes assumed by the notions of organization and organizations, and all are relevant to the Handbook.

In the Handbook, the first of its kind in specifically addressing the relations of men, masculinities, organizations and organizing, we bring together contemporary work by scholars, both well-established and emerging, from all major world regions. The collection considers a range of theoretical and methodological approaches, and engages with multiple topics on both formal organizations, such as businesses and state organizations, and processes of organizing within and beyond organizations. The volume addresses emergent and future issues on men, masculinities and organizations, such as men's violences, tech masculinities, animal advocacy and environmental issues, and men and masculinities in pandemics. The Handbook provides a resource for scholars, policymakers, practitioners and students interested in links between men, masculinities, organizations and organizing, and working in and beyond such fields as gender studies, organization, leadership and management studies, political science, sociology, social and public policy, and social movement studies.

A growing body of studies

While there are a host of texts, including some so-called classics, not least *The Organization Man* (Whyte, 1956), in studies of organizations and organizing that are all about men and masculinities, the explicit gendering of men and masculinities has often been absent. In the wake of Second Wave feminism, and particularly from the late 1970s and 1980s onwards, a growing body of studies by women, men and further genders has focused on men and masculinities in and around organizations in explicitly critical, gendered and sometimes intersectional ways.

Kanter's (1977) *Men and Women of the Corporation* was a landmark study, addressing social dynamics within men's leadership and management (also see Kanter, 1993; Collinson & Hearn, 1995, 2005, 2014) and managerial homosociality. The area of research has become more consolidated in and since the 1990s, with many more specific sub-fields of study. Wide-ranging collections include *Men as Managers, Managers as Men* (Collinson & Hearn, 1996), the special journal issue of *Social Problems* on masculine contest cultures (Berdahl et al., 2018, also this volume), and *Making it Like a Man: Men, Masculinities and the Modern Career* (Aavik et al., 2020).

Among the many questions that were addressed relatively early in the 1980s and 1990s included men and masculinities in bureaucracies (Bologh, 1990; Morgan, 1996), on the factory shop floor, and in management–labour relations (Collinson, 1992), along with their intersections with class inequalities (Cockburn, 1983) and national contexts (Reis, 2004; Tienari et al., 2010); the historical relations and transformations in reproducing patriarchies (Hearn, 1992; Collinson & Hearn, 1994; Roper, 1994; Wajcman, 1998); diverse occupational, managerial and professional identities formations (Kerfoot & Knights, 1993; Barrett, 1996; Kerfoot & Whitehead, 2000), and men's sexualities at work (Metcalf & Humphries, 1985; Roper, 1996) and in leisure time (Allison, 1994). Many of these studies have been framed within analysis of gendered inequalities and inequalities regimes (Acker, 2006), including unequal pay and reward systems, largest pay gaps often at managerial levels, and more specific studies of discrimination against women in selection (Collinson et al., 1990), and (mis)management of sexual harassment cases (Collinson & Collinson, 1989, 1996).

Of the many more focused and more recent examples of studies on men and masculinities, examples include those in the finance sector (Thym, 2019, 2020; Blomberg, 2009; Ho, 2009; Zaloom, 2006; Knights & Tullberg, 2014); use of masculine metaphors (McCabe & Knights, 2016); the "masculinization" of ethical leadership (Lui, 2017, 2021; Knights, 2022); intersectional analysis of interviews with managers (Aavik, 2015); workplace surveillance regimes (Payne, 2018); men opting out of mainstream work (Thym, 2019, 2020; Biese, 2021); impacts of neoliberalism (Cornwall et al., 2016; Garlick, 2020; Wolfman et al., 2021); danger and disaster (Messerschmidt, 1995; Maier & Messerschmidt, 1998; Collinson, 1999); diversity and diversity management (Hearn & Collinson, 2006, 2009); possibilities for men's non-oppressive, even profeminist, organizing, management and leadership (Hearn, 1989; Luyt & Starck, 2020); and global value chains and inter-organizational relations (McCarthy et al., 2021; also this volume). Men and masculinities in organizations also need to be understood in terms of the relations of home and work, and domestic situations. For example, some men managers can be usefully understood as "father-managers" (Hearn & Niemistö, 2012) sometimes distancing themselves from children and family, showing corporate commitment, yet reinforcing gendered stresses in families, with their own gendered power relations (Collinson & Collinson, 1997). This Handbook builds on these and many other earlier research studies.

In addition, management, and indeed management studies, especially corporate management, have often assumed to be consistent with characteristics traditionally valued in men, despite contrary evidence. Indeed not all versions of men's (dominating) leadership rely on what might be seen as heroic models of leadership and management; in some contexts, there seem to be movements towards the post-heroic, and the development of subordinates' capabilities within distributed, project and network organizing; such shifts do not, however, necessarily reduce men's power at the structural level. While much of the research on men and masculinities has been driven by critical, feminist(ic) scholarship concerned with the analysis of gender power relations in workplaces, organizations and management, some are linked to more corporate agendas, such as that on "talent management", management development and diversity management.

Yet, despite all of this, the taken-for-grantedness of men and certain organizational masculinities, as unmarked categories, is very widespread in both everyday organizational practice and policy, and studies thereon. Men's domination of leadership, management, organizations and organizing is still not an explicitly gendered topic of concern in mainstream social science, and not even in much critical social science. Most mainstream studies of organizations, leadership and management do not seem to notice they are very often talking about men and masculinities: they generally do not gender men.

Theories, disciplines and methodologies

In focusing on men, masculinities, organizations and organizing, the Handbook brings together and creates dialogue between various critical approaches and disciplines. These diverse fields of research, such as gender, feminist and queer studies, leadership and management studies, organization studies, business studies, social movement studies, decolonial and postcolonial approaches, internet studies, science and technology studies (STS), and research in education and higher education, have not necessarily engaged with each other significantly, as well as sociology, political science, economics, cultural studies, psychology and social psychology.

In studying these questions, a wide range of methodological approaches and research methods have been employed (on men, masculinities and methodologies, see Pini & Pease, 2013). Quantitative methods have been important in addressing the numerical dominance of men, especially at the highest levels, and pay and reward systems and outcomes. Qualitative methods, including case studies, often drawing on feminist methodologies, have been more widely used, for example, in examining gendered organizational processes. Discursive and textual methods of various kinds have become more popular in recent years. There has been a consistent impact of feminist theories, and a persistent concern with the intersections of gender with class, racialization and ethnicity, occupation, and organizational position and status.

More recent work inspired by posthumanist and feminist new materialist approaches, as well as affect theory (see Mellström & Pease, 2023) highlights the material, including embodied, affective and relational dimensions pertaining to men and masculinities, contesting the centrality of the discursive. These perspectives have methodological implications for the study of men and masculinities, including in the context of organizations and organizing. Existing methodologies and methods in critical studies on men and masculinities (CSMM), however, are predominantly focused on studying men and masculinities through discursive representations which have significant limitations for accessing the non-discursive. Thus, new methodological approaches could be considered and developed in studying men, masculinities, organizations and organizing that go beyond textual analysis to capture elements of life such as affects, embodiment, performances, relations, the more-than-human and their entanglements (Vannini, 2015).

Critical studies on men and masculinities

Further to various disciplines and disciplinary contexts and influences noted, particular mention needs to be made of CSMM, as a sub-field of feminist and gender studies. These studies examine men, boys and masculinities critically in the light of feminist, gender, queer and kindred studies. Though theoretically and methodologically diverse, these studies are generally historical, cultural, relational, materialist, deconstructive, anti-essentialist (Hearn, 1997) and indeed critical studies on men and masculinities. In some cases, there is more emphasis on homogenizations, generalizations and categoricalism in talking about "men", without taking into account differences among men and struggles, but often there has been close attention to context, specificity and difference. These two tendencies have also often been held in creative tension.

Accordingly, in talking about "men" and "masculinities", the terms and their usage always need to be contextualized, including the differences and struggles among and between men as well as other genders and transgressions towards non-binary genders (Aultman, 2019;

Köllen, 2016). In many situations and societies, men are assumed to contrast with women, to be seen as adult cis-males, and to be the "foundation" of masculinities. But that is not always so. Some societies, probably an increasing number, recognize third, or fourth, sexes and genders, non-cis and trans men.

Masculinities can be understood variously as, for example, the traits, identities, psychodynamics and individual and collective practices of men, and boys, but masculinities can also be taken up by women, female-identified people, and non-binary, agender and queer people. To talk about men and masculinities, it is necessary to recognize structural gendered power relations at local, institutional, societal, transnational and global levels, as well as how differently positioned men's and boys' experiences vary and relate to ideals of masculinity differently. This is part of the attempt to avoid simplified or distorted accounts of men, masculinities and gender relations.

Intersectionality in studying men and masculinities

In addition, intersectional perspectives to studying men are imperative. Indeed, intersectionality has been present implicitly and more explicitly in much of the key theoretical and empirical works in CSMM. For instance, the concept of hegemonic masculinity is theorized in relation to other, marginalized and subordinated masculinities (see Connell, 1987; Connell & Messerschmidt, 2005), thus distinguishing more privileged forms of masculinity from less privileged ones and considering their interactions. Scholarship on the notion of hybrid masculinities (Bridges & Pascoe, 2014) primarily concerns young white heterosexual men and intersections between these categories.

Approaching men and masculinities through intersectionality, however, poses a number of conceptual difficulties and dilemmas, including those related to definitions of the concept of intersectionality itself. Debates in existing literature concern, for example, questions of what intersects and how, and the difficulties of analysing several categories simultaneously (Hearn & Louvrier, 2015; Meyer, 2017). More fundamental disagreements involve questions of how intersectionality should be used and by whom. For instance, some scholars argue that the concept of intersectionality was often blind to practices of the dominant groups and their effects (Rommelspacher, 2009; Walgenbach, 2007), while others link intersectionality specifically to Black feminist thought and anti-racist commitments (Crenshaw, 1989; Nash, 2019), and therefore any analysis using an intersectional approach should always consider how the categories of race and racialization are used and to be used, along with the insights of Critical Race Theory more generally. Others, however, propose that intersectionality could be used as a tool to examine any intersections, including among dominant social groupings.

A number of authors want to steer away from some of the challenges related to the concept of intersectionality, as with the problem of referring to identity categories and additivity (when social categories are added, but without attending to their intersectional mutual constitution and possible tensions), which do not assist in grasping the complexity of power relations. Alternative terms include "multidimensionality" to focus on the constitutive connection between different dimensions of power and domination within individuals and social fields,[4] grids and assemblages (Puar, 2012), or "matrix of domination" (Collins, 2008). Given these debates, any approach chosen has theoretical, methodological and political implications and challenges.

With regard to the use of the term, intersectionality, we find it insightful to draw on scholars who emphasize that what matters most is the purpose for which intersectionality is used, arguing that central to any use of intersectionality should be a commitment to social justice and an intent to challenge social inequalities (Bilge, 2013; Collins & Bilge, 2020). Thus, intersectionality could be understood as a form of critical inquiry, as well as praxis. In this sense, critically examining the practices of men and dominant forms of masculinity adheres to these commitments.

Histories, power, men, masculinities, organizations and organizing

The notion of organization is historical, and deeply associated with forms of power, that is, intersectional gendered power. Large organizations are not a specifically modern phenomenon, as evidenced in the ancient hydraulic societies and the Chinese, Egyptian and Sumerian bureaucracies. Across many centuries, complex organization and organizing have been promoted by military, land-owning, economic and religious interests. In recent history, a pervasive image of an organization has been that of a factory, office, building that may appear to function within four walls, but in practice is not isolated from its environment, however defined. In some cases, supposed organizational isolation depended on, and still depends on, global relations of colonialism, slavery, imperialism and of course capitalism. Interestingly, such a visualization of the organization does not derive from the conglomerations of the Industrial Revolution heyday but rather from the industrial mill that could be *seen*. Paradoxically, organization and organization theory became constituted through the passing of that organizational form to the multiple-unit organization, which could not be fully seen, and required less immediate means of control.

With many organizations growing in size, and becoming more consolidated and more powerful (intersectional gendered) concentrations of resources, expansion occurred through horizontal and vertical connection and integration, and geographical and temporal expansion and diffusion. During Fordism, the largest organizations operated more nationally, more in industry than finance and tech, more under the power of the state, and had much smaller revenues than during neoliberalism. In 1960, for example, the largest companies were General Motors, Exxon Mobil and Ford Motor, which are all in the fossil fuel and automobile industry, all from the United States, with annual revenues up to US$11.2 billion, and assets up to US$9.8 billion (CNN Money, 2021). In 2022, despite the pandemic and the ongoing war by Russia on Ukraine, the world's largest public companies managed to increase sales and profits (Murphy & Contreras, 2022). The largest organizations, measured by sales, profits, assets and market value, were the US multinational conglomerate Berkshire Hathaway with the main business and source of capital in insurance as number one, followed by the Industrial and Commercial Bank of China which dropped to number two after nine consecutive years at the top of the list. Third is the Saudi Arabian Oil company. Tech companies such as Amazon, Apple, Alphabet (including Google), and Microsoft range between numbers 6 and 12. In 2022, the top company reached US$958 billion in assets, which is almost 100 times more than in 1960. They operate transnationally and have increasing influence in relation to and over states, while at the same time inequality is growing for more than 70% of the global population, exacerbating the risks of divisions and hampering economic and social development (UN, 2020).

All those companies are directly or indirectly owned, operated or chaired by men, now from not only the United States but also China, Hong Kong, Japan and Saudi Arabia. For Fordism, hegemonic masculinity in organizations has been described as paternalistic and fatherly (Kerfoot & Knights, 1993). During neoliberalism, however, hegemonic transnational business masculinities are pictured as more ruthless, less loyal and more focused on individual profits (Connell & Wood, 2005). For these new global business masculinities, big tech has played an increasing role, also in social media and films.[5] Thereby, not only the gender of those men in power but also the organizing of global capitalism and the capitalist ruling class are gendered and configured through key transnational players, with increasingly close connections between politics and economics (Hearn, 2015, p. 135ff.). Women in the Global South who work informally and/or for little pay serve as "resource for globalizing capital" (ibid., 141). At the same time, there seems to be a development towards respecting characteristics and social fields that have been associated with women in bourgeois societies, such as care, responsibility, relationships and childcare. The Global Workforce Report 2022 (KellyOCG, 2022) refers to a survey of 1,000 senior executives across 12 countries and 10 industries which shows that "leading employers are moving to meet employees' expectations for greater flexibility in how they integrate work in their lives, supporting their mental health, and showing greater authenticity and urgency in engaging with diversity, equity and inclusion". This seems to mark an important difference from previous hegemonic forms of masculinity, which required men to prioritize their career and work requirements above personal and family issues.

In all these various ways, notions of organization, organizations and organizing have become increasingly complex, diverse, differentiated, dispersed and networked, now operating globally and glocally. Organizations encompass multi-organizations, meta-organizations, transnational organizations, inter-organizational relations, network organizations, net-organizations and cyberorganizations, not existing in one specific time–place reality. In some parts of the world, economies have shifted and are shifting from primary and secondary production to tertiary and quaternary production, and their associated changing forms of post-Fordist organizations and organizing, including what has been called surveillance capitalism (Zuboff, 2019). These historical conditions also create many more possible forms of gender power, predominantly, though not exclusively, for men (Little & Winch, 2021). In different ways, these material and immaterial shifts are formed by and form men, masculinities and gender relations in organizations. Meanwhile, the metaphorical conceptualization of organization simply as the organizational building or organizational chart can easily neglect the multiple views from below and from the margins, including women's experiences. Seeing organizations as collections of more complex and diffuse relations of ruling (Smith, 1990) also underlines the importance of knowledge from the margins.

Overview of the volume

Developing the Handbook has been an extended process, with some obvious topics, some less obvious and the recognition that even across 30 chapters with almost 60 authors there were bound to be gaps and omissions. The book has grown organically, with some sought-after chapters not emerging, some new ideas for chapters added, and others developing in new ways from their initial conceptualization, taking a broader, more open-ended approach to organizations and organizing. In one initial draft of the contents, from early 2020, we had 45 possible chapters, including, for example, those on homosociality, hierarchy, resources, and communication and group processes. In the final contents, Part I, "Theories and Frameworks", Part III, "Organizational Settings", and Part IV, "Current and Future Issues", emerged as relatively similar to that plan. Part II, "Structures and Processes of Organizing", underwent much more selective focusing on areas that are still relatively neglected.

The final contents are a negotiation between the state of knowledge and research, the wish to explore new perspectives, and the practicalities of producing the Handbook. Inevitably, some topics and sectors have been studied well and are represented here, others much less, such as agriculture, heavy industry, dangerous work and extreme contexts, Indigenous men and masculinities, trans/gender identities, and some aspects of internal organizational dynamics like recruitment, socialization, negotiation, resistance and dissent. These are important topics for further research, along with the broader questions of ethics, politics and social change. Additionally, we have tried to include a wide range of perspectives, both geographically and theoretically, and attend to questions of location, context and geopolitics.

Overall, in many different ways, the chapters of this Handbook engage in debates between: first, gender, gender relations, men and masculinities; second, organizations and organizing; and, third, the topic in focus, whether it is more theoretical, more concerned with an organizational form, sector, structure or process, or certain social or societal trends or tendencies. Moreover, these theoretical, societal and organizational concerns themselves interconnect in multiple ways.

Part I, "Theories and Frameworks", situates the Handbook in terms of the range of different theoretical positions and influences that have been and are important in examining men, masculinities, organizations and organizing. These include theoretical positions focusing on historical studies, social theory, feminist, gender and queer studies, organization studies, social movement studies, and global and transnational studies. Additionally, gender, men, masculinities and organizations are considered through intersectional perspectives.

The part opens with a broad contemporary global overview, Chapter 2, "New maps of struggle for gender justice: locating men, masculinities and organizations in feminist research on organizations and work", by Raewyn Connell. This is especially fitting, as Connell's work has, in a whole range of ways, inspired this area of theory, practice and politics. The chapter reviews succinctly recent developments in studies of gender, organizations and gender studies, in organizations, organizing and technologies in the world, and in geopolitics more broadly. The following chapter, Chapter 3, by Tigist Shewarega Hussen and Tamara Shefer, titled "Conditional solidarity: men and masculinities in social justice activist movements", provides a somewhat contrasting feminist intervention, in itself, in its topic focus, and its analysis, focusing on the practices and processes of organizing, specifically through the lens of gender and sexuality social movement organizing, including men supporters of feminist causes in public activism. Two movements in South Africa are examined, both feminist activist responses to challenge the larger activist movement: #PatriarchyMustFall, against masculinist structures in the #FeesMustFall (FMF) movement; and #MbokodoLead, feminist activism focused on enhancing the visibility and impact of female leaders in the #FMF movement. The gendering of social movements is shown, whether progressive, regressive or ambiguous in their aims.

The next two chapters are more historical and more theoretical in tone. First, Chapter 4, "Social theory and critical theory", by Richard Howson, delves into the historical connections of critical theory and theorizing, broadly from the Enlightenment. Focusing on Marx, Weber and Gramsci, Howson examines how critical and/or feminist approaches to masculinity contribute to critical studies of organizations and organizing. These issues and arguments are relevant for not only critical theorizing on organizations and organizing but also critical theorizing on gender, masculinity and many strands of feminism, as well as the intersections of organization theory and critical studies on men and masculinities, and feminist theory and critical theory. The chapter is, in many ways, complemented by the next, Chapter 5,

"Paradigms, gender and the making of men and masculinities in organization theory" by Albert J. Mills, Jean Helms Mills and Liela A. Jamjoom. This takes up the more recent history of paradigmatic developments in organization theory, including detailed activities and artefacts, such as textbooks, professional associations and "schools" of thought, seen explicitly or implicitly in gender terms, and then extends that analysis to the social place and power of men and masculinities. This chapter also moves the analysis further on by raising the important issue of intersectional gendering, including in relation to decolonial and critical race perspectives.

This latter focus is taken up more directly and at greater length in the last three chapters of Part I of the Handbook. Banu Ozkazanc-Pan's chapter, Chapter 6, "Decolonizing masculinities: a decolonial and transnational perspective", is a more focused examination of these very issues, with their various emphases and trajectories spelt out in relation to men, masculinities, organizations and organizing. This includes not only addressing coloniality, postcolonialism and decolonizing but also Indigenous perspectives on and ontologies of the matters at hand. Importantly, this arena is not just one theory but encompasses a range of different approaches, theories and practices that do not necessarily coincide. This applies to both organization studies and substantive organizations and organizing. The following chapter, Chapter 7, "Masculinities in the wasteland: (Post)colonial capitalism in the West, China, and Africa", by Sofia Aboim, Mabel Machado and Ling Eleanor Zhang, follows through on these very themes, more substantively with a focus on three world regions. This entails more detailed attention to the interplay between such issues as gender, masculinities, migration and trade, and how they bear on organizations and organizing. It also necessarily attends to the importance of specificities and locationalities, rather than sticking with the homogenization that accompanies some references to "internationalization" and "international" perspectives. The last chapter continues some of these themes. In Chapter 8, "Global, transnational, national and "local" organizations and organizing: the case of space and place", Jeff Hearn considers how spaces and places figure in understanding the differential relations and mutual construction of men, masculinities, organizations and organizing, transnationally, across localities and national contexts. This is even while the transnational and the global also operate locally and with local specificities. While much of the focus is on the macro-picture and historical picture of global and transnational organizations and organizing, including growing concentrations and inequalities, some implications of the transnational social-spatial lens for migration, nation and location are noted.

Organizations operate internally and externally, at one and the same time. Part II, "Structures and Processes of Organizing", delves deep inside organizations to examine how their internal workings continue to reflect and reinforce gendered assumptions and dominant discourses that privilege men and masculinities. The chapters "open the lid" on these dynamics to reveal how organizational processes continue to be "saturated" with masculine values and assumptions in ways that inform men's persistent domination of power and authority. These chapters examine how men's hegemony in many organizations and sectors is experienced and reproduced by organizational members and employees, not only men, and explores the effects, both intended and unwitting, of such gendered organizational asymmetries.

Internally, organizations are characterized by both formal and informal processes. Formal processes present an idealized version of how an organization operates, whereas informal dynamics occur in the shadow world of the formal, sometimes offering a contrary view. Formal hierarchical positions, for example, in leadership and management can facilitate the reproduction of men's power, privilege, status and identity in organizations through processes such as recruitment and selection, promotion, job design, training and development, and even work–life balance programmes. While distinctions can be made between the formal and informal, in practice there is often considerable overlap and interaction between these processes. In addition, managers, leaders and organizations are also outward-facing, as with externally oriented organizational practices such as corporate strategy, marketing, selling and organizational reputation/identity management.

The chapters in Part II address an array of different themes related to men and masculinities in organizations and organizing. These range from leadership, contest cultures, careers and work–life balance issues to caring work, emotions and affect, heterosexuality and homosexuality as well as violence and abuse (mainly) against women and girls in organizations and organizing. In the first chapter of Part II, Chapter 9, "Critical dialectical perspectives on men, masculinities and leadership", David L. Collinson argues that leadership is an important but often taken-for-granted source of men's power, privilege and status within organizations. He suggests that the combined insights of critical studies of men and masculinities and critical leadership studies help to reveal how power is exercised through men's leadership discourses, decisions and practices. Questioning overly deterministic perspectives and highlighting the value of dialectical approaches, the chapter discusses some of the paradoxical, contradictory and self-defeating consequences that can emerge when men leaders' decisions and discursive practices are informed by hypermasculine ways of thinking and acting. The following chapter, Chapter 10, "Workplace masculinity contests and culture", by Jennifer L. Berdahl, Marianne Cooper, Peter Glick, Robert W. Livingston and Joan C. Williams argues that many workplace cultures continue to be sites of "masculinity contests" in which men feel pressured to prove themselves as "real men". The authors identify different dimensions of masculinity along which men compete and they show how this competition differs by work context. The authors contend that organizations with "Masculinity Contest Cultures" are characterized by dysfunctional organizational climates (e.g. toxic leadership, bullying, and harassment) and poor individual outcomes for men as well as women (e.g. burnout, low organizational dedication, lower well-being).

The next two chapters raise further questions about men and careers, highlighting various pressures that can ensue from intense career aspirations. In Chapter 11, "Doing meta-work to navigate conventionally masculinist careers and work norms in professional workplaces", Marta Choroszewicz and Ingrid Biese highlight the hidden, invisible and laborious organizational work (i.e. "meta-work") professionals often have to perform in seeking to live up to the ideals surrounding socially prestigious careers and identities. Meta-work is also an important coping mechanism through which professionals deal with feelings of inadequacy, dilemmas and disappointments surrounding their conventionally masculinist careers. Drawing on two empirical case studies of white, professional men in Finland, Canada and the United States, the authors demonstrate that living up to masculinist careers and work norms requires continuous meta-work. Career aspirations can also impact on work–life balance (WLB). Chapter 12, "Changing and challenging work–life negotiations for men and organizations", by Majda Hrženjak, examines men's negotiations over WLB. In WLB research, men have primarily been viewed as fathers in heterosexual nuclear families of dual-career middle-class couples in rich countries. Men have been found to be stretched between work-centred and breadwinning norms of masculinity, and gendered norms of the carefree, ideal employee. By expanding paid work into private time and space neoliberal corporate colonization undermines the search for work–life balance. Hrženjak recommends that WLB studies widen their scope to explore intersectional locations and multicultural contexts, new developments, such as the gig economy and digitalization, broader understandings of care, diverse family arrangements and life-course stages.

Building on this focus on new understandings of care, the following two chapters address various connections between men, organizations and caring work. In Chapter 13, "Bodies, embodiment, bodywork, care, caring and self-care", Henri Hyvönen questions the findings of recent studies in post-industrialized labour markets which suggest that many men now practise seemingly "softer" forms of "healthy" and "caring" masculinity in organizations. Hyvönen's research on caring work in social services and healthcare finds that although men have adapted to changes in working life, care has also been redefined in masculine terms. His chapter seeks to deconstruct the dichotomy between men's power, often associated with dominance, harm and inequality, and men's caring capabilities. It reveals how caring relations are also power relations that can produce dominance, harm and inequality. Contemporary discourses around "softening" and "caring" masculinity are also central to the following chapter, Chapter 14, by Sam de Boise titled "Emotions and affect in organizing men and masculinity/ies" which addresses how men express emotions within and in relation to organizations. This chapter identifies differences between approaches to emotions and affect and discusses the tendency to view emotions within organizations as inherently gendered, including a focus on men's unemotionality. It also indicates how thinking about men's organizational behaviour and organizing as structured through affective practice may help to avoid the progressive/regressive binary associated with a focus on men's emotional expression while still foregrounding emotional experience.

The next chapter highlights issues of sexuality, desexualization in organizations and the persistent workplace dominance of hegemonic heterosexual masculinity. In Chapter 15, "Mingle with men: sexuality and gay men in organizations", Laura Eigenmann addresses the mutually constitutive relationship between masculinity, sexuality, heteronormativity and organizations, and investigates the negative implications for gay men of this inherent heteronormativity. Her chapter also acknowledges the empowering aspects of shared gay male identities, for example, in constructing closer workplace relationships, mutual support and strong informal networks, all of which help to compensate for gay men's marginalization. This is illustrated through research on informal networks among gay male EU employees in Brussels' LGBTIQ+ advocacy community. The final chapter in Part II "Men's violence and abuse in organizations and workplaces" by Nicole Westmarland examines the complex relations of men, masculinities and violence within organizations and organizing. Drawing on empirical research, the author shows how men's violence can operate within policing, higher education and residential care homes for children looked after by the state. All three empirical contexts have been sites of major UK investigations in recent years. While the chapter focuses on men's violence and abuse against women and girls, the conclusion also highlights some of the harms that men and boys experience within institutions where cultures of violence against women and girls are ingrained.

Part III, "Organizational Settings", captures differences in organizational settings and the importance of men and masculinities in them. Organizations play different roles in society, for example, concerning the economy, politics, securitization, sports and education, to mention the ones mostly covered here. These separate fields, which are connected in many ways, operate with various institutional apparatuses and imply different normative requirements concerning men and masculinities. Without taking into account the multifaceted gendered aspects of organizational settings, they cannot be understood adequately. At the same time, these different settings may deal with similar contemporary dynamics and challenges in human resources, career paths, concerning wealth distribution, work–life balance and care work. These chapters focus on men and masculinities in these organizational settings.

Part III begins with a focus on organizations and organizing in the economy. Chapter 17, "Hegemonic masculinities and the hegemony of men in business and finance organizations: persistence of and challenges to patriarchal power", by Anika Thym, Helen Longlands and Richard Collier looks at how institutions of law, business and finance interact with a range of discourses around masculinities. Particularly, it investigates how patriarchal power is maintained as well as questioned in hegemonic masculinity discourses in those fields. The chapter contributes to understanding the contradictory developments of masculinity discourses, which may have more authoritarian, more emancipatory or paradoxical outcomes. However, developments will turn out, men and masculinity discourses not only impact but also are – for now – constitutively connected with changes in the economy.

The following four chapters focus more explicitly on politics, the state, political organizations and organizing. In her chapter, Chapter 18, "Masculinity of the modern Western state and of state institutions", Birgit Sauer provides an overview of different dimensions of state masculinism. Informed by feminist-materialist as well as Foucauldian concepts, she elaborates on relations of gender and the state. She describes how organizational masculinity manifests itself in masculine procedures, norms and ideas and how they are embedded in the state-bureaucratic apparatus. In addition, she discusses current transformations of state masculinism by using the example of empirical research on the increasing importance of affects and emotions in the actions of street-level bureaucrats. The following chapter, Chapter 19, by F. Oya Aktaş, David L. Collinson, Jeff Hearn and Nurseli Yeşim Sünbüloğlu, is titled "Men, masculinities and military organizations". Modern states could not be imagined without the military including its mechanisms of largely securing the status quo also by repressive means, securitization and surveillance, protection and self-defence as well as expansion of territory – all of which are connected to military masculinities. Military organizations are among the most obviously gendered of all organizational activities. Indeed the military is also one of the clearest arenas of social power, violence and killing in their many guises; military matters are urgent, powerful and lethal, literally questions of life and death for all concerned. This chapter examines the place of men and masculinities in some key organizational issues in military organization and militarism, most notably recruitment, hierarchies and segregations, disability and veterans, and the impacts of these organizations on civilians, before concluding remarks on wider processes and impacts, on research, scientific and technological organizations, on international relations and geopolitics, and on the environment. The chapter thus brings together studies on men and masculinities with those in the military and military organizations.

The next chapter, Chapter 20, by Kopano Ratele, Nick Malherbe, Josephine Cornell and Shahnaaz Suffla, titled "Masculinities, political organizations and political organizing: queering anti-apartheid struggle", approaches politics and political organizations through a social movement perspective. The chapter highlights organizing as a political activity, and with a particular emphasis on queer masculinities. While clearly located in a more specific location and political context, the chapter points to a wider range of possible interconnections between men, masculinities, gender, sexuality, racialization, organizations and organizing. Chapter 21, by Michele Rene Gregory and Daniel Alsarve, titled "Beyond the public light: political strongmen, masculine embodiment and sports organizations", focuses on men, masculinities and sports organizations, while also highlighting the relevance of sports metaphors in politics and how they are used by so-called political strongmen. The chapter illustrates how discourses around masculinity and sport are connected with social discourses more generally, pointing to how different social fields and discourses overlap and interplay with one another. By drawing upon high-profile events, research on male-dominated sports, and arguments on sports and hegemonic masculinities, they illustrate how so-called strongmen create locker room spaces to reinforce white, male, heterosexual supremacy and thereby devalue "others". They illustrate how such demeaning behaviour is connected to the fragility of hegemonic masculinity.

The final three chapters in Part III discuss aspects of education at different stages of learning – including nurseries, kindergartens, schools and higher education – in various fields and contexts. Chapter 22, "(Un)doing masculinity? Men working in women's occupations", by Julia Nentwich and Chieh Hsu, provides an overview of studies on men in women's occupations in different parts of the world, particularly Asian contexts, while taking an intersectional perspective. They illustrate how across studies, men engage in "boundary work" that reaffirms their masculinity or how they develop "alternative masculinities" to reconcile any dissonance between their personal and professional identities. The chapter engages with complicated inter-relations of marginalization, privilege and hegemony within these men. While many men in "women's occupations" often develop alternative masculinities, Nentwich and Chieh show how more often than not, men in women's occupations reinforce central aspects of hegemonic masculinity. The following chapter, Chapter 23, by Ann Phoenix, titled "Boys and schooling: intersectional perspectives", examines schools from gender and intersectional perspectives, focusing specifically on boys, masculinities and schooling. Drawing on empirical insights from Denmark, Finland and the United Kingdom, the chapter considers how dominant masculinity scripts are reproduced as well as resisted in the everyday practices of boys at school. Part III closes with a chapter, Chapter 24, on higher education by Ana Luisa Muñoz-García, Mara Silva Hope, Gabriela Bard Wigdor and Liisa Husu. In their chapter titled "Men, gender and knowledge construction in higher education", the authors critically investigate gender-equality efforts in higher education with a focus on Latin America or *Nuestra América* (Viveros Vigoya, 2023) by studying the university discipline of education studies, characterized by the presence of a majority of women in the lower hierarchical levels. Based on a qualitative study in Chile, they emphasize that it is not enough to "count heads", that is the proportion of women especially in top positions and in certain fields. Rather they make a case for questioning, critically engaging with and transforming structures of hegemonic masculinity, institutionalized sexism and men's privilege even in historically feminized spaces.

Finally, Part IV, "Current and Future Issues", addresses some emergent and future issues pertaining to men, masculinities and organizations, for both research and activism. Organizations and organizing operate in the context of various crises that currently characterize various societies, and which are likely to escalate in the near future, such as global environmental and health crises, and with new and developing technologies shaping organizations, organizing and their futures.

Part IV begins with the neglected question of men, masculinities and gender relations in international trade organizations. Chapter 25, "The hegemony of men in global value chains: insights for intersectional labour governance", by Lauren McCarthy, Vivek Soundararajan and Scott Taylor, problematizes substandard labour practices in global value chains (GVCs), even in contexts with strong legal frameworks and where ethical accreditation schemes exist. They attribute these poor labour relations practices in part to the insufficient attention paid to the interplay of men, masculinities and GVC operations. They highlight the need to recognize the social category of "men" with its material and discursive effects on GVCs and to take an intersectional perspective to improve governance mechanisms in GVCs.

This is followed by a theoretical engagement with crises. Following an introductory framing text by Anika Thym, Chapter 26, "Multiple crisis, crisis of gender relations and crisis of masculinity", by Alex Demirović and Andrea Maihofer, offers a social theoretical framework to understand the constitutive connection as well as specific logic and relative autonomy of the different crises. Rather than intersectionality, they suggest using the term multidimensionality to conceptualize the interconnectedness of relations of power and domination therein. The authors highlight the familial sphere and men's subjectivities as important sites of change. From this perspective, they state and elaborate on the ongoing crisis of masculinity, which questions core aspects of bourgeois masculinity.

The subsequent chapters in Part IV deal with themes and highlight specific issues which are likely to become increasingly relevant to organizational dynamics and processes in the (near) future. The first two of these deal with violences. The issue of men's violence against women remains a key ongoing and future issue to be tackled both practically and theoretically, including in organizational contexts. In Chapter 27, titled "Allyship and accountability in organizations engaging men in violence prevention: principles, practices and political dilemmas", Bob Pease considers questions of men's allyship and accountability to women in organizations engaging men in violence prevention. The chapter examines personal, interpersonal and organizational forms of accountability, various models of accountability and ways to implement them. The author discusses several political dilemmas related to men's allyship in the context of men's violence prevention efforts, such as decisions about which strand of feminism to engage with and how to deal with social divisions between men in violence prevention efforts. Pease suggests that for this anti-violence work to succeed, men must move beyond dominant forms of masculinity, to embrace greater humility.

The global ecological crisis, and notably climate change, has brought increasing critical attention to humanity's exploitative relationship with the more-than-human world. In response to current violent and unsustainable ways of relating to other species and ecosystems, social movements and activisms to reimagine these relationships are becoming increasingly vocal and visible. In Chapter 28, "Men and masculinities in animal advocacy organizations and organizing: from men's domination and masculinized strategies towards an ethics of care and intersectional activism", Kadri Aavik focuses on animal advocacy organizations and organizing, examining how men and masculinities figure in these gendered sites and processes. She argues for the importance of moving beyond masculinized values and strategies that have shaped the movement and its exclusions, towards intersectional activism and building alliances with other progressive social movements. Finally, the chapter considers the potential of vegan men and masculinities in developing less exploitative human–animal relations and more sustainable masculinities.

Given the significance of men and masculinities in the now ubiquitous technologization of society and predominance of global capitalism, men's practices and masculinities in these spheres continue to shape gendered and other power relations on global and local scales. In Chapter 29, titled "Tracing the superheroes of our time: contemporary and emergent masculinities in tech entrepreneurship", Ulf Mellström, Dag Balkmar and Anne-Charlott Callerstig examine masculinity in relation to technology, entrepreneurship and organizations in these areas. The chapter discusses how masculinity features in the configuration of tech entrepreneurship and the predominance of this masculinity in cultural representations. The authors consider the intersection of gender with race in the construction of a hegemonic geek masculinity.

The recent global COVID-19 pandemic can be considered a manifestation of various social and ecological crises that humanity has brought upon itself. Notably, in large part, many unsustainable practices of privileged white Western men and hegemonic masculinities can be identified as the originators of these crises. In Chapter 30, "Men and COVID-19: pandemics and organizing in the 'new normal'", focusing on organizing in the context of pandemics, Stephen Burrell and Sandy Ruxton draw connections between men, masculinities and the COVID-19 crises, underscoring how gender has shaped both the crisis and efforts to mitigate it in three sites of organizing – work, governmentality and social movements. The authors argue for an intersectional approach to understanding and responding to COVID-19 and future pandemics as sites of reconfiguration of social norms.

***

Finally, we need to highlight how men, masculinities, organizations and organizing are themselves intensely relevant for understanding, and critiquing, the activities of research and academia, and indeed writing and authorship (Hearn, 2020). Men's contribution to academic knowledge production is frequently elevated over women's through dominant authorial and citational practices. For instance, men are more likely to refer to the work of other male scholars (Dion et al., 2018) and cite their own work 70% more than women (King et al., 2017). These practices produce and exacerbate "gender gaps" in academic knowledge production, or more specifically, what are known as the "Matthew effect" (men's contributions to a research field are considered the most prominent) and the "Matilda effect" (women's work is regarded as less valuable or even attributed to originate with men) (see Dion et al., 2018). Taking the insights of critical studies of men, masculinities, organizations and organizing to the heart of academia and knowledge production would indeed be transformative not just for research, publishing, universities and higher education but for the planet.

Notes

1 On men, masculinities and militarism, see Aktaş et al. (Chapter 19), this volume.
2 On the links between men, masculinities and sustainability, see Aavik (Chapter 28), this volume.
3 On global concentrations and inequalities, see Hearn (Chapter 8), this volume.
4 On the term multidimensionality as an alternative for intersectionality, see Demirović and Maihofer (Chapter 26), this volume.
5 On media and technology, see Mellström et al. (Chapter 29), this volume.

References

Aavik, K. (2015). *Intersectional Disadvantage and Privilege in the Estonian Labour Market: An Analysis of Work Narratives of Russian-speaking Women and Estonian Men*. PhD dissertation, Tallinn University, Tallinn.

Aavik, K., Bland, C., Hoegaerts, J., & Salminen, J. (2020). *Men, Masculinities and the Modern Career. Contemporary and Historical Perspectives*. Oldenbourg: De Gruyter.

Acker, J. (2006). Inequality regimes: Gender, class, and race in organizations. *Gender & Society*, *20*(4), 441–464. doi: 10.1177/0891243206289499

Allison, A. (1994). *Nightwork: Sexuality, Pleasure, and Corporate Masculinity in a Tokyo Hostess Club*. Chicago: University of Chicago Press.

Ashcraft, K. L. (2022). *Wronged and Dangerous: Viral Masculinity and the Populist Pandemic*. Bristol: Bristol University Press.

Aultman, B. L. (2019). Nonbinary trans identities. In D. Haider-Markel (Ed.), *The Oxford Encyclopedia of LGBT Politics and Policy* (p. 23). New York: Oxford University Press. doi: 10.1093/acrefore/9780190228637.013.1195

Barrett, F. (1996). The organizational construction of hegemonic masculinity: The case of the U.S. Navy. *Gender, Work and Organization*, *3*(3), 129–142. doi: 10.1177/0891243205278639

Berdahl, J. L., Cooper, M., Glick, P., Livingston, R. W., & Williams, J. C. (Eds.). (2018). Work as a masculinity contest. Special issue. *Journal of Social Issues*, *74*(3).

Biese, I. (2021). *Men Do It Too: Opting Out and In*. Oldenbourg: de Gruyter.

Bilge, S. (2013). Intersectionality undone: Saving intersectionality from feminist intersectionality studies. *Du Bois Review: Social Science Research on Race*, *10*(2), 405–424. doi: 10.1017/S1742058X13000283

Blomberg, J. (2009). Gendering finance: Masculinities and hierarchies at the Stockholm stock exchange. *Organization*, *16*(2), 203–225. doi: 10.1177/1350508408100475

Bologh, R. W. (1990). *Love or Greatness: Max Weber and Masculine Thinking. Feminist Inquiry*. London: Unwin Hyman.

Bridges, T., & Pascoe, C. J. (2014). Hybrid masculinities: New directions in the sociology of men and masculinities. *Sociology Compass*, *8*(3), 246–258. doi: 10.1111/soc4.12134

Carrington, D. (2023). Revealed: 1,000 super-emitting Methane leaks Risk Triggering Climate Tipping Points. Retrieved 6 March, from The Guardian: www.theguardian.com/environment/2023/mar/06/revealed-1000-super-emitting-methane-leaks-risk-triggering-climate-tipping-points?CMP=share_btn_link

CNN Money (2021). Fortune 500: 1960 Archive Full List 1–100. Retrieved 13 February 2023, from https://money.cnn.com/magazines/fortune/fortune500_archive/full/1960/

Cockburn, C. K. (1983). *Brothers*. London: Pluto Press.

Collins, P. H. (2008). *Black Feminist thought: Knowledge, Consciousness, and the Politics of Empowerment*. New York: Routledge.

Collins, P. H., & Bilge, S. (2020). *Intersectionality*. New York: Wiley.

Collinson, D. L. (1992). *Managing the Shopfloor: Subjectivity, Masculinity and Workplace Culture*. Berlin: Walter de Gruyter.

Collinson, D. L. (1999). Surviving the rigs: Safety and surveillance on North Sea oil installations. *Organization Studies*, *20*(4), 579–600. doi: 10.1177/0170840699204003.

Collinson, D. L., & Collinson, M. (1997). Delayering managers, time space surveillance and its gendered effects. *Organization*, *4*(3), 373–405. doi: 10.1177/135050849743005

Collinson, D. L., & Hearn, J. (1994). Naming men as men: Implications for work, organizations and management. *Gender, Work and Organization*, *1*(1), 2–22. doi: 10.1111/j.1468-0432.1994.tb00002.x

Collinson, D. L., & Hearn, J. (1995). Men managing leadership? 'Men and Women of the Corporation' revisited. *International Review of Women and Leadership*, *1*(2), 1–24.

Collinson, D. L., & Hearn, J. (Eds.). (1996). *Men as Managers, Managers as Men: Critical Perspectives on Men, Masculinities and Managements*. London: Sage.

Collinson, D. L., & Hearn, J. (2005). Men and masculinities in work, organizations and management. In M. Kimmel, J. Hearn & R. W. Connell (Eds.), *Handbook of Studies on Men and Masculinities* (pp. 289–310). Thousand Oaks, CA: Sage.

Collinson, D. L., & Hearn, J. (2014). Taking the obvious apart: Men, masculinities and the dynamics of gendered leadership. In R. J. Burke & D. A. Major (Eds.), *Gender in Organizations: Are Men Allies or Adversaries to Women's Career Advancement?* (pp. 73–92). Cheltenham: Edward Elgar Press.

Collinson, D. L., Knights, D., & Collinson, M. (1990). *Managing to Discriminate*. London: Routledge.

Collinson, M., & Collinson, D. L. (1989). Sexuality in the workplace: The domination of men's sexuality. In J. Hearn, D. Sheppard, P. Tancred-Sheriff & G. Burrell (Eds.), *The Sexuality of Organization* (pp. 91–109). London: Sage.

Collinson, M., & Collinson, D. L. (1996). It's only Dick: The sexual harassment of women managers in insurance sales. *Work, Employment and Society*, *10*(1), 29–56. doi: 10.1177/0950017096101002

Connell, R. (1987). *Gender and Power*. Sydney: Allen and Unwin.

Connell, R., & Messerschmidt, J. W. (2005). Hegemonic masculinity: Rethinking the concept. *Gender and Society*, *19*(6), 829–859. doi: 10.1177/0891243205278639

Connell, R., & Wood, J. (2005). Globalization and business masculinities. *Men and Masculinities, 7*(4), 347–364. doi: 10.1177/1097184X03260969

Cornwall, A., Karioris, F. G., & Lindisfarne, N. (Eds.). (2016). *Masculinities under Neoliberalism.* London: Zed.

Crenshaw, K. (1989). Demarginalizing the intersection of race and sex: A Black feminist critique of antidiscrimination doctrine, feminist theory and antiracist politics. *University of Chicago Legal Forum, 1989*(1), 139–167. doi: http://chicagounbound.uchicago.edu/uclf/vol1989/iss1/8

Dion, M. L., Sumner, J. L., & Mitchell, S. M. (2018). Gendered citation patterns across political science and social science methodology fields. *Political Analysis, 26*(3), 312–327. doi: 10.1017/pan.2018.12

Garlick, S. (2020). The nature of markets: On the affinity between masculinity and (neo)liberalism. *Journal of Cultural Economy, 13*(5), 548–560. doi: /10.1080/17530350.2020.1741017

Hearn, J. (1989). Leading questions for men: Men's leadership, feminist challenges and men's responses. *Equal Opportunities International, 8*(1), 3–11. doi: 10.1108/eb010495

Hearn, J. (1992). *Men in the Public Eye: The Construction and Deconstruction of Public Men and Public Patriarchies.* London: Routledge.

Hearn, J. (1997). The implications of critical studies on men. *NORA – Nordic Journal of Feminist and Gender Research, 5*(1), 48–60. doi: 10.1080/08038740.1997.9959706

Hearn, J. (2015). *Men of the World: Genders, Globalizations, Transnational Times.* London: Sage.

Hearn, J. (2020). Men and masculinities in academe: Extending gender-sensitive perspectives, processes, policies and practices. In E. Drew & S. Canavan (Eds.), *The Gender-Sensitive University: A Contradiction in Terms* (pp. 97–109). London: Routledge.

Hearn, J., & Collinson, D. L. (2006). Men, masculinities and workplace diversity/diversion: Power, intersections and contradictions. In A. Konrad, P. Prasad & J. Pringle (Eds.), *Handbook of Workplace Diversity* (pp. 299–322). London: Sage.

Hearn, J., & Collinson, D. L. (2009). Men, diversity at work, and diversity management. In M. Özbilgin (Ed.), *Equality, Diversity and Inclusion at Work: A Research Companion* (pp. 383–398). Cheltenham: Edward Elgar.

Hearn, J., & Louvrier, J. (2015). Theories of difference, diversity, and intersectionality: What do they bring to diversity management? In R. Bendl, I. Bleijenbergh, E. Henttonen & A. J. Mills (Eds.), *The Oxford Handbook of Diversity in Organizations* (pp. 1–27). Oxford: Oxford University Press. doi: 10.1093/oxfordhb/9780199679805.013.28

Hearn, J., & Niemistö, C. (2012). Men, 'father managers' and home-work relations: Complexities and contradictions in national policy corporations and individual lives. In P. McDonald & E. Jeanes (Eds.), *Men, Wage Work and Family* (pp. 95–113). Abingdon: Routledge.

Ho, K. (2009). *Liquidated: An Ethnography of Wall Street.* Durham: Duke University Press.

Kanter, R. M. (1977). *Men and Women of the Corporation.* New York: Basic.

Kanter, R. M. (1993). *Men and Women of the Corporation*, 2nd edition. New York: Basic.

KellyOCG. (2022). Re:work Calibrating to Power the Life-work Shift. Retrieved 27 September 2022, from KellyOCG Global Workforce Report 2022: www.kellyocg.com/insights/featured-content/whitepapers/rework-calibrating-to-power-the-life-work-shift/

Kerfoot, D., & Knights, D. (1993). Management, manipulation and masculinity: From paternalism to corporate strategy in financial services in Britain. *Journal of Management Studies, 30*(4), 659–677. doi: 10.1111/j.1467-6486.1993.tb00320.x

Kerfoot, D., & Whitehead, S. (2000). Keeping all the balls in the air: Further education and the masculine/managerial subject. *Journal of Further and Higher Education, 24*(2), 183–201.

King, M. M., Bergstrom, C. T., Correll, S. J., Jacquet, J., & West, J. D. (2017). Men set their own cites high: Gender and self-citation across fields and over time. *Socius, 3*, 2378023117738903. doi: 10.1177/2378023117738903Knights, D. (2022). *Leadership, Gender and Ethics: Embodied Reason in Challenging Masculinities.* London: Routledge.

Knights, D., & Tullberg, M. (2014). Masculinity in the financial sector. In S. Kumra, R. Simpson & R. J. Burke (Eds.), *The Handbook of Gender in Organizations* (pp. 499–518). Oxford: Oxford University Press.

Köllen, T. (Ed.). (2016). *Sexual Orientation and Transgender Issues in Organizations: Global Perspectives on LGBT Workforce Diversity.* New York: Springer.

Kűhne, K., Bartsch, N., Tate, R. D., Higson, J., & Habet, A. (2022). "Carbon bombs" – Mapping key fossil fuel projects. *Energy Policy, 166*, 112950. doi: 10.1016/j.enpol.2022.112950

Little, B., & Winch, A. (2021). *The New Patriarchs of Digital Capitalism: Celebrity Tech Founders and Networks of Power*. London: Routledge.

Liu, H. (2021). *Redeeming Leadership*. Bristol: Bristol University Press.

Lui, H. (2017). The masculinisation of ethical leadership dis/embodiment. *Journal of Business Ethics, 144*(2), 263–278. doi: 10.1007/s10551-015-2831-x

Luyt, R., & Starck, K. (Eds.). (2020). *Masculine Power and Gender Equality: Political Masculinities as Agents of Change*. Berlin: Springer.

Maier, M., & Messerschmidt, J. W. (1998). Commonalities, conflicts and contradictions in organizational masculinities: Exploring the gendered genesis of the challenger disaster. *Canadian Review of Sociology and Anthropology, 35*(3), 325–344. doi: 10.1111/j.1755-618x.1998.tb00726.x

McCabe, D., & Knights, D. (2016). Learning to listen? Exploring discourses and images of masculine leadership through corporate videos. *Management Learning, 47*(2), 179–198. doi: 10.1177/1350507615586334

McCarthy, L., Soundararajan, V., & Taylor, S. (2021). The hegemony of men in global value chains: Why it matters for labour governance. *Human Relations, 74*(12), 2051–2074. doi: 10.1177/0018726720950816

Mellström, U., & Pease, B. (Eds.). (2023). *Beyond Anthropocentric Masculinities: Posthumanism, New Materialism and the Man Question*. London: Routledge.

Messerschmidt, J. W. (1995). Managing to kill: Masculinities and the space shuttle challenger explosion. *Masculinities, 3*(4), 1–22. doi: 10.1177/0891243205278639

Metcalf, A., & Humphries, M. (Eds.). (1985). *The Sexuality of Men*. London: Pluto.

Meyer, K. (2017). *Theorien der Intersektionalität zur Einführung*. Hamburg: Junius Hamburg.

Morgan, D. H. J. (1996). The gender of bureaucracy. In D. L. Collinson & J. Hearn (Eds.), *Men as Managers, Managers as Men: Critical Perspectives on Men, Masculinities and Managements* (pp. 43–60). London: Sage.

Murphy, A., & Contreras, I. (2022, December 5). The Global 2000 2022. Retrieved 13 February 2023, from Forbes website: www.forbes.com/lists/global2000/

Nash, J. (2019). *Black Feminism Reimagined after Intersectionality*. Durham: Duke University Press.

Payne, J. (2018). Manufacturing masculinity: Exploring gender and workplace surveillance. *Work and Occupations, 45*(3), 346–383. doi: 10.1177/0730888418780969

Pini, B., & Pease, B. (Eds.). (2013). *Men, Masculinities and Methodologies*. London: Palgrave Macmillan.

Puar, J. K. (2012). 'I would Rather be a Cyborg than a Goddess'. Becoming-intersectional in Assemblage Theory. Retrieved 14 February 2023, from Transversal Texts website: https://transversal.at/transversal/0811/puar/en

Pulé, P. M. H., & Hultman, M. (Eds.). (2021). *Men, Masculinities, and Earth*. Berlin: Springer.

Reis, C. (2004). *Men Managers in a European Multinational Company*. Mering: Rainer Humpp Verlag.

Rommelspacher, B. (2009). Intersektionalität – Über die Wechselwirkung von Machtverhältnissen. In I. Kurz-Scherf, J. Lepperhoff & A. Scheele (Eds.), *Feminismus: Kritik und Intervention* (pp. 81–96). Münster: Westfälisches Dampfboot.

Roper, M. (1994). *Masculinity and the British Organization Man since 1945*. Oxford: Oxford University Press.

Roper, M. (1996). 'Seduction and succession': Homosocial circuits of desire in management. In D. L. Collinson & J. Hearn (Eds.), *Men as Managers, Managers as Men: Critical Perspectives on Men, Masculinities and Managements* (pp. 210–226). London: Sage.

Smith, D. E. (1990). *Texts, Facts and Femininity: Exploring the Relations of Ruling*. London: Routledge.

Sugiura, L. (2021). *The Incel Rebellion: The Rise of the Manosphere and the Virtual War against Women*. Bingley: Emerald.

Thym, A. (2019). Hegemony self-critique: How men in finance question aspects of masculine and economic hegemony from within. In J. Hearn, E. Vasquez del Aquila & M. Hughson (Eds.), *Unsustainable Institutions of Men: Transnational Dispersed Centres, Gender Power, Contradictions* (pp. 71–86). New York: Routledge.

Thym, A. (2020). Men in finance for emancipatory social change? In R. Luyt & K. Starck (Eds.), *Masculine Power and Gender Equality: Masculinities as Change Agents* (pp. 81–88). Cham: Springer.

Tienari, J., Vaara, E., & Meriläinen, S. (2010). Becoming an international man: Top manager masculinities in the making of a multinational corporation. *Equal Opportunities International, 29*(1), 38–52.
United Nations. (2020, January 21). Rising Inequality Affecting More than Two-thirds of the Globe, but it's Not Inevitable: New UN Report. Retrieved 13 February 2023, from UN News website: https://news.un.org/en/story/2020/01/1055681
Vannini, P. (Ed.) (2015). *Non-Representational Methodologies: Re-envisioning Research.* New York: Routledge.
Viveros Vigoya, M. (2023). The colors of masculinity: Experiences of power and intersectionality in Nuestra América. *Men and Masculinities.* doi: 1097184X231151824.
Wajcman, J. (1998). *Managing like a Man: Women and Men in Corporate Management.* Cambridge: Polity.
Walgenbach, K. (2007). Gender als interdependente Kategorie. In K. Walgenbach, G. Dietze, A. Hornscheidt & K. Palm (Eds.). *Gender als interdependente Kategorie. Neue Perspektiven auf Intersektionalität, Diversität und Heterogenität* (pp. 23–64). Opladen: B. Budrich.
Whyte, W. H. (1956). *The Organization Man.* New York: Simon & Schuster.
Wolfman, G., Hearn, J., & Yeadon-Lee, T. (2021). Hollow femininities: The emerging faces of neoliberal masculinities. *NORMA: International Journal for Masculinity Studies, 16*(4), 217–234. doi: 10.1080/18902138.2021.1996829
Zaloom, C. (2006). *Out of the Pits: Traders and Technology from Chicago to London.* Chicago: University of Chicago Press.
Zuboff, S. (2019). *The Age of Surveillance Capitalism: The Fight for a Human Future at the New Frontier of Power.* New York: Simon & Schuster.

PART I

Theories and frameworks

2

NEW MAPS OF STRUGGLE FOR GENDER JUSTICE

Locating men, masculinities and organizations in feminist research on organizations and work[1]

Raewyn Connell

Introduction

Studies on men, masculinities, organizations and organizing need to be located within broader feminist, gender, queer and postcolonial scholarship and activism on organizations and organizing. This chapter places studies on men, masculinities, organizations and organizing within an agenda of feminist research, relevant to the new circumstances and the continuing struggles for gender equality.

Gender studies has changed much over the last 30 years, especially with growing recognition of feminist thought and activism in the Global South. There have been changes in the object of knowledge, for example, work and organization, especially managerial transformation of organizations and global economic restructuring. There are related changes in the political arena, most recently the rise of an authoritarian populism with new patterns of masculinity politics.

Looking back more than 30 years, Joan Acker's famous article "Hierarchies, jobs, bodies: A theory of gendered organizations" (1990) had been published in the United States. Activists, scholars and femocrats such as Clare Burton (see Burton et al., 1987) in Australia had accumulated experience, not just of equal pay campaigns but also of equal worth and anti-discrimination struggles. Even the US government had just set up its "Glass Ceiling Commission", mandated by a 1991 Act of Congress to investigate barriers to the advancement of women and minorities to managerial positions in the business world (Federal Glass Ceiling Commission, 1995).

Women's movements in many countries were gearing up for the next United Nations World Conference on Women, to be held in Beijing in 1995. From that preparation came new gender-equality research initiatives, such as the continent-wide ICC (*Indice de compromiso cumplido*, Index of achieved commitments) in South America (Grupo Iniciativa Mujeres, 2002; Valdés, 2001). The massive World Conference itself linked feminist groups globally and produced the Beijing Declaration and Platform for Action, to which most governments around the world signed up.

What we didn't recognize at that time was that a second wave of market-dominated politics was rising. India had just begun its turn towards a market regime; European social-democratic

DOI: 10.4324/9781003193579-3

parties under Blair and Schröder now moved fast in the same direction; the Clinton presidency set about abolishing "welfare as we know it" in the United States. At the same time, the women's-liberation model of politics, including the portfolio of affirmative-action and anti-discrimination gender reforms in organizations, was coming under unexpected challenge – from changes in gender theory itself, and from social movements. To understand our current possibilities, we must consider the changes over the last 30 years in gender analysis, organizational life and the political arena.

Changes in gender studies

The field of research, teaching and intellectual debate that was one of the main legacies of the new feminism had already changed a lot and continued to change. New fields of research expanded; theoretical languages changed; and a project that had been launched in elite institutions of the Global North met sharp challenges from the wider world and became a complex of regional projects taking different shapes.

Women's Studies was launched as a critique of men's domination of academic life, the masculinity of curricula and canons, and the way women's experience was excluded from almost all academic disciplines. There was every reason for this critique. I have just been re-reading an important book of literary criticism published in the 1960s.[2] It is astonishing *now* to see how totally the world of literature in the author's mind then was occupied by Men, and only Men, from Homer to Horace to Heine to Hemingway. The book has a short essay on Sylvia Plath, putting her firmly in her place as a talented minor poet; elsewhere there is one reference to Sappho, who is declared "shrill". The rest of the whole heavy book is Men, who evidently were assumed to make all the cultural statements that really matter.

Understandably, then, the feminist impulse was to declare that we too exist and matter and to document in enormous detail the enormous world of women's writing and filmmaking, women's culture, women's bodies and women's relationships. That is still worth doing, because the patriarchy has not withered away.

But to fill out the picture of the "gender relations" and the "organization of gender" that Knights and Rubery (1994, p. 1) invoked in launching the journal, *Gender, Work & Organization* in 1994, it was necessary also to *study up*, to look at the holders of power and privilege. During the 1980s, a research focus on men and masculinities was developing in several countries, and from the 1990s it was active on a world scale (e.g. Tomsen & Donaldson, 2003). The very first issue of *Gender, Work and Organization* opened with a notable paper from this movement: Collinson and Hearn's (1994) "Naming men as men: Implications for work, organization and management". As this title shows, research and theory about men and masculinities very quickly turned to practical applications. The new knowledge was applied not just in organizational life but also in anti-violence programmes, in education, in counselling, in health professions, and more.

Gender studies has broadened in other directions, too. The curiously linked problems of technology and embodiment – metal and flesh – have yielded very creative work. Since I'm citing Australian researchers, I can't resist mentioning the enormous contribution to studies of organizations and technologies by Judy Wajcman, including her splendid manifesto *TechnoFeminism* (2004). Studies of embodiment steadily moved beyond the old "nature vs. nurture" arguments that were central for feminism in the 1960s and 1970s, towards models of the co-construction of the biological and the social (Roberts, 2000). Research on embodiment blends into studies of sexuality, of sport, of child development, of health and of body modification, and in all these areas feminist-influenced research has expanded.

These areas were not just accumulations of empirical research. They were strongly influenced by changes in theory that were happening at the time. Feminism in the humanities and social sciences was already impacted by post-structuralist and deconstructionist thought. Much of this in the 1980s consisted of more or less direct applications of the French masters, notably Foucault, Derrida and Lacan, to troublesome problems about gender.

But in time the impulse was transformed into new agendas of research and practice. An excellent example is work in policy studies – once a peculiarly boring sub-field of political science. Through the 1990s, in texts such as *The Politics of Affirmative Action* (1996), Carol Bacchi turned this field into a subtle exploration of the policymakers' presuppositions and the way the world was imagined and represented in political discourse.

Even more influential was the convergence, in the United States, of post-structuralist thought and sexual politics that produced queer studies and, a recent offshoot, trans studies. This is easily misinterpreted, since so much of the practical work of the movements takes the shape of identity politics, that is, mobilizations around a shared self-image, being or experience. That infuriating and incoherent acronym LGBT, invented as a euphemism in US homosexual politics, makes the point even without the additional TTIQQ. For what are T, L and G here except the names of identity groups, assembled in a tactical alliance that has become strangely reified? So it is worth recalling that the subtitle of *Gender Trouble* (1990) was *Feminism and the Subversion of Identity*. Poor Judith Butler has been reminding people of that "subversion" ever since.

The popular version of her argument is the claim that gender and sexuality are fluid, or at least very multiple, with lots of variants and fragments. Documenting the variants and fragments has become a whole genre of qualitative research in gender studies, a popular topic for PhD dissertations. Curiously, this version of deconstructive feminism has been picked up by feminism's opponents, especially in the Catholic Church (Garbagnoli & Prearo, 2017). They have mobilized against "gender theory", the term right-wing publicists use to designate the idea of fluid identities and negotiable relationships. This has already had toxic political effects in several countries.

To my mind, the most important change in the field of gender studies has happened outside the United States and Europe. It is the growing presence and influence of feminist thought, practice and research from the postcolonial world. Sixteen years ago, it was still possible to publish a book about feminist theory that mentioned no theorists outside the Global North, except a few White feminists in Australia. It wasn't very credible then, and I wish it were impossible now. Unfortunately, I have read a new book on queer and trans theory that selects in the same way – for good measure, omitting the Australians as well.

Academic work in a global economy of knowledge centred on the elite institutions of the Global North, which produce the prestigious frameworks, theories and methodology. The postcolonial world, where most humans live, functions in this economy as a vast data mine, which ships the raw material of information to the North and receives processed disciplinary knowledge in return. This is as true of gender studies as it is of botany, geology or climate science. European and North American writing about gender has been replete with historical, ethnographic, mythic, literary, medical, sexological and political detail that has come from the colonized world. But not theory. In the mainstream economy of knowledge, the majority world is not expected to produce theory. Hence, the geography of the theoretical reviews is just mentioned.

This is not a reflection of reality; it is an effect of power, controlling recognition and circulation of knowledge. Actually, theories, methods, interpretations, concepts and world outlooks *are* produced around the Global South – and always have been. Indigenous knowledges, alternative universalisms (such as Islamic science and jurisprudence), Southern theory arising from the colonial encounter and informal local knowledges contain a wealth of ideas about gender. Some concern matters usually overlooked in Northern theory, such as the land, colonization itself and postcolonial gender orders. Some provide alternative perspectives on familiar matters, such as embodiment, sexuality, children, personhood, family relations and violence. Seeing multiple knowledge formations reveals a wealth of ideas that can enrich the whole field of gender analysis.

I have written about this elsewhere (Connell, 2014, 2015), so I won't labour the point. Recognizing multiple knowledge formations raises the question of how, indeed whether, they can be connected. Chilla Bulbeck's *Re-orienting Western Feminisms* (1998) argues that they can, and Wendy Harcourt's *Body Politics in Development* (2009) explores the complications involved in making connections through political practice. The legacy of colonial domination and contemporary world inequality make these projects difficult. Bulbeck speaks of "braiding at the borders" to suggest the delicacy of the task.

Changes in the object of knowledge

The feminist project assumes that gender relations in the realm of work and organizations can be changed. But other dynamics too have been at work. The most discussed, I think, have been the deepening impact of neoliberal market politics, and the "third industrial revolution" of information technology. In the first wave of neoliberal restructuring, attention was focused on dismantling, or at least weakening, the state's regulatory machinery – currency controls, regulation of banks, economic planning, tariffs and so on. In the second wave of neoliberal restructuring from the 1990s, more attention was given to changing the character of the state itself: commodifying its services, outsourcing its functions to profit-driven companies and reshaping public-sector organizations on a corporate model. The classic bureaucratic elite, risen from the ranks, was increasingly replaced by generic managers, often brought from outside, on contracts with bonuses for achieving goals. In-house research units were replaced by contracts with market research firms and management consultants. This did not mean a loosening of control. Indeed, management became more intrusive, through electronic surveillance and above all the extraordinary expansion of "audit" mechanisms, performance indicators and institutionalized distrust (Power, 1999).

What has happened in government departments has also been happening in civil society and independent public-sector institutions such as universities. Academics are all too familiar with this process, and there are some excellent organizational ethnographies of the ruthless corporatization of public universities (e.g. Tuchman, 2009). What the label "corporate" does not fully catch is the resulting change in labour markets. There has been a striking shift in higher education from a permanent labour force to a highly insecure one. The majority of undergraduate teaching in Australian universities is now done by insecure workers on short-term contracts. Even this damaged public sector is increasingly outweighed, on a world scale. In Brazil, a large majority of higher education students are now in private universities and colleges, and in India about half. Most of these institutions are for-profit; effectively, they are vocational training companies.

Some private universities are now transnational corporations in their own right and so have joined the dominant form of economic organization in our time. Transnational corporations (TNCs) are not simply an expanded version of the tightly integrated manufacturing behemoths of the Global North – U. S. Steel, Ford and so forth – that provide our main images of monopoly capitalism. They are hybrid, and in some respects decentralized, institutions. How they work is illuminated by Juanita Elias' (2008) study of the garment sector in Malaysia. Factory management is done by local men who deploy family networks and political connections, and sustain an ideology of docile, productive femininity for their workers. Overall investment and international trade are in the hands of elite managers, who come from outside Malaysia and whose working world is very different. At this level, the TNC is tied into global finance markets, to retailers and media in the Global North, and to the powerful states that subsidize, tax or restrict their operations.

The transnational managers are a key power group on a world scale, though not the only one. Almost all of them are men. They embody a strongly masculinized culture, though one serviced by women. They travel frequently, living in a climate-controlled environment of hotels, airports and offices. Their labour process is deeply enmeshed with digital technology. They are constantly on the iPhone or the computer, they are linked to databases and audit mechanisms, they follow templates for business operations that are embedded in the corporate intranet, and their work is immediately visible to higher management. The social controls here are fierce. And the pay-off has become very large. CEO packages at big corporations in the United States in 2016 were calculated to be more than 250 times the income of typical workers (Mishel & Schieder, 2017).

It is familiar that the turn to neoliberal market politics has been accompanied by an enormous growth of finance capital. Perhaps less recognized is the enormous expansion of international trade. Consider the volume and value of bulk shipments of oil from the Gulf, coal from Australia, garments from China, electronic components from Southeast Asia, cars from Korea, fruit from Chile, soya beans from Brazil and so on. Trade expansion, in fact, has driven the neoliberal turn across the Global South, as local ruling classes abandoned import-replacement industrialization for a search for comparative advantage in global markets (Connell & Dados, 2014). Both finance and trade have supported a process in which global power has moved away from the territorial containers where it used to be located, that is, the nation-states of the Global North, into transnational spaces.

The restless movement of TNC executives around the world is accompanied by strange migrations of profit, as the firms use transfer pricing and other devices to evade tax and conceal their operations. How much corporate wealth ends up in tax havens is very hard to judge but the Panama Papers and other disclosures suggest it is a lot. The intricate, layered and shifting structure of corporate organization today is partly designed to be opaque. But it also partly reflects what information technology been doing in markets, businesses and states. There are now very important businesses that do not just depend on corporate intranets but operate through an Internet platform with very large numbers of users, and a proprietary and secret algorithm that governs it. Nick Srnicek in *Platform Capitalism* (2017) warns against seeing these firms as inevitably devouring the world – there is instability in many of them – but there is no doubt of their importance.

They imply a strange division in organizational life. On the one hand, it is an enormous amount of labour being done online, by masses of people who are unpaid. These are the "users" who supply content to the platforms, yielding the data which the firms monetize. On the other hand, they are the dark satanic mills that produce the equipment the Internet economy needs. Where there is Apple, there is also Foxconn – the huge manufacturer of iPhones and more, whose fiercely authoritarian operations have driven some Chinese workers to suicide (Qiu, 2016). Here, the division of organizational forms is drawn between two large corporations, each depending on the other. The gender dimensions of these new forms of organization are still working out. However, it is clear already that the masculinization of corporate management has been little disturbed by the advent of large Chinese or Indian firms, the offshoring of global power or the new technologies. It seems we are confronted with new forms of patriarchal power rather than a gender revolution.

Changes in the political arena

By the time the journal, *Gender, Work and Organization*, was launched in the mid-1990s, the women's liberation movement, gay liberation, the student movement and the counterculture of the 1960s and 1970s were well over. Though there has been talk of third-wave and even fourth-wave feminism, no mobilization comparable in depth or continuity has occurred since. Feminism has continued in other ways. I think the metaphor of "waves" is not very helpful. We might think, rather, of changes in form, and the co-existence of different pathways, as the political environment has changed.

Changes in form include striking innovations, such as the emergence of digital feminism. The Internet is used as a means of research and documentation, as a site for cultural expression, as a powerful organizing tool, or for all of these at once. For a splendid example, look at the website of the Bolivian feminist group, Mujeres Creando (*www.mujerescreando.org/*). The anti-harassment movement of 2017–18 spread far and fast via the #MeToo hashtag on social media. Anti-feminist groups also use the Internet extensively, as we see in the hostile trolling that so many women experience online.

Since the 1970s, another current of feminism has followed the long march through the institutions. Australia was perhaps the birthplace of the "femocrat" strategy, certainly one of the pioneers. Feminists worked inside the state bureaucracy to institute equal opportunity and anti-discrimination policies, fund women's health centres, defend employment rights, develop non-sexist curricula for schools and mount anti-violence programmes, as Hester Eisenstein narrates in her admirable *Inside Agitators* (1996). This pathway narrowed as the market agenda took control and was effectively blocked in Australia by right-wing governments in the new century. In other parts of the world, it has remained open. Prominent examples are UN Women and its related agencies, and the European Union with its gender-equality measures.

Most policy work is now done, not by feminists within the state but by non-governmental organizations. There has been angst about the NGO-ization of feminism, the replacement of social movements by non-profits. The issue is a real one. Like public-sector organizations, NGOs have been subjected to managerialism and audit regimes, and they are very vulnerable to authoritarian governments. But at this point they are the prevalent form of organized gender politics. Groups like DAWN (Development Alternatives with Women for a New Era, founded as far back as 1984) operate in transnational spaces, which on the aforementioned argument is vital for feminism now (Moghadam, 2005).

There are doubtless thousands of NGOs working on gender issues, if you add them up: in research, health services, lobbying, media, counselling, public advocacy, education and more. The international network of profeminist men's groups, MenEngage Alliance (www.menengage.org), which works on violence prevention and changing attitudes among men, claims 600 or 700 affiliates. There is impressive creativity in the NGO terrain.

One cannot say, however, that this form of activism has generated a particular kind of *theory*, in the way women's liberation generated radical feminism and socialist feminism, and a later generation produced queer theory and trans feminism. Most NGOs I know of, and most contemporary public-sector agencies concerned with gender issues, seem to work comfortably with a loose liberal feminism. That is to say, they presume a simple dichotomy between women and men; they celebrate the advancement of individual women into management and political office; their rhetoric centres on the idea of equal rights; they hope for, and sometimes work for, a change in men's attitudes. "Women's rights are human rights" is a familiar principle – as if human rights were unassailable.

These ideas have practical value. They justify funding for women's health services, equal educational provision for girls, anti-discrimination measures and campaigns against domestic violence. But they do not address gross economic disparities, and they do not give much grip on the new power structures of transnational corporate management. And in the face of the masculinity politics represented by Putin, Duterte, Orban, Trump, Temer, Sisi, Erdoğan, Modi and Xi – who care not a fig for human rights and who treat opposition with contempt or brutality – these ideas offer no more than a cry in the wind.

Thirty years ago, there was talk about "backlash" against feminism. What we are looking at now is more formidable. Political power in many parts of the world has been grasped by groups of men – there are no women in this list – who operate a strategy of authoritarian populism. Of course, there are large differences among them; but also important similarities, including their gender politics. Most mobilize racism and nationalism, most have cashed in on border protection and fear of terrorism, most are anti-feminist, homophobic, and celebrate strong conventional masculinity. They are not anti-capitalist; indeed, most are cosily tied to big businessmen in networks of crony capitalism, and most of the men just listed would be multimillionaires by now. But this is not recognizably neoliberal politics any more. Actual neoliberal politicians – Merkel, Macron, the Clintons, Blair, Obama, Trudeau and Turnbull – have found themselves on the other side of an increasingly obvious division within the global ruling class. It is already possible that the European Union will be a casualty.

Where now?

New problems for research have come into view. Prominent among them is the continued growth of global markets, global trade and global finance. Even when one is doing ethnography in a local organization or interviewing a local businessman, the tendrils of international connection can be detected. They include share markets that depend on Wall Street, price fluctuations that depend on the Gulf, migrant workforces, technological "solutions" from MYOB on (the Internet bulges with lists of the 30 Best Apps for Small Business) and more.

Transnational corporations themselves need to be more central in the research effort, if we are to catch up with reality. There are fine studies already – I have cited Juanita Elias's – but the world economy is now so big and diverse that a library of such work will be hardly enough. It won't be easy, where a corporation operates in 50 countries and conceals its profit from the taxman. This may require changes in the way we organize research: international teams or networks with online and forensic skills will be needed.

There are heaps of studies on new technologies and the online world. But the consequences in labour and organizational life are less studied, and the gender issues in these consequences are even less. I have mentioned Judy Wajcman's work, and there is room for much more. Here too new research methods may be important. But they need to be thought through. One familiar example is, I think, a trap: the online survey where some forced-choice questions are dreamed up, entered in a web-based template, and netizens are invited to drop in and answer them. It's too easy. No one really knows who or what the findings represent.

The reorganization of power as well as the reorganization of economies on a world scale creates a range of new research needs, such as state structures in the Global South. There are some classic studies in this area to bounce off. Achille Mbembe's amazing *On the Postcolony* (2001) is not to be missed, though I have hardly ever seen it cited in gender studies. Mbembe deals with the postcolonial national state. Bina Agarwal's classic *A Field of One's Own* (1994) looks at the local state as an arena of gender politics – among the many other themes in this monumental work.

Moving to the largest possible scale, the gender structures of North/South interactions are very much in need of examination. Imperial expansion, from the fifteenth to twentieth centuries, was carried out by masculinized workforces of sailors, soldiers, merchants, missionaries, pirates, governors and, eventually, farmers. But what are the gender dynamics of influence, coercion, supremacy, challenge and response in the world of atomic weapons, bulk ore carriers, continent-spanning pipelines and container ships? We get pointers from work such as James Messerschmidt's study of gender rhetoric in the US wars in Iraq, *Hegemonic Masculinities and Camouflaged Politics* (2010). There is much more to be done.

And lurking in most of these issues is the question of gender relations in the offshore world of corporate intranets, world-travelling executives, tax havens, credit and stateless finance. So much contemporary economic power seems to be located – or unlocated – here, answerable to no electorate or judiciary. It is not a completely virtual world. It seems to touch down in Panama, Basel, Davos and the Bahamas, but even that may be largely a smokescreen for Dallas, Riyadh, Guangdong and Mumbai. This could be a dangerous field to research. One can say for certain that it is really, really important. So, there is new fieldwork and data-gathering to be done. But there is also intellectual work to be done, rethinking gender theory. Here, the issue that stands out is decolonization.

Conceptual frameworks for feminist research on work and organization, and the methods used in it, come overwhelmingly from the Global North. But most of the world's work – we need to say this again and again – is done outside Europe and North America. And the postcolonial world, like the colonized world before it, does think, does theorize, does pay attention to what is happening and does work out methods for understanding. At the very least, Global North researchers who do not engage with this issue are missing out on important intellectual resources. At the worst, they perpetuate cognitive injustices that have considerable effects on the rest of the world, given the centrality and influence of Northern academic and policymaking institutions, from Harvard to the OECD.

What is involved in moving to a postcolonial perspective is not the narrowing of research to a single Southern paradigm, because no such thing exists. Rather, it means opening to a wider range of perspectives, concepts and methods. It is a mistake to think that postcolonial social science must all be qualitative, interpretive or postmodern-fragmented. There are important possibilities in quantitative work too, as we see in Maggie Walter and Chris Anderson's *Indigenous Statistics* (2013). The struggle for data sovereignty by Indigenous people applies across the whole spectrum of official, corporate and academic data-gathering.

Here, the point is not research for the sake of research but research for a purpose, in support of a struggle for social justice. That was, notably, the point of Women's Studies 40 years ago, a rectification of knowledge that supported a struggle to equalize respect and resources.

The principle applies today in an even broader sense, as we think on a world scale, and recognize how toxic power structures are laying waste to the natural world as well as the social world.

The current interest in "intersectional" research is a move in the right direction, but a limited one. In this framework, it is common to think of race, class, gender and sexuality simply as categorical distinctions or identities within the society of a nation-state, especially the society of the United States. We need to go far beyond this. When we think "class", we need to think of global power centres and global poverty. When we think "race", we need to think of coloniality, indigeneity, enslavement and the whole vile legacy of imperial divide-and-rule. When we think "gender", we need to think beyond the four walls of home to the people who have no home, and the world-scale dynamics this chapter has been gesturing at. That will not be easy. It will need imagination, hard and sustained work. As an old practitioner – age too is a dimension of intersectionality! – I urge the new generation of scholars to be bold. Don't get stuck in familiar models of gender, not even mine. Share your ideas and findings, and work cooperatively. Feminist movements have flourished the more they have worked as collectives, however, informal or imperfect. And however closely you are scrutinizing statistics, texts, images or situations, connect them with visions of the better world that we know is possible. There is a reason why the big billionaires and strongmen spend so much energy on propaganda, surveillance and repression, and why the little patriarchs bash women so often. They are afraid of equality. The right thing to do is make them more afraid.

Notes

1 This chapter is based on a keynote address given at the *Gender, Work and Organization* conference in Sydney in June 2018, later published in the journal of that name. At the start of the conference, we observed a ceremony called "Welcome to Country" or "Acknowledgment of Country", now common in Australian academic and political life. This registered the fact that we were meeting on land that had been occupied for tens of thousands of years by its Indigenous people. The land was never ceded. There was no treaty under which the British colonists of 1788 occupied it: they simply invaded it. Within two years of their arrival, about half the Aboriginal population of the Sydney area were dead or dying, from an epidemic brought by the British and from loss of food sources (Attenbrow, 2010).

2 In the following years, Aboriginal deaths from settler violence, social disruption and poverty mounted. Frontier warfare, forced removal and the seizing of productive land, with genocidal effects – strenuously denied in right-wing politics today – continued for the next 140 years, as the colonies expanded across the continent.

My family migrated from Scotland, Ireland and Wales to south-eastern Australia while this was happening. As a child, I heard a family memory of Aboriginal people camping on the banks of the Yarra River just below the block of land on which my paternal great-grandfather, then a prosperous merchant, built the family house. I guess that the people camping there had been displaced not just from that block but from the whole area where the eastern suburbs of Marvellous Melbourne were being built for White people, in the great boom of the 1880s.

Modern Australia is still governed by a settler-colonial state which has continued to reject the idea of a treaty: most recently rejecting the Uluru Statement of 2017 (www.clc.org.au/files/pdf/Uluru-Statement-3.pdf). Nevertheless, in the last half-century there has been a powerful revival of Aboriginal culture and politics. The Acknowledgment of Country is a part of this.

The 2018 *GWO* conference was held at the Western end of the beautiful stretch of land and water of which the Gadigal people are custodians. The area is now the plate-glass CBD of a corrupt capitalist metropolis, Australia's main link to global markets, finance and power. It is the site of a new and changing gender order.

References

Acker, J. (1990). Hierarchies, jobs, bodies: A theory of gendered organizations. *Gender and Society, 4*(2), 139–158. doi: 10.1177/089124390004002002

Agarwal, B. (1994). *A Field of One's Own: Gender and Land Rights in South Asia.* Cambridge: Cambridge University Press.

Attenbrow, V. (2010). *Sydney's Aboriginal Past: Investigating the Archaeological and Historical Records*, 2nd edition. Sydney: University of New South Wales Press.

Bacchi, C. L. (1996). *The Politics of Affirmative Action: 'Women', Equality and Category Politics.* London: Sage.

Bulbeck, C. (1998). *Re-orienting Western Feminisms: Women's Diversity in a Postcolonial World.* Cambridge: Cambridge University Press.

Burton, C., & others. (1987). *Women's Worth: Pay Equity and Job Evaluation in Australia.* Canberra: Australian Government Printing Service.

Butler, J. (1990). *Gender Trouble: Feminism and the Subversion of Identity.* New York: Routledge.

Collinson, D., & Hearn, J. (1994). Naming men as men: Implications for work, organization and management. *Gender, Work and Organization, 1*(1), 2–22. doi: 10.1111/j.1468-0432.1994.tb00002.x

Connell, R. (2014). Rethinking gender from the South. *Feminist Studies, 40*(3), 518–539.

Connell, R. (2015). Meeting at the edge of fear: Theory on a world scale. *Feminist Theory, 16*(1), 49–66. doi: 10.1177/1464700114562531

Connell, R., & Dados, N. (2014). Where in the world does neoliberalism come from? The market agenda in southern perspective. *Theory & Society, 43*(2), 117–138. doi: 10.1007/s11186-014-9212-9

Eisenstein, H. (1996). *Inside Agitators: Australian Femocrats and the State.* Sydney: Allen & Unwin.

Elias, J. (2008). Hegemonic masculinities, the multinational corporation, and the developmental state: Constructing gender in 'progressive' firms. *Men and Masculinities, 10*(4), 405–421. doi: 10.1177/1097184X07306747

Federal Glass Ceiling Commission (1995). *Good for Business: Making Full Use of the Nation's Human Capital. The Environmental Scan.* Washington, DC: Federal Glass Ceiling Commission.

Garbagnoli, S., & Prearo, M. (2017). *La croisade 'anti-genre': Du Vatican aux manifs pour tous.* Paris: Textuel.

Grupo Iniciativa Mujeres (2002). *ICC – Indice de compromiso cumplido Chile, 1995–2000: Una estrategia para el control ciudadano de la equidad de género.* Santiago: FLACSO-Chile.

Harcourt, W. (2009). *Body Politics in Development: Critical Debates in Gender and Development.* London: Zed.

Knights, D., & Rubery, J. (1994). Editors' Introduction. *Gender, Work and Organization, 1*(1), 1.

Mbembe, A. (2001). *On the Postcolony.* Berkeley, CA: University of California Press.

Messerschmidt, J. W. (2010). *Hegemonic Masculinities and Camouflaged Politics.* Boulder, CO: Paradigm.

Mishel, L., & Schieder, J. (2017). *CEO Pay Remains High Relative to the Pay of Typical Workers and High-wage Earners.* Washington, DC: Economic Policy Institute. www.epi.org/files/pdf/130354.pdf.

Moghadam, V. M. (2005). *Globalizing Women: Transnational Feminist Networks.* Baltimore, MD: Johns Hopkins University Press.

Power, M. (1999). *The Audit Society*, 2nd edition. Oxford: Oxford University Press.

Qiu, J. L. (2016). *Goodbye iSlave: A Manifesto for Digital Abolition.* Urbana: University of Illinois Press.

Roberts, C. (2000). Biological behavior? Hormones, psychology, and sex. *NWSA Journal, 12*(3), 1–20. doi: 10.1353/nwsa.2000.0061

Srnicek, N. (2017). *Platform Capitalism.* Cambridge: Polity.

Tomsen, S., & Donaldson, M. (Eds.). (2003). *Male Trouble: Looking at Australian Masculinities.* Melbourne: Pluto.

Tuchman, G. (2009). *Wannabe U: Inside the Corporate University.* Chicago, IL: University of Chicago Press.

Valdés, T. (Ed.). (2001). *El índice de Compromiso Cumplido – ICC: Una Estrategia Para el Control Ciudadano de la Equidad de Género.* Santiago de Chile: FLACSO.

Wajcman, J. (2004). *TechnoFeminism.* Cambridge: Polity.

Walter, M., & Anderson, C. (2013). *Indigenous Statistics: A Quantitative Research Methodology.* Walnut Creek, CA: Left Coast Press.

3

CONDITIONAL SOLIDARITY

Men and masculinities in social justice activist movements

Tigist Shewarega Hussen and Tamara Shefer

Introduction

This chapter approaches men, masculinities, organizations and organizing through the lens of social movement organizing. Social movements are characteristically gendered, as are all organizations. Some are overwhelmingly inhabited by men, indeed sometimes of certain ages and other social categories. Some are overwhelmingly inhabited by women, of certain ages and other social categories; some are occupied by those of different gender identities and sexualities. Sometimes their gendering is linked explicitly to their aims, whether progressive, regressive or ambiguous.

In particular, in this chapter, we focus on these matters of social movement organizing, social divisions and allyship (or not) through thinking about the possibilities and challenges related to profeminist male allies and coalition partners in activist organizations across geo-political contexts, particularly in relation to the sustainability of gender justice concerns. The chapter considers the challenges mitigating a more authentic engagement of cisgender men, in particular, in social justice activism that includes gender justice goals. We are interested here to ask questions about the way in which men, women and non-binary people work together towards justice and why an exclusion of a feminist agenda is so often the outcome of such collaborative agendas even when those aims are strong in a social movement. We are also concerned with how men and masculinities are implicated in such a challenge.

We draw in our arguments on two feminist counter-movements located in the South African context during the most active years of decolonial activism among students and civil society.

This chapter draws on two examples of resistance, protest and activism by a group of South African feminists related to masculinity and men's practices in activist social movement organizations and resulting in the erasure of feminist agendas and subverting women's leadership. We seek to illustrate how these feminist articulations of struggle, agency, identity and freedom open up an understanding of the boundaries and limitations of masculinist and nationalist orientations in social movement-building (McFadden, 2018). The two movements we draw on here are both feminist activist responses to challenge the larger activist movement: #PatriarchyMustFall, a movement against masculinist structures in the #FeesMustFall (FMF) movement; and #MbokodoLead, feminist activism that focused on enhancing the visibility and impact of female leaders in the #FMF movement.

DOI: 10.4324/9781003193579-4

We think with these two case studies as a way of interrogating the pitfalls and opportunities that are offered by social activist movements, with respect to both challenging the patriarchal nature of mobilization and organizing, including ICTs, and their extension of patriarchal, and dominant forms of being a man and working towards gender and other forms of inequality. Both of these cases speak to strong feminist resistance against deep-seated masculinized structures that threatened to dismantle feminist and queer voices in this social movement. Developing an understanding of how activists succinctly conveyed knowledge, raised awareness and mobilized feminist and queer groups, this chapter explores men as profeminist allies and coalition partners as played out in one context.

This retrospective and reflexive analysis of the learnings from these two organizational instances attempts to throw light in general on men's allyship, collaboration and solidarity with feminist struggles in organized activism and understand why and in what ways such support and commitment appear always precarious, partial and conditional. Our project here is to explore the way in which patriarchal power and hegemonic masculinities resist, in subtle and more overt ways, a firm commitment to gender and sexual justice while at the same time benefiting from women's contributions to activist or political goals. There is little work that asks questions about why male allies in feminist movements and male collaborators in social justice movements more broadly find themselves unable to sustain a support for gender justice efforts. Such understandings may open up more fruitful and constructive forms of activism and social movements that include reflexive collaborations across gender divides towards ensuring gender justice goals are not lost or subverted by the dominance of particular forms of masculinity and particular male investments in patriarchal dividends.

Social movements and the challenges of profeminist men and men as partners in gender justice efforts

Social movement organizing, and civil society organizing more generally, is one major route and root to the formation and development of more formal organizations, such as associations, NGOs, new parts of the state and businesses. Indeed, this is the case in many postcolonial and post-conflict societies when the organization of activist movements during the struggle for democracy or change is then strongly implicated in and shapes the politics of and around the state. Usually, men and women and other genders work together in such struggles, as evident in the anti-apartheid movements in South Africa, but the emerging state and leadership is not always reflective of such collective engagements. South Africa, for example, notwithstanding an impressive Constitution and Bill of rights, continues to be racked by intersectional gender, race and class inequalities and injustices, including high rates of violence against women and non-conforming, non-binary sexualities and gender, and privileged men still dominate in leadership in political and civil society. Such a scenario has been evident in many current decolonial efforts in postcolonial societies, where feminist and queer activists have brought an intersectional lens and focus to the larger project of change and justice.

However, as well documented in past anti-colonial struggles, feminist goals have not always been valued in the larger activist or struggle organizations, and post-revolutionary or post-conflict societies often return to gender normative "business as usual", despite women's active role in achieving hard-won gains (Dlakavu, 2017; Khalil, 2014; Newsom & Lengel, 2012; Xaba, 2017). Thus, while feminist interventions in online and physical activisms for social justice provide a space for subjugated knowledges of women and non-binary people to be part of the bigger narrative, these very spaces may also reproduce such subjugation and marginalization.

In some circumstances, it is appropriate and understandable that certain social and activist groups and individuals are allies rather than partners. Cisgender men can be allies, arguably should, but often are not, of feminist, women's LGBTQIA+ and further emancipatory organizations and organizing. However, what we are concerned with here is how social movements, activist movements in this case, may take on a particular feminist or queer lens, and draw on women and queer activists labour and commitments to take forward struggles. Yet this all too often devolves into a strategic, rather than long-term, commitment.

Social movements occur offline, online and online–offline. While the chapter is focused on social movements in general and the challenges particular men and masculine dominance pose, in current contexts of global virtual engagements it necessarily includes an emphasis on ICT activism, especially given the proliferation of hashtag movements that have been deployed globally as a mode of feminist and other social activist organization (such as #MeToo, see Chandra & Erlingsdóttir, 2020; Falkof et al., 2022; Hearn, 2018). Notably, online social engagement has dramatically multiplied and diversified in an increasingly technological cyber-communicating world, the conversations between critical masculinities studies and the internet as a global, regional and local organization/s remain relatively marginal (Hearn & Hall, 2017). Yet it is both a necessary and productive space in which to study contemporary globalized hegemonic masculinities and the hegemonies of men, since:

> Seeing men and masculinities through the lens of virtuality and ICTs suggests new and changing transnational forms and processes of hegemonic masculinity and the hegemony of men in many locales, operating partly very much in the flesh, but also very much virtually too.
>
> *(Hearn & Hall, 2017, p. 64)*

Feminist, queer and critical masculinities scholars have increasingly highlighted the role of the internet and social media in shaping and reinscribing normative genders and sexualities, and interrogated the complexities and nuances of sexual and gendered violence through cyberbullying, sexting and Internet Pornography (IP) (Hall et al., 2022; Harvey & Ringrose, 2015). Yet there is also a growing acknowledgement of the possibilities of the virtual world for agency, resistances, transgressions and alternative imaginaries of genders and sexualities (Baer, 2016; Fotopoulou, 2016; Hearn, 2006; Hussen, 2018; Miraftab, 2004).

The online space of activist organization is arguably a productive organizational space, in tandem with and to bolster material activisms, and may play an important role in challenging patriarchy, heteronormativity, gender injustices and violences, as intersected with other forms of inequality. While some scholarship has foregrounded the way that online spaces of activism, art and social media may trouble normativities and binaries of sexuality and gender (e.g. Pather & Boulle, 2019), there remains a lack of work that specifically dialogues from a critical masculinities perspective on ICTs, and that further thinks about virtuality as a complex space for gender activism and men as profeminist allies in this respect (Hearn, 2020; Henry-White, 2015). As Hearn and Hall (2017, p. 69) have argued:

> Much more needs to be done to consider the complex online/offline, fleshy/virtual occurrences of men, masculinities and ICTs. This is likely to become ever more urgent, with technological advances, indeed socio-technological transformations . . . The extent to which this can become a feminist moment remains unclear, stemming in part from the unfinished undecidability of ICTs. In their ubiquitous, decentralized,

destabilized forms beyond differentiation/de-differentiation, ICTs can even seem ontologically queer, potentially changing what humans/men/masculinities are and can be, perhaps within possible postgender scenarios.

There has been a noticeable and productive growth of mass and digital activism globally, and in global Southern and African contexts against social injustices over the last few decades, in which men and women have worked together against oppressive regimes and social inequalities and violences (Chiumbu, 2015; Iosifidis & Wheeler, 2016; Mutsvairo, 2016). However, gender dynamics and inequalities, as well as intersecting raced, classed and global geopolitical power relations, continue to inhabit these digital activisms, despite a shared agenda and commitment to the struggle at hand (Ajayi, 2018; Bonilla & Rosa; Hussen & Shefer, 2023; Lewis, 2019; Lukose, 2018; Mendes et al., 2018; Onwuachi-Willig, 2018; Raiva & Sariola, 2018; Shefer & Hussen, 2020).

In many forms of organized activism, including contemporary online activisms, women are very active and often seek to bring a feminist agenda to bear on the larger struggle. However, it appears that men's support, particularly cisgender men who are more invested in male power, for gender justice and feminist causes is always conditional and often undermined by the hegemony of men and hegemonic forms of masculinity (Hearn, 2004). Notably, there is a growing body of work that seeks to understand the challenges of profeminist cisgender male allies, in both feminist organizations and other activist organizations, such as the ways in which patterns of male dominance or an erasure of a feminist agenda insidiously (re)appear (Carrington, 2017; Droogendyk et al., 2016; Flood & Howson, 2015; Linder & Johnson, 2015; Pease, 2017; Peretz, 2020a, 2020b; Wiley & Dunne, 2019). We seek to contribute to this literature and extend critical scholarship on activist and social movement organizations, by exploring intersecting patterns of gendered power dynamics that often destabilize and trouble movements and organizations. We raise questions not only about men as allies to feminist causes but also the capacity of cisgender men to be fully committed to an intersectional justice project that includes disrupting normative gender and particular groups of men's power.

The case of #Feesmustfall (FMF) movement in South Africa

The #FeesMustFall (#FMF) and #RhodesMustFall movements in South Africa from 2015 to 2016, collectively called the Fallist movement, were a catalyst for the resurfacing of questions that had been deeply buried in the neoliberal and capitalist postapartheid public imaginary (Lewis & Hendricks, 2017; Molefe, 2016; Naicker, 2016). The movement articulated the paradoxical social and political realities of Black students in Higher Education (HE) institutions, and challenged multiple forms of injustice within the postcolonial state – the right to free education, decolonization of the HE system, revisiting curriculum design, feminist struggles against sexual violence, and tackling multifaceted social, economic and symbolic violence. The movement included mass-based activism which was enhanced and popularized through digital platforms. The movement was primarily led by Black students, civil society partners and workers, with both men and women very active. Given the history and current context of racial capitalism,[1] many in the movement, especially #FMF which had a stronger focus on poverty and class inequalities, were also those from poor, working-class communities.

A key characteristic of the larger #FMF movement was the insistence on an *intersectional* perspective on the multiple social, economic and political issues that contribute to the complex experiences of subjugation of marginalized communities, historically and in contemporary contexts. This was made public through generic catchwords and powerful emotionally charged slogans and images to raise awareness and mobilization. For instance, #EndOutsourcing movement tackled policies that are discriminatory and exploitative against workers in universities. #Shakeville was a movement that exposed the racialization of residence or housing access in universities, specifically the struggle Black students go through to get university residence. Likewise, #BringBackOurCadres was a movement that challenged higher education to reinstitute leaders of #FeesMustFall movement in the university. #PathriarchyMustFall was a movement that erupted within the #FeesMustFall movement because of patriarchal and misogynist leadership styles of male leaders of the movement. Last but not least, the #RapeMustFall online movements drew attention and exposed the rape culture in universities.

Throughout these protests, ***Feminist intersectionality*** and ***decolonization*** narratives were taken up rapidly in rallies and protests, and on diverse digital media platforms (Dlakavu, 2017; Gouws, 2017, 2018; Khan, 2017; Xaba, 2017). Thus, decolonial and Black radical feminist ideologies entered into a general public discourse where Black consciousness and pan-Africanism have a long historical and political significance, particularly during the mobilization of students against apartheid. However, while using feminist slogans and supporting queer and gender justice agendas, it is noteworthy that both men and women activists were sceptical about the concept of ***feminism*** in #FMF. A frequently held assumption was that feminism and feminist principles of mobilization are more divisive than other schools of thought, which may also relate to its conflation "with a white, Northern, Western" project (Shefer & Hussen, 2020, p. 403). Embedded in this assumption is a desire to maintain the gender *status quo* and frame efforts at gender justice as disruptive and damaging to social justice movements focused on class and race. The subtext is, of course, the desire to use marginalized communities' voice for the benefit of the movement to create a hype and symbolic performance that shows an inclusive movement while retaining the gendered hierarchy. Thus, male leaders, who retained the majority of leadership in the movement, arguably used the language of Black radical feminism without being politically invested in applying it in activism or taking it on board in informing their political philosophy. In relation to this, Hussen (2022, p. 139) argues that:

> The idea of feminism being "not really political" (in the way that class or anti-colonial struggles are), or not really being intellectually rigorous (unlike Marxist analysis), surfaces again and again in responses to black radical feminism, and in responses to many other African feminist movements. By attacking feminists' dignity or existential sense of self and belonging, these charges can severely erode the confidence, sense of purpose, commitment and solidarity of feminist organizing and activism.

It is in this context that cisgender male allies in the #FMF movement initially performed a solidarity with feminist and queer activists, as a way of creating an inclusive movement that appeared to pay attention to multi-layered and intersectional marginalities at both individual and collective levels. At the same time, by using popular feminist slogans and publicly advocating for feminist principles and goals, the student movement managed to galvanize massive support from students in South Africa and gain publicity as one of the most progressive movements at the level of the international community. These practices and processes of strategic inclusion and subsequent exclusion are most clearly illustrated through the efforts to expose and resist these by the two forms of activism we explore here. We draw on the narratives of these two activist responses as represented in Twitter, online and public spaces, to highlight the extent and nature of the resilience of patriarchal practices and particular men's resistances to a long-term and full commitment to gender and sexual justice.

#PatriarchyMustFall: taking intersectionality seriously

The hashtag #PatriarchyMustFall explicitly challenged masculinist and nationalist practices within the movement that gave the agency and power to cisgender men to take control and lead the Fallist movement, while at the same time claiming that the movement was "intersectional". #PatriarchyMustFall, as a counter-movement, served to shake up the normative power structure, and was deployed to underline the contradictions between the promise of the movement to liberate all unjustly treated citizens, and the practical experiences of many who remained marginalized in the movement.

> Not interested in phased liberation . . . we were fooled about this two & three stage liberation model – NO MORE #PatriarchyMustFall.

This tweet captures the essence of #FMF feminist activists' revolt against the insistence on "phased liberation" strategies in the #FMF movement that excluded and deprioritized gendered and feminist struggles (Dlakavu, 2017; Jacobs, 2019; Matandela, 2017). This practice and logic was a central argument within national democratic and anti-racist struggles from the 1960s to the early 1990s in South Africa and other colonized countries, and within new millennium movements such as the Arab Spring, that "one struggle should be concluded before patriarchy and its bedfellows' sexism and misogyny are addressed" (Malebye, 2020, p. 76). It is primarily male leaders, and at times female leaders, who make this assumption and make decisions that impact the future of feminist mobilizing, and sidelines certain voices from the liberation movement discourse.

It was important for #FMF feminist collectives to employ an explicit strategy of calling out misogyny and patriarchy, while at the same time actively contributing to the national student movement's struggle for free and decolonial education (Khan, 2017). The tone of overt and confrontational messages, as conveyed in the aforementioned tweet, intentionally created a specific feminist politics that promoted the visibility of feminist causes and activism in the movement.

One can observe that #PatriarchyMustFall insisted on addressing multi-layered and intersecting repressions in the face of the silencing of feminism, and especially the strategic marginalization or selective use of Black radical feminism by men. Interestingly, exposing these "internal issues" to the public was considered a threat to the political coherence and success of the movement by many male and anti-feminist activists. Such silencing of what are viewed as more radical voices is not uncommon in social movements in general. Yet feminist activists found it important to publicly air these "issues" as sites of struggle within the movement, as it had the potential to create wider and shifting awareness of what a meaningful intersectional decolonial struggle could be. Far from being irresponsible, they demonstrated accountability to the project of an intersectional struggle involving gender, racism, colonialism and neoliberalism.

TW1[2]*: #PatriarchyMustFall started because Queers and Womxn have been systematically excluded from FMF &RMF*

TW2: I'm so disappointed in #FeesMustFall. If your politics don't include feminists and Queers then Fuck Off!!!!

Another tweet, TW3, stating "*Feminists and queer bodies or no movement at all*", reveals the determination of the marginalized collective in the movement to fight its patriarchal structure. Embedded in this tweet is a refusal to cover up for masculinist leadership, and for feminists and queer folks to refuse to become complicit as "handmaidens" or silenced followers in anti-feminist and homophobic structures. Additionally, TW4's "*The system must go first #Patriarchymustfall*", shows a determination to dismantle the system that is threatening the movement and diverse bodies, genders and sexualities in the collective. It also challenges the normalized assumption and expectation of "phased liberation" by prioritizing the national protest demands of Black women and queer folks.

It is therefore clear that the succinct messages and slogans used by feminists conveyed astute analysis of patriarchal power in a particular context, as well as a deft way of communicating with and inspiring other feminists. Consequently, these tweets functioned not only to criticize and resist but also to underscore the erasure of feminist activists (Hussen, 2022).

#PatriarchyMustFall posed an outspoken and effective feminist provocation to male entitlement and that of activists who found it politically necessary to use feminism instrumentally yet ignore its fundamental principles. The determination of #PatriarchyMustFall may well have led to a backlash of digital and activist activity, since it was at this time that cases of violence against women, particularly among #FMF feminist activists, increasingly were made public (Pilane, 2015).[3] Such violence reveals the desperate efforts to discipline what were viewed as unruly and disobedient female bodies in the movement. Feminist activists who challenged the status quo were "seen as a distraction to Black liberation when they challenge violent, cisnormative Black masculinities that want to maintain power within the movement" (Xaba, 2017, p. 7). Yet Pilane (2015, n.p.) argues, "black women calling out that patriarchy and misogyny within the movement is not an attack, it is a protection of their humanity – including their blackness and womanhood – in its entirety". In fact, as numerous publications by #FeesMustFall feminist activists (Dlakavu, 2017; Xaba, 2017; Jacobs, 2019; Matandela, 2017) show, the real distraction in the movement and for Black liberation is the reactionary patriarchal belief that "we won't be told by women". Several incidents exposed the patriarchal backlash against feminists, particularly led by men who initially claimed to endorse and be allies in using a feminist intersectional lens for the liberation of Black women and queer individuals in the #RMF and #FMF movements. One of the infamous incidents that exposed the patriarchal backlash against feminists was the attack on Black feminist and queer activist Thenjiwe Mswane by Chumani Maxwele – a renowned activist in the #RMF and #FMF movements (Shange, 2017). Although the details of this event were contested, Thenjiwe Mswane was allegedly physically assaulted for raising "the issue of sexual violence in the movement, as well as the side-lining of lesbian, gay, bisexual and transgender (LGBT) members of the movement and their issues" (Bashonga & Khuzwayo, 2017, p. 8). Mswane's experience solidified the feminist voices and embodied the vulnerability of feminists in public rallies, as they were often physically intimidated by men (Hussen, 2022).

Women must lead: #MbokodoLead

The other feminist counter-movement erupted from within the #FMF movement was #MbokodoLead. The emergence of #MbokodoLead that loosely translates to "women must lead" was an initiative to insert Black feminist leadership into what were quickly becoming normalized masculinist leadership structures. Ironically, male members of the #FMF movement were considered strong and visionary because "they fit into the existing narrative of political jargon, tone, and linguistic, which on its own is hypermasculine" (Pilane, 2015, n.p.). Consequently, the leadership of Black women, LGBTQIA+ folk and persons with disabilities was often undermined as "they are depicted as naturally inferior and subordinate, as eternal victims of male oppression" (Zeleza, 2005, p. 207).

At the same time, these activists insisted on a different strategy from the "accommodative" activism pursued by women activists in previous struggles, especially anti-apartheid resistance. While South African women were active in the national liberation movement, they "have rarely achieved visible leadership roles" (Seidman, 1993, p. 293), and women's and feminist struggles were treated as less significant by, for example, the ANC (Hassim, 2002). Thus, the idea of a postapartheid nation that has accomplished the promises of a just and equal society was questioned in the #FMF movement in general, and the feminist movements such as #MbokodoLead and #PatriarchyMustFall in particular.

As the #MbokodoLead digital activism became more visible and noticeable, another strategy employed by feminists in the movement was a rally against patriarchal leadership where Black women presented themselves in ways that defied masculinist leadership and conditional support for feminist goals from men. Black women as a collective therefore decided on a dress code, which included the prescribed wearing of African print headscarves (see Fig. 3.1).

Figure 3.1 Women came out the next day wearing different colour docks, plain white t-shirts and blue/black jeans

Source: Image accessed from Wits PYA[4] Twitter page

Here, it is worth paying attention to the performed femininity, rebellious and reminiscent of local culturally constructed performances of femininities, that the *doek*, a local term for headscarf – also known as *iqhiya* in isiXhosa – came to represent. In many Black South African cultures, doek-wearing is considered a sign of a "good" woman, who is respectful of her culture and tradition. It is particularly encouraged for married women, as it symbolizes her social status in the community. Since the world of most students is often far-removed from these cultural settings, the meaning of the doek might be expected to be rejected. However, many young women appropriated the headscarf to signify their refusal of patriarchy. Notably, both in South Africa and elsewhere in Africa, as well as in the United States (especially in the #BlackLivesMatter movement), many Black African women reclaimed headscarves and wore them as fashion, or to reaffirm their African identity and as a symbol of anti-colonial sentiment.[5]

In her essay, "How South African women are reclaiming the headscarf", Fihlani (2016, n.p) argued that, since a range of headwraps with African prints and texture can be found in different parts of Africa, doek-wearing is also "an expression of what it is to be African". Building on these diverse meanings, the call for Black #FMF feminists to wear the doeks in a #MbokodoLead rally is not a simple act of performed femininity; rather, it is a subversive gender performance that reclaims women's power and leadership in the movement while also gesturing to women's strength in social movements across time and space. The following tweets also suggest this:

TW1: *How gorgeous are the women in this movement? Doing the damn thing in these headwraps. How are we not magic. #MbokodoLead #NationalShutDown*

TW2: *Black women carry on slaying and refuse to be silenced by men that are intimidated by you. #Womandla #MbokodoLead*

These two tweets mark the intricate balance between a subversive performance of compliance while rebelling against repressive male power. TW1 – "doing this damn thing in these headwraps" – is indicative of how Black women negotiated power in #FMF, despite deeply ingrained social constructions of heteronormative and patriarchal society. TW2 portrayed the rebellious intentions of #MbokodoLead – "refuse to be silenced by men" – by asserting women's power to equally lead with men.

Mabaso (2017, p. 102), similarly, in her intersectional analysis, problematized Black women's interactions in the movement, as well as the power dynamics that constrained Black women's agency through relying on a stereotypic femininity, and therefore stereotyped masculinity, that resonated with the deep-seated patriarchal belief that women "should know their place". Mabaso (2017, pp. 102–103) shared her personal experience of being a #FMF feminist activist as follows:

> Prior to the rise of #MbokodoLead, (that is, the moment when the women of #WitsFeesMustFall came to the forefront by asserting the legitimacy of femininity within the movement) I felt the oppression and discipline of patriarchy within the movement itself. I had to discipline my body by dressing as "unfeminine" as possible in order to assimilate and to avoid exposing my body while we were moving around. I also had to discipline my tongue, and to teach it the proper grammatical rules of "comrade speak", which is basically a variant of tsotsi taal[6] predominantly used by working class black males in the township. Thirdly, I had to discipline my movement, to forbid my feet

> from ever carrying me to the front or to the centre where I could lead a song or an address because as many said, that is a man's job. So as a Black woman, in that moment and time, I was subject to double jeopardy.

Mabaso's reflection highlights the persistence of the impulse to keep patriarchal structures in place. First, it was expected that, in these public-occupied spaces, Black women should wear "unfeminine" clothing to hide their sexuality and avoid exposing their bodies. This put the responsibility for sexual assault on women, as well as the responsibility to discipline their own bodies through a preventive measure, which in turn relieved rapist men from taking responsibility for the violence they had inflicted on women. Second, in order to play the supportive role in the movement, women had to learn a few key languages, such as "comrade speak", that sustained the power held by the male leaders, while silencing their own voices. Third, Black women had to obey the idea that they were expected to follow, not lead. Their bodies were forbidden from occupying the centre but were meant to hold the movement together from the margins, "faceless and nameless" (Dlakavu, 2017, p. 118), with unrecognized gendered labour. Here, it has to be recognized that these power struggles got more complicated when it came to self-identified Black queer feminist and transgendered activists (Xaba, 2017).

Similarly, Kamohelo Mabogwane's argument, presented in a collective piece (Lewin et al., 2019, p. 8), is powerfully expressive of the power dynamics at that time. She writes:

> Against the backdrop of the recent surges of student activism in South Africa, we find ourselves living in a world of cishet Fanonian patriarchs who have somehow decided that they form the discourse on activism, (activist) academia, and sometimes even feminism. These are men who see and treat Black women as decoration – necessary figures who can stand in front of a crowd, preferably in a doek (head wrap), but only for a few seconds. To these men, *Black women are leaders, yes – but the power they hold is, to them, fragile, laughable, and will never amount to the kind of serious leadership that they are invested in: "questions of national importance".*
>
> *(our emphasis)*

Mabogwane shows how those with a vested interest in maintaining deeply entrenched gendered power dynamics required women to be symbols of inclusivity, and possibly leadership, without being confused with the "real" leadership figures – the men. Mabogwane here used the "doek" ironically to show the flawed assumptions of those in positions of power in patriarchal structures, who are often fooled by a show of submissive gendered performance and femininity.

> Black women, even when they step up to leadership roles, are expected to adhere to social and cultural power norms. They should be seen, but not for long; they should challenge the status quo, but in a way that supports the male leaders. They should be heard, but not really use their own voice.
>
> *(Hussen, 2022, p. 156)*

Of relevance to Mabogwane's critique, Ratele (2018, p. 94), on the basis of dialogue with a group of such Fallist activist men, argues:

> As it turns out, it is not easy to turn men into profeminists. This is ironically true even for those men who may have experienced oppression. An experience of colonial white

> patriarchal domination is not a sufficient condition to change one into a non-sexist decolonialist. The experience of social injustice is not on its own adequate to radicalize a subject against that particular injustice – or any other form of social injustice.

Ratele's observation indicates that the knowledge of social inequality does not guarantee a social movement or organization organizing that works to actively undo unequal power structures. Instead, there is a higher possibility of recreating hierarchical structure that reproduces a power structure that further marginalizes those at the bottom of the structure.

Overall, #MbokodoLead was effective in foregrounding Black women as leaders and highlighting male activists' apparent lack of investment in and resistance to gender justice issues as well as systematic antagonism and intimidation of women in the movement by male leaders. For many Black women who participated in #MbokodoLead, it would have been easier to keep quiet, to be in the shadows, giving power to the patriarchs, and avoiding being labelled as "a feminist that derails the movement" – an accusation frequently used to demoralize and demonize feminists by male leaders (Xaba, 2017).

Concluding thoughts

The arguments made here are based on activist social movements located in the postcolonial, postapartheid context of South Africa. It should be appreciated in this context that the men who led and participated in this movement are located in centuries of racist and classed subjugation and dehumanization, and the complexities of layers of intersectional violations need to be appreciated. As Ratele (2020, p. 127) advises:

> Attempts to understand black masculinities that fail to consider the acts of men and ideologies of manhood against the dark historical trauma of colonialism, slavery, apartheid and global racism may inadvertently reproduce coloniality of masculinity categories.

On the other hand, we suggest that a number of key issues that emerge here also speak to global and other local challenges of progressive social movements, and specifically men as allies and co-activists in contemporary activism directed at or including feminist and justice goals. First, men frequently position themselves as the vanguards of culturally or nation-state-coded morality; while they stand with women and feminist causes in moments, they often resist shifting normative masculinist and heteronormative representation of leadership and movements. We suggest that this organizational "habit" be understood within both subjective socialization and institutionalized practices which promote stereotyped binary versions of what it means to be a man (and a woman) in a patriarchal society. Second, we have illustrated, on the basis of historical and current evidence in our case studies, that men frequently "take charge" and control of public responses, and often gatekeep "the women's question" and feminist issues in general.

Thus, while feminist scholarship continues to critique anti-feminist backlashes or toxic masculinist leaderships, it remains difficult to visibilize the power dynamics within social movements that are directed towards gender and other justice. Such commitments are frequently shown to be short-lived, with men showing partial, often strategy-based, interest in understanding feminist issues and working side-by-side with feminists, while effectively obfuscating gender and queer justice goals and re-directing the movement at other moments. We have witnessed this in the feminist writings in the Arab Spring movements – Egypt,

Tunisia, Libya and Yemen (Johansson-Nogués, 2013; Maravankin, 2017), in many postcolonial feminist writings in Africa (Hassim, 2002; McFadden, 2005). Solidarities then remain conditional, based on investments in support for the movement, yet fail to offer more sustained resistance to gender justice at a personal and political level. Cisgender, heterosexual male allyship with feminist activists emerges as primarily strategic, and quickly unravels when individual and structural male powers, or men's implications in violence/s, are put on the agenda.

The dynamics exposed here are not peculiar to African or South African digital or public activism and social movements but persist in global online and public activisms and other organizations. However, we argue the importance of raising these issues to problematize the continued erasure of gender struggles in larger justice goals, and go beyond lip service and the strategic deployment of women and queer bodies in activisms, towards a radical engagement with intersectional justice efforts. We suggest that more attention to the gendering of male activists and the masculinization of activism organizations is imperative for current (digital) activism to make a difference. Notably, while our arguments here are primarily grounded in particular social activist movements, relying mostly on narratives from online activist sites, these concerns also speak to wider challenges and are of relevance to larger feminist and social justice activist organizational spaces. Activist organizations, as with the majority of organizational and institutional spaces, remain underpinned by patriarchal logics and normative gendered power dynamics, which undermine solidarities and impede possibilities for change.

Acknowledgements

Thanks to the editors, particularly Jeff Hearn, for helpful and supportive direction on this chapter, and Kadri Aavik and Anika Thym for constructive feedback. Appreciation also to the Andrew W. Mellon Foundation [grant number 31700714] *New Imaginaries for Gender and Sexual Justice project*, Women's and Gender Studies Department, University of the Western Cape.

Notes

1 Racial capitalism, coined by Robinson (1983), while particularly resonant in apartheid South Africa through a Marxist analysis in left-wing scholarship, is understood as a global phenomenon and speaks to the complex intersections of racist ideology with capitalist exploitation. It is widely recognized that South Africa through apartheid legislation and policies of racist segregation of residence, education, transport and all areas of lived experience, was characterized by a particular form of racial capitalism which persists in contemporary postapartheid through the continuities and entanglements of racialized and class inequalities (see, for example, Alexander, 1979, 2002; O'Meara, 1983; Wolpe, 1990).

2 TW refers to Tweets which we number to ensure anonymity. They were selected from Twitter over the time period of 2015–2017 following responses to the #FeesMustFall and #RhodesMustFall movements, as illustrative of the arguments made here. Similar arguments were made on various social media platforms, such as Facebook and Instagram. However, due to the scope of this work, we opted to use a few extracts from Twitter publicly available digital archives.

3 For instance, #TotalShutDown was used by #FMF feminist activists together with other hashtags, such as #PatriarchyMustFall, to advocate against violence against women. #TotalShutDown was a particularly strong movement evident in its sustained use in the aftermath of the #FMF student movement, in South Africa and other African countries.

4 Wits PYA: The Wits Progressive Youth Alliance Comprised of the ANCYL, SASCO and YCL – tried and tested leadership, and the first line of defence for students.
5 Feminists from the 1980s in Africa have done this for a while, although the trend was fairly new to South Africa.
6 Tstositaals are a variety of mixed languages mainly viewed as spoken in townships, historically Black urban areas in segregated apartheid, and also in other agglomerations of languages over South Africa. The word Tsotsi is a Sesotho slang word for "thug" or "robber", while "taal" is the Afrikaans word for "language". A tsotsitaal is "a permanent work of language-mix, language-switch, and terms-coining". Educalingo, https://educalingo.com/en/dic-en/tsotsitaal. Accessed 14 June 2022.

References

Ajayi, T. F. (2018, June 7). #MeToo, Africa and the Politics of Transnational Activism. Retrieved from Africa is a Country: https://africasacountry.com/2018/07/metoo-africa-and-the-politics-of-transnational-activism.

Alexander, N (1979). *One Azania, One Nation*. London: Zed Press.

Alexander, N. (2002). *An Ordinary Country: Issues in the Transition from Apartheid to Democracy in South Africa*. Pietermaritzburg: University of Natal Press.

Baer, H. (2016). Redoing feminism: Digital activism, body politics, and neoliberalism. *Feminist Media Studies*, *16*(1), 17–34.

Bashonga, R., & Khuzwayo, Z. (2017). "This thing of the victim has to prove that the perp intended to assault is kak!": Social media responses to sexual violence on South African university campuses. *Agenda*, *31*(3–4), 35–49.

Carrington, A. (2017). *Accountability: Whose Responsibility Is It? A Commentary on 'Men as Allies in Preventing Men's Violence against Women: Principles and Practices for Promoting Accountability'.* Sydney: White Ribbon Australia.

Chandra, G., & Erlingsdóttir, I. (Eds.). (2020). *The Routledge Handbook of the Politics of the #MeToo Movement*. New York: Routledge.

Chiumbu, S. (2015). Social movements, media practices and radical democracy in South Africa. *French Journal for Media Research*, *4*, 1–20.

Dlakavu, S. (2017). #Feesmustfall: Black women, building a movement and the refusal to be erased. In C. Chinguno, M. Kgoroba, S. Mashibini, B. N. Masilela, B. Maubane, N. Moyo & H. Ndlovu (Eds.), *Rioting and Writing: Diaries of the Wits Fallists* (pp. 110–115). Johannesburg: Society Work and Development Institute (SWOP), University of Witwatersrand.

Droogendyk, L., Wright, S. C., Lubensky, M., & Louis, W. R. (2016). Acting in solidarity: Cross-group contact between disadvantaged group members and advantaged group allies. *Journal of Social Issues*, *72*(2), 315–334. doi: 10.1111/josi.12168.

Falkof, N., Roy, S., & Phadke, S. (2022). *Intimacy and Injury: In the Wake of #MeToo in India and South Africa*. Manchester: Manchester University Press.

Fihlani, P. (2016, June 11). How South African Women are Reclaiming the Headscarf. Retrieved from BBC News: www.bbc.com/news/world-africa-36461213

Flood, M., & Howson, R. (Eds.). (2015). *Engaging with Men in Gender Equality*. Newcastle upon Tyne: Cambridge Scholars.

Fotopoulou, A. (2016). *Feminist Activism and Digital Networks: Between Empowerment and Vulnerability*. London: Palgrave Macmillan.

Gouws, A. (2017). Feminist intersectionality and the matrix of domination in South Africa. *Agenda*, *31*(1), 19–27.

Gouws, A. (2018). #EndRapeCulture Campaign in South Africa: Resisting sexual violence through protest and the politics of experience. *Politikon*, *54*(1), 3–15.

Hall, M., Hearn, J., & Lewis, R. (2022). *Digital Gender-sexual Violations*. London: Routledge.

Harvey, L., & Ringrose, J. (2015). Sexting, ratings and (mis)recognition: Teen boys performing classed and racialized masculinities in digitally networked publics. In E. Renold, J. Ringrose & R. D. Egan (Eds.), *Children, Sexuality and Sexualization* (pp. 352–367). London: Palgrave Macmillan.

Hassim, S. (2002). A conspiracy of women: The women's movement in South Africa's transition to democracy. *Social Research: An International Quarterly*, *69*(3), 693–732.

Hearn, J. (2004). From hegemonic masculinity to the hegemony of men. *Feminist Theory*, *5*(1), 49–72. doi: 10.1177/1464700104040813

Hearn, J. (2006). The implications of information and communication technologies for sexualities and sexualised violences: Contradictions of sexual citizenships. *Political Geography*, *25*(8), 944–963.

Hearn, J. (2018). You, them, us, we, too? . . . online – offline, individual – collective, forgotten – remembered, harassment – violence. *European Journal of Women's Studies*, *25*(2), 228–235.

Hearn, J. (2020). The politics of absent men or political masculinities without the polis. In R. Luyt & K. Starck (Eds.), *Masculine Power and Gender Equality: Masculinities as Change Agents* (pp. 15–34). Cham: Springer.

Hearn, J., & Hall, M. (2017). Looking at men and masculinities through information and communication technologies, and vice versa. In U. Kempf & B. Wrede (Eds.), *Gender-Effekte. Wie Frauen die Technik von morgen gestalten* (pp. 61–73). Bielefeld: Universität Bielefeld.

Henry-White, J. (2015). *Gender Equality?: A Transnational Feminist Analysis of the UN HeForShe Campaign as a Global "Solidarity" Movement for Men*. Doctoral dissertation. University of Missouri-Columbia, Columbia.

Hussen, T. S. (2018). Social media and feminist activism: #RapeMustFall, #NakedProtest and #RUReferenceList movements in South Africa. In T. Shefer. J. Hearn, K. Ratele & F. Boonzaier (Eds.), *Engaging Youth in Activism, Research, and Pedagogical Praxis* (pp. 199–214). London: Routledge.

Hussen, T. S. (2022). *Radical Possibilities at the Crossroads of African Feminism and Digital Activism*. Unpublished PhD thesis, University of the Western Cape, Cape Town.

Hussen, T. S., & Shefer, T. (2023). #MeToo through a decolonial feminist lens: Critical reflections on transnational online activism against sexual violence. In N. Lykke, S. Arora, P. Bakos-Jarrett, R. Koobak & K. Mohamed (Eds.), *Pluriversal Conversations on Transnational Feminisms: And Words Collide from a Place*. London: Routledge.

Iosifidis, P., & Wheeler, M. (2016). Social media, public sphere and democracy. In P. Iosifidis & M. Wheeler (Eds.), *Public Spheres and Mediated Social Networks in the Western Context and Beyond* (pp. 13–37). London: Palgrave Macmillan.

Jacobs, C. A. (2019). Revisiting authoritative accounts of #FeesMustFall movement and LGBTI silencing. In S. N. Nyeck (Ed.), *Routledge Handbook of Queer African Studies* (pp. 185–199). London: Routledge.

Johansson-Nogués, E. (2013). Gendering the Arab Spring? Rights and (in)security of Tunisian, Egyptian and Libyan women. *Security Dialogue*, *44*(5–6), 393–409.

Khalil, A. (2014). Gender paradoxes of the Arab Spring. *The Journal of North African Studies*, *19*(2), 131–136.

Khan, K. (2017). Intersectionality in student movements: Black queer womxn and nonbinary activists in South Africa's 2015–2016 Protests. *Agenda*, *31*(3–4), 110–121. doi: 10.1080/10130950.2017.1396011.

Lewin, J., Mabogwane, K., Smit, A., Alexander, A., Mokoena, A., & Nyaruwata, C. (2019). What is Blackwom?nhood: An intersectional dialogue with the Young Wom?n's Leadership Project. *Agenda*, *33*(2), 61–73. doi: 10.1080/10130950.2019.1603424

Lewis, D. (2019). The politics and ethics of #MeToo in South Africa. *Paper presented at Intimacy & Injury: In the wake of #MeToo in India and South Africa*, Wits Club, University of the Witwatersrand, Witwatersrand, 14–15 February.

Lewis, D., & Hendricks, C. M. (2017). Epistemic ruptures in South African standpoint knowledge-making: Academic feminism and the #FeesMustFall movement. *Gender Questions*, *4*(1), 18.

Linder, C., & Johnson, R. C. (2015). Exploring the complexities of men as allies in feminist movements. *Journal of Critical Thought and Praxis*, *4*(1). doi: 10.31274/jctp-180810-37.

Lukose, R. (2018). Decolonizing feminism in the #MeToo era. *The Cambridge Journal of Anthropology*, *36*(2), 34–52.

Mabaso, N. (2017). Being Black inside #WFMF. In C. Chinguno, M. Kgoroba, S. Mashibini, B. N. Masilela, B. Maubane, N. Moyo & H. Ndlovu (Eds.), *Rioting and Writing: Diaries of Wits Fallists* (pp. 116–120). Johannesburg: Society Work and Development Institute (SWOP), University of Witwatersrand.

Malebye, P. M. (2020). Fallist feminist futures in South Africa. In A. Okech (Ed.), *Gender, Protests and Political Change in Africa* (pp. 61–80). Cham: Palgrave Macmillan.

Maravankin, S. (2017). Arab feminism in the Arab Spring: Discourses on solidarity, the socio-cultural revolution, and the political revolution in Egypt, Tunisia, and Yemen. *Clocks and Clouds*, *7*(2).
Matandela, M. (2017). Redefining black consciousness and resistance: The intersection of black consciousness and black feminist thought. *Agenda*, *31*(3–4), 10–28.
McFadden, P. (2005). Becoming postcolonial: African women changing the meaning of citizenship. *Meridians*, *6*(1), 1–22.
McFadden, P. (2018). Contemporarity: Sufficiency in a radical African feminist life. *Meridians*, *17*(2), 415–431.
Mendes, K., Ringrose, J., & Keller, J. (2018). #MeToo and the promise and pitfalls of challenging rape culture through digital feminist activism. *European Journal of Women's Studies*, *25*(2), 236–246.
Miraftab, F. (2004). Invited and invented spaces of participation: Neoliberal citizenship and feminists' expanded notion of politics. *Wagadu*, *1*(1), 1–7.
Molefe, T. O. (2016). Oppression must fall: South Africa's revolution in theory. *World Policy Journal*, *33*(1), 30–37.
Mutsvairo, B. (2016). *Digital Activism in the Social Media Era*. Cham: Springer Nature.
Naicker, C. (2016). From Marikana to #feesmustfall: The praxis of popular politics in South Africa. *Urbanization*, *1*(1), 53–61.
Newsom, V. A., & Lengel, L. (2012). Arab women, social media, and the Arab Spring: Applying the framework of digital reflexivity to analyze gender and online activism. *Journal of International Women's Studies*, *13*(5), 31–45.
O'Meara, D. (1983). *Volkskapitalisme: Class, Capital and Ideology in the Development of Afrikaner Nationalism, 1934–1948*. Cambridge: Cambridge University Press.
Onwuachi-Willig, A. (2018). What About #UsToo: The invisibility of race in the #MeToo movement. *The Yale Law Journal*, *128*. https://scholarship.law.bu.edu/faculty_scholarship/331
Pather, J., & Boulle, C. (Eds.). (2019). *Acts of Transgression: Contemporary Live Art in South Africa*. Johannesburg: Wits University Press.
Pease, B. (2017). *Men as Allies in Preventing Violence against Women: Principles and Practice*. Sydney: White Ribbon Australia.
Peretz, T. (2020a). Seeing the invisible knapsack: Feminist men's strategic responses to the continuation of male privilege in feminist spaces. *Men and Masculinities*, *23*(3–4), 447–475. doi: 10.1177/1097184X18784990
Peretz, T. (2020b). Trends and trajectories in engaging men for gender justice. In L. Gottzén, U. Mellström & T. Shefer (Eds.), *The International Handbook of Masculinity Studies* (pp. 498–507). London: Routledge.
Pilane, P. (2015, October 25). Patriarchy Must Fall. Retrieved from City Press Magazine. www.news24.com/citypress/voices/THE-STUDENT-Patriarchy-must-fall-20151025
Raiva, M., & Sariola, S. (2018). #Metoo & feminist activism in India. *EASST Review*, *37*(3). https://easst.net/article/metoo-feminist-activism-in-india/
Ratele, K. (2018). Engaging young male university towards a situated, social-psychological profeminist praxis. In T. Shefer, J. Hearn, K. Ratele & F. Boonzaier (Eds.), *Engaging Youth in Activism, Research, and Pedagogical Praxis* (pp. 93–109). London: Routledge.
Ratele, K. (2020). African and Black Men and Masculinities. In L. Gottzén, U. Mellström & T. Shefer (Eds.), *The International Handbook of Masculinity Studies* (pp. 125–134). London: Routledge.
Robinson, C. J. (1983). *Black Marxism: The Making of the Black Radical Tradition*. London: Zed Books.
Seidman, G. W. (1993). "No freedom without the women": Mobilization and gender in South Africa, 1970–1992. *Signs: Journal of Women in Culture and Society*, *18*(2), 291–320.
Shange, N. (2017). Mappings of feminist/womanist resistance within student movements across the African continent. *Agenda*, *31*(3–4), 60–67.
Shefer, T., & Hussen, T. S. (2020). Critical reflections on #MeToo in contemporary South Africa through an African feminist lens. In G. Chandra & I. Erlingsdóttir (Eds.), *The Routledge Handbook of the Politics of the #MeToo Movement* (pp. 397–409). New York: Routledge.
Wiley, S., & Dunne, C. (2019). Comrades in the struggle? Feminist women prefer male allies who offer autonomy- not dependency-oriented Help. *Sex Roles*, *80*(11–12), 656–666. doi: 10.1007/s11199-018-0970-0

Wolpe, H. (1990). *Race, Class and the Apartheid State*. Trenton: Africa World Press.
Xaba, W. (2017). Challenging Fanon: A Black radical feminist perspective on violence and the Fees Must Fall movement. *Agenda*, *31*(3–4), 96104. doi: 10.1080/10130950.2017.1392786.
Zeleza, P. T. (2005). Gender biases in African historiography. In O. Oyěwùmí (Ed.), *African Gender Studies: A Reader* (pp. 207–232). New York: Palgrave Macmillan.

4
SOCIAL THEORY AND CRITICAL THEORY

Richard Howson

Introduction

Thinking about society, its inherent roles and responsibilities, and the way it functions and changes, is foundational to questions that are ineluctably part of considering the future. As the world becomes ever more diverse yet integrated, through expanding and complex communication networks and the organizations they enable that can *inter alia* transform the real into the virtual and the virtual into the real (see Castells, 2010), as well as rearrange gendered social relations, it is more important than ever that there is not only a way to understand better how, why and what is occurring to our world but also the impact these changes have on us and our relations. This task is central to the social science project but more specifically as Clegg and Pina e Cunha (2019, p. 1) argue, it is social theorists that "speculate" about these "large-scale social questions" of which, the gendered or more specifically, the operation of masculinity within the new forms of organizing and their organizations becomes key:

> Contemporary social theory laces through all the concerns of contemporary management and organization theory: it offers not so much theory for management or theory for organizations, but theory that is addressed not only to the social practices that constitute these theories but that also has implications for what these theories take for granted.
>
> *(Clegg & Pina e Cunha, 2019, p. 1)*

In this chapter, the task is to extend the aforementioned position and offer analysis that goes beyond the importance of *social theory* per se so as to provide a foundation from which to critically consider the operation of masculinity within organizations by developing the alignment between "social theory" and its close but younger theoretical partner, "critical theory". It is in this way that we can expand the scope of social theory and incorporate a critical and/or feminist approach to masculinity that contributes to what might be referred to as *critical studies of organizations and organizing* that in turn will usefully expose their various interconnections. Moreover, the issues and arguments addressed in this chapter are relevant for not only critical theorizing on organizations and organizing but also critical theorizing on

DOI: 10.4324/9781003193579-5

gender, masculinity and for many strands of feminism, as well as the intersections of, for example, organization theory and critical studies on men and masculinities, and feminist theory and critical theory (for example, Fraser, 2020; McNay, 2022; Meehan, 1995).

Following Ian Craib (1992, p. 7), a working definition of theory is a mechanism that represents an attempt to explain our everyday experience of the world in a "systematic" way. This systematicity is what Harrington (2004) means by scientific. Though science is a broad field, in purely analytical terms our interest is in the "social" rather than the "natural" sciences. In making this distinction, it is recognized that the term "natural" directs attention to the natural world, while "social" focuses on the world of human relations, organizations and society more broadly. However, emphasis on one does not necessarily exclude the other, as is evident in the way the world must now organize to address issues such as climate change. Nevertheless, theory, or more specifically social theory here, represents a mechanism that provides a framework in which to explore and explain aspects of our social world in a systematic way.

The Enlightenment and the emergence of social theory

Historically, social theory could be argued to have had its foundations in the European Enlightenment of the 1700s and the political and philosophical work of the time which introduced such ideas as reason as a human quality, religion as "tradition", the citizen, civil society, the nation-state, as were inherent in the 1789 declaration by Lafayette and Jefferson on the pursuit of human happiness via rights. Following Collinson and Hearn (2005, p. 291), it is also about this time in history when the organization was transitioning from a single standalone structure to what the authors refer to as "multiple-unit" organizations that the idea of the organization which we identify with today emerged and with it so too, organization theory.[1]

The Enlightenment has been described as a lot of things, but for the purposes of this chapter it represents the historical period between the early 1700s to the French Revolution and/or the death of Immanuel Kant about a decade later (that is, 1804). At the beginning of the Enlightenment, sociology and its specific social theory did not exist as a discipline/perspective in its own right. However, by the turn of the century, a number of philosophers such as Montesquieu, Hume, Smith, Rousseau and Hobbes had written about issues that we now understand as appropriately sociological, not least of which include humanity, rationality, critique of (religious) tradition, citizenship, civil society and republics. These ideas and their development occurred on the back of a rejection of a priori knowledge and a simultaneous embrace of reason as a condition that was grounded in knowledge, freedom and happiness, which in turn was argued, could advance the condition of the life of a society. However, while reason became the foundation of knowledge, and thus theory, it was not equally applied or considered to be exercised at the level of gender. Indeed, through appeals to reason and rationality (often associated with privileged men and masculinities), women and racialized people, among others, have been excluded from many spheres, as they have been considered "irrational" and thus inferior. This was particularly evident in Mary Wollstonecraft's (2004) work *A Vindication of the Rights of Woman* originally published in 1792 and which remains fundamental to feminist critiques of gender relations and equality. This is not least because here the practice of reason as education was key and not just for the desired emancipation of women within gender relations but also for the building of a sustainable form of masculinity.

Thus, Wollstonecraft exposed the reality that although reason was central to the new forms of knowledge as theory it was not considered gender-neutral.[2]

Nevertheless, reason or more specifically "objective rationality" organized the development of social theory but in the early development of sociology it was subordinated to a positivist methodology. Having said that, some care needs to be taken in accepting this position completely and particularly with respect to the ongoing development of social theory through modernity and into postmodernity. Certainly, the historical position presented here is not altogether a complete misrepresentation of the original intent of sociology, that is, as a positivist science that seeks to discover and apply the foundational and essential principles of human society. Park and Burgess (1921, p. 87) in their textbook *Introduction to the Science of Sociology* (often regarded as one of the most influential texts about sociology) refer to sociology as "the last science" in their attempt to show how and why the early sociologists promoted the social over the political. Using the sciences of physics and chemistry as a platform, Park and Burgess (1921, p. 83) are able to clarify the claims by the early sociologists to show how sociology first gained recognition as an "independent science" with Auguste Comte's (original between 1830 and 1842) publication of *Cours de Philosophie Positive* (2012; also see Comte, 1970). However, if Comte's work can be regarded as central to the development of a positive model, he was not the first. In Montesquieu's *The Spirit of Laws* (first published during the Enlightenment in 1747), Durkheim (1965, p. 1) argues that the principles of the new science were set out or could be developed via the particular "social phenomena" referred to as "laws". The aim of the positivist inductive methodology was inter alia to produce social theory underpinned by three key epistemological, ontological and teleological objectives central to the new sociology: to abandon metaphysical ideals for grounded and observable reality; to ensure that political conceptions are no longer absolute and that they exist only in relation to civic society; and to ensure that the purpose of political action be limited by determined laws emergent from the positive model.

In addition, the positive sociological methodology sought to emphasize the failure of politics at the ontological and teleological levels. In other words, a key societal organization of the time, that is, the state and its practices failed to provide the natural and moral laws that could purposively lead to a new order and, second, overcome existing societal antagonisms. Thus, for the early positivists, only sociology could become an integral part of the new scientific study of society that we now know is concerned with the large-scale organizational and gendered transformations emerging through the development of capitalism and modernity. Transformations enable sociologists such as Anthony Giddens (1990, p. 13) to point out that when sociologists speak of society within the framework of modernity, that is, of modern society, then what they speak of is the importance of all forms of *organization and institutionalization* within the "nation-state". The development of modernity and the consequent emergence of its organizations within the nation-state was (and continues to be) of key sociological importance primarily because history and politics had failed to provide the complete stocks of knowledge that would, in turn, provide for social order and cohesion within a new "boundedness" that the "organizationalism" of capitalism had produced and that had not been experienced before even though Marx (Marx & Engels, 1950, p. 225) pointed to it in his claim that men make their own history, but that they do not make it in the way that they please. Indeed, boundedness is particularly relevant not just in the context of modernity but also for theoretically understanding organizations and/or masculinity, as it enables recognition that human agency is bounded insofar that actors operate within contexts (clearly including organizational and gender contexts) that are not intended or fully comprehended by each actor (see Giddens, 1990, p. 14).

From social to critical theory

The development of social theory in sociology during the early 1800s importantly developed many of these ideas and critiques but took the position that knowledge is only valid and reliable where theory itself is based on an ineluctable critical materiality and/or *a posteriori* focus that, in turn, reflects objective rationality and an inductively based method. This broad positivist methodology by the early to mid-twentieth century had become operational not just in sociology but many disciplines that included, for example, politics, social psychology, anthropology, gender studies (including critical studies on men and masculinities), studies of organization and management as well as social philosophical investigations within an expanding social science. The influence of these disciplines would have a dramatic impact on the development of social theory. However, arguably one of the most important developments in terms of the operation and application of theory within the broad social science came via a series of essays primarily written by Max Horkheimer, a sociologist/philosopher and member of the Institute for Social Research (or Frankfurt School) in the 1930s. In particular, the essays, "Traditional and Critical Theory" and "Postscript" (Horkheimer, 1972) explicitly name "Critical Theory" and whose purpose enabled the utilization of "critique" for "change". In saying this, it is not the case that critique and change had not existed in social theory prior to Horkheimer's intervention, as we will see later in this chapter. Indeed, Connerton (1976) traces the much earlier Enlightenment development of critique, as both reflection on the conditions of knowledge (reconstruction) and reflection on the system of constraints that humanly produced (criticism). However, as a standalone development, this critical theory was a new and unique initiative.

The uniqueness of Horkheimer's (1972, pp. 188–243) approach stems from the distinction its development makes with "traditional" theory that operates in the sciences (natural and social) and here sociology, or more specifically positivism, was the methodological protagonist. Critical theory sets a new opposite path in theorization and on which objectivity gives way to subjectivity, the ahistorical gives way to history and the new emphasis is the location of critical theory within society. Thus, critical theory does not accept that the set of propositions that constitute the theory are ossified in time and space but that a "critical theory of society" sets its object as "men as producers of their own historical way of life in its totality" (Horkheimer, 1972, p. 244). The use of "men" here could itself be critically interrogated. In this context, to assume that within society and its social relations there exist concepts, principles and identities that are independent of our own subjective understanding is rejected and must instead be understood as illusory and ideological. A critical theoretical approach to masculinity, for example, would emphasize that it is simply ideological and illusory to posit that the concept produces men without, in turn, recognizing that masculinity is produced by men themselves. This is the foundational social theoretical aspect of critical theory because to explore how and why men produce concepts that produce themselves it is important to explore the organizations in which social relations are themselves organized across society.

Thus, in turn, critical theory, both in general and as Frankfurt School Critical Theory, enables the exposure of the invisibility of the construction of masculinity by men and the taken-for-grantedness of masculine identity and the meanings attached. As suggested earlier,

Wollstonecraft in the late eighteenth century began the exposure of the taken-for-granted nature of gendered identity and meanings arguing that as reason becomes axiomatic it must apply to women, as well as men, and that the taken-for-grantedness of femininity, by men at least, will ultimately fail society. This was taken up and developed in later forms of feminist discourse in which critique that included but also went beyond reason and education addressed other crucial issues such as work, the workplace, paid and unpaid labour that became central to various critiques such as the feminist "domestic labour debate" in the 1970s and 1980s that sought to tie the importance of housework to the market economy and more recently, the issue of the gender pay gap. Similarly, within the critical studies on men and masculinities (CSMM, a key focus is how gendering practices produce an absent presence of men and masculinities in organizations and relations of gender power and domination that draws from these feminist discourses and critiques.

The alignment of social theory with critical theory and its synthesis – critical social theory – has become significant in the development of the social sciences but in many respects remains grounded in key theoretical constructs drawn from philosophy. Notwithstanding the disciplinary differences, for example, critical studies of men and masculinities and critical organization studies, it is appropriate here to offer some examination of these constructs, because, by doing so, it is possible to gain insight into why social and critical theory are so important to our understanding of organizations and their social and gendered relations as well as our position within them. It is also important to add here that Horkheimer (1972, p. 247) made clear that critical (social) theory is also a philosophical exercise. The best place to start then is with knowledge and reality or *epistemology* and *ontology*.

As Kienzle (1970, p. 414) points out, both epistemology and ontology represent key philosophical issues that relate to different problems and therefore ask different questions. Notwithstanding their philosophical background, both have been used by sociologists and other social scientists to inter alia identify the limits of their sociological perspectives. Epistemology represents a concern about knowledge, and in the context of social and critical theory it attempts to answer questions such as what does knowledge look like and how do we know what we know? How do we know it is "real"? In other words, what is truth as well as why and where does truth fail? By identifying epistemological presuppositions, social and critical theories question certain taken-for-grantednesses that may well shake beliefs and common sense about the social world and its organization. Ontology, on the other hand, is concerned with reality. Both social and critical theories make assumptions about the nature of reality, such as the ways in which social life is organized and transformed. They question the everyday assumptions that shape our experiences as well as the experiences that shape our assumptions. Ontological propositions examine such things as the division of labour and power, the nature and expression of identity, the operation of agency and structure, rationality, freedom, and how our relations are socially organized and institutionalized.

In addition to epistemology and ontology is teleology and though the latter may not be as evident or explicit in social and critical theory, Hindess (1977, p. 157) argues that its importance can be seen in, for example, conceptions such as industrialization, economic growth, economic development and organizations because these emphasize the importance of capitalism to our society. Teleology itself posits that a social phenomenon can be explained by taking into consideration not just the cause but also the purpose to which that phenomenon is directed. Thus, the purpose of some activity and/or the intentions held by individuals and/or collectives is inexorably gendered but also key to critique and change.

Critical social theory and mediation

Critical social theory has the task of explaining the large-scale societal issues and phenomena in a systematic way. In this context, sociology has played an important and critical role. In line with Clegg and Pina e Cunha (see 2019, pp. 1–2), the following section examines specific aspects of the theories of both Marx (particularly the critical focus on ownership and the nature of the relations produced) and Weber (particularly the transformational contradiction between rationality and irrationality). Both are recognized as "classical" theorists but are nevertheless key to the development of critical organization theory and management of relations, as well as offering a critical evaluative approach to the nature of agency and structure with respect to social phenomena emerging and developing in the new capitalist society. Both social theorists also offer a single, albeit different, overriding cause–consequence relation within their social theories that can help explain this new historical boundedness as expressed as capitalism–industrialism–patriarchy–rationalism. Within each component though can be seen emerging new forms of social and gendered relations tied ineluctably to new forms or organizations and technologies that give life to new forms of social networks that produce new forms of rationality that, in turn, incorporate new positive characteristics, such as trust, morality, reciprocity and communication that now provide new resources and values within organizations and their relations. However, operating simultaneously are the negative characteristics both theorists exposed that included alienation, subordination, irrationality and false consciousness. Within this dynamic boundedness can be found the basis for the modern organization. However, not often recognized in the theoretical analyses of the bounded organization is the mechanism of "mediation" that sits at its centre. Mediation is often interpreted as a "fundamentally dialectic notion" (see Silverstone, 2005, p. 189) because it refers to the reconciliation of positive and negative characteristics/elements within society. Marx began the critical analysis of the modern social world and in particular questioned the possibility of mediation by claiming that there is an underlying contradiction in the organization of production relations. In so doing, Marx critically exposed the existence but antagonism within the mediatory processes of capitalist organizations. In Weber's work, we see mediation most clearly operating within bureaucratic organizations and equally in the forms of authority, particularly new forms that require mediation between rationality and irrationality and then how the agent attempts to manage this tension.

Mediation in Marxism is crucially important for understanding social meaning because it shows that the purity of identities and relations cannot be expressed via formal reason and therefore will express antagonism and be ineluctably in tension. This critical approach to mediation culminated in *Capital* (Volume I), where the nature and operation of the "commodity" were analysed because it more than anything else is the embodiment of the capitalist organization. Here, commodities are referred to as "masses of congealed labour-time" (Marx, 1974, p. 47) suggesting that labour has social value and this, in turn, is manifested in the opposition between its use and exchange values. In effect, a commodity comes into the world with a "physical or natural form" that expresses a usefulness or use value (UV). But as a commodity its character is twofold and so it is also a "depositor[y] of value" expressed as a "value-form" or exchange value (EV) (Marx, 1974, p. 54). In exposing the dualism of labour and value within the commodity, Marx is also alluding to the tensions within the production and identity of the commodity. In other words, a situation in which EV must work to mediate the evidence of UV via money. It is money that supplies "commodities with the material for the expression of their values" and "represent[s] their values as magnitudes of the same denomination, qualitatively equal and quantitatively comparable" (Marx, 1974, p. 97). Thus, money acts as a mediator, forcing commodities to take on a form/value as a "price or money-form". This new money form does not equate to the physical or natural form of the commodity and its UV but instead reflects an "ideal form" as EV (Marx, 1974, p. 98). Money then transforms the commodities produced by real activity in real social relations into an exchange process that creates a negative reality (Wilde, 1989, p. 70). In other words, a reality in which EV and UV are caught in an "alienated form of differentiation" (following Plumwood, 1993, p. 443).

The importance of this analysis by Marx is that it exposed a new critical theoretical approach that emphasized the antagonism and tension within identifications and relations that would otherwise have been taken-for-granted as at best neutral. Therefore, EV cannot simply content itself with defining itself in terms of labour per se or in tension with UV but instead must include in its identification social meanings, such as subjectivity, marketing and desire. Although Marxist concepts and ideas are today not as predominant as in the past, their significance for our understanding of the operation of men and masculinity within organization and management relations remains. In effect, feminism has shown that in gender relations it is problematic to assume that identity exists as an ideal form independent of the identities and relations they operate within. In other words, masculinity within organizations cannot be taken-for-granted in ideal form *but rather exists within constant tension within gender relations*. Overcoming this tension, albeit incompletely, is part of the hegemonic process whose "task" is to ensure the privilege of an ideal masculinity, that is, hegemonic masculinity.

In a different but not less important approach, Weber's critical social theory moves the mediation project away from the more structural relational material emphases given by Marxism in two important ways. First, by questioning the ontological importance of social structure over agency, it thereby gives particular focus to social action and an emphasis on teleology. Social action, then, can be described as any human action that is intentional and has a purpose or meaning attached to it. If we accidentally do something, then there is no intention and our purpose is unclear as to what we have done, and so it is devoid of preconceived meaning. Therefore, it is not an example of social action. Second, Weber questioned the epistemological emphasis on objective rational knowledge over subjective and very often irrational knowledge as capable of explaining action. *The Protestant Ethic and the Spirit of Capitalism* (1989) was Weber's attempt to introduce the object of his broad sociological investigations, that is, how social meaning/identity becomes operational in social action. It develops a "balance" between the rational and the irrational, and between the secular and the profane to produce what might be understood as the "spirit of capitalism". What Weber sees as being emphasized here is a transformation in the nascent capitalist ethics or moral system evident in the societies of Europe and the early colonies of North America. A key aspect of this new ethic is that it develops from and through a new expression of rationality that itself is based on a particular form of irrationality (Weber, 1989, p. 53).

The spirit of capitalism was the point of departure for further social transformations particularly in the type(s) of authority that was now seen as coming to dominate capitalist organizations. In *Economy and Society* (1978, p. 215), Weber sets out the relationship between rationality and irrationality in a particularly important context that of the three "pure" or ideal types of authority. Traditional authority rests on the established belief in the sanctity of immemorial traditions and the legitimacy of the status of those exercising authority under these traditions. This form of authority holds the historical expressions of rationality that in the current moment would appear no longer applicable and thereby its adherents would be seen as acting irrationally. Charismatic authority rests on the devotion to the specific and exceptional sanctity, heroism or exemplary character of an individual person and of the normative patterns or order revealed or ordained by him. Here too, the operation of rationality sits solely within the individual's acceptance of the charismatic exceptionalism which may not be evident for others and thus may be viewed as a form of irrationality. Rational(-legal) authority rests on the law and in the legality of patterns of normative rules organized within the structures of society, as well as the right of those elevated to positions under such rules to issue commands. Here, the emergence of bureaucratic organizations was of particular importance and represented a set of social and gender relations in which the task was the removal of all forms of irrationality from social action because this form of "gender-neutral" authority gives focus to the current legal/moral structure and less on the historical rules (tradition) or the efficacy (charisma) of the individual (see Bologh, 1990; Ferguson, 1984, for feminist commentaries on bureaucracy). This is the ideal-type organization and is represented in Weber's (quoted in Haveman & Wetts, 2019, p. 4) own words:

> The decisive reason for the advancement of bureaucratic organization has always been its purely technical superiority over any other form of organization. The fully developed bureaucratic apparatus compares with other organizations exactly as does the machine with the non-mechanical modes of production. Precision, speed, unambiguity, knowledge of the files, continuity, discretion, unity, strict subordination, reduction of friction and of material and personal costs – these are raised to the optimum point in the strictly bureaucratic administration.

Setting aside charismatic authority for the moment, the spirit of capitalism becomes the catalyst for the transformation from traditional forms of authority and organization to a more rational-legal authority and bureaucratic organization. But the authority of rationality and intellectuality, Weber argued, leads ineluctably to new forms of social disenchantment. In other words, Weber's ontological position is certainly critical of the new social reality that capitalism creates because it leads the agent towards a dreary, flattened utilitarian existence the consequence of which is that human nature becomes trapped and ultimately, constrained. This, in turn, exposes an interesting and contradictory phenomenon that underpins the rational ontology of the Weberian modern society and, that is, that the rational spirit is underpinned by a substantive irrationality, that is, while the actions appear rational their causes and consequences are far less tangible or reasonable for people in their everyday life. In effect, Weber argues that the capitalist system based as it is on a particular spirit or set of beliefs supports a teleology of rational objective processes as its immediate morality but which when juxtaposed to the broader fundamentals for the facilitation of human nature appears as irrational.

Capitalism and its bureaucratic organization were underpinned by new ethical and moral demands that included an obligation that we must invest in our work in a way that enables a desire to fulfil ourselves through it. The obligation and desire to work and become part of the bureaucracy and assume its underlying morality becomes a part of not just our personal but also our moral development. So, for Weber, the modern capitalist system requires us to think in a way that goes beyond simple business astuteness and instead to feel a devotion to something that transcends each of us. In this context, Weber is in line with Marxism, that is, given the construction of this new rational-legal authority and value-rational action, people's commercial and social practices now influence, even determine, their ideologies.

Hegemony and common sense as critical social theory

The previous section offered a brief explication of the operation of mediation as a theoretical mechanism that explains the nature of boundedness. In extending this critical social theoretical approach to understandings of such social phenomena as organizations, and their relations and practices, the theory of hegemony developed by Antonio Gramsci in the early twentieth century may also be considered classical theory, but equally as representative of a critical social theory, and an important contribution in bringing together social and organization theories. In particular, Gramsci's application of the concepts: "common sense" as a form of hegemonic *particularity* and "good sense" as its conversion to *universality*.

In this context, the place to begin is to challenge the argument that Gramsci's theorization of hegemony developed it as a form of domination. This is a very common interpretation of Gramsci's conceptualization which misunderstands the complex intentions for hegemony in his broader theory. In Buttigieg's (2005, pp. 37–38) critical assessment of those interpretations of hegemony, which claim it as something "imposed" or, in other words, as domination, the level and specificity of the misrepresentation are clarified.

> Hegemony, as theorized by Gramsci, is not imposed; quite the opposite, the governing class achieves hegemony (i.e., becomes hegemonic) through leadership and persuasion, so that instead of imposing itself on the subordinate or subaltern classes, it acquires their consensus. This leadership is not exercised solely or even primarily from the seat of government, but also and much more importantly within the sphere of civil society where consensus is generated.
>
> *(Buttigieg, 2005, pp. 37–38)*

The implications of Buttigieg's critique are clear. First, hegemony is *not* imposed and, therefore, cannot be assumed to achieve completion, but rather is enabled because of processes of leadership, which always contains the potential for coercion and consensus-building, both of which are ongoing. Second, hegemony does not emerge from the government, but rather from civil society, that is, from the sphere of society we might reasonably assume is the expression of the social. In the theory of hegemony, Gramsci emphasized that the social also includes the social relations of production that, in turn, include what we saw in Weber as bureaucratic organizations linked to politics and production, as well as the economy, but also the forms of organizations that operate within civil society (what we might call today as the third sector). But even more crucially, in Gramsci's theory of hegemony, civil society was never disconnected from political society or the economy, and through this ongoing relationship is produced the "State" or more specifically within the theory of hegemony: the Integral State (Gramsci, 1971, p. 263). These foundational ideas set out the movement from common sense to good sense, that is, from particularity to universality from disorganization to organization.

In Gramsci's development of the theory of hegemony, the operation of the concepts, common sense and good sense, reflects the way that hegemony is produced and maintained. Both common sense and good sense are underpinned by the importance of leadership and consensus as well as civil society and both represent different phases in the development and emergence of hegemony. Common sense represents a particular conception of the world but one that is linked to the subaltern groups who lack the ability to create and sustain hegemony. In other words, Gramsci (1971, p. 323) refers to subaltern common sense as "folklore", that is, the incoherent and spontaneous beliefs and thinking of certain collectives of people within society. Folklore as common sense suggests tradition and is expressed as a localized philosophy of sorts insofar as it is a spontaneous form of knowledge that contains practical empirical facts of the given and immediate social world and as such, it becomes the subaltern's view of society. In this context, it acts as the basis of their alternative world view that often has contradictory fragments and, in many ways, can only represent an incomplete understanding of society. Common sense then represents localized sedimented knowledge and configurations of practice that are passively imposed and absorbed as natural. Thus, it can often lead to oppression and inequality that appear as the "order of things" (Gramsci, 1971, pp. 323–326) or as Marx would argue a class-in-itself. Politically, common sense remains infiltrated by power but its knowledge and practices are generally unchallenged.

> Commonsense is not a single unique conception, identical in time and space. It is the "folklore" of philosophy, and, like folklore, it takes countless different forms. Its most fundamental characteristic is that it is a conception which, even in the brain of one individual, is fragmentary, incoherent and inconsequential, in conformity with the social and cultural position of those masses whose philosophy it is. At those times in history when a homogenous social group is brought into being, there comes into being also, in opposition to commonsense, a homogenous – in other words coherent and systematic – philosophy.
>
> *(Gramsci, 1971, p. 419)*

The notes on the "Study of Philosophy" and, in particular, his "Preliminary Points of Reference" in the *Selection from the Prison Notebooks* (1971) develop common sense in conjunction with language, religion and philosophy (Gramsci, 1971, p. 323). In reference to philosophy, he argues the connection between religion and common sense does not coincide but rather religion acts "as an element of fragmented commonsense" (Gramsci, 1971, p. 325). There can be many particular forms and expressions of common sense even within a society but as philosophy supersedes and aggregates these forms and expressions of common sense, it coincides with the constitution of good sense. Davidson (2008, p. 66) makes this point when offering an example of the emergence and nature of good sense.

Good sense incorporates into itself those parts of the common sense and religion it seeks to supplant and rejects/represses others. It resonates with the force of universality because the particularity of common sense and religion "cannot be reduced to unity and coherence even within an individual consciousness, let alone collective consciousness" (Gramsci, 1971, p. 326). Good sense then is part of the political development of hegemony because it "supposes an intellectual unity and an ethic in conformity with a conception of reality that has gone beyond commonsense and has become, if only within narrow limits, a critical conception" (Gramsci, 1971, pp. 333–334). Most importantly, however, unlike classical Marxism, Gramsci viewed common sense not as a purely negative form of consciousness but rather, as the site of potential politics. Indeed, Gramsci argues that both common sense and good sense are bound by historical and social factors and so neither are ever operating as rigid and immobile forms of epistemology but rather it continually transforms itself, enriching itself with new ideas and with opinions that are now into part of ordinary life (Gramsci, 1971, p. 326, footnote 5).

While Gramsci was critical of common sense primarily because on its own it was incapable of producing organized and broad collective action, he did not completely dismiss its efficacy. In fact, throughout his pre-prison writings, which culminated in the unfinished essay, "Some Aspects of the Southern Question", there is the development of a strategy for hegemony that not only gives recognition to common sense but also takes seriously its reconfiguration and elaboration through practical ideas such as "hegemony of the proletariat", which at the time were striking and radical (Gramsci, 1971, pp. 339–343). So, what we see in this brief exploration of Gramsci's common sense and good sense is the basis for the transformation and aggregation of various particularities into hegemony.

A key objective of this hegemonic logic is to arrive at a point where moral and intellectual interests are mediated into a synthesis, rather than negated by economic and political interests. In turn, it produces a "historical bloc" through which there is organized a "collective will" (Gramsci, 1985, pp. 206–212) to set new imperatives for hegemony that give it a "popular" and "national" character. The idea of "popular" is perhaps key here, though, because through it Gramsci seeks to emphasize the need to eschew the knowledge and ethics of any one dominant, identity for example, proletariat as the privileged determiners of a good sense. Instead, knowledge and ethics must be drawn from the society in its broadest sense (Gramsci, 1971, pp. 125–133). Hegemony then is the movement from common sense to good sense but in a way that does not see the obliteration of common sense. Instead, it is incorporation into good sense, and it is this type of movement that produces hegemony as ethico-political or as the highest synthesis.

Conclusion

The task set out for this chapter was to present a discussion of social theory and critical theory that also included the question of hegemony and bring this back at some level to the operation of masculinity within organizations. The approach taken here was predominantly sociological but in a way that began with a diachronic analysis that located social theory in its first sociological iteration as aligned closely to the positivist method with its own objective and ahistorical imperative. The emergence of a specifically articulated critical theory particularly as it was developed in the Frankfurt School questioned the positivist model by emphasizing subjectivity and history.

The second part of the chapter presented analysis of a feature of organizations and organizing, that is, the interconnection between boundedness and mediation through the theories of Marx, Weber and then hegemony through Gramsci. Notwithstanding the difference in these two sections, the main theme that moves through the chapter is the interconnections between critical social theory and feminism, and also how the product of this interconnection has been able to inform the critical studies of men and masculinities, as well as to a lesser degree critical organization studies.

There is still much work to be done with respect to the critical study of men and masculinities in organizations, for example, while hegemonic masculinity is axiomatic in the CSMM and an important focus for future research. Another significant focus would be to examine the development and maintenance of a dominative masculine hegemony across organizations that genders forms of work and undermines the mediatory potentials within bounded contexts. In this context, social theory and critical theory are imperative to the dynamic and continuing task of developing critical knowledge of men and masculinities in organizations and organizing.

Notes

1 This author recognizes the potential eurocentrism inherent to the analysis offered here, and also that there are other non-eurocentric histories and approaches to the Enlightenment, social theory and critical theory. However, because the task is to develop and analyse the interconnections between social and critical theory to organization and critical organization theory in the context of gender and masculinity, and given that organization theory has been identified as located in the transition of the organization pointed to by Collinson and Hearn (as discussed later) but also the epistemological foundation, as argued by Clegg and Pina e Cunha (2019, p. 1), that is expressed through the work of *inter alia* Adam Smith, Karl Marx, Max Weber and Frederick Taylor, there is a justification to focus attention in this way. However, this justification does not seek to "dominatively hegemonize" (see Howson, 2005) this focus, but rather offer a contribution to the broader discussion in this volume which looks beyond particular centrisms, and considers the relations between local, regional and global forms.

2 The importance of this recognition remains within contemporary feminist theory/discourse and particularly with respect to the conception of "work" as public or private, "productive" or "reproductive", and in the context of the critical theorization of organizations (see Collinson & Hearn, 2005, pp. 290–292) through the development of capitalism and the new forms of organizations and work it produced.

References

Bologh, R. W. (1990). *Love or Greatness: Max Weber and Masculine Thinking*. New York: Routledge.

Buttigieg, J. (2005). The contemporary discourse on civil society: A Gramscian critique. *Boundary 2*, *32*(1), 33–52. doi: 10.1215/01903659-32-1-33

Castells, M. (2010). *The Rise of the Network Society*. West Sussex: Wiley-Blackwell.

Clegg, S., & Pina e Cunha, M. (2019). Management, organizations and contemporary social theory. In S. Clegg & M. Pina e Cunha (Eds.), *Management, Organizations and Contemporary Social Theory* (pp. 1–18). Milton Keynes: Routledge.

Collinson, D. L., & Hearn, J. (2005). Men and masculinities in work, organizations and management. In M. Kimmel, J. Hearn & R. Connell (Eds.), *Handbook of Studies on Men and Masculinities* (pp. 289–310). London: Sage.

Comte, A. (1970). *Introduction to Positive Philosophy*. Indianapolis: Bobbs-Merrill.

Comte, A. (2012). *Cours de Philosophie Positive – Leçons 46–51*. Édition réalisée et commentée par M. Bourdeau, L. Clauzade et F. Dupin. Original between 1830 and 1842. Paris: Hermann.

Connerton, P. (Ed.). (1976). *Critical Sociology*. Harmondsworth: Penguin.

Craib, I. (1992). *Modern Social Theory*. New York: Routledge.

Davidson, A. (2008). Hegemony, language, and popular wisdom in the Asia-pacific. In R. Howson & K. Smith, K. (Eds.), *Hegemony, Studies in Consensus and Coercion* (pp. 63–79). New York: Routledge.

Durkheim, E. (1965). *Montesquieu and Rousseau: Forerunners of Sociology*. Michigan: University of Michigan Press.

Ferguson, K. E. (1984). *The Feminist Case against Bureaucracy*. Philadelphia, PA: Temple University Press.

Fraser, N. (2020). *Fortunes of Feminism: From State-Managed Capitalism to Neoliberal Crisis*. London: Verso.

Giddens, A. (1990). *The Consequences of Modernity*. Stanford: Stanford University Press.

Gramsci, A. (1971). *Selections from the Prison Notebooks*. London: Lawrence and Wishart.

Gramsci, A. (1985). *Selections from Cultural Writings*. Cambridge: Harvard University Press.

Harrington, A. (2004). *Modern Social Theory: An Introduction*. Oxford: Oxford University Press.

Haveman, H. A., & Wetts, R. (2019). Organizational theory: From classical sociology to the 1970s. *Sociology Compass*, *13*(3), 1–14. doi: 10.1111/soc4.12627

Hindess, B. (1977). Humanism and teleology in sociological theory. In B. Hindess (Ed.), *Sociological Theories of the Economy* (pp. 157–189). London: Palgrave Macmillan.

Horkheimer, M. (1972). *Critical Theory: Selected Essays*. New York: Continuum.

Howson, R. (2005). *Challenging Hegemonic Masculinity*. London: Routledge

Kienzle, H. J. (1970). Epistemology and sociology. *The British Journal of Sociology*, *21*(4), 413–424.

Marx, K. (1974). *Capital, A Critical Analysis of Capitalist Production Volume I.* Moscow: Progress Publishers.
Marx, K., & Engels, F. (1950). *Selected Works Volume I.* Moscow: Foreign Languages Publishing House.
McNay, L. (2022). *The Gender of Critical Theory: On the Experiential Grounds of Critique.* Oxford: Oxford University Press.
Meehan, E. (1995). *Feminists Read Habermas: Gendering the Subject of Discourse.* London: Routledge.
Park, R. E., & Burgess, E. W. (1921). *Introduction to the Science of Sociology.* Chicago: The University of Chicago Press.
Plumwood, V. (1993). The politics of reason: Towards a feminist logic. *Australasian Journal of Philosophy*, *71*(4), 436–462. doi: 10.1080/00048409312345432
Silverstone, R. (2005). The Sociology of Mediation and Communication. In C. Calhoun, C. Rojek & B. Turner (Eds.), *Handbook of Sociology* (pp. 188–207). London: Sage.
Weber, M. (1978). *Economy and Society Volume One.* Berkeley, CA: University of California Press.
Weber, M. (1989). *The Protestant Ethic and the Spirit of Capitalism.* London: Unwin Hyman.
Wilde, L. (1989). *Marx and Contradiction.* Aldershot: Avebury.
Wollstonecraft, M. (2004). *A Vindication of the Rights of Woman.* 1st pub. 1792. London: Penguin.

5

PARADIGMS, GENDER AND THE MAKING OF MEN AND MASCULINITIES IN ORGANIZATION THEORY

Albert J. Mills, Jean Helms Mills and Liela A. Jamjoom

Introduction

In addressing the broad question of the link between paradigmatic thinking and the making of men and masculinities, we explore the role of paradigms in the gendering of the field of Organization Theory, in particular, the sub-field of Management and Organization Theory. We argue that the development of the study and theorizing of organizations has a lot to do with men and masculinities, as well as, arguably, impacting back on the organization(s) and organizing of men and masculinities. We begin with an outline of Burrell and Morgan's notion of paradigms, their characterization of four main paradigms – Functionalism, Interpretivism, Radical Structuralism, and Radical Humanism, and the implications of these paradigms for feminist theory. We then draw on Hearn and Parkin's (1983) critique of the gendered characterization of paradigms. From there, we trace the roots of the paradigm debate in Kuhn's theory of *The Structure of Scientific Revolutions* (1962) to reveal the profoundly gendered character of the underlying philosophy and its influence on the constitution of the field of Organization Theory (OT). Drawing on Kuhn's notion of paradigmatic development, we examine early gendered trends in the making of the field of OT.

Those gendered trends include the influence of World War II military practices on the development of post-war behaviourism, with its objectivist focus on observable and quantifiable behaviour (Robin, 2001); the early post-war establishment of the US military research and development think tank – the RAND Corporation – and the militarization of theories of organization including the privileging of masculinist notions of organization (see Abella, 2008); the advent of the Cold War and its links to gendered notions of the workplace and the male character of management (Cooke et al., 2005; Whitfield, 1996); the immediate post-war revival of the US Academy of Management (AoM) as an important, male only, academic association in the field of OT (Grant & Mills, 2006; Myrick et al., 2013; Wrege, 1986); examination of debates among leading male professors around a "unified theory of management" (Koontz, 1964); analysis of the role of male-centred histories (George, 1968; Wren, 1972) and textbooks (Mills & Helms Hatfield, 1999); and the Americanization of OT and the role of colonialist narratives in the development of OT (Ibarra-Colado, 2006;

 DOI: 10.4324/9781003193579-6

Wanderley & Barros, 2019). The chapter concludes with recent critiques of the gendered character of OT and alternative ways of viewing organizing.

From functionalism to radical structuralism: Burrell and Morgan's four paradigms

In a number of ways, the notion of OT has come to be understood as a more or less fixed, unified, scientific field of knowledge production (Burrell & Morgan, 1979). According to Burrell and Morgan (1979), the character of this field of knowledge is "a concern for providing explanations of *the status quo*, *social order*, *consensus*, *social integration*, *solidarity*, *need satisfaction* and *actuality*" (p. 26). In the process, it "tends to be *realist*, *positivist*, *determinist*, and *nomothetic*" (p. 26). As such, it can be viewed as "a functionalist paradigm [that] has provided the dominant framework . . . for the study of organizations [and is] at the forefront of . . . management and organization studies" (pp. 25–26). Writing in the late 1970s, Burrell and Morgan (1979) saw OT as constituting a "powerful managerialist worldview" with influence over the theories and practices over what and who gets published, hired and promoted in the academic and gendered world of the business school. As such, OT has, at least until recently, tended to neglect other forms of organizations and organizing.

In developing their characterization of the functionalist paradigm and its dominance, Burrell and Morgan (1979) contended that there were potentially three other paradigmatic communities of scholars in the field of OT– communities that were markedly different from the functionalist paradigm, namely, radical structuralists, radical humanists and interpretivists. The Interpretivist paradigm referred to communities of scholars whose epistemological notion of evidence is grounded in concern to seek "explanation within the realm of individual consciousness and subjectivity, within the frame of the participant as opposed to the observer of action" (Burrell & Morgan, 1979, p. 28). Radical Humanists, on the other hand, while sharing a subjectivist approach with the Interpretivist paradigm, adopts "a frame of reference . . . committed to overthrowing the limitations of existing social arrangements" (p. 32). Radical Structuralists share the Radical Humanist focus on social change but "from an objectivist standpoint" (p. 33). Burrell and Morgan's (1979) characterization of OT and its role in the development of Management and Organization Studies (MOS) strongly influenced how management scholars were to understand OT.[1]

Following Kuhn's *Structure of Scientific Revolutions* to deal with gender imbalances

In attempting to understand changing knowledge in the social sciences, Burrell and Morgan (1979) were drawn to Kuhn's (1962) notion of paradigms. To that end, they sought to discover those factors that contribute to unities of thought and ways of producing knowledge. Burrell and Morgan (1979) argue that Kuhn defined paradigms "as universally recognised scientific achievements that for a time provide model problems and solutions to a community of practitioners" (Kuhn, 1970, p. viii, cited in Burrell & Morgan, 1979, pp. 35–36). However, Burrell and Morgan go on to point out that they are "using the term 'paradigm' in a broader sense than that intended by Kuhn" (p. 36). While Kuhn sets out to understand how communities of practice constitute a unity of thought, Burrell and Morgan (1979) set out to focus more on the processes of change in the social sciences – seeking to understand how "scientific revolution occurs when a new paradigm emerges, and becomes accepted by the scientific community" (Keat & Urry, 1975 p. 55, cited in Burrell & Morgan, 1979, p. 36). Another interesting difference between Burrell and Morgan and Kuhn is that while the latter lays out key factors that reveal the processes of unification, the former focus on what a foundational paradigm looks like. Burrell and Morgan's world is one where fully formed paradigms exist. We do not know how a particular paradigm got there but we know what they look like. Kuhn's world, on the other hand, is one of various processes in an as-yet-formed paradigmatic environment. We know some of the processes involved in the unification of thought, but we do not know what direction they are going in. If Kuhn is at the beginning of the formation of paradigmatic thinking, Burrell and Morgan are at the foundational end of the journey. Yet, despite the lack of focus on gendered processes and paradigms, both Burrell and Morgan (1979) and Kuhn (1962) provide an interesting method for exposing and dealing with gender imbalances at work.

In the following sections, we shall visit several of Kuhn's key concepts, including the role of history, textbooks, normal science, dogmatism, scientific revolutions; a disunified array of schools, interactions, consensus, techniques of interpretation, simplification and the taken-for-granted, which we address in the making of a stable paradigm. In each case, we will examine the potential influence of gender.

From gender neglect to gendered organizations

Burrell and Morgan's (1979) characterization was not without contention, particularly among feminist organizational scholars (Mills, 1988). An important challenge came from Hearn and Parkin (1983) who critiqued Burrell and Morgan's "neglect" of gender. As Hearn and Parkin went on to argue, examples of gender issues and findings are clearly discernible across all four paradigms. In the process, Hearn and Parkin's critique was an early contribution to an emergent "gendered organizations . . . field of study" (Martin & Collinson, 2002, p. 244). In the process of attempting to identify the leading theorists in each paradigm, Burrell and Morgan contributed to the sense of each paradigm as male-centred.[2] For example, only three female scholars are referenced in the entire book – Mary Parker Follett, Joan Woodward and Simone de Beauvoir (with the latter two only included in the references). It would be decades after the publication of Burrell and Morgan's (1979) book before Parker Follett and Woodward gained recognition (Tancred-Sheriff & Campbell, 1992) in the OT literature, and we continue to wait for serious attention to de Beauvoir in the OT field (Bettin & Mills, 2018).

Arguably, the relative absence of women's power in a particular field leaves a potential gap for male leaders and theorists to be associated with dominant forms of maleness and masculinity in OT or some kind of "hegemonic masculinity" (Connell, 1995). A good example here is bureaucracy where the major theorists are usually identified as men (e.g. Weber, 1947) and the major values include rationality, objectivity, and a lack of emotionality (Ferguson, 1984).

Paradigms

A paradigm can be viewed as an end game; namely, the development of shared ways of thinking and practices in the creation of a community of scholars. It is a point in the development of scientific knowledge where the "scientist's work is devoted to the articulation and wider application of the accepted paradigm, which is not itself questioned or criticized" (Keat &

Urry, 1975, p. 55, cited by Burrell & Morgan, 1979, p. 36). Kuhn (1962) lays out a series of socio-psychological factors that influence consensus and how it is sustained. He argues that the paradigm is marked by "normal science".

Normal science

Normal science refers to a series of relatively stable and related scientific activities that develop through consensus around such things as methods and evidentiary practices. Such activities are sustained through such behaviours as consensus and dogmatism, which allows scientists to "take the conceptual, experimental and instrumental bases of their field for granted and direct their attention to the peripheral areas" (Kuhn, 1962, cited in Reisch, 2019). In particular, Kuhn (1962)

> focuses on a scientific community's more or less shared understanding of the character of the field and what counts as "preferred techniques of interpretation". Kuhn [goes on to argue] that, while members of the community may disagree on certain things, they share some level of consensus around what is to count as evidence and knowledge-building.
>
> *(Mills et al., 2021, p. 143)*

However, Kuhn's objectivist approach to science does not allow for the gender influences on the development of so-called scientific activities. As Rosabeth Moss Kanter (1977) and other feminist organizational theorists (e.g. Ferguson, 1984) have argued, the sheer percentage of male employees shapes the association of scientific activities with forms of masculinity. In this case, the notion of *normal* science needs to take into account the way that gender imbalances are an integral part of the normalization processes (Hearn & Parkin, 1983).

Joan Acker (1990) provides a comprehensive analysis of how gendered paradigmatic thinking and normal science come together to contribute to gendered organizational work. This involves five levels of analysis that work together: (1) *Gendering practices/structures*, which include the division of labour where men and women are often assigned to different positions of work, power and authority. This can be seen as a normalization of gendered work; (2) *Gendering cultures* through the creation of certain symbols, images and forms of consciousness that serve to associate certain activities with male and/or female employees. For example, until recently commercial aircraft piloting was associated with men – through the exclusion of female pilots and supporting symbols such as military-like uniforms, technical prowess and military experience (Mills, 2006); (3) *Gendering interactions*, between women and women, men and men, and men and women that enact dominance and subordination at various organizational levels and may lend themselves to the development of a series of micro-behaviours and understandings; (4) *Internal gender constructions*, where the various individual actors come to reflect on their workplace activities and their selves in the process; and (5) *Organizational logic*, where certain activities cohere to form understandings of the normal way of working and being. This latter process comes close to the notion of paradigmatic thinking where accepted practices are objectified and taken-for-granted as knowledge of the field. Here, organizational logic forms a lens through which to assess the extent to which accepted practices are being followed. In the process, this contributes to and maintains acceptance of gendered practices in ways that seem normalized.

Acker's (2006) later work expands on the concept of the gendered organization and takes into account how organizations have inequality regimes, "practices, processes, actions, and meanings that result in and maintain class, gender, and racial inequalities within particular organizations" (p. 443). The patterns of complex organizational inequalities are fundamentally complicated by not only gender but also class, race/ethnicity and other differences. We will later discuss the importance of intersectional research in not only broadening the scope and depth to which we study organizations but also having the capacity to push the boundaries of the Western academy (Liu, 2018).

To return to the commercial airline example, the issue for female employees was not simply one of employment practices but also about how their identities were created through a series of symbols (O'Connor, 1997) and interactions (Hochschild, 1983). Two of the most enduring identities in airline cultures are the "heroic male pilot" and the "sexy female flight attendant" (Kane, 1974). The first case is a particular form of masculinity focused on danger, adventure and a "rugged" form of heterosexuality, while the second case is a specific form of femininity focused on (hetero) sexual attraction and the objectification of the female body (Vantoch, 2013). In later years, the increasing numbers of male stewards saw the emergence of a new form of homosexual masculinity as airline commentators sought new ways of making sense of men doing work that was previously associated with female employees (Vantoch, 2013). Various changes in male and female work associations, over time, have served to normalize the gendered character of airline practices and new understandings of the "new normal" organizational logic.

Textbooks

In the field of science, Kuhn (1962) draws attention to the role of the textbook in normalizing a particular way of viewing the world and ways of relating to it. He goes on to contend that socialization and popular writing contribute to the building of professional identity. Here, he explains that the socialization of new entrants (e.g. students and junior faculty) to the field is influenced by contact with those who come to teach and research with them, as well as exposure to lectures, popular writings, speeches and textbooks about science. In the latter case, "textbooks are reinforced and elaborated by teachers in their lectures and speeches and are 'made nearly rigid by the rigors of professional intercourse and publication'" (Kuhn, 1962, as cited in Reisch, 2019, p. 219). Furthermore, textbooks serve "to make scientific revolutions invisible by providing a false rewritten history of how the paradigm came to be established" (Ibid.). For example, in a study of "two of the most cited and used North American management textbooks", the treatment of the relationship between men, women and management cast men in various exemplary leading positions, while casting women, not only as unfit for leadership but also as problematic employees (Williams & Mills, p. 7). This gave the impression that male leadership and problematic female employees were normal aspects of work life – see also Richard et al., 2021, whose study of leading OT textbooks found that discourses of entrepreneurship characterized female entrepreneurs as "damsels in distress" (p. 281).

History

Historical accounts of the development of organizational theory can be found throughout management textbooks over much of the period of the early 1920s to the end of the twentieth century (see, for example, Balderston et al., 1937; George & Jones, 1996). These accounts served to legitimize the field of OT and reinforce selected events (e.g. the Hawthorne Studies), theorists (e.g. Elton Mayo), approved methods and theories (Human Relations theory; Scientific Management), foci (e.g. efficiency; for-profit), and iconic images of men (e.g. the steelworker Schmidt in Taylor, 1911; also see Benschop & Doorewaard, 1998) and women (e.g. in Hawthorne's Relay Assembly Test Room – Acker & Van Houten, 1974) at work. Meantime, in the early 1970s, the Management History Division of the Academy of Management was founded and two of its members – Claude George (1968, 1972) and Daniel Wren (1972) – published histories of management theory. While George only published a second edition of his original 1968 book, Wren's book has been published in several editions through to the present time. George's history includes only four women – Mary Parker Follett, Lilian Gilbreth, Florence N. Trefethen and Ann Robert Jacques Turgot. Only a few words were devoted to Gilbreth and Parker Follett, while the other two were only included as footnote references. Wren, on the other hand, was a bit more generous with his inclusion of 21 female theorists, from a list of more than 600 theorists. The roughly 3% of female theorists included Mary Parker Follett, Mary Barnett Gilson and Lillian Gilbreth – each of whom has been the subject of research into their neglect by management historians (Phipps, 2011; Tancred-Sheriff & Campbell, 1992); Regina Greenwood, Karen Horney, Ida Tarbell, Florence N. Trefethen and Joan Woodward: only Follett, Gilbreth and Trefethen were cited by both historians. Neither history book, beyond the mention of female theorists, had anything to say about women's work at any level.

Scientific revolutions

Scientific revolutions are almost mythical in Kuhn's (1962) framework and refer to changes in the dominant way of thinking. Those changes are difficult in the face of the various activities that come to constitute and black box (Latour, 2005) them as "normal". Historical accounts, for example, can serve to lend credibility to certain practices by suggesting that they are well established over time. Kuhn (1962), however, believes that change in the dominant way of thinking can and does occur "as doubts emerge and grow [as] the community enters a period of 'crisis' that concludes with the sudden, revolutionary transition to a new paradigm" (Reisch, 2019, p. 126). While Kuhn (1962) sees this as part of knowledge production, Burrell and Morgan (1979, pp. 24–25) see this as highly unlikely, arguing that for a theorist to switch paradigms "calls for a change in meta-theoretical assumptions, which, although manifestly possible, is not often achievable in practice" (Mills et al., 2021, p. 143). Nonetheless, in a study of gendered practices in Pan American Airlines, Dye and Mills (2011) found a major change in the characterization of male and female employees over a period of two decades. In the first decade (1950s) studied, there was a dominant "family" discourse in the organization, with men being treated as father figures, favourite uncles, etc., and women, regardless of age, characterized as daughters. In the second decade (1960s), the dominant discourse was enjoined by a competing discourse of women's liberation that was growing in influence in the company. This led to the opening up of jobs and increased support for women, with men and women similarly cast as competing for jobs. Dye and Mills (2011) contend that the availability of competing discourses allowed for greater identity choices and associated job choices. Another case in point is the issue of gender and business history discussed later.

Moving beyond Kuhn's (1962) framework there are at least two other major phenomena that influence the character of a particular paradigm – socio-political context and controversy.

Here, controversy refers to growing and profound differences in fundamental issues of the character of the paradigm. This would include issues of sexuality, acceptable forms of masculinity and of femininity, and the role the employee would be playing in the organization. For example, homosexuality was prohibited across a number of organizations where it was felt that this would somehow affect the potential customer base.

Socio-political context – the Cold War

It has been argued elsewhere that the development of the functionalist paradigm largely took place in the context of the Cold War (Cooke, 1999; Cooke et al., 2005; Kelley et al., 2006). There were arguably two major influences – the militarization of management theory and the politics of McCarthyism. The first case refers to post-war military support for behaviourism (Robin, 2001), including the establishment of the RAND Corporation (Abella, 2008). The latter case refers to the dampening down of progressive influences on the workplace, including feminists (Horowitz, 1998; Runté & Mills, 2006; Rupp & Taylor, 1987), race equality groups (Foner, 1976; Zinn, 1999), organized labour (Filippelli & McColloch, 1995), educators and academics (McLaren & Mills, 2008; Schrecker, 1986), and people of the so-called Global South (see later). However, in another socio-political context, the development of the second wave of feminism (Steinem, 1992) challenged the then-dominant masculinist attitude to women at work, trying to undercut the deep paradigmatic thinking that was inhibiting women from pursuing workplace positions and careers.

Gendered controversy

Kuhn (1962) contended that, prior to the foundation of a paradigm, some level of consensus needs to be established. In the process, he outlines the various ways (e.g. histories, textbooks, dogmatism, etc.) that consensus and normal science are achieved. He said less about how and why consensus may fail or be slow to develop. The development of OT as a functionalist paradigm offers some clues. In the late 1940s and 1950s, there were at least two groups of management scholars concerned with the development of a "Unified Theory" of Management (Koontz, 1964). On the one hand, there was a group of scholars at the Graduate School of Industrial Administration (GSIA), Carnegie Institute of Technology, led by James March and Herbert Simon. On the other hand, there was Harold Koontz and his associates in the Academy of Management.

In 1958, March and Simon published their book *Organizations*, in which they set out to produce

> a comprehensive volume that brings together into a single framework the diverse approaches that have been taken to this subject by sociologists, followers of Taylor's scientific management, business and public administration theorists, social psychologists, and economists interested in the theory of the firm.
>
> *(March & Simon, 1958, p. inside front cover)*

Laying out the disparate work in a so-called emergent field, *Organizations* "was if anything, a reaction to behavioral science disciplines [that] were not only fragmented [but] in 'startling disorder'" (Tadajewski, 2009, p. 738). However, the disparate work identified by March and Simon did not address gender dynamics at work nor recognize or acknowledge the contributions of female organizational scholars. Of roughly 875 authors referenced in the bibliography, only a handful of female organizational scholars are listed, including Mary Parker Follett, Lillian Gilbreth and Marie Jahoda. There were no references to people of the so-called Global South (see later). Of the 34 members of the Carnegie organization research group whose contribution to the book was acknowledged, only three women were mentioned – Edith M. Lentz, Sylvia Sebulsky and Evelyn L. Adams. Lentz was acknowledged as part of the organization research group; Sebulsky for providing "both thoughtful comments on the text and substantial assistance in preparing the bibliography" (p. vi); and "Mrs. Adams . . . [who] typed the manuscript and performed a variety of other tasks connected with the book that are both too diverse and too numerous to be enumerated here" (p. vi). However, the book had a modest reception in the late 1950s. It arguably did not gain any real attention until early in the 1960s and, even then, interest has faded over the past 60 years (Weick, 2017, p. 1527). Along the way, the book's citation count has varied considerably (Anderson & Lemken, 2019). Nonetheless, Weick (2017) felt that March and Simon remained a "durable set of foundations", and Burrell and Morgan (1979) contend that March and Simon's work made an important contribution to the establishment of the functionalist OT paradigm.

Around the same time as *Organizations* was being published, Harold Koontz, a University of California, Los Angeles (UCLA) professor, was expressing similar concerns about the fragmented character of the emergent field of management studies. Characterizing the state of the field as a "management theory jungle" (Koontz, 1961), Koontz set out to make sense of management theory (Koontz, 1962) and developed a unified theory of management (Koontz, 1964). In the process, he outlined what he saw as six major schools of thought that contributed to a jungle of ideas. Those schools consisted of "The Management Process School", "the Empirical School", "The Human Behavior School", "The Decision Theory School", "The Mathematical School" and "The Social System School", in which he included March and Simon. Here, he notes that "this school has made many noteworthy contributions to management" (p. 180) but expresses serious concerns about the role of competing management theories, characterizing them as "intellectual cults" (p. 182).

Koontz's initial way to deal with the problem was to publish his views on the idea of a united theory of management (Koontz, 1961) and then to hold a symposium around the theme. The symposium, planned for two days in November 1962, would consist of leading management theorists and practitioners. The sponsorship and title of the symposium was to be the "University of California Los Angeles (UCLA) Symposium: Toward a Unified Theory of Management". Of the 61 invitees who attended, only 6 were from industry and 55 from academia. The latter included Koontz's colleague at UCLA Neil Jacoby; Fritz Roethlisberger (Harvard); Harry M. Markowitz (RAND); and James March, Herbert Simon and Richard Cyert from the Carnegie Institute of Technology. The largest group consisted of 17 scholars who were all associated with the Academy of Management (AoM). They included Koontz who would become AoM President in 1963; R.C. Davis (AoM President, 1948), John Mc (1952), Ronald Shuman (1955), Billy Geotz (1958), Keith Davis (1964), Donald McFarland (1965), Preston Le Breton (1966), Earnest Dale (1968), William Wolf (1971) and George Steiner (1972). None of the 61 participants was woman. The AoM did not directly exclude women as members, but they had a recruitment strategy that effectively did so. Basically, existing AoM members invited new members to join and, however, intended, this effectively excluded female membership. Thus, while the AoM was re-established in 1948, it was 1956 before it had its first female member: Mrs. M. A. Miles was listed as one of the 123 paid-up members (Grant & Mills, 2006). It took three more years before a second woman – Ruth E. Troy, of Steubenville College, Ohio – was recruited, but with 337 paid-up members, she was part of a smaller percentage of female members, a trend that carried through 1961 when Koontz was planning the UCLA Symposium. It would be a further 18 years, in 1979, that the AoM elected its first female President – Rosemary Pledger (Grant & Mills, 2006).

Business history as an example of a gendered paradigm within OT

The field of business history provides a perfect example of a gendered paradigm. To begin with, the great majority of North American management textbooks have either little or nothing to say about women, gender or sex differences (Mills & Helms Hatfield, 1999) and/or problematize women (Williams & Mills, 2019). A 1999 review of "107 widely used North American business texts published between 1959 and 1996 concluded that the typical business textbook constitutes a narrative that is built around a white, male, liberal American view of reality" (Mills, 2004, p. 33). Most recently, Kim et al.'s (2022) study published in *Research Policy* explored over one million doctoral dissertations from 1980 to 2010 to discover a bias against topics and research designs that are "feminized". The authors reveal how feminized knowledge reduces the PhD holder's career prospects in their respective fields. Accordingly, "masculinized" research focusing on algorithm, control, efficiency or structure is rewarded, whereas a focus on feminine research, methods and theory is often penalized.

Furthermore, a 2004 study comparing the influence of feminist and malestream theories of organization indicated that whereas "the average feminist theory takes about seven years to be cited [in textbooks], mainstream approaches are recognized in almost half that time" (Mills, 2004, p. 41). Therefore, the citing of feminist organizational theory "has been pitifully slow and inadequate" (Ibid.). For example, it took 24 years before Acker and Van Houten's (1974) study of sex power differentials was cited in a management textbook, and 12 years from publication for Hochschild's (1983) study of emotion to be noticed there. Williams and Mills' (2019) study of the portrayal of women in management textbooks revealed that the notion of women as problematic changed over time to reflect broad stereotypical characterizations of women at a given time. Thus, at one very important layer – textbooks – authorship, content and impact are very limiting in terms of women's contributions. Phillips and Rippin (2010) introduce a second crucial layer, noting that there is "little if any work taking place on the part played by women in the construction of management practices" (p. 283). They go on to link this to authorship (a third level) that they view as "privileged through such things as organizational focus (e.g. male-dominated work) and the exclusion of non-paid work from the study of organizing and managing" (Mills & Novicevic, 2020, p. 62). To that end, Phillips and Rippin (2010) "challenge the marginalization of women's work and the role of women in history, including the marginalization of female management theorists and historians" (Mills & Novicevic, 2020, p. 62). They went on to co-edit a Special Issue on "Women in Management and Organizational History" in the journal *Management & Organizational History*. Nonetheless, a decade later, feminist scholars were still trying to make the case against the marginalization of women historians and the domination of male historians and masculinist narratives (see Hannah Dean, Linda Perriton, Scott Taylor and Mary Yeager's 2020 call for a Special Issue on "Gender, Feminism, and Business History: From periphery to centre" in the journal *Business History*).

Decolonial and critical race perspectives in OT

Taking the discussion away from solely looking at the pervasive masculinity of OT, OT has also been critiqued for neglecting knowledge from different historical and geographical contexts (Ibarra-Colado, 2006; Mignolo, 2009; Mohanty, 1988; Nkomo, 2011; Spivak, 1988; Wanderley & Barros, 2019). The masculinity of OT is compounded with the Anglo-Saxon frame of reference (Frenkel & Shenhav, 2006), which does not position itself as such but as knowledge that is Global/Universal and all-encompassing. Mignolo (2009) argues that the zero-point epistemology prevalent within OT assumes some kind of neutrality, where a privileged knowing "Western" body occupies a detached and neutral point of observation, and expects "the importation, translation, and repetition of knowledge produced in the Anglo-Saxon world" (Ibarra-Colado, 2006, p. 465). This, Ibarra-Colado (2006) argues, is a false discourse, where the very idea of "organization" has been invented as an artifice that "homogenizes different realities" (p. 465), effaces history (Mignolo, 2009; Wanderley & Barros, 2019), suppresses different modes of organizing (Pal, 2016) and subverts locally generated ideas towards a universal conception of "organization" (Prasad, 2003).

Orientalist discourses embedded in OT are used as mechanisms of controlling the Other (Frenkel & Shenhav, 2006; Said, 1978), while also constructing the boundaries of the field: Western, masculine and based on scientific and positivist ways of knowing. The colonial aspect of management views other ways of knowing as inferior to the dominant Western perspective. This binary epistemology excludes ethnic and racial voices from OT and justifies universal claims under the pretext of its civilizing mission (Dirlik, 2002). Therefore, the field of MOS has been built upon a system of omissions, where it capitalizes on a binary distinction between the West and Non-West (Frenkel & Shenhav, 2006). For example, Ashis Nandy (1983) describes the colonial encounter between the British and Indian people(s) as a contradictory one, where the language of the colonizer used hypermasculine descriptors to glorify colonialism, whereas infantilized and effeminized the Indian people(s) to only emphasize their need to be controlled. The fantasy of re-masculinization not only transcends in territorial control and expansion but also has been used as methods to legitimate positive, scientific, "evidence-based" knowledge over oral histories, Indigenous wisdoms, religious and spiritual stories, alternative knowledge and intersectional perspectives (Doucette et al., 2021; Jamjoom, 2021; Jamjoom & Mills, 2022; Karam & Afiouni, 2021; Mahmood, 2005; Manning, 2021). The language of colonial ideology is deeply tinted with masculinization and Westernization.

Fanon (1967) in *Black Skin, White Masks* famously said: "The white man is locked in his whiteness" (p. xiii). This white solipsism, the tendency to think, imagine and speak as if whiteness described the world (Swan, 2017) is entrenched in OT. Iranian writer and philosopher Al-i Ahmad (1984) described the West's power on intellectual autonomy as a disease called "Occidentosis", which calls on a ubiquitous conformity to Western ideals and desires. As such, decolonial thinking emerged as a process of unveiling the "epistemic silences of the racially devalued" (Mignolo, 2009, p. 162), where it defamiliarizes "common" organizational phenomena (Prasad, 2003) towards original emancipated creation (Ibarra-Colado, 2006). It decouples the useless dependency of the Non-West to the West, while revealing colonialist ways of thinking in business (Jack et al., 2011; Jammulamadaka et al., 2021).

There have been thoughtful efforts to include other geographic insights into OT disrupting the "Americanization" and masculinization of OT (e.g. Nkomo, 2011; Sidani, 2008). Indigenous frames of reference have proven to granulate the study of organizations. Concepts such as border-thinking (Anzaldúa, 1987; Mignolo, 1999, 2011), Two-Eyed Seeing (Colbourne et al., 2020) and hybrid epistemologies (Bhabha, 1994; Frenkel & Shenhav, 2006) have been used as hyphenated spaces merging between Western and Non-Western knowledge, decolonizing praxis and offering an alternative to the rigid, masculine and Western conventions of the academy. While at first efforts to balance the masculinity of OT were justified by adding voices of White, middle-class women to MOS, following the important postcolonial feminist work of Spivak (1988) and Mohanty (1988), the 1990s saw the emergence of postcolonial feminist writing in MOS seeking to reveal the heterogeneity of women's experiences in organizations. "The simple addition of women to the research process no longer seemed adequate" (McCall, 2005, p. 1775) to counter the masculinity of the field, and research which showcased the intersectional identity categories of women (e.g. race, ethnicity, gender, religion, etc.) and interlocking systems of oppression gained prominence (e.g. Calás et al., 2013; Collins, 1990; Grillo, 1995; Ludvig, 2006; Sanchez-Hucles & Davis, 2010). Therefore, postcolonial interrogative spaces in OT "contribute to the development of a more critical and heterodox examination of organizations and organizing" (Jack et al., 2011, p. 275).

Conclusion

This chapter provides an outline of the role and impact of paradigms on gendered practices and in particular masculine dominance of organizational theory. Drawing on Thomas Kuhn's notion of paradigm thinking, we have outlined how certain practices combine to produce normal science that serves to normalize ways of doing gender, men and masculinity in an organizational context. We have argued that through detailed accounts of the practices and activities that encourage masculinity, particularly hegemonic masculinity, we can also provide detailed strategies for challenging various forms of masculinity. Our starting point is to ask the question: "Is there a feminist organizational paradigm" or, if not, "What would a feminist organizational paradigm look like?" and "What lessons can we learn from exploring these possibilities?" (see Mills & Murgatroyd, 1991).

Notes

1 According to Google Scholar, the book has to date been referenced, cited and similarly noted 19,000 times.
2 We use the term, male-centred, here to refer to the perception of reality seen through a male-centred lens; we use masculinity to refer to a set of attributes, behaviours and roles associated with men and boys.

References

Abella, A. (2008). *Soldiers of Reason. The Rand Corporation and the Rise of the American Empire.* New York: Harcourt.
Acker, J. (1990). Hierarchies, jobs, bodies: A theory of gendered organizations. *Gender & Society*, *4*(2), 139–158. doi: 10.1177/089124390004002002
Acker, J. (2006). Inequality regimes: Gender, class, and race in organizations. *Gender & Society*, *20*(4), 441–464. doi: 10.1177/0891243206289499
Acker, J., & Van Houten, D. R. (1974). Differential recruitment and control: The sex structuring of organizations. *Administrative Science Quarterly*, *9*(2), 152–163. doi: 10.2307/2393886
Al-i Ahmad, J. (1984). *Occidentosis: A Plague from the West.* Jakarta: Mizan Press Berkeley.

Anderson, M. H., & Lemken, R. K. (2019). An empirical assessment of the influence of March and Simon's organizations: The realized contribution and unfulfilled promise of a masterpiece. *Journal of Management Studies, 56*(8), 1537–1569. doi: 10.1111/joms.12527

Anzaldúa, G. 1987. *Borderlands/La Frontera: The New Mestiza.* San Francisco: Aunt Lute Books.

Balderston, C. C., Karabasz, V. S., & Brecht, R. P. (1937). *Management of an Enterprise.* New York: Prentice-Hall.

Benschop, Y., & Doorewaard, H. (1998). Six of one and half a dozen of the other: The gender subtext of Taylorism and team-based work. *Gender, Work & Organization, 5*(1), 5–18. doi: 10.1111/1468-0432.00042

Bettin, C., & Mills, A. J. (2018). She came and stayed: A De Beauvorean approach to organizing. In T. Peltonen, H. Gaggiotti & P. Case (Eds.), *Origins of Organizing* (pp. 69–88). London: Edward Elgar.

Bhabha, H. K. (1994). *The Location of Culture.* New York: Routledge.

Burrell, G., & Morgan, G. (1979). *Sociological Paradigms and Organisational Analysis.* Burlington, VT: Ashgate.

Calás, M. B., Ou, H., & Smircich, L. (2013). "Woman" on the move: Mobile subjectivities after intersectionality. *Equality, Diversity and Inclusion: An International Journal, 32*(8), 708–731. doi: 10.1108/EDI-05-2012-0037

Colbourne, R., Moroz, P., Hall, C., Lendsay, K., & Anderson, R. B. (2020). Indigenous works and two eyed seeing: Mapping the case for indigenous-led research. *Qualitative Research in Organizations and Management: An International Journal, 15*(1), 68–86. doi: 10.1108/QROM-04-2019-1754

Collins, P. H. (1990). *Black Feminist thought: Knowledge, Consciousness and the Politics of Empowerment.* Boston, MA: Unwin Hyman.

Connell, R. W. (1995). *Masculinities.* Berkeley, CA: University of California Press.

Cooke, B. (1999). Writing the left out of management theory: The historiography of the management of change. *Organization, 6*(1), 81–105. doi: 10.1177/135050849961004

Cooke, B., Mills, A. J., & Kelley, E. (2005). Situating Maslow in Cold War America: A recontextualization of management theory. *Group & Organization Management, 30*, 129–152. doi: 10.1177/1059601104273062

Dirlik, A. (2002). Rethinking colonialism: Globalization, postcolonialism, and the nation. *Interventional Journal of Postcolonial Studies, 4*(3), 428–448. doi: 10.1080/136980102200001383

Doucette, M. B., Gladstone, J. S., & Carter, T. (2021). Indigenous conversational approach to history and business education. *Academy of Management Learning & Education, 20*(3), 473–484. doi: 10.5465/amle.2020.0530

Dye, K. E., & Mills, A. J. (2011). Dueling discourses at work: Upsetting the gender order. *Canadian Journal of Administrative Science, 28*(4), 427–439.

Fanon, F. (1967). *Black Skin, White Masks.* London: Grove Press Inc.

Ferguson, K. E. (1984). *The Feminist Case against Bureaucracy.* Philadelphia, PA: Temple University Press.

Filippelli, R. L., & McColloch, M. D. (1995). *Cold War in the Working Class. The Rise and Decline of the United Electrical Workers.* Albany, NY: State University of New York.

Foner, P. S. (1976). *Organized Labor & the Black Worker 1619–1973.* New York: International Publishers.

Frenkel, M., & Shenhav, Y. (2006). From binarism back to hybridity: A postcolonial reading of management and organization studies. *Organization Studies, 27*(6), 855–876. doi: 10.1177/0170840606064086

George, C. S. (1968). *The History of Management Thought.* Englewood Cliffs, NJ: Prentice-Hall.

George, C. S. (1972). *The History of Management Thought*, 2nd edition. Englewood Cliffs, NJ: Prentice-Hall.

George, J. M., & Jones, G. R. (1996). *Understanding and Managing Organizational Behavior.* Reading, MA: Addison-Wesley.

Grant, J. D., & Mills, A. J. (2006). The quiet Americans: Formative context, the Academy of Management leadership, and the management textbook, 1936–1960. *Management & Organizational History, 1*(2), 201–224. doi: 10.1177/1744935906064088

Grillo, T. (1995). Anti-essentialism and intersectionality: Tools to dismantle the master's house. *Berkeley Women's Law Journal, 10*(1), 16–30.

Hearn, J., & Parkin, P. W. (1983). Gender and organizations: A selective review and a critique of a neglected area. *Organization Studies*, *4*(3), 219–242. doi: 10.1177/017084068300400302
Hochschild, A. R. (1983). *The Managed Heart*. Berkeley, CA: University of California Press.
Horowitz, D. (1998). *Betty Friedan and the Making of the Feminine Mystique*. Amherst, MA: University of Massachusetts Press.
Ibarra-Colado, E. (2006). Organization studies and epistemic coloniality in Latin America: Thinking otherness from the margins. *Organization*, *13*(4), 463–488. doi: 10.1177/1350508406065851
Jack, G., Westwood, R., Srinivas, N., & Sardar, Z. (2011). Deepening, broadening and re-asserting a postcolonial interrogative space in organization studies. *Organization*, *18*(3), 275–302. doi: 10.1177/1350508411398996
Jamjoom, L. A. (2021). A spectacle of otherness: An autoethnography of a conference presentation. *Qualitative Research in Organizations and Management: An International Journal*, *16*(1), 261–277. doi: 10.1108/QROM-12-2018-1708
Jamjoom, L. A., & Mills, A. J. (2022). Narratives of workplace resistance: Reframing Saudi women in leadership. *Human Relations*. doi: 10.1177/00187267221087593
Jammulamadaka, N., Faria, A., Jack, G., & Ruggunan, S. (2021). Decolonising management and organisational knowledge (MOK): Praxistical theorising for potential worlds. *Organization*, *28*(5), 717–740. doi: 10.1177/13505084211020463
Kane, P. (1974). *Sex Objects in the Sky*. Chicago: Follett.
Kanter, R. M. (1977). *Men and Women of the Corporation*. New York: Basic Books.
Karam, C. M., & Afiouni, F. (2021). Career constructions and a feminist standpoint on the meaning of context. *Gender, Work and Organization*, *28*(2), 672–700. doi: 10.1111/gwao.12607
Keat, R., & Urry, J. (1975). *Social Theory as Science*. London: Routledge and Kegan Paul.
Kelley, E. S., Mills, A. J., & Cooke, B. (2006). Management as a Cold War phenomenon? *Human Relations*, *59*(5), 603–610. doi: 10.1177/0018726706066437
Kim, L., Smith, D. S., Hofstra, B., & McFarland, D. A. (2022). Gendered knowledge in fields and academic careers. *Research Policy*, *51*, 1–15. doi: 10.1016/j.respol.2021.104411
Koontz, H. D. (1961). The management theory jungle. *Journal of the Academy of Management*, *4*(3), 174–188. doi: 10.2307/254541
Koontz, H. D. (1962). Making sense of management theory. *Harvard Business Review*, *40*(4), 24–48.
Koontz, H. D. (Ed.). (1964). *Toward a Unified Theory of Management*. New York: McGraw-Hill.
Kuhn, T. S. (1962). *The Structure of Scientific Revolutions*. Chicago: University of Chicago Press.
Kuhn, T. S. (1970). *The Structure of Scientific Revolutions*, 2nd edition. Chicago: University of Chicago Press.
Latour, B. (2005). *Reassembling the Social: An Introduction to Actor-Network-Theory*. Oxford: Oxford University Press.
Liu, H. (2018). Re-radicalising intersectionality in organisation studies. *Ephemera: Theory & Politics in Organizations*, *18*(1), 81–101.
Ludvig, A. (2006). Differences between women? Intersecting voices in a female narrative. *European Journal of Women's Studies*, *13*(3), 245–258. doi: 10.1177/1350506806065755
Mahmood, S. (2005). *Politics of Piety: The Islamic Revival and the Feminist Subject*. Princeton, NJ: Princeton University Press.
Manning, J. (2021). Decolonial feminist theory: Embracing the gendered colonial difference in management and organisation studies. *Gender, Work and Organization*, *28*(4), 1203–1219. doi: 10.1111/gwao.12673
March, J. G., & Simon, H. A. (1958). *Organizations*. New York: John Wiley & Sons.
Martin, P. Y., & Collinson, D. (2002). 'Over the pond and across the water': Developing the field of 'gendered organizations'. *Gender, Work & Organization*, *9*(3), 244–265. doi: 10.1111/1468-0432.00159
McCall, L. (2005). The complexity of intersectionality. *Signs: Journal of Women in Culture and Society*, *30*(3), 1771–1800. doi: 10.1086/426800
McLaren, P. G., & Mills, A. J. (2008). A product of 'his' time? Exploring the construct of managers in the Cold War era. *Journal of Management History*, *14*(4), 386–403. doi: 10.1108/17511340810893126
Mignolo, W. D. (1999). I am where I think: Epistemology and the colonial difference. *Journal of Latin American Cultural Studies*, *8*(2), 235–245. doi: 10.1080/13569329909361962
Mignolo, W. D. (2009). Epistemic disobedience, independent thought and decolonial freedom. *Theory, Culture & Society*, *26*(8), 159–181. doi: 10.1177/0263276409349275

Mignolo, W. D. (2011). Geopolitics of sensing and knowing: On (de)coloniality, border thinking and epistemic disobedience. *Postcolonial Studies, 14*(3), 273–283. doi: 10.3384/confero.2001-4562.13v1i1129
Mills, A. J. (1988). Gareth Morgan: An interview. *Aurora, 11*(2).
Mills, A. J. (2004). Feminist organizational analysis and the business textbook. In D. E. Hodgson & C. Carter (Eds.), *Management Knowledge and the New Employee* (pp. 30–48). London: Ashgate.
Mills, A. J. (2006). *Sex, Strategy and the Stratosphere: Airlines and the Gendering of Organizational Culture*. London: Palgrave Macmillan.
Mills, A. J., & Helms Hatfield, J. C. (1999). From imperialism to globalization: Internationalization and the management text. In S. R. Clegg, E. Ibarra & L. Bueno (Eds.), *Global Management: Universal Theories and Local Realities* (pp. 37–67). Thousand Oaks, CA: Sage.
Mills, A. J., & Murgatroyd, S. J. (1991). *Organizational Rules: A Framework for Understanding Organizational Action*. Milton Keynes: Open University Press.
Mills, A. J., & Novicevic, M. M. (2020). *Management and Organizational History: A Research Overview*. London: Routledge.
Mills, A. J., Novicevic, M. M., & Roberts, F. (2021). ANTi-History of the functionalist paradigm in organization theory: Using the lens of March and Simon's Organizations. *Journal of Management History, 28*(1), 134–155. doi: 10.1108/jmh-03-2021-0021
Mohanty, C. T. (1988). Under Western eyes: Feminist scholarship and colonial discourses. *Feminist Review, 30*, 333–359. doi: 10.1057/fr.1988.42
Myrick, K., Helms Mills, J., & Mills, A. J. (2013). History-making and the Academy of Management: An ANTi-History perspective. *Management & Organizational History, 8*(4), 345–370. doi: 10.1080/17449359.2013.821662
Nandy, A. (1983). *The Intimate Enemy: Loss and Recovery of Self under Colonialism*. New Delhi: Oxford University Press.
Nkomo, S. M. (2011). A postcolonial and anti-colonial reading of "African" leadership and management in organization studies: Tensions, contradictions and possibilities. *Organization, 18*(3), 365–386. doi: 10.1177/1350508411398731
O'Connor, E. S. (1997). Gender, culture and organizational change. *Organisation Studies, 18*(1), 157–162.
Pal, M. (2016). Organization at the margins: Subaltern resistance of Singur. *Human Relations, 69*(2), 419–438. doi: 10.1177/0018726715589797
Phillips, M., & Rippin, A. (2010). Striving to uncover a lost heritage: Reclaiming women in management and organization history. *Management & Organizational History, 5*(3–4), 283–295. doi: 10.1177/1744935910368333
Phipps, S. T. A. (2011). Mary, Mary, quite contrary. *Journal of Management History, 17*(3), 270 281. doi: 10.1108/17511341111141350
Prasad, A. (2003). The gaze of the other: Postcolonial theory and organizational analysis. In A. Prasad (Ed.), *Postcolonial Theory and Organizational Analysis: A Critical Engagement* (pp. 3–43). New York: Palgrave Macmillan.
Reisch, G. A. (2019). *The Politics of Paradigms. Thomas S. Kuhn, James B. Conant and the Cold War "Struggle for Men's Minds"*. Albany, NY: State University of New York Press.
Richard, T., Deal, N., & Mills, A. J. (2021). Damsels in distress: Discourses of entrepreneurship in management textbooks. *Industry and Higher Education, 35*(4), 281–292.
Robin, R. (2001). *The Making of the Cold War Enemy*. Princeton, NJ: Princeton University Press.
Runté, M., & Mills, A. J. (2006). Cold War, chilly climate: Exploring the roots of gendered discourse in organization and management theory. *Human Relations, 59*(5), 695–720. doi: 10.1177/0018726706066174
Rupp, L. J., & Taylor, V. (1987). *Survival in the Doldrums: The American Women's Rights Movement, 1945 to the 1960s*. New York: Oxford University Press.
Said, E. (1978). *Orientalism*. New York: Pantheon Books.
Sanchez-Hucles, J. V., & Davis, D. D. (2010). Women and women of color in leadership: Complexity, identity, and intersectionality. *The American Psychologist, 65*(3), 171–181. doi: 10.1037/a0017459
Schrecker, E. (1986). *No Ivory Tower. McCarthyism & the Universities*. New York: Oxford University Press.
Sidani, Y. M. (2008). Ibn Khaldun of North Africa: An AD 1377 theory of leadership. *Journal of Management History, 14*(1), 73–86. doi: 10.1108/17511340810845499

Spivak, G. C. (1988). Can the subaltern speak? In C. Nelson & L. Grossberg (Eds.), *Marxism and the Interpretation of Culture* (pp. 271–313). London: Macmillan Education.

Steinem, G. (1992). *Revolution from Within: A Book of Self-Esteem*, 1st edition. Boston: Little, Brown and Co.

Swan, E. (2017). What are white people to do? Listening, challenging ignorance, generous encounters and the 'not yet' as diversity research praxis. *Gender, Work and Organization*, *24*(5), 547–563. doi: 10.1111/gwao.12165.

Tadajewski, M. (2009). The politics of the behavioural revolution in organization studies. *Organization*, *16*(5), 733–754. doi: 10.1177/1350508409338882

Tancred-Sheriff, P., & Campbell, E. J. (1992). Room for women: A case study in the sociology of organizations. In A. J. Mills & P. Tancred (Eds.), *Gendering Organizational Analysis* (pp. 31–45). Newbury Park, CA: Sage.

Taylor, F. (1911). *The Principles of Scientific Management*. New York: Harper & Brothers.

Vantoch, V. (2013). *The Jet Sex: Airline Stewardesses and the Making of an American Icon*. Philadelphia, PA: University of Pennsylvania Press.

Wanderley, S., & Barros, A. (2019). Decoloniality, geopolitics of knowledge and historic turn: Towards a Latin American agenda. *Management & Organizational History*, *14*(1), 79–97. doi: 10.1080/17449359.2018.1431551

Weber, M. (1947). *The Theory of Social and Economic Organization* (A. R. Henderson & T. Parsons, Trans.). London: Free Press.

Weick, K. E. (2017). Evolving reactions: 60 years with March and Simon's 'organizations'. *Journal of Management Studies*, *56*(8), 1527–1536. doi: 10.1111/joms.12289

Whitfield, S. J. (1996). *The Culture of the Cold War*, 2nd edition. Baltimore, MD: Johns Hopkins University Press.

Williams, K. S., & Mills, A. J. (2019). The problem with women: A feminist interrogation of management textbooks. *Management & Organizational History*, *14*(2), 148–166. doi: 10.1080/17449359.2019.1598436

Wrege, C. D. (1986). The inception, early struggles, and flowering of the Academy of Management. In *Academy of Management Archives*. Ithaca, NY: Kheel Center for Labor-Management Documentation and Archives, Martin P. Catherwood Library, Cornell University.

Wren, D. A. (1972). *The Evolution of Management Thought*. New York: The Ronald Press.

Zinn, H. (1999). *A People's History of the United States. 1492-Present*. New York: Harper Collins.

6
DECOLONIZING MASCULINITIES
A decolonial and transnational perspective

Banu Ozkazanc-Pan

Introduction

While traditional[1] and non-critical notions of masculinities have coupled the concept with maleness, this chapter delves into the transnational and decolonial ways (see Hearn et al., 2013, 2019; Hearn, 2015) in which gender "gets done" to offer an anti-colonial reading (see Nkomo, 2011) of masculinities. Within the context of management and organization studies (MOS), a critical approach to the study of masculinities can offer insights into the oft-rendered invisible ways in which gender assumptions and expectations are embedded in managerial perspectives and practices. Moreover, given the global nature of businesses in contemporary economies today, understanding how masculinities shape the gendering of organizational life is quite relevant to addressing inequities of various kinds, including those taking shape across gender relations.

To accomplish this, the chapter offers insights from transnational and decolonial perspectives that allow consideration of the geographically relational, gender fluid and non-binary ways in which masculinities take shape including in the context of work and organizational life. Doing so provides epistemological complexity around the concept of masculinities in line with calls to make explicit the male-centric focus of much management research (Kimmel et al., 2005), including more recent engagements as elaborated in this Handbook (Hearn et al., 2023). At the same time, the chapter contributes to a growing body of writing on critical studies on men and masculinities (CSMM) that expands beyond extant frameworks to the study of masculinities including those arriving from non-Western traditions (Hearn, 2019). Altogether, the chapter provides insights arriving from transnational and decolonial traditions to expand the repertoire of research focus, epistemologies and methods available to understand, study and even challenge masculinities within certain contexts.

In line with growing calls to decolonize imposed epistemologies, often from Western and Northern nations, this chapter contributes some insights into rethinking the social world from the perspective of those who have been colonized. Specifically, it offers some examples of new possibilities in thinking about masculinity in Western contexts through the experiences of those who arrive from former colonies and in non-Western contexts by focusing on the *hijra* communities of India, and the Native American *Two-Spirit people.*[2] As such, the chapter proposes how a particular kind of masculinity was remade in different communities and contexts in the

DOI: 10.4324/9781003193579-7

aftermath of arrival, encounters and colonization. As these communities "re-emerge", or rather start becoming recognized in the wake of global conversations around LGBTQIA+ rights, they also allow us to reconceptualize masculinities from diverse ontological premises and positions. In doing so, they open up opportunities to rethink masculinities beyond colonizer perspectives and epistemological foundations including dominant concepts, such as hegemonic masculinity (Howson & Hearn, 2019), that tend to mask other ways of conceptualizing masculinities. By rethinking masculinities through the complexity of decoloniality and transnationalism, the scholarship that attends to organizations and organizing can broaden its theoretical frameworks in the domains of identities, leadership and management. These areas are relevant to engaging with critical and non-Western perspectives about masculinities, particularly as they relate to identity formation, how leadership becomes enacted and gendered, and finally, in terms of how the management of people that are "different" takes shape. While critical engagement with and transformation away from the hegemonic position is one central aspect of CSMM, the field can nonetheless expand to include theoretical insights from communities whose experiences, identities and practices are not neatly explained or confined to the axioms of Western epistemological formations in regard to masculinity.

Exploring the foundations of masculinities

As a theoretical framework, masculinities have a long and rich history in informing our understanding of men (see Brod & Kaufman, 1994; Connell, 1998; Hearn & Howson, 2019; Kahn, 2009), particularly in relation to organizational life and realities (Kimmel et al., 2005) and in the global context given different social, economic and political norms (Connell, 2016). While there are multiple iterations of how to conceptualize and define masculinities, this chapter adopts the definition proposed by Connell (2020):

> pattern or configuration of social practices linked to the position of men in the gender order, and socially distinguished from practices linked to the position of women. Masculinity is not a pre-social category. Masculinity constantly refers to male bodies (sometimes symbolically and indirectly), but is not determined by male biology. One can, therefore, speak of masculine women, and feminine men; of gender ambivalences and contradictions.
>
> *(p. 40)*

To this end, the notion of hegemonic masculinity (Connell, 1987; also see Donaldson, 1993) has become an important and debated/contested approach to qualifying different types of masculinities which may emerge, be rewarded and/or be seen as creating harm or subordinating other types of masculinities (and femininities).

As Connell and Messerschmidt suggest,

> Men who received the benefits of patriarchy without enacting a strong version of masculine dominance could be regarded as showing complicit masculinity. It was in relation to this group, and to compliance among white heterosexual women, that the concept of hegemony was most powerful. Hegemony did not mean violence, although it could be supported by force; it meant ascendancy achieved through culture, institutions, and persuasion.
>
> *(2005, p. 832)*

And while particular kinds of masculinities may be dominant in specific contexts and even in certain approaches to the study of masculinity, this chapter argues that an anti-colonial/decolonial reading of hegemonic masculinities can foster new space for rethinking this concept and framework beyond the purview of Western epistemological approaches. As Stanovsky (2007, p. 494) suggests, this is an important endeavour in that

> First World discourses about Third World masculinities often produce and maintain representations that serve to create, perpetuate, and reinforce First World norms of masculinity and heterosexuality by way of the boundaries and contrasts provided by these "other" Third World masculinities and sexualities.

Thus, rather than only offering insights into non-Western contexts, a transnational decolonial approach can provide the opportunity to understand how masculinities are formed relationally across historic hierarchies, such as those between colonizer nation-states and colonized societies. These relational aspects of masculinity are quite relevant in the context of global organizational life and cross-border work arrangements as different bodies and identities intersect.

In such instances, there can be insights to be gained from understanding how subjects of former non-Western colonies arrive and enact particular types of masculinities that simultaneously affirm and resist assigned gendered identities in contemporary Western contexts. Similarly, there can be much to learn from non-Western contexts where the aftermath of colonialism has allowed some engagement and conversation around masculinities that were erased or even prohibited under colonial rule. At the same time, it is important to acknowledge that history is rarely neat and that the complexity of gender, race and other relations of difference and power were just as likely present. In other words, the world did not exist neatly in pre- and postcolonial terms but rather in a state of at times contradictory relationships between and among those who arrived and those who were already there.

Culture and gender are not necessarily easily categorized especially when one is "looking back" on history and more importantly, neither are cross-cultural and cross-gender relations. And as Russell suggests,

> Dichotomies are programmable and formalizable – in order to break free of their hold we can opt for another view that of "undecidability". Undecidability refers to the (im) possibility of deciding between discrepant and often contradictory orders of meaning and yet it should not be confused with indecision.
>
> *(2005, p. 34)*

Thus, it is likely that forms of domination across gender and other dimensions existed in precolonial societies and were not necessarily the invention of the colonizer. While these are important reminders about the difficulties of "knowing" history, the goal of the chapter is to address the complexity of those gender relations in postcolonial conditions with a particular emphasis on masculinity. And "seeing" such masculinities emerge and become enacted requires moving beyond the epistemological purview of Western traditions (Savci, 2016) and relying on anti-colonial and decolonial traditions. In all, decolonization is an ongoing process rather than an outcome with different iterations, practices and focal points throughout the varied postcolonial spaces and places that individuals inhabit.

To this end, decolonial perspectives have an established tradition in disciplines outside of organization studies as a means to uncover those ideas, practices and epistemological approaches that were effaced under colonization (see Mignolo, 2007; Mignolo & Escobar, 2013; Bhambra, 2014). This approach can be defined as follows:

> Decolonial theory is concerned with confronting, challenging, and undoing the dominative and assimilative force of colonialism as a historical and contemporary process, and the cultural and epistemological Eurocentrism that underwrites it. Decolonial theory might be said to extend the anticolonial project into considerations of the domains of being and knowing; at the same time, it draws from the complex account of cultural discontinuity and imposition offered by postcolonial studies.
>
> *(De Lissovoy, 2010, p. 280)*

Such an approach has also found resonance within organizational studies as scholars have deployed postcolonial and anti-colonial approaches to interrogate the underlying assumptions of organizational studies, particularly in relation to international management research (Ozkazanc-Pan, 2008), leadership and management studies in African contexts (Nkomo, 2011; Zoogah & Nkomo, 2013), management theories in Tunisia (Yousfi, 2014), and more broadly, critiqued organization studies as a discipline (Jack et al., 2011; Manning, 2021). These interventions question the consequences of how "internationalization", neoliberalism or Western business scholarship as a form of coloniality can erase Indigenous or local knowledge around and about management, leadership and other considerations usually examined within the context of organization studies (see Faria et al., 2010; Murphy & Zhu, 2012). Thus, while not all contexts or people have experienced explicit colonization through military conquest, epistemic conquest via dominant forms of knowledge, practice and ideas also reflects a form of erasure, a form of coloniality. Both material and epistemic violence (Spivak, 1988) are drivers of how individuals may come to understand themselves, their context and the remaking of identities as they inhabit environments that foreground the psychological and physical remnants of empire and coloniality.

Thus, it is important to understand the contributions of decolonial approaches to masculinity studies as a means to expose those ways of being and belonging to the social world (see Levitt & Schiller, 2004) that arrive from traditions and contexts entwined with transnational colonial histories. To this end, there is already work within postcolonial and decolonial feminisms that challenge taken-for-granted gender norms and gender relations as they are manifest within geographies with colonial histories (see Lugones, 2010). Such work aims to not only expose the living and working conditions for many "Global South" women globally but also examine extant gendering processes within these contexts that lead to the formation of the nation-state (Butler & Spivak, 2007). To understand these contributions among others, the next section uncovers approaches to the study of masculinities that arrive from anti-colonial and decolonial perspectives. In all these examples, there are similarities in terms of the role and importance of historical social hierarchies, racialized identities and the emergence of bodies and people whose enactment of gender cannot be neatly or clearly categorized as belonging to male or female – perhaps best understood as Indigenous and localized forms of being queer (see Savci, 2020 for a discussion on queer identity under neoliberal Islam). And while there may be some overlap between decolonial, transnational modes of being inclusive of non-binary forms of self, the difference between these approaches and queer theory is the explicit focus on coloniality and its historic and contemporary consequences, engagement with social fields and attendant forms of resistance.

Questioning coloniality: postcolonial interventions

In one of the first engagements with postcolonial thinking and masculinities, Ouzgane and Coleman (1998) offer an opportunity to understand how postcolonial studies qualify and challenge the assumptions of masculinity in regard to racialized hierarchies between and among men and allow consideration for the discussion of emergent masculinities in postcolonial contexts. Moreover, such an approach can yield insights into how masculinities become made and remade in postcolonial contexts. They suggest, "A careful sifting of the mixture of regressive inhibitions and progressive innovations among the intercultural, refracted masculinities of postcolonial locations could provide models for the combination of strategic coalition-building and reflexive critique fundamental to postcolonial theorizing and anticolonial activism" (Ouzgane & Coleman, 1998, p. 1).

The complexity of postcoloniality as context, as epistemological intervention and as a historic moment provides an opportunity to reconsider how masculinities continue to emerge and be remade in contemporary contexts. But more importantly, it provides an opportunity to understand how the intersections of postcoloniality and profeminist masculinities frameworks alter sedimented ways in which the analytics of masculinity research may need to shift. To this end, feminist engagements with masculinities provide three considerations that become relevant to a rethinking of masculinities through postcolonial frameworks.

> First, they [feminist frameworks] can contribute to the feminist critique of the sexist and homophobic practices that have often derailed movements towards liberation and decolonization. Second, along with feminist critique, they bring a balance to the Marxian arrogation of class over gender, sexuality, and race as primary domains of social struggle. And, third, the analytical apparatus of a hierarchy of masculinities (hegemonic, complicitous, marginalized, and subordinated) refines the accuracy of our understanding of the complex range of positions between dominance and resistance that characterize postcolonial societies.
>
> *(Ouzgane & Coleman, 1998, p. 2)*

As pointed out by other postcolonial scholars such as Edward Said (1985, 2012) and Homi Bhabha (1984, 2012), the making of an empire required a subordination and feminization of male colonial subjects and a simultaneous endeavour to "save" female colonial subjects (see Mohanty, 2003). More pointedly, Spivak (1988, p. 297) suggests that such endeavours are representative of "White men saving brown women from brown men". Consequently, these conversations raise awareness around the intertwined ways in which histories of coloniality impact modern-day forms of masculinities. As such, there is no "getting away" from the past when considering and analysing masculinities as they emerge within contexts that have histories of colonialism. Moreover, colonization requires transgressions across established boundaries, such as those traditionally associated with nation-states or with First Nations – in this sense, coloniality always requires an understanding of and engagement with transnational perspectives.

In other words, postcolonial analytics requires not only historicizing the different forms of masculinities as they emerged through the trauma, violence and conflict of colonization but also their transnational histories. These colonization efforts, whether material, psychological or epistemological, did not end with the end of colonization but rather continued and became manifest in present-day encounters between and among people with shared histories. In this sense, one of the main contributions of postcolonial frameworks to masculinity studies is to provide historicization of the forms of encounter as "hegemonic, complicitous, marginalized, and subordinated" (Ouzgane & Coleman, 1998, p. 2) between people across space and time. And the ways in which these histories impact how masculinities emerge not only in previous colonies but also in present-day colonizer states. These considerations are taken up next to explain how decolonial and deconstruction efforts allow for the emergence of new masculinities and ways of being in the world.

Decolonizing masculinities: new and emergent forms of being

Here, I outline examples from research that have broadened our understanding of masculinities by bringing in transnational, migration and decolonial perspectives to research on men and masculinities. In doing so, the work shared here opens up opportunities to think about dominant concepts such as hegemonic masculinity as these concepts get challenged, transformed and even affirmed. The general mechanisms through which such changes and shifts take shape are related to different identity formation narratives and practices that become manifest as individuals move back and forth between different contexts and social fields through migration or other forms of mobility. In addressing these issues, new forms of organizing can be manifest, particularly in relation to the formation of nations, national identities and organizational structures that are foundational to societies and economies. Or as Ramirez and Munar (2022) suggest, new ways to understand how Indigenous knowledge on/about gender can be brought to bear upon colonial forms of organizing, resulting in challenges but also different forms of violence.

Mobile masculinities

As an example of mobile masculinities that challenge extant notions of the gendered division of labour in homes, Sinatti (2014) examines the everyday talk and gender performance of Senegalese men who have emigrated to Italy. As former European/French subjects, Wolof (Indigenous) men from Senegal migrate to become primary breadwinners but, in doing so, have to renegotiate their own understanding of masculinity and gendered hierarchy within family and society. Her research finds that while in Senegal, the traditional ascendancy of men is to become heads of extended families and offer advice and leadership to their community, the lack of such a figurehead in the newly emigrated context requires new and emergent forms of masculinity. Thus, while traditional gender norms may help define a sense of self for such men within their home context, migration changes this dynamic as they have to craft a new sense of identity and self within "the colony". To this end, Sinatti suggests:

> Migrants build trust relationships with relatives as they share or fully delegate decision-making with fathers, mothers, wives, siblings, or children, depending on the family structure. Although this may lead to greater complicity and equity in such interpersonal relations, it nonetheless also results in the migrant's own male authority being

> diminished. In particular, those with a short migration history who are still young and unmarried (and as a result more easily exposed to economic pressures from relatives back home) struggle to find ways of affirming their own position as men in their families beyond the breadwinning role.
>
> *(Sinatti, 2014, p. 222)*

This example provides a nuanced understanding of the ways masculinities get redone by postcolonial subjects who end up travelling to former colony contexts. Rebuilding a sense of identity that is no longer based on gender norms in their home context, these men simultaneously become "Senegalese" and "men" by virtue of occupying the colonizer's space. In other words, if in Senegal they self-stratify according to Wolof traditions, these gendered hierarchies get remade in the context of not only becoming an ethnic identity but a male one as well. The research provides insights into the ways masculinities are forced to be remade within communities, in relation to the new context and in addition, how social mobility is possible when those who migrated find themselves more eligible and desirable so as to be able to marry into a higher social class upon return.

In a similar vein, Stoltz (2019) suggests that past colonial trauma is relived through narratives and stories that impact how first- and second-generation postcolonial migrants come to understand themselves, focusing on examples of Indonesian migrants in the Netherlands. The role of transnational memories of violent trauma and conflict becomes quite relevant for contemporary notions of masculinity and self within these generations. Thus, rather than a sedentary or binary notion of immigration, Stoltz (2019) suggests that the intergenerational transmission of lived trauma impacts modern-day masculinities in migrant populations, and without both a transnational/mobility perspective and a postcolonial lens, the complexity of new identities that emerge under conditions of migration can be flattened.

Stoltz coins "postcolonial memory politics" as a way to understand and examine "which actors and societies collectively deal with memories of past injustices related to colonialism and/or related wars and their effects upon notions of equality and justice in the present and the future" (Stoltz, 2019, p. 154; see also Stoltz, 2020). By expanding the analytics of masculinities beyond individual identities to historic events and experiences as they relate to coloniality, Stoltz (2019) challenges whether we can understand the emergence of masculinity as an individual activity. Rather, her analysis demonstrates that the emergence of masculinities is made possible through the repository of the lived experiences of our communities rather than the choices we make in the present day. Moreover, it also highlights the ways in which immigration and ethnicity are ever present in how individuals forge identities in the present even though coloniality may be "officially" over. In other words, the consequences of coloniality live further in the ways nation-states have been organized around particular identities while marginalizing or leaving others out.

In all, these examples of mobility in postcolonial contexts demonstrate that the formation of masculinities is not only located in a particular site but also across space, time and memory – an important consideration that highlights the relevance and role of transnational modes of postcolonial analysis as they relate to the formation of masculinities. These examples also show the importance to bring together decolonial/postcolonial, anti-racist, feminist, anti-capitalist and other perspectives given they are related albeit have different analytic focuses. Doing so will allow more robust consideration of how forms of organizing, as they relate to societies and economies, rely on particular social, cultural and historic hierarchies that then become manifest in everyday practices, and performances inclusive of those around self and identities. To this end, any analysis of masculinities in contemporary contexts including those in organizations must be sensitive to how historic power relations, gendered norms and epistemic violence impact the lives and lived experiences of individuals. The application of these ideas within the context of organization studies is taken up in the final section of the chapter.

Remaking empire and self in modernity

In a similar research agenda that focuses distinctly on the remaking of masculinity for men struggling financially, Aboim and Vasconcelos (2021, pp. 324–325) suggest that

> our analysis of financially disadvantaged migrant men in Lisbon privileges an intersectional perspective towards the reconstruction of masculinities, which implies renegotiating the valued traits and symbols of masculinity. These strategies are linked to the history of Portuguese colonialism and the ways men hailing from diverse and contrasting colonial and postcolonial histories within the geographies of the Portuguese Empire (Brazil, Mozambique and Cape Verde) rediscover their subordination in the Portuguese context.

Hence, their research uncovers the importance and value of historicizing transnational colonial relations among and between nations as a means to understand the contemporary making and remaking of masculinities as people move between nation-states. As previous colonial bodies encounter the sites, spaces, and people of the colony, Portugal in this specific case, the relevance, and role of historical context giving way to contemporary forms of masculinities become quite important. Consequently, it is not possible to understand the modern-day encounter between previous colonizers and those they colonized without a sense of the transnational modes of being and belonging. These modes or notions emerged in the histories of two peoples and as such, masculinities understood within this context cannot be neatly summarized as colonizer and colonized. Rather, it must be understood and analysed in a manner that offers insights into the ways ongoing engagements and encounters remake new forms of masculinity across space and place. Beyond gender and power, Aboim and Vasconcelos' analysis highlights the role and importance of modernity *and* postcoloniality in any analysis of contemporary masculinities.

Their findings focus on the emergence of subaltern masculinity that is slightly different and distinct depending on the original set of hierarchies formed during colonization between Portugal and each of the colonial states. Hence, the subaltern forms of masculinities that emerge for each group of men upon their arrival in Portugal can be understood based on the specific historic relationship of nation-states. In this sense, individual notions of identity and identity formation practices cannot be decoupled from the historic context in which they are taking shape. The men each engage in different forms of resistance against the sexualizing tropes of the colonial gaze that subjugate them upon arrival. They also engaged in resistance against dominant forms of masculinity that were intertwined with racialized discrimination related to Whiteness and European ancestry and dominant forms of masculinity that feminized them as being unable to become strong, family men.

As the researchers suggest,

> Despite the commonalities, not just amongst themselves but also in relation to working-class forms of resistance, specific categories of subalternization and empowerment are

forged upon nomenclatures of past colonial oppression. However, despite all the diversity we encountered and sought to interpret, one element of the hegemonic order occupies center stage. Alongside inherited categories, the postcolonial present does not escape the imposition of the capitalist neoliberal order.

(Aboim & Vasconcelos, 2021, p. 339)

In all, the complexity of masculinities when intersecting with historical colonialization and contemporary neoliberalism highlights the importance of understanding aspiration alongside disenchantment and mimicry[3] alongside mockery as strategies for resistance (Aboim & Vasconcelos, 2021).

Epistemic violence and masculinities: non-Western approaches

While the previous sections pointed out ways in which masculinities can be made and remade through ongoing encounters between colonizers and people they colonized in contemporary Western contexts, a similar approach must be taken to understand masculinities that existed in non-Western contexts prior to "arrival" and colonization. Acknowledging these encounters and associated non-Western traditions can provide rich insights into the ways people and groups not only self-identify but how they organize their social and professional lives. To this end, in this section, I focus on those ways of being and belonging by using examples from the *hijra* communities of India, and the Native American *Two-Spirit people*. These are only a handful of examples, but they demonstrate that gender, gender relations and sexualities were not singular or the same across contexts that eventually were colonized and/or were forced to integrate and assimilate Western values, practices and ideologies. By demonstrating differences in how masculinities were manifest in different non-Western contexts, the aim here is to showcase the range of possibilities around gender and identities that defy categorization by Western norms and labels.

Hijra communities: non-binary

In South East Asia, hijra communities have a long history and tradition of both being ostracized for not following established gender norms and also being accepted as existing alongside more traditional gender identities, such as male and female. For the purposes of clarification, hijra can be defined as those people who identify as both male and female but also beyond the dichotomy such that their sense of self is not limited by the available language of masculinities (see Khan et al., 2009). One must ask why the only available language to identify oneself arrives from established norms and words associated with male and female – yet, as pointed out by postcolonial scholars, the arrival of colonialism to South East Asia and, in particular, communities that already had individuals who could be described as non-binary (in contemporary terms) resulted in the creation of epistemic categories and hence violence (see Dasgupta & Gokulsing, 2013).

For example, Gannon (2009) points out the ways in which hijra come to be conceptualized and defined in ways that reflected more the mindset of the colonizers than the existing epistemologies and embodiments of the time. He states:

Consequently, the hijra represent a key point . . . in the anchoring of a field of meaning that enabled colonial governance in both a diachronic and synchronic fashion; in other

> words, the figure of the hijra was translated by the colonial writers in such a way as to facilitate the creation of an ideology that privileged British understandings of sexuality and masculinity, not to mention civility, modernity, and, to a degree, religiosity, establishing British authority in the region.
>
> *(Gannon, 2009, p. ii)*

Other scholars point out that becoming a member of the *hijra* community is more than a particular embodiment of masculinity or sexuality. Rather, it is a label conferred after the individual has attained knowledge and skills related to certain rituals, arts and even a language. Hossain elaborates further on this point as, "only those male-bodied persons with a desire for masculine-identified men qualify to receive the training to become a *hijra* under the auspices of a senior *hijra*" (Hossain, 2017, p. 420). In other words, there is a performative and embodied aspect of becoming *hijra* in a particular cultural and social context. This conceptualization of a non-binary identity expands the repertoire of identities associated with masculinities as it requires an understanding not only of historic, social and cultural contexts but also an understanding of the performative aspects of one's identity. In other words, identity is tied to body *and* performativity.

Yet in the context of colonial rule and epistemic violence, such identities and nuances were often erased, often violently and through physical and psychological means. By voicing these histories of identities that do not fall neatly within Western classifications including masculinities, it is possible to expand not only the concepts we have available to understand both identities but also diversity of people that are part of the social fabric of organizations. These points are addressed more fully in the concluding section in terms of application and relevance for organizations and organizing. Next, I focus on another masculinity that exists beyond Western categorizations, *two-spirited people*.

Two-spirited people in Native American/Indigenous traditions

Similar to observations around masculinities that are outside the realm of Western concepts (Innes & Anderson, 2015), here I focus on *two-spirited people*, a tradition of identifying individuals arising from Native American or Indigenous traditions, whereby deities were not seen as male or female (see Jacobs et al., 1997; also Tafoya & Wirth, 1996). Wilson suggests that this term exemplifies how the experience of sexuality is inseparable from the experience of one's culture and community (1996). In fact, she outlines that such individuals were referred to as *berdache* by Western anthropologists, a concept borrowed from Arabic meaning "effeminate" as a way to impose categories upon male "subjects" who didn't fit neatly into existing identity categories (Wilson, 1996, p. 303). By doing so, the nuance and experiences of such individuals were not only erased but they were cut off from the historic context of the culture and community in which they lived. The imposition of Western identity categories enabled not only control over such people and their lands simultaneously but also silenced differences between different understandings of identities, including masculinities.

To this end, by acknowledging *two-spirited people* as grounded in the historical experiences of Indigenous peoples, we can begin to understand the historic, intergenerational trauma that has been central to the experience of self in Native communities. Weaver (2019) suggests that only a social justice perspective that is right and sovereignty-based can address the ongoing trauma and violence that is manifest in Native peoples as they continue to feel the impact of historic and contemporary colonial structures in their lives including epistemic violence related to identity and psychological well-being. Understanding how imposed identity categories, such as gay or *berdache*, not only cut off an individual from their cultural past, but these approaches also centre a Western perspective on masculinities/gender(s) that not only are inappropriate for the context in question but also create further harm. Ultimately, masculinities arising from Native American traditions, such as *two-spirited people*, challenge Western contemporary notions of sexuality and identity by connecting one's self to one's history, culture and community. This generational link is integral for understanding masculinities in contexts where the imposition of identity categories resulted in generations of trauma and, as such, requires that scholars attend to the nuances of the cultural context in investigating and addressing non-Western identities.

Implications for organizations and organizing

Masculinities offer a rich perspective on expanding our understanding of identities as they relate to organizational experience and phenomena. Yet addressing masculinities from a non-Western, decolonial and transnational perspective can inform three areas within the field of organizations and organizing. I address these points herein as they relate to identity formation, diversity management and cross-cultural business.

First, non-Western perspectives on masculinities expand the language and concepts we have available in relation to identities particularly as they relate to sexualities across history, space and contemporary organizational contexts. In doing so, non-Western perspectives open up conversations around how individuals whose identities do not fit or are not represented by Western perspectives on male behaviours, performativity and sexuality can be included in scholarship on and around organizational experiences. These approaches bridge together identity formation literature with masculinity studies by offering insights into the processes through which individuals embody particular identities that are not readily rendered visible or knowable by extant approaches in these areas. These processes through which individuals are forced to inhabit spaces and/or be rendered visible through concepts that are often imposed upon them can be quite violent. Coercive physical means coupled with epistemic violence has resulted in particular people and gender identities that are rooted in historic coloniality as being acceptable in state-building endeavours.

Second, by addressing non-Western approaches to masculinities, the field of diversity management would expand upon the kinds of people, behaviours and identities that are relevant and important for managing in today's contemporary organizational settings. While gender, race and sexuality have been hallmark considerations in most US-based diversity literature, non-Western perspectives that arrive from decolonial and transnational perspectives open up possibilities for understanding the complexity of experiences individuals have within organizations. That is, diversity management as a field can benefit from an expanded understanding of diversity by including those individuals and experiences that are traditionally not considered within the purview of diversity literature given the complexity of their histories. By intersecting diversity literature with concepts arriving from critical non-Western perspectives on men and masculinities, scholars can expand the repertoire of (violent) Western knowledge that currently dominates how we talk about and research differences. By addressing and valuing non-Western experiences and individuals, diversity management research can become richer and more accurate in addressing and understanding the lived experiences of people in a historic context. This approach can also expand the contributions of masculinity studies to the field of diversity management as the performative aspects of sexuality can expand upon the ways in which we have come to understand workplace behaviours that lead to both positive and negative outcomes for various groups of people.

Finally, non-Western perspectives on masculinities can expand upon the limited ways migration and cross-cultural business experiences have been theorized and researched within management and organization studies. Often, migration is seen as a movement from one place to another, but our engagement with decolonial, postcolonial and transnational perspectives opens up the possibilities of living in multiple cultures, social and cultural contexts and within different generations (as is the custom in Native American communities). To this end, cross-cultural considerations in organizational scholarship must attend to the complex experiences and realities of individuals whose lives span across boundaries, time and cultures, challenging binary concepts, such as host versus expatriate or native versus immigrant to name a few dichotomies, that are foundational to the field today.

In all, decolonial, postcolonial and transnational approaches to critical studies on men and masculinities expand the concepts available to study and understand the lives and lived experiences of individuals whose notions of self defy simple categorization. They offer perspectives that provide opportunities for expanding scholarly work not only in critical masculinity studies but also in the areas of identity formation, diversity management and cross-cultural business. Masculinity studies informed by such non-Western views can offer new insights into the ways in which historic formations of self and ongoing-related performativity take shape in today's contemporary organizations as these organizations span nations, communities and lives.

Notes

1 Here, "traditional" is a reference to Western epistemological perspectives that centre the biological male in conceptualizing masculinities. The aim of this chapter is to decouple this concept not only from biology but also from its Western foundations and assumptions on and around gender relations.

2 As a non-Native outsider, my positionality in discussing Native American perspectives is limited, but I want to acknowledge that these concepts and conversations are relevant to discussions on masculinities. In particular, they allow discussion of concepts and traditions that have a rich history in communities who have been the subject of violence and dispossession. And they require acknowledgement and attention in scholarship that often replicates the same oppression through epistemic means.

3 The notion of mimicry is perhaps best addressed by the work of Homi Bhabha and Franz Fanon, among other anti-racist and postcolonial scholars. This concept focuses on the ways colonizers attempt to reframe and force those they colonized in ways and epistemic terms that eschew prior identity categories, Indigenous knowledge and extant hierarchies – yet trying to get the colonized to mimic the colonizer often ends up with versions that are not exact replicas but rather exist in a state of liminality, potentially further threatening the dominance of the colonizer.

References

Aboim, S., & Vasconcelos, P. (2021). Migration after empire. Postcolonial masculinities and the transnational dynamics of subalternity. *Postcolonial Studies*, *24*(3), 323–344. doi: 10.1080/13688790.2020.1846848

Bhabha, H. K. (1984). Of mimicry and man: The ambivalence of colonial discourse. *October*, *28*, 125–133. doi: 10.2307/778467

Bhabha, H. K. (2012). *The Location of Culture*. New York: Routledge.

Bhambra, G. K. (2014). Postcolonial and decolonial dialogues. *Postcolonial Studies*, *17*(2), 115–121. doi: 10.1080/13688790.2014.966414

Brod, H., & Kaufman, M. (Eds.). (1994). *Theorizing Masculinities*. Thousand Oaks, CA: Sage.

Butler, J., & Spivak, G. C. (2007). *Who Sings the Nation-state*. London: Seagull Books.

Connell, R. (2016). Masculinities in global perspective: Hegemony, contestation, and changing structures of power. *Theory and Society*, *45*(4), 303–318. doi: 10.1007/s11186-016-9275-x
Connell, R. (2020). Masculinities: The field of knowledge. In S. Horlacher (Ed.), *Configuring Masculinity in Theory and Literary Practice* (pp. 39–51). Leiden: Brill. doi: 10.1163/9789004299009_004
Connell, R. W. (1987). *Gender and Power*. Sydney, Australia: Allen and Unwin.
Connell, R. W. (1998). Masculinities and globalization. *Men and Masculinities*, *1*(1), 3–23. 10.1177/1097184X98001001001
Connell, R. W., & Messerschmidt, J. W. (2005). Hegemonic masculinity: Rethinking the concept. *Gender & Society*, *19*(6), 829–859. doi: 10.1177/0891243205278639
Dasgupta, R. K., & Gokulsing, K. M., (2013). Introduction: Perceptions of masculinity and challenges to the Indian male. In R. K. Dasgupta & K. M. Gokulsing (Eds.), *Masculinity and its Challenges in India: Essays on Changing Perceptions* (pp. 5–26). Jefferson, NC: Jefferson Publishers.
De Lissovoy, N. (2010). Decolonial pedagogy and the ethics of the global. *Discourse: Studies in the Cultural Politics of Education*, *31*(3), 279–293. doi: 10.1080/01596301003786886
Donaldson, M. (1993). What is hegemonic masculinity? *Theory and Society*, *22*(5), 643–657. doi: 10.1007/BF00993540
Faria, A., Ibarra-Colado, E., & Guedes, A. (2010). Internationalization of management, neoliberalism and the Latin America challenge. *Critical Perspectives on International Business*, *6*(2–3), 97–115. doi: 10.1108/17422041011049932
Gannon, S. (2009). Translating the Hijra: The Symbolic Reconstruction of the British Empire in India. Retrieved from https://central.bac-lac.gc.ca/.item?id=TC-AEU-435&op=pdf&app=Library&oclc_number=428728635
Hearn, J. (2015). *Men of the World: Genders, Globalizations, Transnational Times*. Thousand Oaks, CA: Sage.
Hearn, J. (2019). So what has been, is, and might be going on in studying men and masculinities?: Some continuities and discontinuities. *Men and Masculinities*, *22*(1), 53–63. doi: 10.1177/1097184X18805550
Hearn, J., Aavik, K., Collinson, D., & Thym, A. (Eds.). (2023). *The Routledge Handbook of Men, Masculinities and Organizations*. London: Routledge.
Hearn, J., Blagojević, M., & Harrison, K. (2013). (Eds.). *Rethinking Transnational Men: Beyond, Between and Within Nations*. London: Routledge.
Hearn, J., & Howson, R. (2019). The institutionalization of (Critical) Studies on men and masculinities: Geopolitical perspectives. In L. Gottzén, U. Mellström & T. Shefer (Eds.), *Routledge International Handbook of Masculinity Studies* (pp. 19–30). London: Routledge.
Hearn, J., Vasquez del Aguila, E., & Hughson, M. (Eds.). (2019). *Unsustainable Institutions of Men: Transnational Dispersed Centres, Gender Power, Contradictions*. London: Routledge.
Hossain, A. (2017). The paradox of recognition: Hijra, third gender and sexual rights in Bangladesh. *Culture, Health & Sexuality*, *19*(12), 1418–1431. doi: 10.1080/13691058.2017.1317831
Howson, R., & Hearn, J. (2019). Hegemony, hegemonic masculinity, and beyond. In L. Gottzén, U. Mellström & T. Shefer (Eds.), *Routledge International Handbook of Masculinity Studies* (pp. 41–51). London: Routledge.
Innes, R. A., & Anderson, K. (Eds.). (2015). *Indigenous Men and Masculinities: Legacies, Identities, Regeneration*. Winnipeg: University of Manitoba Press.
Jack, G., Westwood, R., Srinivas, N., & Sardar, Z. (2011). Deepening, broadening and re-asserting a postcolonial interrogative space in organization studies. *Organization*, *18*(3), 275–302. doi: 10.1177/1350508411398996
Jacobs, S. E., Thomas, W., & Lang, S. (Eds.). (1997). *Two-spirit People: Native American Gender Identity, Sexuality, and Spirituality*. Urbana, IL: University of Illinois Press.
Kahn, J. S. (2009). *An Introduction to Masculinities*. New York: John Wiley & Sons.
Khan, S. I., Hussain, M. I., Parveen, S., et al. (2009). Living on the extreme margin: Social exclusion of the transgender population (hijra) in Bangladesh. *Journal of Health, Population, and Nutrition*, *27*(4), 441–451. doi: 10.3329/jhpn.v27i4.3388
Kimmel, M. S., Hearn, J., & Connell, R. W. (Eds.). (2005). *Handbook of Studies on Men and Masculinities*. Thousand Oaks, CA: Sage.
Levitt, P., & Schiller, N. G. (2004). Conceptualizing simultaneity: A transnational social field perspective on society 1. *International Migration Review*, *38*(3), 1002–1039. doi: 10.1111/j.1747-7379.2004.tb00227.x

Lugones, M. (2010). Toward a decolonial feminism. *Hypatia, 25*(4), 742–759. doi: 10.1111/j.1527-2001.2010.01137.x
Manning, J. (2021). Decolonial feminist theory: Embracing the gendered colonial difference in management and organisation studies. *Gender, Work & Organization, 28*(4), 1203–1219. doi: 10.1111/gwao.12673
Mignolo, W. D. (2007). Introduction: Coloniality of power and de-colonial thinking. *Cultural Studies, 21*(2–3), 155–167. doi: 10.1080/09502380601162498
Mignolo, W. D., & Escobar, A. (Eds.). (2013). *Globalization and the Decolonial Option.* London: Routledge.
Mohanty, C. T. (2003). "Under western eyes" revisited: Feminist solidarity through anticapitalist struggles. *Signs: Journal of Women in Culture and Society, 28*(2), 499–535. doi: 10.1086/342914
Murphy, J., & Zhu, J. (2012). Neo-colonialism in the academy? Anglo-American domination in management journals. *Organization, 19*(6), 915–927. doi: 10.1177/1350508412453097
Nkomo, S. M. (2011). A postcolonial and anti-colonial reading of 'African' leadership and management in organization studies: Tensions, contradictions and possibilities. *Organization, 18*(3), 365–386. doi: 10.1177/1350508411398731
Ouzgane, L., & Coleman, D. (1998). Postcolonial masculinities: Introduction. *Jouvert: A Journal of Postcolonial Studies, 2*(1), 1–10.
Ozkazanc-Pan, B. (2008). International management research meets "the rest of the world". *Academy of Management Review, 33*(4), 964–974. doi: 10.5465/amr.2008.34422014
Ramirez, J., & Munar, A. M. (2022). Hybrid gender colonization: The case of muxes. *Gender, Work & Organization, 29*(6), 1868–1889. doi: 10.1111/gwao.12884
Russell, L. (2005). "Either, or, neither nor": Resisting the production of gender, race and class dichotomies in the pre-colonial period. In E. C. Cassella & C. Fowler (Eds.), *The Archaeology of Plural and Changing Identities* (pp. 33–51). Boston, MA: Springer.
Said, E. W. (1985). Orientalism reconsidered. *Cultural Critique, 1*(Autumn), 89–107. doi: 10.2307/1354282.
Said, E. W. (2012). *Culture and Imperialism.* New York: Vintage.
Savci, E. (2016). Who speaks the language of queer politics? Western knowledge, politico-cultural capital and belonging among urban queers in Turkey. *Sexualities, 19*(3), 369–387. doi: 10.1177/1363460715613288
Savci, E. (2020). *Queer in Translation: Sexual Politics under Neoliberal Islam.* Durham, NC: Duke University Press.
Sinatti, G. (2014). Masculinities and intersectionality in migration: Transnational Wolof migrants negotiating manhood and gendered family roles. In T. D. Truong, D. Gasper, J. Handmaker & S. I. Bergh (Eds.), *Migration, Gender and Social Justice* (pp. 215–226). Berlin: Springer.
Spivak, G. C. (1988). Can the subaltern speak? In C. Nelson & L. Grossberg (Eds.), *Marxism and the Interpretation of Culture* (pp. 21–78). Urbana. IL: University of Illinois Press
Stanovsky, D. (2007). Postcolonial masculinities. In M. Flood, J. K. Gardiner, B. Pease & K. Pringle (Eds.), *International Encyclopedia of Men and Masculinities* (pp. 493–496) London: Routledge.
Stoltz, P. (2019). Masculinities, postcolonialism and transnational memories of violent conflicts. *NORMA, 14*(3), 152–167. doi: 10.1080/18902138.2019.1569395
Stoltz, P. (2020). *Gender, Resistance and Transnational Memories of Violent Conflicts.* Cham: Springer Nature.
Tafoya, T., & Wirth, D. (1996). Native American two-spirit men. *Journal of Gay & Lesbian Social Services, 5*(2–3), 51–68. doi: 10.1300/J041v05n02_03
Weaver, H. N. (2019). *Trauma and Resilience in the Lives of Contemporary Native Americans: Reclaiming Our Balance, Restoring Our Wellbeing.* New York: Routledge.
Wilson, A. (1996). How we find ourselves: Identity development and two spirit people. *Harvard Educational Review, 66*(2), 303–318. doi: 10.17763/haer.66.2.n551658577h927h4
Yousfi, H. (2014). Rethinking hybridity in postcolonial contexts: What changes and what persists? The Tunisian case of Poulina's managers. *Organization Studies, 35*(3), 393–421. doi: 10.1177/0170840613499751
Zoogah, D. B., & Nkomo, S. (2013). Management in Africa: Past, present and future. Macro and micro perspectives. In T. Lituchy, B. J. Punnett & B. B. Puplampu (Eds.), *Management Research in Africa: Macro and Micro Perspectives* (pp. 9–31). New York: Routledge.

7

MASCULINITIES IN THE WASTELAND

(Post)colonial capitalism in the West, China and Africa

Sofia Aboim, Mabel Machado and Ling Eleanor Zhang

Introduction: capitalism, organizations and hegemonic masculinity

Powerful masculinities and men's domination have been historically indissociable from labour regimes, management practices and the organizational cultures of transnational capitalism (Hearn & Collinson, 1998), from corporate financialization to high-tech imperialism. The organizing power of capitalism was recognized in critical masculinity studies since Raewyn Connell elaborated her model of hegemonic masculinity in the 1980s. Frequently coupled with the powerful corporate managers of global neoliberal capitalism (Connell, 1995), hegemonic masculinity has become, most often, a shorthand for whiteness, Western-ness, heterosexuality and breadwinning.[1] Furthermore, men's financial success and capacity for entrepreneurship are still greatly measured against prevailing Western-centric models. In and out of the corporate world, for more than two centuries, organizations have been moulded by the expansion of global capitalism (Széll, 2018) and its gendered power relations (Connell, 2016). The effects of capitalism upon organizations and masculinities are, therefore, determinant. After all, much economic and social inequality is due to capitalist exploitation of the labour power of disadvantaged workers, which spreads and grows interwoven with multiple inequalities, from imperialism and racism to sexism and patriarchy (Therborn, 2013).

Capitalism emerged in Europe at the same time as colonial empires established long-lasting hierarchies along lines of gender, race and class, with non-white and working-class men enduring marginalization and injustice. The interconnection between the two systems – capitalism and colonialism – is stronger than commonly theorized by standard political economy, which disregards the relevance of the latter (Bhambra, 2021; Bhambra & Holmwood, 2021). In the same vein, Hardt and Negri (2001) had already claimed that large-scale colonial slave production underpinned the European capitalist economy. Dominant forms of organization imply much more than economic ownership or control of resources, including human labour power (Marx, 1847). Multiple forms of extra-economic coercion (Ince, 2018) are fundamental.

In this chapter, we acknowledge the historical entanglement between capitalism and colonialism and inquire about its impact upon the class and racial hierarchies of masculinity. Old European colonial and postcolonial dynamics produced organizations and models set for

DOI: 10.4324/9781003193579-8

reproducing ideals and practices of white masculine power and Western supremacy. Therefore, the hegemony of white-upper-class and some forms of white-middle-class masculinities is as much an inheritance of colonial oppression as the subalternity of non-white-poor migrants. From this angle, we argue that renderings of capitalism as a *colonial* (Ince, 2018), *racial* (Robinson & Quan, 2019) or *postcolonial* (Sanyal, 2013) enterprise incite a critical departure from Western-centric depictions of globalization and transnationalism, while offering the critical tools to address the organizational violence of capitalism, whether past or present. Proposing an alternative reading of capitalist development, the Indian economist Kalyan Sanyal argues that postcolonial capitalism is analogous to that of proto-modern England[2] and continuously produces a "wasteland of the dispossessed" (Sanyal, 2013, p. 58), which are largely excluded from the very own circuits of capitalist exploitation. Sanyal's postcolonial conceptualization of capitalism offers an important critical view. In the postcolonial world, capitalism is essentially a regime of profit and non-profit, where various organizations and institutions work (through various channels, including the action of the State or international and non-governmental agents) to produce a precarious and subalternized "reserve army" of migrants, outsiders and the poor.

Following Sanyal and in conversation with the decolonial perspective (Quijano, 2007; Mignolo, 2007), we consider all colonial and postcolonial experiences as constitutive elements of modernity, capitalism and *organizations*, at large. Moreover, we examine how masculinity and masculine power are linked to different forms of epistemic and organizational violence in different geographic locations. In this way, we claim that under post/colonial forms of capitalism, organizational practices and cultures contribute to producing forms of social classification that uphold both the inequality between men and women and, within the realm of masculinity, a hierarchical system, with some masculinities over and above others (e.g. Connell, 2016). Despite the unequal power of nations in the global arena, recent research has demonstrated how the connection between organizations and male dominance is steadily marked in different locations. A study of management cultures in organizations comparing Pakistan, Mexico and the United States (Khan & Law, 2018) revealed that the reinforcement of the breadwinning was the most consistent trait of organizations across countries. The dominance of US capitalist organizations and a US-centred corporate elite is nonetheless evident. Examining the complex relationship between Mexico and the United States, Akers Chacón (2021) denounces the transnational complicity of elites (or the capitalist class) in denying migrants fair work conditions. As Chacón critically argues, capitalism is only expanding the state violence and class warfare inherited from colonialism and imperialism.

Inspired by these critical approaches, in the coming sections, we use "decolonial lenses" to examine three exemplary dynamics of masculinity and organizations in postcolonial societies. First, we observe the legacies of European imperialism and show how the expansion of colonial capitalism forged in Western metropolises fostered the racialization and precariousness of workers under regimes of racial capitalism (as coined by Robinson in 1983 and subsequently developed, for example, Robinson & Quan, 2019).[3] Second, we turn to Asia and examine how contemporary capitalism reproduces, across nations and beyond the west, the hierarchies of hegemonic masculinity. More specifically, we investigate China as an exemplary case focusing on masculinities in Chinese organizations, domestically and abroad in its capitalist expansion in Africa. Finally, we zoom in to Southern Africa and highlight how capitalist organizations work until today to oppress and dispossess subaltern men at the intersection of gender, class and race. While our chapter focuses on the violence and exploitation reproducing a "wasteland" of disenfranchised masculinities, we also highlight the power of localized strategies of resistance against oppression, and alternative organizational cultures (e.g. Seremani & Clegg, 2016). We conclude with an assessment of why postcolonial theories and criticism matter for analysing masculinities in organizations.

Organizing masculinities from colonial to postcolonial capitalism

Income inequality has been on the rise for several decades and peaked at unprecedented levels during the COVID-19 pandemic (Deshmukh, 2021). In 2020 alone, global billionaire wealth increased by US$3.9 trillion, while global workers' combined earnings collapsed and fell by US$3.7 trillion (see the Global Inequality Report of 2022 by Chancel et al., 2021). The richest 1% owns today almost half (45.8%) of the world's wealth and the number of billionaires on Forbes' 35th annual list reached a maximum (2,755, which is 660 more than in 2020). The United States still leads the list, but China is drawing closer and closer (Dolan et al., 2021). In sharp contrast, the number of billionaires who made it to the Forbes' list from the African continent was as few as 18 (out of the total sum of 2,755). Overall, merely a tenth of the wealthiest are women (315). Despite visible transformations in the geographies of global power relations brought about by the rise of the BRICS (Brazil, Russia, India, China and South Africa), income and wealth are increasingly concentrated. According to the Global Inequality Report, in 2021, the contrast between world regions is striking. While the average income of North America is 315% of the world's average income, sub-Saharan Africa receives only a meagre 31% of the world's average income. Within and beyond world regions, (mostly male) transnational elites are prospering in the higher echelons of capitalist organizations.

The vast majority of men, however, make ends meet in precarious occupations and navigate a harsh labour market set upon a dense web of inequalities. Organizations and organizational practices and cultures produce disparities based on gender, class and race (Holvino, 2010). One fundamental example derives from critical examinations of recent economic developments. Digital platforms, and the *uberization* of work to respond to demand, contribute to reproducing these inequalities (Grau-Sarabia & Fuster-Morell, 2021). The development of platform capitalism has raised an intense debate concerning precarious and low-wage workers. However, as Dinh and Tienari (2022) rightly alert, Western-centric debates often forget that the majority of low-skilled jobs have always been precarious in the Global South. Dinh and Tienari's critical contribution bridges a relevant gap in the literature. By focusing on Vietnamese drivers' enactment of masculinities through expressing their emotions via social media interactions, the authors show how men deal with precarity when exposed to the ambivalences of platform economy. Navigating the contradictions of their work conditions – where exploitation appears disguised and redressed under ideals or partnership and labour independence – Vietnamese drivers display an array of negative emotions (Dinh & Tienari, 2022, pp. 8–10): bitterness, helplessness, despair, anger, hatred humiliation and shame. A sense of community of "brotherhood" emerges to compensate and resist, though not without tensions and disputes, the authors conclude. At the same time, wealthy Vietnamese businessmen engage in ritualized displays of their status as breadwinners and financially successful elites.

Class inequality is a stamp of masculinities across nations and world regions. The examples abound. Research about the reactions of young South Asian men to their economic and social exclusion in England (McDowell et al., 2014) revealed high levels of unrest and protest[4] among racialized minorities. Alongside class, racial inequalities play a key role. Whether in the Global North or the Global South, many men are unable to convey a sense of positive masculinity, accomplishment or dignity (Williams, 2017). In the United States, African American professional men holding mid-management or higher positions in their companies describe how structural gendered racism hinders their careers (Cornileus, 2013). The theoretical contribution of Critical Race Theory (CRT) has been key for evidencing the enduring strength and reach of the tentacles of racial discrimination. Mobilizing the lenses of CRT to challenge organization studies' colour-blind examinations of working-class men, Bohonos (2021) offers evidence of ambivalence and complexity by conducting participant observation in a US Midwest small construction company employing 15 to 20 semi-skilled white men. Barred from class privileges and facing bleak prospects, these men envied upper-class White men "while excluding women and racial minorities from the organization". Working-class White men sought to "protect the property value of Whiteness" (Bohonos, 2021, p. 69). The combination of class marginalization with racial privilege contributes to maintaining the hierarchy of masculinity intact, with toxic practices targeting Black men and women rather than the owners and managers of the organization.

The roots of the problem are old and not surprisingly take us back to European colonialism. Since the inception of modernity and European imperialism (Sunanda & Marcuzzo, 2019), the colonial endeavour engendered processes of exploitation that long after the end of formal colonial empires continue to imprint global inequalities with the marks of past regimes of oppression. Racialized and non-Western masculinities represented either child-like archetypes of ignorance or the dangers of unregulated savagery (Forth, 2008). The Western white male colonizers would, instead, rule, regulate and exploit the colonized, producing long-lasting forms of colonial capitalism. Colonialism was, as Matlon (2016) points out, a project of racial capitalism, which justifies looking at masculinities "in relation to capitalism" (Matlon, 2016, p. 1017). The centrality awarded to capitalism has consequences for Black masculinities that have not been foreseen by Connell's (1995) theorization. Matlon suggests that expressions of dominance from a marginal location (often expressed via consumerist practices and identities) "serve to legitimize capitalism among Black men generally, even if their structural location remains unchanged". In this sense, we add, regional hegemonies become instrumental in producing patterns of global dominance of capitalist elite masculinities. The project of racial capitalism brought about by colonialism persists in the postcolonial world. Whether in the West or at large, across the globe, masculinities are hierarchically organized. After all, class, racial or ethnic marginalizations feed each other to reproduce patterns of practice favouring hegemonic masculinity.

Nowadays, as before, dominance and subalternity remain forged by harsh capitalist dynamics that cut across different regions of the world and have been developing since the birth of modernity in Western metropolises and their former empires. After all, "colonial capitalism" (Ince, 2018) grew through empires, enslavement and racial subordination first, and globalization afterwards. Transnational relations carry the legacy of colonial oppression and are embedded in a history of gender, class and race marginalization. In this sense, masculinities are inherently postcolonial. As suggested by Aboim and Vasconcelos (2021, p. 327), "the notion of postcolonial masculinities is fitted to signal the continuous subalternization of those subjected to hegemonic powers from imperial days to nowadays".

Critical approaches to organizations and organization theories have established a close conversation with postcolonial theory. As Seremani and Clegg (2016) emphasize, we need more "epistemological third spaces" that enable discussions beyond Western epistemologies. The authors exemplify their argument by discussing Ubuntu accounts of organization and management in Southern Africa. Indigenous to sub-Saharan Africa, Ubuntu is an elusive word with multiple meanings, such as humanity, solidarity, cooperation, respect, or generosity. The late Archbishop Desmond Tutu and the late former South African president Nelson Mandela were advocates of the Ubuntu humanist philosophy.

Organizational cultures flourish outside the West as the centres of economic power shift and expand beyond Western borders. In face of changing geopolitical dynamics, the value of the postcolonial critique has raised key debates. Jackson (2012) interrogates the adequacy of critical theory in international and cross-cultural management studies. Examining, in particular, China's relationship with Africa, Jackson re-interrogates postcolonial theory, which was born out of the West's relationship with the non-West. Postcolonial lenses would then be more adjusted to observe North–South dynamics than South–South relations. Commercial cooperation between China and the countries of the African continent has marked a renaissance of relations for South–South development, outside European and American influence. While reshaping geopolitical relations, South–South dynamics also represent a challenge to critical theorizations of organizations as well as critical masculinity studies.

In the following sections, we turn our attention to masculinity in Chinese organization cultures, both in China and in Africa. Afterwards, we focus on African men's accounts of domination and reassess the relevance of working with concepts of postcolonial and racial capitalism.

(Beyond the West) masculinity in Chinese organizational cultures: at home and in Africa

Chinese cultural traditions and contemporary organizational practices in international business challenge Western assumptions around gendered practices and the construction of masculine identities in the workplace in many ways (Lin & Mac an Ghaill, 2013, p. 508; Song & Liang, 2019). Lin and Mac an Ghaill's (2013) exploration of work and management practices of rural migrant workers in Chinese urban organizational settings, for instance, demonstrates how Confucian ethics and culture play an important role in contemporary working environments in the context of China's modernization project (Lin & Mac an Ghaill, 2013, p. 508; see also Horwitz, 2017). A gendered division of society is consubstantial to Confucian ideology that represents men as morally superior to women and entitled to personal development in the public domain, while women are seen as responsible for domestic tasks and believed to be undependable (Song & Liang, 2019, p. 554; Lin & Mac an Ghaill, 2013, p. 500). In addition, the hierarchical father–son relation in Confucianism is translated into organizations and impacts other interpersonal interactions (Lin & Mac an Ghaill, 2013, p. 505).

In contemporary China, the workplace constitutes "an alternative cultural institution" where new family ties without kin proliferate (Lin & Mac an Ghaill, 2013, 505). The reproduction of father–son relations within organizations (e.g. between factory workers and managers) is key in the construction of masculine identities around paternal responsibilities as prescribed by Confucian values (Lin & Mac an Ghaill, 2013, p. 508). Moreover, masculinity is negotiated through the reproduction of familial gender divisions in workplaces where men typically conduct heavy tasks or are entitled to make important decisions (Lin & Mac an Ghaill, 2013, pp. 505–506).

The situated experiences of Chinese men, and common understandings of masculinity, are also constructed around the concepts of *wen* and *wu*, two Indigenous terms related to cultural attainment and marital value that describe ideal male subjects in China (Louie, 2012,

p. 929; Lin & Mac an Ghaill, 2013, p. 508). *Wen* refers to men's intellectual and cultural virtues, while *wu* refers to physical qualities, the martial and the military (Jiang et al., 2020; Song & Liang, 2019; Lin & Mac an Ghaill, 2013, p. 499; Louie, 2012, 2000). Although Confucian texts describe men as possessing both *wen* and *wu* (Louie, 2000, p. 1065), Chinese culture tends to favour *wen* over *wu* (Song & Liang, 2019, p. 559).

Evolving Chinese masculine identities and representations are linked to historical developments by which women have gained more prominence in public life. Among such developments, the closure of the gender education gap as a result of the One-Child Policy is quite prominent (Song & Liang, 2019, p. 554). Hybrid masculinities (Bridges & Pascoe, 2014) that synthesize elements of historically subordinated femininities and characteristics of other groups are emerging in contemporary China and are becoming typical of privileged man's gender performance and identity (Jiang et al., 2020, p. 725). Although these hybrid masculinities take precedence over Western and traditional representations of masculinity, the notion of *wen* continues to have a strong importance in Chinese society (Jiang et al., 2020, p. 725).

Another key element in the formation and negotiation of Chinese masculinities is that *wen* and *wu* are largely regarded as "attributes normally attainable only by Chinese and not by foreign men" (Louie, 2000, p. 1065). Such distinction between foreignness and Chineseness, which is essentially an issue of race, needs to be noted when examining how ideals of masculinity are constructed and negotiated in an international business setting, especially in Chinese business operations in Africa. As Louie (2000, pp. 1071–1072) has shown, Chinese masculinities, shaped by the interplay of *wen-wu*, gender, class and race, are reaffirmed in relation to foreign men, who remain "out of masculinity stakes" (Louie, 2000, p. 1075). Foreign men are also perceived in Chinese traditional culture as "no match" for the locals (Louie, 2000, p. 1075). It is only when the factor of class is considered (i.e. middle and upper-class men are superior to working-class men) that the masculine identities of foreign men are unchallenged within the Chinese traditional framework (Louie, 2000, p. 1075).

The rise of Chinese multinational corporations (MNCs) in Africa in recent decades is changing the landscape of international business and politics (Alden & Davies, 2006). How Chinese MNCs have attained key resources across the developing world, and in Africa, in particular, has captured the attention of international business academics as well as analysts of Chinese foreign economic policy. China's businesses in Africa predominantly comprise sectors that are labour-intensive and male-dominant (Cooke et al., 2018).

Chinese cultural traditions and masculinity patterns often transpire in international business relations in the form of hierarchical management style. Although emotional ties are rarely created, father–son relations in the workplace become apparent between Chinese managers and African employees (Akorsu & Cooke, 2011). In a study of labour standards in Chinese MNCs in Ghana, Akorsu and Cooke (2011) found signs of discrimination against workers on grounds of gender. Moreover, the authors observed that, because of their nationality, highly educated African managers are given little room for exercising their agency at work (Akorsu & Cooke, 2011). African men in managerial positions tend to implement the Chinese managers' decisions, while workers only recognize the Chinese in decision-making positions as "real" managers (Akorsu and Cooke (2011, p. 2741)). Discrimination also materializes in fewer opportunities for African men to obtain promotions in MNCs, and cooption of their desire to manifest non-conformity with the managers' disrespect for workers (Akorsu & Cooke, 2011, p. 2741).

Another form in which Chinese male dominance is established in international business is through dispatched workers and casual contracting. In Chinese construction firms in Africa, for instance, dispatched personnel are seen as "easier to control" and "more skilled/experienced than local workers" (Cooke et al., 2018, p. 85; Gadzala, 2010). Dispatched workers usually live in controlled spaces such as company dormitories. Hiring these workers presupposes less cultural and language barriers. These are seen as advantages by which many Chinese companies justify their indifference towards regulations establishing caps on overseas employees contracting in various African countries (Cooke et al., 2018, p. 85). Dispatched employees are involved in middle-level processes of identity regulation and company strategies that respond to national discourses aiming at demonstrating China's ascent to power in an economic system historically dominated by the West (Lai et al., 2020).

Processes of identity regulation at the firm level include nurturing and celebrating the ethics of enduring hardship and making sacrifices that are typical of urban migrants, such as staying away from family members and getting by alone in big cities in China or abroad (Lai et al., 2020). By accepting hard-working conditions, MNCs' dispatched employees reinforce China's national pride as a rising industrial power. National values and pride are affirmed at the expense of the well-being of local employees and the workforce in general. In the case of Chinese businesses in Africa, China's superiority is established by contrasting Chinese traditional values with African casual workers' "limited commitment to show up for work" (Cooke et al., 2018, p. 87). Employment and managerial practices based on traditional Chinese values contribute to the increasing precarity of African men and reinforce a particular set of identities that discriminate against them. The contingent nature of employment, the use of dispatched workers and practices of close supervision (Wang et al., 2017) may have a role in the construction and negotiations of subordinate masculinities among African employees.

Authors such as Xing et al. (2016) call for a "less exportive" portrayal of Chinese operations in Africa, by highlighting how foreign managers, especially in private-owned companies, consider local cultural practices. Among those factors, we find the centrality of human relationships and networks in the Chinese Guanxi and the African Ubuntu systems of beliefs (Abodohoui et al., 2020). The fact that these philosophical traditions value social networks is seen as an element of crossvergence (Xing et al., 2016) of managerial practices in China and Africa. Social networks are instrumental in business development for both Chinese and African ventures (Abodohoui et al., 2020, p. 305). However, Chinese economic advantage over most African countries implies that networks can be used to expand Asian firms, while for many African businesses, networking strategies are simply not enough to operate outside the informal sector (Gadzala, 2010).

A focus on Ubuntu and Guanxi sheds more light on the reproduction and contestation of masculine ideals within organizations. The expansion of social networks is typically achieved through activities that are largely considered masculine in both China and Africa. Furthermore, having broad social networks is commonly associated with masculine behaviour. Zhu et al.' s (2016) study, for instance, demonstrated that gendered networking behaviours are prevalent among Chinese individuals. They observe that networking with men can be "disadvantageous" for Chinese female managers because this signals a strength of character that subverts Confucian and Taoist portrayals of women as servile and obedient. By contrast, this practice has positive connotations and consequences when deployed by male managers who do not have to fulfil expectations of femininity (Zhu et al., 2016, p. 60). Women are stereotyped as undependable managers in general (Bowen et al., 2007), which has further prevented them from developing business relationships, especially with men in management roles (Zhu et al., 2016).

Although cultural, historic and religious factors allow women in management positions in African countries to produce "effective" professional and social identities as middle- and upper-class successful individuals, obstacles to their career development associated with a gendered division of labour and patriarchal structures remain in place (Primecz & Karjalainen, 2019). A greater dominance of Chinese men in economic affairs in Africa and proportional discrimination and isolation of women is thus hardly surprising. The gendered character of networking practices is further reflected in accounts of expatriate managers, who are typically men, who find relationship building as unproblematic in host countries because business relationships are mostly cultivated between men in predominantly patriarchal societies (Wang et al., 2017).

Masculinity and work in African contexts: marginalization and resistance

Since the days of European colonialism, Africa has been the stage of intense power struggles and continuous processes of exploitation. Present-day dynamics of transnational neoliberal capitalism continued to constrain local masculinities and the aspirations to build a valued masculinity, thereby perpetuating the subalternization of African men and masculinities (Aboim & Vasconcelos, 2021). African men have been commonly depicted in very stereotypically uniform manners (Ammann & Staudacher, 2021). Most often, the image is not positive either. As Ratele (2008) notes, African men are associated with violence, irresponsibility, promiscuity, because of the focus on African men "being the problem". Ratele (2021) further calls for a decolonial attitude on the work of African men and masculinities, that is to examine African boys, men *qua* Africa and not succumb to the pressures to subscribe to colonial ideas about men and masculinities. The discourse on the crisis of masculinity among African men – particularly, the poor and disenfranchised – fuelled negative views. Men's relationship with the labour market and breadwinning is particularly targeted.

The legacies of colonialism remained strong and impacted men's access to breadwinning, a disputed but central feature of responsible masculinity. Research carried out in Mozambique revealed that, though stemming from precolonial custom, normative breadwinning was altered by colonial rule. Portuguese colonial policies disseminated ideals of the male breadwinner but limited Mozambican men's access to effective breadwinning roles (Isaacman, 1992). Through over a hundred years, colonial policy of forced labour and heavy taxation, men in the south of Mozambique tended to migrate for work, either to nearby towns, where they were mainly employed as domestic servants, or to South Africa to work in the mines. This legacy still informs masculinity. Men are no longer bound to occupations in housekeeping as in colonial days. However, job scarcity led many men to seek professional occupations in traditionally feminine street-vending activities (Agadjanian, 2002; Aboim, 2009).

Across Africa, economic adversity constrained men's enactments of masculinity. In the slums of Nairobi, Kenya's capital city, poor men strive to gain value and seek to reconstitute their "un-masculine" actions as macho (Izugbara, 2015). Many men complain about their own marginalization. As Musariri and Moyer (2021, p. 889) write about migrant men in Johannesburg, South Africa: "In articulating their multiple marginalized positions, our participants often referred to themselves as 'being cornered'". Musariri and Moyer draw on ethnographic research to develop the notion of becoming cornered as a spatial metaphor of marginalization, which is useful to account for men in precarious post-migration contexts.

Reflecting upon their work conditions, Ugandan wage labourers who live in Kampala feel condemned to live in poverty by both their Ugandan and Chinese bosses (Arsene, 2014). Even if resorting to *enjawulo* (an Indigenous word for "difference" that conveys the locally embedded notions of work and labour) and operating with a sense of conviviality, Ugandan workers see Chinese employers occupy, as Arsene writes, a "strangely familiar place". In fact, Chinese and Ugandan employers occupy a similar place in the context of capitalist economy, whereas workers fight to avoid losing their agency. *Enjawulo* strategies translate into a number of practices using the economic logic of markets and profit to overcome the consequences of low wages. Ugandan workers seek every opportunity to be creative beyond the rigidity of formal economic practices.

Kamoche and Siebers (2015, p. 2725) claim that "post-colonial theory casts African countries, and African workers, as victims". Scholars have put postcolonial contributions to the test, pointing out the need to consider agency and resistance as well as the shifts in economic relations (see also Jackson, 2012; Lee, 2009). As we have argued, the interest in Chinese presence in Africa raised concerns about renewed forms of "imperialism" or "neocolonialism", which interrogate (but also expand) postcolonial approaches. Focusing on the perceptions of workers in Kenya, Kamoche and Siebers conclude that their Chinese employers tend most often to see them as "inefficient", "inferior", "backward" or "lacking a work ethic". On the basis of this depiction, the authors consider that the hierarchical dynamics of power (between inferior and superior nations) are consistent with and can be better addressed from a postcolonial perspective.

Certainly, men's agency is not absent. Whether emerging from the mobilization of traditions like *Ubuntu* philosophy in Southern Africa or *enjawulo* strategies in East Africa, African men's agency and resistance demonstrate how local organizational cultures can work to produce hybridity and creative third spaces against negative stereotypes and marginalization. In this sense, local African cultures play an important role in relation to Western or Chinese management. Local masculinities are not just passively thrown into the margins of society; rather, marginalized men are capable of resistance and empowerment. As noted by Murgia and Poggio (2009), apropos their research in Italy, the ability to construct narratives that are alternative to hegemonic masculinity and engage in storytelling is fundamental for changing masculinity in organizations. For example, when men take parental leave, organizations tend to consider them exceptional and try to limit their significance and visibility. However, despite the fact that narratives by men who stay at home to care for children are marginal stories, they are nevertheless important devices and tools to disrupt the dominant organizational narratives (Rhodes, 2001). Stories can thus become very powerful tools given that masculinity might be seen also as a sub-text. Mobilizing alternative personal and cultural narratives of African men is a form of active resistance against hegemonic work models.

It is also true, however, that in African contexts, the hierarchy of masculinity contained in the hegemonic model materializes through a complex web of economic and cultural relations. In turn, these localized relations are part of a wider transnational and global system. Following Connell (2016, pp. 8–9), this global order (with its local and regional regimes) is structured by the power of specific groups, namely corporate managers, who control financial institutions; wealthy oligarchs; dictators controlling authoritarian states; and the state elites of neoliberal governments. At the other end of the spectrum, poor and racialized men continue to suffer from major structural disadvantages, rendering visible how the intersection of class and race conspire to produce an effective "wasteland" of dispossessed precarious workers, as Indian economist Sanyal (2013) argued. In the sense that the gap between the wealthy and the poor, the powerful and the subaltern has been widening at a fast pace, conceptualizations of postcolonial masculinities and postcolonial capitalism gain increased relevance to understand masculinities and organizations locally, regionally and globally.

Conclusion: why postcolonialism matters for masculinities and organizations?

We conclude this chapter by emphasizing the importance of the dialogue between critical masculinity studies, critical organization studies and postcolonial theorizations. As the economic power and geopolitical dynamics shift away from the monopoly of the West, postcolonial approaches offer indispensable lenses for deconstructing current regimes of gender, class and racial inequality. From an epistemological perspective, Edward Said's *Orientalism* is still very well up to date. Thus far, we have not broken away from "a style of thought based upon an ontological and epistemological distinction made between 'the Orient' and (most of the time) 'the Occident'" (Said, 1978, p. 3). Alongside the epistemological deconstruction of Western-centric theorizations, there are other very important reasons for not dismissing the postcolonial contribution.

From the point of view of critical examinations of masculinities, working with notions of postcolonial masculinity enables us to move towards historical and geographical contextualization. Both hegemonic and marginalized masculinities are produced by specific regimes of inequality, in particular, historical conditions. Masculinity emerges, therefore, from contextualized forms of agency and practice. Colonialism and imperialism or financial and platform capitalism configure historical contexts where masculinities take multiple shapes. Organizations and organizational cultures intermediate men's position and power or marginalization.

Throughout the chapter, we paid particular attention to regimes of labour and men's relationships with employment, breadwinner norms and work conditions in the West, China and across Africa. Work and employment remain central amid other forms of inequality and discrimination. Economic and income disparity increased so sharply that looking at inequalities of wealth is unavoidable. One sombre conclusion is that class inequality remains a strong divide. Across nations and world regions, elite masculinities appear associated with money, capitalism and power, while the poor and marginalized appear deprived and very often unable to prosper in local economies. Further inquiring about the connections between masculinities and capitalism (Matlon, 2016) implies then that we award centrality to global regimes of economic inequality and the ways formations of racial or postcolonial capitalism continue to divide men according to their position in the system. Intersections of gender, class and race are above all reproduced by structural orders of inequality and are embedded in localized organizations.

For certain, despite the growing precariousness and exclusion in the "wasteland", agency and resistance still matter for men in organizations. Mobilizing alternative Indigenous traditions, local strategies and engaging in storytelling to promote organizational change offered hopeful insights into the possibilities of change. Through these creative third spaces, new masculinities can emerge. Rather than the deception of hybrid masculinities that disguise hegemonic power (Bridges, 2014), these positive masculinities would effectively "contribute to legitimating egalitarian relations between men and women, masculinity and femininity, and among masculinities" (Messerschmidt & Messner, 2018, p. 32).

Notes

1 Recently, rather than synonymous with transnational business masculinity (Connell, 1998; Connell & Wood, 2005), hegemonic masculinity has been theorized as an empty signifier of the gender system requiring further discussions on the constitutions of many different hegemonic masculinities in global, transnational contexts (Howson & Hearn, 2019).
2 For Marx, the violent process of expulsion of peasants from the land generated the preconditions for capitalism in rural England, promoting the transformation of the social means of subsistence into capital and of its producers into wage workers. For Sanyal, this primitive accumulation, though similar, is different. In the postcolonial world, the dispossessed are never incorporated into the system.
3 The connection between racial oppression and capitalism has raised an intense debate, and both divided opinions and gained centre stage. In a re-reading of Marx, Cedric Robinson, professor of political science and race studies (Black Studies) at the University of California Santa Barbara, saw racism and capitalism expanding in tandem, initially in Europe, where the first practices of colonization emerged. Thus, integrated racism and capitalism gave rise to a new world system, which Robinson calls racial capitalism, a system based on slavery, violence, expropriation, imperialism.
4 The notion of "protest masculinities" is defined by Connell and Messerschmidt (2005, pp. 848–849) as "a pattern of masculinity constructed in local working-class settings, sometimes among ethnically marginalized men which embodies the claim to power typical of regional hegemonic masculinities in Western countries, but which lacks the economic resources and institutional authority that underpins the regional and global patterns".

References

Abodohoui, A., Fhinde, C., Mayuto, T., & Zhan, S. (2020). Moderating effects of networks on the relationship between acculturation and entrepreneurial skills development: Evidence from Africans trained in China. *International Journal of Cross Cultural Management*, *20*(3), 301–328. doi: 10.1177/1470595820970577

Aboim, S. (2009). Men between worlds: Changing masculinities in urban Maputo. *Men and Masculinities*, *12*(2), 201–224. doi: 10.1177/1097184X07313360

Aboim, S., & Vasconcelos, P. (2021). Migration after empire: Postcolonial masculinities and the transnational dynamics of subalternity. *Postcolonial Studies*, *24*(3), 323–344. doi: 10.1080/13688790.2020.1846848

Agadjanian, V. (2002). Men Doing "Women's work": Masculinity and gender relations among street vendors in Maputo, Mozambique. *The Journal of Men's Studies*, *10*(3), 329–342. doi: 10.3149/jms.1003.329

Akorsu, A. D., & Cooke, F. L. (2011). Labour standards application among Chinese and Indian firms in Ghana: Typical or atypical? *International Journal of Human Resource Management*, *22*(13), 2730–2748. doi: 10.1080/09585192.2011.599941

Alden, C., & Davies, M. (2006). Chinese multinational corporations in Africa. *Africa Institute of South Africa*, *3–4*, 1–11.

Ammann, C., & Staudacher, S. (2021). Masculinities in Africa beyond crisis: Complexity, fluidity, and intersectionality. *Gender, Place & Culture*, *28*(6), 759–768. doi: 10.1080/0966369X.2020.1846019

Arsene, C. (2014). Chinese employers and their Ugandan workers: Tensions, frictions and cooperation in an African city. *Journal of Current Chinese Affairs*. *43*(1), 139–176. doi: 10.1177/186810261404300106

Bhambra, G. K. (2021). Colonial global economy: Towards a theoretical reorientation of political economy. *Review of International Political Economy*, *28*(2), 307–322. doi: 10.1080/09692290.2020.1830831

Bhambra, G. K., & Holmwood, J. (2021). *Colonialism and Modern Social Theory*. London: John Wiley & Sons.

Bohonos, J. W. (2021). Critical race theory and working-class White men: Exploring race privilege and lower-class work-life. *Gender, Work & Organizations*, *28*, 54–66. doi: 10.1111/gwao.12512

Bowen, C-C., Wu, Y., Hwang, C., & Scherer, R. F. (2007). Holding up half of the sky? Attitudes toward women as managers in the People's Republic of China. *International Journal of Human Resource Management*. *18*(2), 268–283. doi: 10.1080/09585190601102455

Bridges, T., & Pascoe, C. J. (2014). Hybrid masculinities: New directions in the sociology of men and masculinities. *Sociology Compass, 8*(3), 246–258. doi: 10.1111/soc4.12134.

Chacón, A. (2021). *The Border Cross Us: The Case for Opening the US-Mexico Border.* Chicago, IL: Haymarket Books.

Chancel, L., Piketty, T., Saez, E., Zucman, G., et al. (2021). World Inequality Report 2022. Retrieved 28 December 2021, from World Inequality Lab: https://wir2022.wid.world/

Connell, R. (2016). 100 Million Kalashnikovs: Gendered power on a world scale. *Debate Feminista, 51*, 3–17. doi: 10.1016/j.df.2016.03.001

Connell, R. W. (1995). *Masculinities.* Cambridge: Polity.

Connell, R. W. (1998). Masculinities and globalisation. *Men and Masculinities, 1*(1), 3–23. doi: 10.1177/1097184X98001001001.

Connell, R. W., & Messerschmidt, J. W. (2005). Hegemonic masculinity: Rethinking the concept. *Gender and Society, 19*(6), 829–859. doi: 10.1177/0891243205278639

Connell, R. W., & Wood, J. (2005). Globalisation and business masculinities. *Men and Masculinities, 7*(4), 347–364. doi: 10.1177/1097184X03260969

Cooke, F. L., Wang, D., & Wang, J. (2018). State capitalism in construction: Staffing practices and labour relations of Chinese construction firms in Africa. *Journal of Industrial Relations, 60*(1), 77–100. doi: 10.1177/0022185617724836.

Cornileus, T. H. (2013). "I'm a black man and I'm doing this job very well": How African American professional men negotiate the impact of racism on their career development. *Journal of African American Studies, 17*(4), 444–460. doi: 10.1007/s12111-012-9225-2

Deshmukh, A. (2021). This Simple Chart Reveals the Distribution of Global Wealth. Retrieved 15 September 2021, from Visual Capitalist: www.visualcapitalist.com/distribution-of-global-wealth-chart/

Dinh, T. T. Q., & Tienari, J. (2022). Brothers and broken dreams: Men, masculinity, and emotions in platform capitalism. *Gender, Work & Organization, 29*(2), 609–625. doi: 10.1111/gwao.12786

Dolan, K. A., Wang, J., & Peterson-Withorn, C. (2021). Forbes World's Billionaires List. Retrieved 10 October 2021, from The Richest in 2021: www.forbes.com/billionaires/

Forth, C. E. (2008). *Masculinity in the Modern West: Gender, Civilization, and the Body.* Basingstoke: Palgrave Macmillan.

Gadzala, A. W. (2010). From formal- to informal-sector employment: Examining the Chinese presence in Zambia, *Review of African Political Economy, 37*(123), 41–59. doi: 10.1080/03056241003637904

Grau-Sarabia, M., Fuster-Morell, M. (2021). Gender approaches in the study of the digital economy: A systematic literature review. *Humanities & Social Sciences Communications, 8*, 201. doi: 10.1057/s41599-021-00875-x

Hardt, M., & Negri, A. (2001). *Empire.* Cambridge, MA: Harvard University Press.

Hearn, J., & Collinson, D. L. (1998). Men, masculinities, managements and organisational culture. *Zeitschrift für Personalforschung, 12*(1), 210–222. doi: 10.1177/239700229801200205

Holvino, E. (2010). Intersections: The simultaneity of race, gender and class in organization studies. *Gender, Work and Organization, 17*(3), 248–277. doi: 10.1111/j.1468-0432.2008.00400.x

Horwitz, F. (2017). International HRM in South African multinational companies. *Journal of International Management, 23*(2), 208–222. doi: 10.1016/j.intman.2017.01.005

Howson, R., & Hearn, J. (2019). Hegemony, hegemonic masculinity and beyond. In L. Gottzén, U. Mellström & T. Shefer (Eds.), *Routledge International Handbook of Masculinity Studies* (pp. 41–51). London: Routledge.

Ince, U. O. (2018). *Colonial Capitalism and the Dilemmas of Liberalism.* Oxford: Oxford University Press.

Isaacman, A. (1992). Coercion, paternalism and the labour process: The Mozambican cotton regime 1938–1961, *Journal of Southern African Studies, 18*(3), 487–526. doi: 10.1080/03057079208708325

Izugbara, C. (2015). 'Life is not designed to be easy for men': Masculinity and poverty among urban marginalized Kenyan men. *Gender Issues, 32*, 121–137. doi: 10.1007/s12147-015-9135-4

Jackson, T. (2012). Postcolonialism and organizational knowledge in the wake of China's presence in Africa: Interrogating South-South relations. *Organization, 19*(2), 181–204. doi: 10.1177/1350508411429395

Jiang, J., Huhmann, B. A., & Hyman, M. R. (2020). Emerging masculinities in Chinese luxury social media marketing. *Asia Pacific Journal of Marketing and Logistics, 32*(3), 721–745. doi: 10.1108/APJML-07-2018-0256

Kamoche, K., & Siebers, L. Q. (2015). Chinese management practices in Kenya: Toward a post-colonial critique. *International Journal of Human Resource Management, 26*(21), 2718–2743. doi: 10.1080/09585192.2014.968185
Khan, M. A., & Law, L. S. (2018). The role of national cultures in shaping the corporate management cultures: A three-country theoretical analysis. In J. Vveinhardt (Ed.), *Organisational Culture* (pp. 35–59). London: IntechOpen. doi: 10.5772/intechopen.78051
Lai, K., Morgan, G., & Morris, J. (2020). 'Eating bitterness' in a Chinese multinational: Identity regulation in context. *Organization Studies, 41*(5), 661–680. doi: 10.1177/0170840619835271
Lee, C. (2009). Raw encounters: Chinese managers, African workers and the politics of casualization in Africa's Chinese enclaves. *The China Quarterly, 199*, 647–666. doi: 10.1017/S0305741009990142
Lin, X., & Mac an Ghaill, M. (2013). Chinese male peasant workers and shifting masculine identities in urban workspaces. *Gender, Work & Organisation, 20*(5), 498–511. doi: 10.1111/j.1468-0432.2012.00598.x
Louie, K. (2012). Popular culture and masculinity ideals in East Asia, with special reference to China. *The Journal of Asian Studies, 71*(4), 929–943. doi: 10.1017/s0021911812001234
Louie, K. (2000). Constructing Chinese masculinity for the modern world: With particular reference to Lao she's the two Mas. *The China Quarterly, 164*, 1062–1078. doi: 10.1017/S0305741000019305
Marx, K. (1946[1847]) *Miséria da Filosofia [The Poverty of Philosophy]*. São Paulo: Flama.
Matlon, J. (2016). Racial capitalism and the crisis of Black masculinity. *American Sociological Review, 81*(5), 1014–1038. doi: 10.1177/0003122416658294
McDowell, L., Rootham, E., & Hardgrove, A. (2014). Precarious work, protest masculinity and communal regulation: South Asian young men in Luton, UK. *Work, Employment and Society, 28*(6), 847–864. doi: 10.1177/0950017013510757
Messerschmidt, J. W., & Messner, M. A. (2018). Hegemonic, nonhegemonic, and 'new' masculinities. In J. W Messerschmidt, P. Y Martin, M. A. Messner & R. Connell (Eds.), *Gender Reckonings: New Social Theory and Research* (pp. 35–56). New York: New York University Press.
Mignolo, W. (2007). 'Delinking: The rhetoric of modernity, the logic of coloniality and the grammar of de-coloniality. *Cultural Studies, 21*(2), 449–514. doi: 10.1080/09502380601162647
Murgia, A., & Poggio, B. (2009). Challenging hegemonic masculinities: Men's stories on gender culture in organizations. *Organization, 16*(3), 407–423. doi: 10.1177/1350508409102303
Musariri. L., & Moyer, E. (2021). A black man is a cornered man: Migration, precarity and masculinities in Johannesburg. *Gender, Place & Culture, 28*(6), 888–905. doi: 10.1080/0966369X.2020.1855122
Primecz, H., & Karjalainen, H. (2019). Gender relations in the workplace: The experience of female managers in African harbours. *International Journal of Cross Cultural Management, 19*(3), 291–314. doi: 10.1177/1470595819884094
Quijano, A. (2007). Coloniality and modernity/rationality. *Cultural Studies*, 21(2), 168–178. doi: 10.1080/09502380601164353
Ratele, K. (2008). Analysing males in Africa: Certain useful elements in considering ruling masculinities. *African and Asian Studies, 7*(4), 515–536. doi: 10.1163/156921008X359641
Ratele, K. (2021). An invitation to decoloniality in work on (African) men and masculinities. *Gender, Place & Culture, 28*(6), 769–785. doi: 10.1080/0966369X.2020.1781794
Rhodes, C. (2001). *Writing Organization: (Re)presentation and Control in Narratives at Work*. Amsterdam: John Benjamins.
Robinson, C., & Quan, H. L. T. (2019). *Cedric J. Robinson: On Racial Capitalism, Black Internationalism, and Cultures of Resistance*. London: Pluto.
Said, E.W. (1978). *Orientalism*. New York: Pantheon.
Sanyal, K. (2013). *Rethinking Capitalist Development: Primitive Accumulation, Governmentality and Post-colonial Capitalism*. London: Routledge.
Seremani, T. W., & Clegg, S. (2016). Postcolonialism, organization, and management theory: The role of "epistemological third spaces". *Journal of Management Inquiry, 25*(2), 171–183. doi: 10.1177/1056492615589973
Song, G., & Liang, C. (2019). Masculine gender role expectations in China: A consensual qualitative research-modified study. *Psychology of Men and Masculinities, 20*(4), 553–563. doi: 10.1037/men0000196
Sunanda, S., & Marcuzzo, M. C. (Eds.). (2019). *The Changing Face of Imperialism Colonialism to Contemporary Capitalism*. New Delhi: Routledge India.

Széll, G. (2018). Western and/or universal social sciences? *Asian Journal of German and European Studies*, *3*(7). doi: 10.1186/s40856-018-0029-6

Therborn, G. (2013). *The Killing Fields of Inequality*. Cambridge: Polity.

Wang, D., Fan, D., Freeman, S., & Jiuhua Zhu, C. (2017). Exploring cross-cultural skills for expatriate managers from Chinese multinationals: Congruence and contextualization. *Asia Pacific Journal of Management*, *34*(1), 123–146. doi: 10.1007/s10490-016-9474-z

Williams, J. C. (2017). *White Working class: Overcoming Class Cluelessness in America*. Boston, MA: Harvard Business Review Press.

Xing, Y., Liu, Y., Tarba, S. Y., & Cooper, C. L. (2016). Intercultural influences on managing African employees of Chinese firms in Africa: Chinese managers' HRM practices. *International Business Review*, *25*(1), 28–41. doi: 10.1016/j.ibusrev.2014.05.003

Zhu, Y., Konrad, A. M., & Jiao, H. (2016). Violation and activation of gender expectations: Do Chinese managerial women face a narrow band of acceptable career guanxi strategies? *Asia Pacific Journal of Management*, *33*(1), 53–86. doi: 10.1007/s10490-015-9435-y

8

GLOBAL, TRANSNATIONAL, NATIONAL AND "LOCAL" ORGANIZATIONS AND ORGANIZING

The case of space and place

Jeff Hearn

Introduction

Place and space are both material-grounded and socially constructed, and social relations are part of the production of space and place (Lefebvre, 1974; Massey, 1994; Cresswell, 2004; Agnew, 2005) – with consequent implications for men, masculinities, organizations and organizing. Spatiality, along with geography, geopolitics and indeed temporality, is a growing focus in both critical studies on men and masculinities (Berg & Longhurst, 2003; Hopkins & Gorman-Murray, 2014, 2019; van Hovan & Hörschelmann, 2005), and studies of organizations and organizing. This chapter considers organizations, organizing, men and masculinities, through a *social-spatial lens*: how men and masculinities in and around organizations and organizing are located within social spaces and places.

Organizations and organizing exist, and change, in space and place – even when they have no physical base. Socio-spatiality is partly about *physical distance*, whether interpersonally or geopolitically, but also *social distance/proximity*, and *virtual distance/proximity, accessibility and remoteness*. The situatedness of organizations and organizing in space and place is, in many ways, fundamental to the situation of men, masculinities and gender relations. In spatial terms, *scale* can mean expansion by size, often spreading an activity across larger geographical areas, while *scope* can mean expanding by diversifying activities, even with a more limited (local, national or regional) area. In practice, scale and scope can go together. Scales and scopes, like spatiality generally, also exist in relation to *time*, and spatial–temporal mobility and movement, or their lack, even impossibility.

Socio-spatiality is an important perspective across many aspects of both men and masculinities, and organizations and organizing, and their intersections. This concerns organizations and organizing on and across the physical planet, but also in virtualization and cyberspace, in the nation, in migration, within specific organizations and organizing, in localities, and in the body spaces of individuals and collectivities. Socio-spatiality intersects with divisions of labour, hierarchy and authority, formal and informal, in organizations and organizing. Many organizational and organizing spaces and places are produced, occupied, populated,

DOI: 10.4324/9781003193579-9

dominated and controlled by men, sometimes by force. Military and religious institutions, big business, financial and information technology corporations, transportation, mass media, organized crime, commercial sexual exploitation, pubs, clubs, sports associations and science itself can all be social spaces and places where not only men may dominate over women and other men but also homosociality can be (re)produced, enacted, often celebrated harmoniously, by and for some at least, along with many further gendered processes.

In this chapter, the primary focus is on how spaces and places figure in understanding the differential relations and mutual construction of men, masculinities, organizations and organizing, *transnationally*, that is, across localities and national contexts. Having said that, it is important from the outset to consider how the transnational, and indeed the global, also operate locally and with local specificities. The chapter begins by considering the macro-picture of global and transnational organizations and organizing, in terms of geographical, historical and contemporary changes, including growing concentrations and inequalities. It continues with some implications of this transnational social–spatial lens on migration, nation and location, before concluding comments.

Some geographies and histories

While critical studies on men and masculinities (CSMM) developed very much in relation to Second Wave feminist debates on patriarchy, as a globalized structure of power, often alongside capitalism, many local and local-national studies on men and masculinities followed, many in the Global North, summed up as "the ethnographic moment" (Connell, 1998). More recently, there has been a shift (back) to a broader, big(ger) picture (Connell, 1993; Hearn, 2003) – the global, globalizing, transnational, postcolonial, decolonial(izing), world-centred (Connell, 2014), addressing Global North–South, de/postcolonial, and metropole/centre-semiperiphery-periphery dynamics and approaches (Blagojević, 2009; Cornwall et al., 2011). Since the 1990s, there has been an important expansion of studies on or from the "Global South" (for example, Cornwall & Lindisfarne, 1994; Pease & Pringle, 2002; Jones, 2006; Ratele, 2021). Moves beyond methodological nationalism (Scott, 1998; Beck, 2000; Lie, 2004), towards recognition of the global and the transnational, as in transnational patriarchies (Hearn, 2015), are urgent and necessary.

Globalizations, imperialisms, colonialisms, adventurisms, trade and movements across borders, typically led by men, frequently patriarchal, are ancient. Both historically and in the contemporary world, from slave trade to mercantile capitalism to neoliberalism, numerous transnational movements of people, things, capital, finance, images, texts and virtual resources have been put into effect by organizations and organizing dominated by certain groups of men and masculinities. In synthesizing such shifts, Connell (1998) specified three broad swathes of "globalizing masculinities": "masculinities of conquest and settlement", "masculinities of empire" and "masculinities of postcolonialism and neoliberalism" (pp. 12–16). There is now, for example, a rather well-established literature on settler masculinities (Phillips, 1987) and growing literature on Indigenous masculinities (Innes & Alexander, 2015). Having said that, globalizations look very different when seen from polar and non-human environmental perspectives rather than from the more usual perspectives, whether Arabic, Chinese or European. In referring to the European explorations of the Antarctic, Pyne (2004, p. 67) writes:

> explorers and the civilization that sent them did not discover The Ice so much as The Ice allowed them to discover themselves. . . . Not even the Arctic offered a comparable

> degree of alienness. . . . The density of its pack ice made maritime exploration impossible for any distance. But the circumpolar Arctic was occupied by native peoples, the technology existed by which to travel over the pack at least seasonally, and the lands themselves provided a ready point of access.

Historical alliances have developed between central imperial powers and semi-autonomous collective and strongly organized male actors, locally or regionally. Obvious examples here are the British East India Company (formally, the Honourable East India Company) and the Dutch East India Company (the Vereenigde Oostindische Compagnie [VOC]) in the seventeenth, eighteenth and nineteenth centuries. These companies expanded their scope, with their own armies, waging war, occupying and establishing colonies, and becoming immensely wealthy. The British East India Company created their own elite private school to train the next generation of male imperial administrators, itself becoming a model for some less elite schools. Such companies and governments allied, through force, pressure, inducement or clientelism, local and regional regimes and leaders, themselves often if not always patriarchal.

A different transnational or supranational example of organizing is found in some large religions and religious organizations, some with very long histories. The Catholic Church is an archetypal hyperpatriarchal[1] institution and collection of organizations, in its gendered structures and maintenance of abusive organizing over long periods. There are, for example, well-documented histories of links between church and fascist dictatorships, and between church and organized crime (Raab, 2006).

The modern industrial revolution(s), especially from the late nineteenth century, brought huge increases in both the vertical and horizontal integrations of organizations – not only in economy and capitalist organizations but also in the state, mass media, science and technology, and international organizations of many kinds. This meant an accompanying extension of power and authority, through large multinational extractive, manufacturing and productive companies and trade, for some more strata of privileged men, especially in the Global North and the imperial centres, subordinating other men, women and children (Humphries, 2010).

The discontinuous spatiality, and temporality, of transnational processes, organizations and organizing were also part of the formation of the modern nation-state, itself a relatively recent historical form, and may yet be a more temporary spatio-political form than often assumed. The modern nation-state resulted from complex historical, transnational forces, often competing empires, and more or less stable alliances. It was fundamental in industrial expansion for more organized capitalism, especially from the latter half of the nineteenth century. The patriarchal capitalist, and in some cases imperialist, state, forged by powerful men and powerful groups of men (Connell, 1990; Nagel, 1998), was and is constituted over specific, typically contiguous, unified territoriality. These territories have dominantly been managed by men in national governments, militaries, security forces, policing, and interior and other ministries, even when, perhaps because, "the nation" is sometimes coded feminine. In nation-building, the national spatial "logic" applied to numerous economic, political, social and cultural associations across the same spatial territory as their more or less taken-for-granted national context, with its own gender hierarchies. In the worst cases, the nation-state can become home to fascist, expansionist nationalisms, whereby space, territory and "the people" (of certain kinds) are conflated, and Others are othered, or worse.

These "new" nationalisms had massive impacts on spatialized politics, and the (potential) separation of economy and government. The contemporary spread, perhaps domination, of neoliberalism and globalism has a longer history in the twentieth century than often assumed. These tendencies can be traced to the Geneva School of neoliberals, beginning from the late 1920s, as elaborated by Slobodian (2018) in *Globalists*:

> [They] . . . reconciled the tension between the world of economy and the world of nations through their own distinct geography. Their global imaginary was sketched by the erstwhile Nazi jurist Carl Schmitt in 1950. Schmitt proposed that there was not one world but two. One was the world partitioned into bounded territorial states where governments ruled over human beings [*imperium*]. . . . The other was the world of property, where people owned things, money, and land scattered across the earth [*dominium*]. . . . The doubled world of modern capitalism coalesced in the nineteenth century.
>
> *(p. 10)*

Influential, high public profile, free marketeers, almost all men, organized against the spread of national democratization, economic nationalism, welfare states, and trade unionism, and later post-war decolonization, arguing for control of the ***imperium*** of nation-states, and their power to impede the market, through provisional supranational trade organizations designed to facilitate the ***dominium*** of market sovereignty. This is a continuing form of transnational organizing for markets and neoliberalism. Entrenched transnational patriarchal organizing persists in and through transnational public worlds, globalization and globalisms.

Global and transnational organizational forms

In speaking of the global and the transnational, it may be useful, at this point, to step back for a moment and say more about these terms. There is a vast literature theorizing on contemporary globalization, much of which has developed from a narrower, unidimensional process towards multi-stranded, contradictory global processes, with movements of people, goods, services and information, through economic/material, political and symbolic exchanges. Economy is recognizably increasingly global, but with immediate production of some goods favoured to an extent, if unevenly, and high transportation costs. The nation-state remains a key unit of political organization, especially so for those who are not citizens. Symbolic exchanges are both global and local, with growing transnational cultures, signs, symbols and visuality.

Such global interdependences do not, however, produce global integration; rather, greater global consciousness is accompanied by promotion or "invention" of difference, with "clashes, conflicts, tensions and so on . . . a pivotal feature of globalization" (Robertson & Khondker, 1998, p. 29). Overall, Waters (1995) defined globalization as: "[a] social process in which the constraints of geography on social and cultural arrangements recede and in which people become increasingly aware that they are receding" (p. 3). Yet this assessment now seems outdated, with the COVID-19 pandemic and environmental crises. Other problems with the concept of globalization are that it can be glossed, be used in quite opposed ways and can play down complex intertwining glocalizing processes, while, paradoxically, few "global" processes (apart from climate change) actually operate globally.

The notion of the transnational raises somewhat different framing, in invoking two elements: first, the ***nation*** or ***national boundaries***, and then, "***trans***" (i.e. across) relations, as opposed to "inter" relations or "intra" relations (Hearn, 2004). With the notion of the transnational, a paradox is raised, or at least in prospect: ***the nation can be simultaneously affirmed and deconstructed***. In short, the element of "trans" refers to three basically different notions, as well as more subtle distinctions between and beyond that:

> *moving across* something or *between* two or more somethings, in this case, across national boundaries or between nations . . . ;
> *metamorphosing*, problematizing, blurring, transgressing, breaking down, even dissolving something(s), in this case, nations or national boundaries – in the most extreme case, leading to the demise of the nation or national boundaries . . . ;
> *creating new configurations*, intensified transnational, supranational, or to different degrees, deterritorialized, dematerialized or virtual entities: structures, institutions, organizations, classes, groups, social movements, capital flows, networks, communities, supra-identities, cultural and public spaces, involving two or more nations, or more often different actors there interacting across national borders.
>
> *(Hearn & Blagojević, 2013, p. 9)*

Paralleling these distinctions, structures of transnational organizations and organizing include, first, ***joint, more or less collaborative organizing*** across national boundaries. This may shift towards a second form, namely ***supranational structures*** over and above the nation or national boundaries. In this sense, organizations, such as the EU or large MNEs, can be part of metamorphosing, problematizing, blurring, transgressing and breaking down specific national boundaries. A third kind of structure comprises, through various forms of ***interconnections and interpenetrations*** of transnational institutions and organizing, new configurations with intensified deterritorialized, dematerialized or virtual entities, beyond nations, as, for example, with transnational polycentric offline/online network organizing. These alternatives bring complex transnational intersectional masculinities. Through such various forms of transnational organizations and organizing, transnational men and masculinities operate beyond, between and within nations (Hearn et al., 2013).

The fact that men continue to dominate many centres of power is both cause and consequence of long-established, global patriarchal patterns of men and masculinity, expressed in hierarchies, oligarchies, plutocracies, competitions and exclusions (Connell, 2016). Some of these forms of transnational organizing entail hierarchical concentrations of resources in corporations and other organizations. Many such organizations, often based in global centres, sometimes in semiperipheries, are still bounded in particular spaces and places, even while seeking expansion in scale and scope. These spatial power dynamics of elite men of the global cities intertwine with local and regional elites.

In some cases, such hierarchically concentrated organizations are concerned with direct extraction of natural and associated resources. There, men, and it is usually men, are in control of, or seek to control, land, seabed or water, drawing directly (hierarchically) from the environment, often at increasing scale across and beneath the Earth's surface. Yet, as natural environments exist across and beyond national borders, some such institutions are sometimes precariously situated and/or necessarily transnational. Examples might be those that profit from oil or waste, and those which address environmental issues. They are marked and restricted by the physical environment and finite sets of natural resources (see Hultman & Pulé, 2019; Pulé & Hultman, 2021).

Under modernity and disorganized capitalism (Harvey, 1989), new organizational forms have developed. For example, one contemporary form of socio-spatial extension of hierarchical organizing is by scaling up, with more of the same, on the model of what has been labelled McDonaldization (Ritzer, 1993). This involves global organizing based on the replication and franchising on a relatively small scale, especially as applied, in *neo-Fordist* style, to the material service-oriented consumer economy. It has become a powerful replicatory model, not least for some young people as contract workers and as consumers, with consequent impacts on both "global" and local cultures.

Going further, and in some contrast, growing digitalization and financialization of political economy facilitates a more intense *post-Fordist* level of contractual dispersal – of business, finance, services, media, information, visual culture and the "immaterial" – spatially extended organizing in cyberspace. With lean flexibilization, projectization, network organizing, and shifting memberships of organizations, rigid organizational forms can no longer be taken-for-granted. Organizations may appear less hierarchical, less segregated, more gender-flexible, but the fungibility of labour (i.e. the extent to which labour can be interchanged with other forms of labour or assets) under neoliberal capitalism (Fraser, 2009; Ong, 2006; Stacey, 1987), makes for new gender hierarchies. Indeed, so-called iCapitalists, who have led the shift to digital capitalism and its immense profits (Huws, 2015), have long been zealots for radical neoliberal capitalism, and often male dominance:

> California's Silicon Valley . . . embodies a value system that merges a counter-cultural 60s romantic individualism with a cold-eyed commitment to free markets . . . this rebellious pose . . . reconciled a whole swath of the educated professional classes . . . to free-market capitalism . . . The iCapitalists . . . presented a far more appealing vision to liberals – one of denimed democracy, of gender-blind and colour-blind egalitarianism.
> *(Priestland, 2013)*

Along with new ethnic/racialized patterns in the tech industry (Poster, 2013), the "new boys' networks" – the new patriarchs of digital capitalism (Little & Winch, 2021) – are in part displacing the "old boys' networks" (cf. Kerfoot and Knights, 1993). Such dispersed organizing may, however, still operate from a main central location, as with Apple, Google, Facebook, Amazon and surveillance capitalism (Zuboff, 2019) more broadly, where exploitation of information about people may be more important, and profitable, than direct exploitation of people. Such polycentric organizational models, or "FiFAization" (Hearn et al., 2019), themselves provide conditions for further financialization, contracting out, outsourcing, offshoring and men's overwhelming domination of finance (Young et al., 2011).

Such transnational processes have further implications for what has been labelled neoliberal masculinities. These may concern the spectral appeal, largely unattainable for many men, of autonomous, sovereign, "successful" masculinity within, yet (supposedly autonomously) outside, the market. One example is the individualized risk-taking masculinity in some, but not all, financial sectors (cf. Hearn, 2015; Salzinger, 2016; Garlick, 2021). A related version is the entrepreneurial self, sustained or not, as a re-formed ideal worker, often supposedly gender-neutral, but in practice highly gendered. Mundane concrete manifestations include uberization and zero-hours contracts, with clear gendered divisions of labour between, for example, delivery work and care work.[2] Individualizing forms pervade and percolate through social and mass media, sports, politics, across social classes, resonating for some men working in low-level, local service or transnational quaternary sectors (Cornwall et al., 2018; Roberts, 2018; Davies & Chisholm, 2018; Walker & Roberts, 2018; Wolfman et al., 2021). They also construct the symbolic realm, with powerful consumer marketing creating conditions such that in some locales young men may kill for a certain brand of T-shirt or trainers (Ratele, 2014).

Concentrations and inequalities

Polycentric and networked/networking patterns of organizing are, however, no democratizing force, and may extend to subsuming not just local businesses but also national democratic institutions. They cannot be divorced from the extraordinary increases and concentrations in the wealth of elites in recent years.

> Almost half of the world's wealth is now owned by just one percent of the population. . . . Seven out of ten people live in countries where economic inequality has increased in the last 30 years. . . . In the US, the wealthiest one percent captured 95 percent of post-financial crisis growth since 2009, while the bottom 90 percent became poorer.
>
> *(Fuentes-Nieva & Galasso, 2014, pp. 2–3; also see Credit Suisse, 2016; Hardoon et al., 2016; Oxfam, 2017, 2020)*[3]

Projections from the UK House of Commons suggest this figure may reach two-thirds of global wealth by 2030 (Savage, 2018). Recently, these figures have become more dramatic still:

> The world's ten richest men more than doubled their fortunes from $700 billion to $1.5 trillion – at a rate of $15,000 per second or $1.3 billion a day – during the first two years of a [COVID] pandemic that has seen the incomes of 99 percent of humanity fall and over 160 million more people forced into poverty.
>
> *(www.oxfam.org/en/press-releases/ten-richest-men-double-their-fortunes-pandemic-while-incomes-99-percent-humanity)*

Or to put this another way:

> Widening economic, gender, and racial inequalities – as well as the inequality that exists between countries – are tearing our world apart. This is not by chance, but choice: "economic violence" is perpetrated when structural policy choices are made for the richest and most powerful people. This causes direct harm to us all, and to the poorest people, women and girls, and racialized groups most. Inequality contributes to the death of at least one person every four seconds [estimated at 21,000].
>
> *(Ahmed, 2022, p. 2)*

Concentrations of capital, along with technological and governmental changes, suggest greater concentrations of power in the hands of finance capital, transnational corporations and the transnational capitalist ruling class. This class (Van der Pijl, 1998; Sklair, 2001; Carroll, 2010) is in practice very much a male transnational capitalist class (Donaldson & Poynting, 2006). Pickett et al. (2014, pp. 4–5) summarize the corporate situation:

> One of the mechanisms explaining the rapid increase of global economic inequality relates to the rise of transnational corporations (TNCs) (mostly based in developed nations) that have accumulated a spectacular amount of wealth in the last few

> decades. . . . 1,318 global companies collectively own, through their shares, the majority of the world's largest manufacturing firms and blue chip companies, representing about 60% of global revenues. . . . [A] "super-entity" of 147 companies, less than 1% of the total, controls about 40% of the entire wealth in the network. When considering global financial actors such as hedge funds, private pension funds, mutual funds, investment banks and insurance companies, concentration of wealth reached even more grotesque proportions. In 2010, 6 banks – Bank of America, JP Morgan Chase, Citigroup, -Wells Fargo, Goldman Sachs and Morgan Stanley – controlled about 60% of the US gross domestic product (GDP).[4]

Transnational institutions are difficult to control and police. Similarly, (ab)use of cyberspace, "alternatives facts" and "deepfake" technologies have facilitated de-democratic tendencies in both the political and symbolic realms, within national borders and transnationally. Taking what no longer seem extreme examples, there is the authoritarianism of Trump, former President of the United States, as part of a populist global ultraconservative alliance, "whose defining characteristics are kleptocracy and dominating masculinity, with the likes of Putin (Russia), el-Sisi (Egypt), Erdogan (Turkey), Salman (Saudi Arabia), Duterte (Philippines) among others" (Messerschmidt & Bridges, 2017). Patriarchal, yet unpredictable and fluid, nationalistic politics is enhanced and matched by the symbolic hegemony of transnational iCapitalism.

Migrations, nations, locations

Transnational processes are not only about what happens above and beyond borders. Men and masculinities – in migration, nations, and specific locations and locales – can all be formed and shifted through transnational processes. The social-spatial lens is important in analysing migrant men's complex, contradictory experiences across borders in organizations, organizing, workplaces and more broadly. Migrants are of many and various kinds and combinations. Migration is one means by which some privileged men's power is extended materially and virtually – for global elites, managers of multinationals, ex/repatriates, skilled workers; yet, for others, transnational processes mean temporary or permanent displacement, whether they are dispossessed, forcibly relocated, asylum seekers, refugees, "illegal migrants" or in precarious forms of labour. In the worst cases, migrants are placed in modern slavery with huge health risks and possible death. For some, "human social formations and processes have always been trans-border and trans-boundary" (Levitt, 2010, p. 139).

Transnational organizations and policy actors, be they recruitment agencies, border and policing organizations, even organized crime, are involved in the organizing and control of migrations. State machineries mediate nation, economic systems and migration, not least through gendered, ethnicized/racialized migration controls, complicated by policies on, say, refugees, and those defined as having "key skills" or in "key sectors"; family, often defined by heterosexual marriage; and international laws and agreements. National-spatial "logics" can also apply in joint ventures which may develop into supra-organizational structures, as with the EU, NATO or other alliances, and their diverse masculinities (cf. Woodward, 1996). Meanwhile, nation-states provide bases for various nationalisms, nationalistic organizations and organizing, and nationalistic men and masculinities, even while, somewhat paradoxically, these are very much part of a transnational political movement.

Globalization of business produces variable permutations of the national and the transnational, with its implications for the everyday life of globally mobile managers (Connell & Wood, 2005). Superseding "bourgeois-rational masculinity", "transnational business masculinity" has been represented as increasingly hegemonic, marked by increasing egocentrism, conditional loyalties (even to the corporation), declining sense of responsibility for others, more libertarian sexuality, with tendencies to commodify relations with women. However, such a characterization is too universalizing. Transnational businessmen managers can have variable spatial attachments to particular locales and place-based lifestyles (Reis, 2004; Tienari et al., 2005), along with conventional marriage-type relations. In a study of mobile Finnish managers, the men had quite different, more conventionally gendered marriages, family relations, and more children, compared to their women manager counterparts, who generally had dual-career marriages and less children (Hearn et al., 2008). Women reported that corporate assignments overseas tended to mean "out of sight, out of mind", while men indicated such moves evidenced broadened experience, with consequent career benefits. Men's working abroad appeared to strengthen separate work/domestic spheres: the more time the father-managers had spent on foreign assignments, the greater probability their women partners stayed as housewives, and less housework was reported when back in Finland (Hearn & Niemistö, 2012).

Migrant men may have to navigate not only plural and hierarchical masculinities but also threatened masculinities. One relatively well-established arena of research concerns the migration of gay, bisexual and transgender men into urban centres, such as Berlin, London, New York or San Francisco (D'Emilio, 1998), leading onto spatialized understandings of gender, sexuality and masculinity. Such research is part of the transnational turn in sexuality and gender identity studies (Povinelli & Chauncey, 1999; Zhou et al., 2021). Related research includes that on how US immigration policies restrict migrations of gay and bisexual Latino men and reinforce dominant heterosexual, white masculinities (Cantú, 2009) and the sexual constructions of migration among Peruvian immigrant gay men (Vasquez del Aguila, 2014). Such migrations may involve personal risks, moving from the home country, and sometimes in the host country too.

Different trajectories are emphasized by Donaldson and colleagues (Donaldson et al., 2009) in studying the renegotiations of masculinity of men migrants to Australia from diverse origins and backgrounds. The volume contributors showed how migrant men considered their authority and power, both "at home" and "overseas" to be based upon their paid work, as a "key element" in their manhood. Men may feel reduced, used and taken-for-granted when performing work beneath their skill level, not to mention the disempowerment unemployment may bring. Their self-conception was also affected by women's greater opportunities in Australia for employment and economic and social independence. Migration to Australia changed household divisions of labour and subverted breadwinner masculinity. Despite those challenges, men migrants generally experienced their masculine identity to be quite solid, transportable and stable (Donaldson & Howson, 2009). These conclusions can be compared to those from a study of educated Estonian men "trailing spouses" to Brussels and Strasbourg who found ways of recreating their status and self-worth in new contexts (Pajumets & Hearn, 2012).

Furthermore, many migrants' lives are "multi-stranded" across economic, political, symbolic and emotional realms (Basch et al., 1994). This may mean building hybrid transnational identities and practical bridges to their new country, not only drawing on political, cultural or religious organizing but also linking to their source country. Importantly, such transnational practices are often intensely local in character: "nations do not migrate, but rather regions and villages do";

> [a]bout 80 per cent of the Pakistanis in Britain are from tiny, fully rural Bihar state. Most of the Poles in Western Europe are from villages in Silesia and the southwest. Mexicans in the United States mostly emerge from a handful of rural regions.
>
> *(Saunders, 2011, p. 29)*

Unsurprisingly, many migrants experience emotional ambivalence: sometimes financial gains but emotional pains; economic, political or personal liberation along with experiences of racism and marginalization. Grzywacz and colleagues' (Grzywacz et al., 2006) study of 60 Mexican migrant farmworker men in North Carolina found three-quarters reported ambivalence about leaving wives and children; two-thirds were torn about leaving parents. Both ambivalences were associated with more symptoms of anxiety and poorer mental health – which can be especially serious with farm or other hazardous work if safety precautions are not in place.

Concluding comments

Transnational change in organizations and organizing affects women, men and further genders in many, often contradictory, ways – in, for example, managing, working, being surveilled, consumption and virtualization. At this historical time, there seem to be profound, contradictory transnational tendencies and forces upon men and masculinities: on one hand, the intensification of patriarchal, anti-feminist politics and practices, as, for example, in far right, militaristic politics and misogynist organizing online; on the other hand, there are more signs than ever for transformative possibilities, for example, in dissatisfaction with narrow work orientations, greater concerns for care, and acknowledgements of vulnerabilities. The contradictions of transnational patriarchal relations are becoming clearer and even more urgent.

Organizationally, there are further contradictions. Post-Fordist organizing is elusive. Ahrne and Brunsson (2010) have suggested that

> It may appear as if organization, often associated with bureaucracy and hierarchy, is a phenomenon of the past, and that contemporary societies are characterized either by less structured forms of interaction among highly autonomous actors, perhaps leading to networks; or by highly structured forms with little freedom of action for individuals and organizations, such as the concept of institution suggests.
>
> *(p. 2)*

Likewise, on one hand, capitalism cares not for the sex, gender or sexuality of managers, workers or customers; on the other, both blatant patriarchalism and "gender-neutral gendering" remain powerful in constructing men and masculinities. Organizations remain contexts and sites for intensely uneven and unequal gendered intersectional relations. Most organizations are doubly gendered: public domains, and organizations within them, are dominantly valued over private domains, and structures and processes within organizations themselves gendered, as in men's managerial domination. Transnational organizations and organizing can be triply gendered, with transnational dimensions adding further intersectional gendered power relations, across space, culture, language, inter-organizational powers and virtual technologies; transnational management and control adds a fourth layer of intersectional gendering. Complex transnational social relations construct men's positionalities based on, for example, racialization, ethnicity, sexuality, migrant status and social class. Differential, intersectional gendered structures and processes make for specific local spatial constructions of transnational men and masculinities, beyond, above, across, within nations and locales. The transnational operates at great distances, with national and local inflections, and in immediate localities, locales and body spaces, with their own specificities.

Notes

1 The term, hyperpatriarchal, is used in several different ways, from psychological assessments to analyses of colonialism (Nandy, 1988) and state development (Han & Ling, 1998). Here, it is employed to convey not only how an institution comprises internal organizational structures and exclusions but also how in shifting "identity from an internally oriented, managerial parent to externally pressured, competitive patriarch, it also transforms the role and status of society", which is thereby hyperfeminized (p. 65).
2 As Liz Truss put it, when UK Conservative Foreign Secretary, apparently without irony: "This generation are *#Uber*-riding *#Airbnb*-ing *#Deliveroo*-eating *#freedomfighters*"! With this economic ideology, Truss went on to become prime minister, leading to market turmoil, with losses of at least £300 billion (US$340 billion) from the value of the nation's stock and bond market, and the distinction of the shortest governmental term as prime minister.
3 Depending on the measures used, about 90 percent of billionaires are men.
4 For charting the interlocking concentrations of large business ownership, see Vitali et al., 2011; Peetz et al., 2013; Compston, 2013, made possible in part by the Orbis company database (www.bvdinfo.com/en-gb/our-products/data/international/orbis).

References

Agnew, J. (2005). Space: Place. In P. Cloke & R. Johnston (Eds.), *Spaces of Geographical Thought: Deconstructing Human Geography's Binaries* (pp. 81–96). London: Sage.

Ahmed, N. (2022). *Equality Kills*. Oxford: Oxfam International. https://oxfamilibrary.openrepository.com/bitstream/handle/10546/621341/bp-inequality-kills-170122-en.pdf?sequence=9

Ahrne, G., & Brunsson, N. (2010). Organization outside organizations: The significance of partial organization. *Organization*, *18*(1), 83–104. doi: 10.1177/1350508410376256

Basch, L. G., Schiller, N. G., & Blanc-Szanton, C. (1994). *Nations Unbound: Transnational Projects, Postcolonial Predicaments, and Deterritorialized Nation-states*. Langhorne, PA: Gordon and Breach.

Beck, U. (2000). *What is Globalization?* Cambridge: Polity.

Berg, L. D., & Longhurst, R. (2003). Placing masculinities and geography. *Gender, Place & Culture*, *10*(4), 351–360. doi: 10.1080/0966369032000153322

Blagojević, M. (2009). *Knowledge Production at the Semiperiphery*. Belgrade: Institut za kriminološka i sociološka istraživanja.

Cantú, L. (2009). *The Sexuality of Migration: Border Crossing and Mexican Immigrant Men*. New York: New York University Press.

Carroll, W. K. (2010). *The Making of a Transnational Capitalist Class: Corporate Power in the 21st Century*. London: Zed.

Compston, H. (2013). The network of global corporate control: Implications for public policy. *Business and Politics*, *15*(3), 357–379. doi: 10.1515/bap-2012-0049

Connell, R. (1990). The state, gender, and sexual politics: Theory and appraisal. *Theory and Society*, *19*(5), 507–544. doi: 10.1007/bf00147025

Connell, R. (1993). The big picture: Masculinities in recent world history. *Theory and Society*, *22*(5), 597–623. doi: 10.1007/bf00993538

Connell, R. (1998). Masculinities and globalization. *Men and Masculinities*, *1*(1), 3–23. doi: 10.1177/1097184X98001001001

Connell, R. (2014). Margin becoming centre: For a world-centred rethinking of masculinities. *NORMA: International Journal for Masculinity Studies*, *9*(4), 217–231. doi: 10.1080/18902138.2014.934078

Connell, R. (2016). 100 Million kalashnikovs: Gendered power on a world scale. *Debate Feminista*, *51*, 3–17. doi: 10.1016/j.df.2016.03.001

Connell, R., & Wood, J. (2005). Globalization and business masculinities. *Men and Masculinities*, *7*(4), 347–364.

Cornwall, A., Edström, J., & Greig, A. (Eds.). (2011). *Men and Development: Politicising Masculinities*. London: Zed.

Cornwall, A., Karioris, F. G., & Lindisfarne, N. (Eds.). (2018). *Masculinities under Neoliberalism*. London: Zed.

Cornwall, A., & Lindisfarne, N. (Eds.). (1994). *Dislocating Masculinity: Comparative Ethnographies*. London: Routledge.

Credit Suisse (2016). Global Wealth Databook 2016. Retrieved from http://publications.credit-suisse.com/tasks/render/file/index.cfm?fileid=AD6F2B43-B17B-345E-E20A1A254A3E24A5

Cresswell, T. (2004). *Place: A Short Introduction*. Oxford: Blackwell.

Davies, M., & Chisholm, A. (2018). Neoliberalism, violence, and the body: *Dollhouse* and the critique of the neoliberal subject. *International Political Sociology*, *12*(3), 274–290. doi: 10.1093/ips/oly001

D'Emilio, J. (1998). *Sexual Politics, Sexual Communities: The Making of a Homosexual Minority in the United States, 1940–1970*, 2nd edition. Chicago: University of Chicago Press.

Donaldson, M., Hibbins, R., Howson, R., & Pease, B. (Eds.). (2009). *Migrant Men: Critical Studies of Masculinities and the Migration Experience*. New York: Routledge.

Donaldson, M., & Howson, R. (2009). Men, migration and hegemonic masculinity. In M. Donaldson, R. Hibbins, R. Howson & B. Pease (Eds.), *Migrant Men: Critical Studies of Masculinities and the Migration Experience* (pp. 210–218). New York: Routledge.

Donaldson, M., & Poynting, S. (2006). *Ruling Class Men: Money, Sex, Power*. Bern: Peter Lang.

Fraser, N. (2009). Feminism, capitalism and the cunning of history. *New Left Review*, *56*, 97–117.

Fuentes-Nieva, R., & Galasso, N. (2014). *Working for the Few: Political Capture and Economic Inequality*. Oxford: Oxfam International.

Garlick, S. (2021). Technologies of (in)security: Masculinity and the complexity of neoliberalism. *Feminist Theory*. doi: 10.1177/14647001211046323

Grzywacz, J. G., Quandt, S. A., Early, J., Tapia, J., Graham, C. N., & Arcury, T. A. (2006). Leaving family for work: Ambivalence among Mexican migrant farmworker men. *Journal of Immigrant and Minority Health*, *8*(1), 85–97. doi: 10.1007/s10903-006-6344-7

Han, J., & Ling, L. H. M. (1998). Authoritarianism in the hypermasculinized state: Hybridity, patriarchy, and capitalism in Korea. *International Studies Quarterly*, *42*(1), 53–78. doi: 10.1111/0020-8833.00069

Hardoon, D., Ayele, S., & Fuentes-Nieva, R. (2016). *An Economy for the 1%*. Oxford: Oxfam International. www.oxfam.org/sites/www.oxfam.org/files/file_attachments/bp210-economy-one-percent-tax-havens-180116-en_0.pdf

Harvey, D. (1989). *The Condition of Postmodernity*. Oxford: Blackwell.

Hearn, J. (2003). Men: Power, challenges of power and the 'big picture' of globalization. In I. Novikova & D. Kambourov (Eds.), *Men and Masculinities in the Global World: Integrating Postsocialist Perspectives* (pp. 45–74). Helsinki: Kikimora/Aleksanteri Institute.

Hearn, J. (2004). Tracking 'the transnational': Studying transnational organizations and managements, and the management of cohesion. *Culture and Organization*, *10*(4), 273–290.

Hearn, J. (2015). *Men of the World: Genders, Globalization, Transnational Times*. London: Sage.

Hearn, J., & Blagojević, M. (2013). Introducing and rethinking transnational men. In J. Hearn, M. Blagojevic & K. Harrison (Eds.), *Rethinking Transnational Men: Beyond, Between and Within Nations* (pp. 1–24). New York: Routledge.

Hearn, J., Blagojevic, M., & Harrison, K. (Eds.). (2013). *Rethinking Transnational Men: Beyond, Between and Within Nations*. New York: Routledge.

Hearn, J., Hughson, M., & Vasquez del Aguila, E. (2019). Introduction: Unsustainable institutions of men: Transnational dispersed centres and immanent contradictions. In J. Hearn, E. Vasquez del Aguila & M. Hughson (Eds.), *Unsustainable Institutions of Men: Transnational Dispersed Centres, Gender Power, Contradictions* (pp. 1–21). London: Routledge.

Hearn, J., & Niemistö, C. (2012). Men, managers, fathers and home-work relations: National context, organisational policies, and individual lives. In P. McDonald & E. Jeanes (Eds.), *Men, Wage Work and Family* (pp. 95–113). London: Routledge.

Hearn, J., Jyrkinen, M., Piekkari, R., & Oinonen, E. (2008) "Women home and away": Transnational managerial work and gender relations. *The Journal of Business Ethics*, *83*(1), 41–54. doi: 10.1007/s10551-007-9655-2
Hopkins, P., & Gorman-Murray, A. (Eds.). (2014). *Masculinities and Place*. Aldershot: Ashgate.
Hopkins, P., & Gorman-Murray, A. (2019). Masculinities and geography, moving forward: Men's bodies, emotions and spiritualities. *Gender, Place & Culture*, *26*(3), 301–314. doi: 10.1080/0966369X.2018.1552560
Hultman, M., & Pulé, P. M. (2019). *Ecological Masculinities*. London: Routledge.
Humphries, J. (2010). *Childhood and Child Labour in the British Industrial Revolution*. Cambridge: Cambridge University Press.
Huws, U. (2015). iCapitalism and the cybertariat: Contradictions of the digital economy. *Monthly Review*, *66*(8), 42–57. doi: 10.14452/MR-066-08-2015-01_7
Innes, R. A., & Alexander, K. (Eds.). (2015). *Indigenous Men and Masculinities: Legacies, Identities, Regeneration*. Winnipeg: University of Manitoba Press.
Jones, A. (Ed.). (2006). *Men of the Global South: A Reader*. London: Zed.
Kerfoot, D., & Knights, D. (1993). Management, masculinity and manipulation: From paternalism to corporate strategy in financial services in Britain. *Journal of Management Studies*, *30*(4), 659–677. doi: 10.1111/j.1467-6486.1993.tb00320.x
Lefebvre, H. (1974). *The Production of Space*. Oxford: Blackwell.
Levitt, P. (2010). Taking culture seriously: The unexplored nexus between migration, incorporation and development. *Revue Européenne des Migrations Internationales*, *26*(2), 139–153. doi: 10.4000/remi.5149
Lie, J. (2004). *Modern Peoplehood*. Cambridge, MA: Harvard University Press.
Little, B., & Winch, A. (2021). *The New Patriarchs of Digital Capitalism: Celebrity Tech Founders and Networks of Power*. London: Routledge.
Massey, D. (1994). *Space, Place and Gender*. Cambridge: Polity.
Messerschmidt, J., & Bridges, T. (2017). Trump and the Politics of Fluid Masculinities. Retrieved 21 July, from https://gendersociety.wordpress.com/2017/07/21/trump-and-the-politics-of-fluid-masculinities/
Nagel, J. (1998). Masculinity and nationalism: Gender and sexuality in the making of nations. *Ethnic and Racial Studies*, *21*(2), 242–269. doi: 10.1080/014198798330007
Nandy, A. (1988). *The Intimate Enemy*. Delhi: Oxford University Press.
Ong, A. (2006). *Neoliberalism as Exception: Mutations in Citizenship and Sovereignty*. Durham, NC: Duke University Press.
Oxfam (2017). *An Economy for the 99%: It's Time to Build a Human Economy that Benefits Everyone, Not Just the Privileged Few*. Oxford: Oxfam. Retrieved from www.oxfam.org/sites/www.oxfam.org/files/file_attachments/bp-economy-for-99-percent-160117-en.pdf
Oxfam (2020). "World's billionaires have more wealth than 4.6 billion people". Oxfam, January 20, Accessed 31 May 2021, www.oxfam.org/en/press-releases/worlds-billionaires-have-more-wealth-46-billion-people
Pajumets, M., & Hearn, J. (2012). Post-socialist fathers 'at home' and 'away from home' in 'Old Europe': Facing the challenge through masculine identity talk. *STSS: Studies of Transition States and Societies*, *4*(1), 31–47. doi: 10.58036/stss.v4i1.89
Pease, B., & Pringle, K. (Eds.). (2002). *A Man's World: Changing Men's Practices in a Globalized World*. London: Zed.
Peetz, D., Murray, G., & Nienhüser, W. (2013). The new structuring of corporate ownership. *Globalizations*, *10*(5), 711–730.
Phillips, J. (1987). *A Man's Country: The Image of the Pākehā Male – A History*. Auckland: Penguin.
Pickett, K., Wilkinson, R., & de Vogli, R. (2014). Equality, Sustainability and Wellbeing, Rapporteur Paper, Francqui International Conference 2014, The EU's Fifth Project: Transitional Governance in the Service of Sustainable Societies. Brussels. Retrieved from www.srfood.org/images/stories/pdf/otherdocuments/Equality2.pdf
Poster, W. (2013). Subversions of techno-masculinity: Indian ICT professionals in the global economy. In J. Hearn, M. Blagojević & K. Harrison (Eds.), *Rethinking Transnational Men: Beyond, Between and Within Nations* (pp. 113–133). New York: Routledge.
Povinelli, E. A., & Chauncey, G. (1999). Thinking sexuality transnationally: An introduction. *GLQ: A Journal of Lesbian and Gay Studies*, *5*(4), 439–449.

Priestland, D. (2013). The Libertarian iCapitalists Wouldn't Have Anything to do with the State . . . Would They? Retrieved 19 June, from The Guardian: www.guardian.co.uk/commentisfree/2013/jun/19/libertarian-icapitalists-silicon-valley

Pulé, P. M., & Hultman, M. (Eds.). (2021). *Men, Masculinities, and the Earth: Contending with the (m) Anthropocene.* Houndmills: Palgrave Macmillan.

Pyne, S. J. (2004). *The Ice.* London: Orion.

Raab, S. (2006). *Five Families: The Rise, Decline, and Resurgence of America's Most Powerful Mafia Empires.* New York: St Martin's.

Ratele, K. (2014). Currents against gender transformation of South African men: Relocating marginality to the centre of research and theory of masculinities. *NORMA: International Journal of Masculinity Studies, 9*(1), 30–44. doi: 10.1080/18902138.2014.892285

Ratele, K. (2021). An invitation to decoloniality in work on (African) men and masculinities. *Gender, Place & Culture, 28*(6), 769–785. doi: 10.1080/0966369X.2020.1781794

Reis, C. (2004). *Men Managers in a European Multinational Company.* Mering: Rainer Humpp Verlag.

Ritzer, G. (1993). *The McDonaldization of Society.* Thousand Oaks, CA: Pine Forge.

Roberts, S. (2018). *Young Working-Class Men in Transition.* Abingdon: Routledge.

Robertson, R., & Khondker, H. H. (1998). Discourses of globalization: Preliminary considerations. *International Sociology, 13*(1), 25–40. doi: 10.1177/026858098013001004

Salzinger, L. (2016). Re-making men: Masculinity as a terrain of the neoliberal economy. *Critical Historical Studies, 3*(1), 1–25. doi: 10.1086/685553

Saunders, D. (2011). *Arrival City: How the Largest Migration in History is Reshaping our World.* London: Random House.

Savage, M. (2018). Richest 1% on Target to Own Two-thirds of All Wealth by 2030. Retrieved 7 April, from The Observer: www.theguardian.com/business/2018/apr/07/global-inequality-tipping-point-2030

Scott, J. (1998). *Seeing Like a State.* New Haven, CT: Yale University Press.

Sklair, L. (2001). *The Transnational Capitalist Class.* Oxford: Blackwell.

Slobodian, Q. (2018). *Globalists: The End of Empire and the Birth of Liberalism.* Cambridge, MA: Harvard University Press.

Stacey, J. (1987). Sexism by a subtler name: Postindustrial conditions and postfeminist consciousness in the Silicon Valley. *Socialist Review, 17*(6), 7–28. doi: 10.7591/9781501720741-024

Tienari, J., Søderberg, A., Holgersson, C., & Vaara, E. (2005). Gender and national identity constructions in the cross-border merger context. *Gender, Work & Organization, 12*(3), 217–241. doi: 10.1111/j.1468-0432.2005.00271.x

Van der Pijl, K. (1998). *Transnational Classes and International Relations.* London: Routledge.

van Hovan, B., & Hörschelmann, K. (Eds.). (2005). *Spaces of Masculinities.* London: Routledge.

Vasquez del Aguila, E. (2014). *Being a Man in a Transnational World: The Masculinity and Sexuality of Migration.* New York: Routledge.

Vitali, S., Glattfelder, J. B., & Battiston, S. (2011). The network of global corporate control. *PLoS ONE, 6*(10), e25995.

Walker, C., & Roberts, S. (Eds.). (2018). *Masculinity, Labour, and Neoliberalism: Working-Class Men in International Perspective.* Cham: Palgrave Macmillan.

Waters, M. (1995). *Globalization.* London: Routledge.

Woodward, A. (1996). Multinational masculinities and European bureaucracies. In D. Collinson & J. Hearn (Eds.), *Men as Managers, Managers as Men* (pp. 167–185). London: Sage.

Wolfman, G., Hearn, J., & Yeadon-Lee, T. (2021). Hollow femininities: The emerging faces of neoliberal masculinities. *NORMA: International Journal for Masculinity Studies, 16*(4), 217–234. doi: 10.1080/18902138.2021.1996829

Young, B., Bakker, I., & Elson, D. (Eds.). (2011). *Questioning Financial Governance from a Feminist Perspective.* London: Routledge.

Zhou, Y. R., Sinding, C., & Goellnicht, D. (Eds.). (2021). *Sexualities, Transnationalism, and Globalization: New Perspectives.* New York: Routledge.

Zuboff, S. (2019). *The Age of Surveillance Capitalism: The Fight for the Future at the New Frontier of Power.* London: Profile.

PART II

Structures and processes of organizing

9

CRITICAL DIALECTICAL PERSPECTIVES ON MEN, MASCULINITIES AND LEADERSHIP[1]

David L. Collinson

Introduction

Historically and across many cultures, leadership has tended to be male-dominated and often assumed to be the preserve of men. In contemporary societies, organizations and public life generally, leadership is still frequently conflated with qualities and behaviours stereotypically associated with men and masculinity, such as rationality, authority and toughness (Galea et al., 2022). Despite well-established equality legislation in Western countries, women continue to comprise a small fraction of those occupying senior leadership and boardroom positions (Fawcett Society, 2022).[2] Typically, when people "think leader", they still "think man".

Men's dominance of senior positions is also evident in the frequent associations of leadership and militarism (Aktaş et al., this volume). The revered leader in many societies is he, only occasionally she, who has led the nation be it in war, as in celebrated figures like Churchill and Eisenhower, or in national struggle, as with Mandela and Gandhi. Even in peacetime, militarism often figures prominently, for example, in men leaders' talk, as in the "war on terror" or "the war on drugs" (Collinson & Hearn, 2020). Men in leadership positions often draw on hypermasculine metaphors that view markets, business and politics through the imagery of war or as highly competitive, masculine sports contests (Gregory & Alsarve, this volume).

While men's persistent colonization of senior positions tends to be taken-for-granted in everyday talk or media coverage, gendered assumptions are also evident in leadership research (Hearn, 1989). The nineteenth-century emphasis on "great men" creating change (Carlyle, 1840) and the twentieth-century focus on heroic (Hook, 1945), charismatic (Shamir et al., 1993) and transformational leaders (Bass, 1985) all tended to conflate leadership with men and masculinity. Research has frequently defined leadership effectiveness in terms of traits like assertiveness, competitiveness and confidence. In many societies, these qualities are not only associated with men but have also become the stereotypical norm against which leaders are typically compared and measured.[3] Accordingly, men's leadership practices, for example, in influencing, negotiating, motivating, persuading, networking and lobbying, are often not recognized or even noticed as being gendered. This is the case not only in mainstream/

DOI: 10.4324/9781003193579-11

malestream leadership studies but also in more critical studies that sometimes treat important questions like power and control, hubris and narcissism as if they were gender-free processes.

Although men and masculinity are often central to the study and practice of leadership, it is remarkable how few studies have examined these gendered dynamics. One exception is Holmes' (2009) research on the social construction of leadership and masculinity. She found that men in New Zealand performed leadership through three specific masculine styles: the authoritative, paternalistic and egalitarian. While acknowledging that women leaders may also draw on similar styles, Holmes found that masculine discourses were more frequently enacted by men leaders. Importantly, all the men selected in Holmes' research were positively evaluated by colleagues as effective leaders.

Yet, leadership is by no means always effective. To address the other side of this coin – where men's leadership may also be dysfunctional and even oppressive – this chapter considers the contributions of critical studies of men and masculinities (CSMM) and critical leadership studies (CLS). It suggests that combining insights from these perspectives highlights the importance of (gendered) power asymmetries, (gendered) control practices and intersectional inequalities – issues frequently under-estimated or neglected in social constructionist perspectives. In different ways, CSMM and CLS address intersecting sources of power, privilege and asymmetry in contemporary organizations and societies.

The chapter begins by considering the contribution of CSMM to understanding men and leadership,[4] focusing on the influential concept of hegemonic masculinity. Addressing the deterministic tendencies of some applications of hegemonic masculinity and highlighting the value of more dialectical approaches, the chapter then explores the insights of CLS, and especially its examination of dialectical power asymmetries and control practices. The final section considers how men and masculinities can shape leadership decision-making – important processes through which leaders exercise power and influence. Recognizing that power is important but rarely all-determining, absolute or fixed, the chapter develops a more dialectical approach to men, masculinities and leadership by discussing some of the contradictory, destructive and self-defeating outcomes that can emerge when men leaders' decision-making is informed by hypermasculine ways of thinking and acting.

Men, masculinities and gendered power

Feminist studies are the major influence in developing critical analyses of gender and leadership (e.g. Husu et al., 2010; Ford & Morgan, 2023). They show how romanticized notions of the "heroic" and "charismatic" leader are often saturated with images and assumptions of men and masculinity (Johnson & Lacerenza, 2019) and how organizational hierarchies typically reflect and reinforce men's gendered power and control (Acker, 1990). Challenging taken-for-granted views that white, middle-aged men are inevitably the people in charge who create visions and make decisions, feminist studies demonstrate that gender is an important source of intersectional power and influence typically embedded in organizational structures, cultures and practices (Liu & Baker, 2016; Liu, 2021). Research has focused, for example, on women's experiences of male-dominated leadership and management cultures (Wajcman, 1999), the barriers they face in climbing hierarchies (Carli & Eagly, 2011), the transformative potential of their leadership (Klenke, 2011) and the possible differences in styles between women and men leaders (Rosener, 1990). Studies have also explored how women leaders navigate between cultures of masculinity and femininity (Hobbins et al., 2022), how they are represented in the media (Elliott & Stead, 2018), and how they can challenge gender stereotypes and binaries (Bowring, 2004).

Informed by feminist research, CSMM adopt a specific and critical rather than implicit or incidental focus on men and masculinities. They examine how, why and with what consequences men and masculinity/ies are produced and reproduced (Kimmel et al., 2005). Rather than viewing masculinit*y* as singular or universal, CSMM recognize that "masculini*ties*" can take multiple, shifting, asymmetrical forms related to intersecting inequalities and varying across time and space (Connell & Wood, 2005). Connell's (1995) focus on hegemonic masculinity has been the conceptual "driving force behind the expanding field of critical masculinities studies" (Messerschmidt, 2019, p. 85). This term draws on Gramsci's theory of hegemony which refers to the dominance of one group over another, typically supported by ideologies and legitimating norms and ideas (Collinson et al., 2023).

Hegemonic masculinity problematizes men's structural dominance and control over women and subordinated men, with particular emphasis on intersectional gendered power relations. Connell argues that gendered power relations are characterized by hegemonic (e.g. white, heterosexual, affluent, neocolonial) and subordinate/non-hegemonic masculinities (e.g. complicit, subordinated and marginalized masculinities, such as Black, gay, working class). Subordinate masculinities are typically constructed as compensatory reactions to social positions lacking economic and political power (Messerschmidt, 2019). Hegemonic and subordinate masculinities describe the unities, differences and asymmetries that characterize gender relations between men and masculinities.

Highlighting the socially constructed and intersectional nature of men and masculinities (Hearn, 2014, 2015), CSMM show how gender relations in organizations are often enacted through power and identity dynamics. For many men, work and career continue to be primary sites for gender identity construction, especially through intense competition for dominance and status (Aavik et al., 2020). In "masculinity contests" (Berdahl et al., 2018, also this volume), men try to prove they are powerful and tough, particularly by showing no weakness, demonstrating strength and stamina, prioritizing work over family and home, and engaging in dog-eat-dog hyper-competition. Workplace ethnographies have documented how men in subordinate positions construct masculine counter-cultures that celebrate male breadwinner identities (Cockburn, 1983; Collinson, 1992). Other studies critically examine business (and transnational) managerial masculinities (Roper, 1994; Collinson & Hearn, 1996; Martin, 2001; Connell & Wood, 2005; Hearn, 2014, 2015).

Although CSMM have generally neglected leadership, there is growing interest in applying hegemonic masculinity to the critical analysis of senior organizational positions (Tienari et al., 2010; Khan et al., 2022), including entrepreneurial founders (Hytti et al., 2023). Matos et al. (2018) argue that masculinity contest cultures create the conditions for abusive leadership to thrive. In addition to hyper-competition, men's hegemony can also be reproduced through collaboration and collusion. Galea et al. (2022) argue that men maintain their power, privilege and overrepresentation in senior positions through homosociality: the informal gendered rules, networks and collaborative processes through which some men cooperate with and support other men. Based on a sense of sameness and affinity, homosocial processes improve certain men's access to networks of power, conferring greater guidance, opportunities and advocacy. This informal system of loyalty and trust benefits men's career progression and reinforces hegemonic masculinity while excluding women and undermining transparency. Poorhosseinzadeh and Strachan (2021) show how "the ideal executive" is typically defined as working long hours, being geographically and internationally mobile, having an unbroken career path and prioritizing career over family. Although presented as gender neutral, these criteria reinforce two forms of hegemonic masculinity – careerism and entrepreneurialism – which legitimize men as ideal candidates, that is, single-minded careerists who avoid/ignore caring and family responsibilities.

This focus on hegemonic masculinity also challenges leadership approaches emphasizing sex differences. Connell and Messerschmidt (2005, p. 836) define masculinities as "configurations of practice that are accomplished in social action and, therefore, can differ according to the gender relations in a particular social setting". Rejecting the idea of masculinity as being embedded in the personality of individuals, these arguments question the view that men are more likely to adopt "transactional" leadership styles and women more likely to enact "transformational" approaches. In practice, research has found little difference between women's and men's leadership styles (Boulgarides, 1984), and some women managers and leaders may be more task or achievement-oriented than men and other women (Donnell & Hall, 1980). Pointing to the importance of asymmetrical gendered power relations, hegemonic masculinity therefore challenges the view that the gendering of men derives from a fixed, inner trait or core.

Dialectics of men and masculinities

Despite its centrality to the field, hegemonic masculinity has been criticized. Researchers have argued that the concept is inter alia: ambiguous and unclear, applied inconsistently, neglects positive aspects of masculinity, may reify toxic practices, and does not address how men can be *simultaneously* both dominant *and* subordinate in relation to intersecting inequalities like class, race and sexual orientation (Martin, 1998; Collinson & Hearn, 1994, 2005; Hearn, 2004, 2014). The term has been interpreted in different ways: as a form of masculinity, as more general social processes, and as a set of personal traits rather than as a structure of gender relations that subordinates women (and some men). Regarding leadership dynamics, it can be unclear whether hegemony refers to leadership through force, via control of resources, by example or through persuasion.

Building on these concerns, this chapter questions the deterministic tendencies of hegemonic masculinity and suggests the value of more dialectical perspectives. While hegemonic masculinity explicitly and valuably focuses on the asymmetrical nature of gender relationships, power relations are rarely, if ever, all determining, monolithic, absolute or fixed. In addition to asymmetries and control practices, gendered dynamics are typically characterized by human agency, ambiguity, paradox, resistance, contradiction, flux and change. Some CSMM writers have addressed these themes by proposing more dialectical understandings of hegemonic masculinity.

Demetriou (2001) questions the recurrent tendency to view masculine power as a "closed, coherent and unified totality that embraces no otherness, no contradiction" (2001, p. 355), whereas he contends, it is precisely through its apparently contradictory content that hegemonic masculinity is reproduced.[5] Rejecting the tendency to separate masculinities from each other, Demetriou contends that different masculinities can appropriate and influence one another through "dialectical pragmatism". Christensen and Qvotrup Jensen (2014) suggest that a critical focus on power relations should also acknowledge the importance of reciprocal influence. They observe that "different social categories mutually constitute each other as overall forms of social differentiation or systems of oppression" (2014, p. 69). Hence, the meaning and experience of gendered power relations will vary for different ethnic groups according to class, age, race, sexuality, religion, etc. Exploring white masculinities in Denmark, the authors argue that intersectional theory provides insights into the complex processes which elevate some masculinities while marginalizing others. They recommend focusing less on deterministic and stable power relations and more on "contradictions, antagonisms, ambivalences, ruptures and ongoing struggles to create hegemonic formations" (2014, p. 67). As elaborated in the next section, this emphasis on dialectical understandings of men and masculinities to some extent mirrors developments in critical dialectical leadership studies which emphasize interplay, interconnections, contradictions and resistance within asymmetrical power dynamics.

The deterministic tendencies of hegemonic masculinity are also revealed by its neglect of non-gender-specific sources of social and organizational power, and how these can reciprocally influence gender dynamics.[6] Concentrating on gendered power dynamics, studies of hegemonic masculinity rarely examine other forms of leadership and management control. Hegemonic masculinity critiques hierarchies of gender but presents little analysis of hierarchy per se. Although the term critically examines men's power and identity as men, there is little attention to the power and identity of leaders as leaders or of managers as managers. While gender and masculinity are crucially important, it is rarely, if ever, possible to reduce complex leadership power relations exclusively to these issues.

Non-gender-specific factors are central to intersectional theories which reveal how gendered inequalities may be shaped by diverse social relations and inequalities (e.g. race, ethnicity, class, sexuality, religion, age, etc.). These non-gender-specific phenomena can become interwoven in dialectical ways with gender categories, to produce gendered effects. Different social divisions can cut across gendered power relations in multiple, mutually reinforcing and/or countervailing ways. Building on intersectional theory, it is argued here that other important sources of social, economic and political power and privilege exist for those in senior positions. For example, men's power as leaders derives not only from being men but also from their hierarchical position. The following section develops this point by drawing on CLS to consider sources of power and privilege that may not be explicitly gendered but which have important implications for the reproduction of gendered leadership relations.

Men, masculinities and leadership dialectics

Many studies of leadership have concentrated on identifying effective leaders' traits, qualities and styles. These leader-centred and heroic perspectives pay less attention to the structural, cultural and discursive conditions and consequences of leadership relations. More recently, post-heroic perspectives focus on relational and collective dynamics, examining processes such as distributed, shared and collaborative leadership (e.g. Pearce & Conger, 2003). Shifting the analytical lens from the individual to the collective, post-heroic perspectives recognize the socially constructed nature of leadership and the importance of followers.[7] Yet, these approaches also tend to neglect the asymmetrical nature of leadership relations and leaders' exercise of power and control. While organizations can be understood as collective endeavours, this sense of community and interdependence may be in tension with how organizational power and privilege are conferred, enacted and legitimized.

Questioning the assumptions of both heroic and post-heroic perspectives, CLS show how power asymmetries and control practices are frequently implicated in the conditions, processes and consequences of leadership dynamics (Collinson, 2005, 2011, 2020; Alvesson & Spicer, 2012; Schedlitzki & Edwards, 2021). CLS is a loose umbrella term for a diverse set of perspectives (drawing on insights from the more established fields of critical management studies, communication studies, postcolonialism and feminism as well as post-structuralism, radical psychology, and psychoanalysis). Sometimes competing and in tension, these perspectives critique the power relations and identity constructions through which leadership and followership dynamics are frequently situated, rationalized and reproduced, sometimes resisted and occasionally transformed. They view questions of power, privilege and inequality as fundamental constructs of leadership dynamics even when the latter are more shared, distributed or democratically established.

Exploring the relational and asymmetrical character of leadership dynamics, critical perspectives argue that leaders' power and privilege are enacted in the decisions, statements and claims they make, in their everyday practices and relationships, in the many ways they influence followers, as well as through the organizational structures, resources, information and technologies over which they have considerable discretion. Some CLS writers have highlighted important links between class inequalities, capital accumulation and leadership (Jones et al., 2021). It is certainly the case that leadership can facilitate, disguise and reinforce capitalist, neoliberal and indeed neocolonial agendas, and that locating these dynamics within economic systems like capitalism is important and requires further research (e.g. Tourish & Willmott, 2023).

Critical perspectives also encourage a concern with dysfunctional, destructive and toxic leadership (Lipman-Blumen, 2005).[8] They aim to show that power is not so much a dependent variable or a commodity to be used or abused at will but rather a deeply embedded and inescapable feature of leadership dynamics and organizational structures, cultures and relations: power is hierarchical, structural, relational *and* practice based (Lumby, 2018). Leaders typically play a key role in defining strategies and change programmes, shaping structures and cultures as well as monitoring work and performance, providing rewards, applying sanctions, and in hiring and firing. Leaders can also exercise power by "managing meaning" and defining situations in ways that suit their purposes (Smircich & Morgan, 1982).

Using communication to enact power, leaders can draw on ideologies seeking to redefine sectional as universal interests and on discourses constructing excessively positive definitions of reality (Collinson, 2012). Spector (2020) documents how "post-truth claims making" has emerged as a defining cultural and political phenomenon, fuelling the rise of autocrats and dictators. It is now an important tool of control for authoritarian political leaders posing as populists. Exploring leaders' manipulation of followers, Ciulla (2020) reveals how leaders can fuel followers' sense of resentment. Ashcraft (2022) highlights how such manipulative processes may be shaped by "aggrieved" masculinity and a dangerous sense of victimized manhood. These studies illustrate how power is often exercised in and through leaders' discourses, decisions and practices.

Leaders' power can also be disguised and concealed. O'Connor et al. (2019) examine the strategies of those in senior positions in higher education institutions in Ireland, Italy and Turkey which, they argue, were specifically designed to obscure the centralization of power. Referring to this as "stealth power", they identify four control practices that seek to obscure leaders' power: rhetorical collegiality, agenda control, in-group loyalty and the invisibility of gendered power. Their findings illustrate how leaders' power can operate covertly and through surveillance. Similarly, Lumby (2018) explores subtle forms of leader power such as "shaping discussion and decisions", "acquiring the support of others", "weakening opposition", "denying power" and "creating a favourable impression".

Power dynamics can also inform localized micro-interactions, for example, in the ways individuals stand or sit, whether they make eye contact, the gestures they make, the words they choose (Wilson & Wedlock, 2023), the jokes they tell, as well as in the physical arrangements and features of rooms and locations in which meetings take place (Dick & Collings, 2014). Equally, the architecture of buildings can convey important symbolic messages about leaders' power and status (Dale & Latham, 2015). Those in senior positions are typically located on the top floors of buildings, well away from subordinates and frontline operations, with highly controlled and often segregated entries and exits. In organizations where the CEO is also the owner (and possibly the founder), power can be especially asymmetrical and gendered. Equally, the ownership of many businesses is often passed from one generation to the next, with sons inheriting firms from fathers. This socially legitimized reproduction of patriarchal authority can thus perpetuate men's dominance of leadership.

The foregoing discussion is illustrative rather than exhaustive of the sources of power available to leaders. Suffice it to say that these (and other) non-gender-specific sources of power can be implicated in the reproduction of men's dominance of leadership. Although issues of power are a central concern in CLS, there are many competing theories about what "it" means, where "it" might be located and how "it" is enacted (Clegg et al., 2023).[9] For example, labour process and critical management theorists tend to concentrate on management and ownership in capitalist societies as key sources of power, while avoiding the study of leadership and leaders. CLS suggest that, for good and/or for ill, leadership, just like management, is a central feature of power and control in organizations and societies.

An emerging CLS approach to understanding power views leadership as a dialectical process (Collinson, 2005, 2011, 2020). Dialectical perspectives[10] challenge dichotomization and determinism (Collinson & Fairhurst, in press). They eschew simple binaries like leader–follower, leader–manager, transformational–transactional and so on, arguing that they oversimplify complex inter-relationships (Fairhurst & Collinson, 2023). Instead, they focus on "interdependent opposites aligned with forces that push-pull on each other like a rubber band and exist in an ongoing dynamic interplay as the poles implicate each other" (Putnam et al., 2016, p. 7). Rather than viewing asymmetrical power relations as all-determining, hegemonic or fixed, critical dialectical perspectives also recognize the importance of agency, resistance, contradictions and change. They view social life as a "dynamic knot of contradictions, a ceaseless interplay between contrary or opposing tendencies" (Baxter & Montgomery, 1996, p. 3).

Critical dialectical approaches argue that asymmetrical power relations typically take multiple, economic, discursive, embodied and shifting forms, interconnecting in ways that are often mutually reinforcing but sometimes in tension (Collinson & Fairhurst, in press). Acknowledging the importance of gender and other intersecting inequalities, critical dialectical perspectives also highlight how leaders' power can have positive, productive, and empowering effects, as well as coercive, corrupt and destructive consequences. From this perspective, leaders' (gendered) power and control can be conferred and legitimized by hierarchical position and/or ownership, as well as enacted, exercised and reinforced more informally through processes, relationships, networks and personal agencies.

In addition to recognizing the importance of asymmetrical control strategies, a distinctive feature of critical dialectical approaches is their contention that followers are frequently more proactive, knowledgeable and oppositional than is often acknowledged in leadership studies. Studies emphasize that leader–led relations always contain the potential for conflict and dissent (Zoller & Fairhurst, 2007). Leaders cannot simply assume followers' obedience or loyalty, indeed their exercise of power and control can provoke resistance. Careful to avoid treating leaders' control and influence as all-determining, monolithic or fixed, dialectical perspectives recognize that different enactments of power can be mutually reinforcing and/or in tension with one another, potentially producing shifting, paradoxical, contradictory and unintended outcomes.

Men, masculinities and leadership decision-making

Decision-making is a key aspect of leadership and an important source of leaders' power and influence. While leaders' decisions are typically assumed to be rational, balanced and impartial, various critical studies indicate that in practice this is by no means always the case. Developing a more gendered, dialectical approach, this section discusses examples of how men and masculinities can shape leadership decision-making, how hypermasculine assumptions may cloud leaders' judgements, and how this can lead to dysfunctional, unethical and sometimes disastrous consequences.

Research shows that men leaders can make non-rational and unlawful selection and promotion decisions that discriminate against highly qualified and experienced women candidates, while privileging less qualified and less experienced male applicants (Collinson, 2000; Poorhosseinzadeh & Strachan, 2021). Kanter (1991) found that men in senior positions frequently select in their own image ("homosocial reproduction") in ways that exclude well-qualified women and reproduce all-male elites. She found that men were appointed to senior positions because they were perceived to be more reliable and committed, supposedly free from conflicting loyalties between home and work. Martin (1990) describes how male corporate leaders expected pregnant women managers to organize caesarean operations to fit in with new product launch dates.

Critical studies reveal how men leaders can misjudge cases of (hetero)sexuality in organizations in ways that reinforce gender asymmetries. In various countries from male-dominated shop floors in the United Kingdom (Collinson, 1992) to managerial work in Japanese corporations (Allison, 1994), research has found that men's (hetero)sexuality often remains dominant, privileged and unchallenged by leaders. Some men in senior positions "turn a blind eye" to men's heterosexuality in the workplace, viewing these dynamics as "normal" and "natural" in ways that can undermine heterosexual women (Collinson & Collinson, 1989, 1996) and marginalize homosexual women and men (Eigenmann, this volume). This can have damaging consequences for employees and organizations when legal cases are lost, damages must be paid and reputations undermined. As the #MeToo movement revealed, in some cases men in senior positions may use their unregulated hierarchical power to initiate and conceal sexual relationships with women subordinates.

Research on sexual harassment reveals how men leaders can misunderstand what constitutes harassment and misjudge the most effective ways to address victims' claims. For example, within the UK police service, research has highlighted a long-standing tendency for senior officers to ignore deeply masculine, heterosexual "warrior" cultures characterized by sexual harassment, misogyny and the abuse of women (Cunningham, 2022; Westmarland, this volume). Rather than deal with sexual harassment claims openly and formally, the initial response of some men leaders in various sectors is to try to protect perpetrators, blame victims and resolve matters informally (Collinson & Collinson, 1992). Women's scepticism that their claims of harassment will be dealt with seriously and professionally remains an important barrier to disclosure. Having said that, the progress made by the #MeToo movement demonstrates the power of women's resistance to challenge men's sexual harassment and its mismanagement.

Critical studies also examine the impact of power on leaders themselves. Conferring greater autonomy, status and privilege, senior positions can encourage leaders' hubris and narcissism (Sadler-Smith, 2019). This, in turn, may inform a failure to consult – even a disregard for others' views – and a desire to hold onto power even after support for a leader fades. Power can become so intoxicating (Owen, 2012) that leaders' decision-making becomes impulsive and risky. Leaders may be less empathetic (Asad & Sadler-Smith, 2020) and unable or unwilling to appreciate other points of view (Useem, 2017). Where men leaders enjoy high degrees of autonomy and low accountability gendered forms of corrupt and unethical practices are more likely to occur (Jones, 2022), as indicated by numerous corporate scandals and political exposés such as those revealed in the Panama Papers, the Paradise Papers and the Pandora Papers (Collinson et al., 2023). The demise of Enron illustrates men leaders' unregulated power abuse through reckless, ego-driven masculinity. Portillo and Molano (2017) identified "three mechanisms of interaction" linking men, masculinities and leadership with corruption. These mechanisms understand corruption as male privilege; male performance of power and domination; and a pathway for men to fulfil society's expectations of them as providers.

The global financial sector is heavily male-dominated (Collier et al., this volume) and men financiers' risky behaviour was implicated in the international financial crash of 2007–2008 (Horton, 2022). Male executives' hubristic masculinities and over-optimism resulted in a collective failure to recognize the significant risks involved in extending credit and loans to people who could not afford to repay and then aggregating these debts into mortgage bonds before selling them onto other financial organizations (Collinson, 2012). The result was huge corporate losses, the collapse of famous, long-standing financial organizations and companies "too big to fail" being bailed out by governments. Due to their overrepresentation among subprime mortgage holders, poor people, African American and Hispanic women, and women in the Global South were particularly impacted (Baker, 2014; Fishbein & Woodall, 2006). In the United Kingdom, the Royal Bank of Scotland's (RBS) acquisition of the Dutch Bank ABN Amro in 2007 exemplifies how hubristic masculinity and excessive risk-taking informed executive decisions. Despite this being the biggest banking takeover in history, senior executives at RBS did not undertake due diligence for the purchase. Accordingly, they failed to recognize ABN's exposure to the US subprime mortgage crisis. Occurring just as the global liquidity crisis began to bite, the deal fundamentally weakened the RBS balance sheet resulting in the company having to be bailed out by the UK government. In 2023, the Bank remained partly state-owned.

Critical studies also reveal that men leaders' hypermasculine risk-taking and decision-making can have lethal consequences (Enarson & Pease, 2016). The tragically flawed decision-making by Morton-Thiokol executives that led to the Challenger disaster is a case in point. Maier and Messerschmidt (1998) found that the all-male executive team overruled specialist engineering advice about the threat to safety in launching the shuttle in very cold conditions, defining this as "an acceptable risk". Executives used previously successful launches to rationalize high risk-taking. Focusing narrowly on the task – "to get Challenger up" – their high-risk decision revealed a reckless indifference to its human consequences. The tragedy of the Challenger shuttle exemplifies the disastrous outcomes that can result from the hypermasculine tendency to downplay or under-estimate risk in decision-making (Messerschmidt, 1996).

Similarly, in response to the recent global pandemic, populist male leaders (e.g. in Belarus, Brazil, Hungary, India, Turkey, the United Kingdom and the United States) sought to reassert their masculine power and to reassure citizens by downplaying COVID-19's threat (Collinson & Hearn, 2020). Defining themselves as virile "strong man leaders" (Ben-Ghiat, 2020), they claimed to be invulnerable to the virus. Paradoxically, their masculine strategies, intended to convey the appearance of control, frequently produced counter-productive outcomes. Their reluctance to take the global pandemic seriously resulted in incoherent policies and practices, confused communication and much higher rates of infection and death (Waylen, 2021). After ignoring medical advice, some of these leaders contracted COVID-19 themselves.

Men leaders' decision-making can backfire in personal ways. Various studies illustrate how men in organizations can become so preoccupied with acquiring status, exercising power and confirming masculine identity that work and career become all-consuming (Aavik et al., 2020). Especially within hypermasculine success-oriented cultures, men may be so driven by the desire for personal achievement (Weiss, 1990) and to validate their masculine selves that they privilege and prioritize career development above all other concerns including family, friends and private life (Berdahl et al., 2018, this volume). Such excessive ambition can be expressed, for example, in long hours working and in expecting subordinates to comply with similar work-intensified patterns (Poorhosseinzadeh & Strachan, 2021). The resulting imbalance between work, life and family (see also Hrženjak, this volume) might negatively impact men's private lives, their health and well-being to such an extent they become disillusioned and even decide to opt out of high-pressure careers (Biese, 2020; Choroszewicz & Biese, this volume). Equally, men leaders' neglect of family and childcare responsibilities can undermine their contribution to families as fathers, partners and carers. Only in later years are such driven men likely to acknowledge regret in missing their children growing up, as well as their indebtedness to women's unpaid work at home which typically supported and enabled their career success in the first place.[11]

Recent CSMM research has revealed how men leaders' decision-making in Western societies has had damaging effects on the planet and other beings (Hultman & Pulé, 2018; Aavik, 2023, and this volume). To a significant extent, the current global ecological crisis has been created and exacerbated by the reckless decisions and actions of privileged, Western white men occupying leadership positions and the underlying ideals of hypermasculinity that inform their values and practices (Aavik, 2021). Privileged men are disproportionately represented in the leadership of polluting companies, in the fossil fuel, meat and war industries, as well as in the national governments and transnational bodies intended to regulate these sectors (Pulé & Hultman, 2021). More research is urgently needed on the impact of men, masculinities and leadership not only in exacerbating and denying but also in resisting and mitigating global warming, climate breakdown and planetary pollution.

The foregoing examples illustrate how excessive forms of masculinity can cloud leaders' judgement in decision-making, particularly when men dominate senior positions and women are either in the minority or absent altogether. These cases also illustrate how men leaders' decision-making can be risky and reckless producing unanticipated, counter-productive and even lethal outcomes. Revealing important cracks and schisms in men's domination of leadership, these examples warn against over-determinism in the critical study of men, masculinities and leadership and indicate the value of dialectical perspectives that acknowledge and explore mutually reinforcing interconnections, tensions, contradictions and the potential for change.

Conclusion

The twenty-first-century re-emergence of so-called strongmen political leaders has once more brought into sharp relief important questions about the inter-relations between men, masculinities and leadership. In addressing these issues, this chapter has highlighted the value of more critical perspectives and questioned the deterministic tendencies of hegemonic masculinity. The combined insights of CSMM and CLS help to reveal how power in all its intersecting, gendered and hierarchical forms can be exercised in and through men's leadership discourses, decisions, relations and practices. Parallel developments in both perspectives also point to the value of more dialectical approaches which suggest that while power may be enacted in oppressive ways, it is rarely all determining, absolute or fixed. Critical dialectical studies reveal some of the destructive, contradictory and self-defeating consequences that can emerge when men leaders' discursive practices are informed by hypermasculine values and ways of thinking. In relation to developing critical dialectical perspectives, space limitations precluded detailed discussion here of the gendered processes of resistance and/or conformity. While feminist studies are relevant (e.g. Westwood, 1984; Kondo, 1990), more research is needed specifically on dissent and compliance in gendered leadership dynamics (Gagnon & Collinson, 2017).

Future critical studies could also explore how, why and with what consequences men leaders construct, enact and legitimize their power and control over others. This might examine men, masculinities and leadership at global and transnational levels, addressing international cultural similarities and differences. It could also consider how men leaders may engage in nepotism, favouritism and other homosocial practices that produce unethical, corrupt and destructive outcomes. Research might address the ways that men as leaders seek to project a youthful, successful, competent and healthy image (e.g. Elfving Hwang, 2020). Informing such concerns to impress others and construct a powerful masculine identity may be anxieties and other emotions that could be examined in more detail (e.g. Ciulla, 2023). Behind "strong man" exteriors may be deep-seated insecurities. It is certainly the case that being a leader not only confers power and privilege but can also be stressful, isolating and unhealthy.

Finally, the changing nature of men, masculinities and leadership, including their "positive", caring and empathetic potential as leaders (Tomkins, 2020), as men (Elliott, 2015; Thym, 2018, 2020) and as fathers (Hytti et al., 2023) are also important themes that could be explored further. It is possible, for example, that social change generally and the "#MeToo" movement in particular may facilitate more gender-sensitive and inclusive leadership practices characterized by much greater transparency and accountability as well as more empowering and compassionate forms of masculinity. This in turn could facilitate innovative leadership practices encouraging subordinates to speak up about their concerns without fear of reprisals, as well as workplace cultures that enable better work/life balance. Conversely, as discussed earlier, in recent times, global, political regimes have seen the reappearance of new forms of so-called strongman leadership. This retrogressive re-emergence of "great man" leadership theory in the guise of global masculine authoritarianism highlights the pressing need for further critical analyses of men, masculinities and leadership.

Notes

1 Thanks to Kadri, Anika and Jeff for helpful comments on an earlier draft of this chapter.
2 In June 2022, the EU announced mandatory quotas to ensure women in member states comprise at least 40% of those on corporate boards (Guardian, June 7, 2022).
3 Women leaders can face contradictory, "no-win" situations (Cockburn, 1991). If they show "feminine" qualities, they may be under-valued and not considered "proper" leaders, but if they adopt "masculinized" qualities, they can be perceived as transgressing gender norms and may be sanctioned. Equally, the same behaviours can be perceived positively when performed by men but

negatively when enacted by women. Mavin and Grandy (2012) recommend that women leaders find a balance between "doing gender well" (meeting gendered expectations of women's feminine behaviour like nurturing) and "doing gender differently" (challenging gender expectations through, for example, risk-taking).

4 Like gender dynamics, leadership and followership practices are socially constructed, taking various forms at different times and places. This chapter focuses primarily on those in elite positions who retain the power to make strategic decisions and set agendas. This includes chief executives, owners, top managers and senior management teams as well as those on boards of directors. Similarly, organizations and organizing are socially constructed and vary in form over time, space and culture. In digital contexts, organizations and organizing may be non-physical. This chapter focuses primarily on conventional physical and hierarchical organizations and organizing.

5 Demetriou's arguments were accepted and incorporated by Connell and Messerschmidt (2005) in their reformulation of hegemonic masculinities.

6 While hierarchies can reinforce gendered assumptions that privilege some men and marginalize women (Acker, 1990), they may also produce other (non-gender-specific) effects.

7 In relation to post-heroic leadership, Fletcher (2004) explored some of its gendered paradoxes. More recently, Khan et al. (2022) argue that Australian business leaders are reinterpreting post-heroic leadership as new forms of masculine heroism. By incorporating "softer masculinities" into their repertoire of heroic leadership, business media leaders reframe and legitimize post-heroic leadership as romanticized masculine heroism that largely excludes women.

8 The possible overlaps between "toxic masculinity" (Flood, 2018) and "toxic leadership" (Pelletier et al., 2018) are under-explored. This may be partly because of the paradigmatic lacunae between CSMM and CLS. It may also be because "toxic masculinity" has been heavily criticized, seen as a reductionist and ahistoric attempt to typologize masculinities and to generalize toxicity to all men/masculinities (Waling, 2019; de Boise, 2019), whereas "toxic leadership" has received far less critique, mainly being used to examine destructive practices. Having said that, in an earlier study (Collinson, 2012) I argued that leaders' excessive positivity might be more helpful (than toxicity) in explaining their routine exercise of power and control. That is to say, "Prozac leadership" may be a more common way leaders exercise power, create compliance and silence dissent (see also the discussion of the global financial crash later in this chapter).

9 Debates between Marxists and Foucauldians illustrate some of these competing perspectives on power. The latter's relational focus on disciplinary power highlights some of the limitations of the former's property-based critique of capitalism and private ownership. Yet Foucault's insistence that power is *always exercised* and *never possessed* seems to underplay structural sources of power where, for example, legally enshrined ownership (e.g. of land, property, organizations, etc.) confers considerable control and prestige on privileged individuals and elites. Rather than perpetuate a binary between "relational" and "proprietorial" views of power (e.g. Knights, 2021), critical dialectical approaches point to their synergies. From this perspective, power can be *both* exercised *and* possessed, producing effects that may be *both* repressive *and* enabling as well as negative *and* positive.

10 While dialectical thinking is often associated with Hegel and Marx, its intellectual roots date back much further, for example, to ancient Greek and ancient Buddhist philosophies (Fairhurst & Collinson, 2023).

11 Women's unpaid care and domestic work can significantly contribute to men's career success as well as resulting in their own under-representation in leadership positions.

References

Aavik, K. (2021). Vegan men: Towards greater care for (non)human others, Earth and self. In P. Pulé & M. Hultman (Eds.), *Men, Masculinities, and Earth: Contending with the (m)Anthropocene* (pp. 329–350). Cham: Palgrave Macmillan.

Aavik, K. (2023). *Contesting Anthropocentric Masculinities through Veganism.* London: Palgrave Macmillan.

Aavik, K., Bland, C., Hoegaerts, J., & Salminen, J. T. V. (Eds.). (2020). *Men, Masculinities and the Modern Career: Contemporary and Historical Perspectives.* Berlin: De Gruyter Oldenbourg.

Acker, J. (1990). Hierarchies, jobs, bodies: A theory of gendered organizations. *Gender and Society, 4*(2) 139–158. www.jstor.org/stable/189609

Allison, A. (1994). *Nightwork: Sexuality, Pleasure and Corporate Masculinity in a Tokyo Hostess Club*. Chicago: University of Chicago Press.
Alvesson, M., & Spicer, A. (2012). Critical leadership studies: The case for critical performativity. *Human Relations*, *65*(3), 367–390. doi: 10.1177/0018726711430555
Asad, S., & Sadler-Smith, E. (2020). Differentiating leader hubris and narcissism on the basis of power. *Leadership*, *16*(1), 39–61. doi: 10.1177/1742715019885763
Ashcraft, K. L. (2022). *Wronged and Dangerous: Viral Masculinity and the Populist Pandemic*. Bristol: Bristol University Press.
Baker, A. C. (2014). Eroding the wealth of women: Gender and the subprime foreclosure crisis. *Social Service Review*, *88*(1), 59–91. doi: 10.1086/675391
Bass, B. M. (1985). *Leadership and Performance Beyond Expectations*. London: Free Press and Collier Macmillan.
Baxter, L. A., & Montgomery, B. M. (1996). *Relating: Dialogues and Dialectics*. New York: Guilford Press.
Ben-Ghiat, R. (2020). *Strongmen: How They Rise, Why They Succeed, How They Fall*. London: Profile Books.
Berdahl, J. L., Cooper, M., Glick, P., Livingston, R. W., & Williams, J. C. (2018). Work as masculinity contest. *Journal of Social Issues*, *74*(3), 422–448. doi: 10.1111/josi.12289
Biese, I. (2020). Men opting out: Disenchantment with corporate cultures and career ideals. In K. Aavik, C. Bland, J. Hoegaerts & J. T. V. Salminen (Eds.), *Men, Masculinities and the Modern Career: Contemporary and Historical Perspectives* (pp. 35–52). Berlin: De Gruyter Oldenbourg.
Boulgarides, J. D. (1984). A comparison of male and female business managers. *Leadership & Organization Development Journal*, *5*(5), 27–31. doi: 10.1108/eb053563
Bowring, M. A. (2004). Resistance is not futile: Liberating Captain Janeway from the masculine – feminine dualism of leadership. *Gender, Work and Organization*, *11*(4), 381–405. doi: 10.1111/j.1468-0432.2004.00239
Carli, L. L., & Eagly, A. H. (2011). Gender and leadership. In A. Bryman, D. L. Collinson, K. Grint, B. Jackson & M. Uhl Bien (Eds.), *The Sage Handbook of Leadership* (pp. 103–117). London: Sage.
Carlyle, T. (1840). *On Heroes, Hero Worship, and the Heroic in History*. London: James Fraser.
Christensen, A. D., & Qvotrup Jensen, S. (2014). Combining hegemonic masculinity and intersectionality. *NORMA*, *9*(1), 60–75. doi: 10.1080/18902138.2014.892289
Ciulla, J. (2020). Leadership and the power of resentment/ressentiment. *Leadership*, *16*(1), 25–38. doi: 10.1177/1742715019885772
Ciulla, J. (2023). The myth of the passions: Reason, emotions and ethics in leadership. In D. Schedlitzki, M. Larsson, B. Carroll, M. C. Bligh & O. Epitropaki (Eds.), *The Sage Handbook of Leadership*, 2nd edition (pp. 202–211). London: Sage.
Clegg, S., Simpson, A. V., Cunha, M. P. E., & Rego, A. (2023). From 'leadership' to 'leading': Power relations, polyarchy and projects. In D. Schedlitzki, M. Larsson, B. Carroll, M. C. Bligh & O. Epitropaki (Eds.), *The Sage Handbook of Leadership*, 2nd edition (pp. 395–405). London: Sage.
Cockburn, C. (1983). *Brothers*. London: Pluto.
Cockburn, C. (1991). *In the Way of Women*. Basingstoke: Macmillan.
Collinson, D. L. (1992). *Managing the Shopfloor: Subjectivity, Masculinity and Workplace Culture*. Berlin: Walter de Gruyter.
Collinson, D. L. (2000). Strategies of resistance: Power, knowledge and subjectivity in the workplace. In K. Grint (Ed.), *Work and Society: A Reader* (pp. 163–198). Cambridge: Polity Press.
Collinson, D. L. (2005). Dialectics of leadership. *Human Relations*, *58*(11), 1419–1442. doi: 10.1177/0018726705060902
Collinson, D. L. (2011). Critical leadership studies. In A. Bryman, D. L. Collinson, K. Grint, B. Jackson & M. Uhl Bien (Eds.), *The Sage Handbook of Leadership* (pp. 179–192). London: Sage.
Collinson, D. L. (2012). Prozac leadership and the limits of positive thinking. *Leadership*, *8*(2), 87–107. doi: 10.1177/1742715011434738
Collinson, D. L. (2020). Only connect: Exploring the critical dialectical turn in leadership studies. *Organization Theory*, *1*(2), 1–22. doi: 10.1177/2631787720913878
Collinson, D. L., Aavik, K., Thym, A., & Hearn, J. (2023). Men, masculinities, and leadership: Emerging issues. In S. J. Tan & L. DeFrank-Cole (Eds.), *A Research Agenda for Gender and Leadership* (pp. 87–106). Cheltenham: Edward Elgar.

Collinson, D. L., & Collinson, M. (1989). Sexuality in the workplace: The domination of men's sexuality. In J. Hearn, D. Sheppard, P. Tancred-Sheriff & G. Burrell (Eds.), *The Sexuality of Organization* (pp. 91–109). London: SAGE.

Collinson, D. L., & Collinson, M. (1992). Mismanaging sexual harassment: Protecting the perpetrator and blaming the victim. *Women in Management Review*, *7*(7), 11–17. doi: 10.1108/09649429210019608

Collinson, D. L., & Fairhurst, G. T. (in press). Critical leadership dialectics. In D. Knights, H. Liu, O. Smolović Jones & S. Wilson (Eds.), *The Routledge Critical Companion on Leadership Studies*. Abingdon: Routledge.

Collinson, D. L., & Hearn, J. (1994). Naming men as men: Implications for work, organizations and management. *Gender, Work and Organization*, *1*(1), 2–22. doi: 10.1111/j.1468-0432.1994.tb00002

Collinson, D. L., & Hearn, J. (Eds.). (1996). *Men as Managers, Managers as Men: Critical Perspectives on Men, Masculinities and Managements*. London: Sage.

Collinson, D. L., & Hearn, J. (2005). Men and masculinities in work, organizations and management. In M. Kimmel, J. Hearn & R. W. Connell (Eds.), *Handbook of Studies on Men and Masculinities* (pp. 289–310). Thousand Oaks, CA: Sage.

Collinson, D. L., & Hearn, J. (2020). Gendering leadership in times of COVID: The case of the 'strong man'. In *International Leadership Association*. Leadership for the Greater Good. Retrieved from https://ilaglobalnetwork.org/gendering-leadership-in-times-of-covid-the-case-of-the-strong-man/

Collinson, M., & Collinson, D. L. (1996). It's only Dick: The sexual harassment of women managers in insurance sales. *Work, Employment and Society*, *10*(1), 29–56. doi: 10.1177/0950017096101002

Connell, R. W. (1995). *Masculinities*. Cambridge: Polity.

Connell, R. W., & Messerschmidt, J. W. (2005). Hegemonic masculinity: Rethinking the concept. *Gender & Society*, *19*(6), 829–859. doi: 10.1177/0891243205278639

Connell, R. W., & Wood, J. (2005). Globalization and business masculinities. *Men and Masculinities*, *7*(4), 347–364. doi: 10.1177/1097184X03260969

Cunningham, E. (2022). *Women in Policing: Feminist Perspectives on Theory and Practice*. London: Routledge.

Dale, K., & Latham, Y. (2015). Ethics and entangled embodiment: Bodies-materialities-organization. *Organization*, *22*, 166–182. doi: 10.1177/1350508414558721

de Boise, S. (2019). Editorial: Is masculinity toxic? *NORMA: International Journal for Masculinity Studies*, *14*(3), 147–151. doi: 10.1080/18902138.2019.1654742

Demetriou, D. Z. (2001). Connell's concept of hegemonic masculinity: A critique. *Theory and Society*, *30*(3), 337–361. doi: 10.1023/A:1017596718715

Dick, P., & Collings, D. (2014). Discipline and punish: Strategy discourse, senior manager subjectivity and contradictory power effects. *Human Relations*, *67*(12), 1513–1536. doi: 10.1177/0018726714525810

Donnell, S. M., & Hall, J. (1980). Men and women as managers: A significant case of no significant difference. *Organizational Dynamics*, *8*(4), 60–77. doi: 10.1016/0090-2616(80)90049-2

Elfving Hwang, J. (2020). Competency as an embodied social practice: Clothing, presentation of self and corporate masculinity in South Korea. In K. Aavik, C. Bland, J. Hoegaerts & J. T. V. Salminen (Eds.), *Men, Masculinities and the Modern Career: Contemporary and Historical Perspectives* (pp. 133–152). Berlin: De Gruyter Oldenbourg.

Elliott, C., & Stead, V. (2018). Constructing women's leadership representation in the UK press during a time of financial crisis: Gender capitals and dialectical tensions. *Organization Studies*, *39*(1), 19–45. doi: 10.1177/0170840617708002

Elliott, K. (2015). Caring masculinities: Theorizing an emerging concept. *Men and Masculinities*, *19*(3), 240–259. doi: 10.1177/1097184X15576203

Enarson, E., & Pease, B. (Eds.). (2016). *Men, Masculinities and Disaster*. London: Routledge.

Fairhurst, G. T., & Collinson, D. L. (2023). Leadership dialectics. In D. Schedlitzki, M. Larsson, B. Carroll, M. C. Bligh & O. Epitropaki (Eds.), *The Sage Handbook of Leadership*, 2nd edition (pp. 484–497). London: Sage.

Fawcett Society (2022). *Sex and Power 2022*. London: Fawcett Society.

Fishbein, A. J., & Woodall, P. (2006). *Women are Prime Targets for Subprime Lending: Women are Disproportionately Represented in High-Cost Mortgage Market*. Consumer Federation of America. Retrieved from www.consumerfed.org.

Flood, M. (2018). Toxic Masculinity: A Primer and Commentary. Retrieved 7 June, from XY: https://xyonline.net/content/toxic-masculinity-primer-and-commentary

Ford, J., & Morgan, J. (2023). Critiquing leadership and gender research through a feminist lens. In D. Schedlitzki, M. Larsson, B. Carroll, M. C. Bligh & O. Epitropaki (Eds.), *The SAGE Handbook of Leadership*, 2nd edition (pp. 247–261). London: Sage.

Gagnon, S., & Collinson, D. L (2017). 'Resistance through difference: The co-constitution of dissent and inclusion. *Organization Studies*, *38*(9), 1253–1276. doi: 10.1177/0170840616685362

Galea, N., Powell, A., & Salignac, F. (2022). The role of homosociality in maintaining men's powerfulness in construction companies. *Construction Management and Economics*. doi: 10.1080/01446193.2022.2151025

Hearn, J. (1989). Leading questions for men: Men's leadership, feminist challenges, and men's responses. *Equal Opportunities International*, *8*(1), 3–11. doi: 10.1108/eb010495

Hearn, J. (2004). From hegemonic masculinity to the hegemony of men. *Feminist Theory*, *5*(1), 49–72. doi: 10.1177/1464700104040813

Hearn, J. (2014). Contextualizing men, masculinities, leadership and management: Gender/intersectionalities, local/transnational, embodied/virtual, theory/practice. In S. Kumra, R. Simpson & R. J. Burke (Eds.), *The Handbook of Gender in Organizations* (pp. 417–437). Oxford: Oxford University Press.

Hearn, J. (2015). *Men of the World: Genders, Globalizations, Transnational Times*. London: Sage.

Hobbins, J., Kristiansen, E., & Carlström, E. (2022). Women, leadership, and change – navigating between contradictory cultures. *NORA: Nordic Journal of Feminist and Gender Research*, 1–13. doi: 10.1080/08038740.2022.2098377

Holmes, J. (2009). Men, masculinities and leadership: Different discourse styles at work. In P. Pichler & E. Eppler (Eds.), *Gender and Spoken Interaction* (pp. 186–210). London: Palgrave Macmillan.

Hook, S. (1945). *The Hero in History*. London: Secker and Walburg.

Horton, L. (2022). *Men of Money: Elite Masculinities and the Neoliberal Project*. Lanham, Maryland: Rowman & Littlefield.

Hultman, M., & Pulé, P. M. (2018). *Ecological Masculinities: Theoretical Foundations and Practical Guidance*. Abingdon: Routledge.

Husu, L., Hearn, J., Lämsä, A. M., & Vanhala, S. (Eds.). (2010). *Leadership through the Gender Lens: Women and Men in Organisations*. Helsinki: Hanken Research Reports.

Hytti, U., Karhunen, P., & Radu-Lefebvre, M. (2023). Entrepreneurial masculinity: A fatherhood perspective. *Entrepreneurship Theory and Practice*. doi: 10.1177/10422587231155863

Johnson. S. K., & Lacerenza, C. N. (2019). Leadership is male-centric. In R. Riggio (Ed.), *What's Wrong with Leadership? (and How to Fix It)* (pp. 107–120). New York: Routledge.

Jones, N. S. (2022). Gaslighting and dispelling: Experiences of non-governmental organization workers in navigating gendered corruption. *Human Relations*. doi: 10.1177/00187267221083274

Jones, O. S., Briley, G., & Woodcock, J. (2021). Exposing and replacing leadership through workers inquiry. *Leadership*, *18*(1), 61–80. doi: 10.1177/17427150211026431

Kanter, R. M. (1991). *Men and Women of the Corporation*, 2nd edition. New York: Basic Books.

Khan, M. H., Williams, J., Williams, P., & French, E. (2022). Post-heroic heroism: Embedded masculinities in media framing of Australian business leadership. *Leadership*, *18*(2), 298–327. doi: 10.1177/17427150211049600.

Kimmel, M., Hearn, J., & Connell, R. (Eds.). (2005). *Handbook of Studies on Men and Masculinities*. Thousand Oaks, CA: Sage.

Klenke, K. (2011). *Women in Leadership: Contextual Dynamics and Boundaries*, 2nd edition. Bingley, UK: Emerald Publishing.

Knights, D. (2021). *Leadership, Gender and Ethics: Embodied Reason in Challenging Masculinities*. London: Routledge.

Kondo, D. (1990). *Crafting Selves: Power, Gender, and Discourses of Identity in a Japanese Workplace*. Chicago: University of Chicago.

Lipman-Blumen, J. (2005). *The Allure of Toxic Leadership*. Oxford: Oxford University Press.

Liu, H. (2021). *Redeeming Leadership*. Bristol: Bristol University Press.

Liu, H., & Baker, C. (2016). White knights: Leadership as the heroicisation of whiteness. *Leadership*, *12*(4), 420–448. doi: 10.1177/1742715014565127

Lumby, J. (2018). Leadership and power in higher education. *Studies in Higher Education*. doi: 10.1080/03075079.2018.1458221

Maier, M., & Messerschmidt, J. (1998). Commonalities, conflicts and contradictions in organizational masculinities: Exploring the gendered genesis of the Challenger disaster. *Canadian Review of Sociology and Anthropology, 35*(3), 325–344. doi: 10.1111/j.1755-618X.1998.tb00726
Martin, J. (1990). Deconstructing organizational taboos: The suppression of gender conflict in organizations. *Organization Science, 1*(4), 339–359. https://psycnet.apa.org/doi/10.1287/orsc.1.4.339
Martin, P. Y. (1998). Why can't a man be more like a woman? Reflections on Connell's masculinities. *Gender and Society, 12*(4), 472–474. doi: 10.1177/089124398012004008
Martin, P. Y. (2001). 'Mobilizing masculinities': Women's experiences of men at work. *Organization, 8*(4), 587–618. doi: 10.1177/135050840184003
Matos, K., O'Neill, O., & Lei, X. (2018). Toxic leadership and the masculinity contest culture: How "win or die" cultures breed abusive leadership. *Journal of Social Issues, 74*(3), 500–528. doi: 10.1111/josi.12284
Mavin, S., & Grandy, G. (2012). Doing gender well and differently in management. *Gender in Management: An International Journal, 27*(4), 218–231. doi: 10.1108/17542411211244768
Messerschmidt, J. W. (1996). Managing to kill: Masculinities and the space shuttle challenger explosion. In C. Cheng (Ed.), *Masculinities in Organizations* (pp. 29–53). London: Sage.
Messerschmidt, J. W. (2019). The salience of hegemonic masculinity. *Men and Masculinities, 22*(1), 85–91. doi: 10.1177/1097184X18805555.
O'Connor, P., Martin, P., Carvalho, T., O'Hagan, C., Veronesi, L., Mich, O., Saglamer, G., Tan, M., & Caglayan, H. (2019). Leadership practices by senior position holders in higher educational research institutes: Stealth power in action? *Leadership, 15*(6), 722–743. doi: 10.1177/1742715019853200
Owen, D. (2012). *The Hubris Syndrome: Bush, Blair and the Intoxication of Power*, 2nd edition. York: Methuen.
Pearce, C. L., & Conger, J. A. (Eds). (2003). *Shared Leadership*. Thousand Oaks, CA: Sage.
Pelletier, K. L., Kottke, J. L., & Sirotnik, B. W. (2018). The toxic triangle in academia: A case analysis of the emergence and manifestation of toxicity in a public university. *Leadership, 15*(4), 405–432. doi: 10.1177/1742715018773828
Poorhosseinzadeh, M., & Strachan, G. (2021). Straightjackets of male domination in senior positions: Revisiting Acker's ideal worker and the construction of the ideal executive. *British Journal of Management, 32*, 1421–1439. doi: 10.1111/1467-8551.12448
Portillo, H., & Molano, S. (2017). Approaching Corruption through the Lens of Masculinities. Retrieved 4 April, from CDA Perspectives Blog: http://cdacollaborative.org/blog/approaching-corruption-lens-masculinities/
Pulé, P. M., & Hultman, M. (Eds.). (2021). *Men, Masculinities, and the Earth: Contending with the (m) Anthropocene*. Cham: Palgrave Macmillan.
Putnam, L., Fairhurst, G., & Banghart, S. (2016). Contradictions, dialectics, and paradoxes in organizations: A constitutive approach. *Academy of Management Annals, 10*, 65–171. doi: 10.1080/19416520.2016.1162421
Roper, M. (1994). *Masculinity and the British Organization Man Since 1945*. Oxford: Oxford University Press.
Rosener, J. (1990). Ways women lead. *Harvard Business Review, 68*(6), 119–125.
Sadler-Smith, E. (2019). *Hubristic Leadership*. London: Sage.
Schedlitzki, D., & Edwards, G. (2021). *Studying Leadership: Traditional and Critical Approaches*, 3rd edition. London: Sage.
Shamir, B., House, R. J., & Arthur, M. B. (1993). The motivational effects of charismatic leadership: A self-concept based theory. *Organization Science, 4*(4), 577–594. https://psycnet.apa.org/doi/10.1287/orsc.4.4.577
Smircich, L., & Morgan, G. (1982). Leadership: The management of meaning. *Journal of Applied Behavioural Science, 18*(3), 257–273. doi: 10.1177/002188638201800303
Spector, B. (2020). Post-truth claims and the wishing away of brute facts. *Leadership, 16*(1), 9–25. doi: 10.1177/1742715019885771
The Guardian (2022). Retrieved 7 June, from www.theguardian.com/business/2022/jun/07/eu-agrees-landmark-40-quota-for-women-on-corporate-boards.
Thym, A. (2018). Hegemony self-critique: How men in finance question aspects of masculine and economic hegemony from within. In J. Hearn, E. Vasquez del Aguila & M. Hughson (Eds.),

Unsustainable Institutions of Men: Transnational Dispersed Centres, Gender Power, Contradictions (pp. 71–86). New York: Routledge.

Thym, A. (2020). Men in finance for emancipatory social change? In R. Luyt & K. Starck (Eds.), *Masculine Power and Gender Equality: Masculinities as Change Agents* (pp. 81–98). Cham: Springer.

Tienari, J., Vaara, E., & Meriläinen, S. (2010). Becoming an international man: Top manager masculinities in the making of a multinational corporation. *Equality, Diversity and Inclusion, 29*(1), 38–52. doi: 10.1108/02610151011019200

Tomkins, L. (Ed.). (2020). *Paradox and Power in Caring Leadership*. Cheltenham: Elgar.

Tourish, D., & Willmott, H. (2023). Despotic leadership and ideological manipulation at Theranos: Towards a theory of hegemonic totalism in the workplace. *Organization Studies*. doi: 10.1177/01708406231171801

Useem, J. (2017). Power Causes Brain Damage. Retrieved July/August, from The Atlantic: https://www.theatlantic.com/magazine/archive/2017/07/power-causes-brain-damage/528711/

Wajcman, J. (1999). *Managing Like a Man: Women and Men in Corporate Management*. Sydney, Australia: Allen & Unwin.

Waling, A. (2019). Problematising 'toxic' and 'healthy' masculinity for addressing gender inequalities. *Australian Feminist Studies, 34*, 362–375. doi: 10.1080/08164649.2019.1679021

Waylen, G. (2021). Gendering political leadership: Hypermasculine leadership and Covid-19, *Journal of European Public Policy, 28*(8), 1153–1173. doi: 10.1080/13501763.2021.1942160

Weiss, R. S. (1990). *Staying the Course: The Emotional and Social Lives of Men Who Do Well at Work*. New York: The Free Press.

Westwood, S. (1984). *All Day, Every Day: Factory, Family, Women's Lives*. London, UK: Pluto.

Wilson, N., & Wedlock, J. (2023). Swearing as a leadership tool. *English Worldwide*. doi: 10.1075/eww.22033.wil

Zoller, H., & Fairhurst, G. T. (2007). Resistance leadership: The overlooked potential in critical organization and leadership studies. *Human Relations, 60*(11), 1331–1360. doi: 10.1177/0018726707082850

10

WORKPLACE MASCULINITY CONTESTS AND CULTURE[1]

Jennifer L. Berdahl, Marianne Cooper, Peter Glick, Robert W. Livingston and Joan C. Williams

Introduction

In this chapter, we propose that a key reason why the workplace gender revolution has stalled is that work remains the site of masculinity contests among men. Accordingly, we provide an overview of relevant studies and outline a theoretical framework for thinking about work as a masculinity contest.

In February 2017, Susan Fowler, an engineer at Uber, published a blog post about serious problems at the company (Fowler, 2017). She documented repeated sexual harassment from her manager and how her attempts to get human resources (HR) to act went nowhere, in part because her manager was considered a "top performer". Fowler's account also described an organization characterized by a "Game-of-Thrones" like environment in which managers actively fought with their peers and sought to one-up and sabotage their own supervisors (e.g. by withholding business-critical information) in attempts to take their supervisor's job. Such behaviour was not hidden but openly bragged about.

These bad behaviours resulted in business paralysis: Priorities were continually reordered, projects were abandoned and employees worried that their teams would be dissolved. Summing up Fowler said, "It was an organization in complete, unrelenting chaos". Subsequent investigation by the *New York Times* unearthed employee accounts describing Uber as a "Hobbesian environment . . . in which workers are pitted against one another and where a blind eye is turned to infractions from top performers" (Isaac, 2017, February 22). After Fowler's viral post, other damaging information came to light. Uber was accused of using a software tool to hide its drivers from regulators to avoid investigation; a video showed CEO Travis Kalanick boasting about Uber's tough company culture and telling an Uber driver who suffered financial losses to take responsibility for his own problems; the CEO and other executives visited an escort bar in South Korea and board member David Bonderman notoriously commented that having more women on Uber's Board of Directors would just lead to "more talking" (Rawlins, 2017). In the end, lawsuits were filed, Travis Kalanick was forced to resign as CEO, and the company suffered major reputational damage. While Uber may be an extreme example, it is certainly not the only organization that has this kind of toxic culture. Indeed, Silicon Valley as a whole has been under attack for its "bro" culture, rule-breaking

 DOI: 10.4324/9781003193579-12

and sexism. Recent examples in other sectors include Fox News, the Weinstein Company and the Trump Administration; all have received considerable negative press for toxic leadership, bullying and sexual harassment.

Masculinity context cultures

Though exposés of rotten administrative and organizational cultures are nothing new, this chapter presents a new framework for understanding what goes wrong in them and why. Our framework centres on toxic masculinity, which "involves the need to aggressively compete and dominate others" (Kupers, 2005, p. 713).[2] Work becomes a masculinity contest when organizations focus not on mission but on masculinity, enacted in endless "mine's bigger than yours" contests to display workloads and long schedules (as in law and medicine) (Blair-Loy, 2005; Kellogg, 2011), cut corners to out-earn everyone else (Roth, 2006), or shoulder unreasonable risks (as in blue-collar jobs or finance) (Iacuone, 2005; Meyerson et al., 2007; Nelson, 2012). The coin of the realm shifts in different industries, but the role of toxic masculinity does not. We argue that much of what simply appears to be neutral practices and what it takes to get ahead at work is actually counter-productive behaviour aimed at proving manhood on the job.

Dropping a bias training, diversity initiative, or work–life programme into workplaces dominated by the masculinity contest does not serve to effect meaningful change (Williams, 2013). This chapter aims to inspire research that will arm practitioners to take more consequential and sustainable steps towards promoting diversity and work–life goals by addressing the underlying issue of the masculinity contest. The result will be workplaces that are more efficient and effective in achieving their business objectives – and are healthier and happier for women and for most men, who are either excluded from the masculinity contest, have no interest in playing it, or are destined to lose. Eliminating the masculinity contest will help organizations focus on efficiency and profitability rather than on macho showmanship and will help all workers who want to be left in peace to do their work with dignity.

Much of our own work has exposed how masculine pressures on men motivate them to engage in "bad but bold" behaviour (Glick et al., 2004) – including sexual harassment (Berdahl, 2007a, 2007b), physical aggression (Bosson et al., 2009) and extreme work hours and cut-throat competition (Cooper, 2014; Williams, 1999). This chapter represents the culmination of a collaborative research project to theorize and study workplace culture as a masculinity contest: a zero-sum competition played according to rules defined by masculine norms (e.g. displaying strength, showing no weakness or doubt).

This chapter outlines a theoretical framework for thinking about Masculinity Contest Cultures (MCCs). Other studies represent initial research into measuring MCCs (Glick et al., 2018), assessing their consequences (Alonso, 2018; Brassel, 2020; Cinelli, 2021; Glick et al., 2018; Jacobson, 2022; Koc et al., 2021; Matos et al., 2018; Miedtank et al., 2020; Rawski & Workman-Stark, 2018; Regina & Allen, 2022; Reid et al., 2018; Robbins, 2022; Williams et al., 2022; Workman-Stark et al., 2021a, 2021b), analysing their ideological underpinnings (Kuchynka et al., 2018; Meluso et al., 2023; Munsch, 2022; Munsch et al., 2018; Vial et al., 2022; Williams et al., 2022; Wu, 2020), and considering potential interventions (Ely & Kimmel, 2018; Rawski & Workman-Stark, 2018; Sattari, 2021).

We begin by considering the connections between masculinity and work, exploring how the workplace is a context in which men feel particular pressure to prove themselves as "men". We identify different dimensions of masculinity along which employees may compete and how the competition may differ by context. We then introduce the concept of MCCs in organizations, and how and why MCCs are likely to be linked to a host of undesirable organizational maladies such as toxic leadership, lack of psychological safety in work groups, reduced employee well-being, lack of work–life balance, sexual harassment and bullying. Throughout, we make connections to other insights into MCCs, including efforts towards changing or eliminating them.

Masculinity at work

Following the insights of critical studies on men and masculinities, we understand gender and gender relations as not biologically determined but as historically, socially and culturally specific. For the work context, this means: a manly way of enacting dominance is being the family breadwinner by doing "men's" work, which also secures economic resources that can be used to gain physical and social resources (e.g. Pratto et al., 2008). And, because dominance over others is achieved by having relative control over valued physical, social and economic resources (e.g. Fiske & Berdahl, 2007), the workplace is a primary location in which men attempt to secure manhood and dominance over women and other men (Britton & Logan, 2008).

Masculinity contests often manifest as contests for resources and emerge in "men's work" domains where resources are up for grabs. Contests occur in various venues: sports provide opportunities to demonstrate physical strength and stamina; in politics, elite institutions and clubs, men vie for and exercise social influence to gain resources. However, the workplace represents the venue in which money – the ultimate resource in modern economies – is to be made, making it a central context for resource acquisition and establishing dominance. Dominance in the workplace comes not only with the ability to control others' attempts to acquire resources through work but also with the ability to control one's own and others' lives outside of work, including financial independence, societal standing and family breadwinner status. Because work is a site where men can acquire valued resources that enable dominance over others, it is a primary site in which men attempt to prove and negotiate their manhood.

Research on gender and work has examined how hegemonic forms of masculinity are embedded in companies, organizations and workplaces. This research has revealed how gender inequalities are built into the organization of work itself (highly paid male jobs, lower-paid female jobs) and how gender is constituted both within occupations and in everyday practices and interactions on the job (Acker, 1992; Ely & Meyerson, 2010; Martin, 2004). We propose that masculinity contests are most prevalent – and vicious – in male-dominated occupations where extreme resources (fame, power, wealth) or precarious resources (risky or dangerous "men's" work; Ely & Meyerson, 2010; Zaloom, 2006) are at stake – where the spoils of winning, or the cost of losing, the contest are particularly high.

Hierarchical structures are also likely to be associated with masculinity contests as contenders compete for favour and promotion up the ranks or seek to topple those above. Finally, external pressures on organizations, such as strong competition or a high risk of failure within their industry, are also likely to feed MCCs. Examples abound, from finance and the start-up world of tech in which billions of dollars are quickly made or lost, to surgeons who perform high-stake operations with no room for error, to military and police units performing risky jobs with strict chains of command.

Investigations of masculinity at work in a wide range of occupations have identified how work norms are often conflated with masculinity and contests for dominance. For example,

Pierce's (1996) ethnography observed that celebrated trial lawyers were those dubbed "Rambo litigators", who behaved in forceful and aggressive ways – those (men) who took control of the courtroom and "destroyed witnesses" on the stand. Studies of corporate settings have identified successful managers as being those who are instrumental, decisive and willing to take big risks – who may well be rewarded even when those risks do not pan out, as in the financial collapse that produced the Great Recession of 2008 (Collinson & Hearn, 1994; Kerfoot & Knights, 1993; Messerschmidt, 1995; Nelson, 2012; Pfeffer, 2010). This conflation of top performance with masculine gender performance means that masculinity and workplace success are often treated as synonymous. Success comes to focus not on meeting performance goals but on proving you are more of a man than the next guy. Thus, being a top performer is tantamount to being a man – or for the winners, "*the* man".

The masculinity contest concept focuses on how the very acts that serve to signify an individual man's masculinity can come to define an organization's culture. In this zero-sum game, men compete at work for dominance by showing no weakness, demonstrating a single-minded focus on professional success, displaying physical endurance and strength, and engaging in cut-throat competition. We characterize a company as having an MCC when these behaviours are not just the isolated acts of a few individual men but become the way work gets done, that is, when masculine norms determine who and what gets rewarded, how colleagues should be treated, and attitudes about work/life balance.

MCC in organizations

Organizations with MCCs valorize hegemonic masculinity, or the traits men "ought" to have – being aggressive, assertive, independent, ambitious, competitive and strong – and disparage femininity, or the traits men "ought not" to have – sensitivity, naivete, weakness, insecurity, gullibility, uncertainty and indecisiveness (Rudman et al., 2012). In short, masculine norms emphasize enacting agency and dominance and avoiding weakness and vulnerability. An MCC exists when an individual's or group's status and power within an organization are associated with the insistent display of masculinity and winning masculinity contests against others.

Psychologically, we view MCC as the organizational manifestation of precarious manhood (Bosson & Vandello, 2011): an environment in which one constantly has to prove one's masculinity to others (specifically, "I have no weaknesses", "I put work above all else", "I'm stronger and have more work stamina than others" and "I'm the dog that eats all other dogs" Glick et al., 2018). As previous research has shown, the constant project to prove manhood creates unspoken anxiety for a "hard-won, easily lost" status (Vandello et al., 2008). Any misstep threatens to puncture the "winner" image that individuals within these organizational cultures strive to cultivate, thus destroying their claims to status and success.

Importantly, in MCCs, men and women alike must play the game to survive or win. There are different roles to be played – to use a masculine metaphor, some will be linebackers, others quarterbacks, some coaches and still others cheerleaders. But to survive in the organization, one must fall in line and adhere to a system in which valued resources are obtained through a willingness to uphold the game – playing as a contender or as someone who supports one. Women and men who are not part of the in-group can play, most acceptably, in supporting roles. Recent studies, for example, suggest that women and people of colour who go into law and engineering are expected to play a very specific role: supporting – but not competing with – the in-group involved in the masculinity contest (typically composed almost exclusively of white men; Williams, 2016, 2018). Thus, studies show that, as compared with white men, women of all races report higher loads of "office housework", and that both women and people of colour report less access to the glamour work, as well as more pressure to let others take the lead. In addition, both women and people of colour are more likely than white men to report pushback for assertiveness, self-promotion and anger, all of which are key weapons in the masculinity contest – thus making it risky and difficult for women and people of colour to vie head-on as contenders themselves (e.g. Berdahl & Min, 2012; Brescoll & Uhlmann, 2008; Rudman, 1998; Williams et al., 2016, 2018). Indeed, the masculinity contest is very much a white masculinity contest to the extent that hegemonic masculinity is defined by and through enacting not only male but also white supremacy.

Trying to win masculinity contests within these cultures comes at a risk for everyone involved: Losing means disgrace and the loss of perceived manhood for men, or of proof that one does not have "what it takes" to succeed (for both men and women). But entering into the fray of masculinity contests is particularly dangerous for women, men of colour and non-hegemonic men with resistant masculinities (Sidanius & Pratto, 2001). For example, Asian Americans (men and women) who display dominance tend to be disliked (Berdahl & Min, 2012), and Asian Americans' cultural deference to authority may be read as weakness; both handicap Asian American men in the masculinity contest (Gee et al., 2015). Class migrants (professionals from working-class families) may be disadvantaged in professional jobs because they are brought up to value interdependence and distrust ambition, whereas the masculinity contest reflects elite white people's intense focus on, and admiration for, individual achievement (Stephens et al., 2012). In all these ways, the masculinity contest is heavily weighted to advantage elite white men, to whom it may feel more natural, and in whom it is seen as more socially appropriate, to engage in the raw ambition, ruthlessness and domination necessary to win masculinity contests.

Finally, to engage in and win masculinity contests often requires not only performing hegemonic masculinity but distancing oneself from other identities. For women and men from subordinated groups, this means distancing oneself from, and putting down, other women and subordinated group members, respectively – for women, this strategic distancing is known as the "Queen Bee" phenomenon (Derks et al., 2011; Faniko et al., 2017). Strategic distancing for people of colour typically consists of pressures to "act white" (Carbado & Gulati, 2013; Kang et al., 2016).

For all these reasons, women and men from marginalized groups, and those whose values strongly reject ruthless dominance competitions, typically do not "win" in MCCs. Women and men with subordinated identities may be well represented at the entry levels of organizations with such cultures but their careers typically stall out. An example follows: a recent study of Silicon Valley found that despite Asian Americans' high representation in the workforce, white people were 154% more likely to be executives (Gee et al., 2015). The women and men from marginalized groups who remain within organizations rife with MCCs are likely to survive by playing supporting roles to the victors.

These "losers" include not only women but also most men, who either lost the masculinity contest or refused to play it. Organizations where the masculinity contest is alive and well often are dominated by a small group of men who control the rules of the game. Sexual harassment provides one example. One study found – no surprise – that only 10% of women enjoyed "ambient sexual behaviour" such as sexualized joking. The surprise is that only 43% of men said they enjoyed it, highlighting that most men feel as uncomfortable with masculinity contest behaviours as women do (Berdahl & Aquino, 2009). Male-on-male harassment based on sex is best understood as an expression of dominance in a masculinity contest (Alonso, 2018).

Dimensions of MCC

To theorize the likely dimensions valorized within organizations with MCCs – that is, the dimensions on which people compete for masculine standing and dominance – we considered the physical, emotional, behavioural and social dimensions that define manhood in contemporary Western cultures. Brannon's (1976) oft-quoted summary proposed the following rules for what it takes to attain adult masculinity: *No Sissy Stuff* (express no "weak", feminine emotions), *Be a Big Wheel* (achieve status, success, power), *Be a Sturdy Oak* (exhibit toughness, self-reliance, strength and stamina) and *Give 'em Hell* (crush the opposition). The most well-researched masculine norm scales reinforce and expand on Brannon's masculine prescriptions. The *Masculine Role Norms Scale* (MNRS; Thompson & Pleck, 1986), the *Masculine Role Norms Inventory* (MNRI; Levant et al., 2010) and the *Conformity to Masculine Norms Inventory* (CMNI; Mahalik et al., 2003) each defines masculinity as involving a preoccupation with attaining status or dominance, exhibiting toughness, and avoiding "soft" or feminine emotions and behaviour. Additional dimensions of both the MNRI and CMNI include self-reliance, restricted emotionality, aggression/violence, anti-homosexual attitudes and sexual conquest. The CMNI also includes risk-taking and exerting power over women.

Importantly, although masculinity contest norms are deeply rooted in masculine prescriptions, once infused in organizational culture they become hegemonic not just for majority men but for women and minority men as well. To continue a metaphor, once women or minority men enter the gladiatorial arena, they must fight by the same rules to survive (or serve someone who will do it for them), even as they are hamstrung (compared to majority men) by social prescriptions that foster distaste and punishment for dominant behaviour by women and minority men (e.g. Livingston & Pearce, 2009; Rudman et al., 2012). Organizational masculinity contest norms favour but do not specifically refer to, men, demands to *show no weakness*, demonstrate *strength and stamina*, *put work first*, and engage in *dog-eat-dog* competition can be enforced just as strongly on women and minority men (despite the double bind these groups face). In short, most everyone, including most majority men, though perhaps women and minority men especially given contradictory demands, may suffer negative consequences in MCCs.

Consequences of MCC

MCCs define work as a zero-sum competition won by those who best adhere to the masculine norms outlined earlier. Such cultures create cascading negative consequences that flow from top down: from the organizational and leadership level to the frequency of negative behaviours in the work environment to undermining individuals' relation to the organization and (more distally) to the general well-being of individual organization members (Glick et al., 2018).

When it comes to workplace behaviours, because winning the masculinity contest depends on exhibiting dominance, these norms increase the likelihood of various problematic behaviours. Organizations with MCCs are rife with bullying (Glick et al., 2018; Xie & Zheng, 2022) as the "strong" exploit the "weak", demonstrate their toughness and show they are not to be crossed (i.e. they are the big dogs who eat the little ones). In addition to promoting workplace bullying and incivility, masculinity contest norms – which incentivize exploiting others' weaknesses – promote exclusion and harassment towards historically disadvantaged groups and men with resistant masculinities (Brassel, 2020; Miedtank et al., 2020; Rawski & Workman-Stark, 2018; Workman-Stark, 2021a; Xie & Zheng, 2022a). Consistent with this reasoning, Glick et al. (2018) found that perceiving one's workplace as high in MCC was associated with greater likelihood of experiencing or witnessing not only sexual or gender harassment but also ethnic harassment as well as a more sexist organizational climate.

These unfavourable organizational consequences create negative effects on individuals. First and foremost, the individual's relationship to the organization and their work suffers. Facing a hypercompetitive workplace rife with toxic leaders as well as bullying and harassment from co-workers negatively affects organizational dedication, engagement, work performance and job satisfaction, while promoting work stress, burnout, emotional exhaustion and turnover (Glick et al., 2018; Regina & Allen, 2022; Robbins, 2022; Williams et al., 2022; Workman-Stark, 2021a; Xie & Zheng, 2022b). In such organizations, exposing any chink in one's armour (e.g. by showing any "soft" emotion) can prove fatal, crumbling a carefully constructed facade presented at work. Therefore, the constant pressure to *show no weakness*, demonstrate *strength and stamina*, *put work first*, and come out on top in *dog-eat-dog* competition exacerbates masculinity contests' negative effects on individuals, increasing burnout and workplace stress. Glick et al. (2018) confirmed that MCC workplace norms are associated with poor individual outcomes, especially those involving the individual's relationship to work: greater burnout, higher turnover intentions and lower organizational dedication.

Munsch et al. (2018) showed that the negative consequences of MCCs are heightened for those who see MCC norms as incompatible with their own ideals about how organizations should function, but who believe (falsely) that their co-workers view MCC norms as ideal (a form of pluralistic ignorance). Specifically, Munsch et al. found that individuals who believed coworkers endorse MCC norms more strongly than they do report reduced job satisfaction, job engagement and mental health, along with increased relationship conflict with their spouse or partner. Although MCCs strongly affect the individual's relationship to work, because work forms such a large part of adult life, they also erode individuals' general well-being, both psychological and physical (i.e. mental and physical health).

Conclusions

Researchers and practitioners have spent decades discussing why women and minorities continue to be so underrepresented in well-paid occupations and positions of leadership, despite legislation outlawing sex and race discrimination at work and decades of diversity initiatives. A proliferation of studies, books, seminars and consultants have offered explanations and solutions for the stalled gender revolution. Ely and Meyerson (2000) summarized three common approaches to addressing the problem. One approach – fixing the women – assumes that women lack the confidence and skills to succeed in male-dominated domains, and need special training to adapt and compete (e.g. Babcock & Laschever, 2003; Kay & Shipman, 2014; Sandberg, 2013). Another – valuing the feminine in women (but not men) – assumes that women have unique qualities to bring to traditionally male domains, leading to interventions that promote the value of diversity in improving creativity and performance (e.g. Bart & McQueen, 2013; Woolley & Malone, 2011) but inadvertently reify stereotypes (e.g. valuing what is stereotyped in different groups). A third approach – addressing implicit bias – assumes the problem lies with unintentional bias in selection and promotion, leading to training sessions for decision-makers who teach them to learn to recognize and avoid their biases when evaluating employees (e.g. Devine et al., 2012; Lebrecht et al., 2009).

Despite the popular and intuitive appeal of these approaches, they have not yielded much progress to date. Some women have made it in male-dominated roles, but women still comprise a small fraction of top leaders and occupations remain highly segregated by sex, with male-dominated occupations paid more than female-dominated ones, even when all else (e.g. education and training) is equal. In other words, women's progress has been uneven, and in many ways it has stalled (England, 2010).

The three popular approaches to addressing the underrepresentation of women in male-dominated occupations and roles – fixing the women, valuing the feminine and reducing bias – have helped some women succeed but have ultimately kept intact organizational cultures that reflect and reinforce norms and values of white and class-privileged men (Ely & Meyerson, 2000; Williams et al., 2016). We propose that a key reason why the workplace gender revolution has stalled is that work remains the site of masculinity contests among men. To the extent that men's status at work depends on perceptions of their masculinity and performance as men, they are motivated to prove their manhood in the workplace, often at the expense and exclusion of women and marginalized men. These workplace gender pressures make organizational culture change difficult, dooming many workplace diversity efforts and making gender equality in caregiving roles elusive (Williams et al., 2016). Methods of proving masculinity are likely to vary across domains and occupations, but the general criteria of physical and social dominance in men, and a lack of weakness and vulnerability, remain highly valued qualities in workplaces marked by an MCC.

Finally, personal experience has shown us that the masculinity contest at work is a touchy subject (Berdahl, 2015; Canadian Association of University Teachers, 2015). Yet it is important to begin the discussion. We hope this chapter encourages readers to look at organizations through a new lens that provides insights for practitioners and organizational leaders as well as academics. Further, we hope that the concepts and tools (especially the MCC scale) provided here spur future research. In both cases, we believe that understanding the MCC better will help practitioners and researchers to find ways to promote healthier workplaces in which people are able to thrive based on genuine and meaningful contributions to work, rather than the ability to win masculinity contests.

Notes

1 This chapter is edited and adapted from the open-access article, Work as a masculinity context, by Jennifer L. Berdahl, Marianne Cooper, Peter Glick, Robert W. Livingston, and Joan C. Williams, in the *Journal of Social Issues*, *28*(3), 2018, 422–448: https://spssi.onlinelibrary.wiley.com/doi/10.1111/josi.12289. The article introduced the Special Issue edited by Jennifer L. Berdahl, Marianne Cooper, and Peter Glick (Special Issue Editors). For a full listing of the Special Issue papers, see http://onlinelibrary.wiley.com/doi/10.1111/josi.2018.74.issue-3/issuetoc. Permission to adapt and reprint extracts of this article was granted by the authors. Thanks to John Wiley & Sons, the *Journal of Social Issues*, and the Society for the Psychological Study of Social Issues.

2 We use "toxic masculinity" to refer to the social phenomenon of competing for dominance in contexts defined by hegemonic masculinity (Connell & Messerschmidt, 2005), not as an essentialized or individual characteristic.

References

Acker, J. (1992). From sex roles to gendered institutions. *Contemporary Sociology*, *21*(5), 565–569.

Alonso, N. (2018). Playing to win: Male-male sex-based harassment and the masculinity contest. *Journal of Social Issues*, *74*(3), 477–499.

Babcock, L., & Laschever, S. (2003). *Women Don't Ask: Negotiation and the Gender Divide*. Princeton, NJ: Princeton University Press.

Bart, C., & McQueen, G. (2013). Why women make better directors. *International Journal of Business Governance and Ethics*, *8*(1), 93–99.

Berdahl, J. L. (2007a). Harassment based on sex: Protecting social status in the context of gender hierarchy. *Academy of Management Review*, *32*(2), 641–658. doi: 10.2307/20159319

Berdahl, J. L. (2007b). The sexual harassment of uppity women. *Journal of Applied Psychology*, *92*(2), 425–437. doi: 10.1037/0021-9010.92.2.425

Berdahl, J. L., & Aquino, K. (2009). Sexual behavior at work: Fun or folly? *Journal of Applied Psychology*, *94*(1), 34–47. doi: 10.1037/a0012981

Berdahl, J. L., & Min, J. A. (2012). Prescriptive stereotypes and workplace consequences for East Asians in North America. *Cultural Diversity and Ethnic Minority Psychology*, *18*(2), 141–152.

Berdahl, J. L. (2015). Academic Freedom and UBC. Retrieved 16 August, from http://jberdahl.blogspot.com/2015/08/academic-freedom-and-ubc.html

Blair-Loy, M. (2005). *Competing Devotions: Career and Family Among Women Executives*. Cambridge, MA: Harvard University Press.

Bosson, J. K., & Vandello, J. A. (2011). Precarious manhood and its links to action and aggression. *Current Directions in Psychological Science*, *20*(2), 82–86. doi: 10.1177/0963721411402669

Bosson, J. K., Vandello, J. A., Burnaford, R. M., Weaver, J. R., & Wasti, S. A. (2009). Precarious manhood and physical aggression. *Personal and Social Psychology Bulletin*, *35*(5), 623–634. doi: 10.1177/0146167208331161

Brannon, R. (1976). The male sex role: And what it's done for us lately. In R. Brannon & D. David (Eds.), *The Forty-Nine Percent Majority 419* (pp. 140). Reading, MA: Addison-Wesley.

Brassel, S. (2020). *It's Not Just "Bad Apples" – It's Also about the Barrel: Critically Analyzing Organizational and Social Factors in Sexual Harassment Rates and Outcomes*. PhD thesis, Department of Psychology, University of Michigan, Michigan. https://hdl.handle.net/2027.42/155160

Brescoll, V. L., & Uhlmann, E. L. (2008). Can an angry woman get ahead? Status conferral, gender, and expression of emotion in the workplace. *Psychological Science*, *19*(3), 268–275. doi: 10.1111/j.1467-9280.2008.02079.x

Britton, D. M., & Logan, L. (2008). Gendered organizations: Progress and prospects. *Sociology Compass*, *2*(1), 107–121. doi: 10.1111/j.1751-9020.2007.00071.x

Canadian Association of University Teachers (2015). Investigation Concludes UBC Leadership Violated Academic Freedom. Retrieved 15 October, from www.caut.ca/latest/2015/10/investigation-concludes-ubc-leadership-violated-academic-freedom

Carbado, D. W., & Gulati, M. (2013). *Acting White? Rethinking Race in "Post-Racial" America*. New York: Oxford University Press.

Cinelli, R. G. (2021). *Career Conversations of Professional Women: A Narrative Research Study Exploring Communication Strategies, Rituals, and Goals of Professional Women who Have Navigated Nontraditional Career Pathways*. Doctor of Education thesis in Organizational Leadership, College of Professional Studies, Boston, MA: Northeastern University.

Collinson, D. L., & Hearn, J. (1994). Naming men as men: Implications for work, organization and management. *Gender, Work and Organization*, *1*(1), 2–22. doi: 10.1111/j.1468-0432.1994.tb00002.x

Connell, R. W., & Messerschmidt, J. (2005). Hegemonic masculinity: Rethinking the concept. *Gender and Society*, *19*(6), 829–859. doi: 10.1177/0891243205278639

Cooper, M. (2014). *Cut Adrift: Families in Insecure Times*. Berkeley, CA: University of California Press.

Derks, B., Ellemers, N., van Laar, C., & de Groot, K. (2011). Do sexist organizational cultures create the Queen Bee? *British Journal of Social Psychology*, *50*(3), 519–535. doi: 10.1348/014466610X525280

Devine, P. G., Forscher, P. S., Austin, A. J., & Cox, W. T. L. (2012). Long-term reduction in implicit race bias: A prejudice habit-breaking intervention. *Journal of Experimental Social Psychology*, *48*(6), 1267–1278. doi: 10.1016/j.jesp.2012.06.003

Ely, R. J., & Kimmel, M. (2018). Thoughts on the workplace as a masculinity contest. *Journal of Social Issues, 74*(3), 628–634.

Ely, R. J., & Meyerson, D. E. (2000). Theories of gender in organizations: A new approach to organizational analysis and change. *Research in Organizational Behavior, 22*, 105–153. doi: 10.1016/S0191-3085(00)22004-2

Ely, R. J., & Meyerson, D. E. (2010). An organizational approach to undoing gender: The unlikely case of offshore oil platforms. *Research in Organizational Behavior, 30*(1), 3–34. doi: 10.1016/j.riob.2010.09.002

England, P. (2010). The gender revolution: Uneven and stalled. *Gender & Society, 24*(2), 149–166.

Faniko, K., Ellemers, N., Derks, B., & Lorenzi-Cioldi, F. (2017). Nothing changes, really: Why women who break the glass ceiling end up reinforcing it. *Personality and Social Psychology Bulletin, 43*(5), 638–651. doi: 10.1177/0146167217695551

Fiske, S. T., & Berdahl, J. L. (2007). Social power. In A. Kruglanski & E. T. Higgins (Eds.), *Social Psychology: A Handbook of Basic Principles*, 2nd edition. (pp. 678–692). New York: Guilford Press.

Fowler, S. (2017). Reflecting On One Very, Very Strange Year at Uber. Retrieved 19 February, from www.susanjfowler.com/blog/2017/2/19/reflecting-on-one-very-strange-year-at-uber

Gee, B., Peck, D., & Wong, J. (2015). Hidden in Plain Sight: Asian American leaders in Silicon Valley. Retrieved from The Ascend Foundation: https://c.ymcdn.com/sites/ascendleadership.site-ym.com/resource/resmgr/Research/HiddenInPlainSight_Paper_042.pdf

Glick, P., Berdahl, J. L., & Alonso, N. M. (2018). Development and validation of the masculinity contest culture scale. *Journal of Social Issues, 74*(3), 449–476.

Glick, P., Lameiras, M., Fiske, S. T., Eckes, T., Masser, B., Volpato, C., Manganelli, A. M., Pek, J., Huang, L., Sakalli-Ugurlu, N., Castro, Y. R., D'Avila Pereira, M. L., Willemsen, T. M., Brunner, A., Six-Materna, I., & Wells, R. (2004). Bad but bold: Ambivalent attitudes toward men predict gender inequality in 16 nations. *Journal of Personality and Social Psychology, 86*(5), 713–728. doi: 10.1037/0022-3514.86.5.713

Iacuone, D. (2005). "Real men are tough guys": Hegemonic masculinity and safety in the construction industry. *The Journal of Men's Studies, 13*(2), 247–266. doi: 10.3149/jms.1302.247

Isaac, M. (2017). Inside Uber's Aggressive, Unrestrained Workplace Culture. Retrieved 22 February, from The New York Times: www.nytimes.com/2017/02/22/technology/uber- workplace-culture.html

Jacobson, J. (2022). *Why Can't People Just Chill? Factors that Encourage and Discourage Psychological Detachment.* M.S thesis, San Diego State University, San Diego.

Kang, S. K, DeCelles, K. A., Tilcsik, A., & Jun, S. (2016). Whitened résumés: Race and self-presentation in the labor market. *Administrative Science Quarterly, 61*(3), 469–502. doi: 10.1177/0001839216639577

Kay, K., & Shipman, C. (2014). *The Confidence Code: The Science and Art of Self-Assurance: What Women Should Know*. New York: HarperCollins.

Kellogg, K. C. (2011). *Challenging Operations: Medical Reform and Resistance in Surgery*. Chicago, IL: University of Chicago Press.

Kerfoot, D., & Knights, D. (1993). Management, masculinity and manipulation: From paternalism to corporate strategy in financial services in Britain. *Journal of Management Studies, 30*(4), 659–678.

Koc, Y, Gulseren, D., & Lyubykh, Z. (2021). Masculinity contest culture reduces organizational citizenship behaviors through decreased organizational identification. *Journal of Experimental Psychology, 27*(2), 408–416.

Kuchynka, S. L., Bosson, J. K., Vandello, J. A., & Puryear, C. (2018). Zero-sum thinking and the masculinity contest: Perceived intergroup competition and workplace gender bias. *Journal of Social Issues, 74*(3), 529–550.

Kupers, K. A. (2005). Toxic masculinity as a barrier to mental health treatment in prison. *Journal of Clinical Psychology, 61*(6), 713–724. doi: 10.1002/jclp.20105

Lebrecht, S., Pierce, L. J., Tarr, M. J., & Tanaka, J. W. (2009). Perceptual other-race training reduces implicit race bias. *PLOS One, 4*(1), e4215. doi: 10.1371/journal.pone.0004215

Levant, R. F., Rankin, T. J., Williams, C. M., Hasan, N. T., & Smalley, K. B. (2010). Evaluation of the factor structure and construct validity of scores on the Male Role Norms Inventory – Revised (MRNI-R). *Psychology of Men & Masculinity, 11*(3), 25–37. doi: 10.1037/a0017637

Livingston, R. W., & Pearce, N. A. (2009). The teddy bear effect: Does having a baby face benefit black chief executive officers? *Psychological Science, 20*(10), 1229–1236. doi: 10.1111/j.1467-9280.2009.02431.x.

Mahalik, J. R., Locke, B. D., Ludlow, L. H., Diemer, M. A., Scott, R. P., Gottfried, M., & Freitas, G. (2003). Development of the conformity to masculine norms inventory. *Psychology of Men & Masculinity, 4*(1), 3–25. doi: 10.1037/1524-9220.4.1.3

Martin, P. (2004). Gender as social institution. *Social Forces, 82*(4), 1249–1273. doi: 10.1353/sof.2004.0081

Matos, K., O'Neill, O., & Lei, X. (2018). Toxic leadership and the masculinity contest culture: How "win or die" cultures breed abusive leadership. *Journal of Social Issues, 74*(3), 500–528.

Meluso, J., Bagrow, J., Hébert-Dufresne, L., & Razzante, R. (2023). Masculinity contest cultures and inclusive cultures. In E. B. King, Q. M. Roberson & M. R. Hebl (Eds.), *The Future of Scholarship on Diversity and Inclusion in Organizations* (pp. 157–198). Information Age Publishing.

Messerschmidt, J. W. (1995). Managing to kill: Masculinities and the space shuttle challenger explosion. *Masculinities, 3*(4), 1–22.

Meyerson, D. E., Ely, R. J., & Wernick, L. (2007). Disrupting gender, revising leadership. In D. Rhode & B. Kellerman (Eds.), *Women and Leadership: The State of Play and Strategies for Change.* San Francisco, CA: Jossey-Bass.

Miedtank, T., Vassilopoulou, J., Takkenberg, H., & Dijkstra, G. (2020). Culture and Working Climate for Women Assessment Report. Retrieved from 2020 Equal4Europe Consortium: https://equal4europe.eu/wp-content/uploads/2021/08/D3.1_Culture-and-Working-Climate-for-Women-Assessment-Report.pdf

Munsch, C. L. (2022). Strength, stamina, and structural violence in the social sciences. *The Journal of Men's Studies, 30*(2), 402–424. doi: 10.1177/10608265221108205

Munsch, C. L., Weaver, J. R., Bosson, J. K., & O'Connor, L. T. (2018). Everybody but me: Pluralistic ignorance and the masculinity contest. *Journal of Social Issues, 74*(3), 551–578.

Nelson, J. A. (2012). Would Women Leaders have Prevented the Global Financial Crisis? Implications for Teaching about Gender, Behavior, and Economics (Working paper No. 11–03). Retrieved from Global Development and Environment Institute: www.ase.tufts.edu/gdae/Pubs/wp/11-03NelsonWomenLeaders.pdf

Pfeffer, J. (2010). *Power: Why Some People Have It and Others Don't.* New York: Harper Business.

Pierce, J. L. (1996). *Gender Trials: Emotional Lives in Contemporary Law Firms.* Berkeley, CA: University of California Press.

Pratto, F., Pearson, A. R., Lee, I., & Saguy, T. (2008). Power dynamics in an experimental game. *Social Justice Research, 21*(3), 377–407. doi: 10.1007/s11211-008-0075-y

Rawlins, A. (2017). Uber Board Member Resigns after Making Sexist Comment at Meeting about Sexism, Cable News Network (CNN). Retrieved from https://money.cnn.com/2017/06/13/technology/business/uber-board-member-resigns/index.html

Rawski, S. L., & Workman-Stark, A. L. (2018). Masculinity contest cultures in policing organizations and recommendations for training interventions. *Journal of Social Issues, 74*(3), 607–627.

Regina, J., & Allen, T. D. (2022). Masculinity contest culture: Harmful for whom? An examination of emotional exhaustion. *Journal of Occupational Health Psychology.* doi: 10.1037/ocp0000344

Reid, E. M., O'Neill, O. A., & Blair-Loy, M. (2018). Masculinity in male-dominated occupations: How teams, time, and tasks shape masculinity contests. *Journal of Social Issues, 74*(3), 579–606.

Robbins, C. (2022). The ivory tower: An intersectional view on gender and ethnicity in academia before and after the transition to online work. All Theses, *3759.* https://tigerprints.clemson.edu/all_theses/3759

Roth, M. L. (2006). *Selling Women Short: Gender and Money on Wall Street.* Princeton, NJ: Princeton University Press.

Rudman, L. A. (1998). Self-promotion as a risk factor for women: The costs and benefits of counterstereotypical impression management. *Journal of Personality and Social Psychology, 74*(3), 629–645.

Rudman, L. A., Moss-Racusin, C. A., Phelan, J. E., & Nauts, S. (2012). Status incongruity and backlash effects: Defending the gender hierarchy motivates prejudice against female leaders. *Journal of Experimental Social Psychology, 48*(1), 165–179. doi: 10.1016/j.jesp.2011.10.008

Sandberg, S. (2013). *Lean In: Women, Work, and the Will to Lead.* New York: Knopf.

Sattari, N. (2021). Masculinity in the workplace: Iranian women engineers' navigations of hyper masculine work cultures. *International Journal of Gender and Women's Studies, 9*(1), 27–40. doi: 10.15640/ijgws.v9n1p3

Sidanius, J., & Pratto, F. (2001). *Social Dominance: An Intergroup Theory of Social Hierarchy and Oppression*. Cambridge: Cambridge University Press.
Stephens, N., Fryberg, S., & Markus, H. R. (2012). It's your choice: How the middle-class model of independence disadvantages working-class Americans. In S. T. Fiske & H. R. Markus (Eds.), *Facing Social Class: How Societal Rank Influences Interaction* (pp. 87–106). New York, NY: Russell Sage Foundation.
Thompson, E. H. Jr., & Pleck, J. H. (1986). The structure of male role norms. *American Behavioral Scientist, 29*(5), 531–543.
Vandello, J. A., Bosson, J. K., Cohen, D., Burnaford, R. M., & Weaver, J. R. (2008). Precarious manhood. *Journal of Personality and Social Psychology, 95*(6), 1325–1339. doi: 10.1037/a0012453
Vial, A. C., Muradoglu, M. Newman, G. E., & Cimpian, A. (2022). An emphasis on brilliance fosters masculinity-contest cultures. *Psychological Science, 33*(4), 595–612. doi: 10.1177/09567976211044133
Williams, J. C. (1999). *Unbending Gender: Why Family and Work Conflict and What to Do About It*. New York: Oxford University Press.
Williams, J. C. (2013). Why Men Work so Many Hours. Retrieved 29 May, from Harvard Business Review: https://hbr.org/2013/05/why-men-work-so-many-hours
Williams, J. C., Berdahl, J. L., & Vandello, J. A. (2016). Beyond work-life "integration". *Annual Review of Psychology, 67*, 515–39. doi: 10.1146/annurev-psych-122414-033710
Williams, J. C., Korn, R. M., & Ghani, A. (2022). Pinning Down the Jellyfish: The Workplace Experiences of Women of Color in Tech. Retrieved from Center for WorkLife Law: https://ssrn.com/abstract=4083914
Williams, J. C., Li, S., Rincon, R., & Finn, P. (2016b). Climate Control: Gender and Racial Bias in Engineering? Retrieved from Center for WorkLife Law. UC Hastings College of the Law: https://research.swe.org/wp-content/uploads/2017/10/16-SWE-020-Work- Study-10_20_16-CP.pdf
Williams, J. C., Multhaup, M., Li, S., Korn, R. M (2018). *You Can't Change What you Can't See: Interrupting Racial & Gender Bias in the Legal Profession*. San Francisco, CA: Center for WorkLife Law. UC Hastings College of the Law.
Woolley, A., & Malone, T. (2011). What makes a team smarter? More women. *Harvard Business Review, 89*(6), 32–33.
Workman-Stark, A. (2021a). Exploring differing experiences of a masculinity contest culture in policing and the impact on individual and organizational outcomes. *Police Quarterly, 24*(3), 298–324. doi: 10.1177/1098611120976090
Workman-Stark, A. (2021b). Countering masculinity contest culture at work: The moderating role of organizational justice. *International Journal of Organization Theory & Behavior, 24*(1), 6–23. doi: 10.1108/IJOTB-11 2019 0132
Wu, T. (2020). The labour of fun: Masculinities and the organisation of labour games in a modern workplace. *New Technology, Work and Employment, 35*, 336–356. doi: 10.1111/ntwe.12180
Xie, L., & Zheng, Y. (2022a). A moderated mediation model of masculinity contest culture and psychological well-being: The role of sexual harassment, bullying, organizational tolerance and position in organization. *Sex Roles*. doi: 10.1007/s11199-022-01342-w
Xie, L., & Zheng, Y. (2022b). Masculinity contest culture and turnover intentions: The roles of work stress and coping styles. *Personality and Individual Differences, 199*. doi: 10.1016/j.paid.2022.111836
Zaloom, C. (2006). *Out of the Pits: Traders and Technology from Chicago to London*. Chicago, IL: University of Chicago Press.

11

DOING META-WORK TO NAVIGATE CONVENTIONALLY MASCULINIST CAREERS AND WORK NORMS IN PROFESSIONAL WORKPLACES

Marta Choroszewicz and Ingrid Biese

Introduction

In most corporate environments, masculinist career models continue to be prevalent, idealized and reproduced through, for example, the promotion systems, which leave few alternatives for individuals who want or need to organize their work differently. This is specifically relevant for high-achieving careers and work environments that are instilled with normative patterns of masculinity (Connell & Wood, 2005; Griffin, 2012; Hearn & Piekkari, 2005). While masculinist career models have been created by men for men, they leave little room for diversity among men (Connell & Messerschmidt, 2005), and even presumed privileged male professionals can experience difficulties relating to prevalent work ideals.

In this chapter, we use the concept of meta-work to advance our understanding of how male privilege continues to dominate today's professional workplaces, to uncover how many men struggle with the normative ideal surrounding socially prestigious careers and work norms and how this may impact negatively on their lives and careers. Meta-work refers to hidden, invisible and laborious work performed by professionals in their striving to live up to the traditional and normative ideals surrounding socially prestigious careers and identities (Choroszewicz & Adams, 2019a, pp. 267–269). While the concept was developed to capture the struggle of non-traditional and disadvantaged professionals such as women, young professionals, and sexual, racial and ethnic minorities, our chapter demonstrates that meta-work is also applicable to assumedly privileged groups of middle-class white men. Through two empirical case studies, male lawyers in Finland and Canada, on the one hand, and professional men (corporate managers and lawyers) from Finland and the United States who opted out of their careers, on the other, we extend the concept of meta-work to cover the ways in which masculinist work environments are problematic also for privileged white men. The two cases are illustrative of the men's struggles and how they deal with feelings of inadequacy as well as dilemmas and disappointments surrounding their conventionally masculine careers.

The two cases of male lawyers and corporate managers consider the issue of meta-work in the context of changing male-dominated professional workplaces. For instance, gender

 DOI: 10.4324/9781003193579-13

inequality, including gender-based occupational segregation, is still persistent in the legal profession despite its numerical feminization in the past 30 years, especially in civil law countries such as French Canada and Finland (see, e.g. Choroszewicz & Kay, 2022). Managerial positions are also dominated by men internationally and despite national gender-equality policies, corporate policies to support fathers and their ability and legislative right to actively partake in the care of their children remain ambiguous, even in a country like Finland which is considered one of the most gender equal in the world (Hearn & Niemistö, 2012; Biese, 2021). In fact, research has shown that organizational cultures often override national legislation regarding for example paternity and parental leave (Tomlinson et al., 2018).

Our chapter unfolds as follows: We start with an extensive literature review to establish a set of attributes and behaviours on which male privilege regarding careers and work norms have historically rested. Next, we introduce the concept of meta-work and its link to male privilege. The chapter then continues with two contemporary case studies that illustrate the workings of meta-work for privileged, white professional men in Finland, Canada and the United States. The first case study of lawyers in Finland and Canada demonstrates how promotion systems in private law practices appear to be rooted in the hierarchy of skill sets where a new skill set, including soft skills, emotional work and the rather unending work-related activities enabled by mobile technologies, became central to career progress to the partnership level. The second case of men from Finland and the United States who opted out of conventional masculinist careers shows that meta-work not only can relate to the entry career stage but also can surface in later career stages as a result of feelings of disenchantment and disillusionment with organizational cultures, practices and career ideals. The second case also illustrates how speaking up and trying to change organizational practices and norms may lead to penalization; even for white, privileged males it may simply be easier to leave. Finally, we conclude with a brief discussion of our findings and the implications they can have for masculinist careers, work norms and professional workplaces going forward.

Masculinist careers and work norms

Masculine career ideals date back to industrialization when the family became a unit of consumption, rather than of production, and mainly men started to work in the industries as their wives typically stayed at home to take care of the children (Kinser, 2010; Greenhaus et al., 2010). The masculinist career model was thus created by men for men. In addition to being modelled off men who had no childcare or household responsibilities, it was built on gendered ideals and male attributes and work behaviours (Williams, 2000; Heppner, 2013). Although the reality today is quite different than it was during the early days of industrialization, contemporary career models continue to be modelled off this masculinist career ideal, especially for those who aim to reach the top echelons of corporate hierarchies (see Biese & Choroszewicz, 2019). This includes a continuous linear and upward progression in a timely fashion, brought about through promotions (Hall, 2002). There is an expectation of dedication and devotion to the organization (Blair-Loy, 2003; Biese & McKie, 2015), and a notion of an ideal worker that is able and expected to prioritize career demands over the demands of private or family life (Acker, 1990). In fact, work hours and career commitment have even been found to increase for men after having children (Fox, 2009).

The masculinist career ideal over-emphasizes progression towards career success, marked by higher income, more authority, social esteem and influence as well as a hypercompetitive and client-demanding culture (Collier, 2015; Thornton, 2014). The promotion system is rigid and competitive, and based on merits that are predominantly visible and easily measurable. Professional development in law firms, for example, is measured through economic revenues, new clients and projects (Sterling & Reichman, 2016). The emphasis is on personal progress and improvement (Connell & Wood, 2005), and employees are individually responsible for their own career advancement through resilience, self-making and self-management (Olakivi & Wrede, 2019). Powerful and resourceful networks, including mentors and sponsors, are central to this type of career success (Adams & Kwon, 2019; Francis, 2015; Kay, 2019), and the acquisition of new skills is not something that is expected only on-the-job, but during free time as well (Corbett, 2019). Personal success in the workplace in the form of salary and promotion has been found to be central to men's identity construction and sense of self (Collinson & Hearn, 1994). However, in law firms "the spectre of de-equitization" – the process in which certain partners are demoted from full equity status – has made partnership and thus career success less secure and increasingly dependent on ongoing performance evaluation (Galanter & Henderson, 2008).

Appearance and self-presentation in the business environment as well as self-care as a means of enhancing work performance have also become central (Haynes, 2012; Elfving-Hwang, 2020; Hyvönen, 2020). For example, physical appearance and the need to look young, fit and strong are considered important among business executives, and connections have been made between virility and superior economic performance (Elliott, 2008; Griffin, 2012; Meriläinen et al., 2013). Workplaces have been found to prize social dominance, physical strength and an avoidance of displays of weakness (Berdahl et al., 2018). Furthermore, employees differ in terms of emotional capital. Specifically, young professionals appear to feel a range of emotions more intensely than their older colleagues, as well as feeling pressured to keep particularly negative emotions hidden (Adams, 2019; Cottingham & Dill, 2019). However, while this can have a detrimental effect on the individual (Chapman et al., 2013), risk-taking, competition and the concept of honour that characterize mainly male social interactions have also been found to have a direct link to cultures of violence, including workplace violence (Wood, 2007; Kessler et al., 2008; Penttinen et al., 2019; see Howard, 2000).

On a global level among the business elite and within global organizations, a transnational business masculinity can be discerned, which comprises certain forms of hegemonic masculinity (Connell, 1998; Griffin, 2012; Hearn & Piekkari, 2005). It does not represent all forms of masculinity in the business world (Hearn et al., 2017) nor do those who hold top power positions in organizations necessarily embody hegemonic masculine norms (Connell & Messerschmidt, 2005). Nevertheless, it remains an influential norm and ideal to be taken into account (see Hearn & Piekkari, 2005; Kangas, 2020). Global organizational cultures dominate, reinforce and reproduce masculine ideals and gender structuring despite national differences in practices, recommendations and legislative support for professionals (Griffin, 2012; Collinson & Hearn, 1996; Hearn & Piekkari, 2005; Biese & Choroszewicz, 2018; Choroszewicz & Tremblay, 2018). Corporate executives have thus been found to have similar experiences globally despite different cultural contexts (Hobson et al., 2011; Biese & Choroszewicz, 2018; Biese, 2017). It is a reaffirmation of dominant groups of men and forms of masculinity (Hearn et al., 2017), and those who do not live up to these norms may be excluded from the group and "[fall] to the bottom of the pecking order" (Holgersson, 2013, p. 456). In short, managers are not only subjects but also objects of masculine organizations (Hearn & Collinson, 1998).

However, it is important to note that masculine careers and work norms are not only about the male gender, men's practices and masculine values and behaviours but also about tacit assumptions around class and race (Acker, 2006; Holvino, 2010; Hearn et al., 2016; Adams & Kwon, 2019). Researchers point out that a concept of "career" implies a particular relationship to work that involves a reputable economic activity and participation in workplaces (Aavik et al., 2020; Cleveland et al., 2000), which has been broadly criticized in the scholarship on women's careers (see, e.g. Biese, 2017; Biese & Choroszewicz, 2018, 2019; Mainiero & Sullivan, 2006; O'Neil & Bilimoria, 2005).

In the past decades, professional workplaces have been exposed to changes as new technologies, including platform work and algorithmic systems, have emerged. This includes continuous connectivity and around-the-clock accessibility through mobile technologies that create a norm of boundary permeability from work to private life (Wajcman & Rose, 2011; MacCormick et al., 2012; Mullan & Wajcman, 2017). New modes of governance are introduced in workplaces through new technologies, and work performance is constantly monitored through technological mediation. Workers thus experience work intensification, increasing expectations and new targets (Moore, 2017; Moore et al., 2018). As a result, there is an increasing invisibility of some workers as they are managed and governed through algorithmic systems (Aneesh, 2009). While technology could be used to free up time and make work easier, it has, ironically, only reinforced the early visible logics of optimization, efficiency and techno-optimism.

Meta-work in professional workplaces: an intersectional perspective

The concept of meta-work enables us to attend to an under-researched facet of the emotional aspects of professional identities, roles and careers. Originally, the concept of meta-work emerged as a result of a book project put together by Choroszewicz and Adams (2019a, pp. 267–269) on young professionals' careers and work experiences in various professions across a number of national contexts. They defined this concept as hidden, invisible and laborious work performed by non-traditional and disadvantaged professionals, through which they endeavour to cope with structural inequalities embedded in their professions and professional workplaces. As the structural inequalities are linked to the conventionally masculin ist ideals surrounding professional roles and identities, meta-work was originally expected to cover individual tactics and strategies through which non-traditional groups of professionals try to develop and maintain their sense of professional self and their feeling of belonging to professional communities (see, e.g. Behtoui & Leivestad, 2019).

Meta-work thus broadly covers different types of professionals' often invisible work that they put into presenting themselves as competent professionals. It can cover emotional work (Hochschild, 1983, 2002) but also earlier mentioned self-presentation work, including work on body and appearance (Haynes, 2012; Elfving-Hwang, 2020; Hyvönen, 2020), which is often taken-for-granted in the professions. It can also be work put into knowing when to say "yes" to colleagues' requests for a favour or assistance, and when to say "no" in order to protect one's core professional identity and role, as well as one's right to downtime and private life. In other words, it involves knowing when new work tasks and socializing activities can lead to recognition and rewards within one's own workplace or professional community, and when they can lead to overwork, abuse and discrimination. The invisibility of meta-work is connected to a lack of its recognition and to the reward systems of organizations and professional communities. It is often not recognized because of prevalent ideals of equality instead of equity. Employees are evaluated against the universalistic expectations of merits and end results are stripped of the differential social circumstances, cultural and social capitals and opportunities for their achievements owing to gender, class, ethnicity and race, just to mention a few. This disadvantage is often normalized by insufficient representation of minority groups at the top level of organizations and professional communities, and thus lack of empathy, understanding and openness to experiences of others outside of one's own reference group. As a result, young professionals and minority groups generally continue to be expected to work harder to prove their ability to conform to traditional assumptions around professional roles and identities tailored for and by dominant groups (Choroszewicz & Adams, 2019a, 2019b).

The concept of meta-work also captures the intersection of disadvantages of age, gender, ethnicity, class and race and their embedding in the current hyper-competitiveness of working life, which can negatively impact larger groups of workers and professionals. After all, careers and their advancement are inherent in certain social locations and temporalities (see Jyrkinen et al., 2017; Choroszewicz & Adams, 2019a, 2019b; Hearn & Husu, 2019). As human resource processes, careers and organizations are still designed for the archetypical worker ideal that is increasingly in contrast with social change in terms of gender roles, family models, education systems, class and the ethnic composition of our societies, all workers are already being pressured to do some meta-work. They are also more likely to experience stress and frustration associated with a hyper-competitive and individualistic working culture that might make a majority of today's workers and professionals feel inadequate in their work environments to some extent.

While the concept was developed to capture the struggle of non-traditional and disadvantaged professionals, the cases discussed in this chapter demonstrate that meta-work is also applicable to assumedly privileged groups of middle-class, white men. This may be especially relevant today due to the competitive, fluctuating, highly flexible and changing work environments where there is not much space for collegiality and mentoring (Cottingham & Dill, 2019; Olakivi & Wrede, 2019; Hearn & Husu, 2019). Thus, this chapter extends the concept of meta-work to the ways in which even those who are assumed to be privileged professionals have to deal with rapidly changing work realities, skills and a lack of collegial support. Professionals and workers of all ages, gender, ethnicity and class background are constantly competing with each other for more recognition, prestige and authority, and thus they might be less willing nor have resources to comply with the informal ideals of collegiality and mentoring.

Two case studies on meta-work in professional workplaces

Case study 1: male lawyers within a competitive promotion system of law firms in Finland and French Canada

The case of Finnish and Canadian male lawyers who pursue a legal career according to conventionally masculinist work norms provides insights into highly competitive promotion systems in the private practice of law in both countries and male lawyers' meta-work around coming to terms with them. For this study, 20 Finnish and 14 Canadian male lawyers were interviewed in 2016. They were middle-class, well-educated professionals between the ages of 32 and 68. The majority of them (21) were law firm partners; others worked as junior or senior associates, Of Counsels or sole practitioners. Most of them (27) worked in mid-size or large law firms. All of them were married or cohabitating and had children, except for one who was planning to have children.

For many of the male lawyers in this study, especially those in their early forties and younger, meta-work appeared to be related to their striving for a more balanced life, composed of a legal career and their active participation as fathers in family life. While being hands-on fathers was more available to lawyers in the early stages of their careers, especially in Finland, all the interviewees felt, to some extent, pressures to contemplate their priorities regarding the work–family interface. Additionally, the study shows that the increased use of mobile technologies, such as smartphones, tablets and laptops, for work-related activities outside of working hours posted a particular challenge to a balanced life (Choroszewicz & Kay, 2020). Even before the COVID-19 pandemic, the rather unlimited availability of work-related activities via mobile technologies functioned as a new informal professional norm that was specifically expected of ambitious lawyers. This norm was legitimized especially by older male lawyers who worked as law firm partners and used the norm to identify young colleagues who were professionally suitable and thus deserving of promotions. The majority of younger male lawyers (i.e. 40 and younger) were sceptical of possibilities to combine their roles as hands-on fathers with requirements for making law firm partner, which included an extremely high number of billing hours per year, enough large and prestigious clients, highly prospective legal expertise with future prospects of openings for partnerships within one's own organization, and powerful mentors or sponsors to support one's own candidature.

Furthermore, this study also demonstrates that career progression in the private practice of law has moved from valuation of purely traditional legal skills rooted in familiarity with legislation and the ability to review legislation critically in written and spoken forms towards the valuation of skills for revenue generation, business development and winning and retaining clients. The new entrepreneurial culture of the legal profession has created a need for more flexible and multi-skilled lawyer-managers who combine legal and business skills (Collier, 2015; Sterling & Reichman, 2016). This was also echoed in the interviews with the male lawyers who argued that law firm partners today no longer need to excel in legal skills as they have "an army of associates" to assist them in legal work but instead have to be excellent business persons from the start of their legal careers. This was especially pronounced in Canadian law firms due to a more individualistic work culture (Choroszewicz & Tremblay, 2018).

The masculinist legal career appears to be reproduced through network-based and gendered soft skills (Choroszewicz, 2020). For instance, the professional demeanour of lawyers has shifted from a traditional emotional detachment and affective neutrality towards the revalorization of emotions and soft skills that enable the development of long-term (and often also personal) relationships with clients, to connect with individuals of different cultural backgrounds as well as to manage emotions in order to appear confident, competent and trustworthy. This utilization of emotions and soft skills differs from the previously identified patterns of gender-appropriate professional behaviour expected predominantly from female lawyers. For instance, in her study on litigators, Pierce (1995) noticed that female litigators were expected to demonstrate an adversarial style of lawyering in the courtrooms and a caring orientation outside them. Now, by contrast, all lawyers are expected to know which networking activities to attend, when and how to speak, and how to set people at ease and thus generate their trust. The expectation of lawyers' multifaceted skills and activities has been supported by organizational monitoring systems where lawyers are asked to report on their self-promotions and pro-bono activities such as conference presentations, publishing, voluntary pro-bono legal services and participation in networking events.

This skill set is tailored for prospective partners and thus bears little resemblance to traditional archetypes of reserved lawyers applying legal expertise to legal problems. Moreover, the development of this skill set appeared, to a large extent, to be left to lawyers' self-development and thus privileges male lawyers from certain socio-economic backgrounds who can more easily gain access to a mentor and sponsor-driven professional ecosystem early in their careers (Francis, 2015; Kay, 2019). This ecosystem determines the distribution of challenging assignments among junior and senior lawyers, as well as carrying significant guidance and information necessary for career advancement within law firms. The distinction between traditional legal skills and a new skill set, including soft skills and emotional work, illuminates the hierarchy of the dispositional attributes expected of prospective candidates for law firm partners. Lawyers who excel predominantly in traditional legal skills appear to be channelled towards positions of salary-based senior lawyers and non-equity status partners. Yet, as researchers have noticed, such lawyers may serve as an easily disposable resource employed to do routine work without many opportunities for career advancement (Sommerlad, 2016; Sterling & Reichman, 2016).

Case study 2: men who opted out of conventionally masculinist careers

The case of men who opt out of masculinist careers to adopt alternative lifestyles and solutions for work, points to two main issues for men pursuing a career according to mainstream masculinist norms. First, it shows that although masculinist careers are created by men for men, they do not necessarily support men's lives nor do they allow for much diversity among men. Second, the case illustrates just how destructive and unhealthy masculinist norms in the workplace can be and the meta-work they do as they struggle to come to terms and cope with this.

In this study, 21 managers and lawyers between the age of 34 and 63 from Finland and the United States (US) were interviewed. All but one were married and all but three had children. One was in a same-sex marriage. These men were part of a larger study of men from Finland, the United Kingdom and the United States who opted out of mainstream career models to adopt alternative lifestyles and solutions for work (see Biese, 2021).

The men in the study all had a clear notion of what they thought was expected of them as men and what was considered a "good" career path to follow before they even embarked on their careers. As they graduated from high school and chose what they wanted to study, issues like tradition, prestige, power, the promise of a high salary and the need to be able to support a family, despite not even having any plans to do so, were primary concerns (see Biese, 2021). In fact, research has shown that despite women increasingly working and participating in public life on the same terms as men, the breadwinner ideal still continues to have a strong influence (Tinsley et al., 2015). This is also true in Finland, considered one of the most gender-equal countries in the world, where historically there has been a tradition of women working (see Biese, 2017). For some, the choice of profession was dictated by what men in their family had traditionally done. For others, peer pressure played a part, and they chose to do what their friends were going to do. Many of the men chose paths with a promise of prestige, power and an ability to make large amounts of money.

After having pursued a career for a number of years, several of the men came to a point when they realized that their jobs simply no longer felt right for them. They started to question the way things were done in the organizations where they worked and no longer felt they wanted to or could embody the masculinist norms that permeated the organizational cultures. Although they were white, privileged, middle-class men (with only one belonging to a sexual minority), they nevertheless struggled to conform to the norms and expectations that were placed on them in the organizational setting.

For example, one man considered himself an introvert, and felt very uncomfortable with the new work expectations that a recent promotion had entailed. In his new role as a partner of the firm, he was expected to bring in new clients, which added substantially to his stress levels. When embarking on his career after graduating from university, he was so focused on what was thought of as a "good" job that he never even considered that this type of work would not be right for him. He simply felt he did not fit into an organizational culture where extroversion seemed to be a preferred trait. For another participant, the pressures associated with performance and responsibility in addition to the hectic pace and extreme hours took a direct toll on his health. He had difficulties coping with the high-stress, high-risk nature of his job. He was successful at what he did and was making large amounts of money; however, he came to a point when he realized that working in this way was simply not sustainable for him. He vomited in the bathroom every morning before going to work.

However, for these men, opting out was not only the result of a realization that they had made the wrong decision and chosen a profession that was ill-suited for them. Several of the men also felt disillusioned and disenchanted by the organizational cultures, practices and career ideals where they worked (Biese, 2020, 2021). Some reported frustration over the individualistic nature of work, which seemed to bring out irrational and even childish behaviour in people, and struggled to find a sense of purpose and meaning. For others, it was the unethical treatment of clients or employees that they felt they simply could not live with (Biese, 2020). One participant felt the expectation of not being completely honest with clients during the sales process regarding what the company could deliver was unethical. He therefore decided to withdraw an offer to an important client and was immediately penalized and taken off the account. Another man was enraged by the age discrimination and illegal treatment of employees at the company where he worked and had several arguments with his boss regarding this, to no avail. Yet another witnessed gender discrimination and harassment of women. When raising the issue with his superior, he was told that if he cannot handle the way things are done at the company, he should consider changing jobs.

Several of the participants were penalized for speaking up and criticizing masculinist expectations and the way things were done. They opted out when they felt they no longer could go on. However, by leaving they did not participate in changing organizational cultures or practices. Despite being white, able-bodied, middle-aged men belonging to the dominant group, when not living up to masculinist behavioural expectations, it was simply easier for them to leave.

Conclusion

In this chapter, we have demonstrated the usefulness of meta-work as an analytical tool to capture the challenges and dilemmas of assumedly privileged groups of white, middle-class professional men as they navigate contemporary careers and work norms. We have presented two empirical cases on men: Finnish and Canadian lawyers embarking on and advancing in legal careers; and professional men from Finland and the United States who opted out of successful, mainstream, masculinist careers to work and live on different terms. These cases illustrate how some men struggle with work norms, the masculinist competition and promotion systems prevalent in organizations today. Our chapter provides three main findings with implications for further research on men and careers in organization.

First, masculinist careers and work norms rest upon certain types of skills, values, traits and behaviours that do not correspond to the diverse skills and personalities among men.

Employees, in this case men, are expected to work in certain ways that do not necessarily suit them and as a result their diverse skill sets are not recognized enough and they may not feel comfortable in their jobs. The organizational promotion systems in professional workplaces appear to favour skills that fall within a more commercial rather than strictly technical-professional ethos (see also Spence & Carter, 2014; Sterling & Reichman, 2016), imposing on men a need for meta-work to keep them moving upwards in their organizational careers if they want to gain more respect, authority, influence and money.

Second, at the beginning of their careers, men can better conform to the masculinist work ideals, but as they advance in their careers it becomes more difficult for them to reconcile what they are doing at work with who they feel they really are. Some men feel a strong mismatch between the skills, goals and values favoured by the organizational promotion systems and their own idea of a "good" job. Not everyone wants to climb the proverbial career ladder, nor does everyone necessarily equate it with success (Biese, 2017). Still, the masculinist work culture appears to be so strong that even men do not always feel capable of changing it. When they do speak up to change the practices, structures and cultures of their workplaces, they risk being penalized (see also Bosak et al., 2018; Burris, 2012), and thus it might be simply easier for them to leave. Yet, by leaving, they manifest their dissatisfaction and frustration with the existing social order in their workplaces (Mainiero & Sullivan, 2006).

Third, similarly to minority professionals (see, e.g. Adams & Kwon, 2019; Behtoui & Leivestad, 2019; Kay, 2019), also privileged, white men struggle to comply with conventionally masculinist careers and work norms sustained and reproduced by masculinist organizational promotion systems. Fathers in particular face barriers to work–life balance that relates to traditional gender views and the hegemonic masculine norms prevalent in organizations unsupportive of more egalitarian gender views (Stovell et al., 2017; Choroszewicz & Tremblay, 2018). Specifically in less-egalitarian countries, having more children is associated with higher job ranks and wages as well as greater job stability for fathers (Baranowska-Rataj & Matysiak, 2022).

This chapter demonstrates that living up to masculinist careers and work norms emerges as a process that requires continuous meta-work to advance one's own position within the internal hierarchical ladder of professional workplaces. Masculinist careers and work norms remain so strong partly because men are not recognized as the diverse group that they are. Masculinist careers have been created by men for men, however not for all men but for the masculinist ideal of what an ideal man ought to be and how he should act. The diversity among men, when it comes to personality, traits, needs and values, just to mention a few, needs to be recognized. It will enhance making professional structures and cultures more flexible and sustainable not only for men but also for all employees.

References

Aavik, K., Hoegaerts, J., & Salminen, J. (2020). Introduction: Why men, masculinities and career(s)? In K. Aavik, C. Bland, J. Hoegaerts & J. Salminen (Eds.), *Men, Masculinities and the Modern Career* (pp. 1–12). Berlin: De Gruyter. doi: 10.1515/9783110651874

Acker, J. (1990). Hierarchies, jobs, bodies: A theory of gendered organisations. *Gender and Society*, *4*(2), 139–158. doi: 10.1177/089124390004002002

Acker, J. (2006). Inequality regimes: Gender, class and race in organizations. *Gender and Society*, *20*(4), 441–464. doi: 10.1177/0891243206289499

Adams, T. L. (2019). Women in engineering: Experiences of discrimination across age cohort. In M. Choroszewicz & T. L. Adams (Eds.), *Gender, Age and Inequality in the Professions* (pp. 244–259). New York: Routledge. doi: 10.3138/9781442670297

Adams, T. L., & Kwon, E. (2019). "Not that many female med students want to pursue surgery": Gender, ethnicity, and the life course in medical students' specialty choices. In M. Choroszewicz & T. L. Adams (Eds.), *Gender, Age and Inequality in the Professions* (pp. 41–57). New York: Routledge. doi: 10.4324/9781351052467-3

Aneesh, A. (2009). Global labor: Algocratic modes of organization. *Sociological Theory*, 27(4), 347–370. doi: 10.1111/j.1467-9558.2009.01352.x

Baranowska-Rataj, A., & Matysiak, A. (2022). Family size and men's labor market outcomes: Do social beliefs about men's roles in the family matter? *Feminist Economics*, *28*(2), 93–118 doi: 10.1080/13545701.2021.2015076

Behtoui, A., & Leivestad, H. H. (2019). The "stranger" among Swedish "homo academicus". *Higher Education*, *77*(2), 213–228. doi: 10.1007/s10734-018-0266-x

Berdahl, J. L., Cooper, M., Glick, P., Livingston, R. W., & Williams, J. C. (2018). Work as a masculinity contest. *Journal of Social Issues*, *74*(3), 422–448. doi: 10.1111/josi.12289

Biese, I. (2017). *Opting Out and In: On Women's Careers and New Lifestyles.* London: Routledge. doi: 10.4324/9781315637006

Biese, I. (2020). Men opting out: Disenchantment with corporate cultures and career ideals. In K. Aavik, C. Bland, J. Hoegaerts & J. Salminen (Eds.), *Men, Masculinities and the Modern Career* (pp. 35–52). Berlin: De Gruyter. doi: 10.1515/9783110651874

Biese, I. (2021). *Men Do It Too: Opting Out and In.* Berlin: De Gruyter. doi: 10.1515/9783110725797

Biese, I., & Choroszewicz, M. (2018). Creating alternative solutions for work: Experiences of women managers and lawyers in Poland and the USA. In S. Taylor & S. Luckman (Eds.), *The 'New Normal' of Working Lives: Critical Studies in Contemporary Work and Employment* (pp. 309–325). London: Palgrave Macmillan. doi: 10.1007/978-3-319-66038-7_15

Biese, I., & Choroszewicz, M. (2019). Opting out: Professional women develop reflexive agency. *Equality, Diversity and Inclusion: An International Journal*, *38*(6), 619–633. doi: *10.1108/EDI-06-2018-0097*

Biese, I., & McKie, L. (2015). Opting out and opting in: Women managers in search of balance, control and wellbeing. In M. Connerley & J. Wu (Eds.), *Handbook on Well-Being of Working Women* (pp. 503–516). London: Springer. doi: 10.1007/978-94-017-9897-6

Blair-Loy, M. (2003). *Competing Devotions: Career and Family among Women Executives.* Cambridge, MA: Harvard University Press.

Bosak, J., Kulich, C., Rudman, L., & Kinahan, M. (2018). Be an advocate for others, unless you are a man: Backlash against gender-atypical male job candidates. *Psychology of Men & Masculinity*, *19*(1), 156–165. doi: 10.1037/men0000085

Burris, E. R. (2012). The risks and rewards of speaking up: Managerial responses to employee voice. *The Academy of Management Journal*, *55*(4), 851–875. doi: 10.5465/amj.2010.0562

Chapman, B. P., Fiscella, K., Kawachi, I., Duberstein, P., & Muennig, P. (2013). Emotion suppression and mortality risk over a 12-year follow-up. *Journal of Psychosomatic Research*, *75*(4), 381–385. doi: 10.1016/j.jpsychores.2013.07.014

Choroszewicz, M. (2020). The centrality of soft skills in sustaining masculine ideals in lawyers' career progression in Finland and Quebec. In K. Aavik, C. Bland, J. Hoegaerts & J. Salminen (Eds.), *Men, Masculinities and the Modern Career* (pp. 89–108). Berlin: De Gruyter. doi: 10.1515/9783110651874

Choroszewicz, M., & Adams, T. L. (2019a). *Gender, Age and Inequality in the Professions.* New York & London: Routledge. doi: 10.4324/9781351052467

Choroszewicz, M., & Adams, T. L. (2019b). Gender and age in the professions: Intersectionality, meta-work, and social change. *Professions and Professionalism*, *9*(2), 1–13. doi: 10.7577/p3432

Choroszewicz, M., & Kay, F. M. (2020). The use of mobile technologies for work-to-family boundary permeability: The case of Finnish and Canadian male lawyers. *Human Relations*, *73*(10), 1388–1414. https://journals.sagepub.com/doi/10.1177/0018726719865762

Choroszewicz, M., & Kay, F. M. (2022). Understanding gender inequality in the legal profession. In R. Abel, H. Sommerlad, O. Hammerslev & U. Schultz (Eds.), *Lawyers in 21st Century Societies: Vol. 2 Comparisons and Theories* (pp. 127–149). Oxford: Hart.

Choroszewicz, M., & Tremblay, D. G. (2018). Parental leave policy by male lawyers in Helsinki and Montreal: Professional and cultural barriers to male lawyers' use of paternity and parental leaves. *International Journal of the Legal Profession*, *25*(3), 303–316. doi: 10.1080/09695958.2018.1456435

Cleveland, J. N., Stockdale, M., & Murphy, K. R. (2000). *Women and Men in Organizations: Sex and Gender Issues at Work.* New York: Lawrence Erlbaum Associates. doi: 10.4324/9781410601384

Collier, R. (2015). Naming men as men in corporate legal practice: Gender and the idea of 'virtually 24/7 commitment' in law. *Fordham Law Review*, *83*(5), 2387–2406. https://ir.lawnet.fordham.edu/flr/vol83/iss5/10

Collinson, D. L., & Hearn, J. (1994). Naming men as men: Implications for work, organization and management. *Gender, Work and Organization*, *1*(1), 2–22. doi: 10.1111/j.1468-0432.1994.tb00002.x

Collinson, D. L., & Hearn, J. (1996). Breaking the silence: On men, masculinities and management. In D. L. Collinson & J. Hearn (Eds.), *Men as Managers, Managers as Men* (pp. 1–24). London: Sage Publications. doi: 10.4135/9781446280102.n1

Connell, R. W. (1998). Masculinities and globalization. *Men and Masculinities*, *1*(1), 3–23. doi: 10.1177/1097184X98001001001

Connell, R. W., & Messerschmidt, J. W. (2005). Hegemonic masculinity: Rethinking the concept. *Gender and Society*, *19*(6), 829–859. www.jstor.org/stable/27640853

Connell, R. W., & Wood, J. (2005). Globalization and business masculinities. *Men and Masculinities*, *7*(4), 347–364. doi: 10.1177/1097184X03260969

Corbett, C. (2019). A young man's game: Age and gender in technology jobs. In M. Choroszewicz & T. L. Adams (Eds.) *Gender, Age and Inequality in the Professions* (pp. 213–243). New York: Routledge. doi: 10.4324/9781351052467-12

Cottingham, M., & Dill, J. (2019). Intergenerational dynamics among women and men in nursing. In M. Choroszewicz & T. L. Adams (Eds.) *Gender, Age and Inequality in the Professions* (pp. 58–75). New York: Routledge. doi: 10.4324/9781351052467-4

Elfving-Hwang, J. (2020). Competency as an embodied social practice: Clothing, presentation of self and corporate masculinity in South Korea. In K. Aavik, C. Bland, J. Hoegaerts & J. Salminen (Eds.), *Men, Masculinities and the Modern Career* (pp. 133–152). Berlin: De Gruyter. doi: 10.1515/9783110651874

Elliott, A. (2008). *Making the Cut: How Cosmetic Surgery Is Transforming Our Lives.* London: Reaktion Books. doi: 10.1111/j.1468-4446.2009.01277_4.x

Fox, B. (2009). *When Couples Become Parents: The Creation of Gender in the Transition to Parenthood.* Toronto: University of Toronto Press. doi: 10.3138/9781442697515

Francis, A. (2015). Legal education, social mobility, and employability: Possible selves, curriculum intervention, and the role of legal work experience. *Journal of Law and Society*, *42*(2), 173–201. doi: 10.1111/j.1467- 6478.2015.00704.x

Galanter, M., & Henderson, W. (2008). The elastic tournament: A second transformation of the big law firm. *Stanford Law Review*, *60*(6), 1867–1930.

Greenhaus, J. H., Callanan, G. A., & Godshalk, V. M. (2010). *Career Management*, 4th edition. Thousand Oaks, CA: SAGE.

Griffin, P. (2012). Gender global finance: Crisis, masculinity, and responsibility. *Men and Masculinities*, *16*(1), 9–34. doi: 10.1177/1097184X12468097

Hall, D. T. (2002). *Careers In and Out of Organisations.* Thousand Oaks, CA: Sage.

Haynes, K. (2012). Body beautiful? Gender, identity and the body in professional service firms. *Gender, Work and Organization*, *19*(5), 489–507. doi: 10.1111/j.1468-0432.2011.00583.x

Hearn, J., Biese, I., Choroszewicz, M., & Husu, L. (2016). Gender, diversity and intersectionality in professions and potential professions: Analytical, historical and contemporary perspectives. In M. Dent, I. Bourgeault, J. L. Denis & E. Kuhlmann (Eds.), *The Routledge Companion in the Professions and Professionalism* (pp. 57–70). London: Routledge. doi: 10.4324/9781315779447

Hearn, J., & Collinson, D. L. (1998). Men, masculinities, managements and organizational culture. *Zeitschrift für Personalforschung*, *12*(2), 210–222. doi: 10.1177/239700229801200205

Hearn, J., & Husu, L. (2019). Age-gender relations in the academic profession: Putting the challenges of entry and early career into context. In M. Choroszewicz & T. L. Adams (Eds.), *Gender, Age and Inequality in the Professions* (pp. 193–212). New York: Routledge. doi: 10.4324/9781351052467-11

Hearn, J., Jyrkinen, M., Karjalainen, M., Niemistö, C., & Piekkari, R. (2017). Top men in transnational companies. In H. Peterson (Ed.), *Gender in Transnational Knowledge Work* (pp. 99–118). Cham: Springer International Publishing. doi: 10.1007/978-3-319-43307-3_6

Hearn, J., & Niemistö, C. (2012). Men, managers, fathers and home-work relations: National context, organisational policies, and individual lives. In P. McDonald & E. Jeanes (Eds.), *Men, Wage Work and Family* (pp. 95–113). London: Routledge. doi: 10.4324/9780203115091

Hearn, J., & Piekkari, R. (2005). Gendered leaderships and leaderships on gender policy: National context, corporate structures, and chief human resource managers in transnational corporations. *Leadership*, *1*(4), 429–454. doi: 10.1177/1742715005057450

Heppner, R. S. (2013). *The Lost Leaders*. New York: Palgrave Macmillan. doi: 10.1057/9781137350701

Hobson, B., Fahlén, S., & Takács, J. (2011). Agency and capabilities to achieve a work-life balance: A comparison of Sweden and Hungary. *Social Politics*, 18(2), 168–198. doi: 10.1093/sp/jxr007

Hochschild, A. (1983). *The Managed Heart: Commercialization of Human Feeling*. Berkley: University of California Press. doi: 10.1002/pam.4050030365

Hochschild, A. (2002). The sociology of emotion as a way of seeing. In G. Bendelow & S. J. Williams (Eds.), *Emotions in Social Life: Critical Themes and Contemporary Issues* (pp. 3–15). London: Routledge. doi: 10.4324/9780203494325

Holgersson, C. (2013). Recruiting managing directors: Doing homosociality. *Gender, Work and Organization*, *20*(4), 454–466. doi: 10.1111/j.1468-0432.2012.00595.x

Holvino, E. (2010). Intersections: The simultaneity of race, gender and class in organization studies. *Gender, Work and Organization*, *17*(3), 248–277. doi: 10.1111/j.1468-0432.2008.00400.x

Howard, J. A. (2000). Social psychology of identities. *Annual Review of Sociology*, *26*(1), 367–393.

Hyvönen, H. (2020). Care for the self – But not for the career? Men's perceptions of work-related self-care. In K. Aavik, C. Bland, J. Hoegaerts & J. Salminen (Eds.), *Men, Masculinities and the Modern Career* (pp. 15–34). Berlin: De Gruyter. doi: 10.1515/9783110651874

Jyrkinen, M., Niemistö, C., & Hearn, J. (2017). Career, care and time: Women top managers in the intersections of age, gender and work/family. In I. Aaltio, A. J. Mills & J. H. Mills (Eds.), *Ageing, Organizations and Management: Constructive Discourses and Critical Perspectives* (pp. 229–252). New York: Palgrave Macmillan. doi: 10.1007/978-3-319-58813-1_11

Kangas, E. (2020). *Discourses of Fatherhood in Leadership and Organisations*. Dissertations, Jyväskylä University, Jyväskylä.

Kay, F. M. (2019). Launching careers in law: Entry to first jobs after law school. In M. Choroszewicz & T. L. Adams (Eds.), *Gender, Age and Inequality in the Professions* (pp. 95–113). New York: Routledge. doi: 10.4324/9781351052467-6

Kessler, S. R., Spector, P. E., Chang, C. H., & Parr, A. D. (2008). Organizational violence and aggression: Development of the three-factor violence climate survey. *Work and Stress*, *22*(2), 108–124. doi: 10.1080/02678370802187926

Kinser, A. E. (2010). *Motherhood and Feminism*. Berkeley, CA: Seal Press.

MacCormick, J. S., Dery, K., & Kolb, D. G. (2012). Engaged or just connected? Smartphones and employee engagement. *Organizational Dynamics*, *41*(3), 194–201. doi: 10.1016/j.orgdyn.2012.03.007

Mainiero, L. A., & Sullivan, S. E. (2006). *The Opt-Out Revolt: Why People are Leaving Companies to Create Kaleidoscope Careers*. Mountain View, CA: Davies Black Publishing.

Meriläinen, S., Tienari, J., & Valtonen, A. (2013). Headhunters and the 'ideal' executive body. *Organization*, *2*(1), 3–23. doi: 10.1177/1350508413496578

Moore, P. V. (2017). *The Quantified Self in Precarity. Work, Technology and What Counts*. New York: Routledge. doi: 10.4324/9781315561523

Moore, P. V., Upchurch, M., & Whittaker, X. (2018). *Humans and Machines at Work: Monitoring, Surveillance and Automation in Contemporary Capitalism*. Cham: Palgrave Macmillan. doi: 10.1007/978-3-319-58232-0

Mullan, K., & Wajcman, J. (2017). Have mobile devices changed working patterns in the 21st century? A time-diary of work extension in the UK. *Work, Employment and Society*, *33*(1), 3–20. doi: 10.1177/0950017017730529

O'Neil, D. A., & Bilimoria, D. (2005). Women's career development phases: Idealism, endurance, and reinvention. *Career Development International*, *10*(3), 168–189. doi: 10.1108/13620430510598300

Olakivi, A., & Wrede, S. (2019). Early career doctors and in/justice in work: The invisibility of gender in a 'male' profession. In M. Choroszewicz & T. L. Adams (Eds.), *Gender, Age and Inequality in the Professions* (pp. 24–40). New York & London: Routledge. doi: 10.4324/9781351052467-2

Penttinen, E., Jyrkinen, M., & Wide, E. (2019). *Emotional Workplace Abuse: A New Research Approach*. Cham: Palgrave Macmillan. doi: 10.1007/978-3-030-19993-7

Pierce, J. (1995). *Gender Trials: Emotional Lives in Contemporary Law Firms*. Berkeley, CA: University of California Press.

Sommerlad, H. (2016). "A pit to put women in": Professionalism, work intensification, sexualisation and work – life balance in the legal profession in England and Wales. *International Journal of the Legal Profession, 23*(1), 61–82. doi: 10.1080/09695958.2016.1140945

Spence, C., & Carter, C. (2014). An exploration of the professional habitus in the Big 4 accounting firms. *Work, Employment & Society, 28*(6), 946–962. doi: 10.1177/0950017013510762

Sterling, J. S., & Reichman, N. (2016). Overlooked and undervalued: Women in private law practice. *Annual Review of Law and Social Science, 12*(1), 373–393. doi: 10.1146/annurev-lawsocsci-120814-121705

Stovell, C., Collinson, D., Gatrell, C., & Radcliffe, L. (2017). Rethinking work-life balance and wellbeing: The perspectives of fathers. In C. L. Cooper & M. P. Leiter (Eds.) *The Routledge Companion to Wellbeing at Work* (pp. 221–234). London: Routledge. doi: 10.4324/9781315665979

Thornton, M. (2014). Hypercompetitiveness or a balanced life? Gendered discourses in the globalization of Australian law firms. *Legal Ethics, 17*(12), 153–176. doi: 10.5235/1460728X.17.2.153

Tinsley, C. H., Taeya, M. H., & Amantullah, E. T. (2015). Who should bring home the bacon? How deterministic views of gender constrain wage preferences. *Organizational Behavior and Human Decision Processes, 23*(1), 37–48. doi: 10.5465/ambpp.2013.11358abstract

Tomlinson, J., Baird, M., Berg, P., & Cooper, R. (2018). Flexible careers across the life course: Advancing theory research and practice. *Human Relations, 71*(1), 4–22.

Wajcman, J., & Rose, E. (2011). Constant connectivity: Rethinking interruptions at work. *Organization Studies, 32*(7), 941–961. doi: 10.1177/0170840611410829

Williams, J. C. (2000). *Unbending Gender: Why Family and Work Conflict and What To Do About It.* New York: Oxford University Press.

Wood, J. C. (2007). Conceptualizing cultures of violence and cultural change. In C. Stuart (Ed.), *Cultures of Violence: Interpersonal Violence in Historical Perspective.* London: Palgrave Macmillan. doi: 10.1057/9780230591820_4

12

CHANGING AND CHALLENGING WORK–LIFE NEGOTIATIONS FOR MEN AND ORGANIZATIONS

Majda Hrženjak

Introduction

This chapter is about how men and masculinities are spotlighted in work–life balance (WLB) studies and policy discourses. It proceeds from the assumption that relations between men and masculinities, WLB and organizations are not simple and straightforward, but complex processes of negotiations and controversial adjustments to diverse challenges of working and private life. Rather than asserting their free choice or being entirely subjected to structural limitations, in pursuing WLB men have to negotiate and juggle organizational and identity constraints (leaving aside here political negotiations with the state and negotiations with intimate partners). The engagement of men in the demand for a better WLB is also a challenge for organizations that need to redefine the masculinized norm of the ideal carefree worker and negotiate more employee-friendly organizational cultures with employees, trade unions and the state.

The notion of WLB evolved mostly in Western countries since 1960, with proliferation in recent decades (Lewis & Cooper, 2005). It has been driven by "radical transitions from modernity to contemporary modernity" (Crespi & Ruspini, 2016), including globalization, deindustrialization and destandardization of increasingly precarious labour which has diversified workplaces, life courses and the organization of households in the twenty-first century (Bianchi & Milkie, 2010). Women's increasing labour market participation, consequent erosion of the male breadwinner and female caretaker family model, and state support for involved fatherhood are just a few of these changes, which in recent decades have been accompanied by structural constraints of the neoliberal economy (Walker & Roberts, 2018).

WLB is a contested concept which is reflected in diverse terminology ranging from individualized notions of work–family conflict, work–life integration, reconciliation of work and family (Gregory & Milner, 2009) to emerging more critical and structural notions like dual agenda (Rapoport et al., 2002), socially sustainable work (Brewster, 2004), healthy organization (Chung & van der Lippe, 2020) and corporate responsibility (Grayson, 2017). As Connell (2005) says, the issues of WLB emerged from the historical weakening of the gender order in which masculinities and femininities were attached to distinct spheres of home and workplace. As such, WLB, even with its critiques, is fundamentally linked with gender justice,

DOI: 10.4324/9781003193579-14

and it is important to make men and masculinities visible in how they shape and are shaped by WLB practices and discourses.

In this brief review of the literature, we follow Felstead et al.'s (2002, p. 56) definition of WLB as "the relationship of institutional and cultural times and spaces of work and non-work in societies where income is predominantly generated and distributed through labour markets". First, we outline theoretical contours of the WLB concept and how it was implemented in critical studies of men and masculinities (CSMM). Next, we overview the main topics that appear in CSMM on WLB. In the conclusion, we point to issues, which would deserve more research attention to critically explore the potentials of the WLB concept.

Contested concept of work/family/life/non-work balance

The initial notion of work and family balance has been seen through the lens of accommodating the growing participation of women, in particular working mothers, in paid work from the 1960s. It highlighted women's unpaid care work in the family by asking who will take care of children if women would work and it opened up the issue of gender equality in the labour market by disclosing the gendered substructure of organizations and labour markets (Acker, 1991). In contrast to work and family reconciliation, WLB terminology is positioned as gender-neutral,[1] thus countering the focus on women and challenging assumptions about separate, gendered spheres of work and family (Lewis et al., 2007). However, despite the gender inclusivity of WLB discourses, in practice in many organizational contexts, the negotiation of work and family still tends to be interpreted as primarily a women's issue. The category of femininity is as taken-for-granted in WLB discourses as the category of masculinity is self-evident, but unproblematized in the areas of work, politics, the military, etc. That is why, as pointed out by CSMM scholars (Puchert et al., 2005; Scambor et al., 2014), explicitly naming and making visible men in WLB debates is important to tackle underlying gendered assumptions, norms and practices that persist in contemporary workplaces.

Some authors point to the limited consideration that has been given to the heterogeneity of contemporary life courses, families and the labour force in the WLB literature. The research constructs WLB as primarily a concern of middle-class, dual-career, heteronormative couples in which caring for dependent children is the relevant load in the life part of the WLB. The majority of the studies about WLB actually continue to account for the work–family balance, which reflects also in studies of men and WLB as they do in large majority pertain to fatherhood. However, pluralization of lifestyles and families is taking place in contemporary modernity, as with, for example, increases in single parenting, after-divorce, re-organized, transnational and extended families, elder couples with a need for extensive spousal care, families with disabled family members, sets of childless adults, LGBT+ couples. In addition to the massive presence of women in the labour market, there is an increasing rate of active older workers, workers with long-standing health problems or disability, migrant and transnational workers, etc. who have diverse needs and interests outside work (Gragnano, 2020; Casper et al., 2017). The diversity of social locations and intersectional inequalities still needs to be taken up by WLB research. Keeney et al. (2013) identified eight non-work domains of relevance in WLB: education, health, leisure, friendships, romantic relationships, family, household management and community involvement. The relative importance of these life domains is likely to change over time within the same person because of changes in interests and life circumstances. Feminist scholarship, however, argues that the domain of care should be given a priority within WLB studies. Strategies equating care with other activities tend to obscure how care is a precondition for social sustainability, is largely (unpaid) work, and in turn tends to conceal gender inequalities. The need for more profound structural changes in organizations and workplaces, to accommodate social reproduction, should not be omitted from the gender-neutral WLB discourse (Lewis et al., 2007).

A shift from a focus on gender equality to one on health and well-being was observed recently in WLB discourse (Bergman & Schiffbänker, 2016). As stated by Keeney et al. (2013), the relevance of health to WLB derives from an increase in the rate of elderly workers, with a higher incidence of health problems. Others emphasize that the growing importance of health and well-being in WLB reflects profound changes in the nature of work and workplaces related to globalization, deregulation, the weakened negotiation power of trade unions, reorganization of working processes and efficiency drives. Digitalization, the 24/7 workplace, new forms of work in many contexts resulted in more demanding, intensified working patterns and environments, long working hours and constant feelings of pressure (White et al., 2003). Concerns about stress and burnout, health and well-being associated with workplace changes in the 1980s and 1990s were brought together with the issues of women's participation and gender equality in the labour market.

As argued by Lewis et al. (2007), the use of the WLB discourse globally masks its culture-specific origin in the United States and the United Kingdom, and uncritical assumptions about the universality of the values of dominant neoliberal forms of capitalism. Scarce research attention has been paid to the transference, adaptation and implementation of WLB practices globally, which would explore the potentials and limitations of the WLB concept in a range of contexts with different types of welfare provisions, diverse histories and approaches to work–life conflicts and in various economic situations. Research that has been conducted points to the complex intersectional situation of intermeshing gender and racialized power inequalities and transnational relationships between Western clients and "third world" workers in relation to gender, race and postcoloniality (Rajan-Rankin, 2016).

How are men and masculinities positioned in WLB studies?

Men are debated in relation to WLB globally and within the gender-equality and health and well-being frameworks. CSMM analyse the complexity of men's inclusion in WLB from the perspective of the social regulation of masculinities in the context of hierarchical and competitive relations among men, outlined in Connell's (1995) concepts of hegemonic and multiple masculinities. The concept of hegemonic masculinity, which describes a culturally dominant position of men, subordinating women and marginalized men and maintaining patriarchal relations, is strongly related to men's status and power in paid work in the public sphere (Collinson & Hearn, 2005). Research on gender and work has examined how hegemonic masculinity is embedded in companies, organizations and workplaces. Gendered organizations reflect the assumption of separate gendered public and private spheres like the male breadwinner family model despite representing an increasing minority in contemporary societies. The anachronistic assumption that ideal workers do not have active family responsibilities and that full-time work and uninterrupted career are the norm underpins the devaluing alternative working patterns (Acker, 1991; Crompton et al., 2007). It has been thoroughly analysed how a notion of abstract worker has been gender-blind and shaped according to the allegedly gender-neutral androcentric norms, not only subordinating women but also putting pressure on men (Acker, 1991). Men who transgress gendered norms of work organizations such as full-time work, overwork or negotiate their availability to the employer because of family responsibilities pose a challenge to conventional attitudes, shake the gendered sub-structure of the organization and in so doing become highly visible (Kanter, 1977; Thompson, 2010).

CSMM have highlighted that social control between men and mutual competition for patriarchal dividend bring costs of masculinity such as stress, burnout, neglect of own health and impoverished intimate relationships (Levtov et al., 2015). In more gender-unequal contexts, health, well-being and self-care are accentuated in WLB discourses related to men as a more appealing gender-neutral approach. Edström et al. (2019) observe that a lack of WLB and its impacts on men's health were expressed in many countries undergoing economic transition, like Ukraine, Turkey, Egypt and Algeria. Health and well-being discourses focus on the costs of hegemonic masculinity and the potential benefits of better WLB for men such as better relationships with less probability of conflict and violence, reduced risk-taking and improved health (van der Gaag et al., 2019).

Hegemonic masculinity has been analysed as closely related to a male norm of the family absent breadwinner, which has been challenged not only by the mass entrance of women into paid work but also by the neoliberal restructuring of the economy (Walker & Roberts, 2018). Industrial working-class-based men have been left adrift as employment in manufacturing and production has decreased. Secure male employment has been displaced by globalization, new technology and the rise of the feminized service economy.

Theoretical accounts of neoliberal reorganization of gender relations (accompanied by a political commitment to gender equality with a focus on labour market equality) call for reimagining masculinity by limiting the centrality of paid work in men's lives and identities and developing a notion of caring masculinity (Hanlon, 2012), which Elliott (2015) defines as identities and practices that reject domination and embrace values of care like positive emotion, interdependence and relationality. Indeed, some empirical studies point to men's practical and attitudinal change with regard to caring. In particular, a shift from an absent, emotionally distant father towards active, nurturing and involved fatherhood was observed (Kaufman, 2013; Scambor et al., 2014), while men's involvement in elder care remains less explored (Björk, 2015; Campbell & Carroll, 2007). Fatherhood is established as a discursive and political terrain, in which negotiations take place about the redefinition of the attitude of men to women, children and the family that presumes also a different attitude to paid work (Williams, 1998; Hobson, 2002). Holter (2007) argues that caring men often confront a traditional norm of corporate masculinity in their job. In this context, research about men's WLB practices related to family, care/parenting and gender equality flourish. In what follows, we overview this quantitatively dominant stream of research, while in the subsequent discussion we outline some emerging themes that widen the framework in which men and WLB can be further explored.

Organizational support and constraints for involved fathers: changes towards employee-friendly and gender-equal workplaces

Hobson (2002) places the establishment of norms and practices of fatherhood within the mutual co-effect of the state, the labour market and the family. The state with its policies is critical for the social regulation of gender relations, especially with policies that regulate family relations, care rights and obligations, including fatherhood. In the European context, with Nordic countries as a role model, the most targeted shift from the father-breadwinner to an involved father has been made through the gender-neutral definition of rights to parental leave, the introduction of specific paternal leave and daddy's quota, driven by gender-equality agendas. However, Plantenga and Remery (2005) emphasize that it is the organizational level of the workplace where the details of the work and private life negotiations are worked out.

A consensus reached in fatherhood scholarship reveals that contemporary fathers confront contrasting expectations to perform well as fathers and as ideal, carefree workers and breadwinners simultaneously which exposes men to complex work–family negotiations (Kaufman, 2013). Research points out that even though most organizations are built on and reproduce traditional gender roles, there has been some diversification in organizational cultures driven by gender-equality and WLB policies (Bergman & Schiffbänker, 2016). On the one hand, organizations driven by caring ethics are committed to family-friendly policies and gender equality and willing to accommodate men's WLB needs like paternity leave and flexible working without sanctioning and devaluing them for not meeting expectations of men as carefree workers. On the other hand, companies with masculine ethics are characterized by long working hours, prioritizing work over family and promoting male breadwinner norms. Sectoral analysis revealed that relatively WLB-friendly workplaces prevail in public female-dominated sectors and large companies with strong collective agreements, while male-dominated sectors, concentrated in the private sector, largely continue to ignore WLB policies.

Berdahl et al. (2018, p. 422, and this volume) argue that "a key reason why the workplace gender revolution has stalled is that work remains a site of masculinity contests among men". Their study shows that masculinity contests are the most prevalent in male-dominated organizations where extreme resources (such as wealth, power, fame) or precarious resources (risky or dangerous "men's" work) are at stake and where men compete at work by demonstrating a single-minded focus on competitiveness, professional success and masculine norms also determine attitudes about WLB (ibid., p. 430). Work as masculinity contests resonates with a notion of transnational business masculinity of contemporary global companies and transnational organizations described as increasingly hegemonic, marked by egocentrism, conditional loyalties and a declining sense of responsibility for others (Connell & Wood, 2005). Research on WLB in transnational and highly professional sites points to flexible working cultures in which organizational norms of high-performance and maximizing profits are internalized by employees who themselves become the motivating force of disciplinary processes (Kvande, 2009; Hearn et al., 2017; Thornton, 2016).

Stovell et al. (2017) argue that concepts of masculine identity and unsupportive organizational cultures are the main and interlinked constraints men confront in their WLB. While negotiating WLB can be viewed as a threat to traditional visions of men as a breadwinner, organizations fail to see men as potential carers with family responsibilities and penalize those who strive for greater WLB. Ewald et al. (2020) point to the invisibility of fatherhood in the workplace, which reproduces the organizational norms that underpin men's reluctance and inability to adopt family-friendly working patterns. However, the picture is complex, involving a range of factors shaping men's attitudes, capacities and opportunities towards WLB arrangements which do not only vary between countries but also between social classes, ethnicity/race, education, age, sexual preferences, citizenship status, diverse family arrangements, etc.

Different occupations, sectors of employment, levels of jobs, etc. have been to some extent spotlighted in research, and they sometimes resonate with class analysis. Administrative and white-collar jobs are by the structure of activities less time restricted and thus more open for flexible working patterns. Production and blue-collar jobs are in many cases highly formalized, which tends to be structurally and, if masculinized, also culturally adverse for carers. Research has pointed out that fathers with a lower level of education and job skills are often juggling multiple jobs to fulfil their provider role and have less access to flexible working arrangements than higher status workers (Ewald et al., 2020). Despite enhancing autonomy at work, being self-employed has been found to create more WLB conflict not less (Craig et al., 2012). Fathers in insecure and precarious employment, often young men, are unlikely to be in a position to reduce their working hours (Hrženjak & Humer, 2018).

Most research has focused on managerial and professional men (Stovell et al., 2017; Kvande, 2009), indicating that they face expectations to fully devote themselves to their career progress, which involve long working hours, constant availability for work, presenteeism and prioritizing work over family. Such expectations clash with involved fathering and seeking WLB arrangements may be seen as deviations from professional and gender norms as work devotion is tightly linked to masculine identity. In particular, for managers the gap between the ideal manager and the involved father might serve as significant sources of conflict in men's lives (Ford & Collinson, 2011; Geszler, 2016). Although managerial and professional men have more access to WLB arrangements and resources to afford them, they are less likely to use them because of the workplace and occupational normative assumptions. However, it could also be related to some men's attachments to particular notions of masculine and career-based identities. Some research points out that managers often turn to paid nannies and cleaners, grandmothers, part-time or stay-at-home partners, rather than pursuing cultural change towards better WLB in the organization which they lead (Hrženjak & Humer, 2018).

A prominent theme in research pertains to men's low take-up of the spatial and temporal flexible working arrangements and parental/paternity leave as the most prevalent WLB measure (Brandth & Kvande, 2016, 2019; Borgkvist et al., 2018). Research suggests that in many organizations there is still a persistent stigma against men taking long periods off and that fathers are more likely than mothers to experience their requests for flexible working being turned down. Alternatively, fathers are expected to prioritize work even when they work flexibly for childcare purposes. The study of gender differences in the perceptions and experiences of flexibility stigma, that is, the belief that workers who use flexible working arrangements for care purposes are less productive and less committed to the workplace, shows that flexibility stigma is gendered. Such perceptions not only are limited to managers but include colleagues and co-workers too and may heavily influence the take-up of flexible working arrangements (Coltrane et al., 2013). Chung (2018) shows that men are more likely to believe that workers who work flexibly are likely to make more work for others and are less likely to get promoted. Men are also more likely to say that they themselves have suffered due to colleagues working flexibly.

Studies indicate that organizational cultures, that is, "rules and expectations for behaviour that arise through both the deliberate actions of leadership and the on-going interaction of group members", have considerable impact on the values, attitudes and actions of employees in both work and non-work domains (Bowen & Orthner, 1991, p. 117). Even in the countries where WLB for men is high on the political agenda and surveys indicate men's willingness to become more involved in parental leave (as in Austria), when men in organizations characterized by a masculine ethic negotiate paternity leave, their main motive is to avoid causing the company any inconvenience and to avoid any risks in terms of career progress, wage reduction or job loss. On the other hand, in more gender-equal and WLB-driven companies, fathers are confident that their employers support the practice of paternity leave and negotiate a longer period of leave without expecting any trouble or obstacles when returning to work (Bergman & Schiffbänker, 2016).

The recent empirical study, *Men in Care: Workplace Support for Caring Masculinities*, conducted in 21 organizations across different sectors in 6 European countries (Austria, Norway, Iceland, Poland, Slovenia and Spain) identified barriers and supportive factors for men's caring involvements and examples of already implemented organizational WLB measures (Gärtner et al., 2021). The study found that companies can be gender-equality driven, care-value driven, productivity-competition driven or progress-innovation driven to introduce WLB measures. These range from tailored-made solutions such as additional paternity/maternity leave, flexitime, tight time schedule, accumulating working hours, a flexible number of work hours during the child's first year, teleworking, formal and informal shift changes, a sabbatical year, child time bonus, financial support for children, to health promotion at the workplace, personal coaching and employees' support networks. The most progressive (and the most rarely implemented) adaptation pertains to a shorter working week without reducing salaries. Research reveals that as a rule organizational WLB measures are gender-neutral and do not specifically address men. Consequently, male employees demonstrate a lack of knowledge about the measures they are entitled to. Because of the gender and organizational norms that construct fathers as workers, rather than as workers and carers, men are often not aware of their rights as carers or they do not perceive themselves as recipients of WLB measures. An identified barrier for men's take-up of WLB measures is also a lack of speak up culture. While it is accepted that women publicly talk about their care-related stress, male employees lack organizational space where they could express their issues related to care without being perceived as "weak".

The evidence proves that unsupportive supervisors (line managers as well as top management) restrict the possibilities for fathers to negotiate WLB measures. A lack of a substitute may also be a reason that male employees do not use WLB measures, because their absence would result in increasing the workload for their colleagues. Due to the feeling of solidarity, a sense of obligation or even a feeling of guilt, men may feel reluctant to negotiate WLB measures. The study points to the importance of WLB measures being included in collective agreements as men generally tend not to take up the measures, which are not regulated in the collective agreements. This resonates with Kvande's (2009) finding that men need formal legitimization for their use of WLB measures. The promotion of women was identified as a supporting factor, as it is often accompanied by more openness to negotiation of active fatherhood at least at the level of organizational culture. That the presence of women can change the organizational culture is proved by studies of extremely masculinized organizations such as professional armies, where a larger share of women enhanced the importance of WLB measures (Vuga Beršnak, 2021).

Finally, some studies raise a question about whether temporal and spatial flexibility is indeed a genuine WLB solution. It has been argued that flexibility increases work–family conflict because of the blurred boundaries between work and private life (Thornton, 2016). Flexible arrangements and home working are often related to the expansion of work, its intensification, multitasking and working longer hours which occur, in particular, in companies with demanding work environments and pressures for career advancement (Gärtner et al., 2021; Lott & Chung, 2016). During the COVID-19 pandemic, the collapse of spatial boundaries between home and work has happened with increasing home working which tends to persist in post-pandemic times because many organizations found home working cost-effective (Lyttelton et al., 2021). This leads to new accommodations between fathering and organization, and some studies show that they are underpinned by a traditional gender division of labour in the household (van der Gaag et al., 2019).

This indicates that change towards more employee-friendly and gender-equal organizational WLB cultures are not simple, one-dimensional and unilineal and that WLB measures in themselves have contradictory effects on men and women. Moreover, some authors argue that, by favouring deregulated markets and the diminution of state involvement in social and economic affairs, the macro-context of global neoliberal developments constrain and even work against more employee-friendly, gender-equal and care-integrated workplaces and organizational cultures (Cornwall et al., 2016; Walker & Roberts, 2018).

Global neoliberalism and entrepreneurial subjectivity: contradictions, inequalities and backlashes in progressing towards employee-friendly and gender-equal workplaces

The global neoliberal economy upholds competitiveness, a culture of long working hours, the criteria of individual performance, the flexibility of working relationships and the erosion of workers' rights. Many companies pursued cost reduction by destandardization of employment patterns, which resulted in the precarisation of work and dualization of labour markets (Vosko, 2010; Kalleberg, 2011). These developments have been uneven across and within the regions and countries, having more detrimental effects at the margins of global capitalism and individual societies. Research from the European semiperiphery, that is, from Balkan, post-Soviet Union and Eastern European countries, reveals that the transition into neoliberal economic and welfare restructuring caused de-development with extensive social side effects such as high and structural unemployment, erosion of workers' rights and shrinking of the middle class (Blagojević, 2013). The rural, old, uneducated, or even the urban, educated, but unemployed were the most affected. In many contexts, it enforced re-traditionalization of the gender roles because in the situation of high unemployment and insecurity the pressure of breadwinning for men is becoming stronger (Cornwall et al., 2016). Ukhova (2020) argues for the importance of applying a class lens to the post-socialist re-traditionalization argument. Her analysis shows that gender inequalities in sharing unpaid care work increased in the early years of the post-socialist transition marked by a harsh economic downturn. However, this was a trajectory typical for lower-class households, because they were not able to buy-in services, which would enable women to participate in paid work.

Besides the class dimension, the transnationalization of livelihoods in many families should also be taken into consideration as a survival strategy in Central and Eastern Europe. The region has experienced large labour emigration in transition. On one hand, this has strengthened the traditional absent male breadwinning father role. On the other hand, the large-scale feminization of migration, which facilitates childcare and eldercare in affluent countries, has pushed many men into being "left-behind" fathers taking the sole responsibility for childcare. How men combine responsibilities for childcare and their work in such transnational family arrangements has received scarce attention in WLB studies (Lutz & Palenga-Möllenbeck, 2012; Parreñas Salazar, 2008).

Neoliberalism brought about new forms of governmentality and subjectivities. Rather than working hierarchically from the management down to the worker, power relations in modern companies now work – as in the Foucauldian notion of neoliberal governmentality – in the subject and through the subject (Walker & Roberts, 2018). Gollmitzer (2014) observes new entrepreneurial subjectivities that are seemingly voluntarily self-regulated and self-disciplined, established as flexible, mobile and agile, constantly upgraded, trained, re-programmed and re-invented, with all his or her interests and duties being subjected to work. The entrepreneurial subject asserts norms of individualism, meritocracy and a systematic denial of the structural power relations that are at work, both between the company and employees and between different categories of employees (Gill, 2014). Cook (2017) shows how the neoliberal turn in Japan after 1990 reduced the share of standard employment on the account of flexible irregular workers, that is, "freeters" that can be easily hired and fired. This prevented young men developing culturally normative work-centred breadwinning masculinities, which can have potentially important repercussions on forming family life. In order to avoid being socially stigmatized as freeters, young men negotiate aspirational masculinities that stress self-determined, self-responsible entrepreneurial masculine identities as coping strategies in precarious labour markets and as attempts to be socially perceived as successful despite their vulnerability.

Entrepreneurial subjectivities establish the normative legitimisation of greedy institutions (Egger de Campo, 2013), in which work is intensified and extensified in space and time also through new technologies that transform workers' potential accessibility into normative demand for his or her unlimited availability (Pajnik & Hrženjak, 2020). At the company level, this is often accompanied by new managerial techniques that proclaim high commitment cultures and cultures of excellence, which establish a connection between the self-fulfilling aspirations of employees and the achievement of organizational objectives that encourage the internalization of employers' demands and re-defines working longer and harder as individual free choice (Crompton et al., 2007). The logic of neoliberal working norms strengthens the imperative of the masculinized work-focused, carefree ideal worker. This has the effect of marginalizing employees who do not surrender to these norms. Though these norms prevail in private-sector companies competing on global markets and in specific working fields (for example, knowledge-based, financial, lawyer, media, and creative industry, gig economy, transport, transnational workplaces), the public sector also experiences these in the cost-cutting strategies of new public management.

A number of studies (for example, Lindisfarne & Neale, 2016; Walker & Roberts, 2018) have pointed to working-class men, young men and migrant men globally, along with women, as being negatively affected by globalization and neoliberalism. Many experience unemployment, work without contracts or long working hours and exploitation. They feel disrespected by others, fear losing their jobs and face uncertainties regarding the future and limited possibilities to survive. Robertson et al. (2018) stress the negative impacts that insecure employment, harsh labour conditions and unemployment have on working-class men and the associated multiple disadvantages on men's health and well-being. Social inequalities are being sharpened under neoliberalism and the approach that is aware of power differentials between men should remain central also in WLB studies.

Conclusion

To sum up, in this chapter, WLB has been discussed as a contested concept. Despite its gender-neutral positioning, it remains gender biased in organizational practices, which calls for expanding the visibility of CSMM in relation to WLB in research and organizational strategies. Existing research continues to be largely focused on parenting and family. It has been argued that from the perspective of the heterogeneity of contemporary life courses, families and labour force demographics, such focus seems too narrow, however, from the gender-equality perspective the focus on care should remain a priority. Given that eldercare is becoming a pressing problem in the Global North and that it remains "women's domain" to an even larger extent than childcare, the scope of care should be expanded in the WLB scholarship. With neoliberal deregulation, intensification and flexibilization of labour, the WLB concept becomes relevant also for employees' health and well-being. Inequalities in WLB between and within the regions and countries globally, including between different sectors, occupations and positions in organizations, deserve more research attention.

Men have been debated in WLB research primarily as fathers, stretched between work-centred, competitive and breadwinning norms of masculinity, and gendered norms of the androcentric, carefree ideal worker persisting in the organizations. Research points to the increasing heterogeneity of organizations with respect to the inclusion of men in WLB measures. Some organizations, mostly in public sectors, large companies and those with strong collective agreements, pursue gender equality. Alternatively, they are diversity, innovation and recruitment driven to implement gender-inclusive WLB measures that enable men to negotiate flexible work arrangements and take-up their statutory right to paternity leave. However, many companies, mostly men-dominated, in the private sector, at specific high demanding professional and managerial positions along with transnational workplaces, not only continue a traditional pattern of breadwinning masculinity as a norm of being "a real man" and worker but enforce the organizational culture which fosters the workplace as an arena for masculine contests. Studies of neoliberal developments, and those exploring non-Western contexts, indicate that the shift towards global neoliberal capitalism brings about contradictions, inequalities and backlashes in progressing towards employee-friendly and gender-equal workplaces. Neoliberalism introduces self-disciplining, competitive, performance-driven entrepreneurial subjectivities enforced by new managerial techniques and destandardization of labour, which is perceived as meritocratic and gender-neutral. These developments impact the re-traditionalization of gender roles, in particular, in less affluent countries and families at the (semi)periphery of capitalism, where working-class, young, racialized and migrant men strive to be able to provide for themselves and their families.

Further efforts in CSMM and WLB studies should widen the scope of research in exploring intersectional locations and multicultural contexts, new developments in labour organizations, such as the gig economy and digitalization, develop broader understandings of care, diverse family arrangements and life-course stages, and investigate WLB experiences as potential sites of resistance.

Note

1 According to the definition of the European Union Institute for Gender Equality (EIGE), the concept "gender-neutral" refers to policy, programme or situation that has no differential positive or negative impact in terms of gender relations or equality between women and men (https://eige.europa.eu/thesaurus/terms/1190). From the perspective of gender equality, this concept can be harmful because it does not take into account that women and gender-diverse people are not in the same "starting position" as men because of historical and social disadvantages. Moreover, feminist citizenship studies point out that the liberal ideal of gender-neutral social order of equal legal opportunities does not resolve the dilemma of equality and difference. They highlight that gender neutrality implies masculinity as a universal norm and as the centre in relation to which "other" genders are established (Sevenhuijsen, 1998).

References

Acker, J. (1991). Hierarchies, jobs, bodies: A theory of gendered organizations. *Gender & Society*, *4*(2), 139–158. doi: 10.1177/089124390004002002

Berdahl, J. L., Cooper, M., Glick, P., Livingston, R. W., & Williams, J. C. (2018). Work as a masculinity contest. *Journal of Social Issues*, *74*(3), 422–448. doi: 10.1111/josi.12289

Bergman, N., & Schiffbänker, H. (2016). Work-life balance and fathers in Austria? Empirical evidence at the company level. In I. Crespi & E. Ruspini (Eds.), *Balancing Work and Family in a Changing Society. The Fathers' Perspective* (pp. 113–128). Hampshire: Palgrave Macmillan.

Bianchi, S. M., & Milkie, M. A. (2010). Work and family research in the first decade of the 21st century. *Journal of Marriage and Family*, *72*(3), 705–725. doi: 10.1111/j.1741-3737.2010.00726.x

Björk, S. (2015). Doing, re-doing or undoing masculinity? Swedish men in the filial care of aging parents. *NORA: Nordic Journal of Feminist and Gender Research*, *23*(1), 20–35. doi: 10.1080/08038740.2014.978369

Blagojević, M. (2013). Transnationalisation and its absence: The Balkan semiperipheral perspective on masculinities. In J. Hearn, M. Blagojević & K. Harrison (Eds.), *Rethinking Transnational Men* (pp. 163–186). London: Routledge.

Borgkvist, A., Moore, V., Eliott, J., & Crabb, S. (2018). I might be a bit of a front runner: An analysis of men's uptake of flexible work arrangements and masculine identity. *Gender, Work and Organization*, *25*(6), 703–717. doi: 10.1111/gwao.12240

Bowen, G., & Orthner, D. (1991). Effects of organizational culture on fatherhood. In F. Bozett & S. Hanson (Eds.), *Fatherhood and Families in Cultural Context* (pp. 187–217). New York, NY: Springer.

Brandth, B., & Kvande, E. (2016). Fathers and flexible parental leave. *Work, Employment and Society*, *30*(2), 275–290. doi: 10.1177/0950017015590749

Brandth, B., & Kvande, E. (2019). Fathers' sense of entitlement to ear-marked and shared parental leave. *The Sociological Review*, *67*(5), 1154–1169. doi: 10.1177/0038026118809002

Brewster, C. (2004). Developing managers in Europe. *Advances in Developing Human Resources*, *6*(4), 399–403. doi: 10.1177/1523422304268379

Campbell, D. L., & Carroll, M. P. (2007). The incomplete revolution: Theorizing gender when studying men who provide care in aging parents. *Men and Masculinities*, *9*(4), 491–508. doi: 10.1177/1097184X05284222

Casper, W. J., Vaziri, H., Wayne, J. H., DeHauw, S., & Greenhaus J. (2017). The jingle-jangle of work-nonwork balance: A comprehensive and meta-analytic review of its meaning and measurement. *Journal of Applied Psychology*, *103*, 182–214. doi: 10.1037/apl0000259

Chung, H. (2018). Gender, flexibility stigma and the perceived negative consequences of flexible working in the UK. *Social Indicators Research*, *151*, 521–545. doi: 10.1007/s11205-018-2036-7

Chung, H., & van der Lippe, T. (2020). Flexible working, work – life balance, and gender equality: Introduction. *Social Indicators Research*, *151*, 365–381. doi: 10.1007/s11205-018-2025-x

Collinson, D. L., & Hearn, J. (2005). Men and masculinities in work, organizations and management. In M. Kimmel, J. Hearn & R. Connell (Eds.), *The Handbook of Studies on Men and Masculinities* (pp. 289–310). Thousand Oaks, CA: Sage.

Coltrane, S., Miller, E. C., DeHaan, T., & Stewart, L. (2013). Fathers and the flexibility stigma. *Journal of Social Issues*, *69*, 279–302. doi: 10.1111/josi.12015

Connell, R. W. (1995). *Masculinities*. Cambridge: Polity Press.

Connell, R. W. (2005). Work/life balance, gender equity and social change. *Australian Journal of Social Issues*, *40*(3), 369–383. doi: 10.1002/j.1839-4655.2005.tb00978.x

Connell, R. W., & Wood, J. (2005). Globalization and business masculinities. *Men and Masculinities*, *7*(4), 347–364. doi:10.1177/1097184X03260969

Cook, E. E. (2017). Aspirational labour, performativity and masculinities in the making. *Intersections: Gender and Sexualities in Asia and Pacific*, 41. www.researchgate.net/publication/320032758_'Aspirational_Labour_Performativity_and_Masculinities_in_the_Making' (November 2021).

Cornwall, A., Karioris, F. G., & Lindisfarne, N. (Eds.). (2016). *Masculinities Under Neoliberalism*. London: Zed.

Craig, L., Powell, A., & Cortis, N. (2012). Self-employment, work-family time and the gender division of labour. *Work, Employment and Society*, *26*(5), 716–734. doi: 10.1177/0950017012451642

Crespi, I., & Ruspini, E. (Eds.). (2016). *Balancing Work and Family in a Changing Society. The Fathers' Perspective*. Hampshire: Palgrave Macmillan.

Crompton, R., Lewis, S., & Lyonette, C. (2007). Continuities, changes and transformations. In R. Crompton, S. Lewis & C. Lyonette (Eds.), *Women, Men, Work and Family in Europe* (pp. 230–244). Hampshire: Palgrave Macmillan.

Edström, J., & Greig, A., with Aly, R., Walker, C., & Müller, C. (2019). *Masculinities and Transition: Summary Brief.* Brighton: IDS.

Egger de Campo, M. (2013). Contemporary greedy institutions: An essay on Lewis Coser's concept in the era of the hive mind. *Czech Sociological Review*, *49*(6), 969–987.

Elliott, K. (2015). Caring masculinities: Theorizing an emerging concept. *Men and Masculinities*, *19*(3), 240–259. doi: 10.1177/1097184X15576203

Ewald, A., Gilbert, E., & Huppatz, K. (2020). Fathering and flexible working arrangements: A systematic interdisciplinary review. *Journal of Family Theory Review*, *12*, 27–40. doi: 10.1111/jftr.12363

Felstead, A., Jewson, N., Phizacklea, A., & Walters, S. (2002). Opportunities to work at home in the context of work-life balance. *Human Resource Management Journal*, *12*(1), 54–76. doi: 10.1111/j.1748-8583.2002.tb00057.x

Ford, J., & Collinson, D. (2011). In search of the perfect manager? Work-life balance and managerial work. *Work, Employment and Society*, *25*(2), 257–273. doi: 10.1177/0950017011398895

Gärtner, M., Scambor, E., & Warat, M. (2021). Transnational Analysis of Studies in Organisations. Men in care. Workplace Support for Caring Masculinities. Retrieved Action Grant VS-2018–0417: MiC_org_transnational_report_april_2022.pdf (men-in-care.eu)

Geszler, N. (2016). Behaviour-based work-family conflict among Hungarian manager fathers. *Intersections. East European Journal of Society and Politics*, *2*(3). doi: 10.17356/ieejsp.v2i3.151

Gill, R. (2014). Unspeakable inequalities: Post feminism, entrepreneurial subjectivity, and repudiation of sexism among cultural workers. *Social Politics: International Studies in Gender, State and Society*, *21*(4), 509–528.

Gollmitzer, M. (2014). Precarious employed watchdogs? Perceptions of working conditions among freelancers and interns. *Journalism Practice*, *8*(6), 826–841.

Gragnano, A., Simbula, S., & Miglioretti, M. (2020). Work-life balance: Weighting the importance of work-family and work-health balance. *International Journal of Environmental Research and Public Health*, *17*(3), 907–919. doi: 10.3390/ijerph17030907.

Grayson, D. (2017). *Take Care. How to Be a Great Employer of Working Carers*. London: Emerald Publishing.

Gregory, A., & Milner, S. (2009). Editorial: Work – life balance: A matter of choice? *Gender, Work & Organization*, *16*(1), 1–13. doi: 10.1111/j.1468-0432.2008.00429.x

Hanlon, N. (2012). *Masculinities, Care and Equality: Identity and Nurture in Men's Lives*. Hampshire: Palgrave Macmillan.

Hearn, J., Jyrkinen, M., Karjalainen, M., Niemistö, C., & Piekkari, R. (2017). Top men in transnational companies. In H. Peterson (Ed.), *Gender in Transnational Knowledge Work. Crossroads of Knowledge* (pp. 99–118). Cham: Springer. doi: 10.1007/978-3-319-43307-3_6

Hobson, B. (Ed.). (2002). *Making Men into Fathers. Men, Masculinities and the Social Politics of Fatherhood*. Cambridge: University Press.

Holter, Ø. G. (2007). Men's work and family reconciliation in Europe. *Men and Masculinities*, *9*(4), 425–456. doi: 10.1177/1097184X06287794

Hrženjak, M., & Humer, Ž. (2018). Caring masculinities and flexibilisation of labour markets: Fathers in precarious and managerial employment in Slovenia. *Gender Questions*, *6*(1), 84–110.

Kalleberg, L. A. (2011). *Good Jobs, Bad Jobs. The Rise of Polarized and Precarious Employment Systems in the United States, 1970s to 2000s*. New York: Russell Sage Foundation.

Kanter, R. M. (1977). Some effects of proportions on group life: Skewed sex ratios and responses to token women. *American Journal of Sociology*, *82*(5), 965–990.

Kaufman, G. (2013). *Superdads. How Fathers Balance Work and Family in the 21st Century*. New York: New York University Press.

Keeney, J., Boyd, E. M., Sinha, R., Westring, A. F., & Ryan, A. M. (2013). From work-family to work-life: Broadening our conceptualization and measurement. *Journal of Vocational Behavior*, *82*(3), 221–237. doi: 10.1016/j.jvb.2013.01.005

Kvande, E. (2009). Work – life balance for fathers in globalized knowledge work. Some insights from the Norwegian context. *Gender, Work & Organization*, *16*(1), 58–72. doi: 10.1111/j.1468-0432.2008.00430.x

Levtov, R., van der Gaag, N., Greene, M., Kaufman, M., & Barker, G. (2015). *State of the World's Fathers: A MenCare Advocacy Publication*. Washington DC: Promundo.

Lewis, S., & Cooper, C. L. (2005). *Work-Life Integration – Case Studies of Organizational Change*. Chichester: John Wiley & Sons.

Lewis, S., Gambles, R., & Rapoport, R. (2007). The constraints of a 'work – life balance' approach: An international perspective. *The International Journal of Human Resource Management*, *18*(3), 360–373. doi: 10.1080/09585190601165577

Lindisfarne, N., & Neale, J. (2016). Masculinities and the lived experiences of neoliberalism. In A. Cornwall, F. G. Karioris & N. Lindisfarne (Eds.), *Masculinities under Neoliberalism* (pp. 29–51). London: Zed.

Lot, Y., & Chung, H. (2016). Gender discrepancies in the outcomes of schedule control on overtime hours and income in Germany, *European Sociological Review*, *32*(6), 752–765. 10.1093/esr/jcw032

Lutz, H., & Palenga-Möllenbeck, E. (2012). Care workers, care drain, and care chains: Reflections on care, migration, and citizenship. *Social Politics: International Studies in Gender, State & Society*, *19*(1), 15–37. doi: 10.1093/sp/jxr026

Lyttelton, T., Zang, E., & Musick, K. (2021). Telecommuting and gender inequalities in parents' paid and unpaid work before and during the COVID-19 pandemic. *Journal of Marriage and Family*, *84*(1), 230–249. doi: 10.1111/jomf.12810

Pajnik M., & Hrženjak, M. (2020). Engendering media work: Institutionalizing the norms of entrepreneurial subjectivity. *Journalism*, *23*(2), 499–516. doi: 10.1177/1464884920922075

Parreñas Salazar, R. (2008). *Children of Global Migration: Transnational Families and Gendered Woes*. Stanford, CA: Stanford University Press.

Plantenga, J., & Remery, C. (2005). Reconciliation of Work and Private Life: A Comparative Review of Thirty European Countries. Retrieved 28 September, from www.researchgate.net/publication/46675255_Reconciliation_of_Work_and_Private_Life_A_Comparative_Review_of_Thirty_European_Countries

Puchert, R., Gärtner, M., & Höyng, S. (Eds.). (2005). *Work Changes Gender. Men and Equality in the Transition of Labour Forms*. Opladen: Barbara Budrich.

Rajan-Rankin, S. (2016). Paternalism and the paradox of work – life balance: Discourse and practice. *Community, Work & Family*, *19*(2), 227–241. doi: 10.1080/13668803.2016.1134131

Rapoport, R., Bailyn, L., Fletcher, J., & Pruitt, B. (2002). *Beyond Work-Family Balance: Advancing Gender Equity and Work Performance*. Chichester: Wiley.

Robertson, S., Gough, B., & Robinson, M. (2018). Masculinities and health inequalities within neoliberal economies. In C. Walker & S. Roberts (Eds.), *Masculinity, Labour, and Neoliberalism. Working-Class Men in International Perspective* (pp. 311–334). London: Palgrave Macmillan.

Scambor, E., Bergmann, N., Wojnicka, K., Belghiti-Mahut, S., Hearn, J., Holter, Ø. G., Gärtner, M., Hrženjak, M., Scambor, C., & White, A. (2014). Men and gender equality: European insights. *Men and Masculinities*, *17*(5), 552–577. doi: 10.1177/1097184X14558239

Sevenhuijsen, S. (1998). *Citizenship and the Ethics of Care: Feminist Considerations on Justice, Morality and Politics*. London: Routledge.

Stovell, C., Collinson, D. L., Gatrell, C., & Radcliffe, L. (2017). Rethinking work-life balance and well-being: The perspectives of fathers. In C. L. Cooper & M. P. Leiter (Eds.), *Routledge Companion to Wellbeing at Work* (pp. 221–234). London: Routledge.

Thompson, A. (2010). Men, Masculinities and Flexible Working. Plenary Speech at International Industrial Relations Association (IIRA) Conference 2010. Retrieved 28 November, from http://irep.ntu.ac.uk/id/eprint/27383/1/PubSub4804_Thompson.pdf

Thornton, M. (2016). Work/life or work/work? Corporate legal practice in the twenty-first century. *International Journal of the Legal Profession*, *23*(1), 13–39.

Ukhova, D. (2020). Gender division of domestic labor in post-socialist Europe (1994–2012): Test of class gradients hypothesis. *Social Inclusion*, *8*(4), 23–34. doi: 10.17645/si.v8i4.2972

van der Gaag, N., Heilman, B., Gupta, T., Nembhard, C., & Barker, G. (2019). *State of the World's Fathers: Unlocking the Power of Men's Care*. Washington DC: Promundo.

Vosko, F. L. (2010). *Managing the Margins. Gender, Citizenship, and the International Regulation of Precarious Employment*. Oxford: Oxford University Press.
Vuga Beršnak, J. (2021). *Kulturne značilnosti slovenske družbe in njen odnos do varnosti: vojska na stičišču zahtev države, pričakovanj družbe in lastne pohlepnosti*. Ljubljana: Založba FDV.
Walker, C., & Roberts, S. (Eds.). (2018). *Masculinity, Labour, and Neoliberalism: Working-Class Men in International Perspective*. London: Palgrave Macmillan.
White, M., Hill, S., McGovern, P., Mills, C., & Smeaton, D. (2003). High performance management practices, working hours and work-life balance. *British Journal of Industrial Relations*, *41*(2), 175–195. doi: 10.1111/1467-8543.00268
Williams, F. (1998). Troubled masculinities in social policy discourses: Fatherhood. In J. Popay, J. Hearn & J. Edwards (Eds.), *Men, Gender Divisions and Welfare* (pp. 63–101). London: Routledge.

13

BODIES, EMBODIMENT, BODYWORK, CARE, CARING AND SELF-CARE

Henri Hyvönen

Introduction

It is an often-repeated claim that men do not care. Current public discussions on conventional masculinities and their "toxicity" in comparison to some alternative performances of manhood often locate men's incapability to love and nurture at the heart of gender inequality (see de Boise, 2018; Waling, 2019). Elliott (2016), when discussing the conceptual and practical possibilities of "caring masculinities", argues that the current economic and sociocultural reality separates men from care both materially and discursively. Unpaid work in the reproductive arena has remained mainly the responsibility of women. Concurrently, men's dominance in the current gender order draws on and has contributed to the dominant forms of masculine ideology, under which men cannot show emotions associated with loving and nurturing interaction.

Care as an ambiguous concept makes it possible to say that men take care of many things. In addition to the "heroic male project" centred on shaping the external world (Whitehead, 2002, pp. 120–123), which motivates men to neglect reproductive labour and become carefree, some men's concern for their own social status motivates them to avoid expressing weakness and makes them strive for the impression of carelessness (Hanlon, 2012). Since the 1970s (Harrison, 1978), it has become an established notion that beliefs and actions about health organize the social hierarchy between men: some men use risky health behaviours to "demonstrate dominant – and hegemonic – masculine ideals that clearly establish them as men" (Courtenay, 2000, p. 1388). The COVID-19 pandemic has further problematized some men's lack of care for themselves and other people around them: when disregarding prevailing safety recommendations, men are at risk and men are a risk (Messerschmidt, 2021). Gilmore (1990) argues that in many cultures, "manhood" is an honorary status earned and maintained through sacrifice for others and by giving other people more than one takes from them. I suggest that constructing masculinity through normative statements on men's responsibilities has intensified as men are expected to become more involved in care. Men's incapability to show concern and care for themselves (Gough, 2018), other people (de Boise, 2018) and the environment (Aavik, 2021) has become the most visible threat to the legitimacy of men's moral and intellectual leadership, thus making care a necessary part of protecting men's collective interests in the current gender order.

DOI: 10.4324/9781003193579-15

Organizational life seems to be increasingly about care. In the post-industrialized labour market, men too are expected to participate in jobs offered and organized as services, in which work is done with other people instead of on a production line (Cottingham, 2017; Wolfman et al., 2021). Across the current Global North, work organizations need to adapt to sudden changes of direction and maintain their ability to produce value through the creativity and enthusiasm of individuals (Morini & Fumagalli, 2010). Hopes for the higher productivity of happy and healthy individuals (Ahmed, 2010; Binkley, 2014; Cederström & Spicer, 2015) are demonstrated in current organizations in both the personal example of managers who regulate the range of possible identities in the organization (Bardon et al., 2021; Johansson et al., 2017) and workplace health promotion including both physical exercise (James & Zoller, 2018) and therapeutic interventions (Karjalainen et al., 2021).

In this chapter, my task is to provide the reader with an account of how the growing importance of manifold types of "care" in current organizations shape and are shaped by men and masculinities. I deliberately stress the two-way nature of this change: I aim to deconstruct the dichotomy between men's power, often associated with dominance, harm and inequality, and men's caring capabilities by showing that caring relations are power relations that can produce dominance, harm and inequality. From a theoretical standpoint, this task is twofold as well. On the one hand, I discuss gender as a social structure (Connell, 2012; Hearn, 2014) by demonstrating changes in men's gender performances that maintain their structural power in times of crisis (Bridges & Pascoe, 2014). On the other hand, I draw on poststructural feminist accounts of agency and emotional reflexivity (Berggren, 2014; Waling, 2019) to discuss the ethos of care as manifold relationships of force that shape men's subjectivity and identity as well as their capabilities to act.

The remainder of this chapter is structured as follows. I begin with a brief discussion of the two main social categories I address in this chapter, namely the social category of men and the social category of care. Thereafter, I address research on (1) caring masculinities and men as caregivers, (2) care affecting men's bodies, and (3) men's work-related self-care, by which I refer to measures taken by individuals to improve their own health, well-being and happiness in the context of work. I conclude this chapter by discussing both new and long-term inequalities produced and reproduced in caring relations in organizations.

The social category of men and the social category of care

Feminist research on men is not entirely unanimous about whether men should be perceived primarily as a material-discursive social category to be analysed as dominant agents of social practices or as an identity category constituted by cultural processes (Hearn, 2014; Waling, 2019). Connell (2012, pp. 1676–1677) argues that "[p]oststructuralist gender theory, focusing on cultural processes, does not have much to say about economic processes, organizational life, material interests, or non-discursive forms of power". I acknowledge that materialist analyses of men and masculinities have been successful in preventing an overemphasis on men's identities and the analysis of symbolic systems at the expense of social reality. However, I also suggest that some critical materialist analyses downplay the relevance of men's identities, using the strategy of "naming men as men" (Hanmer, 1990; Hearn, 2014, p. 14), not as a necessary expansion of research focusing on discourse and identity, but as a critique of it. I argue that the relations between men and care not only are about men's interests that are already out there to be found but they are also produced, not simply reflected, by norms, wishes and fantasies expressed in public discussion (Elliott, 2016) and in the day-to-day management of men's work (Cottingham, 2017).

While uses of the concept of man vary, most scholars agree on who can be counted as members of the social category of men. The same cannot be said of the concept of care: just because feminist scholars work on care does not mean they speak about the same social phenomenon. Echoing Elliott (2016), I suggest that in the discussion on the relations between men and care, two separate theoretical families can be outlined. The first approach focuses on men as a relatively carefree social category in the current institutionalized division of labour (Niemistö et al., 2021; Tronto, 1993). Here, care is perceived as invisible, poorly rewarded and yet life-sustaining and necessary labour for society. The second approach perceives men as a social category whose members are not used to caring because their ability to experience and express feelings is limited. Theorists choosing this route emphasize care as an affect: by experiencing more care and letting themselves be affected and moved by caring moments, men could distance themselves from their will to dominate.

Hanlon, one of the key scholars on men and care, puts a lot of weight on care as an attitude and affect. Drawing from the relational theory of the gender order and the concept of hegemonic masculinity (see Connell, 2012), Hanlon (2012, p. 65) argues that in the current gender order, men remain "conflicted about the role of love and care, both in terms of recognising their own emotional needs and meeting them, and in terms of meeting the needs of significant others". This way of discussing care contrasts two ways of being a man: one of which is an identity complying with hegemonic masculinity, and the other, which is an emancipated caring masculinity that offers men ways of resisting and eventually knocking current hegemonic masculinity off its pedestal. The scholars emphasizing care as a positive and much-needed affect recognize that men can care and have cared before but in slightly the wrong way. Elliott (2016, pp. 248–249) makes use of a distinction between the practical tasks of care and the affective relations of care, suggesting that the latter is more valuable in reforming current gender relations as well as harder for men to achieve in the current political reality.

However, I argue that both care-as-labour and care-as-affect approaches reproduce a problematic take on men's power and hide it from the analytical gaze. They ignore one central standpoint, namely caring relations as power relations. As many critical perspectives point out, in critical studies on men and masculinities there has been over-optimism about the direct gender-progressive effects of men's changed practices and men's softer identities. In other words, caring relations are not understood as power relations but as a vehicle for undoing power relations (de Boise, 2018; Waling, 2019). When care is not viewed as an absolute value but as labour in which the subject of care is affected and transformed, the picture changes.

In the context of professional work done within permanent contracts, organizational power relations have started to develop in a seemingly more humane direction. The number of wellness initiatives in workplaces is growing globally (Cederström & Spicer, 2015; James & Zoller, 2018; Karjalainen et al., 2021), which can be taken as a sign of the "softening" of capitalism: management interferes with an individual's life not so much with a stick but with a carrot (Costea et al., 2008). Caring relations are currently turning into the most legitimized power relations. This situation forces men to adapt, but men's increased interest in care also affects the everyday meanings given to the concept of care. As de Boise (2018) points out, despite some men's seemingly feminized vocabulary focusing on emotions and their self-understanding as a "nice guy", their subjectivity is only partially constituted by the discourse aiming at subverting gender relations. Focusing only on what men say, how they judge themselves, and what their actions look like may overlook men's material, embodied and affective attachments to less progressive trends.

The partial reconfiguration of men's identities and practices, in which "toxic" behavioural traits make room for "healthy" ones (Waling, 2019), does not erase the masculinist characteristics of paid work and the institutionalized division of labour. Even in organizations where management is shifting away from the production line and onto individual lives, the objects of management are still viewed as projects. Well-being has become a measurable and optimizable proxy for high performance at work (Bardon et al., 2021; Karjalainen et al., 2021). Concurrently, the pursuit of happiness at work has become a way of encouraging individuals to put work before non-work (Binkley, 2014; Cederström & Spicer, 2015; Dailey et al., 2018). Even if more men are working in social services and healthcare, they have also started to describe the care they can and should provide as assertive, controlling and problem-solving in comparison to feminine modes of care that are considered "soft" (Jyrkinen et al., 2020).

The understandings of care as both an affective relation and compulsory, feminized labour in the current gender order have been fruitful in showing the ideological dilemma between men and care. As care is increasingly organized into paid work in which men too participate (Cottingham, 2017) and the word "care" has become a fashionable catchphrase and synonymous with ethical organizational practices (see Cederström & Spicer, 2015, pp. 45–47; Costea et al., 2008; Dailey et al., 2018), I suggest it is time to focus on how men as a dominant social group in current working life do things within caring relations and the concept of care, and how differences in caring capabilities shape inequalities among men and between masculinities. Therefore, I propose an understanding of care as a productive power relation: care is physical, mental, and emotional labour that maintains life and increases the quality of life. The definition of a good life is always a political question about what the purpose of human life is (Foucault, 2008). To say that organizations care about individual lives may be true and yet vague; rather, it may be more accurate to say that organizations implement *regimes of living* to affect the quality of individual life and to achieve certain purposes. Collier and Lakoff define a "regime of living" as

> a tentative and situated configuration of normative, technical, and political elements that are brought into alignment in situations that present ethical problems – that is, situations in which the question of how to live is at stake. Here the word regime suggests a "manner, method, or system of rule or government", including principles of reasoning, valuation, and practice that have a provisional consistency or coherence.
> *(Collier & Lakoff, 2005, p. 23)*

The relation between caring men and regimes of living is twofold. On the one hand, men are subject to these regimes in which their ability to care for the self and others is produced (Elliott, 2016; James & Zoller, 2018). On the other hand, caring relations, understood as realizing certain regimes of living, constitute a legitimate and accessible way for men to participate in working life in situations where men's visibly dominant gender performances characterized by aggression, conquering, hierarchy and emotional distance become more often noticed in a negative light (Connell & Wood, 2005; Cottingham, 2017; Messerschmidt, 2021; Wolfman et al., 2021). The question here is no longer whether men care, but rather what the productive effects are of the actions of men called "care".

Caring masculinities and men in organizations of care

To date, most scholars in the field of critical studies on men and masculinities have used the concept of masculinity and the framework of plural masculinities to depict differences within the social category of men. That approach to men and masculinities "that gives a central place to the patterned relations between women and men (and among women and among men) that constitute gender as a social structure" (Connell, 2012, p. 1677) has dominated this debate despite its critiques (Berggren, 2014; Hearn, 2012; Waling, 2019). Echoing Whitehead (2002, p. 99), I suggest that relational takes on men have repeatedly put forward a conception of men as "rational actors" who are excluded from the ideological forces that "they deploy". This "oppressor–victim" dualism has obscured the multiple processes of subjectivity and self-identity.

Elliott (2016, p. 240) defines caring masculinities as "masculine identities that reject domination and its associated traits and embrace values of care such as positive emotion, interdependence, and relationality". Elliott encourages a focus on men as subjects of power relations: policies, debates and directives in the EU encourage European societies to redefine nurturing as normal for boys and men and to promote the emergence of new forms of normal and normative masculinities. Concurrently, public images of men acting as emotionally secure caregivers have been commercialized and co-opted by many projects affecting men. Due to increased perceptions of conventional masculinities as "toxic" (Waling, 2019; Wolfman et al., 2021), public images of "healthy" masculinities are persuading men to believe that their "strength is not for hurting" (Masters, 2010), that they can support women by walking "a mile in her shoes" (Bridges & Pascoe, 2014, p. 250) and that they should act as "advocates and allies" for women, gay men and gender minorities (Gough, 2018, p. 66). Current "ethical entertainment" repeatedly shows images of strong men doing good deeds for weaker ones and extends "masculine expertise" to the areas of care and intimacy (Nikunen, 2016, p. 172). In these narratives about men who do good, masculinities are hybrid in nature: despite their references to a wide range of femininities, men are represented as heroes: strong, independent and problem-solving. As Waling (2019) points out, despite supporting boys and men to engage with emotion and vulnerability, the distinction between favourable and unfavourable masculinities works towards the depoliticization of men: gender difference is reconfigured and re-legitimized, rather than deconstructed, and the critique of men's social position in comparison to other genders is jeopardized.

The public discussions on caring masculinities aim at reinventing men's self-understandings and re-orienting their interests. The ideal of caring masculinity has succeeded in discursively challenging masculinism that binds men to workplaces. In the United States (Randles, 2018), Central Europe (Tanquerel & Grau-Grau, 2020) and the Nordic countries (Kangas & Lämsä, 2021), men are now searching for opportunities to relocate themselves closer to the emotional core of the family. The change in men's outspoken ethos does not, however, necessarily affect material practices, and therefore the scope of these changes must be seen as limited: recent studies on the ratio of time spent in unpaid to paid work for men and women do not show an abrupt change in men's participation in unpaid care (Niemistö et al., 2021). Also middle-class men living in a socio-cultural environment embracing participatory fatherhood struggle and feel ambivalent as they form their own ideas about masculinity and identity (Lund et al., 2019).

"For most men, any 'heroic project' begins when they leave for work" (Whitehead, 2002, p. 123), and this project is increasingly located in the field of care work. Public discussions on the need for caregivers have legitimized men's presence in, for example, social services and healthcare. Cottingham (2017) argues that in nursing, a reconfiguration of men's practices better suited to an era of post-industrialization is taking place. Cottingham also warns against the exclusiveness of this redefinition of masculinity: the possibility of perceiving the self and being perceived as "the emotionally adept man" is most often available to white, middle-class men, who are already associated with security and reliability and who have the most cultural capital and resources to review and redefine their own activities.

According to Drange and Karlsen (2016), ethnicity, alongside gender, is an important intersecting difference organizing the positions of different men in the healthcare sector. Ethnic majority men tend to work in organizations they perceive as more congruent with their identities as men: hospitals and psychiatric care. Men with disadvantaged identities, such as ethnic minority men, may be less able to avoid or move out of jobs considered low-level or feminized: under the intra-occupational segregation of care work, minority ethnic male nurses cluster in long-term care. White and heterosexual men are able to make more satisfying compromises in the current socio-economic situation: they seek out care labour that is compatible with their self-understandings and identities as men. In line with Bridges and Pascoe (2014, p. 246), I suggest that their incorporation of performances and identity elements associated with femininities is "selective": care is an arena in which men strive to demonstrate that they are both valuable employees and credible men. Men who feel they have chosen their job and experience agency in their work also find ways of legitimating their presence in care work by stressing assertiveness, being in control, and showing fearlessness in the face of risks as virtues in their line of work (Jyrkinen et al., 2020; Martínez-Morato et al., 2021).

Bodies, embodiment and bodywork

Siltala (2020) perceives the current emotional landscape of risks, stress and uncertainty in Western Europe and the United States as an outcome of their recent economic history. Since the 1970s, collective bargaining and trade unions have withered, and the freedom of capital movement has encouraged national politics to adapt to global competition. In the Global North, automation and global cheap labour have increased the supply of both high-paid expert work and service work. Morini and Fumagalli (2010) argue that the change in the mode of production affects value creation. In the Fordist model of production, the object of exchange was labour consisting of work input and the professional skills applied to it. In the contemporary bio-capitalist model of production, value binds to subjectivity itself and its creative potential. I deliberately start this section by focusing mainly on men as managers of knowledge-intensive work and the capillary effects of their work on their own bodies. Thereafter, I focus on their subordinates as well as men working in sectors less affected by the shift towards bio-capitalism.

Even if the value of the work has become blurred, the indicators of the value of the individual doing the work are becoming clearer and more concrete. Innovativeness, enthusiasm for work, and high tolerance for stress are increasingly associated with health-signalling bodies. There is a reformed perception among privileged men that there is a dichotomy between civilized and rational men and men who are seen as inferior due to their ethnic and/or class background. Farrimond (2012) argues that among men of higher socio-economic status, the conceptual reconstruction of the dominant masculine code in relation to health, a shift from "Neanderthal Man" to "Action Man", is an effort to maintain control and moral leadership in a situation where these qualities are increasingly associated with health and healthiness.

In contemporary organizations, bodies signalling unhealthy lifestyles are increasingly stigmatized. Doing visible work on one's own health is widely perceived as a way of expressing professionalism, loyalty to the organization and commitment to work. The ideological dilemma between masculinity and health awareness (Harrison, 1978; Courtenay, 2000) has been partially replaced by men's "hollow femininities": the neoliberal subject is coded, at least in part, as feminine (Wolfman et al., 2021), albeit men have also found ways of reconstructing their seemingly feminine behaviours in "masculine terms" (Gough, 2018, p. 19). Although men's identities as men and many masculinisms of working life have not withered, some men now define themselves through self-control rather than self-neglect. Siltala (2020) argues that in the current socio-economic reality, the continuities offered by class status are perceived as increasingly uncertain. Those who seek refuge from status threats pursue a sense of individual self-worth and moral superiority by demonstrating flexibility and conscientiousness and by blaming less adaptable individuals, organizations and identity groups for their weakness. Also Connell and Wood (2005) predicted this change as they separated "older bourgeois masculinities" characterized by snobbery, social authority and patriotism from the ascending "managerial masculinities" characterized by anxiety and heightened uncertainty about one's place in the world and gender order.

The shift towards bio-capitalism also shifts the gaze away from the production line and onto individuals, changing managers from controllers to role models. A healthy, fit and athletic body plays an essential role in contemporary managerial identities. Only "managerial bodies" that are found to be convincing enough are invited into organizations: Meriläinen et al. (2015, p. 3) demonstrate this by citing an executive search consultant who assumes that an organization looking for a manager wants a man who resembles "a hunting hound" and not "a St Bernard". As Giazitzoglu and Muzio (2021) point out, "corporate masculinity" is actively learned by men entering professional settings from non-privileged backgrounds. Managers who already have the necessary skills to offset any negative perceptions about their worth in the labour market actively perform their identities as competitive actors: the managerial body must be observed, the current condition of the body must be maintained, and certain characteristics of the body must be developed through eating habits and exercise (Bardon et al., 2021; Johansson et al., 2017; Riach & Cutcher, 2014).

Utilizing the notion of care as labour that consumes time and resources, care for one's own body can also be seen as work. In addition to informal organizational discourses that motivate people to do unpaid work on their bodies to maintain their aesthetic qualities (Mears, 2014), an increasing number of tasks on the organization's premises and during working hours have begun to sort, examine, and directly affect individual bodies. Basing recruitment decisions on body weight and appearance as an indication of health to avoid workers' sickness absence (Huzell & Larsson, 2012); by stigmatizing those who do not obediently participate in the health discourse (James & Zoller, 2018); and by naturalizing the connection between exercise and good results at work through scientific vocabulary (Karjalainen et al., 2021), healthism has turned into a norm that employees must embody in their daily working life in order to appear as credible professionals.

The relationship between managers and subordinates has a capillary quality: it does not consist so much of discipline as of highlighting positive opportunities and justifying the meaningfulness of seizing them. Even if the company "cannot command employees to eat properly", it can create "far-reaching norms about how they should work but also how they should live and relate to themselves in order to remain healthy and productive" (Cederström & Spicer, 2015, pp. 38–39). Differing from the Fordist management of life that relies on standardization, repression of subjectivity in its self-expressive mode and externally imposed control, contemporary healthist care for individual life encourages self-expression and authenticity while processes of self-examination, evaluation and reflection are kept under control (ibid., p. 18; Costea et al., 2008, p. 9). In contemporary organizational culture, care for the self is also care for one's own self-worth compared to others. By theorizing care as an exercise of power over individual life (Collier & Lakoff, 2005; Foucault, 2008) and "care" as a recurring slogan in organizations (Cederström & Spicer, 2015; Costea et al., 2008; Dailey et al., 2018), I argue that "domination" and "values of care" (Elliott, 2016, p. 241) often coincide, rather than oppose each other, in men's organizational lives.

So far, I have discussed men's health behaviour focusing mainly on middle-class men in knowledge-intensive work, ignoring the cultural and material environments in which working-class masculinities are constructed. In some of them, the body does not only signal performance, but to succeed at work in material terms, a man must embody endurance and strength even if talking about one's own health and expressing one's own feelings may appear to be a sign of weakness and inability (Courtenay, 2000). As Hanna et al. (2020, p. 632) point out, both health-neglecting and health-aware masculinities draw from the ideal of speed, strength and stamina, and therefore constitute " 'rational' individualized responses to structural deregulation and insecurity". Drawing on the example of the construction industry in the United Kingdom, these authors suggest that this congruence between two seemingly opposite gender performances has helped younger men shift towards some more health-conscious practices, even if they run alongside a widespread cultural tendency to demonstrate stoicism in the face of ill and use alcohol to ease work-related aches and pains.

Drawing on Ahmed's (2010) argument regarding "happiness duty", the expectation that we will be made happy by taking part in that which is deemed good, I suggest that health is a "happy object" (de Boise, 2018) that is part of more and more men's perceptions of a good life and respectable citizenship. On the other hand, the omnipresent healthism of contemporary working life also locates the body and the self in the centre of one's agency, judgement and action. The self that is being taken care of does not necessarily align with organizational discourses.

Self-care

Recent theoretical discussion in feminist research has focused on the problematics surrounding the naïve ideal of emancipation: as individuals are urged to practise self-care through such positive associations as "well-being", "wellness" and "loving your body", someone or something is already exercising power over those individuals (Gill & Elias, 2014). To illustrate this point, Heyes (2007, p. 82) turns the focus on how subjectivity is constituted, rather than liberated, in practices of self-care: "That is, we should not understand ourselves as seeking to liberate a self that was always there, but rather to invent ourselves as something new that is not yet imagined". As Gough (2018) points out, men's current health behaviours draw on a combination of long-standing beliefs about men and seemingly new conceptual, mental and spatial tools, rather than solving the ideological dilemma between masculinity and health by cessation of performances of manhood.

Men's awareness of their own health has increased their "positive emotion, interdependence, and relationality" (Elliott, 2016, p. 252), but these performances and identity elements are only a necessary and not yet sufficient condition for men's alignment with gender equality. Drawing on Hearn's (2015) vast critique on separating men's health and well-being as a men's equality problem distinct from all the other equality problems, I suggest that the organizational culture that makes men's selves surface is problematic for gender equality. To begin with, it draws men's attention once again to men themselves. Instead of care for others, "managerial athleticism" (Johansson et al., 2017) motivates men to sacrifice their personal time and resources to become valuable in their workplaces (Bardon et al., 2021). Even if men's work-related self-care does not proactively support maintaining gender difference, it does not necessarily oppose neoliberal competition between individuals and the masculinist will to perceive the self as a winner in comparison to others (Bardon et al., 2021; Siltala, 2020), classist statements against groups with health problems (Farrimond, 2012; Riach & Cutcher, 2014) and men's emotional and material distance to caring responsibilities outside paid labour (Lund et al., 2019; Niemistö et al., 2021; Tanquerel & Grau-Grau, 2020).

I recognize the risk of fatalism and pessimism about men. By prioritizing gendered working life and organizations as a source of certain masculinity and an explanatory factor behind men's behaviours, one continues to position men as victims of masculinity rather than highlighting their agency in the reproduction of masculinity (Waling, 2019; Whitehead, 2002). Although studies on masculinist organizations and men's masculinities in those organizations have done well in exploring the institutionalized norms affecting men, they do not necessarily illuminate men's agentive and affective encounters with gendered expectations.

In past work, I have theorized work-related self-care as a site of "co-optation and resistance" for men (Hyvönen, 2020a, p. 18). Although many regimes of living are now constructed and maintained in the context of work, many of them are located outside organizations, or even work outright against work-centred values. As the self and one's own life history are increasingly rendered important in feminist, medical, therapeutic and commercial cultures of self-care that are not necessarily tied to work organizations (Gough, 2018), men can, paradoxically, prioritize the self and simultaneously deconstruct their relations to conventional role expectations for men. Refusal of the values of organizations built upon "masculinist" notions of career and work (Biese, 2020) also hinders men's collective dominance in organizations and the labour market in general. However, I suggest that this should not be understood as a binary choice between masculinist and non masculinist careers. Despite men's self-assessed commitment to dual-career families (Lund et al., 2019) and the "aspiration to balance" repeatedly occurring in their speech when they compare themselves to work-centred men of past generations (Hyvönen, 2020a, p. 24), their actions in the material realm may still reflect and reproduce the institutionalized division of labour between genders.

I continue my project of deconstructing dichotomies in this chapter by pointing out the problems with the dichotomy between the career-oriented masculinity performed in gendered organizations being the only problematic masculinity, and its inevitable counterpart being a "healthy" masculinity realized in distant and critical relationships with the employer. Instead, I suggest that even if the growth of freelance work and the increasing relevance of aesthetic bodywork code men, at least in part, as more feminine than before (Wolfman et al., 2021), this particular situation also makes them capable of damaging behaviours that stem from their identities as men.

Kotzé and Antonopoulos (2021) argue that the traditional markers of masculinity, such as size, strength and security, have not lost their general prestige even in the context of a service-based, post-industrialized economy where family background, social class and tradition have lost their unifying effect on working-class men. Informed by ethnographic work on steroid use, these authors point out that masculine aesthetics are now a product of consumption for both men who pursue aesthetic pleasure and employers who see commercial potential in large male bodies. Drawing on this finding, I suggest that intentional care for one's own body and neglecting one's own health may occur simultaneously. For example, door supervisors or "doormen", whose work is often organized as temporary freelance work, often intentionally choose to maintain their ability to work in ways that are compatible with their identities as men and aesthetically pleasing in that they do not intercept the solid perception of oneself as a hard man who is not afraid of risks. Concurrently, emotional regulation through addictive behaviours and the continuous increase in body size are harmful to their health and the operational capacity of the organization in the long run (Hyvönen, 2020b; Kotzé & Antonopoulos, 2021; Monaghan, 2002).

Conclusion: caring relations as uses and abuses of power

The social role of men as providers, protectors, solvers of problems threatening society, and symbols of hope is attributed to men before their socialization into any particular configuration of labour markets. Drawing on the analyses of historical developments of representations of men (Whitehead, 2002) and the long-term institutionalized division of labour between genders (Connell, 2012; Gilmore, 1990), it can be pointed out that men's bodies carry certain meanings that are relatively stable and static in comparison to the ever-changing flux in socio-economic and labour market contexts in which men's moral and intellectual dominance is reproduced. In contemporary organizations, the most widely accepted form of leadership has adopted either the name or form of care: men exercise power by producing health and well-being. By theorizing care as a legitimized way of exercising organizational power, I have been able to show the ways in which men continue to adapt to the demands of both the rise in gender-equality discourse and the contemporary mode of production. Concurrently, I have demonstrated the limitations of excessive optimism with regard to the subversion of gender relations: men's increased interest in care responds to various crises threatening the legitimacy of men's social dominance in order "to conceal systems of power and inequality in historically new ways" (Bridges & Pascoe, 2014, p. 246).

Even though caring masculinity (Elliott, 2016) has become intelligible for men, not all care is equally masculinized. In organizations that provide care for patients and clients as well as in organizations in which care is a part of management, men seek a compromise between their identities as men and care. Men incorporate bits and pieces of care, previously associated with femininity, into their own identity and, on the other hand, care through their own embodied identity, attaching meanings to care that enable positive self-understanding. In addition to understandings of care as feminized labour neglected by men and care as an affect lacking in men's lives, I propose an analytical view on men's care that does not simply focus on the amount of care provided by men or whether men call their actions "care". In addition to and instead of these approaches, I recommend focusing on the material and discursive consequences of the caring relations in which men participate.

In the context of management and workplace health promotion, care for the self and others is, in addition to demonstrating social responsibility (Dailey et al., 2018), an investment that seeks instrumental benefits (Karjalainen et al., 2021). By rendering the promotion of health and well-being as both humane and useful, necessary, and essentially rational governance, men in working life have managed to feminize and depoliticize themselves and the power they exercise despite the strong connection between healthism and the competitive, masculinist work culture present in many organizations. When assessing the care provided by men, one should look at who is cared for and who is excluded from care. In work organizations, individual human life is subjected to caring attention more often than ever before: by showing employers a model for favourable health behaviours, management shows its humane face and interest in their workers' ability to feel good. Concurrently, the ideal worker to be taken care of is already a docile body willing to be cared for and capable of benefiting from the care it receives. Concern for worker health, well-being, and happiness has also contributed to inequality by structuring some people's lives as more valuable and developable than others.

I conclude by arguing that even if manifold "cares" for others and the self have entered hegemonic masculinity, not all caring masculinities are equally achievable for all men. Achieving a "masculine" job in social services and healthcare (Drange & Karlsen, 2016) or embodying "managerial atheism" (Johansson et al., 2017) require certain kinds of personal capital that are not evenly distributed. Even if some men find ways of combining bodywork and care for others by, for example, exercising with their children (Bardon et al., 2021), care for the body and the performance of the body has also strengthened men's obligation to devote their personal time and resources to their work organization outside working hours. Men's bodywork and care for the self maintains the obligation of non-men to take care of others.

Acknowledgements

This work was supported by the Finnish Work Environment Fund (grant number 200493) and the Kone Foundation (grant number 202103931).

References

Aavik, K. (2021). Vegan men: Towards greater care for (non)human others, earth and self. In P. Pulé & M. Hultman (Eds.), *Men, Masculinities, and Earth: Contending with the (m)Anthropocene* (pp. 329 – 350). Cham: Palgrave Macmillan. doi: 10.1007/978-3-030-54486-7

Ahmed, S. (2010). *The Promise of Happiness*. London: Duke University Press.

Bardon, T., Brown, A., & Puyou, F. (2021). Citius, altius, fortius: Managers' quest for heroic leader identities. *Organization*. doi: 10.1177/13505084211030644

Berggren, K. (2014). Sticky masculinity: Post-structuralism, phenomenology and subjectivity in critical studies on men. *Men and Masculinities*, *17*(3), 231–252. doi: 10.1177/1097184X14539510

Biese, I. (2020). Men opting out: Disenchantment with corporate cultures and career ideals. In K. Aavik, C. Bland, J. Hoegaerts & J. Salminen (Eds.), *Men, Masculinities and the Modern Career: Contemporary and Historical Perspectives* (pp. 35–52). Berlin: De Gruyter. doi: 10.1515/9783110651874

Binkley, S. (2014). *Happiness as Enterprise: An Essay on Neoliberal Life*. Albany: SUNY Press.

Bridges, T., & Pascoe, C. (2014). Hybrid masculinities: New directions in the sociology of men and masculinities. *Sociology Compass*, *8*(3), 246–258. doi: 10.1111/soc4.12134

Cederström, C., & Spicer, A. (2015). *The Wellness Syndrome*. Cambridge: Polity Press.

Collier, S., & Lakoff, A. (2005). On regimes of living. In A. Ong, & S. Collier (Eds.), *Global Assemblages: Technology, Politics, and Ethics as Anthropological Problems* (pp. 22–39). Malden, MA: Blackwell. doi: 10.1002/9780470696569

Connell, R. (2012). Gender, health and theory: Conceptualizing the issue, in local and world perspective. *Social Science & Medicine*, *74*(11), 1675–1683. doi: 10.1016/j.socscimed.2011.06.006

Connell, R., & Wood J. (2005). Globalization and business masculinities. *Men and Masculinities*, *7*(4), 347–364. doi: 10.1177/1097184X03260969

Costea, B., Crump, N., & Amiridis, K. (2008). Managerialism, the therapeutic habitus and the self in contemporary organizing. *Human Relations*, *61*(5), 661–685. doi: 10.1177/0018726708091763

Cottingham, M. (2017). Caring moments and their men: Masculine emotion practice in nursing. *NORMA: International Journal for Masculinity Studies*, *12*(3–4), 270–285. doi: 10.1080/18902138.2017.1312954

Courtenay, W. (2000). Constructions of masculinity and their influence on men's well-being: A theory of gender and health. *Social Science & Medicine*, *50*(10), 1385–1401. doi: 10.1016/s0277-9536(99)00390-1

Dailey, S., Burke, T., & Carberry, E. (2018). For better or for work: Dual discourses in a workplace wellness program. *Management Communication Quarterly*, *32*(4), 612–626. doi: 10.1177/0893318917746018

de Boise, S. (2018). The personal is political . . . just not always progressive: Affective interruptions and their promise for CSMM. *NORMA: International Journal for Masculinity Studies*, *13*(3–4), 158–174. doi: 10.1080/18902138.2017.1325098

Drange, I., & Karlsen, H. (2016). Simply a matter of being male? Nurses' employment outcomes in the Norwegian labour market. *NORA*, *24*(2), 76–94. doi: 10.1080/08038740.2016.1165732

Elliott, K. (2016). Caring masculinities: Theorizing an emerging concept. *Men and Masculinities*, *19*(3), 240–259. doi: 10.1177/1097184X15576203

Farrimond, H. (2012). Beyond the caveman: Rethinking masculinity in relation to men's help seeking. *Health*, *16*(2), 208–225. doi: 10.1177/1363459311403943

Foucault, M. (2008). *The Birth of Biopolitics: Lectures at the Collège de France, 1978–1979*. Basingstoke: Palgrave Macmillan. doi: 10.1057/9780230594180

Giazitzoglu, A., & Muzio, D. (2021). Learning the rules of the game: How is corporate masculinity learned and enacted by male professionals from nonprivileged backgrounds? *Gender, Work & Organization*, *28*(1), 67–84. doi: 10.1111/gwao.12561

Gill, R., & Elias, A. (2014). "Awaken your incredible": Love your body discourses and postfeminist contradictions. *International Journal of Media and Cultural Politics*, *10*(2), 179–188. doi: 10.1386/MACP.10.2.179_1

Gilmore, D. (1990). *Manhood in the Making: Cultural Concepts of Masculinity*. New Haven & London: Yale University Press. doi: 10.12987/9780300157253

Gough, B. (2018). *Contemporary Masculinities: Embodiment, Emotion and Wellbeing*. Cham: Palgrave Pivot. doi: 10.1007/978-3-319-78819-7

Hanlon, N. (2012). *Masculinities, Care and Equality. Identity and Nurture in Men's Lives*. Basingstoke, UK: Palgrave Macmillan. doi: 10.1057/9781137264879

Hanmer, J. (1990). Men, power and the exploitation of women. In J. Hearn, & D. Morgan (Eds.), *Men, Masculinities and Social Theory* (pp. 21–42). London: Unwin Hyman/Routledge. doi: 10.4324/9781315762272

Hanna, E., Gough, B., & Markham S. (2020). Masculinities in the construction industry: A double edged sword for health and wellbeing? *Gender, Work & Organization*, *27*(4), 632–646. doi: 10.1111/gwao.12429

Harrison, J. (1978). Warning: The male sex role may be dangerous to your health. *Journal of Social Issues*, *34*(1), 65–86. doi: 10.1111/j.1540-4560.1978.tb02541.x

Hearn, J. (2012). A multi-faceted power analysis of men's violence to known women: From hegemonic masculinity to the hegemony of men. *Sociological Review*, *60*(4), 589–610. doi: 10.1111/j.1467-954X.2012.02125.x

Hearn, J. (2014). Men, masculinities and the material(-)discursive. *NORMA: International Journal for Masculinity Studies*, *9*(1), 5–17. doi: 10.1080/18902138.2014.892281

Hearn, J. (2015). Men's health and well-being: The case against a separate field. *International Journal of Men's Health*, *14*(3), 301–314.

Heyes, C. (2007). *Self-Transformations: Foucault, Ethics, and Normalized Bodies*. New York: Oxford University Press. doi: 10.1093/acprof:oso/9780195310535.001.0001

Huzell, H., & Larsson, P. (2012). Aesthetic and athletic employees: The negative outcome of employers assuming responsibility for sickness benefits. *Economic and Industrial Democracy*, *33*(11), 103–123. doi: 10.1177/0143831X11427590

Hyvönen, H. (2020a). Care for the self – but not for the career? Men's perceptions of work-related self-care. In K. Aavik, C. Bland, J. Hoegaerts, & J. Salminen (Eds.), *Men, Masculinities and the Modern Career: Contemporary and Historical Perspectives* (pp. 15–34). Berlin: De Gruyter. doi: 10.1515/9783110651874

Hyvönen, H. (2020b). Care of the self, somaesthetics, and men affected by eating disorders: Rethinking the focus on men's beauty ideals. *Journal of Somaesthetics*, *6*(2), 64–81. doi: 10.5278/ojs.jos.v6i2.3654

James, E., & Zoller, H. (2018). Resistance training: (Re)shaping extreme forms of workplace health promotion. *Management Communication Quarterly*, *32*(1), 60–89. doi: 10.1177/0893318917696990

Johansson, J., Tienari, J., & Valtonen, A. (2017). The body, identity and gender in managerial athleticism. *Human Relations*, *70*(9), 1141–1167. doi: 10.1177/0018726716685161

Jyrkinen, M., Väkiparta, M., & Lämsä, A. (2020). Care and gendered work in reception centers in Finland. *Equality, Diversity and Inclusion*, *39*(2), 166–180. doi: 10.1108/EDI-102018-0192

Kangas, E., & Lämsä, A. (2021). Leadership practices in relation to men's work-family balance in Finnish organizations. *Community, Work & Family*, *24*(5), 567–585. doi: 10.1080/13668803.2020.1728231

Karjalainen, M., Islam, G., & Holm, M. (2021). Scientization, instrumentalization, and commodification of mindfulness in a professional services firm. *Organization*, *28*(3), 610–627. doi: 10.1177/1350508419883388

Kotzé, J., & Antonopoulos, G. (2021). Boosting bodily capital: Maintaining masculinity, aesthetic pleasure and instrumental utility through the consumption of steroids. *Journal of Consumer Culture*, *21*(3), 683–700. doi: 10.1177/1469540519846196

Lund, R., Meriläinen, S., & Tienari, J. (2019). New masculinities in universities? Discourses, ambivalence and potential change. *Gender, Work & Organization*, *26*(10), 1376–1397. doi: 10.1111/gwao.12383

Martínez-Morato, S., Feijoo-Cid, M., Galbany-Estragués, P., Fernández-Cano, M., & Marañón, A. (2021). Emotion management and stereotypes about emotions among male nurses: A qualitative study. *BMC Nursing*, *20*(114). doi: 10.1186/s12912-021-00641-z

Masters, N. (2010). 'My strength is not for hurting': Men's anti-rape websites and their construction of masculinity and male sexuality. *Sexualities*, *13*(1), 33–46. doi: 10.1177/1363460709346115

Mears, A. (2014). Aesthetic labor for the sociologies of work, gender, and beauty. *Sociology Compass*, *8*(12), 1330–1343. doi: 10.1111/soc4.12211

Meriläinen, S., Tienari, J., & Valtonen, A. (2015). Headhunters and the "ideal" executive body. *Organization*, *22*(1), 3 - 22. doi: 10.1177/1350508413496578

Messerschmidt, J. (2021). Donald Trump, dominating masculine necropolitics, and COVID-19. *Men and Masculinities*, *24*(1), 189–194. doi: 10.1177/1097184X20984816

Monaghan, L. (2002). Hard men, shop boys and others: Embodying competence in a masculinist occupation. *The Sociological Review*, *50*(3), 334–355. doi: 10.1111/1467954X.00386

Morini, C., & Fumagalli, A. (2010). Life put to work: Towards a life theory of value. *Ephemera*, *10*(3–4), 234–252.

Niemistö, C., Hearn, J., & Kehn, C. (2021). Care and work matter: A social sustainability approach. In C. Binswanger & A. Zimmermann (Eds.), *Transitioning to Gender Equality* (pp. 179–195). Basel: MDPI. doi: 10.3390/books978-3-03897-867-1

Nikunen, K. (2016). Doing good reality, masculine care, and affective capitalism. *Ephemera*, *16*(4), 163–184.

Randles, J. (2018). "Manning up" to be a good father: Hybrid fatherhood, masculinity, and U.S. responsible fatherhood policy. *Gender & Society*, *32*(4), 516–539. doi: 10.1177/0891243218770364

Riach, K., & Cutcher, L. (2014). Built to last: Ageing, class and the masculine body in a UK hedge fund. *Work, Employment and Society*, *28*(5), 771–787. doi: 10.1177/0950017013506773

Siltala, J. (2020). In search of the missing links between economic insecurity and political protest: Why does neoliberalism evoke identity politics instead of class interests? *Frontiers in Sociology*, *5*(28). doi: 10.3389/fsoc.2020.00028

Tanquerel, S., & Grau-Grau, M. (2020). Unmasking work-family balance barriers and strategies among working fathers in the workplace. *Organization*, *27*(5), 680–700. doi: 10.1177/1350508419838692

Tronto, J. (1993). *Moral Boundaries: A Political Argument for an Ethic of Care*. New York: Routledge.

Waling, A. (2019). Problematising 'toxic' and 'healthy' masculinity for addressing gender inequalities. *Australian Feminist Studies*, *34*(101), 362375. doi: 10.1177/1060826518782980

Whitehead, S. (2002). *Men and Masculinities: Key Themes and New Directions*. Cambridge: Polity Press.

Wolfman, G., Hearn, J., & Yeadon-Lee, T. (2021). Hollow femininities: The emerging faces of neoliberal masculinities. *NORMA: International Journal for Masculinity Studies*, *16*(4), 217–234. doi: 10.1080/18902138.2021.1996829

14

EMOTIONS AND AFFECT IN ORGANIZING MEN AND MASCULINITY/IES

Sam de Boise

Introduction

The issue of whether cisgendered men are more or less emotional than people of other genders, and specifically cisgendered women, have been debated since Antiquity (Lloyd, 1984). Men's capacity for supposedly unemotional (i.e. rational) behaviour has been identified as both a reason for cis-men's social privilege (Sattel, 1976) and one of the main "costs of masculinity" (Messner, 1997, pp. 5–6; Hanisch, 1969). Given emotions' link to behaviour, how men understand, experience and express emotions is important to explore. However, while emotions have often been perceived as biologically hardwired and easily quantifiable into levels of "more" or "less", what is perceived as rational or emotional behaviour is context dependent. Furthermore, how emotions are defined and constructed has an impact on how they are experienced in relation to masculinity; anger and rage have been historically compatible with stereotypical ideas of Western masculinity, while fear and sadness have not. In fact, some have suggested that what is perceived as rational action is not even possible without emotions (Damasio, 1995). This has implications for thinking about which types of action are positively or negatively evaluated in organizations when they are performed by people of different genders. It also raises the question of how organizations themselves reproduce gendered hierarchies of emotion.

This chapter explores how emotions and affect have been understood in understanding the relationship between men, masculinity and organizations/organizing. It does so from a predominantly sociological perspective, including some approaches from cultural studies and social psychology. The chapter begins by defining emotions and affect, and the relevance of these for studying men and masculinity/ies before moving on to discuss how emotions have been studied in relation to organizations. Taking a broad definition of organizations in their economic and social forms, the chapter highlights how academic research has theorized the relationship between men, masculinity, emotions and organizations largely in terms of an "old-fashioned", unemotive masculinity which is gradually being replaced by more emotionally expressive, caring forms. It then moves on to discuss the way in which approaches to masculinity and affect might help to retain the initial promise of focusing on masculinity and emotions, without losing sight of the political implications of more critical approaches in studies on men and masculinities (CSMM).

DOI: 10.4324/9781003193579-16

Emotions

There are different theoretical approaches to understanding emotions, which in turn have different methodological implications. Some posit evidence for the existence of a number (ranging between 4 and 10, even 12 in some cases) of hardwired "basic emotions", which tends to draw on evolutionary theories (Darwin, 2009 [1872]; Ekman & Friesen, 1971). These treat different emotions as either activated or deactivated, and easily definable into discrete categories. According to such basic emotions approaches, emotions are objectively defined qualities of experience. Valence-arousal approaches look at intensity as well as groupings of emotional experiences (Barrett, 2006), placing a greater role on subjective experience but which still distinguish between types of emotions. Anthropological and interactional approaches have looked more at exhibition and subjective interpretation *in interaction* with others (Goffman, 1956; Hochschild, 1979, 1983; Turner & Stets, 2005), while constructionist approaches focus on how emotional experience is mediated and understood culturally (Barbalet, 2001; Reddy, 2001; Solomon, 1993). In the latter case, questions as to how language and culture shape the experience, expression and understanding of emotions mean that we cannot take concepts such as "positive" or "negative" emotions as objective terms and need to understand them in terms of the culturally constructed meanings attached to them.

For sociological audiences, the key to an emotion is often the ability to articulate it in language and apply culturally recognized labels to the term (Thoits, 1989; Turner & Stets, 2005). Sociologists are often more interested in what is articulated or displayed, and less able, due to methodological and disciplinary differences, to study what goes on "inside" the body. For this reason, sociologists often employ self-report or observational measures, focusing on the externalization, expression or discursive construction of emotions, even if many still argue that biological factors are important to the physiological stimulation or experience of emotions (Turner, 1999). Importantly, sociologists see emotions as something which are shaped by societies, but which do not determine (even if they influence) behaviour. Hochschild (1979, 1983), whose work has continued to influence the sociology of emotions, also famously dismissed the idea that emotions were simply stimuli which drove action. Her concept of "feeling" and "display" rules, developed from Goffman (1969), demonstrated that women working as flight attendants and men working as tax collectors trained and often developed in line with economic or social norms, but that their expression was largely dependent on a socially informed judgement as to whether the social context was appropriate.

The idea that emotions have to be expressed or articulated in order to be understood *as* emotions raises some empirical and conceptual issues for the study of men and masculinities. Some have argued that in order to adhere to Western expressions of masculinity men learn to "control" or "repress" emotions (Berger et al., 2005; Duncombe & Marsden, 1993, 1995; Firestone, 1979 [1970]; Fischer & Manstead, 2000; Sattel, 1976; Wong et al., 2006) because they are regarded as the opposite of rational or reasonable action (Connell, 1995; Seidler, 1994; Thompson et al., 1985). The idea that men are socialized into not showing or discussing emotions has often been equated with the idea that men are unemotional, lack emotional empathy or are unable to recognize their own emotions. Social psychologists have even gone so far as to label the inability to recognize or display emotions (*alexithymia*) as a specific psychological *disorder* affecting men in the majority (Berger et al., 2005; Wong et al., 2006). Yet this creates a confirmation bias in research in that it treats men as unemotional because the frameworks used to understand and study emotions rely on a model of emotions defined through displays historically associated with social expectations around an appositional "femininity" (see Branney & White, 2008).

By contrast, Barbalet (2001), for instance, has shown that the concept of reason, which has often been seen as the cornerstone of Western expressions of idealized masculinity (Seidler, 1994), is not, in fact, the actual suppression of emotion. Emotions, physiologically, not only make "reasonable" or "rational" action possible (Damasio, 1995), because emotions guide decisions, but the concept of rationality is dependent on the idea of (emotional) irrationality and unreason to give rationality and reason their meaning. Even philosophers credited with forming a highly psychologistic and mechanistic view of basic emotions such as Descartes (Descartes, 2001 [1637/1641]) or James (1884), made the case for emotions as important for the exercise of rational decision-making (Descartes, 1989 [1649]; James, 1879). On the other hand, there is also the idea that men are socialized to display so-called negative emotions – most famously anger, rage and jealousy – at the expense of others (happiness, sadness, joy, fear). Furthermore, what gets labelled as "rational" or "emotional" tends to differ dependent on the perception of the audience and the person exhibiting certain displays (Fischer et al., 2013); emotions are integral to both individual and social action but what "counts" as an emotion is highly gendered (Warner & Shields, 2009). This means that while there has been a commonly held idea that men are unwilling to display emotions, context, interaction and history are all important in shaping how emotions are experienced and labelled. Importantly, the shame, fear and anxiety (which are types of emotional experience) associated with being considered "emotional", motivate men's attachments to displays of rationality (de Boise, 2018).

Affect

Affect is a similarly elusive concept, open to different interpretations. Indeed, the line between emotions and affect is not always clearly demarcated. Some use the terms emotion and affect interchangeably (Ahmed, 2010b; Gorton, 2007), while others make a clear distinction between emotion and affect (Turner & Stets, 2005; Wetherell, 2012). Thoits (1989, p. 318), for example, states:

> emotions can be distinguished from feelings, moods, and sentiments . . . the term *feelings* includes the experience of physical drive states (e.g. hunger, pain, fatigue) as well as emotional states. *Affects* refer to positive and negative evaluations (liking/disliking) of an object, behaviour, or idea: affects also have intensity and activity dimensions.

The concept of affect is also divided into more experiential approaches which look at affects (plural) in terms of subjective experience, and those indebted to philosophical or cultural theory which see affect as a means of understanding collective action, rather than empirically studying the experiences of individual social actors.

The latter, which might be understood more as "affect theory" builds on Descartes' contemporary Spinoza, via Deleuze and Guattari. Spinoza makes a distinction between the Latin term *affectus* and *affectio*, suggesting the capacity to be affected *by* as well as *to* affect which has important consequences for both experience and acting on that experience. This approach suggests that affect is an "intensity" (Massumi, 2002) which exists "beyond emotion" (Gregg & Siegworth, 2010, p. 1), and something which circulates in-between bodies rather than is confined to the experiences of individual bodies. Affect from a cultural theory perspective is a dynamic relation which "signifies potential" (Pedwell & Whitehead, 2012, p. 116) and the focus ranges from political movements as affective to the relationship between viewer and cultural text. For instance, sweaty palms, discomfort and heart palpitations might occur when watching a climber on TV climbing thousands of feet without a rope; the intensity or "affective entrainment" felt emerges in interaction. In this respect, affect as a precursor to political action, especially, is important.

In more phenomenological approaches, drawing from the work on affect by psychologists (Tomkins, 1962), the experience of affect is central to how it is conceptualized, though these may also focus on cultural texts (Ahmed, 2010a; Gorton, 2007; Probyn, 2004; Sedgwick, 2003). The clearest divide between affect and emotions is often made by those adopting more psychological perspectives (Wetherell, 2012), while cultural theorists often tend to treat the two interchangeably. There is also the question of methodology and studying the corporeal but linguistically inexpressible. Some measure changes in heart rate, skin conductivity, more empirically oriented sociological approaches look at self-report studies or interviews while cultural theory approaches place an emphasis on the interpretation of cultural texts or social phenomena (for instance, literature, music, political events) as deciphering affect. According to these approaches, texts themselves might be said to be affective or to have a certain intensity. Crucially, while the literature on emotions has often looked at emotions as properties of individuals, which can be "worked on", approaches to affect have conceptualized embodied responses more in terms of how affect circulates and shapes relations between people (Gregg & Siegworth, 2010) as a "structure of feeling" (Williams, 1958). Importantly affect implies a two-way relationship whereby one is affected *by* as well as affect*ing* others (Pedwell & Whitehead, 2012).

The ambiguity of the term, affect, has been seen as both a strength and a weakness. Wetherell (2012), for instance, has argued that in affect theory, there is a tendency to resort to the pitfalls inherent to stimulus-response models, most obvious in the idea of basic emotions as hardwired motivators of actions, as well as models of crowd psychology dating back to a conservative interpretation of the French Revolution (see Blackman, 2008). One particular issue in considering the relations of affect and masculinity is methodological. The issue is how to render affective experience intelligible in a way that adequately captures the immediate and non-linguistic aspects of experience. Focusing on affect *only* as circulation loses sight of how individuals are affected by affect! At its most extreme, affect theory may arguably lapse into the same notion of disembodiment about which feminist and critical masculinities scholars have been critical when theorizing emotions (Reeser, 2020): affect becomes a catch-all term which means everything. Though there is a shared agreement that affect (a) circulates between individuals; (b) involves elements of non-discursive and non-linguistic experience; (c) is pre- or non-conscious; and (d) is indeterminate and cannot be neatly categorized into binary models of emotional experience as either absent or present.

Gendered organizations: unemotive masculinity

With regard to masculinity and emotions in organizations, there has been a tendency to focus on how "emotion work", in relation to organizational cultures, is gendered, with an emphasis on how men and women *display* emotions within organizations. These approaches are drawn from the idea that feeling and display rules surround socialization into cultural norms around masculinity. Thus, the way in which emotions themselves are gendered helps to maintain the separation between masculinity and unemotional, on the one hand, and femininity and emotions, on the other. These differences in emotion work give organizations their gendered character. Duncombe and Marsden (1993, 1995) pointed to what they saw as a "gender asymmetry" and imbalance in terms of who was doing the emotional labour at home because men were too invested in their occupations. Utilizing Hochschild's (1979) notion of emotion work, they argued that men's lack of emotional investment in family life, documented by numerous scholars (Brody, 1999; Thompson et al., 1985), emerges from structural inequalities relating to patriarchal society and greater investment in their work–life as a result of economic and social advantages. They concluded, therefore, that norms around masculinity and emotional inarticulacy were not simply personal traits but systemic problems arising from the patriarchal division of emotion work (see also Sattel, 1976), with men's behaviour in both public and private spheres defined through the exercise of unemotionality.

Putnam and Mumby (1993), similarly, using Hochschild's framework, highlight how organizations themselves take on the gendered characteristics of rationality, with a devaluing of the emotional and the personal as "feminine". This manifests itself, among other things, in the devaluing of childcare concerns (p. 43) and the highly gendered boss–secretary relationship, where secretaries take on the role of emotional supporter (p. 45). Hochschild's original work also divided emotional, organizational cultures by gender whereby the women flight attendants she observed were expected to be caring and compassionate, whereas the tax collectors who were all men were taught to be unsympathetic and distrustful (Hochschild, 1983, p. 143). The concept of emotional intelligence or "EQ" (Goleman, 1995) has also been employed in relation to organizations in order to emphasize interpersonal qualities which are desirable in both employees and managers. While Goleman focused very little on gender, subsequent studies have argued that men, as managers both have lower (Mandell & Pherwani, 2003) and relatively similar levels of EQ to women (Furnham & Taylor, 2020). Although the concept of EQ, much like IQ, has been heavily critiqued; not least for its separation of emotions from cognitive abilities, for its categorization of emotions into objective levels of lower and higher (which fails to account for context) and for its "masculinist" bias in the emphasis of emotional mastery (Petersen, 2004, p. 130).

In contrast to this notion of unemotional men, Hearn (1993, p. 148) argued that within organizations, men have historically been expected not to display *certain* emotions, in line with display rules concerning masculinity. Rather than men as being unemotion*al*, he suggests they are instead encouraged to be unemot*ive* within organizations, noting that what is taken to be an expression of emotion is highly gendered. As he observed "what is remarkable is not so much that men cry [in organisations], but that this crying itself is seen as remarkable" (1993, p. 143), going on to observe that displays of anger and aggression were (and still are) socially sanctioned within workplaces but that displays of more "feminine"-coded emotions are not. Context thus plays a role in how men's emotions are constructed as unemotional within organizations (Hearn, 1993, p. 146). Related to the notion of emotions as context- and viewer-dependent, Lewis (2000) similarly argues that the behaviour of men and women bosses is treated very differently depending on who is exhibiting the behaviour. Using an experimental research design, she argues that the perception of leaders' effectiveness is more clearly negative when women bosses display anger than with men. Again, this indicates that emotions are not simply what is felt but what is perceived.

Roper (2003) has also suggested that this culture of rationality is inherently gendered in the hierarchical structure of British managerial organizations given that:

> The bureaucrat's power is vested in the ability to act, as Max Weber put it "without regard to persons". Yet despite its meritocratic ring, the expression has a deeply gendered significance. The image of a certain ***kind*** of man: single minded in his pursuit of career success but a responsible breadwinner and loyal servant of the company. It reflects a clear division between men and women.
>
> *(Roper, 2003, p. 1)*

This echoes arguments put forward by Hearn and Parkin (1983) and Hochschild with regard to the rational/emotional division within workplaces as a specifically gendered logic. P. Lewis (2008), in addition, has argued in relation to caring types of organization, the public space of organizational management is dominated by masculine (i.e. "unemotional") values while the actual work of care, which is based on emotion work, is in fact feminized. She suggests that in order to challenge this hierarchy, values from the personal and private need to be imported into organizations but still maintain a distinction between unemotional men in management and emotional women workers. Despite taking a different approach, Nixon (2009), too, makes the case that the form of emotional labour expected in many service sector industries is "incompatible with working masculine habitus", and thus a reason for many men rejecting employment opportunities. This, again, maintains a distinction between a masculinity premised on unemotionality and service sector and care work as premised on "feminine" emotionality.

There is also a health aspect to this gendered exercise of unemotionality, given that burnout and stress, drug abuse and long-term health damage have been linked to the dangers of emotional stoicism as a component of the occupational cultures which sustain hegemonic masculinity (see Berdahl et al., 2018, and this volume; Lohan, 2007). This fatalistic approach to masculinity as necessarily risky also means that workplace-related deaths are often regarded as inevitable rather than preventable (Ericson, 2021). The health consequences of adherence to stoic, "uncomplaining" forms of masculinity in the workplace also have a specific class dynamic. Ironically, the fear of being seen as overly "emotional" leads to both physical and psychological damage to men's bodies, particularly among subordinated and marginalized groups of men (Ward et al., 2017). For instance, Robertson and Monaghan (2012) demonstrate that there are significantly higher long-term health impacts of physical labour on working-class men as well as higher suicide rates among men from areas of high unemployment and low wages. Men, who have historically been less likely to seek help for health-related issues, such as back pain and joint pain, early onset arthritis or physical impairment, have been more likely to die of work-related health problems such as black lung, asbestos poisoning, related to the type of work men are more likely to engage in. This suggests that unemotive masculinity is both a source of privilege and a problem for men within organizations at large.

Softening masculinity?

The notion that men practise emotional repression as part of an adherence to an idealized form of masculinity has seen a number of critiques. One centres on the taken-for-granted assumption that men are unemotional, citing the lack of empirical evidence exploring how men understand and construct emotions (Galasinski, 2004; Holmes, 2015; Seidler, 2007). Another focuses on the methodological problems of taking what counts as an emotion as premised on "feminine" displays (see Branney & White, 2008), whereas historical accounts have demonstrated how masculinity/ies have actually been constructed and corroborated through forms of emotional expression (Ekenstam, 1998; Forth, 2008).

With respect to organizations, the emphasis on men's emotions has seen a turn to focus on men's experiences of workplace-related stress (Berdahl et al., 2018), as well as looking at men's insecurities and anxieties that arise as a result of work (Kelan, 2008) or lack thereof (see McDowell, 2011). Interestingly, cultural depictions of "men at work" have also undergone significant changes which indicate a devaluation of the kind of unemotive masculinity in organizational and occupational cultures, outlined earlier. For instance, in the AMC series, *Mad Men*, set in the world of 1960s advertising on Madison Avenue, the lead character, despite enjoying high status within the intensely patriarchal work culture, as well as being closed off emotionally from colleagues and partners, suffers a series of debilitating anxieties arising from his inability to discuss these problems. Oliver Stone's *Wall Street: Money Never Sleeps*, released in 2010, and, to a lesser extent, Scorsese's 2013 *The Wolf of Wall Street*, also focuses more on the harmful consequences caused by a lack of emotional investment in family life, in contrast with Stone's more morally ambiguous *Wall Street*, released in 1985. HBO's the Sopranos (1999–2007) by contrast depicts a modern-day head of a Mafia crime family who struggles with anxiety and depression, as well as anger and rage, but who actually seeks help from a therapist.

Crucially, due in part to feminist emphases on the centrality of men's emotional communication for gender equality (see Hanisch, 1969), there have also been those who claim that idealized notions of masculinity have undergone a significant transformation which have implications for organizational cultures. Indicative of this is the growth in focus on men in relation to caring organizations such as nursing (Hanlon, 2012; Simpson, 2009), or primary teaching, and the concept of "caring masculinity" (Scambor et al., 2014) which has been expanded by Elliott (2015, 2020). While emotions are seldom defined explicitly in these approaches, as Elliott suggests, what she regards as "softer" and more emotionally attuned forms of new masculinities means both that men are more willing to take on caring roles in which emotions are seen as an asset rather than a hindrance to their occupational life (see also Roberts, 2011). These authors argue that service sector work, which requires greater emotional empathy with customers and colleagues, is compatible with and evidence of changes in masculinity as a form of social organization.

At the same time, there seems to be evidence from both qualitative and quantitative research (particularly from research based on the European Social Survey) that men are less willing to prioritize work and tie their identity to their occupations due to a greater investment in familial care and responsibility. Nevertheless, the degree to which men engage with shared parental care vary by national context depending on social policies for shared parental leave (see Edlund & Öun, 2016; Salin et al., 2018; Geisler & Kreyenfeld, 2018). There have been several studies, from different countries, which have documented changing ideas around fatherhood in conjunction with a more "emotionally invested" role in the home (see Allan et al., 2021; Johansson & Klinth, 2008; Lin, 2019) and a diminishing interest in defining masculinity through work, something linked to interrelated social, cultural and economic shifts (Kilkey, 2006; Montes, 2013), although fathers spending more time with their children does not necessarily mean a more equitably gendered distribution of labour at home (see Craig et al., 2012).

The turn towards demonstrating men's greater emotional investment, in work and at home, is part of a broader discourse around "softening masculinity" (see de Boise & Hearn, 2017) in which men from the largely Anglophone Global North are seen as both more emotionally engaged with other aspects of their life – especially friendship, familial and romantic relationships – and more likely to display and communicate emotions. Nevertheless, the ability to take parental leave and time off to care for one's children is as much a structural issue as it is a personal choice. Men from dual-income, high-earner families and particularly those working white-collar professions where flexible working is possible, or those living in countries with subsidized childcare or parental leave are more freely able to participate in childcare. One aspect that is often overlooked in the idea of "softening masculinity" is also the extent to which this represents a fundamentally *new* shift and the extent to which it is one which affects all men. Indeed, while fairly one-sided caricatures of men as either explosively angry (Hochschild, 2018; Kimmel, 2013) or incompetent emotional articulators (see earlier) have been common, the historically emotionally intimate aspects of homosociality in fraternities, sports clubs and companies have tended to be unexplored through a lens of emotionality. Sports clubs and events have been one of the areas in which it has been historically acceptable for self-defined straight men to hug, kiss and cry at winning (or losing) without being deemed "effeminate" (Robertson, 2003). In this respect, while emotions can be positive in the sense that feelings of loyalty, love, admiration and respect for other men can be subjectively experienced as positive, given their role in homosocial "bonding", emotions can also contribute to exclusionary forms of practice. For this reason, a critical perspective on the ends to which emotions are put is also important (Pease, 2012).

The extent to which these trends have emerged in the past 20 or so years is also questionable. As noted already, historical approaches have shown that men's capacity to express emotions has been valorized in art and cultural organizations – especially in music from Antiquity through to the 2020s – as well as societies at large (Ekenstam, 1998; Forth, 2008). Men of colour, particularly, have historically been defined as "more emotional" (Segal, 1990, p. 188), and simultaneously both "hypermasculine" and "irrationally feminine" in line with racist, colonialist projects since the 1700s. Emotions were also important in organizing men in feminist consciousness-raising groups in the 1960s, 1970s and 1980s (Hearn, 1987; Kimmel, 1995; Seidler, 1991), during which time discussions of the "new man" were as present as they are today (Edwards, 2006; Gill, 2003). Furthermore, while the profeminist men's movement centred on a discussion of emotions, insecurities and patterns of care, the Mythopoetic men's movement which splintered off took a distinctly more ambiguous and even anti-feminist, essentialist turn. Men in this movement placed notions of fraternal love and emotional expression at the movement's core, attempting to "reclaim" an essence masculinity which, in some cases, was seen as having been lost or put under threat by modernism and feminism (see Kimmel, 1995). In this case, the "positive emotions" experienced by men in these movements were not always progressive in terms of furthering a commitment to gender equality because they maintained an essential distinction between men's and women's natural roles.

Affective and affecting masculinity

A focus on men as previously unemotional but becoming "softer" tends to reinforce the idea that emotions are the opposite of a "cold, unfeeling, rationality" characteristic of modernist capitalism (Illouz, 2007, p. 1) towards a more egalitarian future. Yet despite moving away from essentialist conceptions of emotions as hardwired, both unemotive and softening approaches treat emotions as discrete objects which can be thought of in terms of more or less. Discrete emotional experiences are hard to pin down given that multiple emotions are experienced simultaneously and, as noted earlier, emotions are discursively and physiologically intertwined with rationality, as well as context-dependent. In addition, while emotions might be thought of as episodic, the way men feel about their occupational or organizational identities, and why, is the outcome of longer periods of attachment to certain normative ideas about what masculinity is and what men *should* do. These experiences are not easily categorized under the rubric of emotion, but they do involve intense feelings of attachment and belonging.

With the "affective turn in feminist theory" (Koivunen, 2010), this has seen a corresponding shift towards examining notions of masculinity itself as affective; as an intensity that circulates between communities and which shape men's embodied experiences, wants, desires, insecurities and anxieties. For instance, Allan (2018) argues that the very idea of masculinity might be thought of as a form of "cruel optimism" (Berlant, 2011), in which discourses about an idealized form of masculinity as something attainable actually operate as a barrier to self-fulfilment (Ahmed, 2010a makes a similar argument with respect to the idea of the ideal of happiness as an end itself, as contributing to unhappiness). This entails thinking about men's actions as corporeally experienced in interaction with the circulation of discourses about ideas of masculinity (de Boise & Hearn, 2017; Reeser & Gottzén, 2018). Rather than arguing that masculinity is defined through the *actual* suppression or expression of emotions, this also allows for the possibility that the ideal of rationality is itself an attachment to an affective history (de Boise & Hearn, 2017) and that expressions of care and emotional expression may also prove fundamentally anti-egalitarian in their ends (de Boise, 2018).

The promise of affect is that it foregrounds the embodied experience of socio-economic factors while retaining a sense of indeterminacy. Walkerdine (2016), for instance, has observed how histories of "masculine" labour have a particularly enduring affective hold on the imagination of communities which were previously organized around heavy industry. As she observes, even after deindustrialization and a depression of wages, men from these communities often regard themselves, and were regarded by women as, the "breadwinner". Dagget (2018) suggests that the affective anxieties associated with what she suggests is white men's declining power, manifests itself in an attachment to petrochemicals as a reaction to environmental catastrophe. What she terms "petromasculinity" entails a deeply ingrained commitment to an idea of particularly gendered organizations (Acker, 1990) – in this case coal mining, the oil industries as well as providing the impetus for organiz*ing* around geopolitical issues tied up with a specific idea of masculinity. Similarly, the notion of "breadwinner masculinity", despite undergoing some transformation (Montes, 2013), is an enduring one which also exercises an affective hold over how men feel that they are supposed to act. While younger men might perceive career satisfaction, a "healthy" work–life balance and emotional fulfilment as more important than financial success (Elliott, 2020), many older in the global North men still retain the idea of their identity as tied to work (Thompson, 2018). Though it is not clear if this is an effect of cohort or ageing generally, this is not necessarily the case in countries with much lower retirement ages (for instance, Greece has the lowest expected retirement age) and socio-cultural expectations play a huge role in how men experience the idea of work–life balance.

The notion of affect as circulatory and relational has implications particularly for thinking about affective attachment to certain ideas of images of organizational success. Work by Berdahl et al. (2018), focusing largely on the United States, indicates that, despite the more positive shifts outlined earlier, there is still a "toxic leadership culture" based on competition between men – what they term "masculinity contest cultures". As they argue, this emphasis on risk-taking leads to unproductive work environments, as well as creating psychosocial barriers to equality within the workplaces. and how men as managers might put others at risk through the distribution of affect which creates a culture of risk (see also Ericson & Mellström, 2016; Mellström & Ericson, 2014). Again, these cultures may be *experienced*, subjectively, in largely positive emotional terms by individual men despite being harmful to both those who participate in them and those who are subject to them.

As already noted, emotions have been central to profeminist organizing among men. This is in terms of men both discussing emotions in relation to their personal lives and doing "emotion work" as a way of understanding their personal lives as political projects (Hearn, 1987; Seidler, 2006, 1991; White & Peretz, 2009). This is especially the case in organizing men around anti-violence against women initiatives (Messner et al., 2015). Foregrounding men's emotional experiences and understanding men's emotions are political projects insofar as emotions motivate – even if they do not determine – action. Emotion work is key to transforming how one feels about changes and how one responds to those changes whether organizational or societal. However, as also noted earlier, discussing and expressing emotions, even the more intimate ones associated with fear, anxiety, sadness and vulnerability, have also provided fertile ground for extreme ideas which appeal overwhelmingly more to men. Indeed, discussing emotions, as well as feelings of insecurities and anxieties associated with the idea of "declining masculinity" or a crisis of masculinity, has been a powerful recruiting tool, especially in the run-up to and following the 2016 election of Donald Trump in the United States (Hochschild, 2018; Kimmel, 2013).

This has seen the emboldening of the far-right among white men in particular and the organization of white men, especially, around the idea of the "threat" to masculinity posed by multiculturalism and feminism (Graff et al., 2019; Grant & MacDonald, 2020; Strick, 2020; Wojnicka, 2016). Most visibly, this culminated in the attack on the Capitol Hill on 6 January where the intersubjectivity of affect, as it related to ideas around masculinity, was on full display. The emphasis on affect as something which is subjectively experienced as well as which affects others is important in that it retains the focus on motivation (Sedgwick, 2003) but situates this motivation as neither fully cognitively conscious nor fully unconscious. In this way, it overcomes the tendency towards rational/emotional binaries which characterizes theorizing around men and masculinity in organizations, while leaving space for exploring the embodied experiences of these constructs.

Conclusion

The idea that cisgendered men in the Global North are unemotive or that occupational cultures in Global Northern countries have been built on "masculine" cultures of unemotionality, characterized research on emotions, men, masculinity and organizations in the 1980s and 1990s. This has given way, for the most part, to research on how changing expectations of men, predominantly in the Global North, have impacted both on men's experiences of organizations in relation to caring responsibilities at home and organizational cultures themselves. Crucially, this research has explored both how men experience, express and understand emotions, as well as demonstrating how emotions are valued or devalued within organizations in relation to cultural constructs of masculinity. Nevertheless, despite the political promise of emotions as a feminist project, the idea of men becoming more emotional has tended to leave the rational/emotional binary intact. With regard to men's organiz*ing*, the idea of softening and even caring masculinities also overlooks the centrality of emotions in homosocial forms of organization. This is a problem particularly when these same emotions are utilized to build and even animate movements aimed at undermining moves towards gender equality.

Affect provides a way of understanding the collective appeal of emotions for organizing men within both regressively extremist as well as progressively egalitarian groups. The indeterminacy of affect means that it is possible to accommodate both progressive moves towards gender equality and moves away from it, in a way that takes men's emotions seriously but does not construe them as ends in themselves. An understanding of affect as intensity and circulatory foregrounds the importance of looking at how intense embodied experiences manifest themselves in practice, rather than thinking in terms of less or more emotional.

References

Acker, J. (1990). Hierarchies, jobs, bodies: A theory of gendered organizations. *Gender & Society*, *4*(2), 139–158.

Ahmed, S. (2010a). Killing Joy: Feminism and the history of happiness. *Paper presented at the Centre for Interdisciplinary Gender Studies Annual Lecture*, University of Leeds, Leeds.

Ahmed, S. (2010b). *The Promise of Happiness*. London: Duke University Press.

Allan, J. A. (2018). Masculinity as cruel optimism. *NORMA: International Journal for Masculinity Studies*, *13*(3–4), 175–190. doi: 10.1080/18902138.2017.1312949

Allan, J. A., Herron, R. V., Ahmadu, M. E., Waddell, C., & Roger, K. (2021). 'I never wanted my children to see their father the way I've seen mine': Caring masculinities and fathering on the Prairies. *NORMA: International Journal for Masculinity Studies*, *16*(1), 23–37. doi: 10.1080/18902138.2020.1866322

Barbalet, J. M. (2001). *Emotion, Social Theory and Social Structure: A Macrosociological Approach*. Cambridge: Cambridge University Press.

Barrett, L. F. (2006). Valence is a basic building block of emotional life. *Journal of Research in Personality*, *40*(1), 35–55.

Berdahl, J. L., Cooper, M., Glick, P., Livingston, R. W., & Williams, J. C. (2018). Work as a masculinity contest. *Journal of Social Issues*, *74*(3), 422–448. doi: 10.1111/josi.12289

Berger, J. M., Levant, R., McMillan, K. K., Kelleher, W., & Sellers, A. (2005). Impact of gender role conflict, traditional masculinity ideology, alexithymia and age on men's attitudes towards psychological help seeking. *Psychology of Men & Masculinity*, *6*, 73–78. doi: 10.1037/1524-9220.6.1.73

Berlant, L. (2011). *Cruel Optimism*. Durham, NC: Duke University Press.

Blackman, L. (2008). Affect, relationality and the 'problem of personality'. *Theory, Culture & Society*, *25*(1), 23–47. doi: 10.1177/0263276407085157

Branney, P., & White, A. (2008). Big boys don't cry: Depression and men. *Advances in Psychiatric Treatment*, *14*(4), 256–262. doi: 10.1192/apt.bp.106.003467

Brody, L. (1999). *Gender, Emotion and the Family*. Cambridge, MA: Harvard University Press.

Connell, R. (1995). *Masculinities*. Cambridge: Polity Press.

Craig, L., Powell, A., & Cortis, N. (2012). Self-employment, work-family time and the gender division of labour. *Work, Employment & Society*, *26*(5), 716–734. doi: 10.1177/0950017012451642

Daggett, C. (2018). Petro-masculinity: Fossil fuels and authoritarian desire. *Millennium*, *47*(1), 25–44. doi: 10.1177/0305829818775817

Damasio, A. (1995). *Descartes' Error: Emotion, Reason and the Human Brain*. New York: Quill.

Darwin, C. (2009 [1872]). *The Expression of the Emotions in Man and Animals*. London: Penguin Classics.

de Boise, S. (2018). The personal is political . . . just not always progressive: Affective interruptions and their promise for CSMM. *NORMA: International Journal for Masculinity Studies*, *13*(3–4), 158–174. doi: 10.1080/18902138.2017.1325098

de Boise, S., & Hearn, J. (2017). Are men getting more emotional? Critical sociological perspectives on men, masculinities and emotions. *The Sociological Review*, *65*(4), 779–796. doi: 10.1177/0038026116686500

Descartes, R. (1989 [1649]). *Passions of the Soul with an Introduction by Geneviéve Rodis Lewis* (S. Voss, Trans.). Indianapolis IN: Hackett.
Descartes, R. (2001 [1637/1641]). *Discourse on Method & The Meditations.* London: Penguin Classics.
Duncombe, J., & Marsden, D. (1993). Love and intimacy: The gender division of emotion and 'emotion work'. *Sociology*, *27*(2), 221–241. doi: 10.1177/0038038593027002003
Duncombe, J., & Marsden, D. (1995). 'Workaholics' and 'whingeing women': Theorising intimacy and emotion work – the last frontier of gender inequality? *The Sociological Review*, *43*(1), 150–169. doi: 10.1111/j.1467-954X.1995.tb02482.x
Edlund, J., & Öun, I. (2016). Who Should work and who should care? Attitudes towards the desirable division of labour between mothers and fathers in five European countries. *Acta Sociologica*, *59*(2), 151–169. doi: 10.1177/0001699316631024
Edwards, T. (2006). *Cultures of Masculinity.* London: Routledge.
Ekenstam, C. (1998). En historia om manlig gråt. In C. Ekenstam, J. Frykman, T. Johansson, J. Kuosmanen, J. Ljunggren & A. Nilsson (Eds.), *Rädd att falla: Studier i manlighet* (pp. 50–123). Stockholm: Gidlund.
Ekman, P., & Friesen, W. V. (1971). Constants across cultures in the face and emotion. *Journal of Personality and Social Psychology*, *17*(2), 124–129. doi: 10.1037/h0030377
Elliott, K. (2015). Caring masculinities: Theorizing an emerging concept. *Men and Masculinities*, *19*(3), 240–259. doi: 10.1177/1097184X15576203
Elliott, K. (2020). *Young Men Navigating Contemporary Masculinities.* London: Palgrave Macmillan.
Ericson, M. (2021). 'It is men who die and all that, so what is new?' Male vulnerability, institutionalised masculinity and the present absence of a problem in Swedish rescue service accident prevention. *NORMA: International Journal for Masculinity Studies*, *16*(3), 159–173. doi: 10.1080/18902138.2021.1908761
Ericson, M., & Mellström, U. (Eds.). (2016). *Masculinities, Gender Equality, and Crisis Management.* London: Ashgate.
Firestone, S. (1979 [1970]). *The Dialectic of Sex: The Case for Feminist Revolution.* London: Women's Press.
Fischer, A., Eagly, A. H., & Oosterwijk, S. (2013). The meaning of tears: Which sex seems emotional depends on the social context. *European Journal of Social Psychology*, *43*(6), 505–515. doi: 10.1002/ejsp.1974
Fischer, A., & Manstead, A. (2000). The relation Between gender and emotions in different cultures. In A. Fischer (Ed.), *Gender and Emotion: Social Psychological Perspectives* (pp. 71–94). Cambridge: Cambridge University Press.
Forth, C. E. (2008). *Masculinity in the Modern West: Gender, Civilization and the Body.* Basingstoke: Palgrave Macmillan
Furnham, A., & Taylor, N. (2020). The relationship between emotional intelligence and occupational personality scales in senior management. *Personality and Individual Differences*, *154*, 109647. doi: 10.1016/j.paid.2019.109647
Galasinski, D. (2004). *Men and the Language of Emotions.* London: Palgrave Macmillan.
Geisler, E., & Kreyenfeld, M. (2018). Policy reform and fathers' use of parental leave in Germany: The role of education and workplace characteristics. *Journal of European Social Policy*, *29*(2), 273–291. doi: 10.1177/0958928718765638
Gill, R. (2003). Power and the production of subjects: A genealogy of the new man and the new lad. In B. Benwell (Ed.), *Masculinity and Men's Lifestyle Magazines* (pp. 34–56). Oxford: Blackwell.
Goffman, E. (1956). Embarrassment and social organization. *The American Journal of Sociology*, *62*(3), 264–271.
Goffman, E. (1969). *The Presentation of Self in Everyday Life.* London: Allen Lane.
Goleman, D. (1995). *Emotional Intelligence: Why it Can Matter more than IQ.* London: Bloomsbury.
Gorton, K. (2007). Theorizing emotion and affect. *Feminist Theory*, *8*(3), 333–348. doi: 10.1177/1464700107082369
Graff, A., Kapur, R., & Walters, S. D. (2019). Introduction: Gender and the rise of the global Right. *Signs: Journal of Women in Culture and Society*, *44*(3), 541–560. doi: 10.1086/701152
Grant, J., & MacDonald, F. (2020). The Alt Right, "toxic" masculinity and violence. In F. MacDonald & A. Dobrowolsky (Eds.), *Turbulent Times, Transformational Possibilities?: Gender and Politics Today* (pp. 368–388). Toronto: University of Toronto Press.

Gregg, M., & Siegworth, G. (Eds.). (2010). *The Affect Theory Reader*. Durham: Duke University Press.

Hanlon, N. (2012). *Masculinities, Care and Equality: Identity and Nurture in Men's Lives*. Basingstoke: Palgrave Macmillan.

Hanisch, C. (1969). The personal is political. In S. Firestone & A. Koedt (Eds.), *Notes from the Second Year*. New York: Radical Feminism.

Hearn, J. (1987). *The Gender of Oppression: Men, Masculinity and the Critique of Marxism*. Brighton: Wheatsheaf.

Hearn, J. (1993). Emotive subjects: Organizational men, organizational masculinities and the (de)construction of 'emotions'. In S. Fineman (Ed.), *Emotion in Organizations* (pp. 148–166). London: Sage.

Hearn, J., & Parkin, P. W. (1983). Gender and organizations: A selective review and a critique of a neglected area. *Organization Studies*, *4*(3), 219–242. doi: 10.1177/017084068300400302

Hochschild, A. (1979). Emotion work, feeling rules, and social structure. *The American Journal of Sociology*, *85*(3), 551–575.

Hochschild, A. (1983). *The Managed Heart: Commercialization of Human Feeling*. Berkeley, CA: University of California Press.

Hochschild, A. (2018). *Strangers in Their Own Land: Anger and Mourning on the American Right*. New York: The New Press.

Holmes, M. (2015). Men's emotions: Heteromasculinity, emotional reflexivity, and intimate relationships. *Men and Masculinities*, *18*(2), 176–192. doi: 10.1177/1097184x14557494

Illouz, E. (2007). *Cold Intimacies: The Making of Emotional Capitalism*. Cambridge: Polity Press.

James, W. (1879). The sentiment of rationality. *Mind*, *4*(15), 317–346. www.jstor.org/stable/2246635

James, W. (1884). What is an emotion? *Mind*, *9*(34), 188–205.

Johansson, T., & Klinth, R. (2008). Caring fathers. *Men and Masculinities*, *11*(1), 42–62. doi: 10.1177/1097184x06291899

Kelan, E. (2008). Gender, risk and employment insecurity: The masculine breadwinner subtext. *Human Relations*, *61*(9), 1171–1202. doi: 10.1177/0018726708094909

Kilkey, M. (2006). New Labour and reconciling work and family Life: Making it fathers' business? *Social Policy and Society*, *5*(02), 167–175. doi: 10.1017/S147474640500285X

Kimmel, M. (Ed.). (1995). *The Politics of Manhood: Profeminist Men Respond to the Mythopoetic Men's Movement (and the Mythopoetic Leader's Answer)*. Philadelphia, PA: Temple University Press.

Kimmel, M. (2013). *Angry White Men: American Masculinity at the End of an Era*. New York: Nation Books.

Koivunen, A. (2010). An affective turn?: Reimagining the subject of feminist theory. In M. Liljeström & S. Paasonen (Eds.), *Working with Affect in Feminist Readings: Disturbing Difference* (pp. 8–28). Abingdon: Routledge.

Lewis, K. (2000). When leaders display emotion: How followers respond to negative emotional expression of male and female leaders. *Journal of Organizational Behavior*, *21*(2), 221–234. doi: 10.1002/(SICI)1099-1379(200003)21:2<221::AID-JOB36>3.0.CO;2-0

Lewis, P. (2008). Emotion work and emotion space: Using a spatial perspective to explore the challenging of masculine emotion management practices. *British Journal of Management*, *19*(s1), S130–S140. doi: 10.1111/j.1467-8551.2008.00578.x

Lin, X. (2019). Young rural – urban migrant fathers in China: Everyday 'China Dream' and the negotiation of masculinity. *NORMA: International Journal for Masculinity Studies*, *14*(3), 168–182. doi: 10.1080/18902138.2019.1574140

Lloyd, G. (1984). *The Man of Reason: Male and Female in Western Philosophy*. London: Routledge.

Lohan, M. (2007). How might we understand men's health better? Integrating explanations from critical studies on men and inequalities in health. *Social Science & Medicine*, *65*(3), 493–504. doi: 10.1016/j.socscimed.2007.04.020

Mandell, B., & Pherwani, S. (2003). Relationship between emotional intelligence and transformational leadership style: A gender comparison. *Journal of Business and Psychology*, *17*(3), 387–404. doi: 10.1023/A:1022816409059

Massumi, B. (2002). *Parables for the Virtual: Movement, Sensation, Affect*. London: Duke University Press.

McDowell, L. (2011). *Redundant Masculinities?: Employment Change and White Working Class Youth*. London: Blackwell.

Mellström, U., & Ericson, M. (2014). Masculinity at risk. *NORMA: International Journal for Masculinity Studies, 9*(3), 147–150. doi: 10.1080/18902138.2014.951181
Messner, M. (1997). *Politics of Masculinities: Men in Movements.* Oxford: Alta Mira.
Messner, M., Greenberg, M., & Peretz, T. (2015). *Some Men: Feminist Allies and the Movement to End Violence against Women.* New York: Oxford University Press.
Montes, V. (2013). The role of emotions in the construction of masculinity: Guatemalan migrant men, transnational migration, and family relations. *Gender & Society, 27*(4), 469–490. doi: 10.1177/0891243212470491
Nixon, D. (2009). 'I can't put a smiley face on': Working-class masculinity, emotional labour and service work in the 'new economy'. *Gender, Work & Organization, 16*(3), 300–322. doi: 10.1111/j.1468-0432.2009.00446.x
Pease, B. (2012). The politics of gendered emotions: Disrupting men's emotional investment in privilege. *Australian Journal of Social Issues, 47*(1), 125–142.
Pedwell, C., & Whitehead, A. (2012). Affecting feminism: Questions of feeling in feminist theory. *Feminist Theory, 13*(2), 115–129. doi: 10.1177/1464700112442635
Petersen, A. (2004). *Engendering Emotions.* Basingstoke: Palgrave Macmillan.
Probyn, E. (2004). Shame in the habitus. *The Sociological Review, 52*(2), 224–248. doi: 10.1111/j.1467-954X.2005.00533.x
Putnam, L., & Mumby, D. (1993). Organizations, emotion and the myth of rationality. In S. Fineman (Ed.), *Emotion in Organizations* (pp. 36–57). London: Sage.
Reddy, W. (2001). *The Navigation of Feeling: A Framework for the History of Emotions.* Cambridge: Cambridge University Press.
Reeser, T. (2020). Approaching affective masculinities. In L. Gottzen, U. Mellström & T. Shefer (Eds.), *The Routledge Handbook of Masculinity Studies* (pp. 103–111). London: Routledge.
Reeser, T., & Gottzén, L. (2018). Masculinity and affect: New possibilities, new agendas. *NORMA: International Journal for Masculinity Studies, 13*(3–4), 145–157. doi: 10.1080/18902138.2018.1528722
Roberts, S. (2011). Men at work? Emerging nuances in young masculinities in the United Kingdom's retail sector. In B. Pini, R. Price & P. McDonald (Eds.), *Young People and Work* (pp. 67–84). Burlington, VT: Ashgate.
Robertson, S. (2003). 'If I let a goal in, I'll get beat up': Contradictions in masculinity, sport and health. *Health Education Research: Theory and Practice, 18*(6), 706–716. doi: 10.1093/her/cyf054
Robertson, S., & Monaghan, L. F. (2012). Embodied heterosexual masculinities, part 2: Foregrounding men's health and emotions. *Sociology Compass, 6*(2), 151–165. doi: 10.1111/j.1751-9020.2011.00443.x
Roper, M. (2003). *Masculinity and the British Organization Man Since 1945.* Oxford: Oxford University Press.
Salin, M., Ylikännö, M., & Hakovirta, M. (2018). How to divide paid work and unpaid care between parents? Comparison of attitudes in 22 Western countries. *Social Sciences, 7*(10). doi: 10.3390/socsci7100188
Sattel, J. W. (1976). The inexpressive male: Tragedy or sexual politics? *Social Problems, 23*(4), 469–477. doi: 10.2307/799856
Scambor, E., Bergmann, N., Wojnicka, K., et al. (2014). Men and gender equality: European Insights. *Men and Masculinities, 17*(5), 552–577. doi: 10.1177/1097184X14558239
Sedgwick, E. (2003). *Touching Feeling: Affect, Pedagogy, Performativity.* Durham, NC: Duke University Press.
Segal, L. (1990). *Slow Motion: Changing Masculinities, Changing Men.* London: Virago.
Seidler, V. (Ed.). (1991). *The Achilles Heel Reader: Men, Sexual Politics and Socialism.* London: Routledge.
Seidler, V. (1994). *Unreasonable Men: Masculinity and Social Theory.* London: Routledge.
Seidler, V. (2006). *Transforming Masculinities: Men, Cultures, Bodies, Power, Sex and Love.* Oxon: Routledge.
Seidler, V. (2007). Masculinities, bodies, and emotional life. *Men and Masculinities, 10*(1), 9–21. doi: 10.1177/1097184x07299636
Simpson, R. (2009). *Men in Caring Occupations: Doing Gender Differently.* Basingstoke: Palgrave Macmillan.

Solomon, R. (1993). *The Passions: Emotions and The Meaning of Life.* Indianapolis IN: Hackett Publishing Company.
Strick, S. (2020). The Alternative Right: Masculinities and ordinary affect. In G. Dietze & J. Roth (Eds.), *Right-Wing Populism and Gender: European Perspectives and beyond.* Bielefeld: Transcript. doi: 10.1515/9783839449806-012
Thoits, P. (1989). The sociology of emotions. *Annual Review of Sociology, 15*, 317–342.
Thompson, E. (2018). *Men, Masculinities, and Aging: The Gendered Lives of Older Men.* London: Rowman and Littlefield.
Thompson, E., Grisanti, C., & Pleck, J. (1985). Attitudes toward the male role and their correlates. *Sex Roles, 13*(7–8), 413–427.
Tomkins, S. (1962). *Affect Imagery Consciousness: Volume 1 The Positive Affects.* New York: Springer.
Turner, J. (1999). The neurology of emotion: Implications for sociological theories of interpersonal behaviour. In D. D. Franks & T. S. Smith (Eds.), *Mind, Brain and Society: Toward a Neurosociology of Emotion* (pp. 81–108). Stanford, CA: JAI Press.
Turner, J. H., & Stets, J. E. (2005). *The Sociology of Emotions.* Cambridge: Cambridge University Press.
Walkerdine, V. (2016). Affective history, working-class communities and self-determination. *The Sociological Review, 64*(4), 699–714. doi: 10.1111/1467-954X.12435
Ward, M. R. M., Tarrant, A., Terry, G., Featherstone, B., Robb, M., & Ruxton, S. (2017). Doing gender locally: The importance of 'place' in understanding marginalised masculinities and young men's transitions to 'safe' and successful futures. *The Sociological Review, 65*(4), 797–815. doi: 10.1177/0038026117725963
Warner, L., & Shields, S. A. (2009). Status, gender, and the politics of emotional authenticity. In M. Samela & V. Mayer (Eds.), *Emotions, Ethics, and Authenticity* (pp. 91–111). Philadelphia, PA: John Benjamins.
Wetherell, M. (2012). *Affect and Emotion: A New Social Science Understanding.* London: Sage.
White, A., & Peretz, T. (2009). Emotions and redefining Black masculinity: Movement narratives of two profeminist organizers. *Men and Masculinities, 12*(4), 403–424. doi: 10.1177/1097184X08326007
Williams, R. (1958). *Culture and Society: 1780–1950.* London: Columbia University Press.
Wojnicka, K. (2016). Masculist groups in Poland: Aids of mainstream Antifeminism. *International Journal for Crime, Justice and Social Democracy, 5*(2), 36–49.
Wong, Y., Pituch, K., & Rochlen, A. (2006). Men's restrictive emotionality: An investigation of associations with other emotion-related constructs, anxiety, and underlying dimensions. *Psychology of Men & Masculinity, 7*(2), 113–126.

15

MINGLE WITH MEN

Sexuality and gay men in organizations

Laura Eigenmann

Introduction

Sexuality – including sexual acts, desires, emotions, verbal interactions, relationships, harassment, jokes, images, identities, rules and norms – plays a central role in constructing masculinities, gendered power relations and hierarchies between men. Therefore, it is also an indispensable element for studying men and masculinity in organizations. Yet, until the 1980s, sexuality did not commonly appear as a topic of analysis in organizational studies (Hearn & Parkin, 1987, p. 4). This way, the field uncritically reproduced the modern bourgeois and capitalist idea of a neat division between the public and the private spheres, which deemed sexuality a purely private affair. From the mid-1970s on, however, feminist scholars (e.g. Farley, 1978) and some organizational scholars (e.g. Quinn, 1977) started to point out the pervasiveness of sexuality in organizations, especially in the form of straight men sexually harassing women and mutual (hetero)sexual relationships. Inspired by this research, organizational studies scholars have since analysed sexuality in and of organizations in its various forms and from multiple perspectives. Hearn and Parkin (1987) were among the earliest to do so, pointing out that "The organizational construction of sexuality and the power of sexuality to reconstruct organizations exist in a dialectical relationship" (Hearn & Parkin, 1987, p. 131).

This chapter sheds light on the complex and mutually constitutive relationship between masculinity, sexuality and organization. It does so by approaching the topic from the perspective of the inherent heteronormativity of organizations, investigating historical, theoretical and empirical aspects and its implications for gay men. In the first part, the chapter reviews relevant literature, focusing on the following aspects: (a) the historical development and alleged de-sexualization of organizations; (b) the close intertwining of the various dynamics, norms and practices of sexuality in organizations with the construction of hegemonic heterosexual masculinity; (c) the negative impacts of the heteronormativity of organizations on gay men in terms of discrimination and career trajectories; and (d) the empowering aspect of gay male identities, especially in terms of how sharing a gay identity provides the potential for closer workplace relationships, mutual support, and building strong informal networks among gay men, which both compensate for their marginalization. To illustrate this last

DOI: 10.4324/9781003193579-17

point, the second part draws from my own research on informal networks among gay male EU employees in Brussel's LGBTIQ+ advocacy community.

Heteronormativity and the historical de-sexualization of organizations

Many organizations have long been regarded as de-sexualized entities that systematically control and suppress sexuality. In one of the earliest articles on the topic, Burrell (1984), using historical examples, argues that in Europe, modern bureaucratic organizations, which emerged from the Middle Ages onwards, sought to eradicate sexuality from religious, work and state institutions, relegating it to the private bedrooms of married, heterosexual couples to maintain order, enforce calculative rationality and increase productivity. From the start, these attempts to de-sexualize organizations have been closely intertwined with the construction of heteronormativity in at least three interrelated ways: through the disciplining of sexuality into its reproductive and, therefore, heterosexual form; through the enforcement of a gendered and heterosexualized public–private divide; and through the suppression of same-sex desire and sex among men in homosocial contexts.

First, as mentioned earlier, Burrell (1984, p. 107f) argues that those in charge of modern organizations hoped that eradicating sexuality from the public sphere would guarantee order and productivity. This became even more important from the late eighteenth century onwards, as the Industrial Revolution and capitalism fundamentally transformed the social and political order. According to Burrell (1984, p. 113), sexuality was perceived as "expressive of nonrational, uncontrollable emotions which must be suppressed in the interest of efficiency and good order". Burrell draws on Foucault's (1978) concept of "Bio-Power". According to Foucault, the nineteenth century witnessed the emergence of a new form of governance that targeted the population's life, health and size, and operated by controlling how every individual used their sexuality. According to this new governmentality, any form of sexuality that did not directly contribute to the biological reproduction of society was an unnecessary waste of energy. Therefore, the heterosexual, monogamous, married and procreating couple became the norm and the only place where sexuality was accepted and considered healthy (ibid.)

Second, attempts to de-sexualize organizations were part of the emerging bourgeois class's efforts to establish a neat division between work and home – or, more generally, between the private and the public spheres. This division was constitutively linked to a new bipolar and heteronormative gender order, in which sex replaced social class as the primary determinant of an individual's place in society (Hausen, 1976). The heterosexual, married couple was the core unit of this new gender order in which men and women were imagined as opposites completing each other. Sexuality – including emotion, love, desire, comfort, instincts – was ascribed to femininity and the private sphere. In contrast, rationality, instrumentality and competitiveness were ascribed to masculinity, work and the public sphere (Burrell, 1984, p. 99; Fleming, 2007, p. 242; Roper, 1996, p. 212).

It is no wonder, then, that homosexual men constituted a threat to this new social and gender order – and nineteenth-century sexologists became obsessed with them. Gay men not only failed to become part of the core unit of bourgeois society – the heterosexual family – they also disturbed the gendered public–private division. By desiring other men – especially when done so at work or in total single-sex institutions such as the military, convents or boarding schools – they brought sexuality into the public sphere and threatened the construction of men as rational actors in control of their emotions and carnal desires (Klapeer,

2014, p. 197; Rastetter, 1994, p. 209). What undermines the construction of self-restrained, rational masculinity even more is that homosexual sexuality is perceived as particularly uncontrollable and excessive (Hall, 1989; Rumens & Kerfoot, 2009, p. 768; Sombart, 1991).

As Steffen et al. (2016, p. 368) point out, this still affects the work experiences of gays and lesbians today. Reportedly, when heterosexual employees disclose their sexual orientation by showing pictures of their partners or telling stories about their weekends, these acts go mostly unnoticed. However, when homosexuals do the same, co-workers often perceive these disclosures as intrusive insights into their private sex life. It is, therefore, not surprising that various studies (Humphrey, 1999; Rumens & Kerfoot, 2009; Woods & Lucas, 1993) found that man gays and lesbians choose to keep their sexual orientation private to come across "more professional".

Third, historically, the de-sexualization of modern organizations seems to be closely related to the de-eroticization of male friendships and the suppression of homoerotic desire and sexuality between men in homosocial institutions. As Mosse (1983, p. 76f) points out, while in the eighteenth century, close and intimate friendships between men were common and often idealized in many European societies, by the end of the nineteenth century, the bourgeois concept of sexual "respectability" started to prevail. "Respectability" tried to counter the threads of the new "nervous age" (ibid., p. 75) of industrialization and urbanization with ideals of control, restraint and hard work. Now, "[t]he free flow of passion and fantasy was seen as a threat to the order of things" (ibid.). As a result, there were growing attempts "to strip male friendships of all erotic content" (ibid., p. 76).

Another reason why homoerotic relationships between men were perceived as threatening was that they seemed to violate the rules and hierarchies of organizations, ignore established divisions across class and nationality, and bypass the principle of competition and concurrence (Rastetter, 1994, pp. 130, 250). Homosexual men were said to stick together in "uncontrollable solidarity" (ibid., p. 130, translated by LE), potentially forming "new alliances and tying together of unforeseen lines of force" (Foucault,1997, p. 136). By the end of the nineteenth century, this gave rise to the violent suppression of same-sex sexuality in homosocial contexts and totalitarian single-sex institutions, such as the military, convents, boarding schools or the German "Männerbünde"[1] (Burrell, 1984; Foucault, 1997; Rastetter, 1994; Theweleit, 1987), as well as to the association of gay men with espionage in the twentieth century (Woods, 2016, p. 8). Therefore, the de-sexualization of organizations via the suppression of same-sex sexuality among men was also a way to introduce standardized hierarchies and increase organizational control via suppressing seemingly non-rational and unpredictable elements of male relationships.

Heteronormativity in dynamics, norms and practices of (work) organization sexuality

Of course, the efforts to de-sexualize modern organizations did not lead to the *de facto* elimination of all forms and aspects of sexuality from them but rather disciplined it into certain forms considered acceptable. As Rumens (2018, p. 39) notes, these efforts are just one example of how organizations deal with sexuality and how organizations and sexuality mutually construct each other. Collinson and Collinson (1989, 1996) caution that analysing organization sexuality exclusively through the lens of management and control was reductionist and tended to neglect its role in reproducing gendered power relations. In their case studies, only *some* managers seemed concerned with the de-sexualization of labour to avoid distractions from work, while others were not. Furthermore, they point out that the pervasiveness of heterosexual men's sexual discourses and practices in organizations – including the acceptance and normalization of sexual harassment – indicates that only some forms of sexuality were regulated and suppressed. Hearn and Parkin (1987), too, emphasize that sexuality was present in organizations in innumerable ways, for example, in the form of fantasies, feelings, flirtations, allusions, relationships, harassment, discrimination, bullying and generally as part of power dynamics.

These various dynamics, practices and norms of sexuality in organizations are deeply gendered and further enforce heteronormativity. To begin, the workplace still is a main avenue where people seek out heterosexual relationships (Hearn, 2011). But more importantly, workplaces are central sites for the construction and reproduction of hegemonic masculinity and gendered power relations, which centrally operate via heterosexual sexual dynamics.

Men and women do not contribute to organization sexuality equally. Organizations continue to be overwhelmingly dominated by heterosexual men and their definitions and practices of sexuality (Collinson & Collinson, 1989, p. 93). In most cases, men's sexual behaviour in organizations is less about finding a sexual or romantic partner and more about power. A range of studies have analysed how men in organizations use sexuality in their everyday practices to strengthen their power and reinforce the subordination of women (Cockburn, 1983, 1991; Collinson & Collinson, 1989; Gutek, 1985; Hearn, 1985; Pringle, 1989). This is especially apparent when men sexually harass women (Cockburn, 1991, p. 141). But asserting power and re-enforcing hierarchies is also a central component of flirtations, innuendos, jokes, women-objectifying talk, the hiring of women based on their attractiveness, the use of attractive secretaries as status symbols, references to sexual metaphors to describe work (Hearn, 1985) and often even of mutual heterosexual romantic relationships (Quinn, 1977).

All these practices relegate women to objects of male sexual desire. Importantly, sexuality here is less a matter of desire and more a matter of conquest and domination. As Cockburn (1991, p. 142) argues, the sexualization of women is often a strategy of men to control and diminish any potential power that women might acquire within an organization, which might threaten their superior position. Hearn (1985, p. 121) describes how women are often driven out of their workplace by sexual harassment or after starting a romantic relationship with a colleague, concluding that "[s]exual harassment can act as a powerful form of economic protection and exclusion from men's territory". Furthermore, men's sexualization of women in the workplace might also more generally be a reaction to women's breach of the "sexual contract" (Pateman, 1988), according to which a women's place is at home. There are, therefore, strong connections between men's (hetero)sexual practices at work, gendered power relations and power relations at work.

Controlling women's bodies and sexuality is also a key component of men's identities and a factor that determines their position vis-à-vis other men (Hearn & Parkin, 1987, p. 132). For example, Hearn (ibid., p. 118) describes how some men appoint sexually attractive secretaries to "excite the envy of your colleagues". Therefore, the sexualization of women is also a strategy to reinforce competition and solidarity between men (ibid.). Both Cockburn (1983) and Collinson and Collinson (1989) come to similar conclusions in their analysis of how women-objectifying talk among working-class men in the newspaper industry and on the shop floor facilitates male bonding and creates class solidarity among them against their exploitative employers.

Another important dimension of sexuality in organizations that reinforces heteronormativity is the complex dynamic of sexual desire *between* men. Hearn and Parkin (1995, p. 158) point out that "[o]rganization sexuality is for men characteristically a mixture of homosociability, latent homosexuality, homophobia and heterosexual phallocentrism". As mentioned earlier, historically, homophobia often intensified in homosocial contexts. The same can be said for contemporary work organizations. Generally, the more an organization provides opportunities for men to socialize with each other, the more it seems to deny and suppress the potential threat of same-sex desire. In such organizations, men often demonstrate emotional detachment, independence, competitiveness and – as discussed earlier – sexualize women (Bird, 1996; Collinson, 1992, p. 114f). These obsessive demonstrations of agency and "*libido dominandi*" (Bourdieu, 2001) underline the denial of any form of passivity – both a central element for the construction of masculinity and an inherent threat imposed by male same-sex desire.

Nonetheless, relationships between men at work are often marked by sexual tensions. Especially insightful here is Roper's (1996) study of managerial masculinities, which investigates intimacies and "circuits of homosocial desire" between men. For example, Roper found that managers often choose their successors based on a feeling of having "the right chemistry" (ibid.) with this person – a feeling he interprets as latent homoeroticism. Men emulating their mentors – including dress, posture, gestures – and "horseplay" are other examples of homoerotic dynamics. Hearn (1985, p. 124) describes horseplay as "intense physical contact" between men, such as playful attacking, hugging, firm hand contact and playfully grabbing each other's genitalia. While Hearn interprets such practices as a demonstration of heterosexual "macho" culture and independence from other men, Roper (1996, p. 224) sees them as a concealed expression of homosocial desire. He argues that men resort to such covert strategies because a continuum between friendship and sexual relations – which seems generally accepted among women – is radically refused by men.

Experiences of discrimination

The heteronormativity of organizations can have a range of negative implications for gay, lesbian and bisexual employees. These include formal discrimination in the hiring, promotion and firing process; informal discriminations such as harassment, physical and psychological violence, or inappropriate jokes; invisibility; or economic disadvantages. Based on anticipated or experienced discrimination, some LGB people might avoid socializing for fear of being forced to come out. Discrimination, fear and invisibility can affect the physical and mental health of LGB workers, their career trajectories and their job satisfaction.

Researchers have investigated these issues since the late 1970s. Levine (1979) provided one of the first systematic reviews of existing research. Other early reviews include Badgett (1996) and Croteau (1996). However, academic studies were extremely scarce in the first two decades, and those interested in the topic had to rely mostly on data generated by public opinion polls or surveys undertaken by gay activist organizations.

The situation started to improve throughout the 1990s. In the past two decades, the field has grown enormously. Recent reviews (Colgan & Rumens, 2015; Ng & Rumens, 2017; Ozeren, 2014; Rumens, 2018) identify over 1000 studies analysing the discrimination of LGBTIQ+ people in employment from various perspectives. These reviews usually identify two (before 1990 and after 1990) or three (before the early 1990s, from the mid-1990s to 2000, and after 2000) "waves" of research on the topic. These waves differ by focus, aim and the political and social context against which they are set. However, this only applies to the context of the United States, the United Kingdom and the EU – on which most studies focus.[2]

"First-wave" research – which started against the background of the radical 1970s "Gay Liberation" – was primarily concerned with providing evidence for the pervasiveness of discrimination against gays and lesbians. It focused on practices of formal and – to a lesser degree – informal discrimination; on how discrimination impeded individuals' careers and opportunities, on strategies employed by gays and lesbians to conceal their sexual orientation, and on the consequences of voluntary and involuntary identity disclosure (Badgett, 1996; Croteau, 1996; Levine, 1979). Early studies investigating the situation of gay men include those by Williams and Weinberg (1971), Escoffier (1975), Beer et al. (1983) and Olson (1987). These studies were set in a context in which homosexuals enjoyed minimal to no legal protection (Badgett, 1996), and overt formal discrimination such as not hiring, not promoting or firing persons because they were known or suspected to be gay was widespread and socially accepted. Levine (1979) reported that in a 1974 public opinion poll by the Kinsey Institute, 77% of the US respondents felt that gay men should not work in high-status occupations and supported barring them from jobs such as court judges, schoolteachers, ministers, doctors or government officials. Many employers had official policies prohibiting the employment of homosexuals and screened employees with polygraph tests or private investigators before granting them a promotion (ibid., p. 156).

Consequently, most gay men concealed their sexual orientation and undertook significant efforts to "pass" as heterosexuals, for example, by inventing girlfriends and ex-wives or feminizing their partner's name when talking about their private life. Others consciously chose careers in industries considered more tolerant or lower-status jobs. Therefore, as Levine (1979, p. 161) points out, gay men often worked in jobs beneath their qualification or potentials.

"Second wave" research in the early to mid-1990s expanded the focus towards informal discrimination such as verbal harassment, bullying and jokes (Ozeren, 2014, p. 1205). Furthermore, studies investigated how discrimination varies in different industries and settings and across different subgroups of the LGBTIQ+ umbrella (Rumens, 2018, p. 45, e.g. Humphrey, 1999 [public sector], Woods & Lucas, 1993 [business], Burke, 1993 [police], Cammermeyer, 1994; Hall, 1995 [military]). There were also more diversified perspectives on "coming out". In addition to strategies for concealing sexual orientation and the relationship between identity disclosure and discrimination, research now also investigated the factors influencing employees' decisions and strategies to come out (Griffin, 1992; Humphrey, 1999; Woods & Lucas, 1993). Undoubtedly, this shift was influenced by the changing social climate and legal situation in parts of the United States, the United Kingdom and the EU. As it slowly became possible for at least some people to come out without seriously threatening their careers, researchers started to emphasize the benefits of coming out (ibid.; Day & Schoenrade, 1997).

With the emergence of new policies and legislation protecting LGBTIQ+ workers in the late 1990s, second- and third-wave research started to evaluate their effectiveness and tried to identify "best practice" examples for supporting LGBTIQ+ workers. In "third-wave" research, this trend was accompanied by new "business case" arguments for non-discrimination. Researchers now emphasized how inclusion was beneficial for the health and well-being of workers and, therefore, "good for business". Many studies since the 2000s refer to the "minority stress model" (Meyer, 2003) to argue that individuals who hide their sexual orientation for fear of discrimination showed lower performance, productivity, job satisfaction and health because they "wasted" energy trying to conceal their sexual identity

(Badgett et al., 2013; Day & Schoenrade, 1997; Griffith & Hebl, 2002; Steffen et al., 2016). According to this argument, supporting the inclusion of LGBTIQ+ workers contributed to optimizing the organization's exploitation of its workforce, helped attract the most competent workers and increased employees' loyalty (Rumens, 2018, p. 57). However, as Badgett et al. (2013) point out, while the "business case for diversity" seems to be one of the main motivations for organizations to adopt LGBTIQ+-friendly policies, empirical evidence is rather weak. While research does show that LGBTIQ+ friendliness improves individuals' job satisfaction, health, motivation and the overall work climate, there is no evidence on whether these changes actually "pay off" *for the organization* in terms of increased creativity and innovation, a larger customer base, greater recruitment or improved stock prices.

More recently, some researchers have started to criticize managerial discourses on "diversity management". Rumens (2018), for example, argues that these discourses might introduce new restrictive norms because they "constitute organizationally desirable LGBT+ subjects, leaving an array of sexual and gendered Others behind". As Williams et al. (2009) found in their research on "gay-friendly" organizations, homosexuals are often only accepted if they comply with traditional gender roles, middle-class values and conservative politics.

Still, there are reasons for a more positive outlook. According to two surveys by the European Agency for Fundamental Rights (FRA) in 2012 and 2019, significantly more LGBTIQ+ people now report being often or always open about their identity (from 36% in 2012 to 52% in 2019) (FRA, 2020, p. 10). While, in contrast, the percentage of LGBTIQ+ people experiencing discrimination at work increased slightly (from 19% in 2012 to 21% in 2019) (ibid.), this might partly be explained by the fact that more people being out also provides more opportunities for discrimination and by a higher awareness of the injustice of discrimination.

Empowering aspects of gay identities and the EU-level advocacy network around LGBTIQ+ rights

While research on sexuality and organization has developed and diversified enormously over the past three decades, Rumens (2018) points out that a striking commonality of most approaches is that they tend to focus on the negative side of sexuality – such as the reproduction of gendered power hierarchies, sexual harassment and experiences of discrimination. Among the few exceptions are case studies demonstrating that in some organizations, certain forms of queerness are encouraged – either because they contribute to the organization's self-image as fun, progressive or unconventional (e.g. Fleming, 2007; Wasser, 2017), or because certain stereotypes about LGBTIQ+ people align with what is expected from employees (e.g. gay men in public relations benefit from being stereotyped as creative (Tindall & Waters, 2012)). Rumens (2008, 2010a) provides another exception. Analysing gay men's friendships at work, he emphasizes the potential of these friendships to overcome the emotional distance which typically characterizes work relationships between straight men. The gay men he interviewed seemed to develop closer, more affectionate relationships, which provided a source of moral support and helped them climb the career ladder.

The remainder of this chapter delves deeper into the empowering potentials of gay men's workplace friendships, drawing on the example of the EU-level advocacy network on LGBTIQ+ rights. It analyses how LGBTIQ+ EU employees have developed a highly effective informal network among each other, enabling them to influence the policy process despite mostly lacking formal power. More precisely, it focuses on two interrelated aspects: first, it describes how shared experiences of marginalization serve as a base for LGBTIQ+ people to develop a common identity, which strengthens mutual solidarity, support and close friendships. Second, it analyses the role of sexual attraction in these networks for, on the one hand, closer relationships between gay men, and on the other hand, the exclusion of women from these networks and the reproduction of gendered hierarchies.

The unifying and empowering potential of marginalization

Over the past three decades, the European Union has increasingly built a reputation as a promoter of LGBTIQ+ rights. While a range of factors has contributed to this development – including the re-conceptualization of the EU's identity as a human rights actor in the 1990s, the neoliberal re-evaluation of diversity and pressure from LGBTIQ+ civil society organizations – policy change also built up through the action of individuals and their networks *within* the EU institutions. As analyses of the EU's LGBTIQ+ policy history show (Mos, 2012; Swiebel, 2009), it was often a very small circle of actors pulling strings behind the scenes which gave the impetus or decisively contributed to change.

Some of these actors were straight MEPs and high-level EU bureaucrats – most of them women politicized in the feminist movement. However, many of the key actors were LGB employees in mid- and low-level positions, who used a range of informal routes and strategies to compensate for their lack of formal power. Some tried to influence and educate their superiors directly. Others contributed by sharing early policy drafts, information about upcoming opportunities or the need for intervention informally with other actors in the LGBTIQ+ advocacy network. Others found ways to incorporate LGBTIQ+ rights into existing institutional structures, "sneak" them into documents, dossiers and agendas, or give them a higher profile.

According to Mahoney and Thelen (2010), such strategies are typically employed by "united subordinate groups" (ibid., p. 10) – marginalized actors who individually do not have the power to change an institution fundamentally. When an institution strongly disadvantages a group of people, this group often tends to "organize and come to identity with one another" (ibid., p. 9), assembling the power and capacities of its members so that the group becomes able to transform the institution. This is also what happened in the case analysed here: LGBTIQ+ EU employees started to form a tightly knit informal network connecting highly dedicated actors, which allowed them to use the little resources available very efficiently. The base on which they "organized and came to identity with one another" was their shared sexual identity. This identity increased the dedication of individuals to the issue and the bonds they formed with each other. It did so in several ways.

First, many influential actors have a background in LGBTIQ+ activism (Paternotte et al., 2011, p. 219; Swiebel, 2009, p. 29). These actors are dedicated to the network because of their deep-rooted political persuasions and visions that drove them towards activism in the first place. Furthermore, like Woodward (2004) observed in the field of gender equality, they are often connected by shared biographies and friendships that they have built over time with fellow activists who now also work for the EU institutions.

Second, others do not have an activist background but simply associate with the network because they identify as LGBT. In these cases, the idea of sharing an identity seems to be enough to create the feeling of belonging to the LGBTIQ+ policy community and inspire solidarity. As Woodward (2004, p. 79) points out, shared identities often have a unifying potential as they "may be powerful activators of personal relations across status and class". For the LGBTIQ+ community, this unifying potential is particularly relevant because the idea of a shared "global gay identity" is particularly popular among European activists. The term "global gay identity" describes the idea that LGBTIQ+ individuals from all over the world are connected via a common identity based on shared experiences of marginalization, which transcends national borders, class hierarchies and cultural differences, and creates a strong bond of solidarity among them (Altman, 1996; Binnie, 2004; Oswin, 2006).

In the case of the EU institutions, this idea is further strengthened by the myth of a "homosexual cosmopolitanism" (Rupp, 2014, p. 34) – the belief that homosexuals are naturally drawn to international organizations. Some argue that because homosexuals have long been excluded from the national imaginary, they tend to identify more with other homosexuals than with their compatriots (Phelan, 2001). Several respondents depict the EU half-jokingly as a bureaucracy literally permeated by homosexuals, especially by gay men (IP 01, 02, 18, 21, 24, 25, 27_3).

Whether or not homosexuals densely populate the EU institutions is hard to prove. In any case, the informal, gleeful and half-joking way respondents bring this claim up indicates that its value lies less in its accuracy but in the way it feels empowering to those holding onto it. It gives them the feeling of being part of a conspirative community, which draws its strength from building dense networks between disparate actors, turning their shared experiences of marginalization into a source of power through solidarity. As Weeks (1996, p. 72) argues,

> The strongest sense of community is, in fact, likely to come from those groups who find the premises of their collective existence threatened, and who construct out of this a community of identity which provides a strong sense of resistance and empowerment.

The unifying and empowering aspect of the idea of a "global gay identity" lies therefore also in how it depicts gays and lesbians as using their shared negative experiences of marginalization and discrimination to "strike back". Ironically, therefore, the accusation against homosexuals of holding together in "uncontrollable solidarity" turns into a self-fulfilling prophecy.

It is important to stress that the "global gay identity" does not work outside global and social power structures – and, therefore, despite its name, it is an idea mainly shared and shaped by Western, white, cisgender gay men. However, these activists are the ones who dominate the lobby politics at the EU level. While "global gay" communities are undoubtedly as imagined as are national communities (Anderson, 2006 [1983]), "this belief has material and cultural effects" (Weeks, 1996, p. 75). It materializes in institutions, practices and cultures, such as international Pride tourism and international LGBTIQ+ organizations (Klapeer & Laskar, 2018) – or the EU-level advocacy network around LGBTIQ+ rights.

"Mingle with men": the dominance of gay men and the role of sexual attraction

A striking feature of the informal networks among LGBTIQ+ EU employees is that they are heavily dominated by cis gay men. Partly, this might be explained by the general underrepresentation of women in the European institutions,[3] partly by the structural dominance of men, from which the LGBTIQ+ movement is not exempt. Several respondents (IPs 01, 05, 27_1, 27_3) observe that white gay cis men dominate most LGBTIQ+ organizations. They speculate that women are turned off by the dominance of men and their interests but also because "the way they [gay men] behave doesn't appeal to these women" (IP 01). One respondent (IP 05), a member of an EU-level feminist civil society organization, speculates that the male dominance of the LGBTIQ+ movement has also contributed to its recent success, as men tended to have more power, better connections to other powerful men, more financial resources and that gay men were generally "very well embedded in patriarchy".

However, another explanation for the dominance of cis gay men has to do with the role of sexual attraction. The "global gay identity" is not only based on shared experiences of discrimination and marginalization but also on sharing the desire for one's own gender. Additionally, members of homosocial subgroups also share the (actual and potential) desire for each other. Given the central role of sexual attraction and sexual relations for the identity construction of gays, lesbians and bisexuals, it seems evident that erotic attraction also influences the relationships of actors in the LGBTIQ+ advocacy network with each other. Friendship research found that sexuality plays a particularly central role in friendships between gay men. According to Nardi (1992, p. 182), "sexual attraction and sexual involvement are salient components in the early stages of friendship for most gay men", and "sexual involvement is often the next step for men in getting to know someone".[4] Donovan et al. (2004, p. 64) argue that shared sexual interests are one reason why gays and lesbians often live in "different social worlds".

In the workplace context, the centrality of sexuality for how gay men relate to each other has ambiguous benefits. On the one hand, Rumens (2010b, p. 1550) argues, the acknowledgement of (potential) sexual attraction "has the capacity to rupture organizational discourses on how men (and women) ought to relate professionally to one another", allowing them to develop work relationships that are closer, more personal and warmer – and, therefore, potentially stronger than norms of heteronormative masculinity would allow. As Kaufman (1994, p. 150) points out, the masculine norm of the "lonely pursuit of power" and the "belief that power requires an ability to be detached and distant" (ibid.) results in friendships between heterosexual men that are often marked by emotional distance and reduced empathy (see also Hearn & Parkin, 1987, p. 127). For gay men, acknowledging (potential) sexual attraction for each other not only mutually confirms their identity but can also help them overcome this distance. On the other hand, the central role of sexual desire for the networking and solidarity practices of gay men might prompt them to overlook women and contribute to reproducing homosocial networks. When gender becomes an "entry card" to gay male networks, and they turn into "Männerbünde" themselves, they often, as Rumens (2010b, p. 1552) observes, reproduce "gendered modes of organizing based on domination and exclusion".

Conclusion

Overall, this chapter has shown that, at heart, various historical as well as current practices, dynamics and norms of the (de-)sexualization of organizations are part of and contribute to the construction of heteronormative masculinity, which is centrally built on the subordination and domination of women via heterosexual sexual dynamics and the suppression of homoerotic desire between men. Therefore, sexuality in organizations is always intertwined with gendered hierarchies and power dynamics and the heteronormativity inherent in these. For gay men and other LGBTIQ+ persons, the heteronormativity of organization has various negative implications. Research has mainly analysed forms and experiences of discrimination at work, consequences and strategies of coming out, and the effectiveness of measures to protect and support LGBTIQ+ employees.

However, over the past two decades, researchers and organizations have also discovered the positive effects of an LGBTI-friendly work climate on individuals' health, motivation and productivity. Some claim it also improves business outcomes – though there is not enough evidence for this. However, a point that has – with a few exceptions – largely been neglected so far are the empowering aspects of LGBTIQ+ identities for workers. Using the example of the EU-level policy network around LGBTIQ+ rights, the last part demonstrated how marginalized actors sometimes build exceptionally strong informal networks, which – in the case analysed here – allowed them to induce change despite a lack of formal power. Ironically, the shared experience of marginalization can provide a base for gay men to develop a common identity that strengthens mutual solidarity, support and close friendships. Often, these close relationships are further strengthened by the potential and actual sexual attraction between gay men. On the one hand, acknowledging sexual attraction re-introduces elements such as emotion, affection and intimacy to the work context, which allows for closer ties, privileges informal relations and makes their networks particularly effective. On the other hand, the central role of sexual attraction contributes to the dominance of gay men in these networks which strengthens their tendency to exclude women and reproduce gendered hierarchies.

Notes

1 See Kreisky (1994) and Remy (1990) for a more general analysis of "Männerbünde".
2 One exception from this Euro-American centrism is the anthology by Steffen et al. (2016), which gathers contributions investigating a range of national contexts.
3 In the European Parliament, the percentage of female MEPs was only 16–19% in the 1980s, 20–30% in the 1990s and 30–35% since 2000 (European Parliament, Equality and Diversity Unit – DG Personnel, 2018). In the other EU institutions, the share of women in senior administration positions was even lower and only increased very recently: In 1999, women occupied 13.6% of senior positions, still only 17.6% in 2005, and 33.3% in 2020 (European Institute for Gender Equality EIGE, 2021).
4 According to Nardi (1992, p. 182) for lesbians, in contrast, "sex follows a period of getting to know a person", and they are more likely to sexualize existing friendships.

References

Altman, D. (1996). Rupture or continuity? The internationalization of gay identities. *Social Text*, *48*, 77–94.
Anderson, B.R. (2006 [1983]). *Imagined Communities: Reflections on the Origin and Spread of Nationalism*, Revised edition. London: Verso.
Badgett, M.L. (1996). Employment and sexual orientation: Disclosure and discrimination in the workplace. *Journal of Gay & Lesbian Social Services*, *4*(4), 29–52. doi: 10.1300/J041v04n04_03
Badgett, M. L., Durso, L. E., Kastanis, A., & Mallory, C. (2013). *The Business Impact of LGBT-Supportive Workplace Policies.* Williams Institute, School of Law, Los Angeles, CA: UCLA. https://williamsinstitute.law.ucla.edu/publications/impact-lgbt-supportive-workplaces/
Beer, C., Jeffery, R., & Munyard, T. (1983). *Gay Workers: Trade Unions and the Law.* London: National Council for Civil Liberties.
Binnie, J. (2004). *The Globalization of Sexuality.* London: Sage.
Bird, S.R. (1996). Welcome to the men's club: Homosociality and the maintenance of hegemonic masculinity. *Gender & Society*, *10*(2), 120–132.
Bourdieu, P. (2001). *Masculine Domination.* Stanford, CA: Stanford University Press.
Burke, M. E. (1993). *Coming Out of the Blue: British Police Officers Talk about their Lives in 'The Job' as Lesbians, Gays and Bisexuals.* London: Cassell.
Burrell, G. (1984). Sex and Organizational Analysis. *Organization Studies*, *5*(2), 97–118. doi: 10.1177/017084068400500201

Cammermeyer, M. (1994). *Serving in Silence*. Harmondsworth: Penguin.
Cockburn, C. (1983). *Brothers: Male Dominance and Technological Change*. London: Pluto Press.
Cockburn, C. (1991). *In the Way of Women: Men's Resistance to Sex Equality in Organizations*. London: Macmillan.
Colgan, F., & Rumens, N. (2015). Understanding sexual orientation at work. In F. Colgan & N. Rumens (Eds.), *Sexual Orientation at Work: Contemporary Issues and Perspectives* (pp. 1–27). London: Routledge.
Collinson, D.L. (1992). *Managing the Shopfloor. Subjectivity, Masculinity and Workplace Culture*. Berlin: de Gruyter.
Collinson, D.L., & Collinson, M. (1989). Sexuality in the workplace: The domination of men's sexuality. In J. Hearn, D. L. Sheppard, P. Tancred-Sheriff & G. Burrell (Eds.), *The Sexuality of Organization* (pp. 91–109). London: Sage.
Collinson, M., & Collinson, D. L. (1996). It's only Dick: The sexual harassment of women managers in insurance sales. *Work, Employment and Society*, *10*(1), 29–56. doi: 10.1177/0950017096101002
Croteau, J.M. (1996). Research on the work experiences of lesbian, gay, and bisexual people: An integrative review of methodology and findings. *Journal of Vocational Behavior*, *48*(2), 195–209. doi: 10.1006/jvbe.1996.0018
Day, N.E., & Schoenrade, P. (1997). Staying in the closet versus coming out: Relationships between communication about sexual orientation and work attitudes. *Personnel Psychology*, *50*(1), 147–163. doi: 10.1111/j.1744-6570.1997.tb00904.x
Donovan, C., Heaphy, B., & Weeks, J. (2004). *Same Sex Intimacies: Families of Choice and Other Life Experiments*. Abingdon: Taylor and Francis.
Escoffier, J. (1975). Stigmas, work environment and economic discrimination against homosexuals. *Homosexual Counselling Journal*, *2*(1), 8–17.
European Institute for Gender Equality EIGE (2021). Gender Statistics Database: European Union Institutions: Senior Administrators. Retrieved from Vilnius: https://eige.europa.eu/gender-statistics/dgs/indicator/wmidm_adm_eur__wmid_euadmin_eurins/line
European Parliament, Equality and Diversity Unit – DG Personnel (2018). *Women in the European Parliament*. Luxembourg: Political Posts.
Farley, L. (1978). *Sexual Shakedown: The Sexual Harassment of Women on the Job*. New York: Warner Books.
Fleming, P. (2007). Sexuality, power and resistance in the workplace. *Organization Studies*, *28*(2), 239–256. doi: 10.1177/0170840606068307
Foucault, M. (1978). *The History of Sexuality: Volume I: An Introduction*. New York: Pantheon Books.
Foucault, M. (1997). Friendship as a way of life. In P. Rabinow & J. D. Faubion (Eds.), *The Essential Works of Foucault, 1954–1984* (Vol. 1, 135–140). New York: New Press (1st published 1981).
FRA European Union Agency for Fundamental Rights (2020). *A Long Way to Go for LGBTI Equality*. Luxembourg: Publications Office of the European Union. doi: 10.2811/7746
Griffin, P. (1992). From hiding out to coming out: Empowering lesbian and gay educators. *Journal of Homosexuality*, *22*(3–4), 167–196. doi: 10.1300/J082v22n03_07
Griffith, K.H., & Hebl, M.R. (2002). The disclosure dilemma for gay men and lesbians: "Coming out" at work. *The Journal of Applied Psychology*, *87*(6), 1191–1199. doi: 10.1037/0021-9010.87.6.1191
Gutek, B.A. (1985). *Sex and the Workplace: Impact of Sexual Behavior and Harassment on Women, Men and Organizations*. San Francisco, CA: Jossey-Bass.
Hall, E. (1995). *We Can't Even March Straight*. London: Vintage.
Hall, M. (1989). Private experiences in the public domain: Lesbians in organizations. In J. Hearn, D. L. Sheppard, P. Tancred-Sheriff & G. Burrell (Eds.), *The Sexuality of Organization* (pp. 125–138). London: Sage.
Hausen, K. (1976). Die Polarisierung der "Geschlechtercharararkter". Eine Spiegelung der Dissoziation von Erwerbs- und Familienleben. In W. Conze (Ed.), *Industrielle Welt: Vol. 21. Sozialgeschichte der Familie in der Neuzeit Europas. Neue Forschungen* (pp. 363–393). Stuttgart: Klett.
Hearn, J. (1985). Men's sexuality at work. In A. Metcalf & M. Humphries (Eds.), *The Sexuality of Men* (pp. 110–128). London: Pluto Press.
Hearn, J. (2011). Sexualities, work, organizations, and managements: Empirical, policy, and theoretical challenges. In E. Jeanes, D. Knights & P. Y. Martin (Eds.), *Handbook of Gender, Work and Organization* (pp. 299–314). London: John Wiley & Sons.

Hearn, J., & Parkin, W. (1987). *"Sex" at "Work": The Power and Paradox of Organisation Sexuality.* London: Prentice Hall/Harvester Wheatsheaf.

Hearn, J., & Parkin, W. (1995). *Sex at Work: The Power and Paradox of Organisation Sexuality*, Revised and updated edition. New York: St. Martin's Press.

Humphrey, J. C. (1999). Organizing sexualities, organizing inequalities: Lesbians and gay men in public service occupations. *Gender, Work & Organization*, *6*(3), 134–151.

Kaufman, M. (1994). Men, feminism, and men's contradictory experiences of power. In H. Brod & M. Kaufman (Eds.), *Theorizing Masculinities* (pp. 142–165). Thousand Oaks, CA: Sage.

Klapeer, C. M. (2014). *Perverse Bürgerinnen: Staatsbürgerschaft und lesbische Existenz. Queer Studies: Band 4.* Bielefeld: Transcript.

Klapeer, C. M., & Laskar, P. (2018). Transnational ways of belonging and queer ways of Being: Exploring transnationalism through the trajectories of the rainbow flag. *Identities*, *25*(5), 524–541. doi: 10.1080/1070289X.2018.1507958

Kreisky, E. (1994). *Das ewig Männerbündische? Zur Standardform von Staat und Politik.* In C. Leggewie (Ed.), *Wozu Politikwissenschaft? Über das Neue in der Politik* (pp. 191–208). Darmstadt: Wissenschaftliche Buchgesellschaft.

Levine, M. P. (1979). Employment discrimination against gay men. *International Review of Modern Sociology*, *9*(2), 151–163.

Mahoney, J., & Thelen, K. (2010). A theory of gradual institutional change. In J. Mahoney & K. A. Thelen (Eds.), *Explaining Institutional Change: Ambiguity, Agency, and Power* (1–37). Cambridge: Cambridge University Press.

Meyer, I. H. (2003). Prejudice, social stress, and mental health in lesbian, gay, and bisexual populations: Conceptual issues and research evidence. *Psychological Bulletin*, *129*(5), 674–697. doi: 10.1037/0033-2909.129.5.674

Mos, M. (2012). *Sexual Orientation and the Norm of Non-discrimination in the European Union, 1980–2010: From Emergence to Internalisation?* Doctoral thesis, University of Oxford, Oxford.

Mosse, G. L. (1983). Nationalism and sexuality in nineteenth-century Europe. *Society*, *20*(5), 75–84. doi: 10.1007/BF02695011

Nardi, P. M. (Ed.). (1992). *Men's Friendships.* Newbury Park, CA: SAGE.

Ng, E. S., & Rumens, N. (2017). Diversity and inclusion for LGBT workers: Current issues and new horizons for research. *Canadian Journal of Administrative Sciences*, *34*(2), 109–120. doi: 10.1002/cjas.1443

Olson, M. R. (1987). A study of gay and lesbian teachers. *Journal of Homosexuality*, *13*(4), 73–81. doi: 10.1300/J082v13n04_04

Oswin, N. (2006). Decentering queer globalization: Diffusion and the 'global gay'. *Environment and Planning D: Society and Space*, *24*(5), 777–790. doi: 10.1068/d63j

Ozeren, E. (2014). Sexual orientation discrimination in the workplace: A systematic review of literature. *Procedia – Social and Behavioral Sciences*, *109*, 1203–1215. doi: 10.1016/j.sbspro.2013.12.613

Pateman, C. (1988). *The Sexual Contract.* Stanford, CA: Stanford University Press.

Paternotte, D., Tremblay, M., & Johnson, C. (2011). Conclusion. In D. Paternotte, M. Tremblay, & C. Johnson (Eds.), *The Lesbian and Gay Movement and the State: Comparative Insights into a Transformed Relationship* (pp. 213–227). Burlington, Vt: Ashgate.

Phelan, S. (2001). *Sexual Strangers: Gays, Lesbians, and Dilemmas of Citizenship. Queer Politics, Queer Theories.* Philadelphia, PA: Temple University Press. doi: 10.2307/j.ctt14bt1tk

Pringle, R. (1989). *Secretaries Talk: Sexuality, Power and Work.* London: Verso.

Quinn, R. W. (1977). Coping with Cupid: The formation, impact, and management of romantic relationships in organizations. *Administrative Science Quarterly*, *22*(1), 30–45.

Rastetter, D. (1994). *Sexualität und Herrschaft in Organisationen: Eine geschlechtervergleichende Analyse. Beiträge zur psychologischen Forschung: Vol. 33.* Wiesbaden: VS Verlag für Sozialwissenschaften.

Remy, J. (1990). Patriarchy and fratriarchy as forms of androcracy. In J. Hearn & D. H. J. Morgan (Eds.), *Men, Masculinities and Social Theory* (pp. 43–54). London: Routledge.

Roper, M. (1996). 'Seduction and succession': Circuits of homosocial desire in management. In D. L. Collinson & J. Hearn (Eds.), *Men as Managers, Managers as Men: Critical Perspectives on Men, Masculinities and Managements* (pp. 210–226). London: SAGE. doi: 10.4135/9781446280102.n11

Rumens, N. (2008). Working at intimacy: Gay men's workplace friendships. *Gender, Work & Organization*, *15*(1), 9–30. doi: 10.1111/j.1468-0432.2007.00364.x

Rumens, N. (2010a). Firm friends: Exploring the supportive components in gay men's workplace friendships. *The Sociological Review*, *58*(1), 135–155. doi: 10.1111/j.1467-954X.2009.01879.x

Rumens, N. (2010b). Workplace friendships between men: Gay men's perspectives and experiences. *Human Relations*, *63*(10), 1541–1562. doi: 10.1177/0018726710361987

Rumens, N. (2018). *Queer Business: Queering Organization Sexualities*. New York: Routledge Taylor & Francis.

Rumens, N., & Kerfoot, D. (2009). Gay men at work: (Re)constructing the self as professional. *Human Relations*, *62*(5), 763–786. doi: 10.1177/0018726709103457

Rupp, L.J. (2014). The European origins of transnational organizing: The International Committee for Sexual Equality. In P. Ayoub & D. Paternotte (Eds.), *Gender and Politics Series. LGBT Activism and the Making of Europe: A Rainbow Europe* (pp. 29–49). London: Palgrave Macmillan.

Sombart, N. (1991). *Die deutschen Männer und ihre Feinde: Carl Schmitt – ein deutsches Schicksal zwischen Männerbund und Matriarchatsmythos*. München: Hanser.

Steffen, M.C., Niedlich, C., & Ehrke, F. (2016). Discrimination at work on the basis of sexual orientation: Subjective experience, experimental evidence, and interventions. In T. Köllen (Ed.), *Sexual Orientation and Transgender Issues in Organizations: Global Perspectives on LGBT Workforce Diversity* (pp. 367–389). Switzerland: Springer.

Swiebel, J. (2009). Lesbian, gay, bisexual and transgender human rights: The search for an international strategy. *Contemporary Politics*, *15*(1), 19–35. doi: 10.1080/13569770802674196

Theweleit, K. (1987). *Male Fantasies*.(vol. 1: Women Floods Bodies History). Minneapolis, MN: University of Minnesota Press.

Tindall, N.T., & Waters, R.D. (2012). Coming out to tell our stories: Using queer theory to understand the career experiences of gay men in public relations. *Journal of Public Relations Research*, *24*(5), 451–475.

Wasser, N. (2017). *The Promise of Diversity: How Brazilian Brand Capitalism Affects Precarious Identities and Work*. Bielefeld: Transcript Verlag.

Weeks, J. (1996). The idea of a sexual community. *Foundings*, *2*, 71–84.

Williams, C.J., & Weinberg, M.S. (1971). *Homosexuals and the Military*. New York: Harper & Row.

Williams, C.L., Giuffre, P.A., & Dellinger, K. (2009). The gay-friendly closet. *Sexuality Research & Social Policy: Journal of NSRC: SR & SP*, 29–45.

Woods, G. (2016). *Homintern: How Gay Culture Liberated the Modern World*. New Haven, CT: Yale University Press.

Woods, J.D., & Lucas, J.H. (1993). *The Corporate Closet: The Professional Lives of Gay Men in America*. New York: The Free Press.

Woodward, A. (2004). Building velvet triangles: Gender and informal governance. In T. Christiansen & S. Piattoni (Eds.), *Informal Governance in the European Union* (pp. 76–93). Cheltenham: Edward Elgar.

16

MEN'S VIOLENCE AND ABUSE IN ORGANIZATIONS AND WORKPLACES

Nicole Westmarland

Introduction

Violence and abuse in organizations and workplaces is difficult to measure, but it is increasingly recognized as a major problem, both for the individuals involved and for increased costs and reduced performance for organizations. The International Labour Organization (ILO) (2021) define violence and harassment in the workplace as:

> a range of unacceptable behaviour and practices, or threats thereof, whether a single occurrence or repeated, that aim at, result in, or are likely to result in physical, psychological, sexual or economic harm, and includes gender-based violence and harassment.
>
> *(Convention No. 190, Article 1a)*

Examples of violence and harassment in the workplace given by the ILO (2021) include bullying, threats, abuse, mobbing, use of offensive language, unwanted physical contact, abusing a position of power, and inappropriate jokes or banter.

While the recognition of and attempts to prevent violence and abuse in the world of work is relatively recent from an international labour law perspective, feminists have been raising the issue of men's violence in workplaces, specifically in the form of sexual harassment since the 1970s. Books such as Lin Farley's *Sexual Shakedown: The Sexual Harassment of Women on the Job* in 1978 resulted in demonstrating the link between sexual harassment and patriarchal workplace cultures (also see MacKinnon, 1979). Activism and research against sexual harassment expanded to such extent that by 1987, there were at least ten *bibliographies* of studies and texts on sexual harassment (Högbacka et al., 1987). Since then, a very wide variety of research has documented the violence, abuse and harassment faced by women in a range of different organizations and workplaces, including healthcare workers (George et al., 2020; Newman et al., 2021), the taxi industry (Westmarland & Anderson, 2001), "informal workers" (for example, floriculture, horticulture, casual home care, food hawkers) (Hivos East Africa, 2020), and higher education and research (UniSAFE, 2022), to name just a few.

DOI: 10.4324/9781003193579-18

What we know about the nature and prevalence of men's violence and abuse in organizations and workplaces

While some organizations and workplaces are fairly well researched, we still know little about the nature and prevalence of men's violences in others. Often a high-profile "scandal" is the "spark" for a focus on doing research into a given institution or profession. We have seen this happen in residential homes for children, in universities, in sports clubs and in media institutions – to name just a few. Many of these scandals have sparked not only research but also social movements and campaigns – such as #MeToo and #EveryonesInvited.

Where there are data about men's violences in organizations and workforces, this is often restricted to the topic of sexual harassment or sometimes a widened framing of sexual violence and "misconduct". The best source of data across Europe on this topic comes from the EU-wide (28 member states at that time) survey on violence against women conducted by the European Union Agency for Fundamental Rights (2014). Based on interviews with 42,000 women, it constitutes the largest survey of its kind and, although now dated, gives us the most comprehensive picture across Europe, thus far. One of the interesting findings from this survey was the extent to which women in professional and/or management positions had experienced sexual harassment. The survey found that 74% of women in the professional occupational category, and 75% in the top management category had experienced sexual harassment at some point in their lives. One in four of these women had experienced it in the past 12 months. This is compared to 44% of women in the category "skilled manual worker". This higher rate for women in professional and top management positions can be interpreted as potentially due to their higher exposure because of the environments and situations within which they work. As such, sexual harassment can also be seen as a form of sexual discrimination and occupational exclusion (cf. Leeds TUCRIC, 1983; Witz, 1992). An alternative interpretation put forward is that professional women and managers may be more alert to what constitutes sexual harassment and therefore may have been more likely than other women to identify their experience as such and report it as part of the survey. The report concluded:

> Employers and other organisations need to raise awareness and take practical initiatives to recognise and address the reality of sexual harassment experienced by women with diverse occupational and educational backgrounds, and in different work settings.
> *(p. 13)*

The same survey shows some of the impacts that violence and abuse in the workplace can have – 3% of women that said that they avoided being alone with a colleague or boss at work because of the fear of being physically or sexually assaulted. In the last quarter of December 2021, 15.52 million women aged 16 and over were in paid employment in the United Kingdom (Irvine et al., 2022). Applying the 3% figure to this UK population would represent nearly half a million women – about 465,600 – who have had to take this action of avoiding being alone with a colleague or boss. This demonstrates that violence and abuse in the workplace continue to have a significant impact on women.

It is important not to see the problem of violence and abuse in organizations and workplaces as distinct from wider society. Instead, it should be seen as both a reflection of and reflecting into wider cultures. As Hearn and Parkin (2001) put it, when overviewing harassment, bullying and physical violence in organizations, largely enacted by men:

> Organizations are not collectivities formed simply by the individual, intentional action of their founders and members. Rather, organizations always occur in the context of pre-existing (organizational) social relations.
>
> *(p. 2)*

Hence, it is necessary to consider the time, space and place in which violence and abuse happen and how this links with a wide range of intersecting social inequalities, both within and across societies. How and where men and masculinities fit into this broader societal picture is complex and varied, as explored in other contributions to this volume. In this chapter, I seek to shine the spotlight on just three different contexts to understand how masculinities and men's violence operate within, first, policing, second, higher education, and third, residential care homes for children looked after by the state. These have been chosen as they have all been sites of major investigations in recent years in the United Kingdom. While the chapter is focused on men's violence and abuse against women and girls, it ends with a summary and conclusion that also brings into view some of the harms that men and boys experience within institutions where cultures of violence against women and girls are ingrained.

Men's violences in policing

Policing is said to be one of the most masculinized occupations in the world (Lockwood & Prohaska, 2015). A range of barriers exist for women entering the police, and particularly for progressing to senior ranks. These have been identified with the idea of an idealized version of manhood, or hegemonic masculinity, seen as synonymous with policing:

> Extreme hegemonic masculinity is valued in policing, wherein men may represent their virility through physical strength, sexual and misogynistic regard for women, and emphasizing interests designated as masculine (e.g., sports and hunting).
>
> *(Angehrn et al., 2021, p. 7628)*

Silvestri (2017) agrees with this view, though also arguing that concepts of "machismo" and a "cult of masculinity" oversimplify the problem. Instead, she argues that there is a multiplicity of gender representations and performances within policing, and a wider range than often appreciated.

Moving to consider violence, it is clear that some police forces still use violence more or less routinely, as well as having violence available as a resource in situations of civil disorder and crowd control, for example (Hodgson, 2001). In some contexts, police forces have strict rules and regulations against misuse of violence, but still abuses occur. There are clear overlaps here with racism, as the Black Lives Matters protests following the killing of George Floyd in Minneapolis, US, in 2020 brought greater mainstream attention to (Peeples, 2020). One example from the United Kingdom and one example from the United States are used in this section to show just some of the ways in which men's violence and abuse in policing link with violence against women and girls.

In the UK context, the culture of harmful masculinity was highlighted 40 years ago, when Smith and Gray (1983) highlighted accounts of fighting, violence, sexual "conquests" and heavy drinking sessions combined together to represent a "cult of masculinity" (p. 87) across the London Metropolitan Police. Today, despite the same police force having appointed its first-ever woman police chief – Cressida Dick – in 2017 (who has since been forced to resign), it is clear that such problems continue. Shockwaves reverberated across the United Kingdom and further afield in 2021 when a serving Metropolitan police officer kidnapped, raped and killed Sarah Everard when she was walking home on a busy London street. It is thought that the killer (whom I do not name in this chapter to avoid giving him additional notoriety) may have used his police credentials to lure Sarah Everard into his car, perhaps under the guise of COVID restrictions which were still in place at the time she was kidnapped.

In the weeks after her murder, it emerged that the murderer had previously been referred to as "the rapist" by his police colleagues. Other misogynistic and racist examples of policing culture also started to flow out of the Metropolitan police. Two officers were found to have taken photographs on their phones which they then edited to superimpose themselves onto the dead bodies of Nicole Smallman and Bibaa Henry when they were supposed to be guarding the crime scene when they were stabbed to death by a man in a London park. Sharing the photos with two WhatsApp groups, they were also found to have risked contamination of the crime scene. They pleaded guilty to misconduct in public office and were jailed.

In the same London force, and still under the spotlight for the two cases outlined earlier, in early 2022 the Independent Office for Police Conduct (IOPC) reported on evidence of a range of hateful and offensive messages between 19 officers that took place between 2016 and 2018. In these messages, officers were found to have "joked" about raping women and bragging about hitting their partners. One example of a conversation that demonstrates the content and tone of the messages is reproduced as follows:

Officer 1: "*I fucking need to take my bird out, won't see her until next Saturday. Then I have to work. Promised to take her out the Friday after. Making it up to her from when I backhanded her*"

Officer 2: "*Grab her by the pussy*"

Officer 1: "*You ever slapped your missus?*"

Officer 1: "*It makes them love you more. Seriously since I did that she won't leave me alone. Now I know why these daft cunts are getting murdered by their spastic boyfriends. Knock a bird about and she will love you. Human nature. They are biologically programmed to like that shit*".

Officer 2: "*Lmao*"

(*IOPC, 2022a, p. 11*)

In Operation Hotton that followed, the report stated that the incidents were not isolated and could not be put down to the behaviour of a few "bad apples". Rather, they reported that there was evidence of a culture of what they referred to as "toxic masculinity", and that "cultural and structural issues that created an environment in which the conduct matters identified were cultivated and able to breed" (p. 4). They found evidence of "macho" officers dominating teams, and that officers who tried to speak out were ostracized, harassed and humiliated. In particular, female officers were told that they should "play the game or stay quiet" if they tried to challenge the culture, which was often dismissed as just "banter". The Metropolitan Police accepted the 15 recommendations made to them by the IOPC, which included the introduction of a mandatory training programme to encourage officers to tackle sexual harassment and misogyny in the workplace, and the creation of a new team focused on investigating sexual misconduct and domestic abuse.

Following the Sarah Everard murder the Metropolitan Police in London has been under intense scrutiny. The subsequent 363-page Casey Report (Casey, 2023) published in

March 2023 is yet another scathing analysis of the sexism and racism of the Metropolitan Police. However, the problem of men, masculinities and violence within the police is of course not limited to London or the United Kingdom. Somvadee and Morash (2008), for example, highlight that despite many policies in US police departments outlawing sexual discrimination and sexual harassment, it continues to be the case that sexual harassment remains a significant problem. They found a range of forms of sexual harassment in their survey, including telling suggestive stories or offensive jokes (83.7% of their self-selecting sample), sexist remarks (51.2%), unwelcome touching (36.7%), implying better treatment for sexual cooperation (5.1%) and being treated badly for refusing to have sex (2.5%). Qualitative data showed a range of experiences. Examples were given of overt, clear forms of sexual harassment which sometimes overlapped with racial harassment and which women police officers felt were clearly unacceptable. They were often made to feel incompetent by male officers. In some cases, women engaged in jokes and even the sharing of sexually explicit materials, believing that this helped them feel part of the "in-group" and saying that they would let the men know if they felt uncomfortable and wanted them to stop. Somvadee and Morash (2008) conclude that some women were willing to tolerate or even engage in certain behaviours as "the price" that must be paid to fit into a male organizational culture. Complaints about such behaviour were rare, with some women feeling that they were able to stop harassment by male colleagues by themselves, because they had concerns about the process, or because they did not want to be questioned about whether they were "up to the job".

Policing then, despite all the changes that have been introduced to encourage more women into positions within forces such as firearms teams and senior management, that have been and still are male-dominated, and despite some women reaching the highest ranks within policing, including leading forces as Chief Constables, still remains a place where gender, power and control have a stronghold. Violence and abuse within policing are likely to persist until cultural problems around sexism and misogyny as well as intersecting problems, including racism and classism, are properly tackled at all levels.

Men's violence and abuse against women staff and students in higher education

When we think about men, masculinities and higher education, we might optimistically think about how these are spaces where alternative masculinities and discussions about gender-based violence and equalities might flourish. Indeed, we know that this sometimes is the case. One of the key "routes" for men becoming involved in activism to end violence against women historically has been higher education. For example, men have been documented as setting up feminist reading groups in the 1970s and 1980s in the United Kingdom, the United States and elsewhere (Messner et al., 2015; Westmarland et al., 2021). In addition, the study of men and masculinities has had a major influence on many teaching and research programmes across the world (Hearn & Howson, 2020). However, substantial problems remain. Research has documented how men in higher education use male privilege, often combined with other structural privileges, to perpetrate a range of violences against women as students and as staff. This has been documented in a number of (particularly Western) countries – sometimes in surveys specific to gender-based violence and abuse and sometimes under the broader umbrella of bullying and harassment (Keashly, 2019).

The largest investigation into gender-based violence[1] in higher education across Europe is the UniSAFE project which conducted a large-scale survey of all academic staff and students in 46 universities and research institutes, with over 42,000 responses (UniSAFE, 2022). The headline figures from this research include that nearly two in three (62%) of respondents said they had experienced at least one form of gender-based violence since they started working or studying at their university. They found that all forms of gender-based violence were higher among people with a disability or chronic illness, for people from a minority ethnic group, and for academic staff compared with non-academic staff. Women were found to be at highest risk of sexual violence and sexual harassment, and men were at highest risk of physical violence. Trans people were more affected by psychological violence and sexual harassment, and there was a higher rate of gender-based violence for homosexual, bisexual or queer people compared to their heterosexual counterparts. Although there was a low response rate in many, if not all of the institutions, and especially from students, these comparative findings between different social groups are likely to be very reliable.

The United Kingdom has been further behind some other countries, such as the United States, in recognizing and responding to violence and abuse – even while student groups, especially feminist student groups, have organized against sexual harassment since the 1980s (for example, Oxford University Student Union Women's Committee, 1984), if not earlier. Thinking about students first, a turning point in the recognition of the scale and seriousness of "lad culture" and the perpetration of violence and abuse was the publication of a report called *Hidden Marks* by the National Union of Students (NUS) in 2010. This study documented more than 2,000 female students' experiences of harassment, stalking, violence and sexual assault. The authors concluded that violence in college and university settings was commonplace, with many women struggling to complete their studies without coming into contact, either directly or indirectly, with some form of violence or harassment. For example, they found that one in four women had been sexually assaulted, and over two-thirds had experienced verbal or physical sexual harassment.

The study also asked about experiences such as "someone making sexual comments that made them feel uncomfortable" and "someone wolf whistling, catcalling or making sexual noises at them". Most often these acts occurred in social spaces around the university, but in a significant minority of cases (16%) they had occurred in a learning environment including libraries and lecture theatres. More than one in ten students said they had felt uncomfortable within a learning environment because of comments being made that had a sexual overtone, and this was even more common outside learning environments (one in five in student unions, and one in three in the university and college environment more broadly). In some cases, these sexual comments were made by staff as well as students. For example, one student told of a lecturer joking about how to cover up spiking a drink with a rape drug, and another who showed a picture of a former student and said he fantasized about what could have happened between them.

There is also an abundance of evidence that demonstrates the existence of "lad culture" that operates within higher education settings. Phipps and Young (2012) were commissioned by the NUS to look at campus culture and the experiences of female students – especially the role of "lad culture". They define "lad culture" as a form of masculinity – a cultural or subcultural practice that can be engaged in by men and/or women. They describe its key characteristics as being young, hedonistic, objectifying women, holding "politically incorrect" views and "having a laugh". Furthermore, they emphasize its links to "raunch culture" – the hyper-sexualized culture that objectifies women (indeed, women themselves might sometimes also contribute to this) and is linked to the mainstreaming and normalizing of the sex industry and sexual violence. Phipps and Young highlight alcohol and sport as major threads that link "lad culture" to universities – a prime example of this being initiation to sports teams that often require high levels of alcohol consumption to demonstrate one's ability to be "one of the lads" (also see Jackson & Sundaram, 2020).

Since the early work in the United Kingdom, and these key studies that sought to raise awareness of the scale of men's violences and abuse within higher education, efforts have been increased by many universities to "tackle" the problem. Some, most, or all of these efforts have been linked to the academic activists within higher education, by student activists, or by both groups working together. Some of these have also raised awareness of the issues faced by staff who misuse their power and privilege within higher education and sexually harass, use violence against and/or enter unequal relationships with students.

One influential and successful academic activist group is the 1752 Group. The 1752 Group was launched in 2015 at the first UK university conference to focus on staff-to-student sexual harassment. The group is named after the amount of money they were given to hold this conference (£1,752, then equivalent to around €2,300) to demonstrate that while this was a much welcome start, far greater investment and long-term work would be needed from this starting point. Their vision, in establishing the group and continuing their ongoing activism, is:

> Higher education institutions in the UK need to be leading the change to prevent cultures of abuse, respond effectively and without inflicting further harm, ensure robust, student-centred reporting and investigation procedures, and implement policies and procedures to eliminate the sexual misconduct of academic, professional services, contracted and temporary staff.
>
> *(https://1752group.com/about-us/)*

In 2018, the 1752 Group worked with the National Union of Students to conduct the first UK survey on staff sexual misconduct in higher education titled *Power in the Academy.* This study reports on a culture within higher education which enables sexism and sexual harassment. In their report, they use the term "sexual misconduct" – a term that has been increasingly used in higher education policies around sexual violence over the last decade. Sexual misconduct refers to "a continuum of sexualised and predatory behaviours of staff towards students" (p. 8) which is argued to pull into the definition "lower level", "boundary-blurring" behaviours of staff that would not reach the threshold of sexual violence *per se*, but would take in the types of behaviour that might happen early in a grooming process, for example. In this study, which was not a representative sample, they found that one in eight current students had been touched in a way that made them feel uncomfortable and that one in ten said that a staff member had attempted to draw them into a discussion about sex. Almost a third (30%) of students reported a staff member making sexualized remarks or jokes.

They found serious consequences stemmed from the existence of this sexual misconduct. Just some of the impacts can be seen from the following quotes from the free text boxes in their study, demonstrating some of the changes that they had made to their lives:

> I avoid any meetings, other than absolutely necessary, with certain members of staff, even though further meetings might have been beneficial for my academic development/network.

> I found it impossible to feel safe at the campus as I had to encounter the lecturer who was asked not to talk to me but was still around.
>
> I had to change my theme of study to avoid him, fear of campus for bumping into him, unable to participate in academic or social events within the department for fear of contact with him.
>
> I have lost half a year of studying towards my PhD as I had to change projects and therefore had to start from the beginning again.
>
> *(p. 28)*

Unfortunately, many of the students saw the violences they experienced or witnessed as "normal" in higher education, and placed little faith in senior leaders within higher education administration to make real change. As one of the participants in the women students' focus groups put it:

> I don't think it's transgressive for old, grey professors to prey on younger women. It's normal, it's normalised. For that reason, rules don't seem to touch them.
>
> *(p. 38)*

These examples and quotes show the need for change to happen, as well as the impact that sexual violence and misconduct can have on women student's education and lives.

It was research studies, such as those described earlier, that led to a series of podcasts called "Degrees of Abuse" being launched by Al Jazeera's Investigative Unit (*https://interactive.aljazeera.com/aje/2021/degrees-of-abuse/index.html*). This series documents the experiences of staff and students – most often those in relatively junior positions where there are high power differentials such as between PhD researchers and professors (see also *www.aljazeera.com/news/2021/10/19/oxford-professors-abused-position-with-sexist-and-drunken-conduct*). It details how British universities have failed to deal with complaints of sexual harassment and how some senior male academics are seemingly able to act with impunity – including cases where multiple complaints against the same member of staff were not taken seriously and where staff have been able to freely move institutions to shrug off serious cases of sexual violence and misconduct.

One of the ways this impunity has been maintained in the HE sector and elsewhere is through the use of Non-Disclosure Agreements (NDAs). A BBC News investigation in 2020 found that nearly a third of universities had used at least 300 NDAs – Non-Disclosure Agreements – as a response to student complaints – many of which were linked to sexual misconduct, bullying and harassment. NDAs are sometimes known as "gagging orders", "hush agreements" or "confidentiality clauses", which are signed by both employees/students and organizations to stop people talking about something that might damage an organization's image and reputation – and so affect recruitment and global rankings, for example. They usually, if not always, have a monetary award attached to them, as a form of compensation for the harm(s) suffered by the employee or student. If someone breaches an NDA by speaking out about their experience having signed an agreement not to, then they can be sued for breaking a contract.

In 2022, steps forward started to be made when a Universities UK report *Changing the Culture: Tackling Staff to Student Sexual Misconduct* was launched. As part of this report, six Vice Chancellors agreed to sign a pledge to not use NDAs in cases of staff-to-student sexual misconduct. Since then, other Universities have agreed to sign up to the pledge.

This represents a step forward in three respects. First, banning the use of NDAs will prevent some of the covering up of sexual misconduct; second, it will stop people who have used sexual misconduct being able to move to other universities with impunity; and, third, it is argued that it sends a normative message about the appropriateness of their use in other organizations.

There are therefore some signs that the tide might be turning in terms of the brushing under the carpet of sexual violence and misconduct at universities in the United Kingdom. International research suggests that it is essential that responses and interventions are located within and guided by the available academic research (Keashly, 2019). It is hoped that the lessons emerging from UniSAFE and evidence from other parts of the world can be used to inform policy and practice to create higher education work and study places that are free from violence and abuse.

Men's violence and abuse against children living in residential care homes

Different countries around the world have different ways of caring for children whose parents are not able or willing to care for them. Many places have a process of making the child a ward of the state – removing responsibility from the parent either temporarily or permanently. In 2017, based on official records from 140 countries, UNICEF estimated that there were at least 2.7 million children living in residential care worldwide (UNICEF, 2017). As of March 2021, there were 80,850 looked-after children in England which is the highest level since records began (Office for National Statistics, 2021). Although boys are slightly more likely to enter the looked-after children system, girls do account for around 44% of the total (Office for National Statistics, 2021). Recent decades have seen a considerable decline in the use of children's residential care homes, with family placements (e.g. fostering and adoption) now seen as a more professional and appropriate way of providing state care for children (Berridge et al., 2012). However, in past decades, residential children's homes were a common way for a local authority to look after children who could not be cared for by a parent – either on a short-term or long-term basis, and it remains the case that looked-after children may stay in a residential placement at some point.

Official statistics record "abuse or neglect" as the primary need for 66% of the children entering the looked-after system (Office for National Statistics, 2021), and this has risen significantly over the last decade (from around 40% in 2011 [Department for Education, 2011]). It is, in part, the high levels of abuse already experienced by looked-after children that make the abuse they sometimes suffer in residential care homes of even more concern. One example of the way children in residential care homes have been specifically targeted by abusive men was the sexual exploitation that happened in Rotherham in the United Kingdom in the 2000s.

In 2014, it was revealed that at least 1,400 children in Rotherham had been sexually abused, some had been raped repeatedly and many of those who spoke out about their abuse did not have their reports appropriately acted upon (Jay Report, 2014). The Jay Report into child sexual exploitation in Rotherham had a wider scope than just looked-after children, but residential children's homes were one of the places specifically targeted for sexual exploitation of children. The report notes that from the mid-1990s onwards, staff in some residential units felt overwhelmed by the problem of sexual abuse of the young women in their care. Jay notes that while some children were exposed to sexual exploitation for the first time when they entered children's homes, in other cases the situation was more fluid, with children having been exploited beforehand and that exploitation continuing or even increasing once they went into children's homes. She was bold in her criticisms of the local authority's lack of responses at the time:

> There was no appropriate management response to the problem of children being exposed to exploitation whilst in the care of the Council. Nor did we find that elected members as corporate parents were advised of the scale and gravity of the problem.
> *(Jay Report, 2014, p. 53)*

Following the Jay report, South Yorkshire Police were referred to the Independent Office for Police Conduct (IOPC) which looked into how the police had handled the allegations.

The subsequent IOPC report (2022b) was largely seen as a disappointment to those victim survivors who had experienced the abuse and by those supporting them. It was criticized for taking too long to conduct its investigation (Operation Linden) and publish its findings (eight years in total), and for not dismissing anyone despite upholding complaints of misconduct against 14 officers. Of the 91 investigations concerning 265 separate allegations from 51 individual complainants that were part of Operation Linden, the only outcomes were two written warnings, three management action and/or words of advice, and seven no further actions. This is despite upholding 43 of the allegations.

This last example of men's violences against girls in residential care homes differs somewhat from that in the first two kinds of institutions discussed – in that care as a profession and specifically the care of children usually takes place within what are often female-dominated institutions (albeit universities also have a duty of care to their students – but care is not their primary purpose). However, and as in other female-dominated institutions, those in lower-grade posts are predominantly female while those in the highest managerial posts are predominantly male. This is also an example of the importance of intersectionality. In the case of the girls who were abused in Rotherham, gender was not the only factor that made them "vulnerable". Also of significance were concerns around racial and religious tensions (the perpetrators were found to be predominantly British Pakistani men abusing white girls) and social class (the girls would undoubtably have been treated differently if they were from middle-class families). Instead, the police were fearful of being accused of racism, and the girls were dismissed as being "difficult", sexually promiscuous, trouble causers instead of the victims of sexualized grooming that they actually were.

Conclusions

This chapter has shown that there exists a culture within policing and within higher education of sexism, intersecting with racism and other inequalities, which contribute towards the continuation and covering up of violence and abuse within these organizations. The third example – of residential care for looked-after children – was slightly different in terms of male-dominated cultures within institutions, but the effect was the same in terms of victims not being taken seriously when they spoke out about their experiences of violence and abuse. Institutions have tended to protect the perpetrators of violence and abuse (see Collinson & Collinson, 1992), often in a misguided attempt to protect their own reputations – for example, using Non-Disclosure Agreements.

The situations described earlier and many others in institutions across the world show that men's violences in institutions cause significant harms to women and girls within them. But this is not to say that there are not also harms to men and boys enveloped within them. Where men are violent towards women and girls, violence towards boys particularly (and sometimes men) is sometimes also present. We see that in examples that have occurred in such institutions as the BBC and the National Health Service where most of the victims of celebrity abusers including Jimmy Savile[2] were women and girls but boys were also abused. We also see the abuse of boys within the residential care system for looked-after children.

It is not just the direct harms of abuse that men's violence can have on other men and boys though. Heavily gendered social norms have been shown to have harmful effects on men's health and well-being, contributing to high levels of depression and suicide among men (Burrell et al., 2019). Dominance and control over women are frequently seen as a key part of the set of attributes and behaviours associated with a shared social idea of "manhood" (Jewkes et al., 2015). There are a range of studies that have found that the stronger a man's adherence to traditional gender norms, the more likely they are to use violence against women (Equimundo, 2022; Schumacher et al., 2001; Murnen et al., 2002; Fleming et al., 2015). This means that we cannot separate sexist attitudes and opinions from the incidence of violence against women and girls. It also means that in seeking change and a future free from violence against women and girls as well as against men and boys, we must continue to work deep within institutions to stamp out sexism as well as those inequalities that co-exist and intersect with sexism. Here, the connections between men, work and workplaces need their connections to be made visible (Collinson & Hearn, 2005). With increasingly globalized workforces, it is important to understand how different cultures manifest violence and abuse in the workplace – such as differences between what is understood as "assertive" behaviour (Blackwood & Jenkins, 2018) – while taking care not to see violence in some cultures or types of organizations or workplaces as a normal "part of the job".

More research is needed into men as perpetrators both within and outside organizations. Blackwood and Jenkins (2018) highlight how in addressing the prevalence and importance of bullying in workplaces more generally, research has often relied upon reports from the victims themselves. This has been important in terms of bringing attention to the problems faced, but as we move towards reducing it a greater perpetrator focus is needed and that requires a closer look at masculinities within these organizations. It is not enough to have standalone, individual initiatives to end violence and abuse within organizations – it is the masculine-dominated sexist cultures that need to change at their very core to make safer places for all.

Notes

1 In the UniSAFE project, gender-based violence encompasses physical violence, sexual violence and sexual harassment, gender harassment, economic and financial violence, stalking, psychological violence, and online violence, abuse and violation, organizational (gender-based) violence, as well as emerging forms of violence.

2 Jimmy Savile was a long-standing famous radio DJ, TV presenter and celebrity fundraiser in the United Kingdom from the 1960s to 1990s. After his death Saville was found to have been a prolific sex offender, abusing up to 500 child and adult victims (Westmarland, 2015).

References

Angehrn, A., Fletcher, A. J., & Carleton, R. N. (2021). "Suck it up, buttercup": Understanding and overcoming gender disparities in policing. *International Journal of Environmental Research and Public Health, 18*(4), 7627. doi: 10.3390/ijerph18147627

Blackwood, K., & Jenkins, M. (2018). 'Me? A bully?' The different faces of the perpetrator in workplace bullying. In P. D'Cruz, E. Noronha, E. Baillien, B. Catley, K. Harlos, A. Hogh & E. Gemzoe Mikkelsen (Eds.), *Pathways of Job-related Negative Behaviour: Handbook of Workplace Bullying, Emotional Abuse and Harassment* (pp. 1–24), Volume 2. Singapore: Springer. doi: 10.1007/978-981-10-6173-8_20-1

Berridge, D., Biehal, N., & Henry, L. (2012). *Living in Children's Residential Homes.* Research Report DFE-RR201. London: Department for Education. https://assets.publishing.service.gov.uk/government/uploads/system/uploads/attachment_data/file/184079/DFE-RR201.pdf

Burrell, S., Ruxton, S., & Westmarland, N. (2019). *Changing Gender Norms: Engaging with Men and Boys.* London: Government Equalities Office. https://assets.publishing.service.gov.uk/government/uploads/system/uploads/attachment_data/file/952527/Changing_Gender_Norms-_Engaging_with_Men_and_Boys.pdf

Casey, B. (2023). *Baroness Casey Review: Final Report. An Independent Review into the Standards of Behaviour and Internal Culture of the Metropolitan Police Service.* March 2023. www.met.police.uk/SysSiteAssets/media/downloads/met/about-us/baroness-casey-review/update-march-2023/baroness-casey-review-march-2023.pdf

Collinson, D. L., & Collinson, M. (1992). Mismanaging sexual harassment: Protecting the perpetrator and blaming the victim. *Women in Management Review, 7*(7). doi: 10.1108/09649429210019608

Collinson, D. L., & Hearn, J. (2005). Men and masculinities in work, organizations, and management. In M. Kimmel, J. Hearn & R. W. Connell (Eds.), *Handbook of Studies on Men and Masculinities* (pp. 289–310), London: Sage.

Equimundo. (2022). *The International Men and Gender Equality Survey: A Status Report on Men, Women, and Gender Equality in 15 Headlines.* Washington, DC: Equimundo. www.unfpa.org/sites/default/files/pub-pdf/International%20Men%20%26%20Gender%20Equality%20Survey%20%28IMAGES%29%20Global%20Report%202022_EN.pdf

European Union Agency for Fundamental Rights (2014). *Violence Against Women: An EU-Wide Survey. Main Results Report.* Vienna, Austria: European Union Agency for Fundamental Rights. https://fra.europa.eu/en/publication/2014/violence-against-women-eu-wide-survey-main-results-report

Farley, L. (1978). *Sexual Shakedown: The Sexual Harassment of Women on the Job.* New York: McGraw-Hill.

Fleming, P. J., McCleary-Sills, J., Morton, M., Levtov, R., Heilman, B., & Barker, G. (2015). Risk factors for men's lifetime perpetration of physical violence against intimate partners: Results from the International Men and Gender Equality Survey (IMAGES) in eight countries. *PLoS One, 10*(3), e0118639. doi: 10.1371/journal.pone.0118639

George, A. S., McConville, F. E., de Vries, S., Nigenda, G., Sarfraz, S., McIsaac, M. (2020). Violence against female health workers is tip of iceberg of gender power imbalances. *British Medical Journal, 371*, m3546. doi: 10.1136/bmj.m3546

Hearn, J., & Howson, R. E. (2020). The institutionalization of (Critical) Studies on Men and Masculinities: Geopolitical perspectives. In L. Gottzén, U. Mellström & T. Shefer (Eds.), *Routledge International Handbook of Masculinity Studies* (pp. 19–30). London: Routledge. doi: 10.4324/9781315165165

Hearn, J., & Parkin, W. (2001). *Gender, Sexuality and Violence in Organizations.* London: Sage.

Hivos East Africa (2020). *Exploring Prevalence of Sexual Harassment within the Informal Sector in Kenya.* Kenya: Hivos East Africa. https://hivos.org/assets/east-africa/2021/04/Hivos-Sexual-Harassment-at-informal-Sector-Workplaces_Report_2021_Ver07_Web-ver.pdf

Hodgson, J. F. (2001). Police violence in Canada and the USA: Analysis and management. *Policing: An International Journal, 24*(4), 520–549.

Högbacka, R., Kandolin, I., Haavio-Mannila, E., & Kauppinen-Toropainen, K. (1987). *Sexual Harassment.* Helsinki: Ministry of Social Affairs.

ILO (International Labour Organization) (2021). *Eliminating Violence and Harassment in the World of Work.* Genèva, Switzerland: ILO. https://www.ilo.org/global/topics/violence-harassment/lang--en/index.htm

IOPC (Independent Office of Police Complaints) (2022a). *Operation Hotton: Learning Report.* London: IOPC. www.policeconduct.gov.uk/sites/default/files/Operation%20Hotton%20Learning%20report%20-%20January%202022.pdf

IOPC (Independent Office of Police Complaints) (2022b). *The Operation Linden Report: The IOPC Independent Investigations of Complaints and Conduct Matters in Relation to South Yorkshire's Handling of Reports into Non-recent Child Sexual Abuse and Exploitation in Rotherham, South Yorkshire, between 1977 and 2013.* London: IOPC. www.policeconduct.gov.uk/sites/default/files/Operation%20Hotton%20Learning%20report%20-%20January%202022.pdf

Irvine, S., Clark, H., Ward, M., & Francis-Devine, B. (2022). *Women and the UK Economy.* London: House of Commons Library. https://researchbriefings.files.parliament.uk/documents/SN06838/SN06838.pdf

Jackson, C., & Sundaram, V. (2020). *Lad Culture in UK HE: Sexism, Sexual Harassment and Violence.* New York: Routledge.

Jay, A. (2014). *Independent Inquiry into Child Sexual Exploitation in Rotherham (1997–2013).* Rotherham: Rotherham Metropolitan Borough Council. https://www.rotherham.gov.uk/downloads/file/279/independent-inquiry-into-child-sexual-exploitation-in-rotherham

Jewkes, R. K., Flood, M., & Lang, J. (2015). From work with men and boys to changes of social norms and reduction of inequities in gender relations: A conceptual shift in prevention of violence against women and girls. *The Lancet, 385*(9977), 1580–1589. doi: 10.1016/S0140-6736(14)61683-4

Keashly, L. (2019). Workplace bullying, mobbing and harassment in academe: Faculty experience. In P. D'Cruz, E. Noronha, L. Keashly & S. Tye-Williams (Eds.), *Special Topics and Particular Occupations, Professions and Sectors: Handbook of Workplace Bullying, Emotional Abuse and Harassment* (vol. 4, pp. 221–297). Singapore: Springer. doi: 10.1007/978-981-10-5308-5_13

Leeds TUCRIC (1983). *Sexual Harassment of Women at Work.* Leeds: Leeds TUCRIC.

Lockwood, D., & Prohaska, A. (2015). Police officer gender and attitudes toward intimate partner violence: How policy can eliminate stereotypes. *International Journal of Criminal Justice Sciences, 10*(1), 77–90.

MacKinnon, C. A. (1979). *The Sexual Harassment of Working Women.* New Haven, CT: Yale University Press.

Messner, M., Greenberg, M., & Peretz, T. (2015). *Some Men – Feminist Allies in the Movement to End Violence against Women.* Oxford: Oxford University Press.

Murnen, S. K., Wright, C., & Kaluzny, G. (2002). If "boys will be boys", then girls will be victims?: A meta-analytic review of the research that relates masculine ideology to sexual aggression. *Sex Roles, 46*(11–12), 359–375. doi: 10.1023/A:1020488928736

National Union of Students (NUS) (2010). *Hidden Marks – A Study of Women Students' Experiences of Harassment, Stalking, Violence and Sexual Assault.* London: NUS.

National Union of Students (NUS) (2018). *Power in the Academy: Staff Sexual Misconduct in UK Higher Education.* London: NUS.

Newman, C., Nayebare, A., Neema, S., et al. (2021). Uganda's response to sexual harassment in the public health sector: From "dying silently" to gender-transformational HRH policy. *Human Resources for Health, 19*(59). doi: 10.1186/s12960-021-00569-0

Office for National Statistics (2021). *Children Looked After in England Including Adoptions.* London: Office for National Statistics. https://explore-education-statistics.service.gov.uk/find-statistics/children-looked-after-in-england-including-adoptions/2021

Oxford University Student Union Women's Committee (1984). *'The Ones Who Just Patronise Seem Genial by Comparison . . . ': An Enquiry into Sexual Harassment of Women in Oxford University.* Oxford: Oxford University Student Union.

Peeples, L. (2020). Brutality and racial bias: What the data say. *Nature, 583*, 22–25. doi: 10.1038/d41586-020-01846-z

Phipps, A., & Young, I. (2012). *That's What She Said – Women Students' Experiences of 'Lad Culture' in Higher Education.* London: NUS.

Schumacher, J. A., Feldbau-Kohn, S., Slep, A. M. S., & Heyman, R. E. (2001). Risk factors for male-to-female partner physical abuse. *Aggression and Violent Behavior, 6*(2–3), 281–352. doi: 10.1016/S1359-1789(00)00027-6

Silvestri, M. (2017). Police culture and gender: Revisiting the 'cult of masculinity'. *Policing: A Journal of Policy and Practice, 11*, 289–300. doi: 10.1093/police/paw052

Smith, D., & Gray J. (1983). *Police and People of London; The PSI Report.* Aldershot: Gower.
Somvadee, C., & Morash, M. (2008). Dynamics of sexual harassment for policewomen working alongside men. *Policing: An International Journal, 31*(3), 485–498. www.ojp.gov/ncjrs/virtual-library/abstracts/dynamics-sexual-harassment-policewomen-working-alongside-men
UNICEF. (2017). Press Release. Retrieved 2 June, from https://www.unicef.org/kyrgyzstan/press-releases/least-27-million-children-are-living-residential-care-worldwide-unicef-says
UniSAFE. (2022). Policy Brief. Retrieved from https://unisafe-gbv.eu/project-news/unisafes-first-policy-brief/
Universities UK (2022). *Changing the Culture: Tackling Staff to Student Sexual Misconduct.* London: UUK. www.universitiesuk.ac.uk/sites/default/files/field/downloads/2022-09/staff-to-student-misconduct-strategic-guide-28-09-22.pdf
Westmarland, N. (2015). *Violence against Women: Criminological Perspectives on Men's Violences.* London: Routledge. doi: 10.4324/9781315768830
Westmarland, N., Almqvist, A., Egeberg-Holmgren, L., Ruxton, S., Burrell, S., & Delgado Valbuena, C. (2021). *Men's Activism to End Violence against Women: Voices from Spain, Sweden and the UK,* Bristol: Policy Press. doi: 10.47674/9781447357971
Westmarland, N., & Anderson, J. (2001). Safe at the wheel? Security issues for female taxi drivers – visions of a feminine future, *Security Journal, 14*(2), 29–40. doi: 10.5555/sj.2001.14.2.29
Witz, A. (1992). *Professions and Patriarchy.* London: Routledge.

PART III

Organizational settings

17

HEGEMONIC MASCULINITIES AND THE HEGEMONY OF MEN IN BUSINESS AND FINANCE ORGANIZATIONS

Persistence of and challenges to patriarchal power

Anika Thym, Helen Longlands and Richard Collier

Introduction

Diverse political, intellectual and institutional influences have shaped the study of masculinities in the area of business and finance. Rather than taking for granted what is meant by the term "masculinity", this chapter explores how the institutions of law, business and finance interact with a range of discourses around masculinities. These discourses are located within particular transnational, national and local settings, producing distinctive configurations of gender relations therein. Taking masculinities – and men – seriously in this field entails paying attention to the heterogeneous and frequently contested practices and ideas about masculinity which dominate within specific professional and institutional contexts.

Business and finance organizations have not always been a "man's world" in the way they have been commonly understood throughout the past 200 years in Western contexts. A complex picture regarding the history of men's dominance in these fields is revealed through a reading of the development of colonial capitalism, law, finance and investment since the seventeenth century (Froide, 2016; Murphy, 2012; Laurence, 2006). This stands in marked contrast to the depiction, for example, of the 2007/2008 Global Financial Crisis (GFC) as a distinctly masculine phenomenon (Sauer, 2010). Although around the seventeenth and eighteenth centuries women (white and of colour, in Europe and colonized areas) often had considerable financial autonomy, this was increasingly denied as bourgeois cis-heteropatriarchal gender relations became generalized in Europe and colonized areas.

In more contemporary times, the finance industry, nonetheless, remains largely a "world of men" and a pivotal location for the reproduction of the "hegemony of men" globally (Hearn, 2004). Leadership positions in law and finance, especially in trading and investment banking, are almost exclusively taken up by men (Hearn, 2015, p. 138f) with the gender pay gap usually higher in the financial sector than in other sectors of the economy (e.g. data from the UK banking industry show an average 44.5 percent gap; Wilson & Dakers, 2021).

DOI: 10.4324/9781003193579-20

Furthermore, as noted in the following, bullying, harassment and sexist behaviours have been widely seen as commonplace across some arenas of finance, banking and the law (International Bar Association, 2019). In trading, for example, a form of "locker room behaviour" has been considered "part of the professional ethic of the trader" (Zaloom, 2006, p. 118). In addition, financial actors within hyper-competitive organizations and cultures in a global economy often position their institutions as superior not just to other institutions but politics more generally (Ho, 2009; Longlands, 2020). In banking, finance and law, wealthy institutions operate with a hegemonic self-stylization that has served to reproduce recruitment of a so-called intellectual and business elite – particularly evident in certain divisions such as investment banking, large corporate commercial law firms (Collier, 2022, 2015) and financial global centres of men's power based in geographic locations such as Wall Street or the City of London (Ho, 2009, p. 40ff.; Longlands & Collier, 2019). Newer management styles in these areas of business and finance, aligned to what Connell and Wood (2005) have termed "transnational business masculinity", are characterized as highly competitive and driven by a "ceaseless striving for material and symbolic success", one in which "conquest and domination become exalted as ways of relating to the world" (Kerfoot & Knights, 1993, p. 672; Klein, 2017). Some financial exponents suggest counteracting the neoliberal processes of deregulation which exacerbate inequalities. They recommend striving for radical changes in the worlds of business and finance that could lead to more equal, free and caring ways of organizing communities (cf. Thym, 2020, p. 94; Rosenblum, 2009).

Despite the persistence of "masculine domination" (Bourdieu, 2001) in this area, significant changes have taken place. Non-male, non-white and non-heterosexual people are still under-represented, particularly in more high-status and highly remunerated divisions. Across organizations of business, finance and law, however, moves have been made towards greater diversity in leadership positions. This is particularly marked in legal professions where equality and inclusion agendas have become increasingly prominent. Some scholars have sought to conceptualize hegemony not only concerning masculinity but also the nature of "hegemonic femininity" (Schippers, 2007) and the pluralization of hegemonic relations (Aulenbacher et al., 2013, p. 30). Hegemony is described as being based "on more complex notions of political pluralism, 'mixed' (capitalist) economy, diversity, 'third ways', and non-radical forms of multiculturalism" (Hearn, 2004, p. 64). Other scholars have investigated the interconnections between changes in the economy, from Fordistic to neoliberal patterns of hegemonic masculinity and men in leadership positions in multinational business and financial institutions and law (Connell & Wood, 2005; Kerfoot & Knights, 1993; Collier, 2022).

A different strand of work has focused on how changes in the family, including shifting discourses around fatherhood and masculinities, may or may not be contesting and changing understandings of hegemonic masculinity more generally as well as in these fields (Collier, 2019, 2013; Demirović & Maihofer, 2013, p. 43; Longlands, 2020). This work highlights the relevance of men's and women's family practices, subjectivities and self-relations for the development and durability of hegemonic masculinities. While many fathers express a desire to spend more time with their families, aligned to ideas of "caring masculinities", some scholars argue that this does not appear to be widely born out in practice, especially in male-dominated areas in the financial sector – areas that, despite a growing number of diversity and inclusion policies, and in law a profound gender transformation at point of entry to the professional field, still seem particularly resistant to change. Studies from a variety of contexts, including Australia, Scandinavia, Chile and the United Kingdom, suggest that while there are varied and complex gender practices among men in management positions, many men still favour traditional ideals of fatherhood and gender relations, based around the notion of the male breadwinner (Connell, 2010; Madrid, 2017, Longlands & Collier, 2019; Collier, 2019).

Longlands (2020), in her research on fathers working as highly paid bankers in the City of London, explores the central and mutually supportive relationship between the private and professional lives of these men. She highlights how workplace and family relations and practices are not static or uniform. Rather, they are negotiated by men and women in ways that not only help shape and perpetuate but also rearticulate and reinforce processes of hegemonic masculinity linked with global finance, illustrating the seductive, dynamic, adaptive and enduring capacity of hegemony. Her research also illustrates how shifting ideals of fatherhood that might problematize unequal gender relations in both family and workplace contexts can instead be *accommodated* within existing yet mutable hegemonic processes in ways that not only perpetuate but also further strengthen individual and institutional notions of worth and forms of gendered privilege.

In contrast, other studies find that significant shifts towards gender equality are happening at the level of subjectivity more generally in law, business and finance organizations. Demirović and Maihofer (2013), for example, analyse how dominant discourses of masculinity shift in ways interlinked to moves towards more gender equality in the family, where, for example, the traditional division of labour is not taken-for-granted but negotiated and desires for present fatherhood are articulated. An ongoing study by Thym (2019) shows the co-existence of discourses maintaining traditional gendered divisions of labour and those supportive of men committing more time to children which can result in some men dropping out and changing careers in this area (Biese, 2020). This is a terrain marked by ambivalent struggles and contradictions between traditionally patriarchal and equality-oriented understandings of fatherhood.

A rare perspective on the critical views of wealthy people about inequality, meanwhile, is presented in Sherman's (2017) study of affluent New Yorkers, including hedge fund financiers. She found that liberal elites who believe in diversity and meritocracy can feel conflicted about their position in a highly unequal society (see further later). Business and finance organizations are spaces, therefore, in which changes or adaptations in forms of hegemony and governance appear marked by, on the one hand, a reinforcing of hierarchies and men's dominance and, on the other, in certain contexts, a cultural questioning of men's power. These contradictions and the co-existence of challenges to and the persistence of patriarchal power interweave through these accounts of masculinity, for example, in the field of law (Collier, 2022). Studying business and finance organizations can help to understand the complexities of these mechanisms of power and domination as well as ways of questioning domination from a specific inside angle.

Three fields of study on men and masculinities in finance and law organizations

When studying men and masculinities in organizations, it is important not to generalize across professions or occupational fields or particular divisions within transnational firms, and we acknowledge the diversity of and the hierarchies between and within institutions. Moreover, from a social justice point of view researching or writing about powerful individuals' or groups' needs, on the one hand, to be mindful not to privilege them further through providing yet more attention to the social practices they help shape, voice and perpetuate (Conti &

O'Neil, 2007). On the other hand, research exploring the everyday practices of the high-status, highly paid managers of global finance, law and other associated industries can help expose how gendered systems of inequality and stratification are developed and sustained or questioned (Connell, 2012, p. 2; Thym, 2020). While this privileged socio-economic class of people, like the institutions they work for, is neither homogenous nor harmonious, they nevertheless are able, collectively, through the power and status associated with their jobs, to assert significant social, cultural, economic and political influence (Connell, 2012; Donaldson & Poynting, 2007). As such, they play an important role in shaping and supporting processes of hegemonic masculinity linked with particular professional and institutional contexts, and as such are an important terrain of research (Hecht, 2017; Madrid, 2017).

We turn now to look at some fields of study concerning finance and law in more detail in order to flesh out the aforementioned themes.

Men, masculinities and legal professions

The institutions of the professional field of law have been historically dominated by men. Law, indeed, can be seen as a centre of men's power *par excellence* (Hearn et al., 2019; Longlands & Collier, 2019), a sector of business and finance marked by a form of masculine domination that has, across jurisdictions, proved profoundly difficult to dislodge. The highly masculinized character of the world's legal professions, notwithstanding the expansion and demographic diversification of legal practice internationally (Abel et al., 2020; Sommerlad, 1994, 2002), is a theme that resonates across areas of contemporary concern around equality, diversity and inclusion; how best to challenge, for example, the persistence of male dominance at senior levels in the law and impact of gendered ideas of "commitment" in law firms (Sommerlad & Sanderson, 1998); the double-bind experienced by many women lawyers seeking to combine a career in law with family life (Wald, 2010; Pinnington & Sandberg, 2013); the sexualized nature of many legal and business workplace cultures and their constitution of women's corporeality as "other" (Thornton, 1996); the scale of men's violence(s), bullying and harassment within legal professions (International Bar Association, 2019) and the potential and limits of flexible working and work–life balance policies as ways of addressing gender inequalities (Cunningham, 2000; Thornton & Bagust, 2007; Drew et al., 2015).

Law is a sector of business and finance that exemplifies how a neoliberal discourse premised on ideas of meritocratic and rational labour markets has historically justified neglect of the systemic structural causes of gender inequalities in the workplace and the continued constraint of women's agency (Sommerlad & Hammerslev, 2020). Yet law is a highly fragmented field and, on closer examination, diverse connections have been made between masculinity and understandings of what it means to practice law and "think like a lawyer" within geographically specific legal communities (Collier, 2022). Legal professions internationally have become increasingly financialized over the past three decades with law's working practices shaped by the rise of hyper-competitive legal–business cultures (Wald, 2010) and a reconstitution of ideas of legal professional*ism* (Muzio, 2004; Webley, 2015).

How is this relevant to masculinity? The cultures and practices enmeshed with this "law as business" model exemplify features of the hegemonic, global transnational business masculinities discussed earlier (see further Elias & Beasley, 2009; Hearn, 2015; Hearn et al., 2013). Men working in the large law firms and industries that dominate the physical space of the cities of financial power and global economy, in particular, illustrate the resonance of the concept of transnational business masculinities in the context of legal services. Corporate commercial law practice at the interface of the legal and financial services sectors, law firms, banks and finance (Longlands & Collier, 2019; Connell, 2010, 2012) is the locus of hegemonic processes and new gendered configurations of professional identity formation that have come to embody the entrepreneurial and market-oriented values of a geopolitical conjuncture associated with neoliberalism (Sommerlad & Hammerslev, 2020; Sommerlad, 2011).

Digging deeper, however, a broader re-gendering of legal professions has occurred in ways aligned to the processes of organizational *adaptation* to shifting gender relations and, significantly, an organizational embrace of formal equality agendas (Sommerlad, 2007). In this process, the embrace of "soft skills", for example, has become a central feature in sustaining masculine ideals in lawyer's career progression (Choroszewicz, 2020). Notwithstanding the expansion of the number of younger women lawyers in some countries (Abel et al., 2020), meanwhile the financial legal services sector has experienced an increasing degree of (gendered) polarization or segmentation (Ashley & Empson, 2012; Bolton & Muzio, 2007; Sommerlad, 2016); a perpetuation of gendered divisions reflected not only in the internationalization and outsourcing of business legal services but also a growing division, in terms of income, status, size and influence, between elite global transnational corporate firms and "the rest" of legal practice. Within the legal profession literature, a set of powerful and culturally resonant ideas about income professional status, along with interlinked ideas about race, ethnicity, social class and social mobility, continues to be hierarchically associated with workplace cultures closely related to transnational business masculinities and power of certain groups of white, able-bodied, middle-upper class men.

Underscoring this narrative is a model of the lawyer as encoded masculine figure entwined with a form of legal professionalism somehow disconnected from the domains of emotion, affect, corporeality and vulnerability; a theme that has come to the fore over recent years as legal professions internationally express growing concern about the well-being and mental health of their lawyers (International Bar Association, 2021); a concern about the social and psychological consequences of living a form of professional life in business and finance akin to what Thornton (2016a, 2016b) has termed a "flexible cyborg".

Grounding new configurations of masculinity in the legal field in the "global tides" of a "market world" (Connell, 2014) neoliberal economic agendas have not only fostered new (gendered) social inequalities and divisions while maintaining the power of male global elites. At a time when "neoliberalism has grown increasingly illiberal producing new mutations of nationalism and deregulation" (Davies, 2021, p. 240), shifts within legal financial and business cultures exemplify features of the dismantling of the liberal-legal state via the replacing of "separate spaces of 'enclosure'" with a "continuous network" as "leisure, work, education, healthcare, intimacy all blended into one, producing an exhausted individual who lacks any downtime or breaks" (Davies, 2021, p. 239). These developments are part of the changes taking place in the lives of lawyers in an era of digital capitalism (Caserta & Madsen, 2019); shifts interlinked to a wider consideration of the human consequences of globalization that reveal much about how forms of working lives in business, finance and law are themselves, on closer examination, suffused with assumptions about masculinity.

In seeking to better understand the role of the finance industry and associated professional services in shaping and deepening local and global socio-economic inequalities (Sassen, 2001; Harvey, 2006), a closer interrogation of the relationship between legal professions and masculinities reveals much about a legal field that has become "everywhere splintered" and in which "the meaning of the profession [is] contested" (Sommerlad & Hammerslev, 2020). The co-existence of a commitment to formal gender-equality and new gendered alignments and structural divisions is a key feature of how the contemporary gendered dynamics of business and finance – and of the global cities in which these centres of men's power are located (Longlands, 2020) – continue to exclude and include, disadvantage and reward businesses and individuals, favouring those men in positions of power and privilege and the forms of masculinity with which they have been historically associated. While ostensibly gender-neutral, the configurations of spatial practices in legal cultures fostered by neoliberal global capitalism interrelate with gendered ideas in ways that continue to reinforce the authority and legitimacy of certain models of masculinity in high-status workplaces (Chow, 2003; McDowell, 2010; Tienari et al., 2010) and help perpetuate, in turn, the gender divisions of labour within the family (Collier, 2015; Longlands & Collier, 2019; Thornton, 2020).

Men and masculinities in finance organizations

Global economic and financial systems are highly complex and in a constant state of adaptation and development (Berman, 2010; Sassen, 2014; Klein, 2017). Yet as sociological research on the global city highlights, despite these dynamics, wealth and power linked with global finance and the diffuse global neoliberal capitalist system is nevertheless concentrated and grounded (as noted earlier) in specific geographic places – global cities (Sassen, 2001, 2014; Massey, 2010; Harvey, 2006, 2012). This body of scholarship underscores the importance of recognizing and understanding hierarchical and hegemonic processes linked with global finance and presents an understanding of space as shaped through constant internal interactions and relations as well as relations and interactions with spaces and people elsewhere (Massey, 2010). This process of "grounded connectedness" (Massey, 2005, p. 188) and recognition of hierarchy allows us to appreciate how gendered interactions and relations between and within the wealthy hubs of global finance and global cities have a bearing on people's lives within and beyond the core. Wealthy financial institutions and associated professional services, as well as the people (mainly men) who control them, play a key active role in shaping, deepening and maintaining local and global socio-spatial and socio-economic inequalities and gendered hierarchies; doing so in ways that deliberately or by default serve their own interests through the appropriation of space in key geographic locations or the dependency on forms of low paid labour (e.g. female migrant office cleaners often working under precarious contractual arrangements) (Sassen, 2014; Massey, 2010; Perrons, 2015; Longlands, 2020).

While much of this scholarship explores the global rather than the local space, research centred on wealthy banks located in key strategic positions within global cities (Ho, 2009; Longlands, 2020; McDowell, 2010) provides important insight into ways in which configurations of space and spatial practices interrelate with gendered ideas and practices to reinforce the authority and legitimacy of forms of hegemonic masculinity. Hegemony is configured in particular situations through social practices and relations and their inter-relationship with one another; sustaining its seductive authority by presenting as natural and beneficial for all an unequal system that rewards a small but powerful minority (Gramsci, 1971). Wealthy financial institutions – ones that enjoy a powerful local and global presence – dominate the desirable outside spaces within global cities and, as such, are a central component of the identity of the place and gain value and legitimacy through the normalization of this identity (Massey, 2010; Longlands, 2020). Within these institutions, high-status divisions of banking and the legal profession dominate City spaces (see Ho, 2009). And within these high-status divisions, men continue to populate the most highly remunerated high-status senior management positions

(HoC, 2018). These distinctive spatial configurations are significant because they both reflect and feed into an ongoing circuit of gendered power that not only sustains and justifies the masculinization of the workplace but also perpetuates wider forms of socio-economic inequality (Sassen, 2001, 2014) and cross-generational privilege (Longlands, 2020).

At the heart of this cyclical process, a key component of the seductive nature of hegemony in this context is the high level of remuneration on offer among the elite positions of banking, law and associated industries, functioning as both status signifier and status reproducer (Cox, 2011). This acts to narrow the space or incentive for individuals to question the system and supports a model of masculinity that rests on an unwavering commitment to the rationality of the market, the primacy of capital and business accumulation and the practices and systems that underpin these (Connell, 2009, 2012; Longlands & Collier, 2019; Hearn, 2015). Working in specific geographic locations (such as the City of London or Wall Street) in high-status positions provides access to high salaries and generous bonus payments that, in turn, encourage and help justify, legitimize and normalize forms of working linked with a hyper-competitive and long hours culture, and the reproduction of certain kinds of lifestyle and consumer choices and practices, including where to live and, for bankers and lawyers who have families, where to send children to school (Longlands & Collier, 2019; Longlands, 2020; Collier, 2019).

When combined with the neoliberal discourse of meritocracy, competitive individualism and self-responsibility, these social practices relating to bankers' public and private lives support a sense of individual, collective and institutional value and rightful belonging in business spaces and hierarchies – one which rests on notions of economic, intellectual and moral superiority; those at the top have *earned* and deserve their success, while those that do not succeed (whether in banking or elsewhere) are not "smart enough", do not work hard enough or are not committed enough to their jobs (Longlands, 2020; Ho, 2009). This deproblematizes the patriarchal, classist, racist, ageist and ableist nature of elite banking. It also helps mask how economic and social inequalities are not simply a matter of chance, or the result of different abilities, efforts or decisions on the part of individuals (Jakopovich, 2014; Friedman & Laurison, 2019).

The durability of gendered processes of hegemony relating to global finance has been heavily tested in contemporary times by deep periods of economic, social, health and environmental crisis. These interconnected crises have starkly exposed and exacerbated the inequalities that this hegemony both shapes and depends on. Individuals and institutions with direct or indirect access to power and privilege are not only much more likely to be able to respond to social and economic constraints but do so in ways that enable them to renegotiate and reframe their sense of worth and entitlement (see Longlands, 2020; Donaldson & Poynting, 2007). Periods of crisis nevertheless cause seismic shifts and may present an opportunity to reimagine, redesign and build anew the systems and ideology of the future in ways that do not simply reward, revalue and re-privilege those who were already advantaged; by redefining, for example, notions of success (Hall et al., 2013; Hearn, 2015; Featherstone, 2016) or fostering new ways of thinking about workplace well-being and mental health. At the macro-level, developing such a future necessitates a creative, radical rethink and widespread mobilization (Wilkinson & Pickett, 2019; Klein, 2017; Connell & Dados, 2014). At the micro-level, dismantling processes of hegemonic masculinity linked with global finance could begin from a coming together of individual and collective acts of resistance and self-critique that expose, challenge and seek to change contradictions and inequalities embedded in and generated by the current system.

Men in finance organizations: cases of self-critique of hegemony

Men in leadership positions in the financial sector, we have seen, are central to the reproduction of masculine and economic hegemonies. Yet there have always been some privileged people who question relations of power and domination for different reasons (Hearn, 1987; Pease, 2010; Luterbach & Thym, 2021). Here, we want to highlight five possible ways in which hegemony concerning places, institutions, ways of thinking that are taken-for-granted as well as career norms may be questioned by individuals in finance. Such self-critique of hegemony refers to the critical reflection of one's own entanglement in relations of power and domination, as individuals and as members of groups, institutions or societies (Thym, 2019). Such insights, even when ambivalent and contradictory, can offer a particular kind of knowledge for emancipatory developments. As Bourdieu stresses, in order to overcome "*all* forms of domination", it is important not only to focus on places where different forms of subordination may be most explicit but also to analyse and change institutions like internationally operating business and finance organizations, "where principles of domination . . . are developed and imposed" (Bourdieu, 2001, p. 4).

An ongoing research project studying critical self-reflections by men in leadership positions in the Swiss financial sector has analysed different starting points of critique from a privileged position (cf. Thym, 2019, 2020). The sample of the study is not representative of men in leadership positions in finance organizations in Switzerland or more generally but gives insights into critique that is shared by some. The desire of participants to share critical views in the financial sector was the main sample criterion for interviewees, so they may be representative of some dominant strands of critique voiced, but not of the financial sector as a whole. The degree and range in which privilege is recognized, problematized and in what way transformation is sought depend on the interview partner and topic (Pease, 2010, p. 185). The investigation is based on 5 autobiographical books and 23 interviews that were conducted by Anika Thym with men in leadership positions from internationally operating Swiss financial institutions.

A first starting point for self-critique of hegemony is a strong sense of justice and empathy with the devaluation and suffering of others. D. Frei (56 years old, top customer consultant), for example, expresses a strong desire to realize gender equality. He describes existing inequalities in Switzerland as "fundamental problem in our society . . . if a society thinks in patriarchal ways, I simply have to say, that is sick". He illustrates how patriarchal thinking is related to institutional discrimination, which means that in many ways, especially in banking, women are "still at a disadvantage", for example, concerning the gender pay gap. He says that he always believed in gender equality, but he describes a heightened sense of injustice, when thinking of his daughter, who also works in a bank. "I really don't want my daughter to experience this. . . . Already from this perspective, I don't find it correct, if a society functions like this". As was shown in several studies on men supporting gender equality (cf. Travis, 2019), his sense of injustice increased because of his empathetic relation to his daughter. Similarly, other interview partners empathetically criticize discrimination against women, homosexuals, and Jews as well as locally and globally increasing economic inequalities.

A second starting point for critique is the personal class background. P. Widmer (68 years old, former CEO of a private bank), for example, grew up in a working-class context and describes how foreign and strange he felt when entering the financial sector. He was not familiar with the predominant expressions, jokes or gestures and felt a discrepancy between his normality and the normalities in the banking world. Even his reason for entering the financial sector is connected to his working-class background: "The whole critique of capitalism was a very central theme for me for my whole life. . . . I looked into the asshole of capitalism because I thought, you have to understand, how it actually works". He collected data, which he is analysing and would like to write a manifesto to encourage people to protest.

Experiences with class difference are mostly connected to questioning economic inequalities but not necessarily gender relations. Patriarchal relations are, however, strongly questioned by men who do not identify with the hegemonic masculinity practices in finance. Especially feminine masculine identity forms a third possible starting point of critique. Some of the interviewed men show a remarkable openness to femininity in their masculine identity, when they describe themselves as "half a woman", "very feminine man" or as "wanting to be a woman". Their gender identity, and the devaluations they experience because of their "feminine" attributes, form a starting point for questioning patriarchal relations and to support gender-equality efforts. Their gender identities are in sharp contrast to traditional bourgeois masculinity, which is defined as "an eminently relational notion, constructed in front of and for other men and against femininity, in a kind of fear of the female, firstly in oneself" (Bourdieu, 2001, p. 53). Together with the women they promote, these men question a specific kind of masculinity and its devaluation of "feminine" qualities. Unlike some literature on "hybrid masculinities" (Bridges & Pascoe, 2014), we see these "gendered modes of existence" (Maihofer, 1995) in relation to their critique of domination as emancipatory aspects of change.

A fourth important starting point for critique is access to specific knowledge that is acquired. This becomes apparent implicitly when contrasting how some have a language to phrase their critique, while others remain with a feeling of discomfort and struggle to understand problems. For example, one interview partner is aware inequalities are increasing but cannot understand or explain why his daughter earns so much less as a doctor than his son who is a banker, although they both work hard and the daughter arguably does the more relevant job. Those who most readily find words for their critique and feelings studied sociology and political sciences or had therapy sessions that enhance technologies of critical self-inspection and reflection. Others gather a sense of societal connections from family members or friends who are social workers or academics and who convey the importance of caring for others and explain socio-economic connections.

While the previously mentioned starting points focus on care for others who are discriminated, devalued or exploited, a fifth starting point for critique in the interviews is one's own suffering from masculinity and work requirements. One former top manager says in hindsight: "in the end it was the loss, the job-related loss, loss of status and the loss of the family or relationship, that lead to a restart. Both were very painful. The professional and the private loss". Although this crisis was challenging for him, it also enabled him to name and question the masculinity norms that he had subjected himself to. He reflects his identification with wage labour and his desire to "become somebody" by making a career. Looking back, he regrets having taken the gendered division of labour for granted, and now wishes he had shared economic and childcare responsibilities with his wife more equally. Many of the interview partners who questioned different relations of domination often were forced to drop out, because their critique was not heard within their organization. Some, however, remain in the financial sector and push for transformations, although exclusively in smaller banks.

These five strands of critique show how there can be different starting points for the questioning of relations of domination: they can be driven by a sense of equality and solidarity with others, by one's own discrimination due to class, by one's gender identity which does not conform with hegemonic masculinity or the suffering that can come from fulfilling masculinity norms (see also Pease, 2010).

Conclusion

At a time when men's practices, power, privilege and accountability are being questioned across the fields of business, finance and law, developing a deeper understanding of the masculine cultures of these institutions remains a key part of understanding the perpetuation of gendered divisions. Echoing Hearn's (2004) focus on the hegemony of men and asking the "man question" (Dowd, 2010; Collier, 2010) in this context reveals underexplored aspects of the gendered dynamics of identity formation as a certain kind of professional across the areas discussed in this chapter. Paradoxically, at the very moment discourses of equality and inclusion are embedded at an organizational level within business, finance and legal professions, the gendered masculine nature of these cultures, forms of embodiment and disciplinary technologies ensure to some degree that the masculinity of super-élite financial institutions is sustained (Garlick, 2018). There also appear new forms of stratification between these super-elites and the rest; new struggles between different legal and capital fractions, each connected to different masculinities which struggle for hegemony. By way of example and looking at "Brexit" and the UK's recent departure from the European Union (EU), many traditional financial institutions wanted the United Kingdom to remain in the EU. Similarly, in Switzerland, traditional banks wanted to commit to the Swiss-EU Institutional Agreement, while hedge fund managers aim to turn Switzerland into an independent Singapore in the Alps. Hedge funds and organizations operating in shadow banking, often connected to right-wing populist groups and masculinities, have opposed international agreements, wanting to avoid legal commitments concerning taxes, company control, environmental protection, digitalization and so on (Benquet & Bourgeron, 2021). Current struggles around law, finance and gender are interlinked to developments in these fields, enmeshed in ambivalent and contradictory ways with directions and outcomes potentially more authoritarian, more emancipatory or perhaps more authoritarian yet disguised as emancipatory or egalitarian, and with different tendencies in different class levels and social fields.

References

Abel, R. L., Hammerslev, O., Sommerlad, H., & Schultz, U. (Eds.). (2020). *Lawyers in 21st-Century Societies*. Oxford: Hart Publishing. doi: 10.5040/9781509915170

Ashley, L., & Empson, L. (2012). Differentiation and discrimination: Understanding social class and social exclusion in leading law firms. *Human Relations*, *66*(2), 219–244. 10.1177/0018726712455833

Aulenbacher, B., Meuser, M., & Riegraf, B. (2013). Hegemonie und Subversion. Zur Pluralisierung hegemonialer Verhältnisse im Verhältnis von Öffentlichkeiten und Privatheit. In B. Riegraf, H. Hacker, H. Kahlert, B. Liebig, M. Peitz & R. Reitsamer (Eds.), *Geschlechterverhältnisse und neue Öffentlichkeiten: Feministische Perspektiven* (pp. 18–36). Münster: Westfälisches Dampfboot.

Benquet, M., & Bourgeron, T. (2021). *La Finance Autoritaire – Vers la fin du néolibéralisme*. Paris RAISONS D AGIR.

Berman, M. (2010). *All That Is Solid Melts into Air: The Experience of Modernity*. London: Verso.

Biese, I. (2020). Men opting out: Disenchantment with corporate cultures and career ideals. In K. Aavik, C. Bland, J. Hoegaerts & J. T. V. Salminen (Eds.), *Men, Masculinities and the Modern Career. Contemporary and Historical Perspectives* (pp. 35–52). Berlin: De Gruyter Oldenbourg. doi: 10.1515/9783110651874-003

Bolton, S. C., & Muzio, D. (2007). Can't live with 'em; can't live without 'em.: Gendered segmentation in the legal profession'. *Sociology 17*, *41*(1), 47–64. doi: 10.1177/0038038507072283

Bourdieu, P. (2001). *Masculine Domination*. Cambridge: Polity Press.
Bridges, T., & Pascoe, C. J. (2014). Hybrid masculinities: New directions in the sociology of men and masculinities. *Sociology Compass, 8*(3), 246–258. doi: 10.1111/soc4.12134
Caserta, S., & Madsen, M. R. (2019). The legal profession in the era of digital capitalism: Disruption or new dawn? *Laws, 8*, 1–17. doi: 10.3390/laws8010001
Choroszewicz, M. (2020). The centrality of soft skills in sustaining masculine ideals in lawyers' career progression in Finland and Quebec. In K. Aavik, C. Bland, J. Hoegaerts & J. Salminen (Ed.), *Men, Masculinities and the Modern Career: Contemporary and Historical Perspectives* (pp. 89–108). Berlin: De Gruyter Oldenbourg. doi: 10.1515/9783110651874-006
Chow, E. N. (2003). Gender matters: Studying globalization and social change in the 21st century. *International Sociology, 18*(3), 443–460. doi: 10.1177/02685809030183001
Collier, R. (2010). *Men, Law and Gender: Essays on the 'Man' of Law*. London: Routledge.
Collier, R. (2013). Rethinking men and masculinities in the contemporary legal profession: The example of fatherhood, transnational business masculinities and work-life balance in large law firms. *Nevada Law Journal, 13*, 101–130.
Collier, R. (2015). Naming men *as men* in corporate legal practice: Gender and the idea of 'virtually 24/7 commitment' in law. *Fordham Law Review, 83*, 2347–2406.
Collier, R. (2019). Fatherhood, gender and the making of professional identity in large law firms: Bringing men into the frame, *International Journal of Law in Context, 15*(1), 68–87. doi: 10.1017/S1744552318000162
Collier, R. (2022). Men, masculinities and the legal professions: Asking the 'man question'. In R. Abel, H. Sommerlad & O. Hammerslev (Eds.), *Lawyers in 21st Century Societies; Vol. 2: Comparisons and Theories* (pp. 151–172). Oxford: Hart Publishing. doi: 10.5040/9781509931248.ch-007
Connell, R. (2009). *Gender*. Cambridge: Polity.
Connell, R. (2010). Lives of the businessmen. Reflections on life-history method and contemporary hegemonic masculinity. *Österreichische Zeitschrift für Soziologie, 35*(2), 54–71. doi: 10.1007/s11614-010-0054-z
Connell, R. (2012). Inside the glass tower: The construction of masculinities in finance capital. In *Men, Wage Work and Family* (pp. 65–79). New York: Routledge.
Connell, R. (2014). Global tides: Market and gender dynamics on a world scale. *Social Currents, 1*(1), 5–12. doi: 10.1177/2329496513513961
Connell, R., & Dados, N. (2014). Where in the world does neoliberalism come from? The market agenda in southern perspective. *Theory and Society, 43*(2), 117–138. doi: 10.1007/s11186-014-9212-9
Connell, R., & Wood, J. (2005). Globalization and business masculinities. *Men and Masculinities, 7*(4), 347–364. doi: 10.1177/1097184X03260969
Conti, J. A., & O'Neil, M. (2007). Studying power: Qualitative methods and the global elite. *Qualitative Research, 7*(1), 63–82. doi: 10.1177/1468794107071421
Cox, K. R. (2011). Commentary. From the new urban politics to the 'new' metropolitan politics. *Urban Studies, 48*(12), 2661–2671. doi: 10.1177/0042098011413947
Cunningham, K. (2000). Father time: Flexible work arrangements and the law firm's failure of the family. *Stanford Law Review, 53*, 967. doi: 10.2307/1229496
Davies, W. (2021). *This Is Not Normal: The Collapse of Liberal Britain*. London: Verso.
Demirović, A., & Maihofer, A. (2013). Vielfachkrise und die Krise der Geschlechterverhältnisse. In H. M. Nickel & A. Heilmann (Eds.), *Krise, Kritik, Allianzen: Arbeits- und geschlechtersoziologische Perspektiven* (pp. 30–48). Weinheim: Beltz Juventa.
Donaldson, M., & Poynting, S. (2007). *Ruling Class Men: Money, Sex, Power*. Oxford: Peter Lang.
Dowd, N. E. (2010). *The Man Question: Male Subordination and Privilege*. New York: New York University Press.
Drew, N. M. C., Datta, D., & Howieson, J. (2015). The holy grail: Work-life balance in the legal profession. *University of New South Wales Law Journal, 38*, 288.
Elias, J., & Beasley, C. (2009). Hegemonic masculinity and globalization: 'Transnational business masculinities' and beyond. *Globalizations, 6*(2), 281–296. doi: 10.1080/14747730902854232
Featherstone, D. (2016). Contested spaces of hegemony: Left alliances after the crisis. *Soundings, 63*(63), 8–24. doi: 10.3898/136266216819377048
Friedman, S., & Laurison, D. (2019). *The Glass Ceiling: Why It Pays to Be Privileged*. Bristol: Policy Press. doi: 10.2307/j.ctv5zftbj

Froide, A. M. (2016). *Silent Partners: Women as Public Investors during Britain's Financial Revolution, 1690–1750*, 1st edition. New York, NY: Oxford University Press.

Garlick, S. (2018). *The Nature of Masculinity: Critical Race Theory. New Materialisms and Technologies of Embodiment*. Vancouver: UBC Press.

Gramsci, A. (1971). *Selections from the Prison Notebooks* (Q. Hoare & G. N. Smith, Trans.). London: Lawrence & Wishart.

Hall, S., Massey, D., & Rustin, M. (2013). After neoliberalism: Analysing the present. *Soundings: A Journal of Politics and Culture*, *53*, 8–22. doi: 10.3898/136266213806045656

Harvey, D. (2006). *Spaces of Global Capitalism: Towards a Theory of Uneven Geographic Development*. London: Verso.

Harvey, D. (2012). *Rebel Cities: From the Right to the City to the Urban Revolution*. London: Verso.

Hearn, J. (1987). *Gender of Oppression: Men, Masculinity and the Critique of Marxism*. Brighton: Prentice Hall/Harvester Wheatsheaf.

Hearn, J. (2004). From hegemonic masculinity to the hegemony of men. *Feminist Theory*, *5*(1), 49–72. doi: 10.1177/1464700104040813

Hearn, J. (2015). *Men of the World: Genders, Globalizations, Transnational Times*. London: Sage. 10.4135/9781473920644

Hearn, J., Blagojević, M., & Harrison, K. (Eds.). (2013). *Rethinking Transnational Men: Beyond, Between and Within Nations*. New York: Routledge. doi: 10.4324/9780203767603

Hearn, J., Vasquez del Aguila, E., & Hughson, M. (Eds.). (2019). *Unsustainable Institutions of Men: Transnational Dispersed Centres, Gender Power, Contradictions*. London: Routledge. doi: 10.4324/9781315107141

Hecht, K. (2017). *A Relational Analysis of Top Incomes and Wealth: Economic Evaluation, Relative (Dis)advantage and the Service to Capital* (Working paper 11). London: London School of Economics and Political Science (LSE) International Inequalities Institute.

Ho, K. (2009). *Liquidated: An Ethnography of Wall Street*. Durham: Duke University Press. doi: 10.2307/j.ctv123x723.14

House of Commons (HoC). (2018). 'Women in finance', *Treasury Committee – Fifteenth Report of Session 2017–19* (Published on 6 June 2018 by authority of the House of Commons). London: The Stationary Office Limited.

International Bar Association (2019). *Us Too? Bullying and Sexual Harassment in the Legal Profession*. London: IBA.

International Bar Association (2021). Mental Wellbeing in the Legal Profession: A Global Study (London, IBA). Retrieved from https://www.ibanet.org/document?id=IBA-report-Mental-Wellbeing-in-the-Legal-Profession-A-Global-Study

Jakopovich, D. (2014). The concept of class. *Cambridge Studies in Social Research*, *14*(1).

Kerfoot, D., & Knights, D. (1993). Management, manipulation and masculinity: From paternalism to corporate strategy in financial services in Britain. *Journal of Management Studies*, *30*(4), 659–677. doi: 10.1111/j.1467-6486.1993.tb00320.x

Klein, N. (2017). *No Is Not Enough: Defeating the New Shock Politics*. London: Penguin Books

Laurence, A. (2006). Women investors, 'that nasty south sea affair' and the rage to speculate in early eighteenth-century England. *Accounting, Business & Financial History*, 245–264. (world). doi: 10.1080/09585200600756274

Longlands, H. (2020). *Gender, Space and City Bankers*. London: Routledge. doi: 10.4324/9781315107226

Longlands, H., & Collier, R. (2019). Interrogating transnational masculinities, fatherhood and the institution of men: Rethinking gender equity in global finance and large international law firms. In Hearn, J., E. Vasquez del Aguila & M. Hughson (Eds), *The Unsustainable Institutions of Men: Interrogating Transnational Centres, Institutions and Power*. London: Routledge. doi: 10.4324/9781315107141-2

Luterbach, M., & Thym, A. (2021). Männer* und Feminismus: Plädoyer für einen emanzipatorischen Dialog. In AG Transformation von Männlichkeiten (Ed.), *Zeitdiagnose Männlichkeiten Schweiz* (pp. 241–273). Zürich: Seismo.

Madrid, S. (2017). The good night kiss: Fatherhood among corporate managers and the reconfiguration of hegemonic masculinity in Chile. *NORMA: International Journal for Masculinity Studies*, *12*(3–4), 240–255. doi: 10.1080/18902138.2017.1362536

Maihofer, A. (1995). *Geschlecht als Existenzweise. Macht, Moral, Recht und Geschlechterdifferenz.* Frankfurt am Main: Ulrike Helmer.

Massey, D. (2005). *For Space.* London: Sage. doi: 10.2514/1.17749

Massey, D. (2010). *World City.* Cambridge: Polity.

McDowell, L. (2010). Capital culture revisited: Sex, testosterone and the city, *International Journal of Urban and Regional Research, 34*(3), 652–658. doi: 10.1111/j.1468-2427.2010.00972.x

Murphy, A. (2012). *The Origins of English Financial Markets: Investment and Speculation Before the South Sea Bubble.* Cambridge: Cambridge University Press.

Muzio, D. (2004). The professional project and the contemporary re-organisation of the legal profession in England and Wales. *International Journal of the Legal Profession, 11*(1–2), 33–50. doi: 10.1080/0969595042000317415

Pease, B. (2010). *Undoing Privilege: Unearned Advantage in a Divided World.* London: Zed. doi: 10.5040/9781350223738

Perrons, D. (2015). Gender inequality in times of inequality, crisis and austerity: Towards gender sensitive macroeconomic policies. In F. Bettio & S. Sansonetti (Eds.), *Visions for Gender Equality.* Luxembourg: Gender Equality, European Commission – Directorate-General for Justice.

Pinnington, A., & Sandberg, J. (2013). Lawyers professional careers: Increasing women's inclusion in the partnership of law Firms, *Gender, Work and Organization, 20*(6), 616–631. doi: 10.1111/j.1468-0432.2012.00610.x

Rosenblum, D. (2009). Feminizing capital: A corporate imperative. *Berkeley Business Law Journal, 6*(1), 55–95. doi: 10.15779/Z388S0H

Sassen, S. (2001). *The Global City: New York, London, Tokyo.* Princeton, NJ: Princeton University Press. doi: 10.1515/9781400847488

Sassen, S. (2014). *Expulsions: Brutality and Complexity in the Global Economy.* London: The Belknap Press of Harvard University Press. doi: 10.2307/j.ctt6wpqz2.4

Sauer, B. (2010). Das Geschlecht der Finanz- und Wirtschaftskrise: Eine Intervention in aktuelle Krisendeutungen. *Kurswechsel : Zeitschrift für gesellschafts-, wirtschafts- und umweltpolitische Alternativen, 1*, 38–46.

Schippers, M. (2007). Recovering the feminine other: Masculinity, femininity, and gender hegemony. *Theory and Society, 36*(1), 85–102. doi: 10.1007/s11186-007-9022-4

Sherman, R. (2017). *Uneasy Street: The Anxieties of Affluence.* Princeton: Princeton University Press. doi: 10.2307/j.ctvc77mgd

Sommerlad, H. (1994). The myth of feminisation: Women and cultural change in the legal profession. *International Journal of the Legal Profession, 1*(1), 31–53. doi: 10.1080/09695958.1994.9960364

Sommerlad, H. (2002). Women solicitors in a fractured profession: Intersections of gender and professionalism in England and Wales. *International Journal of the Legal Profession, 9*(3), 213–234. doi: 10.1080/0969595032000071761

Sommerlad, H. (2007). Researching and theorizing the processes of professional identity formation. *Journal of Law and Society, 34*(2), 190–217. doi: 10.1111/j.1467-6478.2007.00388.x

Sommerlad, H. (2011). The commercialisation of law and the enterprising legal practitioner: Continuity and change. *International Journal of the Legal Profession, 18*(1–2), 73–108. doi: 10.1080/09695958.2011.619852

Sommerlad, H. (2016). "A pit to put women in": Professionalism, work intensification, sexualisation and work – life balance in the legal profession in England and Wales. *International Journal of the Legal Profession, 23*(1), 61–82. doi: 10.1080/09695958.2016.1140945

Sommerlad, H., & Hammerslev, O. (2020). Lawyers in a new geopolitical conjuncture: Continuity and change. In R. L. Abel, O., Hammerslev, with H. Sommerlad & U. Schultz (Eds), *Lawyers in 21st-Century Societies: Vol. 1* (pp. 1–41). Oxford: Hart Publishing. doi: 10.5040/9781509915170.ch-001

Sommerlad, H., & Sanderson. P (1998). *Gender Choice and Commitment: Women Solicitors in England and Wales and the Struggle for Equal Status.* Aldershot: Ashgate.

Thornton, M. (1996). *Dissonance and Distrust: Women in the Legal Profession.* Oxford: Oxford University Press.

Thornton, M. (2016a). The flexible cyborg: Work-life balance in legal practice. *Sydney Law Review, 38*, 1–21.

Thornton, M. (2016b). Work/life or work/work? Corporate legal practice in the twenty-first century. *International Journal of the Legal Profession, 23*(1), 13–39. doi: 10.1080/09695958.2015.1093939

Thornton, M. (2020). Who cares?: The conundrum for gender equality in legal practice. *UNSW Law Journal, 43*(4), 1473–1493. doi: 10.53637/FWLM2244

Thornton, M., & Bagust, J. (2007). The gender trap: Flexible work in corporate legal practice. *Osgoode Hall Law Journal, 45*, 773–811.

Thym, A. (2019). Hegemony self-critique: How men in finance question aspects of masculine and economic hegemony from within. In J. Hearn, E. Vasquez del Aguila & M. Hughson (Eds.), *Unsustainable Institutions of Men: Transnational Dispersed Centres, Gender Power, Contradictions* (pp. 71–86). New York: Routledge. doi: 10.4324/9781315107141-5

Thym, A. (2020). Men in finance for emancipatory social change? In R. Luyt & K. Starck (Eds.), *Masculine Power and Gender Equality: Masculinities as Change Agents* (pp. 81–98). Cham: Springer. doi: 10.1007/978-3-030-35162-5_5

Tienari, J., Vaara, E., & Meriläinen, S. (2010). Becoming an international man: Top manager masculinities in the making of a multinational corporation. *Equality, Diversity and Inclusion: An International Journal, 29*(1), 38–52. doi: 10.1108/02610151011019200

Travis, M. (2019). How and Why Dads of Daughters Are Leaders in Women's Advancement. Retrieved 21 June 2021, from The Way Women Work website: https://thewaywomenwork.com/2019/11/how-and-why-dads-of-daughters-are-leaders-in-womens-advancement/

Wald, E. (2010). Glass ceilings and dead ends: Professional ideologies: Gender stereotypes, and the future of women lawyers at large law firms. *Fordham Law Review, 78*, 2245.

Webley, L. (2015). Legal professional de (re) regulation, equality, and inclusion, and the contested space of professionalism within the legal market in England and Wales. *Fordham Law Review, 83*, 2349–2367.

Wilkinson, R., & Pickett, K. (2019). *The Inner Level: How More Equal Societies Reduce Stress, Restore Sanity and Improve Everyone's Well-being*. London: Allen Lane.

Wilson, H., & Dakers, M. (2021). U.K. Investment Banks Pay Women 56% of What Male Colleagues Make. Retrieved 28 September 28, from Bloomberg.Com: www.bloomberg.com/news/articles/2021-09-28/u-k-investment-banks-pay-women-56-of-what-male-colleagues-make

Zaloom, C. (2006). *Out of the Pits: Traders and Technology from Chicago to London*. Chicago: University of Chicago Press.

18

MASCULINITY OF THE MODERN WESTERN STATE AND OF STATE INSTITUTIONS

Birgit Sauer

Introduction

"The state is patriarchal!" It is an institution of "male bonding"! These were slogans of the women's movements in Western Europe in the 1960s and 1970s to criticize repressive state policies such as the prohibition of abortion. It took nearly two decades, however, before feminist research approached the phenomenon of the state and began to conceptualize its masculinity theoretically and to systematically explore it empirically. Topics such as women's underrepresentation in decision-making bodies like parliaments or in governments, the role of welfare state institutions for women's lives – the "public patriarchy" (Borchorst & Siim, 1987) – were put on the research agenda. The aim of this early research was to make women visible in political organizations and state institutions and to scandalize their invisibility.

Today, we are again confronted with a new variation of the masculinist state: the COVID-19 pandemic state while strengthening the "left hand", the (re-)distributive aspects of the state (Bourdieu, 2000) after a long period of (welfare) state retrenchment, but simultaneously resisting to acknowledge the fundamental importance of care, reproduces state masculinity.

In 1989, legal scholar Catharine MacKinnon (1989, p. 157) stated that feminism lacked a *theory* of the state. She made an initial proposal for how to conceptualize statehood – namely, similar to Marxist theory, as male domination over women or, more precisely, over the female body. Since the second half of the 1980s, substantive feminist theorizing of the connection between state, gender, men and masculinity started. In the 1990s, inspired by neo-Marxist materialist thinking, by Michel Foucault's (1991, 2008) poststructural and discursive approach to the state and his concept of governmentality feminist state theorists explained the genderedness of the modern state and of masculinist state apparatuses. These concepts were stimulated by critical men and masculinity studies (e.g. Connell, 1987; Hearn, 1987) and thus shifted the focus away from women to gender relations and to gender as a discourse. Masculinity and male-centredness of the Western state therefore refers to the discursive dimension of male domination beyond biological men occupying state institutions (Burstyn, 1983).

Since the 1980s, reflections on the masculinity of the modern Western state developed into two strands: *First*, a more theoretical approach to explain the origin and legitimation of state masculinity stresses that the state can no longer be understood as monolithically

DOI: 10.4324/9781003193579-21

masculinist despite the overrepresentation of men in state institutions. Both state and masculinity are now perceived as flexible and contingent, co-constituting each other as hegemonic discourses beyond the biological sex of state representatives. This emphasizes also differences between men (Hearn, 2004, p. 5; Connell, 1987; Hearn, 1987). *Second*, conceptual and empirical studies on the male-centredness of modern-state bureaucracies unearth their formal and informal masculinity, again beyond a mere focus on men. The overall aim of detecting the masculinity of the state is to understand the transformative character of the state and masculinity as co-constitutive power relations in order to address the role of the state in not only re-producing but also dissolving a hierarchical gender binary engrained in modern Western states.

This chapter will first give an overview of existing literature on the gendered nature and masculinity of the modern Western state. The focus lies on tracing a certain set of discussions, which are mainly northern and Western and look at the development of the bourgeois state around the eighteenth century. The text therefore does not deal with the wide variety of historical and geographical forms of states but highlights the bourgeois-capitalist order of societies. It then focuses on a feminist-materialist-discursive state theory and its conceptualization of hegemonic state masculinity, which are able to grasp the masculinist ambivalences of the modern Western state. Subsequently, I will present approaches to understand the masculinity of state bureaucracies. Finally, I will discuss studies on affective transformations of state bureaucracies and the changing role of masculinity in these processes. The conclusion will point out paths to transform state masculinity and future research directions.

From the patriarchal to the fraternal, masculinist and postmodern state

This section intends to give a brief historical overview of feminist conceptualizations of the gendered modern Western state or better: what we might call "stateness", referring to the "principle" of statehood, namely the demand to order social relations. The aim is to carve out the development towards a poststructural and discursive theory of the state.

The key text of feminist state theory, Carole Pateman's (1988) *The Sexual Contract*[1] explained how contract theories since the seventeenth century legitimized the modern secular state against patriarchal traditions with the idea of fraternity, the fraternal contract, and at the same time excluded women from this contract. Pateman argued that a concealed sexual contract that subjugates women is underlying the fictional social contract, which establishes and justifies the modern state. This fraternal narrative legitimized the state and public sphere as male terrains of power which exclude women on the basis of gender, property, and labour. Ten years later, Charles W. Mills, following Pateman's approach, criticized the racialized and racist foundations of modern statehood. The "racial contract", as Mills (1997) argues, makes non-white men only "subcontractors" like white women, while non-white women are not contracting parties at all, that is, they are constructed as "noncontractors" and therefore fundamentally excluded from the state, public sphere, and rights (Mills, 2007, p. 173). Mill's theory echoed intersectional feminist positions. Following Mills, an intersectional state theory, which, however, still needs to be elaborated, should conceptualize how gender, race, ethnicity, nationality, and religion are institutionalized in state institutions and norms.

Catharine MacKinnon (1989) criticized Marxist theory for not addressing gender inequality. However, following the idea of Marx and Engels that the state maintains the relations of production in the interest of the capitalist class, MacKinnon postulated that the function of the patriarchal state is to guarantee male power over the female body and access to female sexuality. The state is male domination over and through female sexuality, MacKinnon (1989, p. 124) writes: "Man fucks woman: subject verb object". She therefore concludes: "Male power is systemic. Coercive, legitimized and epistemic, it is the regime" (ibid., p. 170).

Without reference to MacKinnon's radical feminist conceptualization of the state and its male-centredness but still in clear distinction from her functionalist approach, explicit poststructural or postmodern explanations of the masculinity of the state emerged since the 1990s. Rather early Raewyn Connell dislocated the monolithic notion of the modern Western state, perpetuated in Marxist as well as feminist thinking of the time: "The patriarchal state can be seen . . . not as the manifestation of a patriarchal essence, but as the centre of a reverberating set of power relations and political processes in which patriarchy is both constructed and contested" (Connell, 1987, p. 130). She further conceptualized the state as "a creative force in the dynamic of gender" (Connell, 1990, p. 529) to highlight the gendered unpredictability of state institutions.

Poststructural feminist authors acknowledged that masculinity and state power reinforce each other. However, as Wendy Brown notes, neither the state nor male domination is unilateral and systemic, and they are certainly not related to each other in a unified amplifying effect. "There is no single thread which, when snapped, unravels the whole of state or masculine dominance" (Brown, 1992, p. 16). Hence, the state is seen as "an intricate grid of often conflicting strategies, technologies, and discourses of power" (ibid., p. 14).

A consensus in feminist state theory developed that the idea of a unitary male state, a set of institutions and norms with the aim of oppressing women must be abandoned:

> [W]hile the state is not unitary in its practices, its intentions or its effects, there is no need to retain the state as a separate sphere, a body of institutions which are centrally organized around the intentionality of control with a given apparatus of enforcement as its command or basis.
>
> *(Yuval-Davis, 1997, p. 13)*

Inspired by Michel Foucault's (1991, 2008) discursive approach, the role of struggles over meaning and knowledge moved to the centre of feminist poststructural state theory:

> It is through discursive strategies, that is, through creating frameworks of meanings, that interests come to be constructed and represented in certain ways . . . The outcomes of particular policies will depend not purely on the limits placed by "structures" but in the range of discursive struggles which define and constitute the state, and specific interest groups, from one moment to the next.
>
> *(Pringle & Watson, 1990, pp. 230–238)*

The discourse-inspired perspective on the state stressed that there is not one single masculinist mechanism – as private ownership of capital, which in Marxist theory constitutes the capitalist character of the state – that creates the masculinist features of the modern state. Rather, homologies between the state and masculine domination exist while simultaneously the power of fathers, politicians, economic bosses, and knowledge producers is always different (Brown, 1992, p. 14ff.). Furthermore, the state consists of different forms of power – discourse, knowledge, information, economic, prerogative, and symbolic-cultural resources – which produce rather different effects. Brown thus concludes that the "domain we call the state is not a thing, system, or subject but a significantly unbounded terrain of powers and techniques, an ensemble of discourses, rules, and practices" (ibid., p. 12).

These poststructural approaches to the masculinity of the modern Western state opened a perspective on transformation: the state's character is contingent and might change over time. The state is – although masculinist on a material, prerogative or symbolic level – not always male-centred, but maleness can be decentred and the state might be de-gendered or changed towards women-friendliness.

A feminist-materialist-discursive state concept: the state as a hegemonic masculinist project

The 1990s were characterized by a neoliberal discourse on the retreat or weakening of the state, while feminist debates about a women-friendly state especially in the Nordic countries stressed the empowering role of welfare state institutions for women's citizenship (Hernes, 1987). However, while Western states changed through neoliberal transformations, the state still possessed all the power resources to regulate women's everyday lives, including the differentiation *between* women along the lines of class, ethnicity, race, nationality, and religion. Furthermore, state masculinity was not in decline but was re-organized in these neoliberal processes. As Wendy Brown remarks:

> The central paradox of the postmodern state thus resembles a central paradox of postmodern masculinity: its power and privilege operate increasingly through disavowal of potency, repudiation of responsibility, diffusion of sites and operations of control.
>
> *(Brown, 1992, p. 29)*

As poststructuralist feminist concepts of the state mainly focus on discourse and meaning, the neoliberal challenge to the state demanded to also take the social and institutional materiality of the state into account and hence to combine materialist, neo-Marxist with discursive state concepts. In the beginning, such a combination was highly contested and questioned as the two theoretical strands were seen to be epistemologically incompatible. However, Marxist-feminist thinkers subscribed to neo-Marxist theories, which were more open to include a gender perspective. According to neo-Marxist ideas – rather similar to poststructural state concepts – the modern Western state is not only an apparatus but foremost a "social relation of forces", and the material condensation of social contradictions, meaning first of all class conflict (Poulantzas, 1978).[2] The state thus consists of different groups of actors, fields, and spaces of action. One of the theoretical innovations with regard to state theory by Marx and Engels is that the state is not seen as the super-structure of economic property relations, not as a rigid skeleton or monolithic structure but as a "flexible" and a "strategic" relationship (Jessop, 1994, p. 43ff.). Therefore, the state has a certain "degree of autonomy" from powerful social forces and actors which dominate social relations. This concept allows a gender perspective to be introduced. As Shirin Rai writes, "The state is a network of economic, political, bureaucratic, legal, cultural and gendered power relations, all of which act with and against each other" (Rai, 1996, p. 5). And feminist forces of all genders might participate in these struggles.

Material interests of women and men and political identities such as gender, sexuality, class, race or religion do not exist outside of the state. They are thus not only represented, ignored, incorporated or denied by the state: rather, they are formed in confrontations, in struggles and discourses of social actors, and in emerging state apparatuses. In the process of condensation, that is, the institutionalization of conflicting social relations, gender and sexuality, practices of race, ethnicity and nationality are inscribed into state institutions and norms. In the contested field of social relations, the state historically was an institutionalization of hierarchical gender relations, of a gender binary, localized in personal status acts, in the gendered division of labour, in the separation of public and private, in the bourgeois family, and hence in a masculinist structure.

State masculinism is inherited from feudal militaristic stateness, but it is grounded in capitalist forces and interest constellations. Therefore, historically state institutionalization had a masculinist bias, based on military or monarchic masculinist traditions even under the rule of law in post-feudal state logics. Colonialism included racist discourses into the emerging capitalist and masculinist state and masculinism had to be re-negotiated along differences between (white and non-white) men. Despite the fact that in the site of social struggles actors have to forge a compromise, which depends on the resources of the different social forces, the welfare state of the nineteenth century was male-centred, it was a masculinist compromise between employers and labour movements to regulate male property and risks of male workers' lives – although women participated in the welfare state negotiations and were part of the emerging labour force. Capitalist interests conjoined with male interests and constructed women as caregivers and hence outside the capitalist labour market. This masculinist "system failure" of the fraternal modern Western state which creates capitalist crises of social reproduction not only in the nineteenth century of Manchester capitalism but also in the COVID-19 pandemic has not been solved until today (similar Hearn, 2022).

Nevertheless, social struggles and their institutionalization in state projects and norms are path-dependent. Therefore, processes of modern-state building differ according to specific constellations of class relations, the strength of feudal groups, religion or the organization of gender relations. Historically, different forms of modern-state masculinity developed. Welfare state masculinity and its interplay with the gender-equality state until today has different variations. The notion of the masculinist state hence refers to the principle of co-constitution of masculinity and state institutions, however with differences according to, for instance, gender regimes.

Nicos Poulantzas and Antonio Gramsci's state concepts allow us to focus on not only material social conditions, relations and resources but also hegemonic processes and on discourse. According to Gramsci, the state is a "field of hegemony" in civil society (Demirović & Pühl, 1998), that is, stateness must be based on hegemonic compromises, and it creates hegemonic relations (Pringle & Watson, 1992, p. 56). Differently put, the state as discourse (Watson, 1990, p. 112) is a product of political contestation over meaning. State compromises need to become hegemonic in the process of state institutionalization. Gender is one of the important resources of meaning and knowledge in modern Western states as is class. State masculinity is nevertheless contingent; it does not merely reflect a prior economic structure of the capitalist gendered division of labour or capitalist property structure. State masculinity is based on discourses about gender, gender relations and gender binary and their connection to capitalist structures.

The materialist theory of hegemony finally builds the link for combining materialist approaches with Foucauldian state theory which stresses the state's power to subjectivate people (Bargetz et al., 2015). Subjectivation as one important governing process targets the body and thus gender and sexuality of people. This is why gender and sexuality developed as important knowledge dimensions of the modern state. Gundula Ludwig (2011) coined the term "heteronormative hegemony" to highlight not only the hetero-patriarchal structure of modern Western states but also the dimension of gendered subjectivation which Foucault's idea of governmentality and self-governance introduced. Heteronormative hegemonic states are simultaneously based on hegemonic masculinity as a compromise forged in social struggles over state hegemony, reflecting a gender binary and thus creating heterosexual and cisgender subjectivities as intelligible but non-heterosexual and transgender subjectivities as insignificant.

Foucault's notion of governmentality furthermore highlights the de-centring of the modern liberal state which is based on the idea of individual freedom. Governing through freedom requires different techniques of governing, namely disciplining *and* self-governing (Foucault, 2008; Sauer, 2001, 2015; Ludwig, 2011). Self-governing points to the fact that state subjects must acquire and embody structures; otherwise these state structures do not exist. State structure and subjectivation processes are based on masculinist power, and they create masculinist power (Connell, 1990, pp. 519–520).

A feminist-materialist-hegemonic perspective stresses that state masculinity is not a pre-given power structure but is always contested and strategically formed. State and masculinity need to become hegemonic in the state field of hegemony by creating male interests, that is, defining those interests outside of the private sphere as male, while interests and experiences disappear in the private sphere as female. Hegemonic masculinity, state masculinity and state power co-constitute each other. State masculinity is a hegemonic compromise, between social forces, equipped with material (power) resources by creating a system of meaning and a discourse based on material relations. Therefore, the state gives men easier access to power (Franzway et al., 1989, p. 10). Nevertheless, states can also shift power away from men and re-create new forms of hegemony.

The modern nation-state created hegemonic masculinity through linking military and citizenship, while the welfare state's class compromise protected the sphere of male wage labour. Ultimately, the modern state has thus incorporated aspects of traditional male dominance in a modified form: physical domination (military, police), economic domination (welfare state), sexual or reproductive domination (abortion regulations, compulsory heterosexuality), discursive and signifying power (designing masculinist state projects) (Brown, 1992, p. 28f).

To conclude, six dimensions are at the centre of a feminist-materialist-discursive conception of the state. *First*, the state is an institutionalization of gender domination and hegemonic masculinity (Franzway et al., 1989, pp. 35, 46), that is, it is an expression of social relations such as a hierarchical division of labour and a strict gender binary. State masculinity, according to Connell, emerges from a relationship between the state and hegemonic masculinity in two ways: "State power is a resource for the struggle for hegemony in gender, as well as hegemonic masculinity being a resource in the struggle for state power" (Connell, 1995, p. 5). State and masculinity are at the same time homologous and contingent; they are mutually constituting discursive formations whose specific modes of interaction and institutionalization take on historically specific forms.

Second, state and civil society are not opposing structures, but the state is civil society's (self-)design for political governance. Power relations are formed in civil society and institutionalized as (state) institutions and norms. The state is as masculinist as civil society. Heterosexual gender binary and masculinist civil society relations constitute masculinist statehood. *Third*, the state is no monolithic structure, but a compromise and thus a flexible arena. State masculinity is not simply the reflection of a hierarchical gender binary, but a heterogeneous constellation of interests, resources, discourses, images and power. State and masculinity are homologous relations of domination, which are co-constituted in social and discursive struggles. In these struggles, different interests are produced in and through the state. The state, therefore, is partly independent of masculinist power. It can pursue its own interests and strategies that might contradict masculinist interests and practices. It is thus not an instrument or agent of men; it does not serve "the" male interests with a masculinist logic, for example, of reproducing a gendered division of labour or of controlling female generativity. The modern state consists of diverse apparatuses and discourses, which preserve masculinity, but in which women might also be represented and which open perspectives of change.

Fourth, the state arena is a hegemonic discourse that prefers certain identities and interests or marginalizes and disarticulates others. Hegemonic state discourses, for example, prefer male life plans – or better: they "normalize" wage labour-centred biographies in contrast to people constructed as only partly or non-employed. Furthermore, bureaucratic discourses – instrumental rationality, hierarchy, abstract rights and the cult of experts (Brown, 1992, p. 14) – reproduce the devaluation of practices related to needs and care. State masculinism, for instance, normalizes female clients of masculinist welfare states as dependents in order to make them administrable and subject to administrative masculinity (ibid., pp. 27, 30). African-American "welfare moms" are an example of such masculinist (classist and racist) state discourses as women are overwhelmed by a double burden of wage labour and care work.

Fifth, masculinity is not the nature or essence of the state; rather the state is historically masculinist "as a matter of concrete social practices" (Connell, 1990, p. 535; Connell, 1995, p. 77ff.; Hearn, 1990, p. 67). Using Bob Jessop's (1990) state theory, it can be claimed that the social basis of statehood is directly linked to hegemonic constructs of masculinity and femininity, which form the foundations of a stable masculinist compromise. Each specific gender regime thus gives rise to a specific state project and practices, a specific form of the state and vice versa. Every state project corresponds with a hegemonic gender project and practices, such as hierarchical heterosexual gender binary, white male supremacy, definitions of public and private, gender-specific division of labour, male welfare state, marriage and family law, and gender-equality policies. Furthermore, the state project corresponds to a gender-specific institutional materiality of the state (male state bureaucracy).

Sixth: State masculinity is based on the materiality of a (gendered) division of labour and emerges in struggles over meaning. It is an ideal, or better: a hegemonic compromise between social forces. Historically, modern-state masculinity inherited soldier masculinity from the feudal state. Feudal soldier masculinity did not simply disappear, but specific apparatuses of the bourgeois-capitalist state such as the military and police continued to be based on soldier masculinity. The generalization of the right to vote for all men towards the end of the nineteenth century was based on the ability to bear arms, which was only granted to men but not to women. The welfare state compromise created workers' masculinity as complicit masculinity, and the neoliberal state was based on competitive, risk-taking and entrepreneurial masculinity. Modern-state masculinity is not only differentiated from women but also in relation to race, affecting the modernization of the state and simultaneously creating marginalized, for example, non-white, racialized Others. However, path-dependent variable forms of masculinist statehood exist that are also capable of representing the interests of specific groups of women or marginalized masculinity. State masculinity is an ongoing process which might include women and other genders in the state, thus transforming the genderedness and masculinity of the state. Whether state masculinity can be overcome in these processes is an empirical question, depending on the constellations of social forces within societies – of class, ethnic and of course feminist forces.

State bureaucracies as masculinist institutions

Camilla Stivers was one of the first researchers who pointed to the necessity of a "feminist approach to public administration theory" (Stivers, 1991, p. 49). Different dimensions of masculinity as a norm have been historically inscribed in state bureaucracies, norms and processes, but concealed and presented as "neutral" (Stivers, 1991, p. 53). The *first* dimension is "positional" (Lovenduski, 1996, p. 5) or "nominal" masculinity (Witz & Savage, 1992, p. 37), that is, a quantitative overrepresentation of men, which has been historically changing but is still evident. Positions in state bureaucracies are occupied by men; bureaucracies are "manned", while women for a long time remained excluded, for example, through occupational bans from positions as state officials. Furthermore, withheld political rights and bans on the political organization of women, as in the cases of Germany and Austria at the turn of the nineteenth century, excluded women from the public sphere and state office.

Second, masculinity is to be understood as "policy" masculinity (Lovenduski, 1996, p. 5). The state is masculinist because state institutions and norms systematically establish male identities, experiences and practices as hegemonic and represent those interests, while female identities and interests are under- or mis-represented (Connell, 1990, p. 535, 2009). In the words of Joni Lovenduski:

> Thus male policy gender bias has at least three manifestations: women may be disadvantaged by a policy; policy initiatives to redress inequalities experienced by women may be poorly funded or lack prestige; and such issues may be marginal to, or absent from, the policy agenda.
>
> *(Lovenduski, 1996, p. 6)*

State bureaucracies can be labelled masculinist because they regulate and produce gender segmentation and inequality through gender-biased policies which reproduce a gender division of labour as well as unequal spheres of masculinity and femininity.

Third, an "organizational" or "substantial masculinity" (Witz & Savage, 1992, p. 37), "masculinity as a system", as the Austrian feminist political scientist Eva Kreisky (2014, p. 19) calls it, refers to invisibly inscribed masculine patterns of state organizations (Vandiver, 2020, p. 158). Historically, modern-state bureaucracy was structured in a similar way to the Taylorized production process of commodities and the bureaucratic work in private enterprises. According to Max Weber, "the state is an 'enterprise' (*Betrieb*) just like a factory. . . . Here as there the authority relations have the same roots", namely "the 'separation' of the worker from the material means of production" (Weber, 1978, p. 1394). Similarly, modern-state bureaucracy "entails the complete separation of state officials from the means of administration", that is, the bureaucrat is separated from actual state power (Brown, 1988, p. 156).

Feminist critiques of Weber's ideal type of state bureaucracy (Bologh, 1990; Kanter, 1993; Ferguson, 1984) showed "that by Weber's own account, the cultivation of instrumental rationality and its development into rationalization in the contemporary age is located in specifically 'masculine' drives" (Brown, 1988, p. 152; Stivers, 1991, p. 54). Wendy Brown therefore claims that the Weberian construction of modern bureaucracy is "rooted in constructions of power and freedom specific to Western manhood" (Brown, 1988, p. 153) or as Camilla Stivers (1991, p. 57) adds: in the connection of maleness and heroism.

Masculinist rules, values and norms shape state institutions and create a "culture of masculinity", which "makes it difficult for most women and some men to pursue and often to perceive their gender interests" (Lovenduski, 1996, p. 6). This masculinist organizational culture is established through a gender division of labour within state bureaucracies, the principle of seniority (which privileges a specific type of masculinity), bureaucratic career path models, authority and hierarchy (Sauer, 2001, p. 54). Furthermore, personal networks of men (whose affective cohesion is denied), sexual attraction and sexual desire as well as sexual harassment and violence shape masculinity within state bureaucracies:

> State organizations were and are important sites of men's sexuality. In these and many other ways the state and private life are intimately related, and form a fundamental, yet neglected, aspect of politics and political change.
>
> *(Hearn, 1990, p. 51)*

In accordance with Weber's ideal type, rationality in the sense of utility, impartiality, objectivity, disinterestedness and the absence of emotions, which is stereotyped as masculinity, characterize state bureaucracy (Hearn, 1994). Accordingly, Paul du Gay (1996, p. 164) refers to an "ethos of office" in the civil service, "with its chief point of honour, the capacity to set aside one's private political, moral, regional and other commitments". With respect to the concept of rationality, the Weberian model of bureaucracy formalised a strong polarization of gender – de-emotionalized men, the bearers of the state, and hyper-emotionalized women, and therefore banished – and externalized affectivity between men from state administration into the private, but also in the realm of masculine and aggressive foreign policy. Recent debates about "feminist foreign policy" aim at changing this long-lasting masculinist state characteristic.

Towards the de-masculinization of state bureaucracies? Neoliberalism and affective activation

In the process of neoliberal restructuring, European masculinist state bureaucracies became more "feminized" in a paradoxical manner: more women entered the public workforce – a process, which started already during the growth of the welfare state in the 1960s and 1970s – salaries went down, and working conditions became more precarious. While some women made it into leading positions in neo-bureaucratic organizations, our empirical research on public employment agencies in Austria, Germany, and Switzerland, and on the Austrian postal services (Penz & Sauer, 2020) revealed persistent forms of hierarchical and horizontal gendered divisions of labour within state bureaucracies and especially at the street level. More women than men work in direct contact with citizens and men do the more prestigious work at street level (ibid.).

Similarly important for the re-structuring of state masculinity since the 1980s is the neoliberal reorganization of state administration towards New Public Management. This includes flat hierarchies, transparency, proximity to citizens, activation of citizens as customers and simultaneously austerity, efficiency, competition, economic rationality and thus growing inequality among public servants and among citizens. Public management reform towards customer-oriented services and the new concept of activation of citizen-customers contributed to an affective turn in parts of the state administration (Penz et al., 2015). Bureaucratic rationality is accompanied by emotionality and affectivity; affective skills, such as friendliness, empathy, patience or politeness – traditionally regarded as female affective capital – are now seen as key competences of male and female state officials. They have to acquire affective labour skills in order to become a functioning element of an activating, touching and affective state. New institutional practices of doing state and doing gender emerged. Furthermore, new modes of state governance and the economization of state administration, that is, orientation towards effectiveness, efficiency and competition, require entrepreneurial capacities in an affective mode.

How do these changes impact state masculinity? Do new affective norms and practices within state bureaucracies lead to a new gender logic and to de-masculinization because affective skills are traditionally associated with femininity? Does affective subjectivation of state officials call traditional concepts of state masculinity into question?

Our studies on the affective transformation of labour market administrations in Germany, Austria and Switzerland (Glinsner et al., 2018) have shown how the neo-bureaucratic constellation of customer orientation, affective activation and entrepreneurialism has led neither to a masculinist re-coding nor to a general feminization of public service work but reveals a more complex picture: we detected strategies of doing and un-doing masculinity as well as femininity through affective strategies by both men and women. Masculinized entrepreneurial practices like aggressive, hierarchical and competitive conduct towards customers or paternalistic behaviour towards female colleagues co-exist and co-develop with affective, empathic service-oriented feminized work practices within state bureaucracies (ibid.).

Overall, our collaborative research (ibid.) results *first* point in the direction of translating emotions into efficiency. Work in public labour agencies has developed as a skilful interplay of "rational" arguments to convince jobseekers about the effectivity of labour market instruments, on the one hand, and to affect them, on the other hand, by creating a trustful atmosphere and giving hope and security. This research revealed the emergence of a new "marginalized masculinity" (Connell, 1995, p. 80) in neoliberal state bureaucracies at the street level, a somewhat "feminized masculinity".

Second, especially experienced male and female employment agents reject the entrepreneurial form of neo-bureaucratic service work but instead draw on notions of stereotypically feminized care work. They disregard disciplinary requirements towards the unemployed and in contrast use supportive measures.

Third, other neo-bureaucrats displayed a rather formal approach towards jobseekers and strongly built on their expertise and professionalism, two elements that traditionally have been gender-typed as masculine. This is an effort to prevent a potential loss of professional status that might occur through the change from traditionally masculinized bureaucratic work to feminized service work. Daniela Rastetter (2008, p. 134) describes such processes as "rationalization of emotion work" and as a masculinist strategy. We interpret this as a result of the contradictory demands of entrepreneurialism and affectivity.

Fourth, our data show that work practices associated with the traditional ideal of a neutral, dispassionate masculinized bureaucracy are still central. We found practices that range from performing the emotionless and detached bureaucrat, following the laws and guidelines rigorously, to hierarchical and authoritarian demonstrations of state power, drawing on stereotypically masculinized aggressive forms of affective labour. In these cases, jobseekers were not gently persuaded or motivated according to the rules of empathic governance, but they were strongly requested to submit themselves to the laws and guidelines of the organization and threatened with sanctions. These practices were performed by mostly young and inexperienced men and women to express and underline the existing hierarchical relationship. Ultimately, our studies unearthed the transformation of masculinist state bureaucracies in three countries with a tradition of strong states. Bureaucratic masculinity did not vanish, but feminized practices supplemented them, and both gendered practices can be used by men and women.

Conclusions

While historically the modern Western state developed as a masculinist idea and reality, feminist conceptualizations pointed out both: the working of masculinism and the transformative potential of the modern state with respect to gender and sexuality. Based on the need for a compromise between conflicting social forces and grounded in governing through freedom, modern states are sites of struggle for equality and emancipation. Since the nineteenth century, women's movements have been included in struggles over state projects and have been successful, although in paradoxical ways: the "public patriarchy" of the welfare state included women in state institutions, pushed for their equality on the labour market and for further equality legislation. In the neoliberal state, project women's inclusion into the labour market was accelerated and gender mainstreaming has been introduced to transform the masculinity of state bureaucracies and policymaking processes. However, despite variations of state masculinity and the development of gender-equality policies across nation-states, women remained "outsiders within" (Hill Collins, 1986) and state masculinity has been restructured albeit in less aggressive and heroic forms. The example of the COVID-19 pandemic is telling: Masculinist neglect of care work remains one of the most important characteristics of Western states. Further research needs to conceptualize and empirically study post-pandemic state masculinity, which has been developing into the extension of the lack of care for the environment. This connection of masculinity, environment and capitalist interest points to the necessity to further explore an intersectional state concept which takes masculinity at the intersection of gender, race, ethnicity and nationality into account. Such a concept might be able to answer the question of the possibility of an emancipatory future of the masculinist patriarchal state. And this concept raises the question of coalitions between all genders to overcome hegemonic (state) masculinity in an emancipatory manner.

Notes

1 Pateman's work has to be located in critical-feminist interrogations of the history of political ideas, such as Clark and Lange's wide-ranging edited collection (1979) and O'Brien's retheorizing of Hegelian-Marxism (1981, 1989).

2 In the paradigmatic debate between Milliband (1969) and Nicos Poulantzas at the end of the 1960s, two controversial analytical perspectives of a "state in capitalist society" (Miliband's instrumentalist or actor-oriented approach) and of a "capitalist state" (Poulantzas' more structuralist approach) were elaborated. Poulantzas (1978) counters Miliband that he underestimates the objectified structure of social class relations in the state apparatus, the "institutional materiality" of the state (see Barrow, 1993, p. 57).

References

Bargetz, B., Ludwig, G., & Sauer, B. (Eds.). (2015). *Gouvernementalität und Geschlecht. Politische Theorie im Anschluss an Michel Foucault*. Frankfurt: Campus.

Barrow, C. W. (1993). *Critical Theories of the State. Marxist, Neo-Marxist, Post-Marxist*. Madison, WI: The University of Wisconsin Press.

Bologh, R. W. (1990). *Love or Greatness. Max Weber and Masculine Thinking. Feminist Inquiry*. Boston, MA: Unwin Hyman.

Borchorst, A., & Siim, B. (1987). Women and the advanced welfare state – a new kind of patriarchal power? In A. S. Sassoon (Ed.), *Women and the State. The shifting boundaries of public and private* (pp. 128–157). London.: Hutchinson. doi: 10.4324/9780429401602-5
Bourdieu, P. (2000). The abdication of the state. In P. Bourdieu, Pierre et al. (Eds), *The Weight of the World: Social Suffering in Contemporary Society* (pp. 181–205). Stanford, CA: Stanford University Press.
Brown, W. (1988). *Manhood and Politics. A Feminist Reading in Political Theory.* Totawa: Rowman and Littlefield.
Brown, W. (1992). Finding the man in the state. *Feminist studies, 18*(1), 7–34. doi: 10.2307/3178212
Burstyn, V. (1983). Masculine dominance and the state. *The Socialist Register, 20*, 45–89.
Clark, L. M., & Lange, L. (Eds.). (1979). *The Sexism of Social and Political Theory: Women and Reproduction from Plato to Nietzsche.* Toronto: University of Toronto Press.
Collins, P. H. (1986). Learning from the outsider within: The sociological significance of Black feminist thought. *Social problems, 33*(6), 14–32. doi: 10.1525/sp.1986.33.6.03a00020
Connell, R. (1987). *Gender and Power. Society, the Person and Sexual Politics.* Cambridge: Polity Press.
Connell, R. (1990). The state, gender, and sexual politics: Theory and appraisal. *Theory and Society, 19*(5), 507–544. doi: 10.1007/BF00147025
Connell, R. (1995). *Masculinities.* Cambridge: Polity Press.
Connell, R. (2009). A thousand miles from kind: Men, masculinities and modern institutions. *The Journal of Men's Studies, 16*(3), 237–252. doi: 10.3149/jms.1603.237
Demirović, A., & Pühl, K. (1998). Identitätspolitik und die Transformation von Staatlichkeit: Geschlechterverhältnisse und Staat als komplexe materielle Relation. In E. Kreisky & B. Sauer (Eds.), *Geschlechterverhältnisse im Kontext politischer Transformation* (pp. 220–240). Opladen: Westdeutscher Verlag.
du Gay, P. (1996). Organizing Identity. Entrepreneurial Governance and Public Management. In S. Hall & P. du Gay (Eds.), *Questions of Cultural Identity* (pp. 151–169). London: Sage. doi: 10.4135/9781446221907.n9
Ferguson, K. E. (1984). *The Feminist Case against Bureaucracy.* Philadelphia, PA: Temple University Press.
Foucault, M. (1991). Governmentality. In G. Burchell et al. (Eds.), *The Foucault Effect. Studies in Governmentality* (pp. 87–104). Chicago: University of Chicago Press.
Foucault, M. (2008). *The Birth of Biopolitics. Lectures at the Collège de France, 1978–1979.* New York: Palgrave Macmillan.
Franzway, S., Court, D., & Connell, R. (1989). *Staking a Claim.* Sydney: Polity Press.
Glinsner, B., Sauer, B., Gaitsch, M., Penz, O., & Hofbauer, J. (2018). Doing gender in public services: Affective labour of employment agents. *Gender, Work and Organization, 26*(7), 983–999. doi: 10.1111/gwao.12263
Hearn, J. (1987). *The Gender of Oppression: Men, Masculinity and the Critique of Marxism.* New York: St. Martin's Press.
Hearn, J. (1990). State organisations and men's sexuality in the public domain, 1870–1920. In L. Jamieson (Ed.), *State, Private Life and Political Change* (pp. 50–72). London: Macmillan. doi: 10.1007/978-1-349-20707-7_4
Hearn, J. (1994). Emotive subjects: Organizational men, organizational masculinities and the (de)construction of "emotions". In S. Fineman (Ed.), *Emotion in Organizations* (pp. 142–166). London: Sage.
Hearn, J. (2004). From hegemonic masculinity to the hegemony of men. *Feminist Theory, 5*(1), 49–72. doi: 10.1177/1464700104040813
Hearn, J. (2022). The place and potential of crisis/crises in critical studies on men and masculinities. *Global Discourse: An Interdisciplinary Journal of Current Affairs and Applied Contemporary thought, 12*(3–4), 563–585. doi: 10.1332/204378921X16334429502843.
Hernes, H. M. (1987). *Welfare State and Women Power. Essays in State Feminism.* Oslo: Norwegian University Press.
Jessop, B. (1990). *State Theory. Putting the Capitalist State in its Place.* Cambridge: Polity Press.
Jessop, B. (1994). Veränderte Staatlichkeit. Veränderungen von Staatlichkeit und Staatsprojekten. In D. Grimm (Ed.), *Staatsaufgaben* (pp. 43–73). Baden-Baden: Nomos.
Kanter, R. M. (1993). *Men and Women of the Corporation.* New York: Basic Books.

Kreisky, E. (2014). Masculinity as an analytical category: Work in progress In K. Starck & B. Sauer (Eds.), *A Man's World? Political Masculinities in Literature and Culture* (pp. 11–23). Cambridge: Cambridge Scholar Publishing.

Lovenduski, J. (1996). Sex, gender and British politics In J. Lovenduski & P. Norris (Eds.), *Women in Politics* (pp. 3–18). Oxford: Oxford University Press.

Ludwig, G. (2011). *Geschlecht regieren. Zum Verhältnis von Staat, Geschlecht und heteronormativer Hegemonie*. Frankfurt am Main: Campus.

MacKinnon, C. (1989). *Toward a Feminist Theory of the State*. Cambridge, MA: Harvard University Press.

Milliband, R. (1969). *The State in Capitalist Society*. London: Weidenfeld & Nicolson.

Mills, C. W. (1997). *The Racial Contract*. Ithaca: Cornell University Press.

Mills, C. W. (2007). Intersecting contracts. In C. Pateman & C. W. Mills (Eds.), *Contract and Domination* (pp. 165–199). Cambridge: Polity Press.

O'Brien, M. (1981). *The Politics of Reproduction*. London: Routledge & Kegan Paul.

O'Brien, M. (1989). *Reproducing the World: Essays in Feminist Theory*. Boulder: Westview Press.

Pateman, C. (1988). *The Sexual Contract*. Cambridge: Polity Press.

Penz, O., Glinsner, B., Gaitsch, M., Hofbauer, J., & Sauer, B. (2015). Affektive Interaktionsarbeit in der öffentlichen Arbeitsvermittlung in Österreich, Deutschland und der Schweiz. *AIS Studien*, *8*(1), 21–36.

Penz, O., & Sauer, B. (2020). *Governing Affects. Neoliberalism, Neo-Bureaucracies, and Service Work*. New York/London: Routledge. 10.4324/9781351212434

Poulantzas, N. (1978). *Staatstheorie. Politischer Überbau, Ideologie, Sozialistische Demokratie*. Hamburg: VSA.

Pringle, R., & Watson, S. (1990). Fathers, brothers, mates: The fraternal state in Australia. In S. Watson (Ed.), *Playing the State. Australian Feminist Interventions* (pp. 229–243). London: Verso.

Pringle, R., & Watson, S. (1992). "Women's Interests" and the Post-Structuralist State. In B. Michèle & A. Phillips (Eds.), *Destabilizing Theory. Contemporary Feminist Debates* (pp. 53–73). Stanford, CA: Stanford University Press.

Rai, S. M. (1996). Women and the state in the third world: Some issues for debate. In S. M. Rai & G. Lievesley (Eds.), *Women and the State. International Perspectives* (pp. 5–22). London: Taylor & Francis.

Rastetter, D. (2008). *Zum Lächeln verpflichtet. Emotionsarbeit im Dienstleistungsbereich*. Frankfurt am Main/New York: Campus.

Sauer, B. (2001). *Die Asche des Souveräns. Staat und Demokratie in der Geschlechterdebatte*. Frankfurt am Main: Campus.

Sauer, B. (2015). Feministische Staatskonzeption als Digestive: Staat im Spätwerk Foucaults. In B. Bargetz, G. Ludwig & B. Sauer (Eds.), *Gouvernementalität und Geschlecht. Politische Theorie im Anschluss an Michel Foucault* (pp. 90–116). Frankfurt am Main: Campus.

Stivers, C. (1991). Toward a feminist perspective in public administration theory. *Women & Politics*, *10*(4), 49–65. doi: 10.1080/1554477X.1990.9970587

Vandiver, J. (2020). Alt-virilities: Masculinism. Rhizomatics, and the contradictions of the American alt-right. *Politics, Religion & Ideology*, *21*(2), 152–176. doi: 10.1080/21567689.2020.1763319

Watson, S. (1990). Unpacking "the state": Reflections on Australian, British and Scandinavian feminist interventions. In M. F. Katzenstein & H. Skjeie (Eds.), *Going Public. National Histories of Women's Enfranchisement and Women's Participation within State Institutions* (pp. 111–140). Oslo: Institute for Social Research.

Weber, M. (1978). Bureaucracy and political leadership, Appendix II-ii. In G. Roth & C. Witig (Eds.), *Economic and Society*. Berkeley, CA: University of California Press.

Witz, A., & Savage, M. (1992). Theoretical introduction. The gender of organizations. In M. Savage & A. Witz (Eds.), *Gender and Bureaucracy* (pp. 3–62). Oxford; Blackwell. doi: 10.1111/j.1467-954X.1991.tb03355.x

Yuval-Davis, N. (1997). Women, citizenship and difference. *Feminist Review*, *57*(1), 4–27. doi: 10.1080/014177897339632

19

MEN, MASCULINITIES AND MILITARY ORGANIZATIONS[1]

F. Oya Aktaş, David L. Collinson, Jeff Hearn and Nurseli Yeşim Sünbüloğlu

Introduction

Militaries and militarism are among the most clearly gendered of all organizational activities. The military is also one of the clearest arenas of social power, violence and killing in their many guises. Military matters are urgent, powerful and lethal, so that the ways armies and those in them are organized and act are literally questions of life and death for all concerned. This applies whether we are talking of "wars of resistance", "just wars", "unjust wars", "peace-keeping" or simply "peacetime". Although there have been several recruitment methods over the centuries, wars, fighting and armies have been almost always associated with men and masculinities. Expenditure and violence in terms of war are organized and enacted largely by men, and, in war and with militarism, even with losses of life, men's collective structural power may be undiminished, even reinforced (Hearn, 2011). Militarism also presents many and various gendered challenges and tensions for those within and around the organizations concerned and for organizing militarily.

Militaries are often part of the state and organized in association with political, economic, administrative power in the highest reaches of the state, including policing, security services, foreign policy and economic interests, as well as imperialist and colonialist interests. The beginnings of current, so-called modern, forms of military connect in many societies to the bourgeois state,[2] and in part to the opposition from aristocratic men who have sought to restrict officer entry to certain kinds of men and masculinities like themselves (related particularly to class, ethnicity and racialization).[3] These gendered, intersectional processes become even more complex with imperialist and colonialist armies, whereby killing and conquering are directed "elsewhere" to "other" lands and people, yet at the same time most of those populating the army and fighting and being killed may be from less-privileged regions, classes or ethnicities of the imperial territory. Thus, while in some contexts military service represents a highly valued form of masculinity and masculinism, in some other situations military service might indicate a lack of elite status, an inability to avoid military service and even a lack of access to corrupt means to such avoidance.

Contemporary military expenditure worldwide is one of the most significant blocks of nation-state expenditure, regardless of the enactment of war(s) or in peacetime. This is not

 DOI: 10.4324/9781003193579-22

only well studied in terms of the military–industrial complex (first used by US President Dwight D. Eisenhower in his Farewell Address, January 17, 1961) and the scientific–military–industrial complex (Boulding, 1967; see Galbraith, 1968) but also highly relevant for analysis of state welfare development, with complex patterns of both warfare/welfare substitution and stimulus (Wilensky, 1975; Gifford, 2006; Obinger et al., 2018). Global military expenditure has been rising constantly over the last decade; it exceeded US$2 trillion in 2021 (Lopes da Silva et al., 2022), which is far more than the development aid. As such, military organizations are some of the largest and most powerful organizations on the planet, with all that this entails in terms of hierarchies, concentration of resources, technological capabilities and potential for corruption. Furthermore, militarism and various moves away from militarism are also fundamental aspects of peace-making and of the relations of men and masculinities to peace-making (Breines et al., 2000; Cockburn & Žarkov, 2002; Hearn et al., 2021; Myrttinen et al., 2017).

This chapter brings together studies on men and masculinities with those in the military and military organizations. Men, militarism and the military are historically, profoundly and blatantly interconnected. Links between men, masculinity and the military have existed for centuries, and are reaffirmed daily, not least in the Russian invasion of Ukraine in 2022. Despite the many obvious connections, these two areas are not always put together. These interconnections have often either been simply accepted or it has gone unnoticed that these military persons are largely men. Indeed, many armies and other fighting forces of the world have been and still are armies composed exclusively of men, young men and boys. It is often young men and boys who are the ones engaged in active combat and direct fighting in wars. While many studies of military organizations and organizing do not acknowledge or emphasize the gender power relations at play, there is now an extensive literature that explicitly genders how men, masculinities and men's practices relate to militarism and war (e.g. Barrett, 1996; Enloe, 1998; Goldstein, 2001; Moser & Clark, 2001; Higate, 2002; Whitworth, 2004; Hopton & Higate, 2005; Duriesmith, 2017; Woodward & Duncanson, 2017; Duncanson, 2019; Fraser, 2019). Hutchings (2008, p. 401) sums up some of these relations:

> war requires the institutionalisation of a range of beliefs, skills, and capacities, which shift according to context. To be grasped and evaluated as a distinctive social practice, war also requires the authorisation of a series of discriminations such as between wars fought well or badly, between good and bad war, between war and other forms of organised violence, and between war and peace. Identifying war with masculinity provides conceptual resources that can authorise such discriminations. At the same time, identifying masculinity with war provides a repertoire of possibilities for what masculinity may mean, which occlude the extent to which masculinity is a genuinely empty signifier.

As Hutchings' final sentence indicates, there are complications to these gendered patterns. First, not all armies are made up of men. Second, even armies and other military institutions that are formally made up of men often have women in servicing or administrative positions. Third, the impact of such military masculinities upon those outside the military – women, men and children – is often huge in educational, national and media projects. Fourth, the exact nature of the connections between men and the military are themselves many, various and sometimes contradictory, as in plural military masculinities, not just a single military masculinity. More theoretically, as with any "type" of masculinity that is theorized and located in specific contexts (such as business masculinities, tech masculinities), all sorts of conceptual issues arise – for instance, what is the relationship between men working in the military and military masculinities, whether in the military or beyond?

In the remainder of the chapter, we address the place of men and masculinities in some key organizational issues in military organization and militarism, most notably recruitment, hierarchies and segregations, disability and veterans, and the impacts of these organizations on civilians, before concluding remarks on wider processes and impacts, on research, scientific and technological organizations, on international relations and geopolitics, and on the environment.

Recruitment

Militaries are mainly composed of soldiers, and for centuries states, rulers or institutions have used many forms of recruitment to mobilize armies. For the last two centuries or more, especially with the foundations of modern nation-states, the militarization of the state was carried out through compulsory military service. Conscription has been used to inculcate social and organizational discipline, construct national identity, reinforce gender, class and racialized hierarchies, define "proper" and "improper" citizenship, and generally re-affirm hierarchy in the society, typically in favour of men and among men. Militaries and recruitment methods have been directly related to gender dominance throughout the centuries, the wars that have been fought, and the large national and international "defence" budgets that have maintained this relation in line with discourses of heroism, valour and self-sacrifice.

Recruitment methods used for the last five centuries can be grouped under four main categories (Lucassen & Zürcher, 2000). The first is the peasant–soldier system where feudal lords or regional administrators train or provide soldiers for wartime in return for taxes or for the right to cultivate the land. The *timar* system in the Ottoman Empire or the *Cossacks* in the Russian Empire are examples here. The second recruitment method is unfree recruitment. In this method, slaves or abducted free people are forcibly recruited. Examples of this method are recruitment of *serfs* in the Russian Empire, *impressment/press-gang* method of British navies, *devshirme* system in the Ottoman Empire and *galley slaves* of several nations' navies. The third recruitment method is individual or collective recruitment on the labour market. In such cases where recruitment is more freely chosen, recruits might be attracted by highly gendered images of tough, rugged military masculinities and appeals to manhood, patriotism and honour, whereas more professional mercenaries are likely to be attracted by explicitly economic incentives such as pay and booty. Indeed, private armies and mercenaries have been present throughout history and also have grown in importance and impact in recent decades. In contemporary times, this has evolved into a relatively large-scale capitalist enterprise, with private armies available for hire.

A further recruitment method is conscription. This can be either indirect or direct. In indirect conscription, town leaders chose soldiers, such as *bunichah* system in Iran, *schutterij* in the Netherlands or the system in Peter the Great's Russian Empire where *mirs* selected eligible soldiers among peasants. In direct conscription, or compulsory military service, every citizen is recruited for a certain period, receives training in the barracks and fights in the war when necessary. Thus, citizenship is defined by recruitment, and the right to citizenship is directly related to military obligation. France is sometimes considered to be the first military nation. After the revolution, conscription and education transformed peasants into citizens and created a citizen army and nation-state (Weber, 1976). Military service has been seen as a duty that men of a certain age, usually as young adults, have to perform and which in turn confers on men the right to vote and participate in politics. The frequent exemption of women[4] and religious or ethnic groups from conscription has resulted in them not being defined as full citizens or in them only partially enjoying their citizenship rights.[5] Through these processes, "ideal citizens" are constructed. Conscription created suitable conditions for the adoption and indoctrination of the nation-state and nationalism. Nationalist projects of the last two centuries, including conscription, are directly related to gender, thus masculinities (Nagel, 1998).

Today, modern armies' human resources consist of conscripted soldiers, professionally hired enlisted soldiers, or both. Through the description of being a soldier and selection procedures of the army, marginalized social groups become visible since armies have been rejecting certain men based on their age, class, ethnicity, sexual orientation or disability. For example, Jewish and Christian men in Islamic countries, as known *dhimmis*, were exempted from compulsory military service especially in the nineteenth century (Ye'or, 1985). Whether recruitment is compulsory or voluntary, armies declare who they will recruit or reject as soldiers, for example, certain categories such as those with disabilities. In some countries, such as Turkey, homosexual men have been exempted from compulsory military service provided they can prove this (Biricik, 2011). Armies of professionally hired enlisted soldiers may recruit certain groups of men if they do not disclose their identity and, for example, embrace the "Don't ask don't tell policy", as is the case in the US military.

Through admission, armies identify and select soldiers, and construct the desirable masculinity with those bodies in the barracks. All the elements of the barracks and the training are there to construct this ideal. These elements work as a laboratory for the creation of the ideal man and the hegemonic masculinity for that society. Conscription has been abandoned as a primary recruitment method by most states; alternatively, states may accept exemption payments from eligible candidates, with professional soldiers preferred. However, there is still a significant number of nation-states that have compulsory military service and from time to time, some nationalist and conservative politicians favour re-introducing conscription.

The history of direct conscription is also the history of deserters and conscientious objectors who refuse to serve in a military because of, for example, political or religious motives. Conscientious objection can be seen as a civil disobedience act (Arendt, 1972) or an organized political movement, as in the case of War Resisters' International. Since hegemonic masculinity is directly related to conscription in at least some societies, being a deserter or an objector challenges the gender roles and the proper citizen ideals.

The recruitment procedures for armies define and construct "physically capable men/people" to join the army, fight, kill and die. In the twenty-first century, armies are still predominantly male, they construct particular masculinities and reemphasize the hierarchy between and among genders and across other social divisions and inequalities. Conscription, as a method for recruitment to the army, is used by the state to construct and prescribe "proper civilians" and "ideal citizens". When military service is compulsory, this is, with some exceptions, mostly so for men, such that militarism and hegemonic masculinity can be closely related.[6] Therefore, deserters and objectors challenge the ideal of hegemonic masculinity as well. Having said that, the act of refusing army service could also be re-interpreted as aligning with certain ideals of hegemonic masculinity – in the sense that a man who objects or deserts could be seen as independently thinking, strong-willed and in some ways heroic.

Hierarchies and segregations

Across the world, men comprise the vast majority of armed personnel. Indeed, the history of the military can be viewed as a relentless preoccupation with valuing and elevating particular forms of disciplined and violent manhood. Heroic and romanticized masculinity is embedded in military leadership, in dominant assumptions about what it means to be a trained fighter and is celebrated in peacetime ceremonies commemorating wartime victories and heroic acts of valour. Typically, in the military an idealized version of manhood pervades organizational structures, cultures and practices, one emphasizing traits stereotypically associated with warrior masculinity, such as courage, strength, toughness, violence, aggression and domination.[7] While a growing number of countries have lifted the combat ban on women, research suggests that women's military integration is limited and constructions of gender difference continue to persist (Eichler, 2014).[8]

Common sense understandings of gender and the military often assume that men are innately violent and women are "naturally" peaceful. More critical perspectives challenge this essentialized and gendered dichotomy, arguing that the links between men, masculinities and militarism are socially constructed rather than biologically determined (Morgan, 1994). Within the burgeoning literature (on men and masculinity in the military), the notion of "militarized masculinity/ies" has become influential (e.g. Ashe, 2012; Belkin, 2012; Eichler, 2012, 2014; Duncanson, 2013; Christensen & Kyed, 2022). Highlighting how militarism and masculinity tend to reinforce each other, this term refers to the idea that "real men" are soldiers and "real soldiers" are men, as also summed up in the term, "soldier masculinity". Moreover, with aged, classed, raced, religious, geographical, national and de/colonial intersections, military masculinities and men's experiences in the army differ between, say, the Russian Federation, the United States or Mozambique. Such gendered assumptions inform and are reproduced in leadership and management practices as well as in more informal socialization processes.[9]

So, for example, military leadership and discipline are typically enacted through hierarchical structures and top-down command and control practices that valorize dominant masculinity. These gendered assumptions tend to inform military HR practices such as recruitment, training, appraisal and promotion as well as more informal, sub-cultural practices like initiation ceremonies for newcomers intended to humiliate and degrade (sometimes known as "hazing"). Frequently, men are recruited through appeals to their masculine identity and their patriotism as citizens, as well as by emphasizing the possibilities of travel, adventure and learning new skills and knowledge. Military training often inculcates exaggerated ideals of manhood while devaluing women and other men/masculinities. As Morgan (1987; also see Morgan, 1994) described in his autobiographical study, military service is concerned to "make a man of you". In sum, notions of masculine heroism are embedded in military leadership styles, management practices and cultural processes.

Yet, these dominant military masculinities are by no means homogenous. Within the literature on men and military, there has also been a growing focus on pluralized military masculinities. These more complex perspectives reveal how militarized masculinities can take many forms in multiple locations and times. These diverse, changing and context-specific military masculinities need to be examined in relation to various constructions of femininity and to other masculinities. They are context-specific and dynamic social constructs. Typically, they are constructed in hierarchical opposition to women and femininities, and other subordinated and marginalized men and masculinities, often intersecting with other differences such as rank, class, ethnicity, race, religion and sexuality.

To give one example, Barrett (1996) describes how the US Navy reproduces a dominant masculinity with multiple forms, valuing toughness, perseverance, aggressiveness, rugged heterosexuality, unemotional logic and a stoic refusal to complain. Women and gay men serve as the differentiated others, against which heterosexual men construct and display gendered identities. But Barrett also outlines how competing occupational sub-cultures, identities and loyalties can equally inform military masculinities in the US Navy. He shows how multiple masculinities co-exist in one organization: aviators emphasized masculinity as risk-taking; surface warfare officers prioritized endurance; supply officers prided themselves on technical rationality. Accordingly, Barrett argues that multiple masculine identities in the US Navy are constructed by differentiating the self through outperforming, discounting, and negating others. Underpinning these concerns, he suggests, is an enduring sense of subjective insecurity that is, paradoxically, not resolved but reinforced by these processes.

Not only are men's dominant military masculinities heterogeneous and pluralized, but they may also incorporate elements of femininity in routine military operations. As Eichler (2014, p. 91) observes,

> It is worth noting that in practice, even as the ideal of militarized masculinity is defined in opposition to femininity, soldiering also includes aspects associated with femininity or the "unmasculine", such as the emphasis on obedience, cleanliness, or caring for fellow soldiers.

Similarly, in times of war, male soldiers may display or express "characteristics more conventionally associated with the feminine than with the masculine" (Morgan, 1994, p. 177). For example, in response to the experience of being under attack or of enacting violence themselves male soldiers may cry or suffer emotionally at the time of the fighting or even much later, for example, with PTSD. Such responses question common sense understandings which automatically view all men as having an innate propensity for violence.

Militarized masculinities constitute a dynamic social construct that is likely to vary and evolve in different times and places, as well as being characterized by multiplicities, complexities and contradictions. While militaries today still tend to be male-dominated, changing gender perceptions may begin to erode these deeply embedded and historical links. Alternatively, it might be that women will be incorporated into specific gendered tasks and functions within the standard military division of labour in ways that reinforce rather than fully challenge dominant military masculinities.

One particularly problematic issue that concerns military, paramilitary and similar organizations is the difficulty of maintaining the potential for and promotion of physical violence (see Johnson, 1986), especially to others outside the organization, while minimizing, or at least reducing, that violence to each other (and the self) within the organization. This classic dilemma for armies is partly the subject of Dixon's (1976) analysis of "the psychology of military incompetence", in which he argues that the primary anxiety of life and death is redirected by and controlled through organizational devices, such as rules and procedures (cf. Menzies, 1960). However, the most important element of organizational process in such organizations is that they produce and reproduce violation, pain and damage. Accordingly, people with such experiences may remain in the organization, be expelled from it or even be killed deliberately or by "friendly fire".

Disability and veterans

Injury, particularly disability, acquired during war complicates the militarist and nationalist ideals of masculinity. Militarist promises to men to experience adventure, build character and stamina, strengthen masculinity, and receive gratitude for their services are, to a large extent, broken with permanent damage to the body. Disabled veterans instead face challenges and even hostility in their everyday lives for various reasons along the lines of the body, masculinity and war. Negative attitudes to the disabled body can partly be explained by the scopic regime of modernity, which produces strangers from those "who disturb its fragile cognitive, moral, and aesthetic boundaries" (Hughes, 1999, p. 157). Physical disability also disturbs the ideals of hegemonic masculinity, which draws heavily on physical capacity and bodily prowess. Disabled male bodies conjure up images of vulnerability, requiring strategies to adjust to the ideals of hegemonic masculinity (Gerschick & Miller, 1997). In addition to, and even further in the background than physical disabilities, are major psychological effects of war and militarism, including emotional trauma, PTSD, depression and even greater probability of suicide (see, for example, Iversen et al., 2005; Goldberg & Willse, 2007).

Nationalism adds a further layer of complexity to the disabled male body as the birth of the modern nation-state is intertwined with modern masculinity. Mosse (1998) points out that during the transition from empires to nation-states masculinity came to symbolize the ideals, anxieties and aspirations for the future. Thus, the healthy, disciplined and well-proportioned male body became a potent signifier of the values the nation-state was built on. To compound the issue, the disabled bodies of ex-soldiers, with the war and violence inscribed on their bodies, became a constant reminder to the society of the war they tried to leave behind (Carden-Coyne, 2007). With these multi-layered meanings associated with the disabled male body, veterans came to be seen as a source of anxiety for the states and societies.[10]

The disabled veteran body generally evokes pity and fear as it is associated with loss of autonomy, dependency, pain, the experience of violence and physical vulnerability (Gerber, 2012, pp. 6–8). Notably, those meanings are not constant. At the height of the war, when upholding soldiers' morale was a priority, injury was akin to a war medal, signifying manly courage (Bourke, 1996, p. 70). In the post-war period, however, entitlements soon eroded (Koven, 1994), veterans lost exclusive access to military facilities serving increasingly more civilians, and even their disability rates were lowered (Sünbüloğlu, 2022). The unruly male bodies of war veterans were thus subject to rigorous regulation by organized efforts in the aftermath of the war. Rehabilitation facilities became the hub of this regulation. Public images of injured soldiers as meticulously arranged bodies in uniforms during their treatment aimed to convey the idea that war damages were under control. Also important was to show the public the disabled veterans during strenuous physical activity. Sports and exercise during rehabilitation became essential instruments to "harness the competitive nature of masculinity in order both to rebuild bodies and restore a sense of the male self" (Anderson, 2011, p. 9). Cricket and polo were particularly favoured in Britain as participation in them defined veterans "not only as full men but as Englishmen" (Koven, 1994, p. 1198). The key to restoring the veterans to their pre-war normalcy was to engage them in work. To alleviate concerns about the war-injured men's dependency on the state and society, as well as to restore their masculinity and citizenship, workshops were made integral to rehabilitative practices (Anderson, 2011; Koven, 1994). The idea that disability "unmade" men was so obviously acknowledged that at the entrance of a renowned UK rehabilitation centre in Chailey was a sign that read "Man Made Here" (Koven, 1994, p. 1176). In societies with rigid class boundaries, such as WWI Germany, the re-making of men prioritized maintaining those boundaries with two kinds of prosthetic arms – the more aesthetic one for middle-class ex-servicemen designed for clerking jobs and the other for working classes which was more suitable for holding machine parts (Perry, 2002).

Organizational care for the disabled veterans is fraught with various norms. For instance, not all types of war disabilities are considered to merit militarist awards, as in the case of the Purple Heart in the United States. This military decoration is awarded only to those who have spilt blood, excluding conditions such as traumatic brain injury (Enloe, 2010, p. 203), thus creating a hierarchy of war damages to the soldiers' bodies and minds. Similarly, not all war-disabled men were considered worthy of care by civilian organizations during the World Wars. Charities and philanthropists "often imposed their own moral codes, picking and choosing men whom they viewed as worthy of treatment in an attempt to mould them into ideal middle-class citizens" (Kowalsky, 2007, p. 577). Current philanthropic efforts may have abandoned such eligibility criteria, but gendered norms still shape the services they provide. Heteronormativity, for instance, is a core element in various details, including house design for veterans, congruent with the heteronormative social attachments the veteran rehabilitation programmes aim to foster (Wool, 2015). Medical professionals, too, explicitly attributed gendered moral values to soldiers' treatment. The willpower of injured men was deemed intertwined with the success of reconstitution of their adult masculine identity (Carden-Coyne, 2007, p. 557) in the rehabilitation programmes. Autonomy over the body was such a valued masculine attribute that medical personnel expressed more respect for those who could endure pain in a manly and stoic manner (Gagen, 2007, p. 530).

These organizational efforts to rehabilitate war injuries and the norms attached to them were not always welcomed by disabled veterans. Some resisted the concept of rehabilitation as they found the state, military and medical authority manifest in rehabilitation more disabling. Others opposed certain aspects of rehabilitation, including vocational training, and claimed rehabilitation under military authority was disempowering and infantilizing, stripping disabled men of their agency (Carden-Coyne, 2007). There was also resentment against being put on display in charity events by these institutions to attract donations (Koven, 1994, p. 1178). Crucially, in some cases, as in post-WWII Canada, veterans exceeded the limits of what was offered to them. Those who returned to civilian life in wheelchairs only to find a physical world designed for the able-bodied propelled change towards more accessible buildings, pioneering to improve conditions also for the broader disabled community (Tremblay, 1996).

Civilian impacts

Militarism has been a huge influence on civilian lives especially for the last two centuries. Militarism, beyond military organizations *per se*, extends the influence of the military onto civilian lives. This influence can be macro such as social, economic, technological and political, meso or micro in scope. For example, male domination and the importance of militarism persists, especially in right-wing populist masculinities, with the notion of being able to defend as a soldier–citizen–man a strong tendency in many places. In this way, the ideal civilian man may be reconstructed in the image of a male soldier and takes his place in the public sphere.

The military and militarism affect civilian lives in many ways. During some wars, more civilians have died, were disabled or injured than military members. Wars result in mass migration and destruction of infrastructures. On the other hand, militarism, an ideology and militarization, a social process, cause civilians to shape their daily lives based on wars (Chenoy,

1998; Enloe, 2004). Militarism is the spread of military values to other public institutions, state policies and social life. These influences on civilian lives may emerge during wartime or peacetime. In peacetime, states organize for future possible wars, while in wartime states mobilize all resources of a certain nation or an international alliance for all-out-war (Mann, 1988). On a micro-level, militarism may result in fast-changing cultural influences, such as survivalism, or fashion trends such as camouflage clothing. Militarism at all levels, whether micro or macro, is a gendered ideology which reconstructs gender, and hierarchies between and among genders through militarization projects with links to nationalism and modernism.

The direct civilian impacts of militaries are their usage of resources to exist and, no doubt, the wars they fight. In 2021 alone, it is estimated that approximately 150,000 people died because of wars. Other crucial and severely damaging effects of wars on civilian populations include food insecurity, humanitarian needs, population displacement, sexual violence and violations of basic human rights (SIPRI, 2022). During wars, mostly men die when serving in the armed forces; however, since civilians die during and after the military conflicts as well, women and children are almost equally likely to die without taking part in killing. The impacts of militaries on civilians can be direct, such as killings and destruction of the ongoing wars or indirect mostly through militarism and militaristic projects. Although wars and politics have changed in form, the influence of militaries and militarism continues to be strong on civilian lives, and especially so with hybrid wars, "image wars", "information wars" (Huhtinen & Rantapelkonen, 2002) and "messy wars" (Huhtinen & Rantapelkonen, 2008), as in attacks on both physical (including water, food and energy systems) and digital infrastructures.

The influence of militaries and militarism on civilian lives, apart from the obvious violence, also exists through militarization of the institutions. Education, especially national education, is one of the institutions where militarism can be most clearly observed. The aim of the nineteenth- and early twentieth-century national educational projects was to construct new citizens, a national identity, the military service ideal for the boys and motherhood ideal for girls (Heywood, 2001; Altinay, 2004). Some features of education make militarism more visible such as school uniforms, hair regulations, respect for and obedience to teachers and senior students, national security classes, military training-like physical education courses. Gender-based implementations of these features strengthen the separation between boys and girls, reconstructing the hierarchy in favour of boys. Today, militarization of education has still been influential. For example, one of the biggest supports for the "Healthy Hunger-Free Kids Act" passed to provide healthy, adequate nutrition for school-age children in the United States came from retired US military members. These supporters pointed out how obesity had become common among children, such that they are "too fat to fight" for their countries and a threat to the nation (Burridge & McSorley, 2013). Therefore, the ideal children's body and behaviour are defined by military standards.

Militarism also has many effects at the micro-level. One of them is undoubtedly fashion. Military-themed clothing and accessories, such as camouflage prints and colours, cargo pants, combat boots, or carrying Swiss army knife, military dog tag, and civilian armaments such as AR-15s and body armours become occasionally popular in the fashion world. Contradictorily, soldier man references in clothing and appearance may sometimes be taken up ironically, in youth culture, as parts of opposition movements, for fashion, or even as a statement for peace. War video games are another area that the effects of militarism on micro-level can be observed. World-renowned games such as Call of Duty or PUBG claim that they offer real-world settings, and the player can experience a realistic war field through narratives and designs. These games position the player on war history and combat or provide game options to allow the player to reconstruct the war history. A further micro-influence of militarism is on lifestyle trends. Survivalist lifestyles have been recently on the rise, especially with the impact of global warming, the COVID-19 pandemic, and due to increasingly polarized national and international policies. "Preppers" or "survivalists" have been preparing for an apocalypse by creating survival plans, stocking food, tools and guns in safe storages, and/ by learning hunter–gatherer-like lifestyles, such as bushcraft (for a post-apocalyptic world). Planning processes include protecting the house, energy generators and food storage units, along with storage of weapons and body armour. These preparations can be counted as "disaster consumerism" (Belmont & Stroud, 2020) and shows one of the links between militarism and capitalism. Apart from stocking the house, all training processes are out of the house, to survive in the wild, mostly in the forests. This lifestyle of survivalism is highly gendered where the bushcraft activities and taking up of arms are done mostly by men as the feature of the "apocalyptic masculinity" (Kelly, 2020), and the food storage and first aid equipment preparation is accepted widely as a woman's job.

Concluding comments: wider processes and impacts

In sum, critical studies highlight the mutually reinforcing connections between men, masculinities, militarism and military organizations. In this chapter, we have focused mainly on the internal organizational dynamics of military organizations, of recruitment, hierarchy, divisions of labour and other segregations, disability and veterans, along with the impacts on civilians. There are, however, many further connections and wider impacts of men, masculinities, militarism and military organizations and organizing across and between societies. One that is of particular relevance for current purposes is how militarism and military organizations have also influenced research and academia, not only in the development of technologies but also in the social sciences. Examples here include the impact of militarism and war on healthcare, psychiatry and rehabilitation, leadership selection, social psychological group process, and organization and management theory.[11]

The wider organizational perspective is important in further respects. Violence, potential violence and the control of violence by men in the military at various stages of war, pre-war and post-war can be conceptualized as "organized violence" and "organizational violence". In this way, the violence and the military extend to many other men including political decision-makers, politicians, diplomats and military suppliers. Men and masculinities have played and continue to play crucial roles in fuelling arms manufacture, including the nuclear arms race and collective violence on a massive global scale. There seems to be an almost insatiable demand for "innovation" with regard to weapon systems and the technologies of war, killing, maiming and violence.

This in turn raises further questions about men and masculinities in shaping some forms of scientific inquiry that are invested in creating scientific knowledges for war and conflict applications, for example, how the work of the male scientists who created the nuclear bomb, dovetail with established ways of doing international relations and geopolitics (Easlea, 1983; Strange, 1983), and the phallic, masculinized symbolism and rhetorics around nuclear weapons (Cohn et al., 2005). Theories of global deterrence, "MAD" (mutual assured destruction), and certain men and masculinities all seem in some ways to perpetuate and escalate hostility, violence and conflicts. Underpinning such (in)security logics are masculine power and control, and the use of the threat of (nuclear and other) violence as a way of trying to retain peace and curb violence. Being "strong" and "powerful" – through owning advanced and superior military hardware – supposedly protects countries from external attack, yet it is often those same masculinities that reproduce insecurities and tensions, and even seem to trigger military conflicts and wars between nation-states. Interconnections persist between male-dominated military, industrial and scientific organizations collaborating to create new and more advanced weapon systems that give nation-states strategic and technological advantage, some scientific research, and men and masculinities.

Finally, links need to be made to the environmental impact of war and the ethics of producing and using military equipment and maintaining militaries at a time of current multiple social and environmental crises. The military–industrial complex has huge negative environmental impact. This is another connection between men, masculinities and climate change and environmental destruction.

Notes

1 Thanks to Keith Grint for helpful comments on an earlier version of this chapter.
2 This chapter focusses primarily on Western states and societies. For example, different dynamics can be traced in the Chinese People's Republic.
3 For example, in the early years of World War II, there were no Black officers in the US military and US Navy (and no Black aviators until the Red Tails were trained and deployed).
4 Today, at least five countries – Israel, Eritrea, North Korea, Sweden, Norway – conscript women. In Norway and Sweden, conscription is not strictly enforced, and conscientious objection is recognized as a right. In Israel, Eritrea and North Korea, conscription is strict and protected by military law, and conscientious objection is not recognized as a right.
5 For example, opponents of suffrage justified their argument by associating the right to vote with compulsory military service in many nation-states, such as Switzerland (Dejung, 2010) and Turkey (Ünder, 2000).
6 An important issue is whether the military service is compulsory and for whom – for instance, in Estonia and Finland it is compulsory for men, but they can choose an alternative civil service which usually involves some kind of feminized care work. Meanings given to the army service can vary – for instance, in Estonia, it is widely supported by the general public, among men and women alike. Part of this has to do with the threat of Russian invasion, as well as constructing the army as a place that "makes boys into men".
7 The elite and special forces within specific militaries typically embody hyper-masculine cultures. These are often represented and reproduced in various television shows describing their selection and training methods.
8 An exception here was the deployment of women agents in European Resistance movements during World War II. The allies recognized that the Germans would automatically tend to assume that women were incapable of violence or acts supporting violence, and would therefore discount them as agents. The German's gendered assumptions could therefore give the women agents an advantage.
9 In earlier times, leadership training in the Swiss financial sector was conducted by the military. If you had not served in the military, you were unlikely to ever get a leadership position.
10 This may well explain why the Allies never published photos of dead allied soldiers until halfway through World War II. It may also explain why after World War I in 1919 many UK cities refused to allow disabled veterans to march on what became Remembrance Sunday, and why in the same year disabled veterans in Luton burned the town hall down in protest (Grint, 2021).
11 Among many examples here, we note the impact of the US Navy, the War Office Selection Boards and the Tavistock Institute (Dicks, 1970) on group process theory, leadership selection, and psychodynamic theory, and of the Cold War on management theory (Runté & Mills, 2006).

References

Altinay, A. G. (2004). *The Myth of the Military-Nation: Militarism, Gender, and Education in Turkey.* New York: Palgrave Macmillan.

Anderson, J. (2011). *War, Disability and Rehabilitation in Britain: Soul of a Nation.* Manchester: Manchester University Press.

Arendt, H. (1972). *Crisis of the Republic: Lying in Politics, Civil Disobedience, On Violence, Thoughts on Politics and Revolution.* New York: Harcourt Brace Jovanovich.

Ashe, F. (2012). Gendering war and peace: Militarized masculinities in Northern Ireland. *Men and Masculinities, 15*(3), 230–248. doi: 10.1177/1097184X12442636

Barrett, F. (1996). The organizational construction of hegemonic masculinity: The case of the US Navy. *Gender, Work and Organization, 3*(3), 129–142. doi: 10.1111/j.1468-0432.1996.tb00054.x

Belkin, A. (2012). *Bring Me Men: Military Masculinity and the Benign Façade of American Empire, 1898–2001.* New York: Columbia University Press.

Belmont, C., & Stroud, A. (2020). Bugging out: Apocalyptic masculinity and disaster consumerism in offgrid magazine. *Feminist Studies, 46*(2), 431–458. doi: 10.1353/fem.2020.0019

Biricik, A. (2011). The 'Rotten Report' and the reproduction of masculinity, nation and security in Turkey. In A. Kronsell & E. Svedberg (Eds.), *Making Gender, Making War: Violence, Military and Peacekeeping Practices* (pp. 95–102). London: Routledge. doi: 10.4324/9780203803202

Boulding, K. E. (1967). The scientific-military-industrial complex. *The Virginia Quarterly Review, 43*(4), 672–679.

Bourke, J. (1996). *Dismembering the Male: Men's Bodies, Britain and the Great War.* London: Reaktion.

Breines, I., Connell, R., & Eide, I. (Eds). (2000). *Male Roles, Masculinities and Violence: A Culture of Peace Perspective.* UNESCO.

Burridge, J., & McSorley, K. (2013). Too fat to fight? Ibesity, bio-politics and the militarisation of children's bodies. In K. McSorley (Ed.), *War and the Body: Militarisation, Practice and Experience* (pp. 62–77). New York: Routledge.

Carden-Coyne, A. (2007). Ungrateful bodies: Rehabilitation, resistance and disabled American veterans of the First World War. *European Review of History – Revue européenne d'Histoire, 14*(4), 543–565. doi: 10.1080/13507480701752185

Chenoy, A. M. (1998). Militarisation, conflict, and women in South Asia. In L. A. Lorentzen & J. Turpin (Eds.), *The Women and War Reader* (pp. 101–110). New York: New York University Press.

Christensen, A.-D., & Kyed, M. (2022). From military to militarizing masculinities. *NORMA, 17*(1), 1–4. doi: 10.1080/18902138.2022.2028428

Cockburn, C., & Žarkov, D. (2002). *The Postwar Moment: Militaries, Masculinities and International Peacekeeping, Bosnia and the Netherlands.* London: Lawrence & Wishart.

Cohn, C., Hill, F., & Ruddick, S. (2005). *The Relevance of Gender for Eliminating Weapons of Mass Destruction.* Stockholm: Weapons of Mass Destruction Commission.

Dejung, C. (2010). "Switzerland must be a special democracy": Compromise military comradeship, and the gender order in 1930s and 1940s Switzerland. *The Journal of Modern History, 82*(1), 101–126. doi:10.1017/S0026749X20000384

Dicks, H. V. (1970). *Fifty Years of the Tavistock Clinic.* London: Routledge & Kegan Paul.

Dixon, N. F. (1976). *On The Psychology of Military Incompetence.* Philadelphia, PA: Basic.

Duncanson, C. (2013). *Forces For Good? Military Masculinities and Peacebuilding in Afghanistan and Iraq.* New York: Palgrave Macmillan.

Duncanson, C. (2019). Masculinities, war and militarism. in L Gottzén, U Mellström & T Shefer (Eds.), *Routledge International Handbook of Masculinity Studies* (pp. 467–476). London: Routledge.

Duriesmith, D. (2017). *Masculinity and New War: The Gendered Dynamics of Contemporary Armed Conflict.* London: Routledge.

Easlea, B. (1983). *Fathering the Unthinkable: Masculinity, Scientists, and the Nuclear Arms Race.* London: Pluto.

Eichler, M. (2012). *Militarising Men: Gender, Conscription, and War in Post-Soviet Russia.* Stanford, CA: Stanford University Press.

Eichler, M. (2014). Militarized masculinities in international relations. *The Brown Journal of World Affairs, 21*(1), 81–93.

Enloe, C. (1998). *Does Khaki Become You?: The Militarisation of Women's Lives.* London: Pandora.

Enloe, C. (2004). *Bananas, Beaches and Bases.* Berkeley, CA: University of California Press. (1st published 1989).

Enloe, C. (2010). *Nimo's War, Emma's War: Making Feminist Sense of the Iraq War.* London: University of California Press.

Fraser, E. L. (2019). *Military Masculinity and Postwar Recovery in the Soviet Union.* Buffalo, NY: University of Toronto Press.

Gagen, W. J. (2007). Remastering the body, renegotiating gender: Physical disability and masculinity during the First World War, the Case of J. B. Middlebrook. *European Review of History: Revue européenne d'histoire, 14*(4), 525–541. doi: 10.1080/13507480701752169

Galbraith, J. K. (1968). *The New Industrial State.* Boston: Houghton Mifflin.

Gerber, D. A. (2012). Introduction: Finding disabled veterans in history. In D. A. Gerber (Ed.), *Disabled Veterans in History* (pp. 1–51). Ann Arbor: The University of Michigan Press.

Gerschick, T. J., & Miller, A. S. (1997). Gender identities at the crossroads of masculinity and physical disability. In M. M. Gergen & S. N. Davis (Eds.), *Toward a New Psychology of Gender* (pp. 455–478). London: Routledge.

Gifford, B. (2006). The camouflaged safety net: The U.S. armed forces as welfare state institution. *Social Politics: International Studies in Gender, State and Society, 13*(3), 372–399. doi: 10.1093/sp/jxl003

Goldberg, G., & Willse, C. (2007). Losses and returns: The soldier in trauma. In P. T. Clough & J. Halley (Eds.), *The Affective Turn: Theorizing the Social* (pp. 264–286). London: Duke University Press.

Goldstein, J. S. (2001). *War and Gender.* Cambridge: Cambridge University Press.

Grint, K. (2021). *Mutiny and Leadership.* Oxford: Oxford University Press.

Hearn, J. (2011). Men/masculinities: War/militarism – searching (for) the obvious connections? In A. Kronsell & E. Svedberg (Eds.), *Making Gender, Making War: Violence, Military and Peacekeeping Practices* (pp. 47–63). London: Routledge. doi: 10.4324/9780203803202

Hearn, J., Ratele, K., Shefer, T., & Rahman Khan, A. (2021). Men, masculinities, peace, and violence: A multi-level overview. In T. Väyrynen, É. Féron, S. Parashar & C. C. Confortini (Eds.), *Routledge Handbook of Feminist Peace Research* (pp. 313–323). London: Routledge.

Heywood, C. (2001). *A History of Childhood: Children and Childhood in the West from Medieval to Modern Times.* Malden, MA: Blackwell.

Higate, P. (Ed.). (2002). *Military Masculinities.* New York: Praeger.

Hopton, J., & Higate, P. (2005). War, militarism and masculinities. In M. Kimmel, J. Hearn & R. Connell (Eds.), *Handbook of Studies on Men and Masculinities* (pp. 432–447). Thousand Oaks, CA: Sage.

Hughes, B. (1999). The constitution of impairment: Modernity and the aesthetic oppression. *Disability & Society, 14*(2), 155–172. doi: 10.1080/09687599926244

Huhtinen, A., & Rantapelkonen, J. (2002). *Image Wars: Beyond the Mask of Information Warfare.* Helsinki: Marshal of Finland Mannerheim's War Studies Fund.

Huhtinen, A., & Rantapelkonen, J. (2008). *Messy Wars.* Helsinki: Finn Lectura.

Hutchings, K. (2008). Making sense of masculinity and war. *Men and Masculinities, 10*(4), 389–404. doi: 10.1177/1097184X07306740

Iversen, A., Dyson, C., Smith, N., & Wessely, S. (2005). 'Goodbye and good luck': The mental health needs and treatment experiences of British ex-service personnel. *The British Journal of Psychiatry, 186*, 480–486. doi: 10.1192/bjp.186.6.480

Johnson, R. (1986). Institutions and the promotion of violence. In A. Campbell & J. J. Gibbs (Eds.), *Violent Transactions* (pp. 181–205). New York: Basil Blackwell.

Kelly, C. R. (2020). *Apocalypse Man: The Death Drive and the Rhetoric of White Masculine Victimhood.* Ohio: The Ohio State University Press.

Koven, S. (1994). Remembering and dismemberment: Crippled children, wounded soldiers, and the Great War in Great Britain. *American Historical Review, 99*(4), 1167–1202. doi: 10.2307/2168773

Kowalsky, M. (2007). 'This honourable obligation': The King's National Roll Scheme for disabled ex-servicemen 1915–1944. *European Review of History: Revue européenne d'histoire, 14*(4), 567–584.

Lopes da Silva, D., Tian, N., Béraud-Sudreau, L., Marksteiner, A, & Liang, X. (2022). Trends in world military expenditure, 2021, SIPRI Fact Sheet. Retrieved April 2022, from www.sipri.org/sites/default/files/2022-04/fs_2204_milex_2021_0.pdf

Lucassen, J., & Zürcher, E. J. (2000). Introduction: Conscription and resistance. The historical content. In E. J. Zürcher (Ed.), *Arming the State: Military Conscription in the Middle East and Central Asia 1775–1925* (pp. 1–19). London: I.B. Tauris.

Mann, M. (1988). *States, War and Capitalism: Studies in Political Sociology*. Oxford: Blackwell.

Menzies, I. (1960). A case-study in the functioning of social systems as a defence against anxiety: A report on a study of the nursing service of a general hospital. *Human Relations*, *13*(2), 95–121. doi: 10.1177/001872676001300201

Morgan, D. (1987). *It Will Make a Man of You: Notes on National Service, Masculinity and Autobiography* (Studies in Sexual Politics 17). Manchester: Department of Sociology, University of Manchester.

Morgan, D. (1994). Theater of war: Combat, the military, and masculinities. In H. Brod & M. Kaufman (Eds.), *Theorizing Masculinities* (pp. 165–182). Thousand Oaks, CA: Sage.

Moser, C. O. N., & Clark, F. (Eds). (2001). *Victims, Perpetrators or Actors?: Gender, Armed Conflict and Political Violence*. London: Zed.

Mosse, G. L. (1998). *The Image of Man: The Creation of Modern Masculinity*. Oxford: Oxford University Press.

Myrttinen, H., Khattab, L., & Naujoks, J. (2017). Re-thinking hegemonic masculinities in conflict-affected contexts. *Critical Military Studies*, *3*(2), 103–119. doi: 10.1080/23337486.2016.1262658

Nagel, J. (1998). Masculinity and nationalism: Gender and sexuality in the making of nations. *Ethnic and Racial Studies*, *21*(2), 242–269. doi: 10.1080/014198798330007

Obinger, H., Petersen, K., & Starke, P. (Eds.). (2018). *Warfare and Welfare: Military Conflict and Welfare State Development in Western Countries*. Oxford: Oxford Academic. doi: 10.1093/oso/9780198779599.001.0001

Perry, H. (2002). Re-arming the disabled veteran: Artificially rebuilding state and society in World War One Germany. In K. Ott, D. Serlin & S. Mihm (Eds.), *Artificial Parts, Practical Lives: Modern Histories of Prosthetics* (pp. 75–101). New York: New York University Press.

Runté, M., & Mills, A. J. (2006). Cold War, chilly climate: Exploring the roots of gendered discourse in organization and management theory. *Human Relations*, *59*(5), 695–720. doi: 10.1177/0018726706066174

SIPRI. (2022). SIPRI Yearbook 2022: Armaments, Disarmament and International Security-Summary. Retrieved 23 August 2022, from SIPRI: Stockholm International Peace Research Institute website: www.sipri.org/sites/default/files/2022-06/yb22_summary_en_v3.pdf

Strange, P. (1983). *It'll Make a Man of You: A Feminist View of the Arms Race*. Nottingham: Mushroom.

Sünbüloğlu, N. Y. (2022). In-between military and civilian: Ongoing conflict, disability, and masculinity. *NORMA*, *17*(1), 35–51. doi: 10.1080/18902138.2021.2009274

Tremblay, M. (1996). Going back to civvy street: A historical account of the impact of the Everest and Jennings wheelchair for Canadian World War II veterans with spinal cord injury. *Disability & Society*, *11*(2), 149–170. doi: 10.1080/09687599650023209

Ünder, H. (2000). Atatürk ve Kadınların Askerliği [Ataturk and the Conscription of Women]. *Tarih ve Toplum*, *195*, 51–58.

Weber, E. (1976). *Peasants into Frenchmen: The Modernisation of Rural France, 1870–1914*. Berkeley, CA: Stanford University Press.

Whitworth, S. (2004). *Men, Militarism, and UN Peacekeeping: A Gendered Analysis*. Boulder, CO: Lynne Rienner.

Wilensky, H. (1975). *The Welfare State and Equality: Structural and Ideological Roots of Public Expenditure*. Berkeley, CA: University of California Press.

Woodward, R., & Duncanson, C. (Eds.). (2017). *The Palgrave International Handbook of Gender and the Military*. London: Palgrave Macmillan.

Wool, Z. H. (2015). *After War: The Weight of Life at Walter Reed*. Durham, NC: Duke University Press.

Ye'or, B. (1985). *The Dhimmi: Jews and Christians under Islam* (D. Maisel Trans.). New York: Associated University Press.

20

MASCULINITIES, POLITICAL ORGANIZATIONS AND POLITICAL ORGANIZING

Queering anti-apartheid struggle

Kopano Ratele, Nick Malherbe, Josephine Cornell and Shahnaaz Suffla

Introduction

Political organizations and political organizing more generally are major sites for the organizational practices and processes of men and masculinities – albeit with many and vastly contrasting political aims, projects and hopes. Accordingly, this chapter focuses on political and social movement settings, which in turn construct men and masculinities in very different and often adversarial ways. Nunes (2021) has contended that organizing politically entails assembling, expanding, coordinating and deploying the collective's capacity to act. However, he goes on to warn, political organizations are oftentimes sites of trauma, and therefore there is a risk that an organization's *power to* manifests as the *power over*. Instead of sites of empowerment, organizations can be oppressive. Men's political organizing and involvement are illustrative of this. Indeed, emerging in the 1960s and 1970s, some men's social movements developed as a backlash to second-wave feminist political organizing and the perceived loss of hegemonic male privilege (Leek & Gerke, 2020; Morrell, 2002). These anti-feminist men's rights movements reject feminist analyses of structural gender power dynamics and construct men as the victims of gender hierarchies that supposedly privilege women (Leek & Gerke, 2020).

Moreover, even organizations with liberatory intentions carry the risk of asserting power over rather than an emancipatory power to. A prescient example here can be noted in how hegemonic supremacist heteropatriarchal masculinities have, in some instances, suppressed heterogeneous gender expression within political organizations with emancipatory goals, whether this be the abolitionists in the United States (Davis, 1983), anti-colonial movements throughout Africa (Kelley, 2002) or the so-called Pink Tide in Latin America (Friedman, 2007). In each of these instances, the hegemonic ideal of masculinity, which, among other figurations, privileges patriarchy and heterosexuality, functioned by and large to foreclose other non-deterministic gender performances within the context of emancipatory political organizing.

However, men's movements have also been enabled by feminist and profeminist politics, formed to organize around sexual and gender-equality, and consciousness-raising, such as

DOI: 10.4324/9781003193579-23

anti-patriarchal and/or queer politics (Leek & Gerke, 2020; Messner, 1997; Morrell, 2002; Peretz, 2017; Ratele et al., 2011). In this chapter, we use "queer" as an umbrella term to denote both an orientation and a community of those who identify as LGBTQI+. Pro/feminist men's organizing could also include organizing against war, racism and environmentalism, and for social justice more broadly. In many instances, these anti-patriarchal men's movements began with groups of men who organized in solidarity with feminist movements to promote gender justice and address violence against women (Leek & Gerke, 2020). While many men came to feminist and profeminist organizing from a position of male privilege, many movements of men from marginalized identities – such as queer men – drew on and allied with feminist aims to understand and resist their own oppression (Leek & Gerke, 2020; Peretz, 2017).

Men's political organizing and involvement in social movements, we might say, take many forms. Leek and Gerke (2020) assert that the boundaries of what constitutes "men's movements" are complex, but generally the term refers to a kind of organizing that is self-consciously focused on mobilizing men as gendered subjects around issues impacting men and boys. Theorists have cautioned, however, against sweepingly labelling men's mobilizations around gender concerns as "movements" as much of this type of organizing is focused on personalized concerns like self-improvement, rather than explicitly political demands (Leek & Gerke, 2020).

In contrast to self-avowed men's movements and organizations, we can think more generally of movements and organizations involving men that comprise political organizing in which men may be dominant in terms of numbers or authority but where gender is not a formal organizing principle (Morrell, 2002). Such movements and organizations that involve men include anti-racist, anti-colonial, decolonization, and more recently, decolonial struggles, groupings and campaigns. In the United States, an example of these kinds of movements can be observed in the broad-based Black Power movement (which included organizations such as the Student Nonviolent Coordinating Committee and the Black Panther Party). Organizing through the Black Power lens flourished in the early 1960s to early 1970s. Prominent figures within the Black Power movement included Malcolm X (who is regarded as the inspiration for the movement), Angela Y. Davis and Stokely Carmichael (later known as Kwame Ture) (see Davis, 1983; Farmer et al., 2019; Nasheed, 2021).

The Black Consciousness Movement (BCM) which gained prominence in South Africa in the mid-1960s to mid-1970s is another example of a movement involving men. Renowned names in the BCM include Steve Biko, Mamphela Ramphele and Barney Pityana (Badat, 2009; Hirschmann, 1990). While women were involved in anti-racist struggles in South Africa and the United States, and evidence exists that there were contestations around gender in anti-racist organizations, these struggles tended to foreground race over other categories of political analysis and engagement. In consequence of this, while men dominated power positions in the anti-racist Black Power movement and BCM, like the anti-apartheid movement and organizations that we discuss later, these were not always movements that aimed at transforming gender relations and masculinities.

In this chapter, we are concerned with examining the masculinized *power over* (in contrast to the enabling form of positive *power to* effect social change) within anti-apartheid organizations in South Africa. In particular, we re/turn to the 1980s – among the most violent and brutally oppressive periods of the apartheid regime (which prevailed from 1948 to 1994), exemplified most sharply in the 1985 State of Emergency (Imma, 2017) – and what hegemonic masculinity meant for anti-apartheid organizations during this time. Our objective is to reflect on what the efforts to *queer* anti-apartheid struggle can teach us about (we might say, among *non-queered*) political commitment, organization and struggle historiography. As such, we consider what studying (usually, also, hetero-patriarchal) masculine performance on the political left, rather than the right – as is so often the case (Oxlund, 2008) – can offer to organization efforts that are concerned with an intersectional, intensively affective approach to liberation.

In what follows, a brief overview of how hegemonic masculinity functioned within anti-apartheid organizations is offered. Attention then turns to queer masculinity and what gender and sexuality meant for (which is to say complexified, disturbed or invited) and within anti-racist anti-apartheid organizing. Central to our attention is a consideration of what the life and letters of Simon Tseko Nkoli (1957–1998), undoubtedly the best-known queer anti-apartheid activist, teach us about organizing within a non-queered broad political movement and masculinity. We conclude by proffering remarks on what Nkoli means for gender liberation today, both within and beyond political organizations.

Masculinity and anti-apartheid organization

Although the history of anti-apartheid organizations is well documented, the gendered and sexual dynamics of these organizations are less so. When examining the anti-apartheid struggle, as Elaine Unterhalter (2000) observed, the construction of masculinities "cannot be understood outside the complex workings of race, class, and formations of the state in different periods" (p. 162). What is especially pertinent in that sentence for us is what is left out, namely sexualities. As Ratele (2009a, 2009b) has shown, sexualities were key in private apartheid as much as public apartheid. Private apartheid involved racism in intimate life, evidenced in laws of racially defined sexual immorality; where public apartheid involved racism in public and work life, for instance, in segregated education, residential areas zoned for different race groups and job reservation for whites (Ratele, 2009b; Shefer & Ratele, 2011; Stevens et al., 2013). For example, regarding racism in sexual life, while an immoral deed is usually taken to refer to a sexual act, Ratele (2009a) has shown that under colonial and apartheid regimes there was "a peculiarly South African idea of immorality" since the laws and mores around immorality in the country paid "very close attention to race relations" (p. 294).

Anti-apartheid resistance, like the anti-colonial and nationalist liberation struggles before it, was undergirded by different images of heteronormative manhood (Suttner, 2005), such as the warrior, the militant and the hero (see Langa & Eagle, 2008; Unterhalter, 2000). Masculinities in these forms were further consolidated when the apartheid government banned anti-apartheid organizations, meaning that there was considerable risk and danger in being associated with these organizations (Suttner, 2005). Linking heroism – and, indeed, a willingness to die for political liberation (Suttner, 2014) – to one's gender identity was, for many Black people (oftentimes men), experienced as empowering because being Black meant the structural and symbolic denial of not "merely" one's manhood but one's humanity.

It needs underlining that although various images of masculinity –militant, militaristic, warrior, or heroic – undergirded many of the most prominent anti-apartheid organizations, such as the South African Students' Organization (SASO), Pan-Africanist Congress (PAC) and African National Congress (ANC), liberatory masculinity was not necessarily associated with violence. For a long time, anti-colonial and anti-apartheid struggles were peaceful, preferring petitions, letters and marches, to other modes of political engagement. At the same time, in denying the right to life and freedom of Black people, colonialism and apartheid systems must be understood as always inherently violent – in economic, cultural, psychical, spiritual and physical senses. From the 1960s though, the apartheid State increasingly relied on overt violence, including the violent removal of Black people from "white South Africa", which included killing Black people (Hallett, 1984; Lodge, 2011; Platzky & Walker for The Surplus People's Project, 1985; Time, 1960). As such, anti-apartheid organizations began to resort to more violent resistance tactics (Davis, 2018). Indeed, it was in 1961, following the Sharpeville massacre[1], that the armed wing of the ANC, known as uMkhonto we Sizwe (MK), as well as that of the PAC, known as the Azanian People's Liberation Army (APLA), was formed (Cornell et al., 2022). Struggle masculinities, resultantly, assumed a more violent character during this time.

In the 1980s, the kinds of struggle masculinity observed in anti-apartheid organizations were especially militaristic (Xaba, 2001). Those anti-apartheid combatants who were involved in armed struggle were expected by their organizations to enact a politically combative masculinity predicated on physical strength, bravery and toughness, with comradeship forged through these masculine values (Langa & Eagle, 2008). The non-comrade – the politically uninvolved man – was, by implication, unconscientized, fearful and disloyal (see Mtebule, 2002, as cited in Langa & Eagle, 2008). Those who refused to, did not, or could not adequately take up this kind of politically combative masculinity were assumed to embody a widely denigrated peaceful character (which was read as acquiescent to or collusive with racist structures) (see Cornell et al., 2022).

However, there was gender trouble even within the most masculinist anti-apartheid organizations. For instance, in both MK and the APLA, female combatants received the same military training as male combatants (Axelsson, 2015). Although the militarized masculine norms meant that these female combatants tended to mute their femininity in whatever ways they could (see Bridger, 2018), they nonetheless challenged the seemingly rigid fixity of anti-apartheid masculinity, thereby demonstrating the fissures within masculinity. Women were also involved in many other organized anti-apartheid struggles, some of which were violent, while others were not (see, e.g. Bonnin, 2000; Cornell et al., 2022).

We can see, then, how a normative struggle masculinity altered not only over time (for more detailed examples here, see Unterhalter, 2000; Xaba, 2001) but was also undermined from within anti-apartheid organizations themselves. Indeed, such masculinity was not embodied in a smooth or predictable way. It underwent shifts, ebbs and flows; at one moment failing and losing, and overcoming and making gains at another – enduring challenges at the very moment it was being consolidated. We might conclude that even in its most hegemonic form, anti-apartheid masculinity was always plural and metamorphosing (Suttner, 2014).

Queer anti-apartheid organization

The history of queer life in apartheid South Africa has, by and large, been written from a metropolitan, predominantly white urban milieu (Batra, 2016). Yet we should not take the limited literature on Black queer life during apartheid to mean that the experience of being Black and queer was uniform during this time (Reddy, 2001). There is a growing body of research that is concerned with this very issue, and in particular how Black queer experiences informed, interacted with and expanded organized anti-apartheid resistance.

Queer anti-apartheid organizing dates back to at least the 1960s. In 1968, for example, the Law Reform Movement was established to fight the apartheid government's attempts to amend its racist legislation (e.g. the Immorality Act) to include queer life (Gevisser &

Cameron, 1995). It was in the 1980s, however, that apartheid forces began to police sexualities with increasing violence, which resultantly saw developments in queer organizing (Currier, 2012; Ngubane, 2016). In 1982, the first lesbian and gay organization in the country, the Gay Association of South Africa (GASA), was established. GASA was a mostly white, middle-class organization. Of significance, GASA refused to support explicitly anti-apartheid organizing (Carolin, 2018). This is not to say that GASA members were not oppressed by apartheid. Indeed, the 1986 GASA convention was raided by the apartheid government's Vice Squad (Batra, 2016). Nonetheless, GASA was plagued with internal white racism and was politically inept. An inference can also be made that GASA did not think of being lesbian or gay as having anything to do with being white or Black. Apparently, there was little conception of multiple jeopardies (King, 1988) or intersectionalities of systemic homophobia and systemic racism (Bowleg, 2013).

In response to the racism within GASA, the Black-led, multiracial Gay and Lesbian Organization of Witwatersrand (GLOW) was founded in 1988 (Imma, 2017; Ngubane, 2016). GLOW's organizational requirements sought to reflect South Africa's most pressing emancipatory requirements, meaning that GLOW responded to the movements and shifts within South Africa's transitionary landscape (Gevisser & Cameron, 1995). GLOW, therefore, took the community education focus of 1980s' queer organizing into an explicitly political activist realm in the 1990s (Batra, 2016).

GLOW's intersectional "queer Afropolitanism"[2] was instrumental in consolidating the so-called gay left in South Africa. By 1991, the organization had branches in Kwa-Thema, Tembisa and Soweto, as well as the city of Johannesburg (Batra, 2021). GLOW played a crucial role in applying pressure on the ANC (and, albeit to a lesser extent, other prominent liberation organizations, such as the PAC and Azanian People's Organization, as well as political parties like the Democratic Party and Inkatha Freedom Party) so that queer rights were incorporated into its political agenda. This pressure helped shift several anti-apartheid activists' understanding of LGBTQI+ issues as white and middle-class issues (Carolin, 2018), and to challenge currents of homophobia and heteronormativity within the ANC (Currier, 2012). Struggle masculinities within the ANC were thus presented with a fundamental challenge and were to some extent expanded through GLOW's attempts to build solidarity by linking together sexual and racial liberation. In the early 1990s, when South Africa underwent a tremendously violent social transition from apartheid, GLOW worked with the ANC and several legal groups to secure LGBTQI+ rights in the country's Constitution (the so-called sexual equality clause, see Chernis, 2016; Gevisser & Cameron, 1995), and in 1996 South Africa became the first nation in the world to constitutionally acknowledge the rights and dignity of queer people (Batra, 2016). Such legislation does not, of course, guarantee that queer lives are valued in South Africa. This is most evident in many of today's ANC leaders' refusal to support LGBTQI+ rights (Ngubane, 2016), along with the appalling rates of violence endured by queer people in contemporary South Africa, especially Black lesbians and trans people (Reid, 2014). As such, queer struggles remain alive in South Africa today, and draw from a considerable – if often neglected – history of struggle in the country (Davids & Matebeni, 2017).

Simon Nkoli and the queering of organized struggle

Histories of anti-apartheid struggle tend to honour the kinds of hegemonic gender ideals that are understood – erroneously, in some cases – to have driven this struggle. The struggle heroes that are remembered most often and most publicly are typically those who embodied these ideals, such as Nelson Mandela, Albert Luthuli, Steve Biko, Robert Sobukwe and Govan Mbeki. While men such as these are undoubtedly important figures, we should not ignore other kinds of gender performances that not only informed anti-apartheid organization but, as we have seen, disrupted hegemonic struggle masculinities, inviting new ways of doing masculinities and being men in the context of struggle. This does not mean that we must turn away from the role of hegemonic masculinities when we write the history of anti-apartheid struggle. Rather, our historiographies can assume a wider lens so that we might broaden our historical consciousness by interrogating how constructions of gender were enacted, struggled over, troubled, stretched and challenged within and between anti-apartheid organizations. In drawing from, as well as adding to, the growing number of studies that have taken up this task (e.g. Batra, 2016; Bonnin, 2000; Bridger, 2018; Carolin, 2018; Cornell et al., 2022; Langa & Eagle, 2008; Imma, 2017; Reddy, 2001), we look in this section to the life and letters of Simon Nkoli, South Africa's best known queer activist.

Who was Simon Nkoli?

Simon Nkoli was born in Soweto in 1957, although he grew up in Sebokeng, a township located in the southern region of South Africa's Gauteng province (Morgan, 2017). He began his activist life in student politics. In addition to being detained for several months when he was 15 years old, he was actively involved in the 1976 Soweto Uprising, where young people protested against the apartheid government's racist Bantu Education Act[3] (Nkoli, 1995). In 1980, Nkoli became regional secretary of the Congress of South African Students[4] (COSAS), which he had joined in the late 1970s. Nkoli (1995) later shared that he came close to losing this position when his sexuality became known.

During the same period, the 1980s, Nkoli was also central in queer activism. He was actively involved in both the UDF and GASA. His political activism halted in 1984, however, when he was arrested – along with around 900 other people – at the funeral of a comrade who was murdered by apartheid State forces for participating in a rent boycott in the township of Sebokeng (Munro, 2012; Ngubane, 2016; Nkoli, 1995). Although most of the arrested were released, Nkoli, as well as 21 other UDF members who were part of the boycott, were not. In what became known as the Delmas Treason Trial, these 22 men were charged with treason, murder and furthering the aims of the ANC. These were serious charges that, under the apartheid regime, carried the death penalty (Gevisser & Cameron, 1995). After four years in prison, Nkoli was acquitted in 1988. He founded GLOW in that same year and soon became a well-known, and internationally beloved, figure of queer liberation (Batra, 2016). On 30 November 1998, a day before World AIDS Day, Nkoli died, aged 41, from an HIV-related illness (Imma, 2017).

For Nkoli, the struggle for racial liberation was not to be considered alongside struggles for gender and sexual liberation. These were all part of the same struggle for human emancipation and thus needed to be considered together. As Reid (2014, n. p.) recalls:

> I remember well the words of the late Simon Nkoli, gay rights and anti-apartheid activist, spoken at Africa's first gay and lesbian march in Johannesburg in 1991: "In South Africa I am oppressed because I am a black man and I am oppressed because I am gay . . . so when I fight for my freedom I must fight against both oppressions".

As Nkoli himself put it: "my baptism in the struggles of the township helped me understand the need for a militant gay rights movement" (Nkoli, 1995, p. 256). His insistence that racial emancipation is always, at the same time, a sexual and a gendered liberation served as an important challenge to hegemonic struggle masculinities.

As the old feminist dictum has it, for Nkoli, the personal was always political. Throughout his life, Nkoli actioned this axiom by ensuring that the personal operated politically by centring queer rights within anti-apartheid struggle. In exploring how Nkoli did this, and what this meant for masculinity in the context of anti-apartheid organizing, we turn to the prison letters he wrote to his romantic partner and comrade, Roy Shepherd.

Although Nkoli wrote many letters in prison – to comrades, friends and family – his letters to Shepherd offer an intimate portrait of how his queer masculinity informed his political organizing. Letters, for Nkoli, were psychologically comforting at a time when little support was available to him. He reflects that while in prison "what helped me most was that I received so many letters" (Nkoli, 1995, p. 255). As Martin (2020) argues, Nkoli's letter writing is indispensable for constructing an "affective historiography" of queer liberation struggles in apartheid South Africa. Many of Nkoli's letters to Shepherd have been archived by the Gay and Lesbian Memory in Action (Morgan, 2017). In what follows, we draw from this particular archive, as well as key moments in Nkoli's activist life, to establish an affective, historiographical consideration of queer anti-apartheid struggle which, for Nkoli, was always also a wider struggle for human emancipation.

The Delmas Treason Trial

At first, many of the UDF comrades with whom Nkoli was imprisoned during the Delmas Treason Trial were not aware that he was queer (Imma, 2017). He writes to Shepherd:

> Johny's girlfriend came on Friday as well, so I was the only one sitting there on the benches looking at other people talking to their friends, parents and lovers, wishing that I could have courage to interfere as they always do when my lover is around. I suppose they all don't recognise him because a gay relationship is not supposed to be real.
>
> *(Morgan, 2017, p. 32)*

Prison guards who were aware of Nkoli's sexual orientation would taunt and mock him (Nkoli, 1995), constantly inferring that his comrades would not accept him. Not being accepted by his comrades was a fear that Nkoli did, indeed, hold (Martin, 2020). However, during the trial, it was discovered by the prison warders that one of the trialists was involved in a sexual relationship with a convicted prisoner (Nkoli, 1995). Upon learning this, several other trialists expressed dismay. One condemned it as "disgusting", while others feared it would delegitimize their struggle in the eyes of the international community (Martin, 2020). It was in response to these reactions that Nkoli told his comrades that he, too, was gay, and condemned their homophobia (see Morgan, 2017).

As expected, many of the trialists did not respond kindly to Nkoli's intervention. Some of them even suggested that Nkoli be tried separately. All of this took a considerable toll on his mental health (Imma, 2017). The most prominent of the trialists, however, came to Nkoli's defence, at first on the basis of his deft organizational skills and political commitment. Eventually, though, these arguments found their rhetorical basis in the fact that the struggle against homophobia could not be separated from struggles against racism (Morgan, 2017). This would become the official stance of the trialists, many of whom had not hitherto considered queer struggles (see Munro, 2012). Later, Patrick "Terror" Lekota, a fellow UDF leader and defendant in the Delmas Treason Trial, was moved by Nkoli to join the fight to incorporate queer liberation into the ANC's political agenda (Imma, 2017). Far from delegitimising their struggle, as many of the trialists had feared, Nkoli brought this struggle much-needed international attention. Imma (2017) recounts that because of Nkoli, several letter-writing campaigns were initiated all over the world, with the Simon Nkoli Anti-Apartheid Committee, founded in Toronto, Canada and Sweden's International Gay and Lesbian Association expressing its unconditional support for Nkoli. He also received support from anti-apartheid organizations based in Britain and Holland (Nkoli, 1995).

Nkoli challenged his comrades' solidarity, rattling it so that it could be consolidated and expanded (Imma, 2017). He did so by undermining the kinds of hegemonic masculine performance that many of his comrades had understood to be synonymous with struggle. By demonstrating how political commitment was dispersed across different masculinities and, indeed, genders and sexual orientations more generally, it became clear that such commitment needed to, in turn, reflect the emancipatory demands of all people. To queer struggle in the manner exemplified by Nkoli builds upon and widens the scope of struggle, opening up new possibilities for solidarity and politicized consciousness.

The Gay and Lesbian Organization of Witwatersrand

Prior to his imprisonment, Nkoli was an active member of GASA (Imma, 2017). He was, however, always dissatisfied with the organization's insufficient political disposition. This was noted early on when he founded the Saturday Group in 1984, wherein gay Black men who were associated with GASA could discuss political issues that pertained to their lives (Martin, 2020). The Saturday Group collapsed soon after Nkoli went to prison (although it re-formed later after his acquittal; Batra, 2021). As he writes to Shepherd, "I am so sad that Saturday Group has vanished to nowhere. But as soon as I come back from Prison – nevermind for how long – I will start a new progressive gay organisation" (Morgan, 2017, p. 17). Even more devastating to Nkoli, though, was GASA's refusal to support him during his imprisonment on the grounds that he was arrested for his anti-apartheid political activity (i.e. the rent boycott), rather than for queer-related activism (Batra, 2021). With GASA being the largest and most influential queer organization in South Africa at that time, Nkoli's sexual identity, which he had always understood and actioned in fundamentally political ways, could only find an organizational form in GASA's politically regressive mandate. Throughout his letters to Shepherd, Nkoli grapples with whether or not he should resign from GASA. In one letter he writes,

> Gasa has done nothing for me since I was arrested . . . That has frustrated me a little and I know you are not going to be happy to hear such a story from me – but however . . . some individual members of Gasa are seeing me – . . . I will remain a member of Gasa always.
>
> *(Morgan, 2017, p. 26)*

Oscillating on this matter for some time, he eventually concedes that

> I don't want it when people start talking about me. That's why I become too scared when Gasa started debating about me as if I USED TO LIVE. I am still living . . . I am sorry to tell you that I have decided to resign from Gasa as soon as I come out.
>
> *(Morgan, 2017, p. 38)*

GASA came to represent an anti-human politics that Nkoli could not bear. However, unlike his anti-apartheid comrades with whom he was imprisoned and whose idea of anti-racist politics had shifted because of Nkoli's queer politics, GASA refused to expand its emancipatory purview, remaining committed to a "single-issue" and thus closing itself off to related struggles (i.e. those against apartheid's racial capitalism) that the majority of queer people in South Africa face (see Munro, 2012). It was for this reason that Nkoli, demonstrating a profound and psychologically demanding political commitment, left GASA. This act is made all the more courageous when we consider that as politically blinkered as GASA was, there were almost no other organizational protections for queer people in South Africa at that time. In leaving GASA, Nkoli presented a different kind of counter-hegemonic heroic masculinity.

After his release from prison in 1988, Nkoli co-founded GLOW, whose non-racial, Black-led and anti-apartheid politics served as a remedy for GASA's ineffectual, "colour-blind" politics. Significantly, GLOW was aligned with the UDF (see Carolin, 2018), which ensured that anti-apartheid struggle organizations were to explicitly engage with and take up the struggles of queer people. As noted earlier, GLOW was instrumental in ensuring that when the ANC assumed governance in South Africa, the rights of queer people would be constitutionally honoured, a pioneering landmark (Gevisser & Cameron, 1995; Martin, 2020). Moreover, Nkoli was involved in founding the National Coalition for Gay and Lesbian Equality, an organization that was also central to ensuring that queer rights were constitutionally enshrined in South Africa (Munro, 2012).

The manner by which Nkoli organized his political commitments emphasizes how organizing must be held to an intersectional politics. A failure to do so need not mean that we accept a one-dimensional view of liberation, or that we resign from politics altogether. These failures point to new, important avenues for organizing struggle, avenues that render struggle in necessarily broad-based (and thus broadly appealing) terms. We saw this with GLOW, which sought to radicalize both queer and anti-apartheid struggles by refusing to pry them apart from one another.

HIV and AIDS activism

Although learning of his HIV-positive status in 1985 while on trial, Nkoli's attentiveness to HIV and AIDS was noted long before he publicly disclosed his own status in 1990 (Munro, 2012). In his prison letters, Nkoli reprimands Shepherd for referring to a man by his HIV status exclusively (Martin, 2020). He also fantasizes about a time when same-sex relations are not, within the popular imagination, associated with AIDS, a time when "Aids will never come as part of our discussion" (Morgan, 2017, p. 44). HIV and AIDS became central to Nkoli's political organizing when he was released from prison and began to notice not only the pervasiveness of the AIDS epidemic but also the kinds of cultural stigmas attached to the disease. From 1990, he led and raised funds for the Township AIDS Project (Batra, 2021), where lawyers and public health advocates worked on community-oriented AIDS education initiatives (Morgan, 2017).

Nkoli (1995) was steadfast in his critique of the ANC government's handling of the AIDS epidemic, demanding always that State policies be attentive to sexual health and the stigmas surrounding sexual health. In his *Open Letter to Nelson Mandela*, Nkoli (1990) connected struggles for HIV and AIDS medical treatment in South Africa with global struggles of this kind, reminding then-president Nelson Mandela (at a time when it was not popular to level critique at his leadership) that in South Africa, the rights of all people were to be secured as per the much-celebrated Constitution (Batra, 2016). Although his letters were now public

– rather than monitored and censored by apartheid prison authorities – Nkoli remained committed to an ethics that sought to politicize the personal. His public disclosure, community education programmes and frank political commentary proved essential for securing funding for, and improving access to, HIV and AIDS medication in South Africa, while also playing an important role in debunking widespread conceptions at the time that AIDS was an "unAfrican" disease (see Martin, 2020).

Organizing against systematized oppression is never a process that is locked in place. It shifts in accordance with the socio-political conjuncture. For Nkoli, his emancipatory organizing extended well beyond the walls of his prison cell and official apartheid legislature. As with all of his organizing, his entry point into post-apartheid activism was the politicization of the personal. He was among the first Black men in South Africa to speak publicly about his experience of living with HIV (Imma, 2017), which was said to have caused him more anxiety than when he disclosed his sexual orientation to his UDF comrades in prison (Martin, 2020). As Imma (2017) argues, Nkoli's was a "precarious visibility" that carried with it possibilities for social change along with immense psychological discomfort and the risk of depoliticizing his message via commodification. Nonetheless, Nkoli's exemplary commitment to liberation was characterized by a willingness to move with history and to organize through a politicization of the personal, no matter how challenging this was.

Struggling masculinities

When looking at Nkoli's life and letters, we are offered a nuanced understanding of how queer masculinities operated within and upon anti-apartheid organizing. Like hegemonic struggle masculinities, we should not consider queer masculinity in a monolithic fashion that ignores the contradictions, concessions and resistances that define how these masculinities were embodied and performed in the struggle against apartheid. Nkoli's queerness was lived out in a plethora of ways. He offered a tender, vulnerable sort of masculinity that is not readily associated with the liberation struggle. As he writes to Shepherd regarding his trial:

> I will try to be a good witness Roy, though I am feeling too scared to stand in the witness box. I don't want the people to look at me when I am giving evidence and the prosecutor shouting at me.
>
> *(Morgan, 2017, p. 29)*

Such vulnerability was not, however, the sole determinant of Nkoli's masculine performance. Indeed, he expresses frustration with such simplistic associations when he writes that:

> I'm getting annoyed everytime, because people keep on saying I am BEAUTIFUL. Handsome – gentle – sweet hearted. They complain about me, for having no fights. They say I never get angry. I'm so polite. Why should I fight – or scream? In fact they are all a bunch of liars – twice I kicked Jacob. Can't they see that I am aggressive – that's why I kicked Jake!
>
> *(Morgan, 2017, p. 23)*

The fluidity of the gender constructions that Nkoli adopted within his queer identity opened him up to a similarly nuanced engagement with struggle. For Nkoli, struggle was absolutely necessary for liberation. However, he repeatedly acknowledged that struggling politically was a taxing necessity, one that could be left behind in a truly liberated society. In other words, although Nkoli's liberatory imagination was undoubtedly shaped by struggle, he appeared to always allow himself space to dream of a world beyond struggle. For example, he is unafraid to acknowledge to Shepherd that his trial, politically important as it was, was also dull ("The trial is quite boring today . . . I am absolutely bored", Morgan, 2017, p. 36), as were many of the political meetings that the trialists held ("after church we had some discussions – heavy political discussion – I hate this kind of discussions sometimes" Morgan, 2017, p. 21). Nkoli's letters are replete with references to jubilation, literature, clothing, love and food as much as they emphasize the importance of emancipatory political organizing. There are many times in his letters that Nkoli expresses an awareness of this tension:

> This is going to be a Marathon trial. Please Roy for my sake, don't ever get yourself into politics. I will die at once if I hear that you detained. Please my Roy, it won't be wise for both of us to be in prison, while now I know that when I am released I am going to fall in your arms.
>
> *(Morgan, 2017, p. 17, sic)*

Nkoli exemplified a sort of queer struggle masculinity that operated alongside, against and within the kinds of hegemonic struggle masculinities that tend to be remembered in most apartheid historiographies. His queer gender identity engaged directly with, and indeed transformed, hegemonic anti-apartheid struggle masculinities, and thus offers insights into how struggle can be extended and consolidated, if also put to the test, when it reckons with a plethora of gendered ways of being and doing.

Conclusion: gender liberation and political organization today

At the beginning of this chapter, it was observed that in contrast to self-conscious antifeminist and profeminist/feminist men's movements and organizations, in more general movements and organizations involving men, gender was usually not the primary category of socio-political engagement. However, even though gender was and is not always privileged in progressive organizations involving men (we gave the example of anti-colonial, Black Power and BCM), since colonialism and anti-Black racism sought to deny the humanity of colonized subjects, we can understand the reclamation of gendered identities as part of reasserting humanity within liberation struggles. The trouble is that the kinds of masculinity that were desired within these struggles were all too often heteropatriarchal. This is where Simon Nkoli's embodied struggle is instructive.

The life and letters of Nkoli point to a different kind of struggle masculinity that has received relatively little official remembrance, but nonetheless played a crucial role in emancipatory organizing in South Africa. If we are to give nuance to apartheid historiography, we are compelled to remember and engage critically with Nkoli's struggles as well as the collective struggles of which he was a part. Certainly, Nkoli was exemplary of how affect and struggle as well as organizational politics and the personal were always part and parcel of the anti-apartheid liberatory imaginary. He writes:

> Well, I am sorry to hear that you cried when you read my first letter. Don't cry over me Roy. I am taking this situation as part of life in the struggle for a better society in the future. Remember that there is no easy walk to FREEDOM.
>
> *(Morgan, 2017, p. 15)*

As Martin (2020) recounts, at Nkoli's funeral, Zackie Achmat – a well-known queer community activist – made a rallying call to "cry, rage, mobilise. Don't only mourn" (p. 685). The conventional, masculinized, liberatory command: "Don't mourn, organize!" is thereby challenged – and extended – in this case. Mourning is, for many, a precondition for organizing and should not simply be dismissed as apolitical. Struggle masculinities that disallow affectivity may in fact hamper collective organization. The kinds of masculinity exhibited by Nkoli throughout his life demonstrate new, potentially more freeing, ways of being within – and also, crucially, beyond – struggle. As such, Nkoli did not limit his gendered identity expression to a narrow understanding of struggle. Instead, he used struggle to imagine, act and organize for a world in which all identities could be free:

> By reading Danielle Steel [an American romance novelist] I learn so much about how some people suffer because of love – but one also learns to be brave, and courage is dwelling in me. I've learnt that I should wait – pray – wait – pray – wait – pray – suffer – communicate with other people – remember – think – recall the past – think of the future – And I am still living.
>
> *(Morgan, 2017, p. 27)*

It is, however, important that Nkoli's remarkable – and, indeed, well-archived – legacy does not eclipse the collective nature of queer struggles in South Africa. As Chernis (2016) argues, the relatively extensive focus that Nkoli's life has received should not diminish efforts to broaden our understanding of the queer personal–political dialectic in South Africa. We are urged to examine the lives of other queer activists during, before and after the 1980s. Doing so may nuance further how identity and struggle – the personal and the political – are able to take form through the registers of one another. In recent years, we have seen several examples of queer and feminist activists challenging hegemonic masculinity within political organizing. In the wave of the student protests that swept South Africa in 2015 and 2016, tensions were evident around the intersections of race, gender and sexuality among student activists (Davids & Matebeni, 2017; Khan, 2017; Mashayamombe & Nomvete, 2021; also see Hussen & Shefer, this volume). Indeed, as the student movements developed, there were noted instances of sexism, homophobia, heterosexism and transphobia that emerged within certain activist spaces (Ndelu et al., 2017). As a student who was involved in the RhodesMustFall movement at UCT reflected, "The fact that I was gay, it was also a problem. I cannot separate my gayness from my blackness, and that is what they are expecting me to do" (Cornell et al., 2018, p. 188). Within the student movements, then, divisions arose between "students who identified as Black, queer and transgender feminists and sections of the movement who identified more explicitly with patriarchy" (Ndelu et al., 2017, p. 2). In response, many queer and feminist activists within these movements disrupted and resisted currents of heterosexist patriarchy and transphobia within their organizing – the Trans Collective at the University of Cape Town, being one notable example here (see Davids & Matebeni, 2017; Khan, 2017; Ndelu et al., 2017).

We might then conclude that by connecting a non-deterministic kind of gender enactment to the ever-shifting demands of political organization – no matter how psychologically burdensome this was (Martin, 2020) – Nkoli was able to undergird his political activism with an astonishing kind of hope; a belief in a better future that was not inevitable, but that was always a horizon of possibility. Nkoli was, of course, not the only person to do this (Chernis, 2016), but the wealth of archived materials makes his life and thought an exemplary instance of queering struggle that extends the purview of liberation in an intersectional manner and that was able to push collective struggle beyond itself. As he put it: "But I think I'll be free at the end of this trial – most of us, maybe all of us. We must keep on hoping Roy" (Morgan, 2017, p. 36).

In this chapter, we have considered the *queering* of anti-apartheid struggles among *non-queered* political organizations and organizing. Our analysis speaks not only to specific queer and anti-racist struggles but to intersectional and affective approaches to liberation more broadly. These issues and challenges are both intensely historical and persistently relevant for gender liberation, within and beyond political organizations and organizing.

Notes

1 In March 1960, the South African Police fired on a crowd of people engaged in a peaceful protest in Sharpeville against oppressive pass laws, killing 69 people, many of whom were children.
2 Refers to the enlargement of the geo-racial spread of gay liberation, described by Batra (2021) as "a worlding of sexualities that was first, simultaneously local, national, and international and next, openly political and community oriented" (p. 143).
3 The Bantu Education Act was a South African segregation law involving the racist compartmentalizing of education. The Act enforced the racial segregation of educational institutions.
4 The student organization was affiliated with the United Democratic Front (UDF), an anti-apartheid coalition group.

References

Axelsson, S. (2015). Gendered struggle for freedom: A narrative inquiry into female ex combatants in South Africa. In S. Shekhawat (Ed.), *Female Combatants in Conflict and Peace: Challenging Gender in Violence and Post-conflict Reintegration* (pp. 167–185). London: Springer. doi: 10.1057/9781137516565_11

Badat, S. (2009). *Black Man, You are on your Own.* Johannesburg: Real African Publishers.

Batra, K. (2016). Worlding sexualities under apartheid: From gay liberation to a queer Afropolitanism. *Postcolonial Studies, 19*(1), 37–52. doi: 10.1080/13688790.2016.1222857

Batra, K. (2021). *Worlding Postcolonial Sexualities: Publics, Counterpublics, Human rights.* London: Routledge. doi: 10.4324/9781003170303

Bonnin, D. (2000). Claiming spaces, changing places: Political violence and women's protests in KwaZulu-Natal. *Journal of Southern African Studies, 26*(2), 301–316. doi: 10.1080/03057070050010138

Bowleg, L. (2013). "Once you've blended the cake, you can't take the parts back to the main ingredients": Black gay and bisexual men's descriptions and experiences of intersectionality. *Sex Roles, 68*(11–12), 754–767.

Bridger, E. (2018). Soweto's female comrades: Gender, youth and violence in South Africa's township uprisings, 1984–1990. *Journal of Southern African Studies, 44*(4), 559–574. doi: 10.1080/03057070.2018.1462591

Carolin, A. (2018). Locating sexual rights in the anti-apartheid movement: Simon Nkoli and the making of post-apartheid protest theatre. *Critical Arts, 32*(5–6), 3550. doi: 10.1080/02560046.2018.1560342

Chernis, L. (2016). Guest Post: Archiving an Icon – GALA's Simon Nkoli Collection. Without Borders Conference, June 22–24, 2016. LGBTQ+ Archives, Libraries, Museums & Special Collections. Retrieved 15 February 2023, from http://lgbtqalms.co.uk/2016/11/11/guest-post-archiving-an-icon-galas-simon-nkoli-collection-by-linda-chernis/

Cornell, J., Kessi, S., & Ratele, K. (2018). Dynamics of Privilege, Identity and Resistance at a Historically White University: A Photovoice Study of Exclusionary Institutional Culture. In *Places of Privilege* (pp. 173–193). Leiden; Boston: Brill. doi: 10.1163/9789004381407_011

Cornell, J., Malherbe, N., Seedat, M., & Suffla, S. (2022). Discourses of gender and political violence in South Africa. *Social Politics: International Studies in Gender, State and Society, 29*(1), 309–332. doi: 10.1093/sp/jxab005

Currier, A. (2012). *Out in Africa: LGBT Organizing in Namibia and South Africa.* Chicago, IL: University of Minnesota Press.
Davids, N., & Matebeni, Z. (2017). Queer politics and intersectionality in South Africa. *Safundi, 18*(2), 161–167. doi: 10.1080/17533171.2016.1270015
Davis, A. Y. (1983). *Women, Race, and Class.* London: Vintage.
Davis, S. R. (2018). *The ANC's war against apartheid: Umkhonto We Sizwe and the liberation of South Africa.* Bloomington, IN: University of Indiana Press.
Farmer, A., Phillips, M., Spencer, R. C., & Yellesetty, L. (2019). Women in the black panther party: A roundtable. *International Socialist Review*, 111.
Friedman, E. J. (2007). How Pink is the 'Pink Tide'? Feminist and LGBT Activists Challenge the Left. Retrieved 15 February 2023, from Nalacs Report of the Americas: https://nacla.org/article/introduction-how-pink-pink-tide
Gevisser, M., & Cameron, E. (Eds.). (1995). *Defiant Desire: Gay and Lesbian Lives in South Africa.* New York: Routledge.
Hallett, R. (1984). Desolation on the veld: Forced removals in South Africa. *African Affairs, 83*(332), 301–320.
Hirschmann, D. (1990). The black consciousness movement in South Africa. *The Journal of Modern African Studies, 28*(1), 1–22. doi: 10.1017/S0022278X00054203
Imma, Z. (2017). Black, queer, and precarious visibilities: Simon Nkoli's activist image in South Africa's Exit newspaper. *Callaloo, 40*(3), 61–74.
Kelley, R. D. G. (2002). *Freedom Dreams: The Black Radical Imagination.* Boston, MA: Beacon Press.
Khan, K. (2017). Intersectionality in student movements: Black queer womxn and non-binary activists in South Africa's 2015–2016 protests. *Agenda, 31*(3–4), 110–121. doi: 10.1080/10130950.2017.1396011
King, D. K. (1988). Multiple jeopardy, multiple consciousness: The context of a Black feminist ideology. *Signs: Journal of Women in Culture and Society, 14*(1), 42–72.
Langa, M., & Eagle, G. (2008). The intractability of militarised masculinity: A case study of former Self-Defence Unit members in the Kathorus area, South Africa. *South African Journal of Psychology, 38*(11), 152–175. doi: 10.10520/EJC98472
Leek, C., & Gerke, M. (2020). Men's movements. In N. A. Naples (Ed.), *Companion to Women's and Gender Studies* (pp. 447–462). Oxford: Wiley Blackwell. doi: 10.1002/9781119315063.ch21
Lodge, T. (2011). *Sharpeville: An Apartheid Massacre and Its Consequences.* Oxford: Oxford University Press.
Martin, Y. (2020). 'Now I am not afraid': Simon Nkoli, queer utopias and transnational solidarity. *Journal of Southern African Studies, 46*(4), 673–687. doi: 10.1080/03057070.2020.1780022
Mashayamombe, J., & Nomvete, S. (2021). Leadership and politics of belonging in a 2015 FeesMust-Fall movement: A case of uprising. *Politikon, 48*(1), 41–56. doi: 10.1080/02589346.2021.1877454
Messner, M. (1997). *Politics of Masculinities: Men in Movements.* Thousand Oaks, CA: Sage.
Morgan, R. (2017). Till the Time of Trial: The Prison Letters of Simon Nkoli. Retrieved 12 February 2023, from GALA Queer Archive: https://bit.ly/2TEihDV
Morrell, R. (2002). Men, movements, and gender transformation in South Africa. *The Journal of Men's Studies, 10*(3), 309–327. doi: 10.3149/jms.1003.309
Mtebule, N. (2002). *Identity in the Making: Researching Young Black Urban Masculine Identity in the Post-apartheid Era.* Unpublished master's dissertation, University of the Witwatersrand, Johannesburg, South Africa.
Munro, B. M. (2012). *South Africa and the Dream of Love to Come: Queer Sexuality and the Struggle for Freedom.* Chicago, IL: University of Minnesota Press.
Nasheed, J. (2021). The Black Power Movement: Understanding Its Origins, Leaders, and Legacy. Retrieved 15 February 2023, from www.teenvogue.com/story/the-black-power-movement-origins-leaders
Ndelu, S., Dlakavu, S., & Boswell, B. (2017). Womxn's and nonbinary activists' contribution to the RhodesMustFall and FeesMustFall student movements: 2015 and 2016. *Agenda, 31*(3–4), 1–4, doi: 10.1080/10130950.2017.1394693
Ngubane, G. S. (2016). *Queer Apartheid in South Africa and the Politics of Representation.* Doctoral dissertation, San Francisco State University. Retrieved 15 February 2012, from https://sfsu-dspace.calstate.edu/bitstream/handle/10211.3/173362/AS362016WOMSTN48.pdf?sequence=1

Nkoli, S. (1990). Simon Nkoli writes an open letter to Nelson Mandela – Reprinted from New York's village voice. *Exit*, 16.
Nkoli, S. (1995). Wardrobes: Coming out as a black gay activist in South Africa. In M. Gevisser & E. Cameron (Eds.), *Defiant Desire: Gay and lesbian lives in South Africa* (pp. 249–257). New York: Routledge.
Nunes, R. (2021). *Neither Vertical Nor Horizontal: A Theory of Political Organization.* London and New York: Verso.
Oxlund, B. (2008). Masculinities in student politics: Gendered discourses of struggle and liberation at the University of Limpopo. *Psychology in Society*, *36*, 60–76.
Peretz, T. (2017). Engaging diverse men: An intersectional analysis of men's pathways to Anti-violence activism. *Gender & Society*, *31*(4), 526–548. doi: 10.1177/0891243217717181
Platzky, L., & Walker, C., For The Surplus People's Project (1985). *The Surplus People: Forced Removals in South Africa.* Johannesburg: Ravan Press.
Ratele, K. (2009a). Apartheid, anti-apartheid and post-apartheid sexualities. In M. Steyn & M. Van Zyl (Eds.), *The Prize and the Price: Shaping Sexualities in South Africa* (pp. 290–306). Cape Town: HSRC Press.
Ratele, K. (2009b). Sexuality as constitutive of whiteness in South Africa. *NORA – Nordic Journal of Feminist and Gender Research*, *17*(3), 158–174. doi: 10.1080/08038740903123784
Ratele, K., Shefer, T., & Botha, M. (2011). Navigating past "the white man's agenda" in South Africa: Organizing men for gendered transformation of society. In E. Ruspini, J. Hearn, B. Pease & K. Pringle (Eds.), *Men and Masculinities Around the World* (pp. 247–260). New York: Palgrave. doi: 10.1057/9780230338005_18
Reddy, V. (2001). Institutionalizing sexuality: Theorizing queer in post-apartheid South Africa. In D. Constantine-Simms (Ed.), *The Greatest Taboo: Homosexuality in Black Communities* (pp. 163–184). Los Angeles, CA: Alyson Books.
Reid, G. (2014). South Africa's Worrying Prevarication on LGBT Rights. Retrieved 15 February 2023, from www.hrw.org/news/2014/09/22/south-africas-worrying-prevarication-lgbt-rights
Shefer, T., & Ratele, K. (2011). Racist sexualisation and sexualised racism in narratives on apartheid. *Psychoanalysis, Culture & Society*, *16*, 27–48. doi: 10.1057/pcs.2010.38
Stevens, G., Duncan, N., & Hook, D. (2013). *Race, Memory and the Apartheid Archive: Towards a Transformative Psychosocial Praxis.* New York: Palgrave Macmillan. doi: 10.1057/9781137263902
Suttner, R. (2005). Masculinities in the African National Congress-led liberation movement: The underground period. *African Historical Review*, *37*(1), 71–106. doi: 10.10520/EJC53427
Suttner, R. (2014). Nelson Mandela's masculinities. *African Identities*, *12*(3–4), 342–356. doi: 10.1080/14725843.2015.1009623
Time (1960). South Africa: The Sharpeville Massacre. Retrieved 15 February 2023, from http://content.time.com/time/subscriber/article/0,33009,869441-1,00.html
Unterhalter, E. (2000). The work of the nation: Heroic masculinity in South African autobiographical writing of the anti-apartheid struggle. *The European Journal of Research*, *12*(2), 157–178. doi: 10.1080/09578810008426770
Xaba, T. (2001). Masculinity and its malcontents: The confrontation between 'struggle masculinity' and 'post-struggle masculinity' (1990–1997). In R. Morrell (Ed.), *Changing Men in Southern Africa* (pp. 105–124). Durban: University of KwaZulu-Natal Press.

21

BEYOND THE PUBLIC LIGHT

Political strongmen, masculine embodiment and sports organizations

Michele Rene Gregory and Daniel Alsarve

Introduction: hegemonic masculinities, locker rooms and sports organizations

And when you're a star they let you do it. You can do anything, whatever you want. Grab them by the pussy. You can do anything.

(Makela, 2016, An audio recording released in 2016 of then Presidential candidate Donald J. Trump)[1]

This quote relates to sports, men/masculinities and power for several reasons. It exemplifies the metaphorical and expanded use of locker room talk. After the recording of Trump boasting that he could grab women "by the pussy" was made public, his attorney, former New York City Mayor Rudy Giuliani, argued that Trump's comments were typical "locker room talk" and not to be taken seriously (Epstein, 2016). Trump's words were not only a reminder of casual locker room behaviour, mostly associated with male-dominated team sports, but also the depth and scope of it in other types of organizational spaces. The episode echoes results that we have found in our own research and exemplifies how some men find locker room banter and jokes about women and other marginalized groups harmless, regardless of the language used (Alsarve & Angelin, 2020; Gregory, 2009, 2011).

The notion of "the locker room", in its twenty-first-century edition, has expanded into social media and other online spaces that enable peers to chat and banter without fear of being judged for "political incorrectness". Paralleling this technological expansion, the possibility of hidden film and voice recording threatens its intimacy and foundation. Trust, loyalty and silence are therefore actualized more explicitly in these homosocial contexts than ever before. Those who downplay the significance of sexist locker room talk in "private spaces" may fail to understand that these actions do not have clearly demarcated boundaries or only involve men using jokes and banter as a form of harmless solidarity. Research illustrates that locker room humour among men is used as a form of ridicule in order to exploit colleagues' weaknesses (Collinson, 1988) and to construct highly skilled women professionals as lacking in ability, thus denying many access to important career opportunities (Gregory, 2009, 2016). Furthermore, despite those who minimized Trump's boasting of "grabbing women by the

DOI: 10.4324/9781003193579-24

pussy", more than a dozen women have accused the former President of sexual misconduct (Keneally, 2020). This does not mean that all sportsmen are homophobic, abusive, misogynist or exploitative, but the "hegemony of men", as Hearn (2004) writes, takes new, hybrid shapes and finds more subtle ways for its domination.

There is a wealth of research on men and masculinities, especially hegemonic masculinity. Scholars such as Carrigan et al. (1985) and Connell and Messerschmidt (2005) have argued that, as there is no singular embodiment of men's experiences, the same applies to hegemonic masculinity. Masculine embodiments fluctuate over men's life cycle as they navigate a range of public and private spaces (Giazitzoglu, 2022), and are therefore diverse, fluid, subjective and shaped by numerous factors, such as culture, ethnicity, class, sexuality, gender identity, body type, religion, age, location, profession and organizational spaces. Hegemonic masculinity is "the currently most honoured way of being a man" (Connell & Messerschmidt, 2005, p. 832) in a particular space and time, and Connell & Messerschmidt argue that what gives it legitimacy is its acceptance and participation by subordinate groups, or as Carrigan et al. argue, "very large numbers of men are complicit in sustaining the hegemonic model" (1985, p. 592). In some instances, accepting "ideal" constructions of masculinity is more important than active participation, as "hegemony works in part through the production of exemplars (e.g., professional sports stars), symbols that have authority despite the fact that most men and boys do not fully live up to them" (Connell & Messerschmidt, 2005, p. 846). For some men in power who are not athletes, male sports that privilege aggression, violence and domination are symbolic of how they operate in their respective fields – a contest between the strong (winners) and the weak (losers).

Consequently, male-dominated sports play an important role in the construction of hegemonic masculinity. This is especially true for contact sports that glorify strength, violence, infliction of pain, risk-taking, and marginalization of women and "non-attractive" men/masculinities (Alsarve, 2022). This includes rugby (Giazitzoglu, 2022), ice hockey (Alsarve & Angelin, 2020) and American football (Butterworth, 2014; Sabo, 2004; Sabo & Panepinto, 1990). Embracing a warrior mentality is acceptable, where the body is used as a weapon in combat on the field or in the arena (Jansen & Sabo, 1994; Messner, 1992), and inflicting pain and playing hurt is revered (Giazitzoglu, 2022). In these and other male-dominated competitive spaces, including sports organizations, living up to "ideal" masculinities requires constant work, especially when there is an identity threat perceived by some men – a threat that requires them to engage in sometimes extreme behaviour to "re-accomplish hegemonic masculinity" (Giazitzoglu, 2022, p. 1).

The most commercialized sports are extremely gendered and dominated by males (Knoppers & Anthonissen, 2008). Such sports gain great social significance as industries where cultural and symbolic ideals of masculinity are constructed, that is, they are leading definers of masculinity (Connell, 2005). Organizations promoting football, ice hockey and other sports thus build their success on being masculinizing businesses. Put differently, men's football clubs can function as protecting and producing white, heterosexual, male dominance in society. Although women are included in such organizations, they are effectively marginalized from the core sports-related areas and employed in positions on the periphery (Bryan et al., 2021). That is, despite an openness to include women and others, change of the hegemonic order in organizations does not necessarily take place. Rather, the (limited) presence of women, an inclusion that might look like progress, can instead be understood as restricted to preserve male dominance (Claringbould & Knoppers, 2012; Knoppers & Anthonissen, 2008). Therefore, it becomes important to understand and explain how male dominance of sports organizations is reproduced – a dominance that is often demonstrated beyond the public light.

Our analysis of certain forms of masculine embodiment, such as the locker room, misogyny and homophobia in sports, is situated within hegemonic masculinity and sports organizations scholarship. In this chapter, we are particularly interested in the power relations between strongmen, an aspect of hegemonic masculinity, in the domain of sports. The term "strongmen" is used to describe heads of state who embrace authoritarianism, such as Jair Bolsonaro, Vladimir Putin and Donald J. Trump, and their embodiment of virility, aggression, dominance, fearlessness, heroism and "traditional" beliefs about gender, which are key in their construction of power and their political legitimacy (Ben-Ghiat, 2021). They are often admirers of elite male sports, especially those that make clear distinctions between the strong and the weak. Hence, similarities exist between strongmen in politics and in sports. We will show not only how competition and hierarchy are central in these relations but also how domination and exclusion techniques are continuously used in these men's positioning and hierarchization. The main point is that positions considered hegemonic are the result of constant, ongoing power games where men's (hegemonic, entitled, marginalized or subordinated) positions are at stake, questioned and in need of justification. Metaphorically speaking, the (seeming) stability of the gender regime should rather be understood as a vibrant complexity with constant, situational negotiations and conflicts (Connell, 2005; Hearn & Howson, 2020).

We argue that the concept of hegemony of men/masculinities is still relevant for critically understanding gendered power. The power expressed in, for example, strongmen's homophobia and misogyny finds expressions in the avenues of the expanded locker room beyond the public light. By drawing on examples from sports research and contemporary media sources, we analyse comments by and informal conversations between strongmen and set them in a broader context of gendered power in organizations. In the following, a review of previous research on hegemonic masculinities in the sports field is presented, which is followed by our analysis of the power of hegemony at work.

Stable and complex: sports, hegemony and gendered power

> *The institutional organization of sport embeds definite social relations: competition and hierarchy among men, exclusion or domination of women. These social relations of gender are both realized and symbolized in the bodily performances. Thus men's greater sporting prowess has become a theme of backlash against feminism. It serves as symbolic proof of men's superiority and right to rule.*
>
> (*Connell, 2005, p. 54*)

Sports' construction of gender actualizes a feminist and organizational challenge. Several sports entail narrower and more exclusionary conditions for women and femininities, while also celebrating dominating and bodily (masculine) ideals that marginalize male practitioners who cannot conform to them (Alsarve, 2022; Alsarve & Tjønndal, 2019; Gilenstam et al., 2008). These conditions, that take the male norm for granted, more intensely affect girls and women involved in male-dominated sports. Media attention, public popularity and financial support help stabilize the current "gender regime" (Connell, 2006). Taken together, these factors serve to uphold men's and masculinities' hegemonic positions in sports institutions.

The concept and perspective of hegemonic masculinity and men as hegemony captures the stability and complexity of patriarchal power (Connell, 2005; Hearn & Howson, 2020). With a departure point in this analytical framework that stems from a Gramscian tradition, several scholars over the past decades have identified how sports construct and recognize men and masculinities as dominating, appealing, and powerful (Bryson, 1990; Cooky et al., 2015; McKay et al., 2000; Messner, 1992, 2007; Messner et al., 2000). The power play between men and critical analysis of men's power exercised over women and other men is still of (feminist) importance to scrutinize. The #MeToo movement is an extremely concrete example of this need. Thanks to this, the recording with Trump was made public. But Trump's words must also be interpreted as a man's attempt to impress other men. A story of sexual assault can have significant importance in the power game between political strongmen. Typically, this game is played beyond the perceived risk of being classified as "politically incorrect". Such processes have occupied our interest in our locker room studies (Alsarve & Angelin, 2020; Gregory, 2009, 2011), and they continue to stimulate our research interest. Beyond the public light, the expected silence and loyalty are at stake, and these circumstances continue to make misogyny, homophobia and racism useful means of power.

As much as locker rooms are places and spaces, they are also a metaphor regarding how certain forms of masculinities are performed (Gregory, 2009). The connection between metaphors such as "blitz" and "sudden death" in certain sports is significant and illustrates how some hypermasculine representations are held in high esteem by some athletes, sports officials and even politicians (Jansen & Sabo, 1994). In addition, playing hurt becomes a metaphor for valour and respect, while those who advocate for health and safety protocols are sometimes accused of not just demasculinizing and queering men's sports but also a nation (Sanderson & Cassilo, 2019). Strongmen have even used COVID-19 as a platform for performing hypermasculinity – "fighting" the disease takes on a militaristic performance, like a highly competitive game (Kurtzleben, 2020). Therefore, we argue that metaphors, power and identity are used to decide not only which men gain access to male-dominated spaces but also how some come to lose their privileged access.

Misogyny in informal spaces: the locker room at work

The expectancy of not making misogyny and homophobia public is of great importance and underlines the meaning of silence in the reproduction of hegemony. That is also why a locker room culture, its masculine embodiments and the downplaying of its importance represent a real challenge to women/femininities and sexual and ethnic minorities, although even some minority men engage in homophobia and sexism, as some gay men are racist and sexist. The locker room is a space, and a metaphor for hegemonic masculinity, dominance, superiority, inclusion and exclusion – a space that has been normalized by many despite rarely being public. Whether the locker room exists in sports organizations or other institutions, such as political and business spaces, key areas consist of banter, bullying, drinking, conformity, sexism, homophobia and racism (Gregory, 2009, 2011). Not all these issues exist all the time in every locker room, as behaviour is fluid and complex. The case study of the United States National Football League (N.F.L.) in this section illustrates how casual certain forms of white heterosexual masculine embodiment operate in elite professional men's team sports organizations.

The N.F.L. has a "Personal Conduct Policy" regarding behaviour considered detrimental to the integrity of public confidence in the organization, a policy that applies to everyone in the league (NFL Owners Endorse New Personal Conduct Policy, 2014). The policy largely focuses on illegal and violent behaviour, such as weapon violations and sexual and domestic abuse, yet there is no mention of sexism, homophobia or racism. Separately, there is also an N.F.L. anti-discrimination policy which forbids discrimination against players due to race, religion, national origin and sexual orientation (Anton, 2011). Gender is not included, probably because only men play in the league, although it is not clear how the current policies would affect a transgendered player. In light of more recent allegations of racism and sexism against those in leadership positions, in 2020 the N.F.L. announced new policies that would "increase employment opportunities and advancement for minorities and women throughout the league", as well as committing US$250.000 over a 10-year period to address systemic racism (Battista, 2020). This amount is incongruent with a billion-dollar industry, in which team valuations range from US$2 billion to US$6.5 billion (Ozanian & Settimi, 2021).[2] Furthermore, the league's "commitment" to diversity and inclusion makes no mention of LGBTQ+ individuals.

In early October 2021, emails containing misogynist, homophobic and racist comments sent by Jon Gruden, one of the most important head coaches and media analysts affiliated with the N.F.L., became public. The emails spanned almost a decade (from 2010 to 2018), and Gruden was working for EPSN during the period that he sent the emails, in between head coaching positions within the N.F.L. Many of the emails released by the N.F.L. Commissioner, Roger Goodell, revealed that Gruden initiated some of the email correspondence with two other powerful men associated with the N.F.L., Bruce Allen, who during the email period was the President of the Commanders,[3] and Jeff Pash, who was and is currently the N.F.L.'s general counsel and executive vice president (see Belson & Rosman, 2021). The emails reveal a locker room, not of players but of powerful white heterosexual men in and associated with the N.F.L. who were in a "safe" white heterosexual men-only space. This was a space where they could banter with each other and express their trust and friendship. It was also a space where they could assert their views on race, including anger and fear about racial justice, women, non-hegemonic men and even well-known white heterosexual men who did not embody the type of dominant hypermasculinity they and others endorsed. The Gruden emails are an example of how exclusive locker rooms form just as easily in cyberspace, online, through emails or other private channels, as they do in person at work, at external events and at clubs.

This case study shows that formal anti-discrimination policy, while important, cannot always address informal behaviour resulting in homophobia, misogyny and racism. In some instances, sports institutions and (con)federations have worked actively since the 1970s to eliminate discrimination, racism and sexism. However, success stories often seem to be enveloped in a deeper, more stable power structure (Antunovic & Linden, 2020). On the one hand, praiseworthy inclusion initiatives are highlighted as successful but, on the other hand, often become "side projects" that ultimately do not thoroughly challenge and change the core problem of patriarchal power in sports (Bryan et al., 2021). This ambivalence between policy and praxis, progression and stability, actualizes the relevance of understanding sports as a complex dynamic of power.

Weaponizing misogyny and homophobia in the locker room

Some of the emails Gruden sent included photos of topless women (Schad & Jones, 2021) and his opposition to women referees in the N.F.L. The Gruden emails were incidental to the N.F.L.'s 2020 investigation into claims (many eventually substantiated) by former and current female employees of the team now called the Commanders and its culture of pervasive sexual harassment and bullying over decades (Belson & Rosman, 2021; Macur, 2018). In his statement regarding the investigation findings, N.F.L. Commissioner Goodell announced that the organization had operated "both generally and particularly for women", in a "highly unprofessional" manner that included "bullying", "intimidation", multiple allegations of "sexual harassment" and a "general lack of respect in the workplace" (Around the NFL Staff, 2021).

In addition to sexist material, homophobic jokes, banter and name-calling were also part of the email exchanges. For example, Gruden joked about the men in his email group performing oral sex on him, mocking gay male sex and defining it as inferior to heterosexual sex. As the locker room is a space full of banter involving sex and sexuality (Alsarve & Angelin, 2020; Gregory, 2009, 2011), the jokes and banter at gay men's expense is not surprising. Banter can also turn coercive, used to feminize and to dominate men who may either be gay or perceived as "weak". Jason Collins, who in 2013 was the first active NBA player to publicly announce that he was gay, spoke about homophobia and humour in the locker room, and argued that a key reason behind the comments was for players to make other players "look small" and you did this by "cut[ing] their masculinity" (Gregory, 2016, p. 165; cf. Collinson, 1988). Gay men, even though sometimes considered inferior in the hegemonic masculine locker room, also find that they are weaponized by hegemonic men to score points by making non-gay men appear weak.

Gruden also called gay men "queers" and straight men who angered him "faggots" and "pussies" (Belson & Rosman, 2021). In addition, Gruden complained that the N.F.L. Commissioner had pressured a head coach to "draft 'queers'" after the team selected Michael Sam (Belson & Rosman, 2021), who in 2014 would have been the first openly gay player in the N.F.L. (Sam was cut before the season began). The sexist and homophobic banter and comments illustrate how certain forms of masculine embodiment are privileged and how hegemonic bodies represent power and superiority. In spaces and organizations where women, LGBTQ+, Asian, Black, brown and immigrant bodies are constructed as inferior, ridiculed and targeted, their bodies are also used as weapons to label and disparage even straight white powerful men.

Locker rooms can be spaces of personal insults, where men embody forms of hegemonic masculinity to claim their "status" over marginalized groups, and, to reduce selected hegemonic men to a marginalized group. The frequency of "gay" and "feminized" personal insults illustrate how fragile hegemonic masculinity is, while at the same time being a condition that many men will fight to maintain. For example, Gruden called Roger Goodell, the N.F.L. Commissioner, who arguably is the most powerful man in American sports, a "faggot" and a "clueless anti-football pussy" (Belson & Rosman, 2021). In addition, even powerful white heterosexual men not associated with the N.F.L., such as then Vice-President Joseph R. Biden in 2012, were called a "nervous clueless pussy" by Gruden. Eventually, Gruden explained that he used these references because he was angry with these men, and regarding Goodell, he was upset over the Commissioner's concussion safety protocols, a move he felt would lead to parents dissuading their "children from playing football" (Mortensen, 2021). In addition, Gruden was angry with the Commissioner's more recent support for Black racial equality initiatives after years of some players' silent protest before games – in a league where approximately 65% of players are Black. Like some men, policies and positions are "queered", and demonized if they do not match up to gendered, racial and sexual hegemonic masculine constructions.

Although research shows how gendered homophobic banter among athletes, with the goal of enhancing one's performance, exists (Adams et al., 2010; Newman et al., 2021), less is known about elite male officials in sports organizations. Even off the field, homophobic comments aimed at other men can illustrate that their masculine performances are not masculine or superior enough. The locker room is a unique space to understand how certain types of hegemonic masculine performance are codified, as well as the responses to men who are seen to have failed at upholding dominant forms of masculinity.

Even though hegemonic masculinity is fluid, temporal and contextual, the lack of elite gay male athletes in professional sports is telling. In 2021, N.F.L. player Carl Nassib (who coincidentally played for Gruden until he resigned) announced he was gay, as did Australian soccer star Josh Cavallo, and the National Hockey League's Luke Prokop. Former N.F.L. player Wade Davis, Jr. argued that "macho" masculine performances clearly involve sexuality: "There's a certain type of macho that one knows that they have to perform in order to attempt to be accepted . . . So I was very conscious of the way that I walked, the way that I talked" (Buchh, 2021). Retired athletes who are gay, such as Davis, Jason Collins and others, acknowledge that now there is greater acceptance of gay people; however, homophobia in the locker room illustrates the challenges in changing pressure to conform. For many, it is easier and safer to wait until they retire and from a chronological distance criticize the culture that once paid, but simultaneously violated, them (cf. Alsarve, 2022).

In their study on sports journalists' views on gay men in sports, Kian et al. (2013) argue that because "homophobia has decrease[d], hegemonic masculinity theory is losing favour among a new generation of sport scholars" (2013, p. 898). Although much has changed since Connell's early scholarship on hegemonic masculinity, it is debatable whether Kian et al.'s assessment of the waning significance of hegemonic masculinity is accurate – at least in certain situations. Gruden's homophobic comments to describe and delegitimize gay and straight men, made during a similar period when Kian et al.'s research was published, suggest that in some circumstances homophobia remains an important feature of hegemonic masculinity, at least in private and informal spaces. Senior officials making public homophobic comments have certainly diminished drastically, although it is less clear how homophobic comments surface in private – hence, the importance of the Gruden emails.

Kian et al. (2013) also found that in the United States some reporters "wonder about the sexual orientations" of "some athletes" such as male figure skaters, because "extreme gender non-conformity" (men being "effeminate") "is stigmatized", but not "homosexuality" (p. 903; cf. McCormack, 2012). However, Gruden's homophobic comments to attack and marginalize heterosexual men in power who are not "effeminate" and who have largely conformed to gendered expectations of masculinity suggest that sometimes homophobic comments are used to disparage gender-conforming men. Furthermore, there are those who have made statements showing they are publicly accepting of gay men but privately make homophobic comments, such as Gruden, illustrating the complexity and non-linear path regarding the social acceptance of the LGBTQ+ community.

Clinging to hegemonic masculinity, even privately, by some strongmen, such as Gruden, is a feature of holding on to the type of power that they, and others, have benefited from. However, the weaponization of gender and sexuality to "diminish" other men illustrates how men can lose their "membership" in the hegemonic masculinity club. Hegemonic masculinity is itself about competition, adhering to certain principles and behaviours so as not to risk being marginalized as a man (Connell, 2005). The next section explores constructions of hypermasculinity and white masculinity through the N.F.L.'s concussion protocol.

However, policies and actions that involve caring about health and safety are "queered" by some strongmen.

Hegemonic masculinity on the ropes: playing while hurt is masculine, concussions are not

When a boxer has an opponent "on the ropes", it means that a boxer has physically manoeuvered the opponent into a defensive position against the ropes and the opponent is in trouble of losing the match. For some men, their membership in the male-dominant club is metaphorically on the ropes because of their (less macho) principles of how American football should be played or governed. Similar tendencies have been noticed in completely different contexts. When a TV reporter in Sweden raised the problem that players in the Swedish Hockey League (SHL) had suffered from several head injuries and suggested that the women's hockey rules (where checking is not allowed) should be introduced, he was met with scornful reactions and laughter from the experts (Karlsson, 2016). Such anxieties echo Connell's (2005) accentuating of the specific situation's importance and how hegemonic notions of masculinities are maintained situationally alongside structural aspects (such as rules, economic conditions, etc.).

American football is a sport that requires as many skills as there are positions, from exceptional athleticism, quickness, flexibility, hand-eye coordination, brute strength, and psychological and mental intelligence and sharpness. It is also a violent game. Additionally, violent metaphors such as "blitz" and "warriors" are synonymous with the sport, as are "motivational" talks by coaches and senior officials. Before a playoff game on 16 January 2022, Steelers' head coach Mike Tomlin told his team that this would not be a game where they could afford to "blink" (lose focus), and he added: "if you're a blinker, cut your eyelids off" (Gaydos, 2022). In addition, Alsarve (2021) shows how ice hockey coaches motivate and instruct players to pick a fight with an opponent to create an advantage through using special teams. The connection between masculinity, ice hockey, football, and other sports and war and the military is decades old (see, for example, Dunning & Maguire, 1996; Messner, 1990; Young, 1993). Displaying courage in a battle, game or war can mean taking risks and being fearless. Football customs represent the "social reproduction of masculinity", including "inflicting pain" on opponents and the ability to "endure pain" (Sabo & Panepinto, 1990, p. 117). Despite the use of "gladiator" references and metaphors to construct the game's identity, not every athlete would agree that playing through injuries is productive.

Yet, playing while hurt is also sometimes part of the construction of hegemonic masculinity. To some, the N.F.L.'s efforts to protect players' bodies and minds are equated with femininity and men who are perceived as weak – those who do not display hypermasculinity and dominance, key elements in the game. American football embodies one of the most physical forms of masculinity: toughness, brutality, fearlessness, domination and risk-taking in the form of men getting hit and hitting hard to the point of sometimes causing life-altering injuries. A concern for players' health that results in minimizing dangerous hits and tackles is constructed as weakness and submission. It is not uncommon to hear football analysts, such as Pro Hall of Famer Troy Aikman, valorize those who play with injuries and through pain. Playing while hurt is a moral feat, an invitation to a prized form of masculinity. It is interpreted as proof of a player's dedication and commitment to winning, qualities attractive to both teammates and coaches (Robidoux, 2001; Young, 2012).

The culture's reproductive force lies in young players being fostered in similar pain-denying and non-whining codes of conduct (Alsarve, 2018, 2022). As in all sports, players can and are replaced with younger, stronger and healthier ones. These athletes must, in turn, prove to be made of the "right stuff". For decades, several examples of ice hockey rookies being humiliated in forced hyper-sexualized and homoerotic hazing rituals have surfaced – abuses committed by teammates with coaches and team management fully aware of its presence (Campbell, 2020; Crow & Macintosh, 2009; Hernqvist, 2021). Besides its degrading and maladaptive dimensions, hazing has been considered a traditional part of athlete socialization where young players or practitioners enter the next stage level of their careers (Waldron & Kowalski, 2009). Most importantly, hazing underscores the culture's power dynamics, where the novice and the peer group learn their lack of power which justifies the veterans' dominance.

These types of actions, values and powers create a system where older or more highly ranked people are given legitimacy to control the subordinated with degrading methods. Therefore, political strongmen also see a value in upholding sports cultures' prevailing hegemonic ideals; change can threaten their own position. In 2016, then Presidential candidate Donald J. Trump mocked the N.F.L.'s concern about concussions, referring to them as "a little ding on the head" (Guarino, 2016). The intersection of sports and masculinity is political, and a country's elite male sports can be interpreted as a reflection of a nation's hegemony, imagined or real, and the men/masculinities who make this possible. The masculinization of injury and illness differentiates the "strong men" from the "weak". Strongmen, either politicians or sports personnel, use what they see as dominant physical masculine embodiment to glorify their "winning" policies and to separate the "winners" from the "losers". In political spaces, the masculinization of illness or injury has also been associated with a tough pro-white masculine nationalistic agenda. Guarino argues that Trump's disparaging comments about "softer" concussion protocols were not the first time he addressed "what he [saw] as weakness in modern football. During a campaign rally . . . he said football has become soft like our country has become soft" (2016). Concussion protocols become a metaphor for the (negative) state of the nation and are used to invoke a loss of national manliness and thus, change of the hegemonic power order.

Sex(ualiti)es are effective components and a reproductive force in sports organizations and in the more general power games between strongmen. Regarding Gruden calling the football commissioner a "faggot" and a "clueless anti-football pussy" because of his concussion protocol, we see how gay men are used as metaphors for "weakness" in a sport. Men who "show" concern about health and safety are feminized, and consequently their dominant status is called into question. In a hypermasculine game, a line demarcates hypermasculine embodiment such as "inflicting pain" and "enduring pain" (Sabo & Panepinto, 1990) from caring about pain and "weaknesses".

A "manly" response to illness and injury becomes part of the dominant forms of masculine embodiment. Publicly making light of a serious illness or brain injury that for some men will result in memory loss, depression, suicide and premature death from degenerative brain disease is similar to a militaristic culture that requires sacrifice in defeat of the enemy. The N.F.L. has finally acknowledged the connection between football and degenerative brain diseases such as CTE (chronic traumatic encephalopathy); one of the most significant studies a few years ago found that approximately 40% of retired N.F.L. players had suffered brain injuries (American Academy of Neurology, 2016). A recent study found that N.F.L. players were four times more likely to develop ALS (amyotrophic lateral sclerosis also known as

Lou Gehrig's disease), which is fatal, than the adult male population (Hernandez, 2021). Similarly, another study of college football players found serious health effects from repeated blows to the head (Moody, 2021).

American football is clearly more than a game, and more health damaging than "a little ding on the head". These "little dings on the head" have racial implications in a sport that is so-called race neutral. In 2021, the N.F.L. stopped using "race-norming" to determine financial awards paid to retired players suffering from dementia and other serious neurological disorders from brain injuries sustained during their careers (Belson, 2021; The Associated Press, 2021). Until the N.F.L. stopped this practice in 2021, which had begun in 2013 when the N.F.L agreed to a landmark US$765 million concussion settlement (Belson, 2013), the cognitive abilities of Black players were deemed "naturally" lower than those of white players, which meant that any cognitive impairment that Black players sustained due to football was assessed as less variable or substantial – the assumption was that they had lower cognitive levels, to begin with. The result was the Black players received less money for the same cognitive declines demonstrated by white players. Even in a sport where Black male athletes dominate the field, they can still end up being penalized for being minorities.

Strong men representing strong men

As we have illustrated, some political strongmen like former President Trump have invoked sports tropes not just as a way of constructing and re-affirming male privilege and superiority but also to address nationalist male fears regarding what they believe is a "softening" (feminizing) of their countries. In Spring 2020, one of the worst periods of the COVID-19 pandemic globally, the Brazilian President, Jair Bolsonaro, advocated for the return of football men's competitions in his country. Bolsonaro argued that: "in the case of o jogador (male player) contracting the virus, the chances of them passing away is infinitesimally small on account of their optimum physical state" (Veja, 2020). Only the bodies of elite male athletes are "seen" as they embody and symbolize a defence against COVID-19, much like footballers mount a game defence. Male Brazilian footballers represent strong men for a strongman. In addition, the references to corporeal hegemony serve as a metaphor for how important men's football is to the country's financial interests, revenues and media attention – not only in Brazil but in most other countries (cf. Bryan et al., 2021). The gendered hierarchy of football in Brazil is in part rooted in the history and legacy of the men's national team, which is one of the most successful in winning World Cups – but also its significance to the nation's identity. The importance of the competitive, athletic male body is symbolic of domination and invincibility – not just in the sport but also in a nation (cf. Allain, 2008, 2011).

Strongmen like Bolsonaro, Gruden and Trump valorize the male athletic body, its achievements, and in the case of Trump, advocate for some of the most extreme aspects of masculinity in sports. Furthermore, men's dominant sports become a metaphor for the nation's identity and dominance. Trump reinforces the militarization aspect of American football but also the masculine identity of the country. Unlike some other elite men who reserve their social and political views for private spaces where they feel safe, Trump expresses his views publicly, validating what many feel that they cannot say in the open. This is an example of how with some strongmen, the private also becomes public.

The role of hegemonic masculinity in sports and in other spaces is complex and nuanced, and for some men, their masculinity is on the ropes. Furthermore, playing violently and while hurt comes at a cost for many, another reminder of the real dangers of embracing the most aggressive aspects of a sport that is both electrifying and brutal.

Conclusion

In this chapter, we have argued for the relevance and continued fruitfulness of critically understanding gendered power as hegemony and men and certain masculinities as hegemonic. By highlighting both contemporary and historical episodes, we have demonstrated how misogynist, homophobic and other disparaging strategies become enduring and useful factors in re-affirming hegemony. We have been interested in how the reproduction of men's power is taking place beyond the public light. In this way, our chapter becomes a contribution to the research on discrepancies between policy and practice pointing to what seemingly progressive and formal policies can achieve in terms of discrimination and humiliation. We have shown not only how a hegemonic culture is stabilized but also how hegemonic positions constantly need to be motivated and secured. In the extended, digitalized and symbolized locker room of power, power resources are always at stake.

In an era of strongmen, in sports and politics, competitive men's sports and sports policies symbolize not only, to some, how masculine, feminine or queer a game is, but also a nation's identity. Gains in gender, racial and LGBTQ+ equality and the resistance to misogyny, racism, and homophobia in sports and society have been remarkable over the past few decades. However, in some places and spaces, there are those who unapologetically advocate for and reinforce a type of white re-masculinization of society, illustrating not just societal and institutional conflict but also the many and varied debates regarding the state of hegemonic masculinities.

Notes

1 This audio recording was used as evidence in a court case where, on 9 May 2023, former President Trump was found liable for the sexual abuse and defamation of plaintiff E. Jean Carroll and was ordered to pay Ms. Carroll US$5 million. In a deposition where Mr. Trump was questioned about his comments in the audio, his response was, "Well, historically, that's true with stars." He further added, ". . . if you look over the last million years, I guess that's been largely true, . . . unfortunately or fortunately" (Weiser et al., 2023).

2 Only one year after Ozanian and Settimi's article was published in 2021, the valuations of the 32 teams increased in range from US$2 billion to US$6.5 billion to US$3 billion to US$8 billion, an increase of between 50% and 23% (Ozanian & Teitelbaum, 2022). This illustrates how the COVID-19 pandemic, while exacerbating economic inequality, was an asset for many of the ultra-wealthy, such as N.F.L. owners.

3 The team's original name, from 1933 to 2019, was the "Washington Redskins", a term that is offensive to many Native Americans. The name was changed to the "Washington Team" in 2020 in response to years of criticism of the original name, and in 2022 the name was changed to the "Commanders" (Belson, 2022).

References

Adams, A., Anderson, E., & McCormack, M. (2010). Establishing and challenging masculinity: The influence of gendered discourses in organized sport. *Journal of Language and Social Psychology*, *29*(3), 278–300. doi: 10.1177/0261927X10368833

Allain, K. A. (2008). "Real fast and tough": The construction of Canadian hockey masculinity. *Sociology of Sport Journal*, 25(4), 462–481. doi: 10.1123/ssj.25.4.462

Allain, K. A. (2011). Kid Crosby or Golden boy: Sidney Crosby, Canadian national identity, and the policing of hockey masculinity. *International Review for the Sociology of Sport*, 46(1), 3–22. doi: 10.1177/1012690210376294

Alsarve, D. (2018). 'Power in the arm, steel in the will and courage in the breast' – a historical approach to ideal norms and men's dominance in Swedish club sports. *Sport in History*, *38*(3), 365–402. doi: 10.1080/17460263.2018.1496948

Alsarve, D. (2021). The need for a violence prevention programme in ice hockey: A case study on how hegemonic masculinity supports and challenges violent behaviour in Swedish ice hockey. *European Sport Management Quarterly*, *21*(2), 218–236. doi: 10.1080/16184742.2020.1737956

Alsarve, D. (2022). Historicizing machoism in Swedish ice hockey. *The International Journal of the History of Sport*, *38*(16), 1688–1709. doi: 10.1080/09523367.2021.2022649

Alsarve, D., & Angelin, M. (2020). 'It's freer and easier in a changing room, because the barriers disappear . . .': A case study of masculinity ideals, language and social status amongst Swedish ice hockey players. *European Journal for Sport and Society*, *17*(1), 26–46. doi: 10.1080/16138171.2019.1706239

Alsarve, D., & Tjønndal, A. (2019). 'The Nordic female fighter': Exploring women's participation in mixed martial arts in Norway and Sweden. *International Review for the Sociology of Sport*, *55*(4), 471–489. doi: 10.1177/1012690218822307

American Academy of Neurology (2016). Study: More than 40 Percent of Retired NFL Players Had Brain Injury. Retrieved 11 April from www.aan.com/pressroom/home/pressrelease/1453

Anton, T. (2011). NFL's Anti Discrimination Policy Includes Sexual Orientation. Retrieved 27 September from https://bleacherreport.com/articles/868038-nfls-anti-discrimination-policy-includes-sexual-orientation

Antunovic, D., & Linden, A. D. (2020). "Powerful lessons" in women's sport: ESPN's nine for IX series. *Journal of Sport and Social Issues*, *44*(6), 534–549. doi: 10.1177/0193723519899245

Around the NFL Staff. (2021). NFL fines Washington Football Team $10M Following Investigation into Team Culture. Retrieved 1 July, from ESPN: www.espn.com/nfl/story/_/id/31745729/nfl-fines-washington-football-team-10m-culture-investigation

Battista, J. (2020). NFL Commits $250M Over 10-year Period to Combat Systemic Racism. Retrieved 11 June from www.nfl.com/news/nfl-commits-250m-over-10-year-period-to-combat-systemic-racism

Belson, K. (2013). N.F.L. Agrees to Settle Concussion Suit for $765 Million. Retrieved 29 August, from The New York Times: www.nytimes.com/2013/08/30/sports/football/judge-announces-settlement-in-nfl-concussion-suit.html

Belson, K. (2021). N.F.L. Concussion Settlement Will Drop Race-Based Assessment for Payouts. Retrieved 2 June, from The New York Times: www.nytimes.com/2021/06/02/sports/football/nfl-concussion-settlement-race.html

Belson, K. (2022). With Commanders, the Washington N. F. L. Franchise Moves Past Old Name. Retrieved 2 February, from The New York Times: www.nytimes.com/2022/02/02/sports/washington-football-team-commanders.html

Belson, K., & Rosman, K. (2021). Raiders Coach Resigns after Homophobic and Misogynistic Emails. Retrieved 11 October, from The New York Times: www.nytimes.com/2021/10/11/sports/football/what-did-jon-gruden-say.html

Ben-Ghiat, R. (2021). *Strongmen: Mussolini to the Present*. New York: W.W. Norton & Company.

Buchh, Z. (2021). Wade Davis Jr. Describes The Fear Of Being Outed While He Was in the NFL. Retrieved 24 June, from NPR: www.npr.org/2021/06/24/1009750956/wade-davis-jr-describes-the-fear-of-being-outed-while-he-was-in-the-nfl

Bryan, A., Pope, S., & Rankin-Wright, A. J. (2021). On the periphery: Examining women's exclusion from core leadership roles in the "extremely gendered" organization of men's club football in England. *Gender & Society*, *35*(6), 940–970. doi: 10.1177/08912432211046318

Bryson, L. (1990). Challenges to male hegemony in sport. In M. A. Messner & D. F. Sabo (Eds.), *Sport, Men, and the Gender Order: Critical Feminist Perspectives* (pp. 173–184). Champaign, IL: Human Kinetics Books.

Butterworth, M. L. (2014). The athlete as citizen: Judgement and rhetorical invention in sport. *Sport in Society*, *17*(7), 867–883. doi: 10.1080/17430437.2013.806033

Campbell, K. (2020). Shocking Allegations in CHL Lawsuit Detail Sexual Abuse and 'a Deviant Culture'. Retrieved 9 December, from The Hockey News: https://thehockeynews.com/news/shocking-allegations-in-chl-lawsuit-detail-sexual-abuse-and-a-deviant-culture

Carrigan, T., Connell, B., & Lee, J. (1985). Toward a new sociology of masculinity. *Theory and Society*, 14(5), 551–604.
Claringbould, I., & Knoppers, A. (2012). Paradoxical practices of gender in sport-related organizations. *Journal of Sport Management*, *26*(5), 404–416. doi: 10.1123/jsm.26.5.404
Collinson, D. L. (1988). 'Engineering humour': Masculinity, joking and conflict in shop-floor relations. *Organization Studies*, *9*(2), 181–199. doi: 10.1177/017084068800900203
Connell, R. (2005). *Masculinities*. Cambridge: Polity Press.
Connell, R. (2006). Glass ceilings or gendered institutions? Mapping the gender regimes of public sector worksites. *Public Administration Review*, *66*(6), 837–849. doi: 10.1111/j.1540-6210.2006.00652.x
Connell, R. W., & Messerschmidt, J. W. (2005). Hegemonic masculinity: Rethinking the concept. *Gender & Society*, *19*(6), 829–859. 10.1177/0891243205278639
Cooky, C., Messner, M. A., & Musto, M. (2015). "It's dude time!": A quarter century of excluding women's sports in televised news and highlight shows. *Communication & Sport*, *3*(3), 261–287. doi: 10.1177/2167479515588761
Crow, R. B., & Macintosh, E. W. (2009). Conceptualizing a meaningful definition of hazing in sport. *European Sport Management Quarterly*, *9*(4), 433–451. doi: 10.1080/16184740903331937
Dunning, E. G., & Maguire, J. (1996). Process-sociological notes on sport, gender relations and violence control. *International Review for the Sociology of Sport*, *31*(3), 295–319. doi: 10.1177/101269029603100305
Epstein, R. J. (2016, October 10). Rudy Giuliani makes 'locker room' Joke at Rally. *The Wall Street Journal*. Retrieved from www.wsj.com/articles/BL-WB-65940
Gaydos, R. (2022). Steelers' Mike Tomlin Reveals Final Message to Team: 'If You're a Blinker, Cut Your Eyelids Off'. Retrieved 16 January, from Fox News: www.foxnews.com/sports/steelers-mike-tomlin-message-blinker-eyelids-off
Giazitzoglu, A. (2022). Masculinity, embodiment and identity-work: How do organisational members use their bodies as identity resources to (re) accomplish hegemonic masculinity? *Organization*, 1–24. doi: 10.1177/13505084221074041
Gilenstam, K., Karp, S., & Henriksson-Larsén, K. (2008). Gender in ice hockey: Women in a male territory. *Scandinavian Journal of Medicine & Science in Sports*, *18*(2), 235–249. doi: 10.1111/j.1600-0838.2007.00665.x
Gregory, M. R. (2009). Inside the locker room: Male homosociability in the advertising industry. *Gender, Work & Organization*, *16*(3), 323–347. https://onlinelibrary.wiley.com/doi/10.1111/j.1468-0432.2009.00447.x
Gregory, M. R. (2011). 'The faggot clause': The embodiment of homophobia in the corporate locker room. *Equality, Diversity and Inclusion: An International Journal*, *30*(8), 651–667. doi: 10.1108/02610151111183180
Gregory, M. R. (2016). *The Face of the Firm: Corporate Hegemonic Masculinity at Work*. New York and London: Routledge.
Guarino, B. (2016). Trump Knocks 'Softer' NFL Rules: 'Concussions – 'Uh Oh Got A Little Ding on the Head?' Retrieved 13 October, from The Washington Post: www.washingtonpost.com/news/morning-mix/wp/2016/10/13/trump-just-criticized-the-nfls-softer-rules-intended-to-help-protect-players-from-traumatic-brain-injury/
Hearn, J. (2004). From hegemonic masculinity to the hegemony of men. *Feminist theory*, *5*(1), 49–72. doi:10.1177/1464700104040813
Hearn, J., & Howson, R. (2020). Hegemony, hegemonic masculinity, and beyond. In L. Gottzén, U. Mellström, & T. Shefer (Eds.), *Routledge International Handbook of Masculinity Studies* (pp. 41–51). New York: Routledge.
Hernandez, J. (2021). NFL Players are Four Times More Likely to Develop ALS, a New Study Shows. Retrieved 16 December, from NPR: www.npr.org/live-updates/morning-edition-2021-12-16#nfl-players-are-four-times-more-likely-to-develop-als-a-new-study-shows
Hernqvist, D. (2021). 'Inkilningar pågår definitivt i dag' ['Hazing is definitely happening today']. Retrieved 6 November, from Svenska Dagbladet: www.svd.se/inkilningar-pagar-definitivt-i-dag
Jansen, S. C., & Sabo, D. F. (1994). The sport/war metaphor: Hegemonic masculinity, the Persian Gulf War, and the New World Order. *Sociology of Sport Journal*, *11*, 1–17. doi: 10.1123/ssj.11.1.1
Karlsson, E. (2016). Wikegårds hån mot damhockeyreglerna [Wikegård's mockery of the women's hockey rules]. Retrieved 4 February, from Aftonbladet: Wikegårds hån mot damhockeyreglerna (aftonbladet.se)

Keneally, M. (2020). List of Trump's Accusers and Their Allegations of Sexual Misconduct. Retrieved 18 September, from ABC News: https://abcnews.go.com/Politics/list-trumps-accusers-allegations-sexual-misconduct/story?id=51956410

Kian, E. M., Anderson, E., Vincent, J., & Murray, R. (2013). Sport journalists' views on gay men in sport, society and within sport media. *International Review for the Sociology of Sport, 50*(8), 895–911. doi: 10.1177/1012690213504101

Knoppers, A., & Anthonissen, A. (2008). Gendered Managerial Discourses in Sport Organizations: Multiplicity and Complexity. *Sex Roles, 58*(1), 93–103. doi: 10.1007/s11199-007-9324-z

Kurtzleben, D. (2020). Trump Has Weaponized Masculinity as President. Here's Why It Matters. Retrieved 28 October, from NPR: www.npr.org/2020/10/28/928336749/trump-has-weaponized-masculinity-as-president-heres-why-it-matters

Macur, J. (2018). Washington Redskins Cheerleaders Describe Topless Photo Shoot and Uneasy Night Out. Retrieved 2 May, from The New York Times: www.nytimes.com/2018/05/02/sports/redskins-cheerleaders-nfl.html

Makela, M. (2016). Transcript: Donald Trump's Taped Comments About Women. Retrieved 16 October, from The New York Times: www.nytimes.com/2016/10/08/us/donald-trump-tape-transcript.html

McCormack, M. (2012). *The Declining Significance of Homophobia: How Teenage Boys are Redefining Masculinity and Heterosexuality.* New York: Oxford University Press. doi: 10.1093/acprof:oso/9780199778249.001.0001

McKay, J., Messner, M. A., & Sabo, D. F. (2000). *Masculinities, Gender Relations, and Sport.* Thousand Oaks, CA: SAGE.

Messner, M. A. (1990). When bodies are weapons: Masculinity and violence in Sport. *International Review for the Sociology of Sport, 25*(3), 203–220. doi: 10.1177/101269029002500303

Messner, M. A. (1992). *Power at Play: Sports and the Problem of Masculinity.* Boston, MA: Beacon Press.

Messner, M. A. (2007). *Out of play: Critical Essays on Gender and Sport.* Albany NY: State University of New York Press.

Messner, M. A., Dunbar, M., & Hunt, D. (2000). The televised sports manhood formula. *Journal of Sport and Social Issues, 24*(4), 380–394. doi:10.1177/0193723500244006

Moody, J. (2021). Study: Football Head Trauma Linked to Health Abnormalities. Retrieved 17 December, from Inside Higher Ed: www.insidehighered.com/quicktakes/2021/12/17/study-football-head-trauma-linked-health-abnormalities

Mortensen, C. (2021). Gruden Disparaged Goodell in 2011 Email. Retrieved 10 October, from ESPN: www.espn.com/video/clip/clip?id=32372800

Newman, J. A., Eccles, A., Rumbold, J. L., & Rhind, D. J. A. (2021). When it is no longer a bit of banter: Coaches' perspectives of bullying in professional soccer. *International Journal of Sport and Exercise Psychology, 20*(6), 1576–1593. doi: 10.1080/1612197X.2021.1987966

NFL Owners Endorse New Personal Conduct Policy. (2014). Retrieved 10 December, from www.nfl.com/news/nfl-owners-endorse-new-personal-conduct-policy-0ap3000000441758

Ozanian, M., & Settimi, C. (2021). The NFL's Most Valuable Teams 2021: Average Team Value Soars to $3.5 Billion As League Shrugs Off Pandemic Year. Retrieved 5 August, from Forbes: www.forbes.com/sites/mikeozanian/2021/08/05/the-nfls-most-valuable-teams-2021-average-team-value-soars-to-35-billion-as-league-shrugs-off-pandemic-year/?sh=51f4fb66654e

Ozanian, M., & Teitelbaum, J. (2022). NFL Team Values 2022: Dallas Cowboys Are The First Franchise Worth $8 Billion. Retrieved 22 August, from Forbes: www.forbes.com/sites/mikeozanian/2022/08/22/nfl-team-values-2022-dallas-cowboys-are-the-first-franchise-worth-8-billion/?sh=1245007f6365

Robidoux, M. A. (2001). *Men at Play: A Working Understanding of Professional Hockey.* Montréal: McGill-Queen's University Press.

Sabo, D. (2004). The politics of sport injury: Hierarchy, power, and the pain principle. In K. Young (Ed.), *Sporting Bodies, Damaged Selves: Sociological Studies of Sports-related Injuries* (pp. 59–80). Bingley, England: Emerald.

Sabo, D. F., & Panepinto, J. (1990). Football ritual and the social reproduction of masculinity. In M. A. Messner & D. F. Sabo (Eds.), *Sport, Men, and the Gender Order: Critical Feminist Perspectives* (pp. 115–126). Champaign, IL: Human Kinetics Books.

Sanderson, J., & Cassilo, D. (2019). "I'm glad I played when the country still had gonads": Pop Warner's kickoff policy change and the framing of health and safety initiatives in football. *Journal of Sports Media*, *14*(1–2), 1–22. doi: 10.1353/jsm.2019.0002

Schad, T., & Jones, M. (2021). Jon Gruden, Raiders coach, resigns as homophobic, misogynistic comments are revealed in emails. Retrieved 11 October, from USA Today: www.usatoday.com/story/sports/nfl/raiders/2021/10/11/jon-gruden-raiders-coach-resigning-homophobic-misogynistic-racist-emails-nfl/6098552001/

The Associated Press. (2021). The NFL Will Stop Assuming Racial Differences When Assessing Brain Injuries. Retrieved 1 June, from NPR: www.npr.org/2021/06/02/1002627309/nfl-says-it-will-halt-race-norming-and-review-brain-injury-claims

Veja (2020). Bolsonaro Defende Volta do Futebol: 'Desemprego bate à porta dos clubes'. Retrieved 1 May, from https://headtopics.com/br/bolsonaro-defende-volta-do-futebol-desemprego-bate-a-porta-dos-clubes-12766798

Waldron, J. J., & Kowalski, C. L. (2009). Crossing the line: Rites of passage, team aspects, and ambiguity of hazing. *Research Quarterly For Exercise And Sport*, *80*(2), 291–302. doi: 10.1080/02701367.2009.10599564

Weiser, B., Fadulu, L., & Christokbek, K. (2023). In Rape Trial Deposition Video, Trump Says Vulgar Tape Simply Reflects Truth. Retrieved 4 May, from The New York Times: www.nytimes.com/2023/05/04/nyregion/e-jean-carroll-trump-rape-trial.html

Young, K. (1993). Violence, risk, and liability in male sports culture. *Sociology of Sport Journal*, *10*(4), 373–396. doi: 10.1123/ssj.10.4.373

Young, K. (2012). *Sport, Violence and Society*. London: Routledge.

22

(UN)DOING MASCULINITY? MEN WORKING IN WOMEN'S OCCUPATIONS

Julia Nentwich and Chieh Hsu

Introduction

Still today occupations are gender-segregated. There are occupations that are predominantly taken up by either women or men. Over the last 30 years, a still-growing body of research has developed, especially in occupations with more established organizational settings. In exploring men's situation in women's occupations, research has mainly focused on healthcare and nursing (Asakura & Watanabe, 2011; Cottingham et al., 2016; Dill et al., 2016; Evans, 2008; McDonald, 2013; McDowell, 2015; Panopio, 2010; Price-Glynn & Rakovski, 2012), care work (Husso & Hirvonen, 2012; Näre, 2010; Nyaga & Torres, 2017), child care and early childhood education (Buschmeyer, 2013; Choi, 2018; Chen, 2019; Chen & Wang, 2020; Hellman et al., 2015; Nentwich et al., 2013; Warin, 2006, 2019), primary school teachers (Cushman, 2005; Simpson, 2004, 2005; Smedley, 2007), body-related professions such as hairdressing (Chen, 2017) and beauty work (Ahmed, 2006), service jobs such as flight attendance (Ferguson & Ayuttacorn, 2019; Simpson, 2004, 2005), administrative support (Van Antwerpen & Ferreira, 2010), as well as domestic labour (Näre, 2010) and cleaning services (Choi, 2018). In terms of less structured work, Agadjanian (2005) investigated the female profession of street vending, and Scott et al. (2021) explored the experiences of male sex workers. Some studies have also compared distinctive situations for men across different female-dominated jobs (Cross & Bagilhole, 2002; Hayes, 1989; Lupton, 2000; Simpson, 2004, 2005, 2012; Ma & Yeh, 2008).

These studies reveal that men working in female-dominated occupations often experience "identity dissonance" (Warin, 2006). They are held accountable as men and at the same time as professionals in their respective fields. Research on men in female-dominated occupations hence sheds light on the significance of context in the construction of gendered identities. Are male identities equally contested for those working across various types of female occupations? How do men cope with these challenges? Do men experience discrimination in similar ways that women experience token status in male-dominated professions? Or are they as men rather in a privileged situation and "riding the glass escalator"? Research on men in female-dominated occupations has provided us with some answers. In a nutshell, findings mainly concern men's ambivalent privilege and their strategies in the face of identity challenges.

DOI: 10.4324/9781003193579-25

First of all, men working in female-dominated professions are often "jockeying for position" (Edley & Wetherell, 1997). They experience "identity dissonance" (Warin, 2006), a feeling of pressure to perform a stable identity that can be particularly stressful in a situation with conflicting norms. As men working in female-dominated jobs need to perform as men and as professionals, they are called into different subject positions (Nentwich et al., 2013). The resulting insecurity needs to be "managed" (Collinson, 2003) and research shows that men are developing different strategies to cope, notably "boundary work" and "alternative masculinities". Engaging in boundary work, men aim at securing a certain masculine identity by distancing themselves from female colleagues and female-connoted tasks in their jobs. This way, their masculinity is secured, and the feeling of identity dissonance is muted. Practicing "alternative" masculinities (Lupton, 2000; Cameron, 2001; Cross & Bagilhole, 2002; Buschmeyer, 2013), men follow a different strategy. By appropriating femininity (Pullen & Simpson, 2009), they create alternative positions for becoming men. In consequence, the conflict between their masculine and professional identities is dissolved by reconsidering the gendered norms at work (Brody, 2015). The two strategies of boundary work and the creation of alternative masculinities allow men to cope with identity dissonance in distinctively different ways (Nentwich et al., 2013).

Furthermore, masculinity is closely connected to status and privilege (Connell, 1995; Williams, 1992; Simpson, 2010; Schwiter et al., 2021). For instance, men earn higher wages compared to women, both in male- and in female-dominated occupations (Budig, 2002; O'Reilly et al., 2015). Evidence suggests that masculine qualities are more appreciated and remunerated even in predominantly female professions (Williams, 2015, p. 390). While masculinities' connection to power and more broadly to hegemony is a constant and rather stable finding, more recent evidence shows that it is nevertheless more complicated and complex than previous studies of the "glass escalator" (Williams, 1992) have suggested.

In this chapter, we provide an overview of this research, systematically exploring the theoretical insights on the performativity of hegemonic masculinity (Connell, 1995; Wetherell & Edley, 2009, 2014; Edley & Wetherell, 1997) and revisiting the possibilities for undoing masculinity, understood here as developing alternative positions (Nentwich et al., 2013; Kelan, 2018). We at the same time look at cases of doing masculinity, such as men engaging in "protest masculinity" (McDowell et al., 2014) when working in precarious jobs. The chapter is structured chronologically, following the development of academic debates, as well as discourses, on men in female-dominated occupations over the last 30 years. We start with those early studies that shed light on men's privilege and the "glass escalator". We then move on to explore insights from studies on marginalized men and from an intersectional perspective highlighting that privilege is often more ambivalent than originally claimed. Lastly, we look at recent research investigating men working in female-dominated occupations from an identity perspective. In particular, we discuss this research's insights into how male identities are formed by hegemonic masculinity, which is highly dependent on the specific context of the female-dominated occupation. We then share some concluding thoughts on the doing and undoing of masculinity.

Token position and the patriarchal dividend: men benefiting from hegemonic masculinity

Research studying men working in women's occupations shows that men typically enjoy certain privileges. This is different from women working in men's occupations. Women often occupy a token position that characterizes them as "the lacking Other" (Mitchell, 1974), as lacking the competences, interests or agency necessary for doing this particular job. Hence, women mainly receive a negative token effect that puts them under additional pressure to perform and conform to gender norms (Kanter, 1977). However, this is different with men in a token position. They seem to benefit from hidden advantages when in the same situation, unlike token women who are subjected to the "male gaze" (Simpson, 2010, p. 221) and would rather aim for invisibility by keeping a low profile. Men in highly visible positions are generally earning higher wages compared to women, both in male- and female-dominated occupations. They also profit from default privileges granted by gender relations in society at large (Budig, 2002). In sum, existing research has sufficiently shown that "qualities associated with men and masculinity were more highly regarded and rewarded than qualities associated with women and femininity, even in predominantly female professions" (Williams, 2015, p. 390). While women face a "glass ceiling", men ride the "glass escalator" (Williams, 1992).

As a matter of fact, the token position has different consequences for women and men. While being perceived as different is often a positive asset for men in female professions, women describe their token position as an uphill battle. This is what Connell (1995) refers to as "the patriarchal dividend". She describes a general privileging effect that is bestowed on men just because they are men. The "patriarchal dividend" is an effect of hegemonic masculinity (Connell, 1995). Hegemonic masculinity is a power relation that produces different hierarchical positions for men and women. Hegemonic masculinity is performed in everyday practices and also in the workplace. She identified specific "performed" masculinities regarded by society as the aspired form of masculinity, such as being competitive and risk-taking (Connell & Messerschmidt, 2005). The performance of hegemonic masculinity is "mobilized" (Martin, 2001), for instance, by exclusively socializing with men, peacocking or competing with other men and displaying heroic forms of masculinity (Kelan & Wratil, 2017). Engaging in what is seen as hegemonic masculinity, men are constituting a hierarchical relation between different men and different masculinities as well as with regard to women and femininities.

Evidence from nursing in East Asia illustrates how men navigate to secure their positions. Examining the occupational experiences of 12 male nurses in rural Japan, Asakura and Watanabe (2011) found that these men prioritized their breadwinner status and the importance of financial security. They cemented their masculinity and male identity by supporting female colleagues and showing masculine strength where their help is needed, while also developing a "positively" dependent relationship with doctors to perpetuate their dominant position. By establishing these ties with female nurses and doctors, they are able to create a stable position and even stand out in a female-dominated profession. Similarly, Tzeng & Chen (2008) have shown that male nurses in Taiwan tend to adapt to initial pressure and would selectively enter medical units or intensive stations that require and value their physical labour, which very much reinforces their masculine qualities. They simultaneously subscribe more to the aspiration of climbing the occupational ladder to match their "breadwinner status". Though a minority in this profession, they enjoy more authority and are on equal ground in their communication with doctors. Paradoxically, social and gendered expectations of men, shaping much of their subjective development at work, are critical to fostering their professional advances while also precipitating their withdrawal from this career. In both instances, instead of toning down their masculinity in a profession associated with feminine caregiving and emotional labour, male nurses in Japan and Taiwan continue to practise the hierarchical dynamics of hegemonic masculinity and exhibit dominance through their alliance with doctors.

While the display of hegemonic masculinity is a norm that is rarely met by men, they nevertheless are granted a privileged position. That is, men do not have to represent the norm of hegemonic masculinity in all their interactions other than to buy into and be supportive of it (Connell & Messerschmidt, 2005; Messerschmidt, 2018). Connell argues that even men who perform masculinity in alternative ways are benefiting from hegemonic masculinity as they do not actively challenge it (Connell, 1995, p. 79; Wetherell & Edley, 1999, p. 337; Connell & Messerschmidt, 2005, p. 836).

Research investigating men's privileged positions in women's occupations additionally shows that men are often very aware of the special treatment they are receiving. With regard to gender, Simpson (2004) demonstrates that the men working in female-dominated occupations she interviewed in the United Kingdom all felt very comfortable about working in female-dominated fields. Furthermore, they describe working with women as something very positive in the context of being "fast tracked" in their careers and receiving special consideration. For example, they report getting away with more mistakes compared to women and recall being granted more authority because they were men, which is often associated with an over-estimation of their expertise. While these effects are not necessarily perceived as positive and men also describe negative effects, Simpson's study suggests that men are indeed aware of the privilege they are granted when working in a female profession.

A recent study by Schwiter et al. (2021) analysed positioning practices by men working in childcare and nursing in Switzerland. Also here, men are very much aware of situations in which they are receiving more positive attention compared to their female colleagues. However, talking about these situations, they do not frame them as an effect of privilege but rather find different explanations for the special treatment they are receiving. For instance, they would attribute the extra attention to the differences of their male bodies and their specific individual competences and skills. Hence, although very much aware of receiving positive attention, they are refusing to interpret this treatment as a result of privilege. Providing different arguments and understandings, they are actively silencing privilege by explaining it away.

Taken together, we often see different effects for women and men working in gender-atypical professions. While men tend to receive positive treatment in token positions, the reaction women are typically receiving is more negative, such as being marginalized or excluded (Williams, 1989). In addition, men rarely actively contest the "pedestal effect" from which they benefit (Peretz, 2018, p. 2). Therefore, various studies reveal that privilege and the "patriarchal dividend" are something actively achieved and maintained by men in women's occupations (Schwiter et al., 2021).

Marginalized masculinities and intersectionality: men experiencing disadvantage and discrimination

It should be noted that male privilege is not granted to all men equally as more recent research on intersectional masculinities, men doing intimate work and those in precarious jobs is pointing out. For instance, gay, disabled or working-class men are often unable to access some of the privileges attributed to their gender (Wingfield & Myles, 2014, p. 1213). In nursing, for example, race, ethnicity and citizenship seem to be more important than gender when explaining wage differences in the United States (Price-Glynn & Rakovski, 2012). For one, Black male nurses are not mistakenly identified as doctors as is often the case with their white counterparts. As Wingfield (2009) revealed, Black male nurses in the United States tended to be mistaken for janitors or housekeeping staff. This attests to how stereotypes of Black men working in unskilled jobs are reproduced and their professional competences denied (Wingfield, 2009, p. 19). In the case of Norway, employment patterns of male immigrant nurses are more similar to native-born women than to native-born men (Karlsen, 2012). This demonstrates that privilege is "not monolithic" but "unevenly distributed" (Coston & Kimmel, 2012, p. 97) and much dependent on the social categorizations of a person, consequently informing whether an individual will experience privilege or rather marginalization.

When denied male privileges and status, men in fact engage in practices that highlight specific forms of masculinity. An example is that male sex workers in Hong Kong focus on the skill aspect of their craft and emphasize professionalism and their adamant adherence to work ethics, substantiating their craftsman masculinity (Yau & Kong, 2021). These men go to great lengths to retitle the nature of their work and redefine an occupation perceived to be feminine to safeguard their masculinity. Similarly, in the field of early childhood education, men working in nurseries in Switzerland emphasize their professional work and career objectives to secure masculinity (Tennhoff et al., 2015). In Mainland China's ongoing developmental context, however, male sex workers focus on the possibilities of grander pursuits their temporary undertaking may provide, as a transitional "steppingstone" that could help them fulfil their entrepreneurial dreams. Understanding their illicit sex work as transient and aspiring to become small business owners by first engaging in "informal employment", these men exhibit an alternative "guerrilla masculinity" (Yau & Kong, 2021, p. 564). Here, guerrilla masculinity characterizes the strategy of dabbling in irregular and transitory work in the hope of achieving something bigger. Either way, these types of strategic masculinity that grant meanings to more marginalized, highly volatile and less organized jobs conform to a repertoire of hegemonic masculinity that is linking maleness to skill, ventures and entrepreneurship.

However, in female occupations with rigid hierarchies, men's positive treatment can be rather qualified. For example, a study (Ma & Yeh, 2008) that investigates men in traditional women's work in Taiwan found that male nurses are often "passed" when it comes to promotion as a result of gender oppression in the workplace and have to accomplish more than their majority female counterparts in order to be considered. Similarly, in the world of hairdressing where tiered internal structures are in place and accreditation is valued, male stylists must strive to advance their skills and earn credentials lest they be "squeezed" out of competition in a female-dominant environment. Contrary to the notion of their riding the glass escalator, men doing service work that requires and entails some degree of intimacy and care risk not only the refusal of service from some clients but also being marginalized in their professions should they fail to climb the occupational ladder.

This is particularly the case with men working in early childhood education. As masculinity is associated with being rational, distant and less emotional and often also connected to physical and sexual violence, men are often perceived as unsuitable carers, particularly if the work involves close physical contact. Not only are their competences sometimes doubted, but they can also be perceived as dangerous. Masculinity as such is perceived as dangerous, a perception that generalizes violence as an important expression of hegemonic masculinity to individual men (Cremers & Krabel, 2012). As the following quote by Sargent (2005, p. 254) puts it: "Women's laps are places of love. Men's are places of danger". Men working with children are at risk of being perceived as potentially dangerous to children, particularly through highlighting their sexuality (Moss-Racusin & Johnson, 2016). For instance, engaging in mundane tasks requiring physical contact with children, such as changing diapers, putting children to sleep, dressing or comforting a child, puts men at risk of being perceived as paedophile, while this is not the case with women (Brody, 2015; Nentwich et al., 2013; Eidevald et al., 2018).

Men in early childhood education are permanently under suspicion of being harmful to children. This is even more severe in cases with weak or no organizational measurements securing child safety in place (Cremers & Krabel, 2012). Being perceived as a potential threat to children limits men's ability to develop professionalism, interferes with their relationships with children and also excludes men from certain tasks (Cremers & Krabel, 2012). Many try to cope with such predicaments by avoiding certain tasks, doing them in a way that minimizes suspicion or engaging in the task while ignoring the personal risk involved (Eidevald et al., 2018). In a similar vein, studies on Indian and Sri Lankan male domestic workers (Chopra, 2006; Näre, 2010) have clearly suggested that they are expected to "mute their maleness" and desexualize encounters to minimize the sense of threat and danger brought to urban households. Stabilizing their positions as professional workers, men in these occupations need to develop strategies that allow them to circumvent the strong discourse of masculinity as sexualized, threatening and potentially dangerous. As a matter of fact, this is how they create images of caring masculinities (Eidevald et al., 2018).

Studies of men in female-dominated occupations have also highlighted that there are particular groups of men experiencing disadvantage and discrimination in their jobs (McDowell et al., 2014; Christensen & Jensen, 2014). That is to say, the privileging effects of masculinity are closely connected to the intersectionality of masculinity with race, class and sexualities (Coston & Kimmel, 2012; Wingfield & Myles, 2014). Understanding intersectionality therefore allows us to understand more clearly "how being a man can be a category of disempowerment and lack of privilege rather than a privileged position" (Christensen & Jensen, 2014, p. 70). A case in point are men from rural villages employed in garment factories in northeast China. They work alongside women workers who constitute over 90% of the workforce in these garment factories. The men are typically tasked with largely unskilled "heavy-lifting" duties as opposed to women's skilled sewing. The replaceable nature of these men's work, compounded by dismal job prospects and exclusion from promotion, resulted in their marginalization which spiralled "into an industrial underclass" (Kim, 2015, p. 151) status. Seeking to neutralize their doubly disadvantaged position, that is, their rural background and their low rank on the internal factory hierarchy, they engage in "protest masculinity" (McDowell et al., 2014). By binge drinking, disruptive behaviours and producing rancour and other anti-social tendencies, they defy norms and orders within the factory, prove their "untamable" character (unlike the female workers) and reclaim their masculinity.

In sum, there is now considerable research showing the complexity of patterns of privilege when gender, race, class, citizenship, etc. are analysed in intersection. Overall, there is a general convergence on how men from different social strata and work circumstances "(hyper)actively" preserve their masculinity in female occupations, albeit to different degrees and adopting various strategies. The type of "female work" men do, depending on whether it pertains more to subservience and taming of the body (e.g. factory work, sex work) or to delivering care (e.g. childcare, nursing, hairdressing), likely determines how they respond to compromised or jeopardized masculinity. Nevertheless, men working in female-dominated professions often need to prove their masculinity, reaffirm the script of hegemonic masculinity and find ways to solve the conflict between their professional and gender identities.

Struggling with identity and searching for alternatives: men engaging in alternative masculinities

As we have already seen, men working in women's occupations are not only positioned as privileged but often actively seek to achieve privilege. This can be understood as resulting from their struggle for position and needs to be interpreted as an effect of power (Collinson, 2003). Men in female-dominated professions are shifting between male and female subject positions and need to constantly manoeuvre between hegemonic and alternative masculinities (Hrženjak, 2013; Tennhoff et al., 2015). In practice, men in nursing do not always emphasize their difference from female colleagues. They might at times also activate a feminine "nursing identity" when talking about their work as nurses (McDowell, 2015). Men engaging in alternative forms of masculinity could also be "embracing" (Wingfield, 2009) or "appropriating femininity" (Pullen & Simpson, 2009). In so doing, they are changing the meaning of masculinity and are coming up with new solutions to the identity dissonance they are experiencing (Nentwich et al., 2013). By practicing "alternative masculinities", men are actively counteracting hegemonic masculinity (Buschmeyer, 2013).

While some men are very engaged in alternative masculinities and also highly motivated to serve as role models for boys (Buschmeyer, 2013), more often they re-do hegemonic masculinity. As engaging in alternative masculinities is often perceived as challenging the norm of hegemonic masculinity, men's legitimacy is at stake. In consequence, men need to engage in various discursive practices to legitimize their position. The variable and highly situative self-positioning that can be observed in these moments can be explained by Gherardi's (1994) concept of "remedial work". Remedial work is performed when the gender order needs to be re-installed and most often this is done by emphasizing hegemonic masculinity. Hence, alternative masculinities are rather fragile and rarely taken up consistently. Rather, men have been described as "jockeying for position" (Edley & Wetherell, 1997), a metaphor highlighting the constant discursive struggle of men aiming at legitimizing their masculinity in both alternative and hegemonic ways.

An example is provided by a study of male sex workers in Hong Kong (Yau & Kong, 2021). It shows in detail how sustaining masculinity while at the same time being expected to retain a certain bodily docility is a risky balancing act for men and requires deliberate efforts. Resonating with what discourse psychological research has already highlighted, accounting work is indispensable to men's manoeuvring of identity dissonance (Wetherell & Edley, 2014). While men do affirm their position of privilege in one situation, they counter or resist it in another (Wetherell & Edley, 2014).

Nentwich et al. (2013) have analysed the positioning practices of men working in early childhood education in Switzerland. Interpreting the constant manoeuvring of nine male early childhood workers in qualitative interviews, they show that men are engaging in hegemonic masculinity as well as alternative forms. More specifically, they engage in the former by building "male niches" (Williams, 1989). By emphasizing the "rougher games" they play or playing football with the kids and by "claiming skills, interests and interaction styles that are stereotypically labelled as masculine" (Nentwich et al., 2013, p. 7), they construct a legitimate position in the female field of early childhood education. A second practice for emphasizing difference is referencing the "symbolic" position of the father. Often prompted by the interviewer's question about differences, referencing the symbolism of the heterosexual "ideal family", as one of the interview partners put it, was adopted by informants as a highly effective reaction that creates legitimacy. Sometimes men also referred to their position as the "male breadwinner" as an important aspect of hegemonic masculinity to bolster their own masculinity, soothing identity dissonance and doubt.

While men resorted to these three practices to construct a masculine identity in a female-dominated field, they at the same time also engaged in practices stressing equality in the sense of equal treatment. A classic example that marks moments of exclusion is when men working in the nursery are not allowed to change nappies. By being excluded from a very common task when taking care of small children, they are becoming the suspicious, "unwanted other". "Emphasizing equality" thus emerges as an important practice men are engaging in "for re-installing men's legitimate position" (Nentwich et al., 2013, p. 337). A second practice that focuses on installing sameness with regard to women is "appropriating femininity". Here, the skills or characteristics male childcare workers need to be competent in and that are traditionally perceived as feminine are brought to the fore and "internalized" as expressing aspects of their personality. For instance, they would describe themselves as rather "calm and sensitive", attenuate the role of football and rough play and emphasize singing and reading out fairy tales as an expression of their true personality (Nentwich et al., 2013, p. 13). As such, these men are creating an alternative form of masculinity that counters the gendered connotation of these tasks and thereby allows them to resolve identity dissonance. Finally, male childcare workers in this study emphasized their professional capacity. On the basis of their pedagogical skills, interests and experience, these men are creating legitimacy for their position. Emphasizing their professional identity, they are bypassing the gendered positions here as they are not referring to gendered differences or sameness. In this case, alternative masculinity is enacted without actually being labelled as such (masculinity). Emphasizing professional identity, both the masculine gender identity and the profession's female connotation are left aside.

Providing biographical accounts for their occupational choice, men often recall the reactions they have received from peers, parents and also their female colleagues or bosses. While these reactions are not necessarily negative, they nevertheless highlight a perceived misfit of professional and gender identity resulting in the feeling of "identity dissonance" (Nentwich et al., 2013). Men's moves of "jockeying for position" (Edley & Wetherell, 1997) are therefore indicative of identity dissonance: there is not just one subject position, and none of the positions available is easy to stabilize. "Alternative masculinity" in Nentwich et al.'s study (2013) is analysed as a specific way of positioning with regard to hegemonic masculinity. Men might claim female traits and competences as being part of their personality or invest in a professional identity that does not reference gender at all. Nonetheless, what is striking with these findings is that it does not seem to be a new type of masculinity but rather a constant shifting of positions. Claiming sameness with their female colleagues in one moment, the very same men are also invested in niche building and as well hegemonic masculinity in another moment of the interview.

Another case in point for the fragility of men's position in female-dominated occupations is the citizenship or migrant status of male workers in female occupations (Nyaga & Torres, 2017; Panopio, 2010). Research by Nyaga and Torres (2017) on Filipino live-in carers in Toronto offers another glimpse of how gender, race/ethnicity, class, citizenship status and skill intersect to affect men doing women's work. Given that Canada's Live-in Caregiver Program only recognizes women as caregivers, its policies are oriented towards disciplining and overseeing "female foreign bodies" in the private space, somehow leaving men "with minimum surveillance" (p. 57). This may be interpreted as reverse male privilege. Despite a "male dividend" from the policy end, the irony is that for men to enter a highly sexualized field of work, more acute scrutiny and screening on the part of the employer during the hiring process are expected. In fact, it is very much due to the ethnic characteristics Canadians project onto Filipinos, primarily being submissive and docile, that Filipino men are even permitted to do caregiving work. Additionally, in comparison with the higher threshold and gatekeeping for alien and racialized bodies to enter the public sphere, live-in services in the private realm constitute a more accessible alternative for Filipino male migrants.

Engaging with femininity, however, does not necessarily mean that femininity is "appropriated" to a male gender identity. In India, where caste divides and stigmatization have defining influences on one's social status, men are willing to redefine their work as not just barbers that are of a lower social rank but as more feminized "beauticians". By detaching themselves from mere hair-cutting practices that are caste-based, they turn to a more modernized, though feminine, profession to liberate themselves from "the status of a polluted caste" (Ahmed, 2006, p. 174). Hence, engaging with female-connoted tasks can also be deliberate strategy men adopt to gain status. In a similar vein but more economically oriented, the often feminized profession of nursing has come to be conceived in the Philippines as an opportunity guaranteeing upward mobility and monetary rewards. Filipino male nurses working in London (Panopio, 2010) regard themselves as global workers with coveted skills meeting global shortages. Such an understanding, placing emphasis on their success and valuable contribution, removed them from visible threats to their masculinity, though nursing is still considered a female occupation in the United Kingdom. More interestingly, Filipino male nurses tend to prioritize the maximization of their earning potentials, even preferring to "stay on the floor" for more shifts (hence boosting their income) and sidestep the opportunity of being groomed into managerial positions, an indicator of male privileges in previous studies. Social mobility can indeed be an important motive also for working-class men to enter a female-dominated profession (Lupton, 2006). It is, however, to be noted these Southeast Asian men (whether Indian barbers and beauticians or Filipino nurses) are often pushed or propelled by an aspiration to be liberated from caste stigma or profit-oriented pragmatism, rather than by a motivation to undo masculinity.

Other examples of how men in domestic service work shift between positions abound. Indian male helpers only have to show femininity in front of their male employers but feel rightly entitled to uphold their masculinity by refusing female bosses' requests, such as "washing women's underwear" (Chopra, 2006, p. 160). On the other hand, whereas Sri Lankan men are perceived as "effeminate and submissive" by their Neapolitan employers, they themselves exploit such false feminized impressions, through which they maintain appropriate hierarchical distance. This strategy, almost a cultural and ethnic "trait" (Näre, 2010, p. 72), consciously deployed by male cleaners and carers, can be interpreted as men "jockeying for position" to secure places in a women's occupation. Meanwhile, to align themselves with images of hegemonic masculinity despite the feminine work they do, Sri Lankan men observe a traditional gendered division of labour in their own household and emphasize their breadwinner status.

Digging deeper into men's strategies to cope with identity dissonance, we can see that context is crucial for the doing of masculinity. Men are navigating norms of masculinity by shifting between positions. Like this, they can either call for alternative masculinities or engage in a more strategic display of femininity while at work. What is crucial across all these studies is that men workers are concerned to constantly re-emphasize their difference from women and femininity by reaffirming masculinity in one way or another. Interestingly, this is often done through an emphasis on the male body. While Asian men working in service jobs or care work in Western households are "muting the maleness" of their body at the workplace (Chopra, 2006; Näre, 2010), the male nurses and childcare workers interviewed in Switzerland actually refer to their male body as a legitimate reason for being different. In light of strong norms of gender equality, differences linked to the body seem more acceptable than benefiting from male privilege (Schwiter et al., 2021).

Conclusion: doing and undoing masculinity at work

Research on men in female-dominated occupations provides some answers to questions of doing and undoing masculinity. First of all, men working in these occupations are experiencing "identity dissonance", and research has highlighted several strategies for coping with this experience. As their occupational identity is connotated with femininity, doing masculinity becomes more complex for them. As we have shown, there are different responses to this challenge. While some men engage in "niche building", others are "appropriating femininity". They either emphasize masculinity and re-interpret aspects of their job to stabilize their masculine identity or re-interpret masculinity to make it fit with the tasks they are engaging. Both strategies help them decrease the experience of identity dissonance. However, it is important to see that both strategies are rather fragile. Building male niches might backfire and make men look like they are not competent to do the job, as the example of male childcare workers and nurses shows. Engaging in alternative masculinities, however, does not result in stable alternative subject positions for these men. Unable to attain a stable alternative position, they have to in turn engage a "jockeying for position". Lacking the stable alternative position aimed for, they have to engage in manoeuvring between positions to stabilize their identity. While there seems to be a strong need for alternative positions, they are not (yet?) available to men. Creating alternative masculinities is rather resulting from the experience of identity dissonance, but not so much a new way of doing masculinity or actually challenging and changing hegemonic masculinity. Having said that, hegemonic masculinity is still a very strong norm governing men's lives.

We have furthermore affirmed that men in women's occupations are often in a privileged situation. White middle-class men from Western societies are riding the glass escalator. This is rather unlike what we know of white middle-class women entering male-dominated occupations, who are excluded from the actual job. While both women and men are experiencing "boundary work", the result is strikingly different. While women are excluded, men are pushed to higher positions or into different fields. Boundary work does not necessarily label them as incompetent but as more competent to do other things. Despite these obviously privileging effects, it would be hasty to conclude that male privilege and the "patriarchal dividend" can be claimed by all men. Expanding the research perspective beyond Western white middle-class masculinity, it becomes obvious that not all men are equally capable of benefiting from hegemonic masculinity. Privilege seems to be "unevenly distributed" as Coston and Kimmel (2012, p. 97) have suggested, and men are also experiencing exclusion and discrimination. Being denied a masculine position, men engage in several practices securing their masculinity. They would emphasize professionalism or entrepreneurialism as important features of hegemonic masculinity or display what has been called "protest masculinity" (McDowell et al., 2014) to reclaim their masculinity. While hegemonic masculinity is a pattern that cuts through situations and is easily available to some men, in other instances, active work and conscious efforts are needed before privilege attached to hegemonic masculinity can be claimed and achieved. Research particularly highlights these explicit instances of doing masculinity by men in a female context.

Having said this, masculinity seems to be highly contextualized in how it is done and also if it is done. Hegemonic masculinity is a norm that is always in the background as soon as men enter the scene (Nentwich & Vogt, 2021). However, research on men working in women's jobs has shown that it is only activated if masculinity or male privilege is at stake. Through doing masculinity in a female-dominated context, men are attempting to reclaim a privileged position. Men are hence achieving status through entering a female-dominated job. As a matter of fact, men in female-dominated jobs are more likely to solidify hegemonic masculinity and the benefits that come with the patriarchal framework. It still holds true that male power is preserved in female-dominated occupations (Williams, 1992). Hegemonic masculinity, although challenged in some moments, is rather re-installed and only rarely contested or challenged.

Although men working in female-dominated occupations are often perceived as undoing gender, this is not necessarily what they are aiming at. Research suggests that alternative masculinities are not as motivating to men in these professions as we might have believed or identified, particularly from a Western perspective. More often men are more prone to stabilize hegemonic masculinity than to undo the norms of hegemonic masculinity. Alternative masculinities hence are not abundantly available and are still in need of being stabilized in the female-dominated context of women's occupations.

References

Agadjanian, V. (2005). Men doing "women's work": Masculinity and gender relations among street vendors in Maputo, Mozambique. In L. Ouzgane & R. Morrell (Eds.), *African Masculinities: Men in Africa from the Late Nineteenth Century to the Present* (pp. 257–269). New York: Palgrave Macmillan. doi: 10.1057/9781403979605_16

Ahmed, S. M. F. (2006). Making beautiful: Male workers in beauty parlors. *Men and Masculinities*, *9*(2), 168–185. doi: 10.1177/1097184X06287763

Asakura, K., & Watanabe, I. (2011). Survival strategies of male nurses in rural areas of Japan. *Japan Journal of Nursing Science*, *8*(2), 194–202. doi: 10.1111/j.1742-7924.2011.00176.x

Brody, D. L. (2015). The construction of masculine identity among men who work with young children, an international perspective. *European Early Childhood Education Research Journal*, *23*(3), 351–361. doi: 10.1080/1350293X.2015.1043809

Budig, M. J. (2002). Male advantage and the gender composition of jobs: Who rides the glass escalator? *Social Problems*, *49*(2), 258–277. doi: 10.1525/sp.2002.49.2.258

Buschmeyer, A. (2013). The construction of 'alternative masculinity' among men in the childcare profession. *International Review of Sociology*, *23*(2), 290–309. doi: 10.1080/03906701.2013.804293

Cameron, C. (2001). Promise or problem? A review of the literature on men working in early childhood services. *Gender, Work & Organization*, *8*(4), 430–453.

Chen, M. H. (2017). Hairdressing as a form of body work: From performing manual labour to negotiating embodied aesthetic labour. *Taiwanese Journal of Sociology*, *62*.

Chen, Y. Z. (2019). Exploring identities and practices of Taiwanese men working in family day care: A tentative typology. *Journal of Gender Studies*, *28*(8), 883–894. doi: 10.1080/09589236.2019.1577131

Chen, Y. Z., & Wang, J. Y. (2020). Doing masculinities: Exploring gender and age in professionalizing family day care in Taiwan. *The Journal of Men's Studies*, *28*(2), 206–222. doi: 10.1177/1060826520901330

Choi, S. Y. (2018). Masculinity and precarity: Male migrant taxi drivers in South China. *Work, Employment and Society*, *32*(3), 493–508. doi: 10.1177/0950017018755652

Chopra, R. (2006). Invisible men: Masculinity, sexuality, and male domestic labor. *Men and Masculinities*, *9*(2), 152–167. doi: 10.1177/1097184X06287766

Christensen, A.-D., & Jensen, S. Q. (2014). Combining hegemonic masculinity and intersectionality. *NORMA: International Journal for Masculinity Studies*, *9*(1), 60–75. doi: 10.1080/18902138.2014.892289

Collinson, D. L. (2003). Identities and Insecurities: Selves at Work. *Organization, 10*(3), 527–547. doi: 10.1177/13505084030103010

Connell, R. W. (1995). *Masculinities*. University of California Press.

Connell, R. W., & Messerschmidt, J. W. (2005). Hegemonic masculinity. Rethinking the concept. *Gender & Society, 19*(6), 829–859. doi: 10.1177/0891243205278639

Coston, B. M., & Kimmel, M. (2012). Seeing privilege where it isn't: Marginalized masculinities and the intersectionality of privilege. *Journal of Social Issues, 68*(1), 97–111. doi: 10.1111/j.1540-4560.2011.01738.x

Cottingham, M. D., Johnson, A. H., & Taylor, T. (2016). Heteronormative labour: Conflicting accountability structures among men in nursing. *Gender, Work & Organization, 23*(6), 535–550. doi: 10.1111/gwao.12140

Cremers, M., & Krabel, J. (2012). Generalverdacht und sexueller Missbrauch in Kitas: Bausteine für ein Schutzkonzept. In M. Cremers, S. Höyng, J. Krabel & T. Rohrmann (Eds.), *Männer in Kitas* (p. 265–285). Barbara Budrich.

Cross, S., & Bagilhole, B. (2002). Girls' jobs for the boys? Men, masculinity and non-traditional occupations. *Gender, Work & Organization, 9*(2), 204–226.

Cushman, P. (2005). It's just not a real bloke's job: Male teachers in the primary school. *Asia-Pacific Journal of Teacher Education, 33*(3), 321–338. doi: 10.1080/13598660500286176

Dill, J. S., Price-Glynn, K., & Rakovski, C. (2016). Does the "glass escalator" compensate for the devaluation of care work occupations?: The careers of men in low- and middle-skill health care jobs. *Gender & Society, 30*(2), 334–360. doi: 10.1177/0891243215624656

Edley, N., & Wetherell, M. (1997). Jockeying for position: The construction of masculine identities. *Discourse & Society, 8*(2), 203–217. doi: 10.1177/0957926597008002004

Eidevald, C., Bergström, H., & Broström, A. W. (2018). Maneuvering suspicions of being a potential pedophile: Experiences of male ECEC-workers in Sweden. *European Early Childhood Education Research Journal, 26*(3), 407–417. doi: 10.1080/1350293X.2018.1463907

Evans, J. (2008). Men in nursing: Issues of gender segregation and hidden advantage. *Journal of Advanced Nursing, 26*(2), 226–231. doi: 10.1046/j.1365-2648.1997.1997026226.x

Ferguson, J. M., & Ayuttacorn, A. (2019). Air male: Exploring flight attendant masculinities in North America and Thailand. *The Asia Pacific Journal of Anthropology, 20*(4), 328–343. doi: 10.1080/14442213.2019.1634137

Gherardi, S. (1994). The gender we think, the gender we do in our everyday organizational lives. *Human Relations, 47*(6), 591–610.

Hayes, R. (1989). Men in female-concentrated occupations. *Journal of Organizational Behavior, 10*(3), 201–212.

Hellman, A., Nakazawa, C., & Kuramochi, K. (2015). Being professional: Norms relating to male pre-school teachers in Japanese kindergartens and nurseries. In S. Brownhill, J. Warin, I. Wernersson (Eds.), *Men, Masculinities and Teaching in Early Childhood Education* (pp. 106–117). London: Routledge.

Hrženjak, M. (2013). Negotiating masculinity in informal paid care work. *International Review of Sociology, 23*(2), 346–362. doi: 10.1080/03906701.2013.804296

Husso, M., & Hirvonen, H. (2012). Gendered agency and emotions in the field of care work. *Gender, Work & Organization, 19*(1), 29–51. doi: 10.1111/j.1468-0432.2011.00565.x

Kanter, R. M. (1977). *Men and Women of the Corporation*. New York: Basic.

Karlsen, H. (2012). Gender and ethnic differences in occupational positions and earnings among nurses and engineers in Norway: Identical educational choices, unequal outcomes. *Work, Employment and Society, 26*(2), 278–295. doi: 10.1177/0950017011432907

Kelan, E. K. (2018). Men doing and undoing gender at work: A review and research agenda. *International Journal of Management Reviews, 20*(2), 544–558. doi: 10.1111/ijmr.12146

Kelan, E. K., & Wratil, P. (2017). Post-heroic leadership, tempered radicalism and senior leaders as change agents for gender equality. *European Management Review, 15*(1), 5–18. doi: 10.1111/emre.12117

Kim, J. (2015). From "country bumpkins" to "tough workers": The pursuit of masculinity among male factory workers in China. *Anthropological Quarterly, 88*(1), 133–161.

Lupton, B. (2000). Maintaining masculinity: Men who do 'women's work'. *British Journal of Management, 11*, 33–48. doi: 10.1111/1467-8551.11.s1.4

Lupton, B. (2006). Explaining men's entry into female-concentrated occupations: Issues of masculinity and social class. *Gender, Work & Organization, 13*(2), 103–128. doi: 10.1111/j.1468-0432.2006.00299.x

Ma, Tsai-Chuan & Yeh, Yu-Ching. (2008). Crossing the Labors' Boundary? An Investigation of Male Workers in Traditional Women's Work. *Taiwan: A Radical Quarterly in Social Studies, 72*, 1–48. doi: 10.29816/TARQSS.200812.0001

Martin, P. Y. (2001). 'Mobilizing masculinities': Women's experiences of men at work. *Organization, 8*(4), 587–618. doi: 10.1177/135050840184003

McDonald, J. (2013). Conforming to and resisting dominant gender norms: How male and female nursing students do and undo gender. *Gender, Work & Organization, 20*(5), 561–579. doi: 10.1111/j.1468-0432.2012.00604.x

McDowell, J. (2015). Masculinity and non-traditional occupations: Men's talk in women's work. *Gender, Work & Organization, 22*(3), 273–291.

McDowell, L., Rootham, E., & Hardgrove, A. (2014). Precarious work, protest masculinity and communal regulation: South Asian young men in Luton, UK. *Work, Employment and Society, 28*(6), 847–864. doi: 10.1177/0950017013510757

Messerschmidt, J. W. (2018). *Hegemonic Masculinity: Formulation, Reformulation, and Amplification.* Lanham, MD: Rowman & Littlefield.

Mitchell, J. (1974). *Psychoanalysis and Feminism.* London: Penguin Books.

Moss-Racusin, C. A., & Johnson, E. R. (2016). Backlash against male elementary educators. *Journal of Applied Social Psychology, 46*(7), 379–393. doi: 10.1111/jasp.12366

Näre, L. (2010). Sri Lankan men working as cleaners and carers: Negotiating masculinity in Naples. *Men and Masculinities, 13*(1), 65–86. doi: 10.1177/1097184X10382881

Nentwich, J. C., Poppen, W., Schälin, S., & Vogt, F. (2013). The same and the other: Male childcare workers managing identity dissonance. *International Review of Sociology, 23*(2), 326–345. doi: 10.1080/03906701.2013.804295

Nentwich, J. C., & Vogt, F. (2021). *(Un)doing gender empirisch erforschen.* In J. C. Nentwich & F. Vogt (Eds.), (Un)doing Gender empirisch: Qualitative Forschung in der Kita (p. 7–50). Cham: Springer. doi: 10.1007/978-3-658-32863-4

Nyaga, D., & Torres, R. A. (2017). Gendered citizenship: A case study of paid Filipino male live-in caregivers in Toronto. *International Journal of Asia-Pacific Studies, 13.* doi: 10.21315/ijaps2017.13.1.3

O'Reilly, J., Smith, M., Deakin, S., & Burchell, B. (2015). Equal pay as a moving target: International perspectives on forty-years of addressing the gender pay gap. *Cambridge Journal of Economics, 39*(2), 299–317. doi: 10.1093/cje/bev010

Panopio, S. (2010). More than masculinity: Experiences of male migrant nurses in London (London School of Economics, Gender Institute). *New Working Paper Series, 26.*

Peretz, T. (2018). Seeing the invisible knapsack: Feminist men's strategic responses to the continuation of male privilege in feminist spaces. *Men and Masculinities, 23*(3–4), 447–475. doi: 10.1177/1097184x18784990

Price-Glynn, K., & Rakovski, C. (2012). Who rides the glass escalator? Gender, race and nationality in the national nursing assistant study. *Work, Employment and Society, 26*(5), 699–715. doi: 10.1177/0950017012451634

Pullen, A., & Simpson, R. (2009). Managing difference in feminized work: Men, otherness and social practice. *Human Relations, 62*(4), 561–587. doi: 10.1177/0018726708101989

Sargent, P. (2005). The gendering of men in early childhood education. *Sex Roles, A Journal of Research, 52*(2), 251–259.

Schwiter, K., Nentwich, J., & Keller, M. (2021). Male privilege revisited: How men in female-dominated occupations notice and actively reframe privilege. *Gender, Work & Organization, 28*(6), 2199–2215. doi: 10.1111/gwao.12731

Scott, J., Grov, C., & Minichiello, V. (Eds.). (2021). *The Routledge Handbook of Male Sex Work, Culture, and Society.* London: Routledge. doi: 10.4324/9781003152835

Simpson, R. (2004). Masculinity at work: The experiences of men in female-dominated occupations. *Work Employment & Society, 18*(2), 349–368. doi: 10.1177/09500172004042773

Simpson, R. (2005). Men in non-traditional occupations: Career entry, career orientation and experience of role strain. *Gender, Work & Organization, 12*(4), 363–380. doi: 10.1111/j.1468-0432.2005.00278.x

Simpson, R. (2010). A reversal of the gaze: Men's experiences of visibility in non-traditional occupations. In *Revealing and Concealing Gender* (pp. 219–232). London: Palgrave Macmillan. doi: 10.1057/9780230285576_12

Simpson, R. (2012). *Men in Caring Occupations: Doing Gender Differently.* Houndmills: Palgrave Macmillan.

Smedley, S. (2007). Learning to be a primary school teacher: Reading one man's story. *Gender and Education, 19*(3), 369–385.

Tennhoff, W., Nentwich, J. C., & Vogt, F. (2015). Doing gender and professionalism: Exploring the intersectionalities of gender and professionalization in early childhood education. *European Early Childhood Education Research Journal, 23*(3), 340–350. doi: 10.1080/1350293X.2015.1043808

Tzeng, Ya-Ling & Chen, Ching-Ju. (2008). The lived experience of male nurses in clinical nursing practice. *Journal of Evidence-Based Nursing, 4*(1), 61–70. doi: 10.6225/JEBN.4.1.61

van Antwerpen, S., & Ferreira, E. (2010). Males in predominantly female-dominated positions: A South-African perspective. *Journal of Contemporary Management, 7*, 363–379.

Warin, J. (2006). Heavy-metal humpty dumpty: Dissonant masculinities within the context of the nursery. *Gender and Education, 18*(5), 523–537.

Warin, J. (2019). Conceptualising the value of male practitioners in early childhood education and care: Gender balance or gender flexibility. *Gender and Education, 31*(3), 293–308. doi: 10.1080/09540253.2017.1380172

Wetherell, M., & Edley, N. (1999). Negotiating hegemonic masculinity: Imaginary positions and psycho-discursive practices. *Feminism & Psychology, 9*(3), 335–356. doi: 10.1177/0959353599009003012

Wetherell, M., & Edley, N. (2009). Masculinity manoevres: Critical discursive psychology and the analysis of identity strategies. In N. Coupland & A. Jaworski (Eds.), *The New Sociolinguistics Reader* (pp. 201–214). New York: Palgrave Macmillan.

Wetherell, M., & Edley, N. (2014). A discursive psychological framework for analyzing men and masculinities. *Psychology of Men & Masculinity, 15*(4), 355–364. doi: 10.1037/a0037148

Williams, C. L. (1989). *Gender Differences at Work: Women and Men in Nontraditional Occupations.* Berkeley, CA: University of California Press.

Williams, C. L. (1992). The glass escalator: Hidden advantages for men in the "female" professions. *Social Problems, 39*(3), 253–267. doi: 10.2307/3096961

Williams, C. L. (2015). Crossing over: Interdisciplinary research on "men who do women's work". *Sex Roles, 72*(7–8), 390–395. doi: 10.1007/s11199-015-0477-x

Wingfield, A. H. (2009). Racializing the glass escalator: Reconsidering men's experiences with women's work. *Gender & Society, 23*(1), 5–26. doi: 10.1177/0891243208323054

Wingfield, A. H., & Myles, R. L. (2014). Still a man's world? Revisiting men who do women's work. *Sociology Compass, 8*(10), 1206–1215. doi: 10.1111/soc4.12206

Yau, A. C. H., & Kong, T. S. K. (2021). Male sex work and masculinities in Hong Kong and Mainland China: "One country, two men". In J. Scott, C. Grov, & V. Minichiello (Eds.), *The Routledge Handbook of Male Sex Work, Culture, and Society* (p. 555–570). London: Routledge. doi: 10.4324/9781003152835

23

BOYS AND SCHOOLING

Intersectional perspectives

Ann Phoenix

Introduction

Over the last 30 years, it has been increasingly recognized that it is only possible to understand organizations by considering the ways in which they are gendered. Rather than viewing gender as a characteristic of individuals that they take into organizations, this view constructs gender as structured into organizations and replicated through gendered processes that, in most organizations, continue to reproduce male advantage. As the pioneering feminist organizational theorist, Joan Acker (1992) suggests, these gendered processes continue to reproduce gendered distinctions, even as understandings of gender shift. They are linked with power relations and emotions. Gender is also a resource for institutions, used sometimes to organize the workforce in implicit ways. For example, the gender pay gap allows organizations to save money on women's pay, while gaining equal or more work from women. In her later work, Acker's analyses (e.g. 2012) focused on the ways in which gender, "race" and social class intersect in organizations. Rather than viewing gender as operating in isolation from other social categories, intersectional analyses are built on theorizations of gender as part of multiple social categories that simultaneously intersect and decentre each other. All social categories are socially located and so involve unequal power relations (Anthias, 2020) and are part of histories that are sedimented into organizations and in which people are positioned (Collins, 2019; Phoenix, 2022). This means that institutions not only have intersections negotiated within them but are part of the intersections. For schools, age, generation, nation and locality all intersect with gender, racialization, ethnicization and social class to (re) produce social inequalities that are negotiated in schools but that are not confined to school premises.

This chapter contributes to developing a holistic understanding of boys, masculinities and organizations by focusing on schools as gendered organizations. There are, for example, numerous studies and analyses that show that the intersection of racialization, social class and gender affect attainment, make a difference to social relations within schools and are an often implicit, but central part of the organization of schools (Hadjar & Buchman, 2016; Hobbs, 2016; Wallace & Joseph-Salisbury, 2022). Masculinities for Black working-class boys are thus different from masculinities for Black middle-class boys, white working-class boys or

 DOI: 10.4324/9781003193579-26

Black working-class girls. A consideration of boys, masculinities and organizations thus needs to take an intersectional approach that simultaneously considers different social categories, positionality and institutional organization (Gross et al., 2016; Strand, 2021).

The chapter is divided into four parts. It first considers the relevance of gender to schooling before discussing the current state of the art in discussions of intersectionality. The third part focuses on masculinities and school organizations. The main part of the chapter then draws on studies of masculinities at school in Denmark, Finland and the United Kingdom to consider a range of everyday practices of masculinities in schools. The chapter foregrounds intersections of gender, sexuality, racialization and migration status and examines the ways in which the (re)production of masculinities is both particular to the organizational sites in which they are practised, differentiated by intersectional positioning and facilitated by an intersectional frame. This issue is increasingly recognized in the literature, where intersections of age, gender, sexuality ethnicity, disability and migration status have all been shown (in different combinations) to be central to masculinities and organizations (e.g. Acker, 2012; Hearn, 2014; Liu, 2018; Rodriguez et al., 2016).

Gender and schooling

While the gendering of organizations is increasingly studied and a growing number of studies focus on boys and masculinities in schools (Ferguson, 2020 [2000]; Joy & Larsson, 2019; Mayeza & Bhana, 2020; Peltola & Phoenix, 2022), there is relatively little work on schools as gendered organizations. Yet, as Connell (2008) suggests, school is an important social arena in which gendered development occurs and masculinities and femininities are constructed. Connell (2008, p. 136) proposes that the gender regimes of organizations encompass "four dimensions: the division of labour (e.g., gendered jobs), power relations (e.g., the nature of authority), emotional relationship (e.g., patterns of antagonism and solidarity), and organizational cultures (e.g., beliefs about gender difference, equal opportunity)". All of these dimensions are subject to change but remain central to the reproduction of gendered power relations and of hegemonic masculinities.

The ways in which schools as institutions are gendered are not, of course, arbitrary. Rather, they are set up with the sanction of states in order to rear citizens and have histories of taking for granted essentialist and binary gendered, racialized, classed, age-differentiated and national divisions. The binarizing notion that girls and boys will grow up to have different destinies is part of the history of schooling, even in countries where formal, widespread education is relatively recent. In countries such as the United Kingdom and the United States, those differences were routinely marked on school architecture in terms of separate girls' and boys' entrances. Some primary schools were also age marked, even placing the infants' entrance (for the youngest children) with the girls' entrance, underlining the fact that girls are expected to be gentler and more caring for little children than boys (see Figure 23.1).

Despite the widespread espousal of gender equality in schools and dawning recognition that school students do not fit into only two genders, it is still the case that in at least 20 countries some schools have some single-sex educational provision (Global Education Monitoring Report, 2022). Indeed, sometimes the argument for single-sex education is to ensure that girls do get equal opportunities at school. Equally, by age 11, if not before, schools, like many public institutions, generally mark gender by demarcating separate toilets and changing rooms. The point is that even the fabric of schools can be patterned by gender, even before teachers and children enter them. However, there is a great deal of evidence

Figure 23.1 Example of primary school with entrances separated by gender and age

Source: Alex Ramsay/Alamy Stock Photo

that children and young people's practices, and sometimes those of their teachers, informally segregate their schools along gendered, and where relevant, racialized and social class lines (Bettencourt et al., 2019; Bonal & Bellei, 2019; Dunne, 2007; Lareau & Calarco, 2012; Peltola, 2020; Reay, 2005).

Equally, the fact that it has long been predominantly women who teach and care for younger children is because care for young children is organized internationally so that women do low-paid care work and men remain under-represented in early childcare (Owen et al., 1999). As Connell (2008, p. 137) points out, this is not accidental but is "embedded in a division of labour at the level of the whole economy, and in a persisting large imbalance between men and women in domestic work and child care in the family". Schools are thus contradictory in that they are built on gendered tradition and intersections that produce inequalities that are imbricated in schools as organizations. Yet they are also about teaching new knowledge and educating for change, including sometimes for equalities. The question thus arises of what kinds of intersectional gendered futures seem likely to be emergent and what possible futures of schools and organizations might help to deliver more gender-equal futures.

Theorizing intersectionality

The term intersectionality was coined by Kimberlé Crenshaw in 1989. However, many scholars and activists had already been attempting to do what are now thought of as intersectional analyses before Crenshaw named the idea. The main idea of intersectionality is that no social category exists in isolation of other social categories. This means that, for example, identities, locations, histories and social structures linked to gender, racialization age, ethnicity and nation all operate simultaneously and need to be analysed as interlinked, even if only one of those categories is being focused on in a particular analysis (Collins & Bilge, 2020).

According to many intersectionality theorists, three other elements are central. First, categories mutually constitute each other when they intersect. They, therefore, do not just add together but help to construct each other in ways that are different from each single category (Collins, 2019). Second, all social categories stand in power relations to others (Anthias, 2020). This means that people might be relatively powerful in relation to one social category and less powerful in relation to others. Working-class boys, for example, may benefit from what Connell (1996a) calls the "patriarchal dividend" and yet be less privileged because they are working class. There is, therefore, the possibility of boys (and, indeed, everyone) being positioned in contradictory and complex ways (Collins & Bilge, 2020). Equally, children stand in power relations to adults, but what it means to be a man, woman or child depends on the power relations between those categories. Third, this means that we have to analyse social identities as complex because they decentre each other as they intersect (Yuval-Davis, 2016). Hankivsky (2014, p. 2) suggests that "according to an intersectionality perspective, inequities are never the result of single distinct factors. Rather, they are the outcome of intersections of different social locations power relations and experiences".

One of the clearest ways in which intersectionality is visible in childhood is in the differential attainment of different groups of children. Steve Strand (2022) explains that accounts of educational achievement framed exclusively in terms of social class, ethnicity or gender are insufficient, and suggests that we need more nuanced accounts of educational success and failure. A nuanced view of school attainment has to recognize that attainment is differentiated not only by gender, ethnicity and social class but by school type and country (Codiroli Mcmaster & Cook, 2019; Gillborn, 2015; Gross et al., 2016). The following section considers schools as institutions and the ways in which gender, in the form of masculinities, is both built into and played out in them.

Masculinities in schools as gendered institutions

Schools are complex in that they are institutions of states and societies as well as individual, local organizations. Berg (2007) employs the distinction between organizations as "the associations through which people act" and institutions as "the interests, group-related norms and conditions for action, which they have to follow". Furthermore, Berg (2007) suggests that schools are both led and steered by the state

> a concept that draws attention to the mandates and activities that the state and society require the school as an institution to perform and undertake. Leading, on the other hand, is a concept that focuses on the tasks and the work that schools as organizations actually carry out.
>
> *(Berg, 2007, p. 581).*

Skelton (2001) points out that schools continually change partly because the relationship between the economy, culture and politics is central to the concerns schools are expected to address. While, of course, schools as organizations are part of schools as institutions, viewing the organization as separate from the institutions can help to explain how masculinities are played out in school organizations in ways that differ from official state and societal mandates about how gender, for example, should be enacted. It also helps to explain that schools are regulatory institutions (Swain, 2000), regulating both the differentiation of children and young people by age, educational qualification and the sort of behaviours, practices and ideologies they are expected to learn in order to fit in with, and contribute to, society.

Schools are gendered institutions. This is not surprising since all societies make distinctions on the basis of gender. Raewyn Connell (2008) suggests that a basic way in which schools as institutions shape patterns of masculinity is by providing a social milieu in which hundreds of children and young people are thrown together for long periods. In consequence, schools create peer forums that foreground particular patterns of masculinity. However, school policies, practices, interactions and ideology are also patterned by gender. Gender differences are reinforced through curricula, teaching styles, dress codes, sports, disciplinary practices (Walkerdine, 1990) and teacher expectations (Walkerdine, 1984) as well as the interactions between students. In addition, there are more male staff in higher education and school administration, while women constitute the majority of nursery (kindergarten) and primary school (elementary) staff (Owen et al., 1999). The knowledge conveyed to children is accredited by patriarchal institutions, and some disciplines are highly gender imbalanced (Connell, 1996a). Children and young people thus enter schools that are structured in gendered ways that, in many cases, privilege the masculine, even as the institutions of school advocate gender equality. The institution of school legitimizes the gendered distribution of opportunities and resources as well as cultural values among the students (Anand, 2020).

From an intersectional perspective, schools as institutions both reproduce inequalities that are patterned by gender, social class and racialization. For example, the construction of good and bad behaviour in schools is gendered, racialized and implicitly social classed so that, for example, school policies and practices of discipline, testing and tracking contribute to what has come to be known as the "school to prison pipeline" for Black boys in the United Kingdom and the United States (Ferguson, 2020/2000). In the United Kingdom, Black boys are more likely than any other groups of students to be strip searched by police in schools (Stone, 2022). In many countries, white working-class boys continue to get formal qualifications at a lower rate than girls or white, middle-class boys (Strand, 2021).

The following sections draw on empirical research to discuss the processes that produce and reproduce intersectional differences within the institution of school and the implications for masculinities.

Living masculinities: gendered practices in schools

Jon Swain (2005) argues that schools afford boys many opportunities to construct versions of masculinities that, as Connell (1996b) suggests, draw on the local resources and strategies available as well as normative cultural constructions. This is because, as Connell makes clear, it is the institution that throws most boys together with other boys of the same age into peer groups. Swain (2005) points out that the English private schools (called "public schools" in the UK) of the nineteenth century were expressly set up with the aim of teaching boys how to be male, involving misogyny, homophobia and emotional repression, so that gender was always central to schools. Berry Mayall (1994) pointed out that schools treat children as projects to be controlled as they are moulded into the future citizens desired and gender is part of what is moulded.

There are numerous ways in which schools as organizations (re)produce gendered positioning and relations. These include the policies and rules that are foregrounded and the ways in which teachers and other school staff implement, or fail to implement, these. It has long been known that schools differ in the ways they implement institutional expectations, and the more effective schools in terms of producing good educational qualifications also tend to have positive school climates (Rutter, 1979). The teaching and expectations from teachers of boys and girls are also central. So too are the ways in which gender is marked on school premises in terms of school spaces, often as part of the "hidden curriculum". However, gender relations among children and young people and between staff and different students are central to the everyday negotiation and (re)production of gender relations in schools. This will be the focus of the rest of the chapter. However, many of the issues identified earlier are addressed in the following studies that examine children's practices and views of schools as organizations.

Schools as spatialized organizations

Schools are differentiated in terms of where they are located and, hence, the numbers of children who attend, the ethnicity of children in the neighbourhood, the practices of the local community, social class and the resources to which they have access (Peltola & Phoenix, 2022; Skelton, 2001). Schools in numerous countries thus differ in terms of socio-economic circumstances and, in some countries like the United Kingdom and the United States, social class differentiates schools so that some are considered working-class and others middle class. The ways in which masculinities are negotiated thus vary by the area in which schools are located. In a study of working-class schools in Northern Ireland where boys were, unlike most working-class boys, educationally successful, Nicola Ingram (2018, p. 133) found that "each school differs in terms of its institutional habitus, . . . the schools, through their taken-for-granted practices and forms of organization, come to shape the habitus of those within in particular ways".

As discussed earlier, the organization of schools in many countries is spatialized in gendered, racialized and social class ways. In relation to gender, this ranges from provision designed to keep boys and girls separate in different schools, to informal segregation that is intersectionally patterned within different school spaces in mixed-gender schools. The space of the classroom, where children are placed in close proximity, is also often informally gender segregated (Hey, 1997; Salmon, 1995). The fact that there are spaces that are deliberately gender segregated, such as toilets and changing rooms, also impacts on social relations and young people's imaginaries of each other. This is illustrated in the following research group interview exchange that comes from a study of masculinities and ethnicities conducted with 12–15-year-old young people in three Helsinki schools selected because they differed in relation to the socio-economic status and ethnic composition of the neighbourhoods in which they are located (see Peltola & Phoenix, 2022). The following focus group discussion was conducted in Finnish, translated by paid student interns and checked by Marja Peltola who conducted the interviews and discussed them with the author whose first language is English. All the names presented in the following are pseudonyms. The boys were not asked about space but about differences in what boys and girls do and spontaneously mentioned spatialization.

Interviewer: Right. Well if you think about what things, or let's continue from here so what things do boys do and are they somehow different from what girls do, so are there some things that a boy can't ever do? Some things what girls would do but boys can't do?

Martin: Well I can't go to the toilet together with my friends because it looks weird. [joint laughter]

Interviewer: Okay well that is a good, concrete example.

Onni: It is exactly, I have at times always asked for example from some friend of mine that why do girls go at the same time to the toilet, but they don't really know how to answer that either. I don't know what's the reason for that, but like. Then again if boys go to the bathroom at the same time, then it feels that there is something.

Martin: Something [has] happened.

Onni: Yeah something actually bad or different is happening, but then again if girls go then no one is interested really.

Lauri: Yeah and then they squeeze into the same toilet stall.

Onni: Yeah we have a joke about that, that are they making some chair there or something, so what happens there. [joint laughter]

(Focus group 5, 5 boys, 14–15 years, four with white Finnish background, one with Estonian parents, Kukkula School)

In the previous example, all the boys are white, although Martin has migrant Estonian parents. Their school is located in an area that is socio-economically mixed and had a minority (approximately one-fifth) of pupils with so-called foreign backgrounds, most of which were Russian or Estonian. The boys co-constructed a narrative that locates girls as spending illegitimately long periods of time in the girls' toilets. The fact that it is a space that excludes boys seemed to feed their curiosity and makes it an imagined space that the boys fill with imagined strange behaviours from girls that they can joke about in the absence of being able to observe girls. Two things are evident from the joint discussion. One is, that while the boys maintain that they do not know what girls do (in the toilets and more generally), they are clearly attentive to what girls do. Second, while they cannot control girls' use of space in the toilets, their denigration of what girls do there, and their construction of them as strange serves to underline Connell's (1996a) point that boys are preoccupied with peer group life and constantly renegotiate their relations in the constantly changing arenas provided by the school. In the previous example, that renegotiation is intersectional in being gendered, located in a particular school and likely to be age-related. The boys' curiosity about girls' mysteriousness gives them the opportunity to do what they both enjoy and identify as central to masculinity, to joke together.

Both boys and girls expect girls to use space differently than boys and, indeed, to take up less space than boys do. Asked in the Helsinki study about the difference between girls and boys, those in a mixed focus group give a range of answers including fighting in the corridors and so taking up public space. In the following extract, a girl speaks first, followed by a boy.

Interviewer: Does something come to mind?

Elsa: A girl is thought to be weird if she, for example, fights. [laughs] Or like that rare you see girls fighting in the school corridors unlike when boys always fight in the school corridors.

Interviewer:	Do boys fight a lot here in the school corridors?
Veeti:	Well it's a bit like– kind of playful, so that you like to take [wrestler's] holds and wrestle and so on. Probably exactly, those kind of cool throws of the films and some these type of [laughing] locks.

(Focus group 2, 2 boys and 2 girls, 12–13 years, Finnish background, Nurmi School) (Peltola & Phoenix, 2022)

A further example comes from an individual interview with a boy from the same school as in the previous example. Liban explained that "all" boys gathered around a ping-pong table to play and to socialize during the breaks. A new development at their age was that girls occasionally came to join the activity. Their presence was tolerated by the boys as strange but acceptable exceptions to what they largely considered masculine activities.

Interviewer:	What about here in school, do you see here, like, different groupings of boys?
Liban:	Well I think that we are all different, but then when we are here in school everybody, like hangs out, like nobody minds even though you are at the same time, or nobody cares what is your opinion, you know. Because, for instance, if we are all like a bit different, for instance, I have my own opinion, but then when the break begins, we all gather around the ping pong table and we all play, you know, so that it doesn't really matter what you think. . . .
Interviewer:	Is it here, is it usually just boys who hang out there around the ping pong table?
Liban:	Well not necessarily. Sometimes some girls come, like, "we want to play", then we are just like, in a fair way, so that everybody queues, so then we are like, "if you go there at the end of the queue then you can play".

(Individual interview Liban, 14 years, Somali background, Kukkula School)

Liban's account makes clear that the ping-pong table is a boys' space where, despite their differences, "all" boys play ping-pong. The repeated joint activity is able to temporarily render individual differences between boys irrelevant. Liban explained that girls who wanted to play ping pong were treated "fairly" and allowed to take a turn, but this is clearly exceptional in that it is "sometimes" that girls come to play and, while all boys play, girls have to explain that they "want to play". Studies on boys and masculinities generally find that joint activities – doing things together – is a marker of masculinity, while interacting through talk is considered more feminine (de Boise & Hearn, 2017; Edwards, 2004; Thorne, 1993). Particular school contexts allow and encourage different activities. Shared activity helped boys to maintain an inclusive masculine sociality, which, according to many boys' accounts, mostly ignored individual differences.

The final example of spatialization in this section comes from a study of 12–13-year-old children in a Danish school. In her ethnographic observation, Jette Kofoed (2006, 2008) observed break times and lessons, studying the communication between pupils during class, mapping their social relations and conducting narrative interviews with all members of the class. The pupils were encouraged to talk about their everyday lives and to reflect on specific events, social relations and positioning, particularly processes of inclusion and exclusion and how "pupilness" was constructed. She found that football dominated the playground at each break and was preceded by a ritual of selecting teams.

> Previous to the actual activity 'playing football', a line of difference has already been drawn. It is a distinction which has implications for the meaning-making processes. The difference is about gender. The canon about football is spoken out loudly. The difference of gender is silenced, however. It is already established. The fact is that actors who are bodily signed as girls do not engage in football. Relevant players are those who are bodily signed as male . . . whether they actually play football or not. Even those boys who have no special skills in handling the ball are considered relevant and legitimate players/participants. Girls – irrespective of their ball-skills – are non-legitimate participants. The difference that separates the pupils in legitimate and non-legitimate players is body signs. Only within the category of male bodily signed actors do football skills become relevant criteria. This difference has implications for both boys and girls. For the feminine signed it implies that they are prevented from playing football. If they intend to play ball, basketball is an option. If they want to be close to football playing, the position as spectator is available. Football skills, familiarity and time do not make any sense if the bodily sign is feminine. For the masculine signed it implies that they have to take part in the game to do appropriate "boyhood" and masculinity.
>
> *(Kofoed, 2006, p. 3)*

Kofoed's (2008) observation showed how space and social relations both play a part in producing and reproducing hegemonic and more marginalized forms of masculinities at school. Kofoed's analysis focused on emergent intersectional complexities. She observed that the informal, but repetitive, ritualized selection of players for football games excluded girls from this dominant activity was taken-for-granted by both girls and boys. However, a more implicit form of policing through this activity was the negotiation of hierarchies and constructed community and otherness through the process of naming boys as chosen for the team. This reiterated notions of who the attractive pupils and the "skilled players" were. These were always male and always white in this Copenhagen playground, without this ever having to be made explicit.

Kofoed's findings show how the organization of the school is both a resource for negotiating and reproducing gender relations and how gender relations are part of both the formal and informal organization of the school. Those gender relations and the negotiation of masculinities are intersectional in that they are racialized as well as gendered and spatialized. This was also found by Swain (2000), who suggested that "boys" networks were saturated by, and structured through, divisions of power, with the hegemonic groups' ability to define what constituted the exalted form of masculinity, policed by its own self-regulation. It may well be that, as women's football teams become ever more successful internationally and more girls play football, the gendered nature of the ritualized use of playground space shifts. However, any snapshot of the spatialization of gender in schools shows how gender is intersectionally part of school organizations and institutionalized into school practices (Berg, 2007).

Teacher practices and negotiations of intersectional masculinities

The Kofoed study dealt with the informal organization of football among boys in a Danish school playground. However, some teachers are also often involved in the organization of football in school. From a study of primary schools, Swain (2000) argues that schools as regulatory institutions had policies and organized football in ways that created forms of disciplinary power designed to control boys. He identified surveillance, classification (and so differentiation of boys) and normalization (and hence Othering) as techniques of power used by the school and various teachers for this purpose. He argued that there were a number of simmering power-related tensions that were produced by the school's policies and organization of football. He observed antagonism both between pupils and between Year 5 and 6 pupils and teachers over, for example, whose turn it was to play football in a particular playground.

In the previous example, Swain describes conflicts produced by the organization of the school. In the following example, from a study conducted by Valerie Walkerdine (1990) with four-year-old boys, the conflict is not so easily explained. It comes from a very rare, and much-cited, example in a UK nursery school where boys talk to their woman teacher in very sexist language. It comes from a study that is more than 30 years old, but, as we shall see, remains relevant.

Annie takes a piece of Lego to add on to a construction she is building. Terry tries to take it away from her to use himself, and she resists. He says: Terry: You're a stupid c – t, Annie. The teacher tells him to stop, and Sean tries to mess up another child's construction. The teacher tells him to stop. Then Sean says:

Sean: Get out of it Miss Baxter paxter.
Terry: Get out of it knickers Miss Baxter.
Sean: Get out of it Miss Baxter paxter.
Terry: Get out of it Miss Baxter the knickers paxter knickers, bum.
Sean: Knickers, shit, bum.
Miss B: Sean, that's enough, you're being silly.
Sean: Miss Baxter, knickers, show your knickers.
Terry: Miss Baxter, show your bum off. [they giggle]
Miss B: I think you're being very silly.
Terry: Shit Miss Baxter, shit Miss Baxter.
Sean: Miss Baxter, show your knickers your bum off. Take all your clothes off, your bra off.
Terry: Yeah, and take your bum off, take your wee -wee off, take your clothes off, your mouth off.
Sean: Take your teeth out, take your head off, take your hair off, take your bum off. Miss Baxter the paxter knickers taxter.
Miss B: Sean, go and find something else to do please.

(Walkerdine, 1990, p. 4)

Walkerdine (1990) suggests that, in the historical period in which she made this observation, the child-centred pedagogy that schools practised, particularly for younger children, made it difficult for the teacher to cut off the boys' sexist joking at her expense. She treats it as an innocent episode where the boys are simply being naughty. However, Walkerdine suggests that the boys are exercising power over a woman teacher in ways that they have learned will give them power over her. Intersectionally, the period, masculinity and the boys' white, working classness are all of relevance here. Given what we know about how young Black boys were treated in the UK schools at the time (and continue to be treated to some extent) (Sewell, 1997), it is highly unlikely that two Black boys would have been treated so leniently.

Seven years after Walkerdine recounts this episode, Miller (1997) interviewed 16 women teachers in the United States about their experiences of having been student teachers. She presents the experiences of five, all of whom described episodes of sexual objectification by boys and young men who commented on their bodies or whistled at them. The organization of schools is of crucial importance here in that the student teachers were particularly subjected to this in the corridors as they moved between lessons and encountered queues of children waiting to go into the next lesson. Miller (1997, p. 27) concludes that

> Some male students feel entitled to exert power in a school context and demean and dehumanize women student teachers through objectification. Others are mute or provide open support to these behaviours, thus undermining the intellectual and egalitarian mission of public schools.

More recently, Variyan and Wilkinson (2022) interviewed 32 women teachers in three élite private boys' only schools in Australia. Variyan and Wilkinson point out that, while there has been increasing recognition of sexual harassment of teachers at school in various continents, there is little recent academic research. In keeping with Miller's (1997) findings, the women teachers in their study also gave accounts of being subjected to sexual harassment from their male students. They found it difficult, however, to make headteachers believe them if they reported it and some who attempted to tackle the harassment directly with the boys sometimes had to deal with boys' complaints to their parents that the women teachers were being sexually inappropriate. In private schools where parents are clients, this could put the women teachers in precarious positions. Variyan and Wilkinson (2022) suggest that offensive and misogynist behaviour is not an aberration, but a "normative but usually hidden manifestation of white privileged heterosexual masculinity" (p. 183). As they point out, this does not mean that all boys harassed women teachers, "but that sexual harassment is the hidden product of heteronormative 'machinery' that organises relational life within elite private boys' schools" (p. 195).

The point well made by Variyan and Wilkinson (2022) is that sexual harassment is an inextricable part of the broader "cultural, social, political and material-economic arrangements that organise their schools" (p. 183). Part of the intersectionality of gender relations at school is thus sedimented into schools' organizational arrangements and, in consequence, implicitly reproduces gendered norms. It is important to recognize, however, that while their findings are produced within Australian élite boys' schools and have features specific to those contexts, the findings fit those from state schools in a number of countries. For example, Lahelma et al. (2000) argue that women teachers in Finland considered that the sexual harassment they faced was a form of resistance against teacher authority and of shifting power relations in boys' favour. Miller (1997), writing from the United States, suggests that schools are perpetrators of patriarchal values. As she points out, not all boys are involved in this, and it is an unintentional aspect of school organization. However, many boys exhibit what Connell (1996a) calls complicit masculinity and do not challenge sexual harassment that they witness.

It has become clear that sexual harassment is extremely common in schools in many countries and that this has been often neither recognized nor treated seriously. In the United Kingdom, the Office for Standards in Education (Ofsted) conducted a review of 32 schools, speaking to 900 schoolchildren and found that 90% of girls and 50% of boys had been sent sexually explicit pictures they did not want to see and 92% of girls reported that sexist name-calling was common (Ofsted, 2021). The ways in which schools are organized and the availability of social media for schoolchildren make sexual harassment a continuing common means of exercising power relations over many girls and some other genders, reinforcing masculine power. In the United Kingdom, the website "Everyone's Invited" was set up in 2020 following publicity about the widespread nature of sexual harassment in schools, by a UK young woman, Soma Sara. It aimed to give schoolchildren who had been sexually assaulted at school the opportunity to document their experiences. After 50,046 submissions, the volunteers were no longer able to manage to upload the submissions to the website. What was painfully clear is that girls from all social groups had experienced sexual harassment and that many hundreds of schools were involved. This chapter thus raises both ethical and political questions that demand action at the level of both practice and policy. In recognizing the prevalence of unwanted sexual references and harassment at school, it is important to recognize, as Shefer and Hearn (2022) point out, that it is important to challenge unequal and unjust practices in ways that do not reflect or reproduce orthodoxies about sexuality, gender and family and that do not essentialize boys and young men as all the same.

The previous discussion has highlighted aspects of teacher practices that not only arise from the organization of schools but are not aimed at particular children. Yet, while most teachers consider that they behave in egalitarian ways and view all children as equal, there is a variety of research evidence that suggests that teachers construct ideal pupils as white, male and middle class (Walkerdine, 1988). Such boys are considered ideal in being loveably naughty in ways that many teachers think "real children" should be. Youdell (2006, p. 2) found from her ethnographic study in Australia and the United Kingdom that:

> "who" a student is – in terms of gender, sexuality, social class, ability, disability, race, ethnicity and religion as well as popular and sub cultural belongings– is inextricably linked with the "sort" of student and learner that s/he gets to be, and the educational inclusions s/he enjoys and/or the exclusions she faces.

From her ethnographic observation in a US primary school, Ann Ferguson (2000) found that school institutional practices were couched in universal terms but maintained a racial order. In particular, white boys who "act out" were considered "naughty", while Black boys who did so were "adultified" as criminals in the making.

> Once a reputation has been established, the boy's behavior is usually refigured within a framework that is no longer about childish misdemeanors but comes to be an ominous portent of things to come. They are tagged with futures: "He's on the fast track to San Quentin Prison", and "That one has a jail-cell with his name on it". For several reasons, these boys are more likely to be singled out and punished than other children. They are more closely watched. They are more likely to be seen as intentionally doing wrong than a boy who is considered to be a Good Bad Boy.
>
> *(Ferguson, 2000, pp. 95–96)*

In the Finnish context and for younger children, Heidi Layne (2016) shows in a range of studies that teachers often view young children from minoritized ethnic groups as problems within Finnish classrooms and as embodying lack (for example, of Finnish language). Teachers sometimes misrecognize the children they see regularly. From analysis of Black boys' care work in her decades-long US research, Wendy Luttrell (2012) suggests that teachers in multicultural schools often did not see that working-class Black boys, for example, sometimes came late because they had caring responsibilities for younger siblings while their parents went to their jobs. Schools as institutions are often inflexible about issues like lateness and this, together with teachers' social constructions of Black boys, makes their moral agency invisible and opens them up to judgement, rather than support, from teachers.

There are multiple intersectional processes at play in such examples. These include implicit processes of in/exclusion where teachers have lower expectations of, for example, Black, Asian or Muslim young people or white, working-class boys (Archer, 2003; Kurki, 2008; Meetoo, 2020; Youdell, 2006). It also involves differential treatment of groups of children that serve to perpetuate "institutional racism" regardless of expectations (Rollock, 2007a, 2007b) and intersectional cultures of masculinity and femininity that impact engagement with schoolwork (Phoenix, 2008). Teachers, as members of society with their own histories, are implicated in racialized/ethnicized/religious positionings that affect their positioning and the positions they create for their pupils to occupy. Michalinos Zembylas (2015), from decades of research on racism in Cyprus schools, borrows from Foucault's notion of "technology" as assemblages of knowledge, practices, techniques and discourses that people use to achieve particular ends. Racism is linked to affect in that constructing people as racialized others involves the deployment of aversive affects. For Zembylas (2015), racism at school is a "technology of affect", a means by which political sentiment pervades a setting and produces attachments, senses of belonging and so insiders and outsiders and differential treatment (Hook, 2005). Racism, and its intersections with other social categories, thus has far-reaching consequences for children's relationships and outcomes.

Negotiating complex masculinities in peer relationships at school

Connell (2008) points out that school gender regimes are differentiated in that there are often parts of school life where gender is strongly marked and other parts where it is not. The substantial body of research on boys, young men and masculinities at school indicates that what Connell calls processes of masculinity formation are intensely active in interactions with peers in schools where they are thrown together.

In the Helsinki study described earlier (Peltola & Phoenix, 2022), as in most studies of young masculinities, boys reported that friendly relations are important to negotiating masculinities. What is different about the Helsinki boys, however, is that they maintained that everyone is friendly with everyone. In other studies, including Barrie Thorne's (1993) classic study of primary school, boys differentiated themselves into groups where one was dominant and had privileged use of the school space for sports and related activities. In the Helsinki study, boys did have particular interests, hobbies outside school and friends they saw outside school. However, they were invested in maintaining friendly relations because if they did not, they felt that they would potentially be subject to teasing interactions and name-calling. Despite claims of everybody being friends with everybody, they reported that teasing and name-calling were common among boys and one of the ways in which they negotiated masculinities. A central part of the boys' masculine sociality and boys' friendships consisted of joking, which boys considered fun and could be inclusive as well as a means of sharing observations and (positive) emotions. However, as found in other studies, joking was also a way to mark difference, to ridicule others and to establish (masculine) hierarchies. The boys indicated that calling other boys gay was the easiest and most common form of joking, and while they suggested that everybody was equal, their accounts showed how gender, racialization, sexuality and socio-economic positioning were all important to constructing inclusions and exclusions as well as how boys were treated. Intersectionality was thus important and introduced complexity to the analysis of boys' everyday practices (Peltola & Phoenix, 2022). In contradiction to notions that joking is simply fun, boys had to be careful not to take offence even when jokes were racist, homophobic or offensive in other ways (Frosh et al., 2002; Huuki et al., 2010). Connell (2008) suggests that for boys in school the struggle for dominance among their peers could produce bullying and exclusion, particularly of those thought to be effeminate or gay.

While the boys in the Helsinki schools did report some playfighting in the lower years, full-blown fights seemed carefully to be avoided. Yet they gave contradictory accounts of bullying, eschewing the notion that it should be taken seriously.

Bikram: I have noticed that in some groups of friends, the strategy is that, for example, someone is being bullied, well even the bullied one does not care 'cause he is in a group in which they bully each other. So he doesn't care, and he starts bullying them too.
Elias: Yea like kind of joking around.
Bikram: Yea like joking around. But then in some, like our group is like this, that we for example call each other names but no one cares. But then some new guys we do not really know what they are like so, they could for example get sad real fast and get offended.
Luka: Yea.
Mikael: Yea.
Bikram: So then in a way we do not know that.
Mikael: And then as we do not get that we just [keep] joking around.
Bikram: Yea we do not get it.
Mikael: Yea.
Bikram: But for example between us we can call each other names, because nobody cares.
Mikael: And it is not even really calling names –
Bikram: No since –
Luka: It is just kind of joking around.
Bikram: Yea joking around. Like we get the joke and so on, but not everyone necessarily does.

(Focus group 6, 5 boys, 12 years, one with Finnish background, two with migrant parents, two mixed parentage, Harju School)

In the previous extract, joking marks the borders of friendships in that "new guys" do not understand the pattern of joking and can be made sad, whereas those who know each other apparently do not care. It was repeatedly stated that boys had to be more on guard with less close acquaintances – and with girls who did not understand when what was being said was a joke. The fact that only Bikram uses the term "bullied" and that the others and Bikram immediately move on to talking about "joking" shows how joking and bullying are imbricated in each other. The dilemmas of joking/bullying fit with Rosen and Nofziger's (2019) argument that bullying is shaped by the gendered patterns of interaction that are both part of the school institution and culture more generally.

A different sort of example is provided by Archer et al. (2019). From their observation of science classes, she found that:

> A dominant performance was identified across the classrooms of "talking science through muscular intellect". . . . [S]uch performances were experienced ambiguously

> by teachers and were viewed negatively by Other students, notably girls and "quiet" boys, due to silencing their contributions and limiting the range of ways that Others might be recognised as intelligible science students.

Academic boys have been reported in other work to use a muscular intellectualism to "beat up" other people (Redman & Mac an Ghaill, 1996). In the Archer et al. (2019) study, it was clearly experienced as bullying by quiet boys and girls but was another way in which school organization afforded possibilities for dominant masculinities to be performed and negotiated.

Concluding comments

Since schools are institutions that are steered by governments and educational authorities as well as being organized and led by school authorities, change can be difficult to enact. At the same time, schools continually change in relation to ideological changes in society and many people are asking for changes, taking the school closures that were part of the COVID-19 pandemic as opportunities for thinking about the changes that would increase social justice (Ladson-Billings, 2021). It is also the case that shifts in the status of women's football might lead more girls to want space in school playgrounds to play football (Roberts et al., 2020). The ways in which such shifts may be racialized and the place of social class in relation to them remains to be seen.

Despite the ferment of movements like Black Lives Matter and #MeToo, there have not been widespread changes in the ways in which gender and racialization are addressed in schools in the United Kingdom and the United States (Wallace & Joseph-Salisbury, 2022). In addition, the "culture wars" being waged in some countries place schools in contradictory positions where some, who do not want social change, denigrate "wokeness". Despite this, and the continued focus on school effectiveness and efficiency in many countries, changes to gender relations and racialization in terms of how teachers address school pupils seem likely, although they cannot be prejudged.

One of the debates about boys, young men and masculinities at school is about whether, and if so how, masculinities are changing. The research discussed earlier shows both the importance of schools as organizations for the negotiation of masculinities and that there are continuing themes and differences in the ways masculinities are negotiated in schools, both over time and across place. What seems to remain consistent is that boys and young men construct gendered hierarchies in which boys are superior to girls and some masculinities are preferable to others. Intersectional differences in racialization with gender and social class are also reiterated in schools. However, some boys simultaneously "do" masculinities in ways that fit with refusals of hegemonic masculinities and maintain that everybody is friendly with everyone and do not fight and make jokes about each other which could be hard to take.

The plurality of the ways in which masculinities are expressed in schools within, and between, societies shows that masculinities are dynamic, changing over time (as well as across place). The complexity, plurality and local specificity of masculine performativity show the importance of intersectional processes in schools. As Langa (2020, p. 14) suggested from his research in South Africa, hegemonic masculinity is characterized by a "constant process of negotiation, translation and reconfiguration in order to adapt to new historical periods and contexts". The future of schools as organizations is, therefore, one of continued change and contestation (Giroux, 2018) that has implications for future masculinities.

References

Acker, J. (1992). From sex roles to gendered institutions. *Contemporary Sociology, 21*(5), 565–569. doi: 10.2307/2075528

Acker, J. (2012). Gendered organizations and intersectionality: Problems and possibilities. *Equality, Diversity and Inclusion: An International Journal, 31*(3), 214–224. doi: 10.1108/02610151211209072

Anand, I. (2020). A Feminist Approach to Masculinity: How Schools Impose Binaries. Retrieved 1 February 2023, from Feminism in India: https://feminisminindia.com/2020/07/21/masculinity-feminist-analysis-schools-gender-binaries/

Anthias, F. (2020). *Translocational Belongings: Intersectional Dilemmas and Social Inequalities*. London: Routledge.

Archer, L. (2003). *Race, Masculinity and Schooling: Muslim Boys and Education*. Maidenhead: Open University Press.

Archer, L., Nomikou, E., Mau, A., et al. (2019). Can the subaltern 'speak 'science? An intersectional analysis of performances of 'talking science through muscular intellect 'by 'subaltern' students in UK urban secondary science classrooms. *Cultural Studies of Science Education, 14*(3), 723–751. doi: 10.1007/s11422-018-9870-4

Berg, G. (2007). From structural dilemmas to institutional imperatives: A descriptive theory of the school as an institution and of school organizations. *Journal of Curriculum Studies, 39*(5), 577–596. doi: 10.1080/00220270600880994

Bettencourt, L., Dixon, J., & Castro, P. (2019). Understanding how and why spatial segregation endures: A systematic review of recent research on intergroup relations at a micro-ecological scale. *Social Psychological Bulletin, 14*(2), e33482. doi: 10.32872/spb.v14i2.33482

Bonal, X., & Bellei, C. (2019). The renaissance of school segregation in a context of globalization. In X. Bonal & C. Bellei (Eds.), *Understanding school Segregation. Patterns, Causes and Consequences of Spatial Inequalities in Education* (pp. 1–28). London: Bloomsbury.

Codiroli Mcmaster, N., & Cook, R. (2019). The contribution of intersectionality to quantitative research into educational inequalities. *Review of Education, 7*(2), 271–292. doi: 10.1002/rev3.3116

Collins, P. H. (2019). *Intersectionality as Critical Social Theory*. Durham, NC: Duke University Press.

Collins, P. H., & Bilge, S. (2020). *Intersectionality*. Cambridge: Polity.

Connell, R. (1996a). New directions in gender theory, masculinity research, and gender politics. *Ethnos, 61*(3–4), 157–176. doi: 10.1080/00141844.1996.9981534

Connell, R. (1996b). Teaching the boys: New research on masculinity, and gender strategies for schools. *Teachers College Record, 98*(2), 206–235. doi: 10.1177/016146819609800203

Connell, R. (2008). Masculinity construction and sports in boys' education: A framework for thinking about the issue. *Sport, Education and Society, 13*(2), 131–145. doi: 10.1080/13573320801957053

de Boise, S., & Hearn, J. (2017). Are men getting more emotional? Critical sociological perspectives on men, masculinities and emotions. *The Sociological Review, 65*(4), 779–796. doi: 10.1177/0038026116686500

Dunne, M. (2007). Gender, sexuality and schooling: Everyday life in junior secondary schools in Botswana and Ghana. *International Journal of Educational Development, 27*(5), 499–511. doi: 10.1016/j.ijedudev.2006.10.009

Edwards, T. (2004). *Cultures of Masculinity*. London: Routledge.

Ferguson, A. A. (2020/2000). *Bad Boys: Public Schools in the Making of Black Masculinity*. Ann Arbor, MI: University of Michigan Press.

Frosh, S., Phoenix, A., & Pattman, R. (2002). *Young Masculinities: Understanding Boys in Contemporary Society*. London: Routledge.

Gillborn, D. (2015). Intersectionality, critical race theory, and the primacy of racism: Race, class, gender, and disability in education. *Qualitative Inquiry, 21*(3), 277–287. doi: 10.1177/1077800414557827

Giroux, H. A. (2018). When schools become dead zones of the imagination: A critical pedagogy manifesto. In K. J. Saltman & A. J. Means (Eds.), *The Wiley Handbook of Global Educational Reform* (pp. 503–515). Hoboken, NJ: Wiley-Blackwell. doi: 10.1002/9781119082316.ch24

Global Education Monitoring Report. (2022). In Which Countries do Children Attend Single-sex Schools? [UNESCO GEM]. Retrieved 1 February 2023, from https://world-education-blog.org/2021/03/29/in-which-countries-do-children-attend-single-sex-schools/?subscribe=success#subscribe-blog-blog_subscription-5

Gross, C., Gottburgsen, A., & Phoenix, A. (2016). Education systems and intersectionality. In A. Hadjar & C. Gross, C. (Eds.), *Education Systems and Inequalities* (pp. 51–72). Bristol: Policy Press.
Hadjar, A., & Buchmann, C. (2016). Education systems and gender inequalities in educational attainment. In A. Hadjar & C. Gross (Eds.), *Education Systems and Inequalities* (pp. 159–184). Bristol: Policy Press.
Hankivsky, O. (2014). *Intersectionality 101.* Canada, BC: The Institute for Intersectionality Research & Policy: Simon Fraser University.
Hearn, J. (2014). On men, organizations and intersectionality. *Equality, Diversity and Inclusion: An International Journal, 33*(5), 414-428. ISSN: 2040-7149.
Hey, V. (1997). *The Company She Keeps: An Ethnography of Girls' Friendships.* Buckingham: Open University Press.
Hobbs, G. (2016). Explaining social class inequalities in educational achievement in the UK: Quantifying the contribution of social class differences in school 'effectiveness'. *Oxford Review of Education, 42*(1), 16–35. doi: 10.1080/03054985.2015.1128889
Hook, D. (2005). Affecting whiteness: Racism as technology of affect (1). *International Journal of Critical Psychology, 16,* 74–99.
Huuki, T., Manninen, S., & Sunnari, V. (2010). Humour as a resource and strategy for boys to gain status in the field of informal school. *Gender and Education, 22*(4), 369–383.
Ingram, N. (2018). *Working-class Boys and Educational Success.* London: Palgrave MacMillan.
Joy, P., & Larsson, H. (2019). Unspoken: Exploring the constitution of masculinities in Swedish physical education classes through body movements. *Physical Education and Sport Pedagogy, 24*(5), 491–505. doi: 10.1080/17408989.2019.1628935
Kofoed, J. (2006). *Selecting the Team: Doing Whiteness and Masculinity.* Aalborg: Akademiet for Migrationsstudier i Danmark, Aalborg Universitet.
Kofoed, J. (2008). Appropriate pupilness: Social categories intersecting in school. *Childhood, 15*(3), 415–430. doi: 10.1177/0907568208091671
Kurki, T. (2008). Sukupuolittuneita ja rodullistettuja koulutusreittejä. *Maahanmuuttajataustaiset Tytöt Siirtymässä Toisen Asteen Koulutuksiin. Nuorisotutkimus, 26*(4), 26–51.
Ladson-Billings, G. (2021). I'm here for the hard re-set: Post pandemic pedagogy to preserve our culture. *Equity & Excellence in Education, 54*(1), 68–78. doi: 10.1080/10665684.2020.1863883
Lahelma, E., Palmu, T., & Gordon, T. (2000). Intersecting power relations in teachers' experiences of being sexualized or harassed by students. *Sexualities, 3*(4), 463–481. 10.1177/136346000003004006
Langa, M. (2020). *Becoming Men: Black Masculinities in a South African Township.* Johannesburg: Wits University Press.
Lareau, A., & Calarco, J. M. (2012). Class, cultural capital, and institutions: The case of families and schools. In S. T. Fiske & H. R. Markus (Eds.), *Facing Social Class: How Societal Rank Influences Interaction* (pp. 61–86). New York, NY: Russell Sage Foundation.
Layne, H. (2016). 'Contact Zones' in Finnish (intercultural) education. Retrieved 1 February 2023 from Ethesis: https://helda.helsinki.fi/bitstream/handle/10138/165072/ContactZ.pdf?sequence=1&isAllowed=y
Liu, H. (2018). Re-radicalising intersectionality in organisation studies. *Ephemera: Theory and Politics in Organization, 18*(1), 81–101.
Luttrell, W. (2012). Making Boys' care worlds visible. *Boyhood Studies, 6*(2), 186–202. doi: 10.3149/thy.0602.186
Mayall, B. (1994). *Children's Childhoods: Observed and Experienced.* London: The Falmer Press.
Mayeza, E., & Bhana, D. (2020). Boys negotiate violence and masculinity in the primary school. *British Journal of Sociology of Education, 41*(3), 426–443. doi: 10.1080/01425692.2020.1721267
Meetoo, V. (2020). Negotiating the diversity of 'everyday' multiculturalism: Teachers' enactments in an inner city secondary school. *Race Ethnicity and Education, 23*(2), 261–279. doi: 10.1080/13613324.2018.1497962
Miller, J. H. (1997). Gender issues embedded in the experience of student teaching: Being treated like a sex object. *Journal of Teacher Education, 48*(1), 19–28. doi: 10.2307/1167280
Ofsted (2021). *Review of Sexual Abuse in Schools and Colleges.* London: Gov.UK. Retrieved 1 February 2023 from Gov.UK website: www.gov.uk/government/publications/review-of-sexual-abuse-in-schools-and-colleges/review-of-sexual-abuse-in-schools-and-colleges

Owen, C., Moss, P., & Cameron, C. (1999). *Men in the Nursery: Gender and Caring Work*. London: Sage.

Peltola, M. (2020). Everyday consequences of selectiveness. Borderwork in the informal sphere of a lower secondary school in the metropolitan area of Helsinki, Finland. *British Journal of Sociology of Education*, *42*(1), 97–112. doi: 10.1080/01425692.2020.1861930

Peltola, M., & Phoenix, A. (2022). *Nuancing Young Masculinities: Helsinki Boys' Intersectional Relationships in New Times* (p. 232). Helsinki: Helsinki University Press. https://library.oapen.org/handle/20.500.12657/53948

Phoenix, A. (2008). Racialised young masculinities: Doing intersectionality at school. In *Ethnische Diversitäten, Gender Und Schule. Geschlechterverhältnisse In Theorie Und Schulischer Praxis* (pp. 19–39). Oldenburg, Germany: BIS-Verlag.

Phoenix, A. (2022). Intersectional pasts haunt intersectional futures. *Global Dialogues*, *12*(3), 17–19.

Reay, D. (2005). Doing the dirty work of social class? Mothers' work in support of their children's schooling. *The Sociological Review*, *53*(2_suppl), 104–115. doi: 10.1111/j.1467-954X.2005.00575.x

Redman, P., & Mac an Ghaill, M. (1996). Schooling sexualities: Heterosexual masculinities, schooling, and the unconscious. *Discourse: Studies in the Cultural Politics of Education*, *17*(2), 243–256. doi: 10.1007/978-94-6209-305-8_11

Roberts, J. S., Gray, S., & Camacho Miñano, M. J. (2020). Exploring the PE contexts and experiences of girls who challenge gender norms in a progressive secondary school. *Curriculum Studies in Health and Physical Education*, *11*(1), 3–17. doi: 10.1080/25742981.2019.1696688

Rodriguez, J. K., Holvino, E., Fletcher, J. K., & Nkomo, S. M. (2016). The theory and praxis of intersectionality in work and organisations: Where do we go from here? *Gender, Work and Organization*, *23*(3), 201–222. doi: 10.1111/gwao.12131

Rollock, N. (2007a). Legitimizing Black academic failure: Deconstructing staff discourses on academic success, appearance and behaviour. *International Studies in Sociology of Education*, *17*(3), 275–287. doi: 10.1080/09620210701543924

Rollock, N. (2007b). Why Black girls don't matter: Exploring how race and gender shape academic success in an inner city school. *Support for Learning*, *22*(4), 197–202. doi: 10.1111/j.1467-9604.2007.00471.x

Rosen, N. L., & Nofziger, S. (2019). Boys, bullying, and gender roles: How hegemonic masculinity shapes bullying behavior. *Gender Issues*, *36*(3), 295–318. doi: 10.1007/s12147-018-9226-0

Rutter, M. (1979). *Fifteen Thousand Hours: Secondary Schools and their Effects on Children*. Cambridge, MA: Harvard University Press.

Salmon, P. (1995). *Psychology in the Classroom: Reconstructing Teachers and Learners*. London: Continuum International Publishing.

Sewell, T. (1997). *Black Masculinities and Schooling. How Black Boys Survive Modern Schooling*. Stoke-on-Trent: Trentham Books.

Shefer, T., & Hearn, J. (2022). *Knowledge, Power and Young Sexualities: A Transnational Feminist Engagement*. London: Routledge.

Skelton, C. (2001). *Schooling the Boys*. Buckingham: Open University Press.

Stone, N. (2022). Stripping and searching children. *Youth Justice*, *22*(3), 339–348. doi: 10.1177/14732254221134195

Strand, S. (2021). Ethnic, Socio-economic and Sex Inequalities in Educational Achievement at Age 16: An Analysis of the Second Longitudinal Study of Young People in England (LSYPE2). Report for the Commission on Ethnic and Racial Disparities (CRED), Department of Education, University of Oxford. Available online at: GOV.UK (www.gov.uk)

Strand, S. (2022). Education and achievement at 16. *Sociology Review*, *31*(3).

Swain, J. (2000). 'The money's good, the fame's good, the girls are good': The role of playground football in the construction of young boys' masculinity in a junior school. *British Journal of Sociology of Education*, *21*(1), 95–109. doi: 10.1080/01425690095180

Swain, J. (2005). Masculinities in education. In M. S. Kimmel, J. Hearn & R. W. Connell (Eds.), *Handbook of Studies on Men and Masculinities* (pp. 213–229). Thousand Oaks, CA: Sage. doi: 10.4135/9781452233833

Thorne, B. (1993). *Gender Play: Girls and Boys in School*. Chicago: Rutgers University Press.

Variyan, G., & Wilkinson, J. (2022). The erasure of sexual harassment in elite private boys' schools. *Gender and Education*, *34*(2), 183–198. doi: 10.1080/09540253.2021.1962516

Walkerdine, V. (1988). *The Mastery of Reason: Cognitive Development and the Production of Rationality.* London: Taylor & Frances/Routledge.
Walkerdine, V. (1990). *Schoolgirl Fictions.* London: Verso.
Wallace, D., & Joseph-Salisbury, R. (2022). How, still, is the Black Caribbean child made educationally subnormal in the English school system? *Ethnic and Racial Studies*, *45*(8), 1426–1452. doi: 10.1080/01419870.2021.1981969
Youdell, D. (2006). *Impossible Bodies, Impossible Selves: Exclusions and Student Subjectivities.* Dordrecht: Springer.
Yuval-Davis, N. (2016). Beyond the recognition and re-distribution dichotomy: Intersectionality and stratification. In H. Lutz, M. T. H. Vivar & L. Supik (Eds), *Framing Intersectionality: Debates on a Multi-Faceted Concept in Gender Studies* (pp. 155–169). London: Routledge.
Zembylas, M. (2015). Rethinking race and racism as technologies of affect: Theorizing the implications for anti-racist politics and practice in education. *Race Ethnicity and Education*, *18*(2), 145–162.

24

MEN, GENDER AND KNOWLEDGE CONSTRUCTION IN HIGHER EDUCATION

Ana Luisa Muñoz-García, Mara Silva Hope, Gabriela Bard Wigdor and Liisa Husu

Introduction

Contemporary, modern universities and higher education may appear to be gender-neutral organizations. Yet decades of research on gender in academia have demonstrated how universities and the scientific community more broadly are gendered social phenomena. Indeed, the very origin of the university is gendered. The university as an institution – but importantly *not* the pursuit of science itself going back thousands of years – was built solely on male privilege and female exclusion (see, for example, Schiebinger, 1999, pp. 21–32). Throughout their history from the eleventh century until the late nineteenth century, with some rare exceptions, universities excluded women based on sex. Only men had the right to teach and hold academic posts. It was not until the nineteenth and twentieth centuries that barriers to women were gradually lifted after they acquired the right to university studies. Meanwhile, some women pursued science elsewhere outside of universities (Schiebinger, 1999).

The entry and increase in women's enrolment in higher education in the twentieth century have been described as "dramatic progress" (Stolte-Heiskanen et al., 1991). Higher education enrolment is approaching gender parity globally but continues to be characterized by gender segregation of disciplinary fields, as well as by vertical segregation (see, for example, Times Higher Education and UNESCO IESALC, 2022). Men's overrepresentation, especially in the professoriate, and gender inequalities in academic careers are persistent and global phenomena (Stolte-Heiskanen et al., 1991; Harding et al., 1995; Caprile, 2012; UNESCO, 2019; European Commission, 2021). Entrenched gendered and male-dominated patterns in academia appear almost regardless of cultural differences or differences in the overall state of gender equality in a given country. Globally, under a third of researchers were women in 2016, with the highest shares of women in Central Asia (48.2%) and Latin America and the Caribbean (45.1%), and lowest, less than two out of ten, in South and West Asia (UNESCO, 2019). Chile, the country this chapter focuses on in more detail, ranks with 33.1% women, 16th among the 20 Latin American countries where women employed in research and development areas were measured (Mandiola, 2021).

These questions have preoccupied feminist scholars in studies in higher education and science studies for a long time. Since the mid-1990s, these issues have been placed prominently

DOI: 10.4324/9781003193579-27

on the agenda in mainstream science and higher education policy, nationally and internationally. This has occurred in universities (see, for example, Fogelberg et al., 1999; MIT, 1999; Drew & Canavan, 2020), national research funding agencies (Husu & de Cheveigné, 2010; European Commission, 2009), high-profile science journals such as *Nature* and *Science*, the United Nations and its specialized agencies such as UNESCO (Harding et al., 1995; UNESCO, 2019, Times Higher Education and UNESCO IESALC, 2022), and the European Union (see, for example, Rees, 2001; European Commission, 2021, 2022).

Academia is about studying, taking degrees, teaching, administration, supervising, grading, writing, researching, publishing, refereeing, mentoring and being mentored, networking, managing resources and people and being managed, fundraising, conferencing, travelling, career advancement, the making of professionals and experts, introducing and fighting for new ideas, production of new knowledge, gatekeeping, outreach, and more. Academia is about intellectual activity and knowledge production but also about competition, recognition and prestige (Bourdieu, 1988). Gender differences have been found in most of these arenas (for example, Caprile, 2012; Fox et al., 2017). These gender differences may vary in extent across cultures and disciplines, but a general tendency is that the differences tend to be for men's advantage and women's disadvantage. An exception is student enrolment where there is now a female majority in many disciplines in many countries in humanities, arts, social sciences and medicine. That women are a majority among students in many countries has often led to misleading claims of "the feminization of the university", ignoring the fact that women continue to be a minority among students in STEM fields (Science, Technology, Engineering and Mathematics), that gender imbalance among the academic staff has changed only very slowly, and that university leaders are mainly men (see, for example, European Commission, 2021; Times Higher Education and UNESCO IESALC, 2022).

Moreover, when speaking about "gender", the term itself and the conceptualization of gender have often mainly referred to women in most studies on gender and higher education, science and academia, as well as in policy development. Where men are named explicitly and included in the analysis, it has been mainly as a comparison group, such as in studies of career progress, scientific productivity and funding success. Problematizing academic masculinities, instead of taking them for granted, and studying academic men as gendered, "as men", is a relatively new development (Hearn, 2020). This includes research on academia as a site of men's power, privilege and mutual support (Bulumulle, 2015), neoliberal university management (Hearn, 2017), diverse academic masculinities (Collier, 1998), constructions of disciplines and research cultures (Gonsalves et al., 2016), gendered processes in publication (Ding et al., 2006), research funding (Bornmann et al., 2007), and assessment of CVs and differential letters of recommendation (Madera et al., 2009).

In this chapter, we emphasize that addressing gender inequalities in academia and higher education primarily or merely as a head count issue is not enough to achieve gender equality. Common narratives of "women taking over academia", "feminization" or there being "too many women" indicate that there is a lack of awareness of hegemonic masculinity norms and gendered hierarchies. When the focus is on counting heads, complex gendered power dynamics in academic structures, cultures and careers are easily ignored, the negative impacts of numerous gendered practices and sexism, gender-based violence and racism in academia are not recognized, and intersectional approaches are neglected. The main argument of this chapter is that when counting heads is prioritized in creating, installing and implementing gender equity policies in higher education, without recognizing complex processes of inclusion, the policies will not address many of the fundamental issues that produce inequality.

To illustrate how systems of knowledge in higher education are deeply rooted in hegemonic masculinity, we focus on discourses about research and knowledge construction within the academic Chilean higher education system.

Hegemonic masculinity and academia in Latin America

This section outlines some broad patterns around gender and academia in Latin America. As in most regions across the globe, higher education institutions in Latin America, such as universities, are social spaces where sexist practices persist in research and teaching policies and in the discourses and practices of people in their daily lives. However, while at the discursive level, institutions often present themselves as a cutting-edge space for gender and inclusion, in reality, hegemonic masculinity norms are prevalent in academic socialization, communities and epistemic regimes, as well as the theoretical and political approaches that govern universities. Buquet (2011) explains that most academic advances in gender issues occurred from university research. Despite various gender studies programmes in Latin America, they work in marginal spaces within the universities and have not profoundly impacted university systems in higher education, neither their institutional policies nor their sexist practices within it.

Likewise, for Morgade (2018), universities may assume that there is gender equality because there is a large mass of female students in the university; however, that it in itself does not necessarily or directly impact the everyday sexist practices or the patriarchal power relations because the concentration of power remains with men. There is a symbolic agreement that the power of high-ranking positions in universities should be for men. In addition, cis-hetero-patriarchal micropolitical practices discourage women from occupying positions in higher ranks. Also, feminine subjectivity fostered by patriarchy often prevents women from seeking senior hierarchical positions because they may be perceived, and even perceive themselves, as less prepared.

Universities are often built on homosocial reproduction, in which men promote like-minded men and mainly interact with other men to produce knowledge or make decisions. Women often organize, request or promote practical or bureaucratic activities called "academic housework" (Mandiola et al., 2019). This can also include care work, such as helping to ease tensions among colleagues and students in a neoliberal university where increasingly high demands are placed on academics and students. Domestic or academic housework in the university includes invisible and unpaid tasks, which do not promote the academic career (Mandiola et al., 2019). This gender division of tasks responds to men's androcentric values and patriarchal subjectivation. Women are predominantly regarded as emotional, not rational and placed on the side of nature and constructed in opposition to reasonable and political men. According to previous analyses of feminism and knowledge production in universities in Latin America, the hegemonic subject of science and technology is male, and women in the field are constructed as objects who listen passively to what men say (Maffia, 2007; Muñoz-Garcia, 2020a).

For the Argentinian context, Morgade (2018) points to the gender imbalance in the distribution of positions, and that research leaders are typically men who assign tasks to women. Therefore, in line with Connell and Messerschmidt (2005), it is relevant to analyse how androcentrism, sexism and hegemonic masculinity are reproduced in this kind of control of women, the prevalent heteronormativity, and practices of competition and surveillance. These dynamics take place between men and towards marginalized groups. The form of patriarchal subjectivity that is dominant in academia is connected to other relations of discrimination, inequality and marginalization, such as class, race, ability and age (Connell, 2005). Hegemonic masculinity is constructed as white, male, heterosexual, economically, socially and culturally powerful and in opposition to women and marginalized and subordinated masculinities such as gay or trans people (Bard Wigdor, 2018, 2020).

Gender and research in higher education in Chile

We now turn more specifically to a case of higher education and research in Chile. Over the last decade, various policies and initiatives related to science and gender were promoted, as part of the reorganization of the key Chilean institution for promoting and financing scientific research, now called the National Agency for Research and Development (ANID – previously called Conicyt), which is now part of the Ministry of Science, Technology, Knowledge, and Innovation (BCN, n.d.). New policies impacting the entire system of research in higher education include the Conicyt Gender Equity Policy (2012), the Institutional Policy for Gender Equity in Science and Technology 2017–2025 (2017), the Gender Equity Policy (2020) and the Gender Bureau that was created to update the Institutional Policy on Gender Equity in Science and Technology (2017–2025). During 2021, roundtables with women researchers and a national survey have been convened throughout the country to create guidelines for a Gender Policy. The National Policy on Gender Equality in Science, Technology, Knowledge and Innovation was published in 2021; this is a document that presents a diagnostic of the current state of the art, setting out objectives and principles associated with its 50/50 by 2030 action plan (MinCTCI, 2021).

The national programme responds to the continuing demand for research from a gender perspective on sexual and labour harassment and abuse of female researchers. These demands have been forcefully articulated, especially since the May 2018 feminist movement in Chile. The May 2018 movement emphasized the need for protocols on sexual harassment, and non-sexist education at all educational levels, as well as demanding an end to patriarchal violence (Hiner & López Dietz, 2021; Muñoz-García et al., 2018; Jackson & Muñoz-García, 2019; Muñoz-Garcia, 2020a; Muñoz-Garcia & Lira, 2020). These sustained efforts were intended to close gender gaps so that women can stay in academia and continue with their careers. In Chile, only 34% of those who work in research are women, only 16% lead Centres of Scientific and Technological Excellence, and 22% of the tenured professors of the Council of Rectors of Chilean Universities (CRUCH) universities are women. Of the 59 universities in the country, only five have a female President (MinCTCI, 2021).

Mandiola (2021) analysed these policies and finds that except for the Institutional Policy of Gender Equity in S&T 2017–2025, the others do not explicitly define what they understand by gender, equity/gender, equality or gender mainstreaming – a trend which often occurs for gender-equality and diversity policies (cf. Callerstig, 2014, p. 115; Verloo & Lombardo, 2007, p. 22). There is little theoretical detail on how gender and sex are used in the documents. Mandiola also points out that in the publications, gender relations are not understood as power relations and that gender mainstreaming does not go beyond "*counting women and men*" (Mandiola, 2021, p. 12). The measures focus on the access of women without questioning why women do not or cannot access these academic spaces: "it is not enough that women enter [to the academic spaces], but we must also question where and what are their possibilities of participation in the spaces they access" (Mandiola, 2021). Some of the data used to illustrate the gender gap in research are the award rate of the national research funding instrument Fondecyt Regular.[1] Between 2017 and 2021, 26% of the Fondecyt Regular grants were held by women and 74% by men (ANID, 2022a). In highly feminized areas such as education, of the 39 total Fondecyt Regular projects awarded in 2022, 19 are led by a woman, and 20 by a man (ANID, 2022b).

Further analyses from feminist perspectives on gender and knowledge (Muñoz-Garcia, 2020a; 2020b) established that although there is parity in access to undergraduate and master's degrees in higher education in Chile, the proportion of women decreases progressively as they advance to doctoral studies (MinCTCI, 2020) and in the academic hierarchy within the university (MinCTCI, 2021). Furthermore, those who obtain a doctorate earn on average 20% less than their male peers, regardless of the work sector (MinCTCI, 2021). According to the Ministry of Science, Technology, Knowledge and Innovation, reasons for the underrepresentation of women on higher levels are gender biases in the evaluation of research projects, the assumption that women take care of children, family and domestic roles, sexist stereotypes, the devaluation of their abilities, and harassment, discrimination and violence.

Based on that context, between 2017 and 2020, it was conducted an extensive study on knowledge policies in the field of education. We found that resistance to gender-equality policies is connected to an idea and understanding of gender equality based solely on the high presence of women. What is neglected and not acknowledged is the gendered division of academic labour that relates to widespread norms around what it means to be a woman and a man in academia. Other important aspects of discrimination identified include the constant delegitimization of women's work and the complex process that many women researchers must face within the university concerning the validation of their knowledge.

Although the focus of this study was knowledge issues, the fieldwork was set during the peak of the feminist movement in May 2018 and before the social uprising in Chile in October 2019. Sixty-two semi-structured interviews were conducted with policymakers, research managers and academics from the educational field. According to the Conicyt research project award databases, academics were selected and contacted by email. Nineteen interviews were conducted during the first year with people participating in national commissions and research reports in Chile and with deputies and Senators active in science and technology commissions. That year, academics who participated in the Conicyt Education Study Group were interviewed. In the second year, we interviewed 43 people, including Vice Chancellors, research directors and scholars working in faculties of Education. Of the 62 interviewees, 31 were women, and 31 men. Interviews were conducted in Spanish; pseudonyms were used to analyse and present the data and translated quotes into English, as in the following extracts.

The analysis involved a data coding process, identifying a set of codes that later were used for a specific analysis on gender issues and the construction of knowledge (Clarke & Braun, 2017), like gender and research, gender and science, and gender and academia. Codes were defined and discussed by the research team inductively from the data collected. Thematic analysis (Clarke & Braun, 2017; Nowell et al., 2017) to analyse policies and practices of research from a feminist perspective was used. Doing a study on research policies in higher education, thematic analysis was useful in understanding emerging themes such as uncovering resistance to extending the research clock for scholars who were mothers and were applying for grants. While thematic analysis allowed us room for emerging themes, a feminist perspective provided the lens to understand and theorize the generated during the first two years of fieldwork. Themes were identified arising from interviews where the participants talked widely on gender policies in research created lately by the National Commission of Science and Technology and the demands of the feminist movement in Chile. This back-and-forth dialogue with the raw data and the social context in which the research was taking place allowed us to reflexively decide the ways each theme fits into the overall story of the large research project. Thus, in the analysis, we paid attention to the ways the gender discourses on research practices were creating tensions within the process of constructing knowledge.

Hegemonic masculinity in the field of education, where men are a minority

Hegemonic masculinity can also perpetuate highly feminized academic spaces. In the educational academic field, a narrow idea of gender equality is based on the majority presence of cisgender women in the discipline at the student and lower faculty levels. However, the idea of overcoming gender discrimination, inequality and gender-based violence is questioned when the academic trajectories and gender differences in knowledge construction are brought into the picture. Indeed, in our own studies, we have observed how research continues to be a space governed by hegemonic masculinity, even in fields with a high numerical presence of women.

We begin with Javier, an academic who works at a private university. When we asked what it means for him to be a man developing research, the look on his face showed profound bewilderment with the question. He considers that we live in a deeply unequal society regarding gender. Yet he thinks it is "*irrelevant*", in his words, to reflect on his participation in producing knowledge in a highly feminized field. He closes his argument with "*perhaps a woman could answer that question with much more sensitivity, I would not know what to tell you*", thus positioning sensitivity as a feminine emotional characteristic, the antithesis of masculine rationality, while also acknowledging the limits of his perception and knowledge of the matter. On the other hand, the statement could be interpreted to mean that women have "much more sensitivity" as a result of their greater knowledge and experience of sex discrimination and marginalization.

Like Javier, Rodrigo, an academic at a private university in the Capital, considers that in education, "*even though I do not have statistical studies, surely the proportion of women investigating must be 60 per cent*". In addition, he is convinced that problems in research have nothing to do with gender but "*with egos*", and that was independent of whether you are a woman or a man. Similarly, Sebastian, an academic who works at another private university, considers that the distinctions between men and women should not be highlighted as a problem. He explains that "*the role of women in research, in the field of education, I do not know if it should be an issue, . . . one should see what he does, and not whose pen it is*". These positions show that the informants are not aware of gendered power relations in the field, and gendered power relations remain, as so often, invisible and taken-for-granted. Also, Sebastian considers that it would seem very wrong to make distinctions in the research arena and "*listen*" more or less based on the idea of being a woman or a man. By the idea of listening, he means reading their work or having a public voice just because someone is a woman. He adds that in the future he expects an "*egalitarian, democratic and participatory academic space, without making distinctions*". On the other hand, he acknowledges that in "*engineering women have been brutally marginalized, in education not*". In various times during the interview, Sebastian insists on his long-standing work with female colleagues, highlighting his colleagues' "*rigorous and impeccable work*", and how rewarding it is to work with them.

For Pedro, an academic from another private university, the issue of gender has become a relevant discussion in recent years, and in his faculty he sees more female researchers than men. He considers that in education there is "*a natural gender balance*", meaning that there is equal number of men and women. In a similar vein, Manuel, an associated academic from a private university, believes that *"fortunately in education there are many female colleagues"*; therefore, it is a privileged space to "*learn from them [women] and in the most educational, pedagogical way possible when one incurs in sexist attitudes or actions that go unnoticed*".

Others, like Cecilia, who works as an academic at a private university are aware of different processes concerning gendered power relations at the university: "*I hadn't mentioned it, but [gender] is a complex issue because research projects, except for some specific programs, are not dominated by women despite being a discipline dominated chiefly by women*". Cecilia analyses the imbalance in the presence of female researchers in the educational area, and how it impacts what she calls "*the perpetual gap*" in academic careers and the positions of full professors in the system. Like many other women academics, she considers that research is disseminated differently between men and women, usually more visibility given to studies by men academics. This imbalance of the academic work that Cecilia draws attention to is also recognized by Felipe, an academic who works in a public university. He describes a strange feeling of knowing that, in education, "*you share mostly with female colleagues, and that gives you a feeling of equality. However, most of the people who make decisions are men*". In addition, Felipe, who has "*brown skin*" and "*experiences racism in multiple ways*" also suggests extending equality work to include aspects of racism, homophobia, ableism and classism.

The responses of these participants illustrate how masculine hegemony can be made invisible by the feminization of a disciplinary field such as education. Beyond the feminization of the discipline, the positionalities occupied by the different corporealities within the academic space are also made invisible. What is problematic about the previous findings is that "*that feeling of equality*" that Cecilia mentions is later contradicted by the gendered validation processes and the gendered division of academic labour, experienced and observed mostly by women researchers in universities.

Academic divisions of labour and processes of differential validation

The high number of women in the academic field of education was understood by most of the interviewed men as an expression of gender equality or as an indicator that men were a minority. In contrast, the interviewed women emphasized how much they struggle to be validated within academic spaces. The academic division of labour could partly explain why women are often absent in senior positions. Tania, an associated professor from a university on the South of Chile, explains that "*things have not changed that much during the past decade*" and that women's situation has changed from being "*homemakers at home to homemakers of the university*". According to Carmen (an academic . . .), this corresponds to a "*logic where knowledge in Chile has been associated with being a masculine domain*". Tania deeply expresses the differences she has to face as a researcher who works in an "*academy that has a heteronormative logic, where women bear the greatest burden of raising children*". As a researcher, she presents everyday examples that allow us to understand hierarchies and gender divisions in academia: who do we ask for authorization to investigate, who carries out the paperwork, who leads a project and who executes it, and also who leads research centres or research grants?

Processes of validation and legitimacy that many female academics go through within university spaces and in doing research put into question the naturalized idea of women's increased participation as a solution to gender discrimination and inequality. An early career academic, Angelica, expands on the idea of barriers and facilitators that make her path an "*uphill*" task. She describes the distribution of scores for authorship in publications and participation in research projects. Before the interview, she thought participating in projects and publications as a second or third author was also valued, from an understanding that knowledge is "*a collective construction*". However, she realized, during the interview, the assigned scores are differentiated depending on where one is listed. To her, "*it seems disastrous to think that one should always go first. It discourages collective work*".

Similarly, Rafaela, an academic from another private university in the capital, an institution more oriented to teaching, described slowness of the processes and difficulties for women to advance in their academic careers at the university. Rafaela explains that women have "*a historical disadvantage, which means permanently demonstrating the capabilities of our male colleagues*". She recognized that "*the world of education is feminine*". She considered that research moves within a masculine logic, and the world of teaching and formation is mainly done by women. According to her, her fellow men researchers are cited and considered in the national discussion on research issues, and "*they have never had to prove what they had attained just for the fact of being a man and being there, so for oneself, it has always been two or three times more difficult to do*".

The existence of high presence on women in the academic field of education is sometimes seen as a sign of equality. However, the idea of equality vanishes when discussing research and knowledge construction. Other conversations related to the processes of validation and the division of academic labour emerge, complicating the questions about who those are who do research, who is advancing in academic careers, and who gradually acquires or end up in roles related to domestic work at the university and position themselves in the hierarchy in a way that gives them less stability, prestige and recognition in the universities. This leads us to think about the sexist structure interwoven in academic spaces that perpetuates hegemonic masculinity, even in highly feminized spaces.

Final remarks: the structure is uneven

Gender positionalities are important in knowledge construction. The widespread lack of awareness of unequal gender norms, and thus of self-reflection from a gender perspective, as shown in this Chilean study, especially among men, naturalizes existing gender relations in universities and omits attention to the sexist structure of academic spaces in which these gendered processes occur. There is a reluctance to talk about masculinity because gender is still widely understood as a women's issue. In the field of education, men are a minority. Therefore, one might imagine that how hegemonic masculinity operates in the research arena might not be a critical or explicit issue.

The result of this study shows a lack of awareness that gender-equality efforts are not only about counting heads but also need to be about countering hierarchical power relations. The valuation of some people over others becomes a problematic aspect in universities because it ignores that the universities work in a capitalist, cis and heteronormative, patriarchal order (Enciso Domínguez et al., 2021). For example, statistically, in Chile, there is a more significant number of women in areas that usually have lower wages, that are less socially valued, and are associated with the patriarchal, feminized roles of women (INE, 2015). Another example of this resistance can be seen in the argumentative fallacy of citing some anecdotes as evidence, or some indirect and specific references to a relationship or knowledge of the few women who occupy positions of power to affirm that gender inequality does not exist. That is an extraordinary situation used to make it a rule (Maffía, 2006) and prop up sexism by undermining or not taking gender studies and the policies that have historically been generated to address this structural inequality seriously (Pereira, 2012, 2017). In this way, androcentrism and scientism, typical of a colonial view of knowledge and its elaboration processes, are evidenced and show that scientific knowledge is not neutral, objective and/or disembodied (Anderson, 1995). We argue that it matters who, how and in what way knowledge is constructed in academia (McShane, 2021). Ignorance of the structural situation of universities regarding gender is the mirage that Gloria Bonder talks about in an interview with Graciela Morgade, as it is challenging to recognize that discrimination exists and does not change automatically with head counts (Morgade, 2015). More complex still, the figures that show equivalence between numbers of men and women in universities in some positions, without being accompanied by feminist analysis, lose focus on the causes of discrimination. We should question those figures: how do women enter these spaces? What are the feminized and gendered trajectories in the university? How is the hierarchical pyramid of the university composed according to gender?

At the same time, one of the most relevant aspects that results of this study invite us to think about is the omission or ignoring of a sexist structure that regulates all aspects of politics and the daily life of universities (Ahmed, 2015). For example, the statement by Manuel, "*There is a lack of more men investigating in education and the classrooms of the school system*", invites us to analyse why men are not in educational spaces of school teaching, and debate the role of masculinity in the educational processes of initial and primary level. Historically, education and training have been associated with motherhood and care, and these educational spaces continue to be associated with the world considered by capitalism as private family sphere. Therefore, they are not so much associated with masculinity and the world of the public and the political. For example, although Manuel mentions, accurately, the proportion of women actively working in schools, it is necessary to consider that this participation is also linked to salary hierarchies where women occupy positions with lower salaries, to a greater extent. To be more specific, in Chile, while a high school teacher earns around US$13 per hour, in Initial Education, a preschool assistant receives around US$7 for the same hour worked. It is no coincidence that 73% of the teaching staff in the Chilean school system are women and 27% are men. Particularly in Early Childhood Education, this percentage of women reaches almost 100%. Data are absent when it comes to recruitment and promotion processes in academia. Nevertheless, despite the numeric balance of men and women in postgraduate studies and early career academics, the number of women decreases as we advance in the academic hierarchy (MinCTCI, 2021).

As women feminist researchers, we reconsider the question posed by Manuel: Is there a lack of men in the educational field? We say yes. They are less numerous at the base of the pyramid, where basic training tasks central to people's socialization are carried out, and where it is said in common sense terms, "*teachers are like second mothers*". Thus, men are less present in the primary classroom because they do not act as "*second parents*". It is not the space assigned for hegemonic masculinity. A similar situation is described in universities, where most women are teaching and doing administrative work, and less in leading educational research (Mandiola et al., 2019). This becomes key to understanding knowledge construction and gender in a context where research circulates as an axis consolidating academic prestige.

Drawing from our Chilean case, the patriarchal structure is fundamental for understanding exclusions and inclusions and the reproduction of sexist logics in the higher education system and, more specifically, in the knowledge construction system. The patriarchal system does not translate into the fact that women have the same opportunities; on the contrary, it shows that the few who arrive, to sustain themselves, must masculinize the exercise of power as a hierarchical and subordinate device. In addition, it involves women learning new practices, discourses and technologies of power and developing support strategies in hostile worlds due to their clear masculinization. On the other hand, an essentialist discourse about what it would be like to be a woman, typically related to care, protection and education, ratifies historical roles in which women are usually positioned (Mandiola et al., 2019). From this essentialist vision, and in addition to the interviews, the binary structuring of Western Cartesian thought is evidenced in assumptions about the existence of two sexes, woman–man, with difficulties perceived in including other sexualities and genders that escape the biological and heteronormative fiction of reality (Mardones et al., 2020). Further, this translates into the materials that are taught, and how they are taught in undergraduate and graduate degrees, perpetuating the colonial binaries of women/men and reflecting on all the oppressed bodies in this academic regime. Indeed, trans corporealities do not even emerge in the academic discourse of our study as possible actors in the university.

To sum up, discourses of the feminization of the field and the "marginalization" of men often overlook the struggles women had to wage regarding their limited historical participation in the political and public world, including the university sphere. We were interested in understanding those critical knots in the research arena in Chilean context, and in the context of a feminist movement that mobilized across an entire country. We encountered resistance woven into university work that limits and complicates the possibilities of advancing a gender-equality agenda. When some claim there were not enough men in a field with a majority of women, that there was gender parity or even accusations of "reversed gender discrimination" (in the words of one of the interviewees), their statements imply that persisting patriarchal inequalities are not taken into account adequately. Feminism and sexual dissidence contribute to creating awareness of existing structural inequalities in society and the higher education system, but that knowledge does not easily become predominant. Furthermore, it would be necessary to incorporate a more complex and nuanced view of gender issues and resistance to gender advances in universities.

Finally, we emphasize that higher education, as a field to produce knowledge and a space for training, cannot be satisfied simply with counting bodies, and favouring the number of women as the only measure of equity. It is necessary to think about how gender figures and gender relations are transformed and/or materialized in concrete action plans, and how the construction and production of knowledge can take place through equal opportunities and conditions. This work also requires an emancipatory transformation of cultures, norms, institutional practices and subjectivities related to hegemonic masculinity.

Note

1 Fondecyt Regular is the Chilean National Fund for Scientific and Technological Development. It aims to encourage and promote the development of basic scientific and technological research. It is the main public fund of this kind in the country.

References

Ahmed, S. (2015). Introduction: Sexism – A problem with a name. *New Formations: A Journal of Culture/Theory/Politics*, *86*, 5–13.

Anderson, E. (1995). Feminist epistemology: An interpretation and a defense. *Hypatia*, *10*(3), 50–84. doi: 10.2307/3810237

ANID (2022a). *Panel Interactivo Compendio Estadístico 2017–2021*. Departamento de Estudios y Gestión Estratégica. Retrieved 15 August 2022, from the MinCTCI's website: https://app.powerbi.com/view?r=eyJrIjoiNjkzMTZhN2YtNTNlMi00ODIxLTkzYjYtN2EwYWM2MTM2MDM0IiwidCI6ImU3M2FmMWRlLWU5ZTYtNGM0OS1iMWUxLWZjNjg3ZjM2MjY0NyIsImMiOjR9

ANID (2022b). *Concurso Nacional de Proyectos Fondecyt Regular 2022. Proyectos seleccionados para adjudicación*. Ministerio de Ciencia, Tecnología, Conocimiento e Innovación. Retrieved 21 June 2022, from MinCTCI's website: https://s3.amazonaws.com/documentos.anid.cl/regular/2022/postulacion/Nomina-Aprobados-Regular-2022.pdf

Bard Wigdor, G. (2018). Las violencias romantizadas: Masculinidades hegemónicas en el capitalismo tardío y heteropatriarcal. *Aposta. Revista de Ciencias Sociales*, *77*, 59–100.

Bard Wigdor, G. (2020). Controversias y reflexiones feministas en el centro del capitalismo tardío. Sudamérica. *Revista de Ciencias Sociales*, *13*, 213–237.

BCN (n.d.). *Ministerio de Ciencia, Tecnología, Conocimiento e Innovación. Ley Fácil*. Biblioteca del Congreso Nacional de Chile. Retrieved 25 September 2022, from BCN's website: www.bcn.cl/leyfacil/recurso/ministerio-de-ciencia,-tecnologia,-conocimiento-e-innovacion

Bornmann, L., Mutz, R., & Daniel, H. D. (2007) Gender differences in grant peer review: A meta-analysis. *Journal of Informetrics*, *1*(3), 226–238. doi: 10.1016/j.joi.2007.03.001

Bourdieu, P. (1988). *Homo Academicus*. Berkeley, CA: Stanford University Press.

Bulumulle, K. S. (2015) *Interrogating What is Male Privilege in the Academy*. Doctoral dissertation, University of Adelaide, Adelaide.

Buquet, A. G. (2011). Transversalización de la perspectiva de género en la educación superior: Problemas conceptuales y prácticos. *Perfiles educativos*, *33*(spe), 211–225.

Callerstig, A. C. (2014). *Making Equality Work: Ambiguities, Conflicts and Change Agents in the Implementation of Equality Policies in Public Sector Organisations*. Linköping: Linkoping University Press. doi: 10.3384/diss.diva-105207

Caprile, M. (Ed.). (2012). *Meta-analysis of Gender and Science Research* (Synthesis report). Brussels: European Commission.

Clarke, V., & Braun, V. (2017). Thematic analysis. *The Journal of Positive Psychology*, *12*(3), 297–298. doi: 10.1080/17439760.2016.1262613

Collier, R. (1998). 'Nutty professors', 'men in suits' and 'new entrepreneurs': Corporeality, subjectivity and change in the law school and legal practice. *Social & Legal Studies*, *7*(1), 27–53. doi: 10.1177/096466399800700

Connell, R. W. (2005). *Masculinities*, 2nd edition. Berkeley, CA: University of California Press.

Connell, R. W., & Messerschmidt, J. W. (2005). Hegemonic masculinity: Rethinking the concept. *Gender & Society*, *19*(6), 829–859. doi: 10.1177/0891243205278639

Ding, W. W., Murray, F., & Stuart, T. E. (2006). Gender differences in patenting in the academic life sciences. *Science*, *313*(5787), 665–667. doi: 10.1126/science.1124832

Drew, E., & Canavan, S. (Eds.). (2020). *The Gender-sensitive University: A Contradiction in Terms?* London: Routledge. doi: 10.4324/9781003001348

Enciso Domínguez, G., González-Yañez, M., & Chiappini, F. (2021). Resistencias y reproducciones de mujeres académicas: Estrategias de supervivencia en la academia patriarcal/neoliberal. *Quaderns de Psicología*, *23*(2). doi: 10.5565/rev/qpsicologia.1603

European Commission, Directorate-General for Research and Innovation (2009). *The Gender Challenge in Research Funding: Assessing the European National Scenes*. Luxembourg: Publications Office of the European Union. doi: 10.2777/36195

European Commission, Directorate-General for Research and Innovation (2021). *She Figures 2021: Gender in Research and Innovation: Statistics and Indicators*. Luxembourg: Publications Office of the European Union. doi: 10.2777/06090

European Commission, Directorate-General for Research and Innovation (2022). *Towards Inclusive Gender Equality in Research and Innovation*. Luxembourg: Publications Office of the European Union. doi: 10.2777/162481

Fogelberg, P., Hearn, J., Husu, L., & Mankkinen, T. (Eds.). (1999). *Hard Work in the Academy: Research and Interventions on Gender Inequalities in Higher Education*. Helsinki: Helsinki University Press.

Fox, M. F., Whittington, K., & Linkova, M. (2017). Gender, (in)equity, and the scientific workforce. In U. Felt, R. Fouché, C. A. Miller & L. Smith-Doerr (Eds.), *Handbook of Science and Technology Studies* (pp. 701–731). Cambridge, MA: MIT Press.

Gonsalves, A. J., Danielsson, A., & Petterson, H. (2016). Masculinities and experimental practices in physics: The view from three case studies. *Physical Review Physics Educational Research, 12*(2). doi: 10.1103/PhysRevPhysEducRes.12.020120

Harding, S., McGregor, E., & Abir-Am, P. G. (1995). *The Gender Dimension of Science and Technology*. Paris: UNESCO.

Hearn, J. (2017). Neoliberal universities, patriarchies, masculinities, and myself: Transnational-personal reflections on and from the Global North. *Gender a výzkum/Gender and Research, 18*(1), 16–41. doi: 10.13060/25706578.2017.18.1.348

Hearn, J. (2020). Men and masculinities in academia: Towards gender-sensitive perspectives, processes, policies and practices. In E. Drew & S. Canavan (Eds.), *The Gender-sensitive University: A Contradiction in Terms?* (pp. 97–109). London: Routledge. doi: 10.1515/9783110651874-014

Hiner, H., & López Dietz, A. (2021). ¡Nunca más solas! Acoso sexual, tsunami feminista, y nuevas coaliciones dentro y fuera de las universidades chilenas. *Polis Revista Latinoamericana, 20*(59), 122–146. doi: 10.32735/S0718-6568/2021-N59-1590

Husu, L., & de Cheveigné, S. (2010). Gender and gatekeeping of excellence in research funding: European perspectives. In B. Riegraf, B. Aulenbacher, E. Kirsch-Auwärter & U. Müller (Eds.), *GenderChange in Academia*. Wiesbaden: VS Verlag für Sozialwissenschaften. doi: 10.1007/978-3-531-92501-1_4

INE (2015). *Mujeres en Chile y mercado del trabajo: Participación laboral femenina y brechas salariales*. Santiago, Chile: Instituto Nacional de Estadísticas.

Jackson, L., & Muñoz-García, A. L. (2019). Reaction is not enough: Decreasing gendered harassment in academic contexts in Chile, Hong Kong, and the United States. *Education Theory, 69*, 17–33. doi: 10.1111/edth.12357

Madera, J. M., Hebl, M. R., & Martin, R. C. (2009). Gender and letters of recommendation for academia: Agentic and communal differences. *Journal of Applied Psychology, 94*(6), 1591–1599. doi: 10.1037/a0016539

Maffía, D. (2006). El vínculo crítico entre género y ciencia. *Clepsydra, 5*, 37–57.

Maffía, D. (2007). Epistemología feminista: La subversión semiótica de las mujeres en la ciencia. *Revista Venezolana de Estudios de la Mujer, 12*(28), 63–98.

Mandiola, M. (2021). Juegos de mesa: Política de género en ciencia. *Observatorio Económico, 156*. doi: 10.11565/oe.vi156.418

Mandiola, M., Ríos, N., & Varas, A. (2019). "Hay un tema que no hemos conversado" La cassata como organización académica generizada en las universidades chilenas. *Pensamiento Educativo. Revista de Investigación Educacional Latinoamericana, 56*(1), 1–16. doi: 10.7764/PEL.56.1.2019.10

Mardones Leiva, K., Apablaza Santis, M., & Vaccari Jiménez, P. (2020). Discursividades binarias en las políticas educativas de género y sexualidad en Chile. *Estudios pedagógicos* (Valdivia), *46*(1), 399–411. doi: 10.4067/S0718-07052020000100399

McShane, J. (2021). What does it mean to 'decolonize' gender studies?: Theorizing the decolonial capacities of gender performativity and intersectionality. *Journal of International Women's Studies, 22*(2), 62–77.

MinCTCI (2020). *Radiografía de Género en Ciencia, Tecnología, Conocimiento e Innovación*. División de Estudios y Estadísticas. Diciembre 2020. Retrieved 21 August 2022, from MinCTCI's website: www.minciencia.gob.cl/uploads/filer_public/ea/43/ea435b1-bf76-4100-85c2-9c0da4ccad4d/radiografia_genero_2020.pdf

MinCTCI (2021). *Política Nacional de Igualdad de Género en Ciencia, Tecnología, Conocimiento e Innovación. Plan de Acción 50/50 para el 2030*. Ministerio de Ciencia, Tecnología, Conocimiento e Innovación (Ministerio CTCI), MinCTCI, Ministerio de la Mujer y la Equidad de Género, Subsecretaría de Educación Superior y Subsecretaría de Comunicaciones.

MIT (1999). A study on the status of women faculty in science at MIT. *The MIT Faculty Newsletter, XI*(4).

Morgade, G. (2015). Entrevista a Gloria Bonder. *Revista Del IICE, 38*, 89–94. doi: 10.34096/riice.n38.3463

Morgade, G. (2018). Las universidades públicas como territorio del patriarcado. *La universidad hoy, a 100 años de la Reforma, 1*, Especial #5.

Muñoz-Garcia, A. L. (2020a). A conversation on sexism in gender policies in research. In S. Strid, D. Balkmar, J. Hearn & L. Morley (Eds.), *Does Knowledge Have a Gender? A Festschrift for Liisa Husu on Gender, Science and Academia* (pp. 210–226). Örebro: Örebro University Press.

Muñoz-Garcia, A. L. (2020b). Reflexiones feministas para otra investigación posible. *Cuadernos de Teoría Social, 12*(12), 14–40.

Muñoz-García, A. L., Follegati, L., & Jackson, L. (2018). Protocolos de acoso sexual en universidades Chilenas: Una deuda pendiente. *Serie de Policy Briefs, 20*, 1–6.

Muñoz-Garcia, A. L., & Lira, A. (2020). Creando políticas feministas en educación. In M. Corvera & G. Muñoz (Eds.), *Horizontes y propuestas para transformar el sistema educativo chileno* (pp. 140–167). Santiago, Chile: Biblioteca del Congreso Nacional de Chile.

Nowell, L. S., Norris, J. M., White, D. E., & Moules, N. J. (2017). Thematic analysis: Striving to meet the trustworthiness criteria. *International Journal of Qualitative Methods, 16*(1). doi: 10.1177/1609406917733847

Pereira, M. D. M. (2012). "Feminist theory is proper knowledge, but . . .": The status of feminist scholarship in the academy. *Feminist Theory, 13*(3), 283–303. doi: 10.1177/1464700112456005

Pereira, M. D. M. (2017). *Power, Feminist Knowledge and Feminist Scholarship: An Ethnography of Academia*. London: Routledge. doi: 10.4324/9781315692623

Rees, T. (2001) Mainstreaming gender equality in science in the European union: The 'ETAN report'. *Gender and Education, 13*(3), 243–260. doi: 10.1080/09540250120063544

Schiebinger, L. (1999). *Has Feminism Changed Science?* Cambridge, MA: Harvard University Press. doi: 10.7788/figurationen.1999.0.0.50

Stolte-Heiskanen, V., Acar, F., & Ananieva, N. (1991). *Women in Science: Token Women or Gender Equality?* Oxford: Berg.

Times Higher Education and UNESCO International Institute for Higher Education in Latin America and the Caribbean (IESALC) (2022). Gender Equality. How Global Universities are Performing, Part 1. Retrieved 25 November 2022, from Times Higher Education's website: www.timeshighereducation.com/digital-editions/gender-equality-how-global-universities-are-performing-part-1

UNESCO (2019). Women in Science. Fact Sheet No 55, June 2019. Retrieved 28 September 2022, from UNESCO's website: https://unesdoc.unesco.org/ark:/48223/pf0000381749?posInSet=7&queryId=N-33cabba6-1973-455e-8c66-ded1055addb5

Verloo, M., & Lombardo, E. (2007). Contested gender equality and policy variety in Europe: Introducing a critical frame analysis approach. In M. Verloo (Ed.), *Multiple Meanings of Gender Equality* (pp. 21–50). Budapest: Central European University Press. doi: 10.1515/9786155211393-005

PART IV

Current and future issues

25

THE HEGEMONY OF MEN IN GLOBAL VALUE CHAINS

Insights for intersectional labour governance[1]

Lauren McCarthy, Vivek Soundararajan and Scott Taylor

Introduction: global value chains, governance and the absence of men

Exploitation, low pay, dangerous sites, unsafe materials, excessively long hours, bullying and sexual harassment are a few of the damaging labour conditions and working practices that persist within the global value chains (GVCs) producing the majority of the world's goods. Labour governance mechanisms such as standards, social audits and worker welfare programmes have all sought to eradicate or modify these conditions, with some success. Notwithstanding, GVCs remain highly problematic with deleterious effects on labour that stretch across the globe.

In this chapter, we argue that labour governance mechanisms, designed to better-working conditions in GVCs, could be significantly enhanced through greater attention to the intersection of practices and narratives of masculinity (Connell, 2005) and the social category of "men" (Hearn, 2004). We draw on Hearn's (2012) conceptual framing of "hegemony of men" as a means of deconstructing and denaturalizing the social construction of what it means to be "a man". Our aim is not to essentialize men as beholden to biology, or to demonize them, but to develop a more complex understanding of "rigidities and movements of and around the taken-for-granted social category of men . . . and hegemony within and among men, whether in terms of ways of being or men's practices" (Hearn, 2004, p. 66). Applying this frame to GVC labour governance research shows how damaging or violent practices are experienced, reproduced and challenged both discursively and materially in GVCs.

Value chains are commonly defined as "the full range of activities that firms and workers perform to bring a product from its conception to end use and beyond . . . [which] includes activities such as design, production, marketing, distribution and support to the final consumer" (Gereffi & Fernandez-Stark, 2011, p. 4). These chains become "GVCs" when they begin to include "inter-firm networks on a global scale" (ibid.). Lead firms tend to be held accountable for substandard labour practices in faraway factories, plantations or mines (Boyd et al., 2007), such that many now incorporate labour conditions into contractual and relational exchanges (Bird & Soundararajan, 2020).

These exchanges rely on two key mechanisms: top-down social auditing programmes and bottom-up welfare or empowerment programmes (Soundararajan & Brown, 2016).

DOI: 10.4324/9781003193579-29

Social audits measure and report on the social and ethical performance of suppliers against an adopted benchmark, usually codes of conduct and sustainability standards/certifications. Codes provide ethical guidelines developed by lead firms to guide stakeholder engagement (Emmelhainz & Adams, 1999), while third-party sustainability standards and certifications, also known as private regulations or multi-stakeholder initiatives (Mena & Palazzo, 2012), are quasi-voluntary benchmarks for monitoring and reporting developed through deliberation between multiple stakeholders (usually firms, civil society and state).

Firm-led welfare and worker empowerment programmes, usually developed alongside non-governmental organizations (NGOs), are designed to govern GVC labour conditions from the "bottom-up" (Prügl, 2015). Examples include Coca-Cola's 5by20 women's empowerment programme, operating across Africa, the Middle East and South America (Tornhill, 2019), which trains women in finance and micro-entrepreneurship skills to "upgrade" them in GVCs, and Gap's PACE programme in India (Nanda et al., 2013), which delivers peer-to-peer health and finance education for women workers in factories. These operate on instrumentally rational logics: educated, empowered workers are said to take fewer sick days, be more loyal and work more efficiently (Nanda et al., 2013), but the extent to which they achieve their aims of empowerment has been questioned (McCarthy, 2017; Tornhill, 2019).

The most important aspect of GVCs, and the labour governance mechanisms therein, is that they are embedded within gendered and racialized forms of capitalism. The term "racial capitalism" (Robinson, 2000 [1983]) highlights how capitalism melded with pre-existing racializing processes of colonization across Europe in feudal times. It has since been developed to show how racial difference is produced within capitalist systems to create ideas of differential value. Racism, as a by-product of racialization, is then utilized within economic processes such as land ownership and labour (Pulido, 2017). We use the term "racialized" as per Bhattacharyya et al. (2016) to emphasize the ongoing processual nature of the phenomenon. Capitalism is gendered and racialized because it seeks to derive value through difference (Pulido, 2017), and gender and race remain two of the most explicit and enduring ways of categorizing difference (Federici, 2004). By emphasizing difference between men–women, Black–white and developed–underdeveloped–undeveloped, higher value is placed on men (and masculinity), whiteness and the Global North.

GVCs are an economic structure where these differences are attenuated, emphasized and wherein some people's value is rewarded while others are exploited (Bonacich et al., 2008). Within GVCs, differences are produced along class, caste, religious and national identities in combination with race and gender. Labour governance mechanisms are known for their lack of attention to differentiated postcolonial contexts (e.g. Özkazanç-Pan, 2019), gender (e.g. Barrientos et al., 2003) and unequal power relations between northern and southern actors (e.g. Khan & Lund-Thomsen, 2011). Our specific contribution is to shine light on the importance of men and masculinities in GVC practice and scholarship.

Men and masculinities disproportionately affect all structures, agents and cultural political economies that GVCs operate through, contexts characterized by organizational violence and force. GVC governance can be understood differently by naming the social category of "men" as a key analytic. This does not mean reproducing gender stereotypes or re-asserting binaries. We use man/woman as categories that have been socially constructed as different, bringing material and political implications for the people living with those categories (Levine, 2015). We also draw on intersectional feminist analysis (Crenshaw, 1989) to understand the power relations that masculinities and men reproduce or resist. This enables a quite different understanding of GVCs, focusing on "multiple differentiated patriarchies" (Hearn,

2004, p. 66) and inequalities that are "the outcome of intersections of different social locations, power relations and experiences" (Hankivsky, 2014, p. 1; see also Mohanty, 2003). This approach to men and masculinities shows how the experiences of less-privileged group members can be erased (Crenshaw, 1989; Liu, 2017). Some men benefit from their assumed gender, while others do not, but dominant forms of patriarchal, racialized masculinity continue to drive exploitative conditions with differentiated intersectional effects within most GVCs. Ignoring this limits the effectiveness of GVC labour governance mechanisms, such as audit programmes and welfare interventions, with real impacts on the lives of all.

Our argument unfolds in three main sections. First, we review some debates in critical studies on men and masculinities (CSMM), emphasizing the analytical potential of the "hegemony of men" framework. We then discuss the two key labour governance mechanisms through dimensions of gender differentiation, power, practice and women's roles, to show how they are inherently limited in ethics and effects because of the lack of attention paid to the social category of men. We conclude by summarizing the implications of our argument and offer a renewed research agenda for analysis of GVCs and labour governance mechanisms.

Masculinities, men and GVCs

Masculinities as a concept developed rapidly during the 1980s and 1990s, especially in the work of Connell with her notion of hegemonic masculinities. Initially, research focused on reasons for gender inequality – or, more precisely, explanations of women's continued subordination to men (Carrigan et al., 1985). Analysis centred on "manhood acts" (Schrock & Schwalbe, 2009, p. 277) and "configurations of practice" (Connell, 2005, p. 44) that position women as different and subordinate across multiple, intersecting social, cultural, political and economic spheres, sometimes but not always drawing on feminist analytics (Schrock & Schwalbe, 2009). This work is often allied with feminist theories and movements, as a way of naming the "dominant centre" in order to deconstruct it (Hearn, 1996), to de-naturalize men's actions and behaviours in order to critique them (Hearn, 2012). In this, it provides a relational lens that derives from an understanding of gender as social construction (Connell, 1987) performed in everyday social life (Butler, 1990). Masculinities are acknowledged as relational, plural, temporally and spatially variable, and differentiated. Structural, material conditions and everyday embodied "doings" and "sayings" provide understandings of power relations and dynamics of resistance (Connell, 2005). As a gender dynamic, masculinities interact with other socially constructed categories such as ethnicity, sexuality, nationality, class and age.

Organizational research often identifies patriarchal or hegemonic masculinities in everyday practices that include control, aggression and violence (Alcadipani & Tonelli, 2014), pathological risk-taking (Knights & Tullberg, 2012), callous competitiveness and emotional detachment (Kerfoot & Knights, 1998), belittlement (Collinson, 1988), direct and indirect discrimination (Slutskaya et al., 2016) and an absence of collaboration and trust (Ely & Meyerson, 2010). However, this research often neglects the places intimately connected to northern organizations through GVCs. This suggests that understanding of the social category of men and the implications of GVC practice lacks insight into global and transnational dynamics (Hearn, 2015), especially in the Global South. This could be remedied by repositioning men as key actors in maintaining the patriarchal structures that hegemonic masculinities seek to explain.

The most conceptually coherent way to do this is through careful reading of Hearn's (2004, 2012) development of ways to see "the hegemony of men", which "seeks to address the double complexity that men are both a *social category formed by the gender system* and *dominant collective and individual agents of social practices*" (Hearn, 2004, p. 59, emphases in original). This highlights discursive and materialist experiences of gender (Hearn, 2012). Hearn's argument draws on a wide range of theoretical influences, including Marxian feminist perspectives on political economy, historical scholarship, poststructuralist and postcolonial theory, queer theory and intersectional feminism, to allow for the development of a wide-ranging empirical agenda. Importantly, Hearn advocates looking critically at "dominant constructions, powers and authorities of men in relation to women, children and other men, both men who are subordinate and those who are superordinate" (Hearn, 2012, pp. 597–598). This shows and deconstructs men's categorical power, a practical action aligned with theoretical development that acknowledges the everyday realities of power relations within GVCs. It also provokes a renewed research agenda for understanding the governance of GVCs, working with four of the categories (amalgamated from the initial seven) that Hearn (2012) proposes.

First, close examination of the system of differentiation shows the social category of men as a binary system of power relations with normative ideals embedded in it (Allen, 1998). This focuses on how and why men are set apart from women, discursively and materially, contributing to the social construction of a hierarchy of status designed to reproduce discriminatory gendered norms (Allen, 1998). This may include "conduct of state and statistical classifications; religious and educational practices; and institutional ways in which people are placed within the social category of men" (Hearn, 2012, p. 597). Such systems of differentiation aid the hegemonic acceptance of a category of men. Within GVC research, it is especially important that race, religion, nationality, caste and migrant status be included in analysis of such systems of differentiation, given how embedded these are within racialized capitalism (Federici, 2004).

Second, detailed examination of which men, and therefore which men's practices, shows how differentiation processes are framed. The category of men is best seen as a spectrum, a "composite, multi-layered hierarchical structure" (Levine, 2015, p. 84) in itself. This spectrum is a political fact defined by dialectics of identity and difference articulated through social assumptions of binary reality. This translates into treating the social category of men as (a) different (from the social category of women, non-binary, trans and intersex people); (b) intersecting with other categorical experiences (e.g. race, religion and caste) in complex ways; and (c) open to material and symbolic differentiation within the broad overall category. This brings together discursive and materialist perspectives, to develop clarity on distinctions between men as individuals and group members, and the social construction of normative, repressive discourses as to how and why identity and membership are achieved/denied.

Third, it suggests more detailed attention to the everyday practices men engage in to maintain, reproduce or disrupt the social categories that patriarchal structures rely on. Hearn (2004) stresses that it is the everyday taken-for-granted naturalized "normal" performances of masculinity that should be detailed, rather than overt displays of "machismo" (although these may also be present).

Finally, we turn to the effects of these systemic forms, power relations and practices on members of the social category of women and vice versa. This is distinctive from the excellent work that has been done on women's experiences of working in GVCs (Barrientos et al., 2003). We start with the specific question of how a hegemony of men affects women and how they can support or undermine men's practices. It is important to avoid any sense of women being responsible for the current dominance of men; however, there are complex responses written into women's experiences, which may contribute to exploitation or resistance, individually or collectively.

Taken together, this shows how analysing the social category of men as a means of critiquing GVC governance structures and practices can provide distinctive accounts of men's agency for the analytical purpose of gaining insight into the power relations of GVCs. Power is a "very significant, pervasive aspect of men's social relations, actions, and experiences" (Hearn, 2004, p. 51) relative to women which, despite the increase in critical analysis of GVCs, corporate governance and labour conditions, continues to be under-theorized and under-analysed (Elias, 2008). Our argument leads to much more nuanced understandings of how key social categories are manufactured and maintained by a dominant group to reproduce social structures and everyday norms of practice. This reorientation towards dominant norms and taken-for-granted ideologies implies more attention to the "of whom and by whom" (Hearn, 2004, p. 55) exercise of power to clarify the form and nature of dominance and resistance. It is also fundamentally practical in relation to lived experience, showing and deconstructing men's power in order to understand and challenge exclusionary authority and patriarchal social systems. In this, it is the beginning of a feminist critical theory of power relations in GVC governance with emancipatory aims, challenging normative concepts and problematizing their effects. We now turn to applying the framework to our field of GVC labour governance.

The hegemony of men in labour governance mechanisms

These four dimensions provoke a series of questions for GVC governance scholars, shown by brief illustrations drawn from our past research into labour governance standards and worker empowerment programmes in the United Kingdom, India and Ghana, alongside contributions from other scholars working in this area. We show how the hegemony of men is embedded in social audit and worker welfare programmes, which currently fail to capture or problematize asymmetries of gendered power manifest in the dominance of men. We raise the possibility that governance is based on (some) men's interests in making the issues and interests of women and (some) men lesser or unimportant, and argue that this is a key research issue for the future.

Systems of differentiation

Hearn (2012) emphasizes the social–structural forms that differentiate men from women, and between different groups of men. GVC governance is clearly structural in the shape of regulations, legislation and rules, and social in the assumptions these forms make about who qualifies as "male" or "female", and differences within this binary (Connell, 1987). Feminist and postcolonial analyses have, to an extent, shown how and why contemporary global trade, commodities and capital flows – the fundamental systems that enable GVCs – are both gendered and racialized (Bhattacharyya et al., 2016). Taking a historical perspective, Clark (1994) details how gender relations between men and women changed during British colonization of Ghana, as women were excluded from the "masculine" cash-crop business of cocoa, and pushed into more informal (and thus "inferior") trading livelihoods. In India, Ramamurthy (2010) shows how the expansion of multinational corporations into cottonseed production relies on the intersection of caste and age to produce new gender roles, as men leave waged employment to grow cottonseed, formerly seen as young girls' work. De Neve (2014) explores the different ways in which men and women within the garment sector in India navigate employment opportunities according to their gendered ages, class and caste statuses. Younger male textile workers are encouraged to compete with one another to produce most in the shortest amount of time, performing patriarchal forms of masculinity to re-assert agency in repetitive and poorly paid work. This in turn sets the benchmark for women workers' performance, often unachievable, leading to gender-based violence. GVCs not only thrive from systems of differentiation but also shape them by associating masculinities and femininities with different forms of work and worth.

Audit programmes which rely on the labour regulations, norms and assumptions of sourcing destinations create similar systems of differentiation. Their baseline is compliance with local regulations; however, state labour regulations act in themselves as a system of differentiation. For example, Indian labour regulations state maximum working hours as 9 hours per day or 48 hours per week; beyond this, workers are entitled to receive overtime wages. These rules apply equally to both women and men; yet in addition, employers are encouraged to permit women to work only between 6 a.m. and 7 p.m. Even under exceptional circumstances, women should never be working between 10 p.m. and 5 a.m.; during working hours, women's breaks are often closely monitored (Nagaraj, 2019). None of these latter restrictions apply to men. These temporal delineations show how labour regulations seek control over women's time and work, and thereby societal position and role.

Norms and assumptions in context also act as systems of differentiation by characterizing the types of work men and women will perform. Within GVCs, women are guided towards so-called lower-skill tasks, such as weeding, weaving, harvesting, fruit and flower picking, embroidery and packaging, positioned as diligent, unquestioning and delicate-fingered (Ahmed, 2018; Elson & Pearson, 1981; Ruwanpura & Hughes, 2016). Men are often found working on more physical tasks: pesticide-spraying, heavy machinery use, shifting, carrying and loading (McCarthy, 2018; Van der Gaag, 2014). Different tasks are socially constructed as suitable for women or men as an extension of normative gendered roles as carers or protectors (Salzinger, 2003), relevant to the spaces in which women and men are "supposed to" be found: women "at home" and men "at work" (Ruwanpura & Hughes, 2016). This segregation affects pay, as roles women are encouraged to command less, or no, material reward (Bain, 2010).

Systems of differentiation are equally present within corporate-led welfare programmes, shown in a very clear distinction between social categories of "male" and "female", and the types of work people thus categorized are encouraged into. Such segregation is especially prevalent in the welfare focus on women's economic empowerment. On one hand, these programmes represent awareness of women's systemic oppression and exploitation; on the other, they reflect women as human capital, a resource for international agencies, governments and corporations (Tornhill, 2019). Women are simultaneously positioned as victims and saviours, with implications for how men are situated in development (Cornwall et al., 2011) and corporate responsibility narratives (Lee & Parpart, 2018). Who is included in worker empowerment programmes, and how they are portrayed, reproduces the persistent, damaging norms that inflect the production of "correct" roles and behaviours of women and men within systems of differentiation that uphold the hegemony of men.

Differentiation is also present in the types of economic activity women are encouraged into. Small-scale trading, baking, mobile phone charging or work designated as "craft" are defined as suitable forms of "micro-entrepreneurship" (Tornhill, 2019). These activities can fill gaps in regular working life, for example, between harvests; however, they can also prevent women being recognized as legitimate agentic individuals. For example, in Ghana, female cocoa farmers were considered "helpers" rather than full members of the profession (McCarthy, 2017). It is instructive to consider what jobs male workers might be encouraged to take if they were participants in a worker empowerment programme. Would they be guided to weave baskets, make jewellery or bake bread? Or would types of work and their attendant socially constructed notions of worth change once men were involved (De Neve, 2005, 2014)? Both audit and welfare programmes neglect as well as contribute to continued systems of differentiation between women and men, and men and men, which in turn serve to maintain a hegemony of men and reproduce oppressive practices.

Powerholders

GVCs are sites of complex power imbalances (Nadvi, 2008), operating within racialized capitalism, which tend to "concentrate power and dominance among particular groups of men" (Patel-Campillo, 2012, p. 275) – white, usually European, Australasian or North American men. Hearn's conceptualization directs us beyond the North–South binary to consider the fluidity of intersectional power relations reproduced by men within a particular space, which we now explore.

Traces of racialized capitalism are found in the design and promotion of audit programmes that suggest southern actors need to be externally monitored, in order to uphold northern righteousness. This leads to the construction of northern consumers having an ethical conscience, and "white-knight" heroic managers helping develop less fortunate local producers (Liu & Baker, 2016). Southern actors are depicted as "developing" rule takers, their experiences or preferences given less importance (Khan et al., 2007). When orientation to change is based on practices of domination and top-down compliance, and when coercion and distrust surround the relationship, southern actors may resist through continuing irresponsible, oppressive practices, producing false evidence of compliance (Soundararajan & Brammer, 2018).

However, northern actors' power can be diluted through the value chain (Soundararajan & Brown, 2016). Power is transient and contextually embedded (McCarthy, 2017) and although audit programmes are designed in the North, implementing actors are southern men who control resources on the ground. Within this, there is additional complexity, in that power and resources do not reside just with one group of southern men. Stratification through religion and caste in India, for example, plays a crucial role. There is uneven dispersion in resource endowment, uneven access to productive resources and opportunities and uneven rewards to resource contributions, making some groups of men more powerful than the others (Bapuji & Chrispal, 2020). Higher value-generating activities in Indian GVCs are often controlled by upper caste Hindu men, while workers and those engaged in so-called lower value-generating activities practice minority religions and "belong" to lower castes (Soundararajan et al., 2018). Migrant men and women are discriminated against and dehumanized by local residents and employers both in the North (Cohen, 2018) and the South (Revathy, 2018). In sum, some men have persistent control over other men and women, and some men are oppressed so that powerholders can retain their position. Unless these nuances are captured, as they are in the hegemony of men framework through its emphasis on men as a social category, audit programmes are unlikely to address oppression shaped by power relations in particular contexts.

Similarly, within corporate-led welfare programmes, power relations should ostensibly be re-balanced given the emphasis on "empowerment" of workers (Tornhill, 2019). Yet defining women as "profitable subjects" (Chatterjee, 2020, p. 10) does little to challenge systemic forms of gender, race and other oppressive social stratification (Özkazanç-Pan, 2019). Participants are often selected based on demonstrations of compliance with programme agendas (Tornhill, 2019); the primary outcome is the promise of economic empowerment, however low quality of the actual work itself. Claims that programmes help in achieving a form of economic independence are contrasted with low returns and high social and economic risks (Dolan & Scott, 2009). While men in the Global North finance and market such programmes (reaping reputational dividends), research suggests it is largely women who implement and run them, without full resources or a voice in the design (McCarthy, 2015). This omission is repeated in neglecting to consult producers', workers' and families' preferences (Tornhill, 2019), as shown in McCarthy's (2017) analysis of how women cocoa farmers were encouraged to work in "craft" groups to supplement their farming income. The women preferred to work alone, resisting the programme's design. Asking "which men" benefit, and "which women" are involved in empowerment programmes, opens up intersectional power relations.

A focus on women workers and the exclusion of men within many corporate welfare programmes serve to reify the repressive system of difference on which the hegemony of men relies. For example, by only teaching women workers about health, nutrition and sanitation (modules offered by Primark's Sustainable Lives or PACE), programmes continue to position women as family and community carers, with men absent, absolved or excluded from these responsibilities. This has considerable effects on allocation of unpaid care work and contributes to male resistance to gender-equality programmes (Van der Gaag, 2014). In combination with the feelings of powerlessness certain groups of men within GVCs may experience, further exclusion in this form may serve to exacerbate, rather than eradicate, inequalities.

Practices

We now direct attention to practices across GVCs through which systems of differentiation and power relations are reproduced. Two particular practices, exclusion and threat, are significant here. While audit programmes may be normatively based on the principle of democratic legitimacy, southern actors, especially women and marginalized men, are often excluded from design and implementation planning (Khan et al., 2007). Southern suppliers, unionists or workers are not fully represented on the standard governing boards (Alamgir & Alakavuklar, 2020); some may enjoy membership for observation, but without voting rights. This limits voice and has implications for the content of the benchmarks. For example, women's specific needs related to working environments (e.g. safe transport, safe toilet facilities, access to breastfeeding space) are absent in part because of the exclusion of women's voices and dominance of (some) men's (Bain, 2010). Simply adding women or marginalized people to these decision-making bodies does not equate to higher levels of equality (Alamgir & Alakavuklar, 2020). Even when appropriate provisions are included, control over resources can give dominant men power to maintain conventional business practices without implementing them.

Threat, another practice that maintains systems of differentiation and reproduces power relations, manifests at various levels in GVCs. At the transnational level, northern lead firms use threat as a tactic to make southern suppliers comply with preferred auditing programmes.

Non-compliance is punished with penalties or order cancellation, encouraging compliance by any means possible. This rule-based approach to GVC labour governance reflects a patriarchal and racist discourse on control and authority. As Knights (2015, p. 212) explains: "[the use of] deontological rules and regulations . . . shores up, rather than threatens masculine phallic and logocentric power at the cost of an ethics of commitment to openness". This helps explain how, despite the development of hundreds of auditing programmes, exploitation and corruption still occur in places that are apparently heavily "regulated" (Connell & Wood, 2005).

As a result of threat, suppliers may engage in "evasion work", everyday practices that appear "to follow the rules while violating the essence of those rules to misdirect the interpretation of others" (Soundararajan et al., 2018, p. 1303). This creates a representation of conformity by, for example, bribing state authorities to obtain false documents or avoid inspection, training workers in "correct responses" to questions, operating multiple facilities under different names and falsifying workforce size for tax evasion purposes. This enables lead organizations and suppliers to satisfy stakeholders while perpetuating damaging or exploitative social and environmental practices. Within factories and service spaces, threat is also used as a tactic to curb resistance and increase obedience. It is manifest in verbal or physical abuse, including sexual abuse of women committed by dominant men such as male owners and supervisors (Global Labor Justice, 2019). Both women and men workers can be frightened away from expressing displeasure, speaking out during auditing practice or joining/forming unions (Anner, 2015). "Disobedient" workers are dismissed or are subjected to further threat or physical violence.

The relationship between women and the hegemony of men

We now draw attention to women, to ask how women are positioned within GVCs in ways that support, or challenge, the production and maintenance of the hegemony of men. Women negotiate positions in GVCs within a system of "patriarchal bargaining" (Kandiyoti, 1988) that is especially significant to relative power within households, and therefore the degree to which women can contest gender relations. This process shapes not only women's rational choices, to remain safe economically and socially while avoiding violence, but also their subjectivity and agency, varying from context to context. Within GVCs, some women make use of "coping mechanisms", which suggests they (appear to) accept ascribed patriarchal practices. For example, women contribute to evading auditing practices by remaining silent or expressing what they were trained or ordered to do (Crane et al., 2019; Soundararajan et al., 2018). Some women (appear to) accept subordinate roles or less well-paid employment, positioning themselves as ignorant, refraining from expressing views or considering certain areas of work beyond their gender status (Kandiyoti, 1988). Women can adopt a "just worldview" (Lerner, 1980) to make sense of gendered power relations, defending powerholders' positions and attributing moral superiority to them. This can lead to intragroup othering: signalling of otherness among women workers, especially when moving up in a role hierarchy as supervisor or manager.

Feminist scholars have long argued that girls' and women's opportunities in terms of education, paid work and leisure are reduced by unpaid caring tasks, which fall overwhelmingly to women (Folbre, 2006). Who performs unpaid care work matters because it contributes to assumptions about personal worth and value related to work (hooks, 2003), which in turn shore up the hegemony of men, and demean or ignore the unpaid labour on which capitalism also depends (Federici, 2004). In GVCs, women are associated with unpaid labour or poorly paid feminized labour, while men are associated with production and paid work (Ramamurthy, 2010). This has not changed as more women have moved into employment; many men still consider domestic work a fundamental subjective challenge to their identity as men (Kato-Wallace et al., 2014). Assumed roles and identities are naturalized such that women may insist they are responsible for these duties that men are "useless" at, or unable to perform. This limits opportunities for men and women to engage in both spheres of experience, which would provide benefits for men, women and society. Men who experience shared caregiving in their childhood homes are more likely to practise this as adults (Levtov et al., 2014), indicating a pressing generational need for change in both attitudes (practices and relations) and structural policies (systems of differentiation) (Kato-Wallace et al., 2014) in the hegemony of men. Yet less than half of all nations provide paternity or shared parental leave, and where it is offered, men often do not use it (Van der Gaag et al., 2019).

GVC welfare programmes can contribute to damaging assumptions about unpaid labour practices, re-positioning women as carers and men as providers within the hegemony of men. When women are guided towards home-based crafts or trading that they can carry out alongside their caring responsibilities, this can be read in two ways. It may be interpreted as a practical way of responding to how life is organized for the majority of women around the world, a corporate-led move to enable women to "bargain" their time. However, these programmes do not challenge the damaging, discriminatory status quo; rather, they make it easier for assertions of appropriate practices for men (paid work, away from home) and women (unpaid or piecemeal work, close to home) to strengthen (McCarthy, 2017). This is problematic for any claims to "empowerment" or "welfare"; without men taking on domestic unpaid labour, women cannot achieve freedom or equality (Folbre, 2006). Equally men's lives are limited when they do not share in home-making and care of others (Van der Gaag et al., 2019). As much as unpaid labour is described as a "burden", it is also an expression of love, belonging and community, that all human beings benefit from (Folbre & Nelson, 2000).

There are of course shifts in women's relation to the hegemony of men. Bargaining connotes a repositioning of power, however small. In the cocoa value chain, some women used training and inclusion to call out inequities between men and women, particularly related to unfair sharing of unpaid labour (McCarthy, 2018). Women organized and vocalized against malpractice within Bangladeshi textile factories through trade unions (Alamgir & Alakavuklar, 2020), co-opted a "business-case" for better treatment in Mexico (Plankey-Videla, 2012) and resisted gender expectations through "hysteric" behaviours in Malaysia (Ong, 2010). Challenges to dominant power are facilitated through feminist NGOs and community groups, some of which work with GVC labour governance mechanisms to do so (Grosser & McCarthy, 2019).

Renewing GVC research

Through this critical review, we offered observations about the relationship between the hegemony of men and two GVC labour governance mechanisms, standards/auditing and welfare programmes. Our argument develops a research agenda that focuses on the social category of men and the complex forms that interact with it. It is important to reiterate how governance of GVCs and mechanisms developed to address labour injustices have produced material change at both producer and consumer ends of the chain. The detailed empirical work and sophisticated conceptual development achieved within feminist work in particular is a model for organization studies, where there is still a tendency to "add women and stir" as a means of demonstrating gender sensitivity, and an apparently unshakeable hostility to feminism, especially in its more radical implications (Bell et al., 2020). GVC governance research approaches gendered analysis in a one-sided way, either presenting men as an absent structural presence or ignoring them altogether. As stressed, men are not automatons and masculinity is not monolithic: there are many men and masculinities, many ways of seeing them, and many manifestations of them among the many communities involved in GVCs.

Nonetheless, hierarchical binaries continue to structure everyday life, abjecting one side of the binary as "other" and therefore subject to subordination in a hierarchy of thought, action and outcome. Within GVC research, we have shown that there is much important work on damaging hierarchies, especially in critical accounts of the social construction of gender and race. In renewing the GVC research agenda, Levine's (2015) argument that hierarchies and binaries are not necessarily inevitably intertwined or mutually reinforcing is significant. For Levine (2015, p. 86), it is possible to take a formalist analytical approach that maintains analytical separation between hierarchy and binary, allowing the possibility of analysis through "multiple overlapping hierarchical binaries" that are finely differentiated internally. We have used this in our argument already in two ways: in considering the significance of intersections of different forms of domination and oppression, and in observing that the social category of men is heterogeneous. This creates empirical and conceptual complexity, but we remain convinced that there is a concise, clear and compelling case to respond to in our review of research in this area. The simple act of seeing and naming men provides focus on the presence of a hegemony of men across the complex inter-connected worlds of work and home embedded in GVCs. With this in mind, we conclude by outlining three routes derived from our analysis, pointing to ways in which research on GVCs and labour governance can be reoriented, with the aim of feeding insights into theory, policy and practice.

Naming men's power in global value chains

Governing GVCs to improve labour practice requires explication of intersecting systems of differentiation, power, practices and women's relationship to them. We know a substantial amount about women workers' experiences, particularly in terms of workplace exploitation and harassment. In centring men as agentic subjects in their own right in discussions of gender, ethnicity, caste, religion, equality and labour relations, researchers can complement the powerful feminist work in this area. Paying more attention to the existence of the hegemony of men within GVCs has implications for everyone. For example, how do socio-cultural expectations of being a primary earner affect day-to-day decisions and behaviours (De Neve, 2014)? How do the pressures of securing and maintaining contracts with buyers in the Global North intersect with localized, intersectional oppressions, and in what ways might this result in exploitative behaviour? What are the similarities and dissimilarities of pressures for "elite" transnational business managers working in the Global North and men working in the South? How is male power reproduced or challenged through social structural divisions in the Global South? These questions viewed through a hegemony of men lens open up more ways of understanding power relations in GVCs, and how they contribute to the success or failure of labour governance. Starting with analysis of men as primary actors in the reproduction of patriarchal gender regimes and other forms of inequalities that sustain the kind of masculinities that have been identified as damaging provokes a very different understanding of GVCs that simultaneously centres and deconstructs men as actors.

Feminist methodologies and intersectional analyses

Rethinking GVC governance mechanisms through a hegemony of men lens also suggests a need to review our methodologies and methods. Greater use of feminist methods has already been suggested a number of times (e.g. Grosser & Moon, 2019) and is perhaps easily ignored by those disinterested in feminism. We would therefore suggest something more relational and contextual: the need to understand, in-situ, complex inter-relations enacted with reference to gender performances. An intersectional analysis is therefore key in surfacing assumptions related to men and masculinities. Understanding how masculinities are enacted in particular contexts, cognizant of the historical impact of global trade and colonization, as well as the ongoing effects of globalization and racialized capitalism (Liu, 2017, 2018) will provide a more nuanced account of how GVCs are structured, organized and governed by and for the social category of men.

This implies researching men-in-contexts, perhaps starting with the feminist principle that embodied, material, physically felt encounters can generate research questions as meaningful as deductive reasoning. This more inductive approach builds on the impressive feminist postcolonial tradition of ethnography in global workspaces (Ong, 2010; Salzinger, 2003). Liu (2018, p. 81) also advocates the use of biographies and histories to "re-radicalize" intersectional research: "Biography compels researchers to align ourselves with the struggles of marginalized subjects. History asks us to locate our subjects in their specific histories of social injustice". This is crucial for research on GVCs and labour rights, in contexts imbued with many levels of practice and dark histories of racist trade and racialized colonization.

Getting physically close, seeing experiences from new angles and listening to people will ensure that the nuances of masculinity, men and resistance to hegemonic practices are noticed. We know that workers' micro-resistance can destabilize the gendered and racialized status quo, but how we think about choice, agency and resistance in these often-constrained spaces needs close attention (Koggel, 2003). In the face of exclusion (Liu, 2017) and unemployment (Fernández-Kelly & Wolf, 2001), some men may re-formulate codes of masculinity, perhaps in ways that enact and embody more collective, humanist principles. Yet such studies are rare, and empirical research which makes space for the stories of women and men in GVCs "doing gender" differently, showing how difference and inclusion can be celebrated, is sorely needed. Recently BSR, a corporate social responsibility consultancy that promotes women's empowerment programmes in GVCs, began including men within their "Respect" programmes addressing sexual and gendered violence in factory settings, in part through raising the issues of male dominance and alternative masculinities (BSR, 2019). How these programmes work, their strengths and weaknesses, and how they fit alongside wider structures and norms are important areas for future research. Practising different ways of inhabiting the social category of men may, for example, involve resisting systems of binary differentiation, as powerholders navigate around or bypass them altogether, which may necessitate unique skills and capabilities.

GVCs and "grand challenges"

We have focused on working conditions and labour abuses in GVCs but exploring broader global challenges, such as the climate emergency, through a hegemony of men and masculinities lens is also obvious. Climate breakdown, pollution and the degradation of nature are all violence against humanity, often related to the social and economic dominance of men and masculinities. Sustainability transitions such as recycling or reducing carbon footprints are held back by some men's perception of environmentalism as "unmanly" and "gay", and the fear that they will be categorized as such (Swim et al., 2020). Patriarchal masculinity, which also encourages avoidance of housework and childcare, considers caring for the planet to be emasculating at worst, and someone else's problem at best (Brough et al., 2016).

In conclusion

Our overarching purpose here is to honour contributions to understanding gendered labour governance mechanisms and GVCs, while outlining a key empirical and conceptual framing that we believe has been overlooked. We have deliberately not presented this outlining as filling a "gap" – given the volume of research in this area gap-spotting is not credible as a way of constructing an argument, nor would it respect the detailed research already published. We have, however, shown that there is a lack of recognition of masculinities and, especially, the social category of men, and suggested that this results in under-conceptualization that affects all aspects of knowledge in the field. This is as true of the context that we work in, the North, as it is for knowledge that provides insight into the South. Masculinities have formed a transparent window through which researchers have looked, and hence made largely invisible. Men qua men have also been for granted in most GVC research, assumed as the norm or obscured. Recognizing this is a first step towards bringing masculinities and men into the light, as central to the governance of GVCs, and therefore integral to analysis. If this can be combined with existing intersectional understanding of women's experiences wherever they live and work, the gendered nature of governance interventions from the North and feminist methodologies, then researchers in any cultural context will be better placed to inform the policy work that seeks to ameliorate labour practices throughout GVCs, while contributing to theoretical developments in gender studies.

Note

1 This chapter is an edited version of the text originally published by McCarthy, L., Soundararajan, V., & Taylor, S. (2021). The hegemony of men in global value chains: Why it matters for labour governance. *Human Relations*, *74*(12), 2051–2074. We are very grateful to the SAGE for permission to edit and republish in this way, and to the book editors for their substantive contribution to that process.

References

Ahmed, F. E. (2018). Voice and power: Feminist governance as transnational justice in the globalized value chain. *Business Ethics: A European Review*, *27*(4), 324–336. doi: 10.1111/beer.12192

Alamgir, F., & Alakavuklar, O. N. (2020). Compliance codes and women workers' (mis)representation and (non)recognition in the apparel industry of Bangladesh. *Journal of Business Ethics*, *165*(2–3), 295–310. doi: 10.1007/s10551-018-4080-2

Alcadipani, R., & Tonelli, M. J. (2014). Imagining gender research: Violence, masculinity, and the shop floor. *Gender, Work and Organization*, *21*(4), 321–339. doi: 10.1111/gwao.12039

Allen, A. (1998). Power trouble: Performativity as critical theory. *Constellations*, *5*(4), 456–471. doi: 10.1111/1467-8675.00108

Anner, M. (2015). Labor control regimes and worker resistance in global supply chains. *Labor History*, *56*(3), 292–307. doi: 10.1080/0023656X.2015.1042771

Bain, C. (2010). Structuring the flexible and feminized labor market: GlobalGAP standards for agricultural labor in Chile. *Signs: Journal of Women in Culture and Society*, *35*(2), 343–370.

Bapuji, H., & Chrispal, S. (2020). Understanding economic inequality through the lens of caste. *Journal of Business Ethics, 162*(3), 533–551. doi: 10.1007/s10551-018-3998-8

Barrientos, S., Dolan, C., & Tallontire, A. (2003). A gendered value chain approach to codes of conduct in African horticulture. *World Development, 31*(9), 1511–1526.

Bell, E., Meriläinen, S., Taylor, S., & Tienari, J. (2020). Dangerous knowledge: The political, personal, and epistemological promise of feminist research in management and organization studies. *International Journal of Management Reviews, 22*(2), 177–192. doi: 10.1111/ijmr.12221

Bhattacharyya, G., Gabriel, J., & Small, S. (2016). *Race and Power: Global Racism in the Twenty First Century*. New York: Routledge.

Bird, R. C., & Soundararajan, V. (2020). The role of precontractual signals in creating sustainable global supply chains. *Journal of Business Ethics, 164*(1), 81–94. doi: 10.1007/s10551-018-4067-z

Bonacich, E., Alimahomed, S., & Wilson, J. B. (2008). The racialization of global labor. *American Behavioral Scientist, 52*(3), 342–355. doi: 10.1177/000276420832351

Boyd, D. E., Spekman, R. E., Kamauff, J. W., & Werhane, P. (2007). Corporate social responsibility in global supply chains: A procedural justice perspective. *Long Range Planning, 40*(3), 341–356. doi: 10.1016/j.lrp.2006.12.007

Brough, A. R., Wilkie, J. E., Ma, J., Isaac, M. S., & Gal, D. (2016). Is eco-friendly unmanly? The green-feminine stereotype and its effect on sustainable consumption. *Journal of Consumer Research, 43*(4), 567–582. doi: 10.1093/jcr/ucw044.

BSR (2019). HERrespect: How Business Can Make a Difference on Violence against Women and Girls. Retrieved 13 August 2020, from: https://herproject.org/files/curriculum/herrespect-program-summary- june2019-rev.pdf

Butler, J. (1990). *Gender Trouble*. London: Routledge.

Carrigan, T. C., Connell, B., & Lee, J. (1985). Toward a new sociology of masculinity. *Theory and Society, 14*(5), 551–604. doi: 10.1007/BF00160017

Chatterjee, S. (2020). A suitable woman: The coming-of-age of the 'third world woman' at the bottom of the pyramid: A critical engagement. *Human Relations, 73*(3), 378–400. doi: 10.1177/0018726719828445

Clark, G. (1994). *Onions Are My Husband: Survival and Accumulation by West African Market Women*. Chicago: University of Chicago Press. doi: 10.7208/chicago/9780226107769.001.0001

Cohen, L. (2018). How America's 'Ground-zero' for Modern Slavery was Cleaned up by Workers' Group. Retrieved 13 August 2020, from CNN Edition: https://edition.cnn.com/2017/05/30/world/ciw-fair-food- program-freedom-project/index.html

Collinson, D. (1988). 'Engineering humour': Masculinity, joking and conflict in shop-floor relations. *Organization Studies, 9*(2), 181–199. doi: 10.1177/017084068800900203

Connell, R. W. (1987). *Gender and Power: Society, the Person and Sexual Politics*. Cambridge: Polity.

Connell, R. W. (2005). *Masculinities*. Cambridge: Polity. doi: 10.1177/1097184X03260969

Connell, R. W., & Wood, J. (2005). Globalization and business masculinities. *Men and masculinities, 7*(4), 347–364. doi: 10.1177/1097184X0326096

Cornwall, A., Edström, E., & Greig, A. (2011). *Men and Development: Politicizing Masculinities*. London: Zed. doi: 10.5040/9781350221352

Crane, A., Soundararajan, V., Bloomfield, M., Spence, L. J., & LeBaron, G. (2019). *Decent Work and Economic Growth in the South Indian Garment Industry*. Bath: University of Bath. Retrieved 05 January 2023, from: www.bath.ac.uk/publications/decent-work-and-economic-growth-in-the-south-india-garment-industry/attachments/decent-work-and-economic-growth-in-the-south-india-garment-industry.pdf

Crenshaw, K. (1989). Demarginalizing the intersection of race and sex: A black feminist critique of antidiscrimination doctrine. *University of Chicago Legal Forum, 1*(8), 139–167.

De Neve, G. (2005). Weaving for IKEA in South India: Subcontracting, labor markets and gender relations in a global value chain. In Y. Assayago & C. J. Fuld (Eds.), *Globalizing India: Perspectives from Below* (pp. 89–115). London: Anthem Press. doi: 10.7135/UPO9781843313823.005

De Neve, G. (2014). Fordism, flexible specialization and CSR: How Indian garment workers critique neoliberal labour regimes. *Ethnography, 15*(2), 184–207. doi: 10.1177/1466138112463801

Dolan, C., & Scott, L. (2009). Lipstick evangelism: Avon trading circles and gender empowerment in South Africa. *Gender & Development, 17*(2), 203–218. doi: 10.1080/13552070903032504

Elias, J. (2008). Hegemonic masculinities, the multinational corporation, and the developmental state: Constructing gender in "progressive" firms. *Men and Masculinities*, *10*(4), 405–421. doi: 10.1177/1097184X07306747
Elson, D., & Pearson, R. (1981). 'Nimble fingers make cheap workers': An analysis of women's employment in third world export manufacturing. *Feminist Review*, *7*(1), 87–107. doi: 10.1057/fr.1981.6
Ely, R. J., & Meyerson, D. E. (2010). An organizational approach to undoing gender: The unlikely case of offshore oil platforms. *Research in Organizational Behavior*, *30*, 3–34. doi: 10.1016/j.riob.2010.09.002
Emmelhainz, M. A., & Adams, R. J. (1999). The apparel industry response to "sweatshop" concerns: A review and analysis of codes of conduct. *Journal of Supply Chain Management*, *35*(2), 51–57. doi: 10.1111/j.1745-493X.1999.tb00062.x
Federici, S. (2004). *Caliban and the Witch: Women, The Body, and Primitive Accumulation*. New York: Autonomedia.
Fernández-Kelly, P., & Wolf, D. (2001). A dialogue on globalization. *Signs: Journal of Women in Culture and Society*, *26*(4), 1243–1249. doi: 10.1086/495655
Folbre, N. (2006). Measuring care: Gender, empowerment, and the care economy. *Journal of human development*, *7*(2), 183–199. doi: 10.1080/14649880600768512
Folbre, N., & Nelson, J. A. (2000). For love or money- or both? *Journal of economic perspectives*, *14*(4), 123–140. doi: 10.1257/jep.14.4.123
Gereffi, G., & Fernandez-Stark, K. (2011). *Global Value Chain Analysis: A Primer*. Durham, NC: Duke University.
Global Labor Justice (2019). *END Gender-based Violence and Harassment: Gender Justice on Garment Global Supply Chains – An Agenda to Transform Fast-Fashion*. Washington, DC: Global Labor Justice. Retrieved 5 January 2023, from www.globallaborjustice.org/wp-content/uploads/2019/11/end-GBV-pillar1_11-19.pdf
Grosser, K., & McCarthy, L. (2019). Imagining new feminist futures: How feminist social movements contest the neoliberalization of feminism in an increasingly corporate-dominated world. *Gender, Work & Organization*, *26*(8), 1100–1116. doi: 10.1111/gwao.12267
Grosser, K., & Moon, J. (2019). CSR and feminist organization studies: Towards an integrated theorization for the analysis of gender issues. *Journal of Business Ethics*, *155*(2), 321–342. doi: 10.1007/s10551-017-3510-x
Hankivsky, O. (2014). *Intersectionality 101*. Vancouver: The Institute for Intersectionality Research & Policy, SFU. Retrieved 5 January 2023, from https://resources.equityinitiative.org/bitstream/handle/ei/433/2014%20Hankivsky%20Intersectionallity%20101.pdf?sequence=1&isAllowed=y
Hearn, J. (1996). Deconstructing the dominant: Making the one(s) the other(s). *Organization*, *3*(4), 611–626. doi: 10.1177/135050849634017
Hearn, J. (2004). From hegemonic masculinity to the hegemony of men. *Feminist Theory*, *5*(1), 49–72. doi: 10.1177/146470010404081
Hearn, J. (2012). A multi-faceted power analysis of men's violence to known women: From hegemonic masculinity to the hegemony of men. *The Sociological Review*, *60*(4), 581–610. doi: 10.1111/j.1467-954X.2012.02125.x
Hearn, J. (2015). *Men of the World: Genders, Globalizations, Transnational Times*. London: Sage. doi: 10.4135/9781473920644
Hooks, b. (2003). *The Will to Change: Men, Masculinity, and Love*. New York: Atria.
Kandiyoti, D. (1988). Bargaining with patriarchy. *Gender and Society*, *2*(3), 274–290. doi: 10.1177/089124388002003004
Kato-Wallace, J., Barker, G., Eads, M., & Levtov, R. (2014). Global pathways to men's caregiving: Mixed methods findings from the International Men and Gender Equality Survey and the Men Who Care study. *Global Public Health*, *9*(6), 706–722. doi: 10.1080/17441692.2014.921829
Kerfoot, D., & Knights, D. (1998). Managing masculinity in contemporary organizational life: A 'man'agerial project. *Organization*, *5*(1), 7–26. doi: 10.1177/135050849851002
Khan, F. R., & Lund-Thomsen, P. (2011). CSR as imperialism: Towards a phenomenological approach to CSR in the developing world. *Journal of Change Management*, *11*(1), 73–90. 10.1080/14697017.2011.548943

Khan, F. R., Munir, K. A., & Willmott, H. (2007). A dark side of institutional entrepreneurship: Soccer balls, child labour and postcolonial impoverishment. *Organization Studies*, *28*(7), 1055–1077. doi: 10.1177/0170840607078114

Knights, D. (2015). Binaries need to shatter for bodies to matter: Do disembodied masculinities undermine organizational ethics?. *Organization*, *22*(2), 200–216. doi: 10.1177/1350508414558724

Knights, D., & Tullberg, M. (2012). Managing masculinity/mismanaging the corporation. *Organization*, *19*(4), 385–404. doi: 10.1177/1350508411408170

Koggel, C. (2003). Globalization and women's paid work: Expanding freedom?. *Feminist Economics*, *9*(2–3), 163–184. doi: 10.1080/1354570022000077935

Lee, J., & Parpart, J. L. (2018). Constructing gender identity through masculinity in CSR reports: The South Korean case. *Business Ethics: A European Review*, *27*(4), 309–323 doi:. 10.1111/beer.12191

Lerner, M. J. (1980). *The Belief in a Just World*. Boston, MA: Springer. doi: 10.1007/978-1-4899-0448-5

Levine, C. (2015). *Forms: Whole, Rhythm, Hierarchy, Network*. Princeton, NJ: Princeton University Press. doi: 10.1515/9781400852604-010

Levtov, R. G., Barker, G., Contreras-Urbina, M., Heilman, B., & Verma, R. (2014). Pathways to gender-equitable men: Findings from the international men and gender equality survey in eight countries. *Men and Masculinities*, *17*(5), 467–501. doi: 10.1177/1097184X14558234

Liu, H. (2017). Sensuality as subversion: Doing masculinity with Chinese Australian professionals. *Gender, Work & Organization*, *24*(2), 194–212. doi: 10.1111/gwao.12158

Liu, H. (2018). Re-radicalising intersectionality in organisation studies. *Ephemera: Theory and Politics in Organization*, *18*(1), 81–101.

Liu, H., & Baker, C. (2016). White Knights: Leadership as the heroicisation of whiteness. *Leadership*, *12*(4), 420–448. doi: 10.1177/1742715014565127

McCarthy, L. (2015). *Organising CSR for Gender Equality: Institutional Work in the Cocoa Value Chain*. PhD thesis, University of Nottingham, Nottingham.

McCarthy, L. (2017). Empowering women through corporate social responsibility: A feminist Foucauldian critique. *Business Ethics Quarterly*, *27*(4), 603–631. doi: 10.1017/beq.2017.28

McCarthy, L. (2018). "There is no time for rest": Gendered CSR, sustainable development and the unpaid care work governance gap. *Business Ethics: A European Review*, *27*(4), 337–349. doi: 10.1111/beer.12190

Mena, S., & Palazzo, G. (2012). Input and output legitimacy of multi-stakeholder initiatives. *Business Ethics Quarterly*, *22*(3), 527–556. doi: 10.5840/beq201222333

Mohanty, C. T. (2003). 'Under western eyes' revisited: Feminist solidarity through anticapitalist struggles. *Signs: Journal of Women in culture and Society*, *28*(2), 499–535. doi: 10.1086/342914

Nadvi, K. (2008). Global standards, global governance and the organization of global value chains. *Journal of Economic Geography*, *8*(3), 323–343. doi: 10.1093/jeg/lbn003

Nagaraj, A. (2019). In Tamil Nadu, Factories are Illegally Giving Women Pills to Keep them Working Through Period Pains. Retrieved 11 July 2023, from Scroll.in: https://scroll.in/article/926794/in-tamil-nadu-factories-are-endangering-female-workers-health-by-illegally-plying-them-with-pills

Nanda, P., Mishra, A., Walia, S., Sharma, S., Weiss, E., & Abrahamson, J. (2013). *Advancing Women, Changing Lives: An Evaluation of Gap Inc.'s P.A.C.E. Program*. Washington, DC: International Center for Research on Women. Retrieved 5 January 2023, from www.icrw.org/wp-content/uploads/2016/10/PACE_Report_PRINT_singles_lo.pdf

Ong, A. (2010). *Spirits of Resistance and Capitalist Discipline: Factory Women in Malaysia*. New York: SUNY Press.

Özkazanç-Pan, B. (2019). CSR as gendered neocoloniality in the Global South. *Journal of Business Ethics*, *160*(4), 851–864. doi: 10.1007/s10551-018-3798-1

Patel-Campillo, A. (2012). The gendered production – consumption relation: Accounting for employment and socioeconomic hierarchies in the Colombian cut flower global commodity chain. *Sociologia Ruralis*, *52*(3), 272–293. doi: 10.1111/j.1467-9523.2012.00569.x

Plankey-Videla, N. (2012). *We Are in This Dance Together: Gender, Power, and Globalization at a Mexican Garment Firm*. New Brunswick, NJ: Rutgers University Press.

Prügl, E. (2015). Neoliberalising feminism. *New Political Economy*, *20*(4), 614–631. doi: 10.1080/13563467.2014.951614

Pulido, L. (2017). Geographies of race and ethnicity II: Environmental racism, racial capitalism and state-sanctioned violence. *Progress in Human Geography*, *41*(4), 524–533. doi: 10.1177/0309132516646495

Ramamurthy, P. (2010). Why are men doing floral sex work? Gender, cultural reproduction, and the feminization of agriculture. *Signs: Journal of Women in Culture and Society*, *35*(2), 397–424. doi: 10.1086/605899

Revathy, L. N. (2018). Migrant Thread in Tirupur Fabric. Retrieved 25 March 2020, from The Hindu Business Line: www.thehindubusinessline.com/specials/india-file/migrant-threads-in-the-tirupur-fabric/article23650435.ece

Robinson, C. J. (1983 [2000]). *Black Marxism: The Making of the Black Radical Tradition*. Chapel Hill, NC: University of North Carolina Press.

Ruwanpura, K. N., & Hughes, A. (2016). Empowered spaces? Management articulations of gendered spaces in apparel factories in Karachi, Pakistan. *Gender, Place & Culture*, *23*(9), 1270–1285. doi: 10.1080/0966369X.2015.1136815

Salzinger, L. (2003). *Genders in Production: Making Workers in Mexico's Global Factories*. Berkeley, CA: University of California Press.

Schrock, D., & Schwalbe, M. (2009). Men, masculinity, and manhood acts. *Annual Review of Sociology*, *35*, 277–295. www.jstor.org/stable/27800079

Slutskaya, N., Simpson, R., Hughes, J., Simpson, A., & Uygur, S. (2016). Masculinity and class in the context of dirty work. *Gender, Work & Organization*, *23*(2), 165–182. doi: 10.1111/gwao.12119

Soundararajan, V., & Brammer, S. (2018). Developing country sub-supplier responses to social sustainability requirements of intermediaries: Exploring the influence of framing on fairness perceptions and reciprocity. *Journal of Operations Management*, *58*, 42–58. doi: 10.1016/j.jom.2018.04.001

Soundararajan, V., & Brown, J. A. (2016). Voluntary governance mechanisms in global supply chains: Beyond CSR to a stakeholder utility perspective. *Journal of Business Ethics*, *134*(1), 83–102. doi: 10.1007/s10551-014-2418-y

Soundararajan, V., Spence, L. J., & Rees, C. (2018). Small business and social irresponsibility in developing countries: Working conditions and "evasion" institutional work. *Business & Society*, *57*(7), 1301–1336. doi: 10.1177/0007650316644261

Swim, J. K., Gillis, A. J., & Hamaty, K. J. (2020). Gender bending and gender conformity: The social consequences of engaging in feminine and masculine pro-environmental behaviors. *Sex Roles*, *82*(5), 363–385. doi: 10.1007/s11199-019-01061-9

Tornhill, S. (2019). *The Business of Women's Empowerment: Corporate Gender Politics in the Global South*. London: Rowman and Littlefield International.

Van der Gaag, N. (2014). *Feminism and Men*. London: Zed. doi: 10.5040/9781350220058

Van der Gaag, N., Heilman, B., Gupta, T., Nembhard, C., & Barker, G. (2019). *State of the World's Fathers: Unlocking the Power of Men's Care*. Washington, DC: Promundo-US. Retrieved 5 January 2023, from file:///C:/Users/sbrt128/Downloads/BLS19063_PRO_SOWF_REPORT_015.pdf

26

MULTIPLE CRISIS, CRISIS OF GENDER RELATIONS AND THE CRISIS OF MASCULINITY

Alex Demirović and Andrea Maihofer

Framing preface — Multiple crisis: contextualizing men, masculinities, organizations and organizing in analyses of crises

Anika Thym

The following chapter, "Multiple crisis, crisis of gender relations and the crisis of masculinity" by Alex Demirović and Andrea Maihofer builds on their earlier work translated from German.[1] This introductory framing preface seeks to contextualize the chapter in relation to the translation, as well as to recent literature on men, masculinities and crises, with a focus on organizations and organizing. The analysis of crises concerning men, masculinities, organizations and organizing can focus on different societal levels. The chapter looks at society as a whole and develops a concept to understand the social organization of the ongoing multiple crisis with a focus on the crisis of masculinity. Other studies investigate crises and organizations in a narrower sense, for example, concerning organizations of crisis management. Some studies discuss the way crisis management in organizations is often gendered male and built on heroic masculinity norms (Alvinius et al., 2020; Ericson & Mellström, 2019), while others demonstrate how crisis management can become more gender equal by focusing on communication and including women (Penttinen, 2011).

An important contextualization concerning language and content refers to the term "multiple crisis" ("Vielfachkrise" in German), which may sound like a grammatical contradiction in English but points to one of the core arguments of the text. Demirović and Maihofer look at society as a whole, which is divided into different segments with their specific inner logic and autonomy. Therefore, crises in the different segments materialize in a specific way, like the crisis of gender relations and masculinity, the crisis of social reproduction, education, the climate and ecological crisis, the crisis of political representation or economic crises. However, within society as a whole, the authors conceptualize these different social segments and crises as connected in the way they are constituted and reproduced within that complex segmented whole. They speak of the "multiple crisis" in the singular to emphasize how current crisis dynamics and processes are not merely connected in an additive way, but internally. In overdetermined more or less expected or surprising ways, one crisis may affect another, or even society as a whole.

This perspective on internal connections of different social segments may help to understand crises which occur on a global scale, yet manifest themselves differently in the various

 DOI: 10.4324/9781003193579-30

contexts. The UN, for example, speaks of a "global crisis", because the climate and ecological crisis, the Russian war on Ukraine and the COVID-19 pandemic entail crises on a global scale (United Nations Conference on Trade and Development, 2022). This global crisis is also a crisis of organizations and organizing because it would have to be solved on a global level, by new forms of organization and organizing. Current national as well as supranational organizations lack either the global scope and/or the means to address the crucial challenges they face. One reason for these struggles and the difficulty to find solutions is the way in which men and masculinities are organizing and organized within global transpatriarchies (cf. Hearn, 2015, p. 77ff.). Such transpatriarchal organizing makes it difficult to organize for and achieve global organizations that operate for a more equal, ecological and sustainable world.

Like Demirović and Maihofer, Fraser conceptualizes the current ongoing crisis in an all-encompassing way and with a focus on the importance of capitalism. Referring to the structure of bourgeois societies with their division of spheres such as the "public" political sphere, the economic sphere of production and the familial private sphere of reproduction, Fraser (2016, p. 116) talks about "boundary struggles" between those spheres. Thereby, she highlights a fundamental crisis of reproduction of capitalist societies. This crisis was caused by capitalist production which is free-riding on its "indispensable background condition[s]", like racist exploitation, reproductive work that is needed for the reproduction of the workforce, but not valued enough, or the ecology, which is increasingly destroyed, although human life depends on these preconditions (Fraser, 2016, p. 102). Fraser ultimately establishes the connections between various crises economically and prioritizes economic aspects. She does so by expanding the concept of labour in such a way that it also includes racist unfree labour and unpaid reproductive labour, in order to summarize the contradictions in a "crisis of capitalism" (Fraser & Zelik, 2022). With this approach, she neglects non-economic or non-labour-related aspects of gender relations, racialization and exploitation related, for example, to specific subjectivities and normative regimes of truth, rationality and emotionality. Thus, she outlines an expanded version of the Marxian contradiction between capital and labour as the one driving force of the crisis. In contrast, Demirović and Maihofer are concerned to conceptualize social segments and multiple crises in a way where no area and no form of discrimination or exploitation is prioritized. They emphasize that because different segments and relations of power and domination are connected internally, they can only be overcome together, by addressing the specific autonomy of each part as well as their constitutive connections.

Demirović and Maihofer emphasize the need for an intersectional, or as they develop it, a multidimensional perspective on the multiple crises, which aims at overcoming all relations of exploitation and discrimination. In addition, some scholars stress the need for interdisciplinary collaborations to gain the knowledge needed to understand the different aspects of crises. Because "crisis as a notion, condition and experience refers to and operates at various societal levels" (Bergman-Rosamond et al., 2020, p. 467), some make a "case for interdisciplinary crisis studies" (Bergman-Rosamond et al., 2020). They state: "Examining the intricate and complex character of crises, their composition, intersections and responses not only requires multi- and cross-disciplinary approaches: there is also something to be gained from developing a genuinely interdisciplinary grammar for thinking and talking about crisis" (Bergman-Rosamond et al., 2020, p. 470).

Concerning the perception and possible solutions of such crises, Demirović and Maihofer emphasize that a crisis can only be called a crisis if it is perceived as such. However, crises are perceived differently and sometimes in contradictory ways, as potentially liberating, or as threatening. Consequently, fundamentally different solutions are proposed by different organizations and forms of organizing. Analysis of the so-called refugee crisis, for example, illustrates how right-wing populists favour authoritarian structures and often organize a specific masculinity around crises narratives (Norocel, 2022, p. 589).

The crisis of masculinity more specifically, which Demirović and Maihofer also diagnose, can be conceptualized in different ways. Yekani focuses on the persistence of patriarchal structures and refers to a "crisis" of masculinity, where the crisis is an expression of the ongoing patriarchal goal to maintain male privilege (Yekani, 2011). Focusing on the subjectivity of masculinity, Tholen makes out a crisis of masculinity in which hegemonic masculinity has become "dysfunctional", because despite the feminist critique of the male heteronormative hegemony, there is a continuing absence of a constructive and authentic culture of dialogue between the genders, which would also have to be initiated and shaped by men (Tholen, 2015, p. 47). Tholen therefore proposes a "dialogical subjectivity", which would have its foundation in conversations, love and care for the self and the other (Tholen, 2015, p. 47f.). Hearn highlights the academic potential when he points out "how crisis can be a driver of critical studies on men and masculinities" (Hearn, 2022, p. 563). As Hearn emphasizes on the topic more generally: "there appears to have been over-recognition of the 'crisis of masculinity', some recognition of crisis tendencies of patriarchal relations and of gender, and under-recognition of crises created or reinforced largely by certain men and masculinities globally and transnationally" (Hearn, 2022, p. 563). This insight highlights how important it is to critically consider powerful people, mostly men, who operate transnationally when thinking about organizing ways out of the multiple crisis.

References

Alvinius, A., Deverell, E., & Hede, S. (2020). A gender perspective on temporary organisations in crisis management. *NORA – Nordic Journal of Feminist and Gender Research*, *28*(4), 273–286. doi: 10.1080/08038740.2020.1785008

Bergman-Rosamond, A., Gammeltoft-Hansen, T., Hamza, M., Hearn, J., Ramasar, V., & Rydstrom, H. (2020). The case for Interdisciplinary Crisis Studies. *Global Discourse: An Interdisciplinary Journal of Current Affairs and Applied Contemporary thought*, *12*(3–4), 465–486. doi: 10.1332/2043789 20X15802967811683

Ericson, M., & Mellström, U. (Eds.). (2019). *Masculinities, Gender Equality and Crisis Management.* London: Routledge.

Fraser, N. (2016). Contradictions of capital and care. *New Left Review*, *100*, 99–117.

Fraser, N., & Zelik, R. (2022). Nancy Fraser: "Wir haben den Begriff der Arbeit viel zu eng gefasst". Retrieved 1 December 2022, from WOZ website: www.woz.ch/!BPF6D9ZDHE61

Hearn, J. (2015). *Men of the World: Genders, Globalizations, Transnational Times.* London: Sage.

Hearn, J. (2022). The place and potential of crisis/crises in critical studies on men and masculinities. *Global Discourse: An Interdisciplinary Journal of Current Affairs and Applied Contemporary thought*, *12*(3–4), 563–585. doi: 10.1332/204378921X16334429502843

Norocel, O. C. (2022). The conceptual imbrications of men, masculinities and crises: A reply to 'The place and potential of crisis/crises in critical studies on men and masculinities' by Jeff Hearn. *Global Discourse: An Interdisciplinary Journal of Current Affairs and Applied Contemporary thought*, *12*(3–4), 586–591. doi: 10.1332/204378921X16421973649174

Penttinen, E. (2011). Nordic women and international crisis management: A Politics of hope. In A. Kronsell & E. Svedberg (Eds.), *Making Gender, Making War: Violence, Military and Peacekeeping Practices* (pp. 175–191). New York: Routledge.

Tholen, T. (Ed.). (2015). 'Krise der Männlichkeit'. Zur Konzeptualisierung eines häufig verwendeten Topos. In *Männlichkeiten in der Literatur. Konzepte und Praktiken zwischen Wandel und Beharrung* (pp. 45–50). Bielefeld: Transcript. doi: 10.1515/9783839430729-004

United Nations Conference on Trade and Development. (2022). Global Crisis. Retrieved 2 December 2022, from UNCTAD website: https://unctad.org/global-crisis

Yekani, E. H. (2011). *The Privilege of Crisis: Narratives of Masculinities in Colonial and Postcolonial Literature, Photography, and Film.* Frankfurt am Main: Campus Verlag.

***

Multiple crisis, crisis of gender relations and the crisis of masculinity

Alex Demirović and Andrea Maihofer

Introduction

Since 2007–2008, large parts of the OECD states, as elsewhere, have been in a comprehensive crisis. Although it does not hit all states equally hard and there are also phases of recovery, it is the deepest economic and financial crisis of capitalist states since 1929. This crisis – and otherwise it would not be such a crisis – has an impact on social relations, and thus on living conditions and political behaviour, as well as the way many people experience life. But besides the economic crisis, which is often seen as the driving force, there are numerous other and differently positioned crisis dynamics. Often mentioned are the energy or climate crisis, the crisis of democracy and political parties, the crisis of education, and the crisis of gender relations.

These crisis developments pose a number of fundamental problems for critical social theory. Even the question of how the current deep economic crisis can be understood in terms of social theory is not easy to answer. Even more difficult seems to be the attempt to adequately grasp this complex bundle of simultaneous and non-contemporaneous, co-existing, mutually influencing or intensifying crises and to critically assess their significance.

In our opinion, a differentiated understanding of crises requires a *society-wide perspective* on the various crisis dynamics and phenomena. With the term multiple crisis, we want to emphasize the inner connection of autonomously running crisis processes – and thus distinguish it from the term "polycrisis" (Tooze, 2023).

Following Marx's "categorical imperative to overthrow all conditions in which man is a debased, enslaved, neglected, contemptible being" (Marx, 2009, p. 137), this implies two things: First, there needs to be a knowledge of *how* these multiple crises are interrelated. This is all the more important because, as we will show, it is a central mechanism of domination to repeatedly prevent precisely this knowledge of internal connections. Closely related to this, it is also necessary to realize that the current various mechanisms of power and domination are also connected in a context of constitution and reproduction beyond their respective inherent logics and their interactions. Because of this connection, we speak of a multiple crisis in the singular. It is not merely an external, additive connection. Rather, the various crisis dynamics and phenomena are internally related, interlocking in a circular fashion, reinforcing and compacting each other. Only with a perspective on society as a whole is there the prospect of developing an emancipatory practice that sustainably overcomes all these different relationships in which people are subjected to domination, exploitation and discrimination.

In terms of social theory, this raises two main problems: How can society be thought of as a comprehensive ensemble (German: Gesamtzusammenhang) without at the same time ontologizing it as a totality? How can the until now prevailing prioritization of *one* social sphere or social dynamic be avoided without ending up in a non-binding pluralism of forms of domination? In order to address these problems, we will first explain in more detail what we mean by crisis and why we think it makes sense to speak of a *multiple crisis* at present. Furthermore, we try to develop a concept of society that not only allows us to grasp the different social spheres and thus also the different crisis dynamics, both in their respective own logics and contradictions and in their common context, but also the different prevailing mechanisms of stratification, disciplining and discrimination. The latter in particular, as we will show, requires an intersectional or, as we suggest, multidimensional perspective. We then focus on the crisis of gender relations, especially the crisis of masculinity. Here, it becomes clear, among other things, that crises have their own logics and cannot simply be traced back to economic processes or dysfunctions or be understood as such, as is often done. Finally, we consider how developments in gender relations are very significant for the further course of the current crisis. After all, the crisis concerns central "cornerstones" of the current social formation.

What is a crisis?

Crisis as crisis trajectories

Crisis usually refers to an open situation of upheaval, a turning point, in which a decision is made: medically the decision about life and death, militarily about victory or defeat (HKWM, 2010, p. 2121; Becker, 2011). That is, the crisis represents a climax that is resolved in one direction or another: things cannot go on as they were, but the new has not yet prevailed. The crisis results from contradictions and tensions that existed before and which lead to a multitude of small crises that, if no decisive countermeasures are taken, can develop into major crises.

A distinction can be made between exogenous and endogenous crises; however, this boundary is blurry at best. For example, because the COVID-19 pandemic seems at first glance to be exogenously caused by a virus, while it is the result of an expansion of human habitats and a related zoonosis. There is no crisis for the virus: the pandemic is a crisis internal to society. What is decisive is how society deals with this external shock. In such a crisis, just as in the case of a tsunami, a flood or a volcanic eruption, society must realize that it is always constituted by a specific social relation to nature. Understood in this way, we are talking about endogenous crises. In other words, they do not enter a functioning system from the outside and block what has been running smoothly up to now. Rather, they reveal already existing internal frictions, incompatibilities and conflicts; they reveal the need for change. However, it is by no means certain that solutions to the crisis(es) will be found.

Marx, for example, is quite cautious about such expectations. According to him, crises are always only momentary violent solutions to existing contradictions, violent eruptions that restore the disturbed equilibrium for the moment (Marx, 1969, p. 259). Similarly, Gramsci emphasizes that crises by no means make large breaches in the normality of bourgeois society and therefore do not result in changes that resolve themselves, as it were. He considers it a misleading empiricism to equate crises with their epiphenomenal outbreak (cf. Gramsci, 1996, p. 1716f), for example, the world economic crisis with Black Friday on Wall Street in 1929.

Crises only create the *possibility of* change in a social pattern of reproduction and regulation but are not themselves this change. They can drag on for a very long time and fundamentally paralyse a society or turn into a destructive dynamic, as in the case of the world economic crisis of 1929, which dragged on for more than 20 years and was associated with dictatorships, war and destruction, with persecution, mass murder and expulsions of large population groups as well as prolonged reconstruction work. It was not until the 1950s that a new equilibrium was found with the Fordist mode of regulation in the capitalist centres.

In view of this, it seems more appropriate to speak of the crisis as a form of autonomous *crisis trajectories*. These crises neither necessarily nor teleologically lead to a radical break or a catastrophe nor to a new equilibrium. Crises always have something contingent about them;

they have a specific character that results from the social conditions and the specific conflicts that accompany them: Crises are always crises of particular social conditions.

Crisis as a connection between objective and subjective moments

Crises are not objective processes (Demirović et al., 2011). A crisis is only a crisis if – as Habermas (1973) rightly pointed out – it is also experienced as a crisis from the internal perspective of the actors involved. In terms of hegemony theory, we argue that crises are always the result of social practices that are internally linked to power and knowledge. However, not all social actors have the same knowledge of crises or are willing to accept the existing knowledge of others. Whether and which social processes and phenomena are determined to be in crisis – such heterogeneous phenomena as sexist exploitation and violence, anthropogenic climate change, low birth rates, overpopulation or the supposed threat of Islam – is rather the subject of mostly long-lasting social conflicts and disputes.

In society, therefore, there is always a specific knowledge of crises and practices for overcoming them among certain individuals, groups or institutions. However, such actors may not initially succeed in generalizing their understanding of things and making it relevant for social action. Hegemonic practices in politics, academia or journalism contribute to this knowledge being considered false or irrelevant in order to invoke normality or bring other crises to bear.

In terms of social theory, this means that crises – be they of the economy, energy, the environment, politics or gender relations – are always concrete crises in particular contexts of domination.

Crisis as multiple crisis

Crisis as part of the social context of domination also includes efforts on the part of the ruling groups not only to bring the crisis under control but also to prevent it from spreading to other areas of society or even to its entirety. But crises are complex phenomena and never just a specific crisis of, for example, the economy, gender relations or the environment. For this reason, crisis analyses of the past decades have explicitly addressed the *connections* between crises. Eugen Varga (1969), for example, already took numerous other crisis dynamics into account in his analyses of the world economic crisis of 1929 and included the crisis of the labour market, politics, world agriculture or colonialism in his diagnosis but was only able to establish the connection itself in economic terms.

In contrast, in their analyses of social development since the 1930s, Horkheimer and Adorno (2002) were less concerned with the economy but rather focused on a diagnosis of the deep crises of the meaning and self-perception of the bourgeois of standing up for happiness, freedom and equality. Accordingly, the crises of reason and the sciences, of the family and sexuality, of the subject and the erosion of culture have been at the centre of their work. In the understanding of Critical Theory, bourgeois society is thus a comprehensive crisis context that could have been overcome through reasonable practice. Instead, however, the available social resources were used to give the crisis itself a specific form: rearmament, war, racist mass murder, sexism and mass consumption to ensure the reproduction of society as a context of domination.

But even in these important analyses, which have contributed a great deal to understanding the complexity of the crisis, it is ultimately the *economic* relations and market processes that form the starting point of destructive and crisis-like processes, whose crisis dynamics continue to expand and *subsequently draw* more and more areas of society into the crisis. In a similar way, crisis-theoretical approaches also currently assume that the economy, freed from political fetters and self-regulating, would colonize society from the outside in a kind of land grab and penetrate all areas with business management calculations (cf. Dörre, 2009; Hufer, 2010; also see Aulenbacher, 2012).

In contrast, we take up Gramsci's emphatic critique of those who give a *single* definition to the event of crisis or who want to find, which is the same thing, a single cause or a single origin (Gramsci, 1996, p. 1716). From our point of view, it cannot be a matter of identifying crisis processes as economic ones, but conversely, it is a matter of *deciphering economic crises as social crises*. However, such a deciphering practice is hegemonically repeatedly attempted to be prevented by reducing the complexity of the interrelationships to certain isolated phenomena such as economics or immigration or feminism (e.g. for incels and masculinists). These isolated areas can then be claimed to be subject to quasi-natural laws. Action is presented as having no alternative, or it is claimed that there is only rational and appropriate, or irrational action.

We consider this strategic parcelling and limitation of knowledge to be a central *mechanism of power and domination*, a targeted form of domination through separation. It contributes to the fact that the various subaltern groups usually claim priority or even exclusivity for their respective perspectives, their critique of the exploitation of nature, social inequality, sexism or racism over the other perspectives of critique. The movements end up in competition with each other instead of productively linking the different perspectives of critique and making the inner connection of all these crisis phenomena visible in order to form emancipatory alliances on this basis.

In contrast, we propose to call the current complex constellation of crises a "*multiple crisis*" (Demirović et al., 2011; Brand, 2009) and to understand the crisis dynamics and phenomena as an internally interconnected context that reproduces itself through contradictions and discharges itself in different crises, which (even if they have specific features) can mutually influence and reinforce each other. In this sense, we argue in the following that the bourgeois social formation, on the basis of the capitalist mode of production, constitutes itself on a whole bundle of social relations of domination and contradictions, which are structured in a specific way and which – although they stand in a constitutive inner connection – cannot be reduced to one another. Rather, it is precisely this inner connection that is the reason for their specific temporality and autonomy, which leads to different types of crisis and, in particular conjunctures, to the phenomenon of the often overdetermined crisis.

How to think of society as ensemble?

Society as a segmented, articulated whole

Unlike the Hegel-Marxist tradition, we do not understand society as a totality, but as a segmented whole consisting of unequal autonomous spheres. Society is therefore an always unstable result of social struggles and a compromise equilibrium between social forces that also struggle over the boundaries between the spheres and the specific divisions of the whole (market/state, city/village, man/woman, top/bottom, companies). Following this, the bourgeois social formation represents a hegemonic totalization that is the result of the success of a certain alliance of actors and their ways of life in these struggles. It is constituted (in contrast to the feudal social formation) as an ensemble of domination in which a certain kind of integration, normalization, individualization and subjectivation of social relations occurs.

With the capitalist mode of production, a society is formed with a multiplicity of autonomous spheres, in which social actors pursue specific practices. Society itself is an ensemble of domination, a totalization that gives the concrete practices of people – that is, the processing of nature, the coordination of cooperation, erotic and generative practices, the physical, psychological or intellectual self-relationship of individuals or the symbolic appropriation of the world – a historically determined form, which is segmented and dividing labour. Conflicts and crisis dynamics form in the respective autonomous spheres, which show a specific non-simultaneity in relation to other spheres and can in turn lead to crises affecting other spheres of society. For example, solidarity with homosexuals can lead to conflicts during the football World Cup and ultimately also attack an organization such as FIFA. These crises reproduce themselves on an ever-higher level. This is because in each crisis, the forces ruling in the relevant field develop means to solve it, which are intended not to overcome the given crises once and for all, but to temporize or displace them. In this way, crisis management contributes to an increasingly complex society that absorbs crisis dynamics and reproduces them on a higher level (cf. Boltanski & Chiapello, 2003; Streeck, 2011).

Instead of totality, which expresses an underlying essential contradiction that unfolds, we use Louis Althusser's (2006) concept of a segmented whole. In this, the disparate processes do not stand additively side by side, but rather they over-determine each other. *The specific ensemble and its arrangement itself becomes causality*. Althusser assumed that these disparate processes reach unity only at a single moment: they then over-determine themselves in such a way that they condense into the unity of a single crisis of rupture.

Against the background of this consideration, we want to understand the current situation as a *multiple crisis constellation* in which the crisis dynamics have not yet condensed into such a unity of a rupture. Crises such as the economic, financial, energy or climate crises are each autonomous in their own specific way and have their own temporal rhythm. This gives the way the crises overdetermine each other an unpredictable, non-linear character: the accident at the Fukushima nuclear power plant leads to the phase-out of nuclear energy in Germany, but not in Japan, Poland or France. A consolidation of the crises into a unity cannot be brought about by political means and just as little can it be prevented in this way.

What is decisive about these considerations for the analysis of the multiple crisis as a determination of the current social constellation is: on the basis of the capitalist mode of production, *none of* the social spheres and *none of* its respective specific crisis dynamics has a priori priority. The particular dominance of the contradictions and crisis moments of one area (economy, environment, state budget, education, religion or gender relations) over others results from processes of displacement and condensation between the social forces within this whole itself. The complexly articulated whole can therefore always be dominated by another crisis constellation. In such a particular crisis constellation, the existence of this whole then condenses and represents the concrete situation. It becomes the, singularly, general: in the specific form of this crisis, its actors, its strategies and perspectives, the generality of specific society and its development alternatives are represented. Besides the economic one, there are consequently not only numerous other crisis processes but also numerous other possible condensations of crisis dynamics and forms in which the social conflicts are carried out and represented (gender, energy, climate, national debt, democratic participation, education or ageing of a population).

If this is the case, it cannot be capitalist property relations alone that justify speaking of capitalist sociality. Why then speak of capitalism at all, why not give priority to another contradiction? In fact, just as in the case of the crisis, there are constant social disputes about how society should be conceived. According to our thesis, society is capitalist precisely as this particular articulated whole of economy and specific forms of the political state, culture, gender relations, natural relations and racialized relations. All these forms constitute the bourgeois social formation and constitute an *overdetermined, complexly segmented whole.*

Multidimensionality as a social theoretical perspective

As mentioned earlier, Marx's "categorical imperative to overthrow all conditions in which man is a debased, enslaved, neglected, contemptible being" (Marx, 2009, p. 137) implies the call to take into account all forms of human discrimination, exploitation and disregard. No social area, no dimension may be overlooked, all mechanisms of power and domination must be critically analysed and included in the process of transformation.

It is an effect of symbolic violence (Bourdieu, 2001) that in critical social analyses of society, it often happens that *one* social sphere and its logic of action, *one* specific mechanism of domination or *one* emancipatory movement is privileged as the key to understanding the whole and as the decisive lever of social change and liberation. One social force then claims to share the emancipatory goals of all other forces, with the fatal consequence of concentrating efforts for emancipation on *one* issue, *one* field of action, *one* emancipatory practice, and to the detriment of other emancipatory aspects. Other central social mechanisms of power and domination, the interconnections as well as the dynamic shifts in dominance between them, are lost from view.

The concepts of intersectionality or interdependence are current attempts to take equal account of different mechanisms of power and domination and to avoid such prioritizations. However, there are a number of problems associated with this.

In the concept of intersectionality (cf. Crenshaw, 1997), race, class, gender and sexuality are often understood merely as *categories of* social processes of differentiation and hierarchization, the use of which is often already understood as the first step towards overcoming the corresponding conditions (cf. critically also Dietze et al., 2007b; Walby, 2007). Moreover, the concept of intersectionality always implies the additive idea of intersecting axes of discrimination and inequality that exist *beyond* the intersection, seemingly unaffected by each other (Dietze, 2007a, p. 9). This not only entails the tendency to search for empirically pure groups (cf. Walby, 2007; Dietze et al., 2007b), which then subsequently "meet" at the intersection in a selective manner, but also the difficulty of how their connection can be concretely conceived.

In addition, "categories" or "axes of *inequality*" are predominantly spoken of (Klinger & Knapp, 2005, p. 73). This reduces the effects of mechanisms of domination and differentiation on the production of inequality. However, race, class, gender and sexuality are complex social practices that encompass economic or political aspects as well as processes of subjectification, disciplining and normalization, and related institutions, norms, ways of thinking, body practices and forms of desire (cf. Walgenbach, 2007; Dietze et al., 2007b; Maihofer, 1995). Finally, the concept of intersectionality is peculiarly blind to domination, as it does not take into account the effects of practices of domination among the dominant themselves (cf. Rommelspacher, 2009; Walgenbach, 2007).

Primarily because of the notion of a genuine core of social categories (Walgenbach, 2007, p. 59), many now advocate speaking of interdependence and understanding the categories themselves as interdependent. In relation to gender, this means always already seeing it as simultaneously racialized, sexualized and localized (Dietze et al., 2007b, p. 108). In our view, this creates its own difficulty. To speak of gender or race as each interdependent category (mis)leads us to focus again on only *one* category as the centre of analysis and to demonstrate that and how all others are interdependently interwoven with gender or race. If we look at social relations or, as in the aforementioned case, individuals, it is not enough to speak of gender as always already racialized or sexualized; in an individual, race/ethnicity, class, gender and sexuality are always constitutively interrelated. They form a unity but do not merge into it. Rather, they also unfold specific dynamics, contradictions and lines of division: subaltern men can be racist, sexist oppressed women can belong to the ruling class.

For all these reasons, we consider the concept of ***multidimensionality*** to be more appropriate than that of intersectionality or interdependence. Although it has been used many times, it has not yet been explicitly elaborated as an alternative (cf. e.g. Meißner, 2011; Walgenbach, 2007; Rommelspacher, 2009). It does, however, represent a social theoretical perspective that makes it possible to take *equal* account of the various mechanisms of power and domination and to understand them both in their respective autonomy and in their *constitutive context*.

Masculinity and the crisis of gender relations

Even though this may be contentious, we think it makes sense to speak of a crisis of gender relations, which is currently visible in a series of contradictions and tensions as well as diverse social disputes about their development. Especially in the context of the crisis of gender relations, it becomes clear that what is called a crisis is as controversial as its evaluation. For some people or groups, a crisis can be one that involves liberation, while others perceive it exclusively as uncertainty or even as a threat. And this can be more than "just" a subjective awareness of crisis, if, for example, as is currently the case, the crisis affects the very modes of subjectification of individuals. The assessment of whether gender relations are in crisis depends on whether various aspects and their mutually reinforcing interplay are taken into account or, as is often the case, only individual phenomena are focused on. Additionally, what is seen as the central cornerstone of the prevailing gender order makes a difference, that is, what exactly has to "happen" in order to be able to justifiably speak of a crisis of gender relations.

In each case, the crisis of gender relations is interwoven with other crisis dynamics in a more or less non-contemporaneous way and represents both a central *effect* and a significant *motor* within the current multiple crisis. It is often difficult to separate cause and effect. For example, the dynamics of financial market capitalism go hand in hand with male-bonding constellations and aggressive patterns of masculinity, which include ruthlessness, monetized performance and competitive orientation, and sexism. Moreover, some of the high-risk business models pursued by banks, which contributed significantly to the outbreak of the financial crisis, particularly targeted African-American and Hispanic women (cf. Fishbein & Woodall, 2006; with regard to microcredit see Wichterich, 2012). In such cases, women are valorized as autonomous economic subjects and at the same time subjected to male-dominated profit strategies. Men in the financial sector also find the common practices problematic in some cases, for example, when economic inequalities are increased, but also personally when the complete dedication to the job makes the desired involved fatherhood impossible (cf. Thym et al., this volume).

To speak of a crisis of gender relations further implies that quite different aspects *within* gender relations can be affected by crisis dynamics, which are closely interconnected, but must nevertheless be distinguished: the crisis of reproduction and care work, sexuality, forms of relationship and life, fertility and generational relations, as well as the binary cis-heteronormative gender order. All these areas are currently characterized by a paradoxical simultaneity of change and persistence and crisis-like tensions (cf. Maihofer, 2007).

Like many others, we believe that the crisis of social reproduction is an essential element in the crisis of gender relations as well as more generally in the current crisis (cf. inter alia Fraser, 2016; Winker, 2012; Wichterich, 2011; Schilliger, 2009). However, we see a danger of a narrowing social theory in the economistic and functionalist choice of terms, which results in particular from privileging the concept of work in the context of the capitalist economy. This conceptual narrowing now emanates from the feminist side and implies not only the loss of a multitude of gender-theoretical insights but also the complexity and multiplicity of contradictions and crisis phenomena in gender relations go out of sight.

In contrast, we want to use the example of the crisis of masculinity to show that it is not only an effect of economic changes or developments in the context of employment. On the contrary, it is rooted in manifold changes within gender relations themselves, which in turn have an impact on the economy and wage labour.

For some in the public discussion, the crisis of masculinity is obvious and is diagnosed as such for more and more areas of society. For others, however, it is a media "ploy" with the purpose of defending male supremacy. There is no doubt that there is quite a broad social debate about this. One sign of this is the growing questioning of hegemonic masculinity. Bourdieu already illustrated how, especially due to the feminist movement, "masculine domination no longer imposes itself with the transparency of something taken for granted", which is why its maintenance requires ever more legitimization (Bourdieu, 2001, p. 88).

In our opinion, this development has intensified in recent years and has reached wider social circles. The crisis of financial market capitalism and state crisis management has played a significant role here. It is the reason why previously positive elements of hegemonic masculinity were "suddenly" re-evaluated as negative factors and criticized as driving moments or even causes of the crisis: pronounced competitive behaviour, high risk-taking, career and success orientation (cf. Wichterich, 2011; Kurz-Scherf & Scheele, 2012; Heilmann, 2012). "Feminist critique of patriarchy" thus received, according to Kurz-Scherf, "new resonance" (2012, p. 90).

However, it is no less significant that in the meantime more and more men themselves not only experience conventional ideas and practices of masculinity as problematic and restrictive: Gainful employment, winner mentality or (sexist) violence – masculinity has thus become "self-reflexive" (Meuser & Scholz, 2011, p. 67) – but also many men live and want to live (more)equal relationships in their partnerships, family arrangements, as well as at work (cf. Baumgarten et al., 2012; Heilmann, 2012; Meuser, 2012; König, 2012). Among men themselves, essential elements of conventional hegemonic masculinity are thus increasingly losing their dominant orientation function and thus their normative power. Alongside them, new forms of masculinity are emerging, which counteract the conventional ones, or at least relativize them, and partly bring new and old practices of masculinity into strong contradiction with each other. This multiplication of masculinity is also reinforced by the growing public and everyday presence of bi- and homosexual as well as trans and queer masculinities. But not only central practices of masculinity but also *male supremacy* itself have lost their self-evidence and persuasiveness for many men.

These developments are attributed, among other things, to the de-securitization and disappearance of the Fordist male normal employment relationship and the associated breadwinner model (cf. e.g. Maihofer, 2004; Meuser & Scholz, 2011; Heilmann, 2012). According to these authors, this is accompanied by a growing insecurity of men in their traditional role as family breadwinner and professional man or, as Wichterich puts it, a crisis of hegemonic breadwinner masculinity (Wichterich, 2011, p. 133). In addition, Heilmann mentions the neoliberal intensification and condensation of subjectivised gainful employment as a cause that is affecting men to have doubts about a one-sided labour-centredness (Heilmann, 2012, p. 63).

As correct as these observations are, they often imply a problematic economistic prioritization of the employment sphere (cf. Aulenbacher, 2012; Janczyk, 2009). In addition, a number of significant processes, for example, in the family sphere, are disregarded or make them appear merely as a *consequence* of the undermining of the male gainful employment model. In our opinion, however, developments have been taking place in the family context for a long time, which, although closely connected to processes in the labour market, have their own logic and dynamics and in turn have an impact on the professional sphere.

For some time now, there has been a steady development towards family arrangements based on partnership (cf. Maihofer, 2004; König, 2012). It is true that the additional burden still lies mostly with women. At the same time, however, the number of men is rising steadily, who are participating more and more self-evidently in child-rearing and care work, but less in housework and nursing, and to very different extents (cf. Baumgarten et al., 2012; König, 2012; Meuser, 2012; Maihofer, 2021). The decisive factor here is that this does not only happen because the female partners expect it but because many fathers themselves want to spend more time at home with the children and the family. In clear distinction from their own absent fathers, they want to be present fathers who want to have and maintain an everyday firm emotional relationship with their children. In an analogous way, this also applies to same-sex parents. However, since gainful employment still has a high significance for men's own identity, many men now also have a reconciliation problem and the various demands and desires come into clear conflict with each other. Furthermore, especially in the (more) equal family arrangements, it is becoming increasingly difficult for parents to find time for rest and their own regeneration: their own reproduction is increasingly coming into crisis (cf. König & Jäger, 2011).

All this leads to an intensification of intra-family disputes about the division of housework, childcare and parenting, as well as gainful employment, because it is no longer conventionally predetermined (cf. König, 2012). At the same time, contradictions and tensions *between* men are also growing, especially between men who increasingly take care of children and those who do not have children or live in traditional family arrangements, both in everyday professional life (through the experience of the devaluation of their employment identity through teasing to mobbing) and in labour market competition (career opportunities, flexibility; cf. Baumgarten et al., 2012; Gesterkamp, 2012). Against this background, newly emerging divisions (Heilmann, 2012) can be observed as well as growing public disputes *between* men about the changes in ideas and practices of masculinity.

According to Meuser and Scholz, however, all this is not (yet) a crisis of masculinity. Men can undoubtedly experience this as "crisis-like" in a negative sense (Meuser & Scholz, 2011, p. 59) and feel fundamental uncertainty and disorientation. According to them, however, one can only speak of a crisis when the "social position of the male gender", that is, the male hegemony itself, is challenged and enters into crisis (ibid.). For this reason, for them, it is only a "structural change of hegemonic masculinity" (ibid.).

In our opinion, however, not only are many aspects of conventional hegemonic masculinity now fundamentally questioned but so is the *social power of men themselves*. In this vein, Heilmann points out that the current processes could be more than a structural change (Heilmann, 2012). After all, a number of social spheres such as the employment sphere, the family, the education system, politics or the media, which have so far been central to the reproduction of traditional hegemonic masculinity, are now undergoing fundamental change. In other words, the *conditions for the reproduction of* traditional hegemonic masculinity are beginning to disappear. Alongside this, according to our thesis, new forms of masculinity are emerging, up to and including the rejection of gender as a specific social relation. This increasingly leads to social conflicts and disputes about dominance between different concepts and practices of masculinity, which are at the same time closely linked to very different ideas of gender and gender relations.

In the context of these disputes, we also see the scandalization of sexual abuse of boys by men in educational institutions, churches and in sports that has been observed for some years, or the increased exposure to child pornography, child trafficking or child abuse. A certain connection between institutional power, sexual violence and masculinity that has existed for generations is obviously no longer accepted by many men either. At the same time, there are fierce counter-reactions: the churches' fight against homosexuality, or the emergence of an anti-feminist movement in which the women's movement, feminism or women generally are held responsible for the crisis of masculinity (cf. Gesterkamp, 2012). In the extreme, this can lead to militarized violence like that of the Norwegian mass murderer Anders Behring Breivik. How these conflicts will end and how fundamentally the gender order will change, however, is itself part of the crisis and depends not insignificantly on which social forces will prevail.

Final remarks

As we have illustrated with regard to some aspects, the crisis of gender relations is about processes that take place over decades, largely in the micro-processes of everyday life, and which in many cases are also emancipatory practices. The contradictions in gender relations are increasingly linked to crises in the prevailing modes of subjectivation and make individuals search for alternative forms of life concerning gender, eroticism, the body, the family, the relations between generations, and in general for emancipatory forms of living together. But it is precisely this clear search and the increased occurrence of alternative ways of existence that at the same time leads to increased counter-reactions, in which it is a matter of defending the prevailing patriarchal heteronormative gender order. This is not least because without it the bourgeois social formation cannot maintain itself. For this reason, too, we consider a broad and detailed analysis of the crisis of gender relations indispensable for the analysis and critical assessment of the current constellation of crisis in society as a whole.

Note

1 The earlier text from which this chapter develops is: Demirović, A., & Maihofer, A. (2013). Vielfachkrise und die Krise der Geschlechterverhältnisse. In H. M. Nickel & A. Heilmann (Eds.), *Krise, Kritik, Allianzen: Arbeits- und geschlechtersoziologische Perspektiven* [*Crisis, Critique, Alliances: Work and Gender Sociological Perspectives*] (pp. 30–48). Weinheim: Beltz Juventa. We thank Quinn Allison for the translation from German and the Rosa Luxemburg Foundation for financial support for the translation.

References

Althusser, L. (2006). *For Marx* (B. Brewster, Trans.). London: New York: Verso.

Aulenbacher, B. (2012). Gegenläufige Blicke auf Kapitalismus und Arbeit – Feministische Kapitalismusanalysen im Verhältnis zu Kapitalismustheorie und Arbeitssoziologie. In K. Dörre, D. Sauer & V. Wittke (Eds.), *Kapitalismustheorie und Arbeit. Neue Ansätze soziologischer Kritik* (pp. 113–126). Frankfurt/New York: Campus.

Baumgarten, D., Kassner, K., Maihofer, A., & Wehner, N. (2012). Warum werden manche Männer Väter, andere nicht? Männlichkeit und Kinderwunsch. In H. Walter & A. Eickhorst (Eds.), *Das Väter-Handbuch. Theorie, Forschung, Praxis* (pp. 415–443). Gießen: Psychosozial-Verlag.

Becker, F. (2011). *Hegemonie und Krise. Zur Analyse von Krisenzusammenhängen in Antonio Gramscis "Gefängnisheften"*. Berlin: Diplomarbeit. Humboldt Universität zu Berlin.

Boltanski, L., & Chiapello, E. (2003). *Der neue Geist des Kapitalismus*. Konstanz: UVK.

Bourdieu, P. (2001). *Masculine Domination*. Cambridge: Polity Press.

Brand, U. (2009). *Die Multiple Krise. Dynamik und Zusammenhang der Krisendimensionen, Anforderungen an politische Institutionen und Chancen progressiver Politik*. Berlin: Heinrich-Böll-Stiftung.

Crenshaw, K. (1997). Demarginalizing the intersection of race and sex: A Black feminist critique of antidiscrimination doctrine. *The University of Chicago Legal Forum*, 139–167.

Demirović, A., Dück, J., Becker, F., & Bader, P. (Eds.). (2011). *VielfachKrise. Im finanzmarktdominierten Kapitalismus*. Hamburg: VSA.

Dietze, G., Hornscheidt, A., Palm, K., & Walgenbach, K. (2007a). Einleitung. In K. Walgenbach, G. Dietze, A. Hornscheidt & K. Palm (Eds.), *Geschlecht als interdependente Kategorie. Neue Perspektiven auf Intersektionalität, Diversität und Heterogenität* (pp. 7–22). Opladen: Verlag Barbara Budrich. doi: 10.2307/j.ctvddzkrr.3

Dietze, G., Yekani, E. H., & Michaelis, B. (2007b). "Checks and balance": Zum Verhältnis von Intersektionalität und Queer Theory. In K. Walgenbach, G. Dietze, A. Hornscheidt & K. Palm (Eds.), *Geschlecht als interdependente Kategorie. Neue Perspektiven auf Intersektionalität, Diversität und Heterogenität* (pp. 107–139). Opladen: Verlag Barbara Budrich. doi: 10.2307/j.ctvddzkrr.6

Dörre, K. (2009). Die neue Landnahme. Dynamiken und Grenzen des Finanzmarktkapitalismus. In K. Dörre, St. Lessenich & H. Rosa (Eds.), *Soziologie – Kapitalismus – Kritik. Eine Debatte* (pp. 21–86). Frankfurt am Main: Suhrkamp.

Fishbein, A. J., & Woodall, P. (2006). Women are Prime Targets for Subprime Lending: Women are Disproportionately Represented in High-cost Mortgage Market. Retrieved from www.consumerfed.org/pdfs/WomenPrimeTargetsStudy120606.pdf

Fraser, N. (2016). Contradictions of capital and care. *New Left Review*, *100*, 99–117.

Gesterkamp, Th. (2012). Für Männer, aber nicht gegen Frauen. *Aus Politik und Zeitgeschichte*, *40*, 3–10.

Gramsci, A. (1996). *Gefängnishefte 7*. Hamburg: Argument.

Habermas, J. (1973). *Legitimationsprobleme im Spätkapitalismus*. Frankfurt am Main: Suhrkamp.

Heilmann. A. (2012). Die Krise männlicher Muster von Erwerbsarbeit – Chance für eine solidarische Arbeits- und Geschlechterpolitik? In I. Kurz-Scherf & A. Scheele (Eds.), *Macht oder ökonomisches Gesetz? Zum Zusammenhang von Krise und Geschlecht* (pp. 52–67). Münster: Westfälisches Dampfboot.

HKWM/Historisch-Kritisches Wörterbuch des Marxismus (2010). *Krise*. Hamburg: Argument.

Horkheimer, M., & Adorno, T. W. (2002). *Dialectic of Enlightenment* (G. S. Noeri, Ed.). Stanford, CA: Cultural Memory in the Present.

Hufer, K. P. (2010). Emanzipation: Gesellschaftliche Veränderungen durch Erziehung und politische Bildung – Ein Rückblick auf eine nach wie vor aktuelle Leitidee. In B. Lösch & A. Thimmel (Eds.), *Kritische politische Bildung. Ein Handbuch* (pp. 13–24). Schwalbach im Taunus: Wochenschau.
Janczyk, S. (2009). *Arbeit und Leben: Eine spannungsreiche Ko-Konstitution. Zur Revision zeitgenössischer Konzepte der Arbeitsforschung.* Münster: Westfälisches Dampfboot.
Klinger, C., & Knapp, G. A. (2005). Achsen der Ungleichheit – Achsen der Differenz. *Transit, 29*, 72–95.
König, T. (2012). *Familie heißt Arbeit teilen. Transformationen der symbolischen Geschlechterordnung.* Konstanz: UVK.
König, T., & Jäger, U. (2011). Reproduktionsarbeit in der Krise und neue Momente der Geschlechterordnung. In A. Demirović, J. Dück, F. Becker & P. Bader (Eds.), *VielfachKrise. Im finanzdominierten Kapitalismus* (pp. 147–164). Hamburg: VSA.
Kurz-Scherf, I. (2012). "The Great Transformation" – Ausstieg aus dem Kapitalismus? Ein Plädoyer für feministischen Eigensinn in den aktuellen Krisen- und Kritikdynamiken. In I. Kurz-Scherf & A. Schelle (Eds.), *Macht oder ökonomisches Gesetz? Zum Zusammenhang von Krise und Geschlecht* (pp. 81–105). Münster: Westfälisches Dampfboot.
Kurz-Scherf, I., & Scheele, A. (Eds.). (2012). Macht oder ökonomisches Gesetz? Einleitung. In *Macht oder ökonomisches Gesetz? Zum Zusammenhang von Krise und Geschlecht* (pp. 7–19). Münster: Westfälisches Dampfboot.
Maihofer, A. (1995). *Geschlecht als Existenzweise. Macht, Moral, Recht und Geschlechterdifferenz.* Frankfurt am Main: Ulrike Helmer.
Maihofer, A. (2004). Was wandelt sich im aktuellen Wandel der Familie? In B. Beerhorst, A. Demirović & M. Guggemos (Eds.), *Kritische Theorie im gesellschaftlichen Strukturwandel* (pp. 384–408). Frankfurt am Main: Suhrkamp.
Maihofer, A. (2007). Gender in Motion. Gesellschaftliche Transformationsprozesse – Umbrüche in den Geschlechterverhältnissen? Eine Problemskizze. In D. Grisard, J. Häberlein, A. Kaiser & S. Saxer (Eds.), *Gender in Motion. Die Konstruktion von Geschlecht in Raum und Erzählung* (pp. 218–315). Frankfurt am Main: Campus.
Maihofer, A. (2021). Wandel und Persistenz hegemonialer Männlichkeit – aktuelle Entwicklungen. In AG Transformation von Männlichkeiten (Eds.), *Zeitdiagnose Männlichkeiten Schweiz* (pp. 31–54). Zürich/Genf: Seismo.
Marx, K. (1969). *Das Kapital. Dritter Band. Karl Marx – Friedrich Engels – Werke 25.* Berlin: Dietz.
Marx, K. (2009). *Critique of Hegel's 'Philosophy of Right'* (J. O'Malley, Ed.). Cambridge: Cambridge University Press.
Meißner, H. (2011). Totalität und Vielfalt – gesellschaftliche Wirklichkeit als multidimensionaler Zusammenhang, *Prokla, 165*, 543–560. doi: 10.32387/prokla.v41i165.331
Meuser, M. (2012). Entgrenzungsdynamiken: Geschlechterverhältnisse im Umbruch. *Aus Politik und Zeitgeschichte, 40*, 17–24.
Meuser, M., & Scholz, S. (2011). Krise oder Strukturwandel hegemonialer Männlichkeit. In M. Bereswill & A. Neuber (Eds.), *In der Krise? Männlichkeiten im 21. Jahrhundert* (pp. 56–79). Münster: Westfälisches Dampfboot.
Rommelspacher, B. (2009). Intersektionalität – über die Wechselwirkung von Machtverhältnissen. In I. Kurz-Scherf, J. Lepperhoff & A. Scheele (Eds.), *Feminismus: Kritik und Intervention* (pp. 81–96). Münster: Westfälisches Dampfboot.
Schilliger, S. (2009). Who cares? Care-Arbeit im neoliberalen Geschlechterregime. *Widerspruch, 56*, 93–106.
Streeck, Wolfgang (2011). Die Krisen des demokratischen Kapitalismus. *Lettre Internationale*, 7–17.
Tooze, A. (2023). Chartbook #192 On Deglobalisation and Polycrisis – ADAM TOOZE. Retrieved March 18, 2023, from Adam Tooze website: https://adamtooze.com/2023/02/01/chartbook-192-on-deglobalisation-and-polycrisis/
Varga, E. (1969). *Die Krise des Kapitalismus und ihre politischen Folgen.* Frankfurt am Main: EVA.
Walby, S. (2007). Complexity theory, systems theory, and multiple intersecting social inequalities. *Philosophy of Social Sciences, 37*(4), 449–470. doi: 10.1177/0048393107307663
Walgenbach, K. (2007). Gender als interdependente Kategorie. In K. Walgenbach, G. Dietze, A. Hornscheidt & K. Palm (Eds.), *Geschlecht als interdependente Kategorie. Neue Perspektiven auf*

Intersektionalität, Diversität und Heterogenität (pp. 23–64). Opladen & Farmington Hills: Verlag Barbara Budrich. doi: 10.2307/j.ctvddzkrr.4
Wichterich, C. (2011). Krise der Ernährermännlichkeit und neoliberale Gleichstellung durch die Krise. In A. Demirović, J. Dück, F. Becker & P. Bader (Eds.), *VielfachKrise. Im finanzmarktdominierten Kapitalismus* (pp. 129–145). Hamburg: VSA.
Wichterich, C. (2012). Mikrokredite und die Entdeckung der Frauen. *Die Beiträge in LuXemburg*, *4*, 28–35.
Winker, G. (2012). Erschöpfung des Sozialen, *Die Beiträge in LuXemburg*, *4*, 6–13.

27

ALLYSHIP AND ACCOUNTABILITY IN ORGANIZATIONS ENGAGING MEN IN VIOLENCE PREVENTION

Principles, practices and political dilemmas

Bob Pease

Introduction

As men have become more prominent in violence against women prevention organizations in recent years, the issue of men's relationship with women against violence services has become a subject of ongoing concern for many feminist anti-violence activists and scholars. This chapter aims to explore the nature of those concerns and the various ways in which activist men and the organizations they work within have responded to them.[1]

A key issue in these discussions is whether men involved in violence prevention organizations should be accountable to women against violence services or feminists involved in violence prevention. Alternatively, should men rely upon their own capacity for self-criticism and their commitment to the ideals and values of emancipation?

If men are to be accountable, to which organizations, women and/or feminists should they be accountable to and what form should that accountability take? In this chapter, I argue why accountability is necessary and I engage with political dilemmas associated with it in the context of the social divisions between men and the reality that most men involved in publicly recognized violence prevention are straight white able-bodied middle-class men. I also explore different levels of accountability including personal, interpersonal and organizational forms and outline different models of accountability and strategies for their implementation.

Accountability is premised upon the notion that it is inappropriate for men to take on leadership roles or work in equal partnership in violence prevention. Being an ally means having a supporting role in relation to campaigns under women's leadership. This is because of men's dominance and the privilege and the structural gender inequalities within which men's violence takes place.

Ayvazian (1995, p. 1) defines an ally as "a member of a dominant group in our society who works to dismantle any form of oppression from which she or he receives the benefit".

 DOI: 10.4324/9781003193579-31

Similarly, Borshuk (2004) defines ally activism as "outgroup activism", where those involved are not direct beneficiaries. This is to differentiate allies from beneficiary activists, which is a term coined by Myers (2008) to describe people whose interests are directly impacted by social movements.

Why accountability is necessary?

The concern about accountability arises from the potential harm that aspiring allies can cause.[2] It is evident from research on social movements that the involvement of dominant group members can reproduce inequalities within movement organizations (Messner et al., 2015). The power and control located in the wider societal context of unequal relationships will often play out within alliances (Margaret, 2010). This includes how decisions are made and whose voices are heard. Consequently, when men and women work together in social movement organizations, they must find ways of addressing their differences and the relations of power within which they are embedded (Tamasese, 1998). Given that men are socialized into a sense of entitlement that goes with their privileged position, how do they counter the likely biases that will come to the fore when they work with women against men's violence? The purpose of accountability processes is to address the sexism and male privilege which men bring with them when they get involved in violence prevention work.

Setting up a dichotomy between male allies and other men

Attempts to broaden the problem of men's violence to include the responsibility of all men invites defensive responses from many men. Men often argue that it is not *all* men who are responsible for men's violence. Rather, it is just a small group of "bad" men. In approaching men as potential allies, the aim of engaging men in violence prevention campaigns is often to pre-empt men's potential defensive responses by emphasizing that "not all men are violent" (Piccigallo et al., 2012).

Strategies have been developed to enable men to feel that by standing up against violence they are the "good men" and that they can demonstrate a healthy masculinity. Goldrick-Jones (2002) refers to these "good men" as "white knights to the rescue", where men take charge on the premise that they know how to "fix" men's violence against women. It is important for men's anti-violence organizations to avoid perpetuating the conception of the good man because it fails to recognize the ways in which all men *are* implicated in male privilege and gender inequality. The language of "good men" does not encourage men to critically self-reflect on how their own behaviour and attitudes are part of the wider systems of dominance and oppression. When men present themselves as the "good guys", they exceptionalize themselves from the wider problem of men's violence and gender inequality. This means that they are likely to be less aware of, and accountable for, their complicity in men's violence.

Depoliticizing anti-violence work

One of the ongoing debates about violence prevention is how explicitly feminist anti-violence campaigns should be. The level of commitment to feminist analyses and the particular form of feminism adopted will shape the ways in which accountability is understood and operationalized. One of the dangers of men's increased involvement in violence prevention is the de-radicalization of feminist analyses of men's violence against women (Pease, 2008).[3]

There is a tension between mainstreaming campaigns against men's violence against women and moving away from social movement politics. This tension is reflected in the differences between professionalized public health approaches to violence prevention and the activist politics of women's movement organizations. Issues have also been raised about men becoming private consultants in violence prevention work and using their involvement in these activities to develop highly paid careers (Messner et al., 2015).

It is also important to be mindful about how organizations that support violence prevention can use their involvement primarily as a public relations exercise rather than seriously tackling the structural causes of men's violence against women. When sporting clubs, military organizations and male-dominated workplaces develop prevention programmes with men, they need to interrogate the ways that gender inequalities are embedded in their structures and cultures, if their practical steps are to contribute to major structural transformation (Messner et al., 2015).

Using traditional masculinity to challenge men's violence against women

The concepts of "real men" not being violent and "being man enough" to stand up against men's violence have been used to engage men in anti-violence work. Thus, some anti-violence organizations use traditional masculinity as a way of getting men involved (Messner et al., 2015; Pease, 2015; Salter, 2016).[4] Although the aim is to redefine masculinity, if masculinity is a contributing cause of violence against women, then reinforcing masculinity to engage men to stop violence seems fraught with problems. Goldrick-Jones (2002) asks the question of whether men can be allies to feminism if they retain their commitment to masculinity which is part of the reproduction of patriarchy.

Within profeminism, there is an important debate about the extent to which men's support of feminism requires a reformulation of masculinity or a rejection of it (Kimmel, 2000; Pease, 2014; Stoltenberg, 1989). Constructing a profeminist subjectivity for men may involve destabilizing men's identities as men and encouraging them to loosen their connection to masculinity and manhood. This debate will play out differently with class-privileged white men compared with racialized, colonized and working-class men who often feel the need to assert their masculinity in the face of marginalization by other social divisions.

Excluding women

Although there is a place for men organizing separately against men's violence and all-male organizations can be sites of progressive personal and social change, all-male groups need to be transparent and responsive to feminist concerns. Many men in the violence prevention sector argue that men need a space without the presence of women to speak authentically about their experience. Piccigallo et al. (2012), for example, talk about the importance of men being comfortable with each other and being able to talk openly without the presence of women.[5]

Marchese (2008) documents accounts of men's anti-violence organizations who exclude women from being involved in their activities. However, why should all-male groups be required for men to have honest conversations? Given what we know about all-male groups producing male peer endorsement of men's violence (DeKeseredy & Schwartz, 2013), men only groups seem more likely to reproduce dominant forms of masculinity than challenge them. How can all-male groups be accountable to women when the exclusion of women reinforces the notion of male authority? Stoltenberg (cited in Marchese, 2008) argues that if men feel uncomfortable speaking about their experience in the presence of women, then this in itself emphasizes the importance of why they need to learn how to communicate outside of traditional frames of masculinity and male sociality.

Gaining more praise and marginalizing women's voices

Men gain more credit and receive more praise when they become involved in violence prevention (Linder & Johnson, 2015). This is particularly problematic when women have done most of the work in organizing an event and men get most of the credit for being involved. It has been noted that in most of the White Ribbon events in Australia, for example, that while men present themselves for photos and interviews,[6] women do most of the administrative and background work in getting the project organized (Pease, 2017).

One of the often-stated concerns about engaging men is that women will be marginalized and silenced (Marchese, 2008). It has been widely noted that when men challenge men's violence they are more likely to be listened to because of their privileged status. Messner et al. (2015) refer to men's unearned praise and the greater likelihood of being listened to as the "pedestal effect". While it means that men's privilege is being used for a progressive outcome of influencing other men, it may further marginalize the voices of women who are less likely to be heard. If men's voices are heard as more authoritative, it may lead to the further suppression of women's voices. It is important when men receive unearned praise to make the point that they would not be doing the work if it was not for feminist women who have mentored and taught them almost everything they know (Atherton-Zeman, 2009).

Impacting on women's space

The presence of even a small number of men in women's organizations and campaigns has an impact on group dynamics. Castelino (2012) explored the issue of how the family violence sector changes when men become engaged in the prevention of violence against women. Men's involvement influences the ways in which violence against women is understood, and it shapes strategies for violence prevention. Men's involvement shifts the focus from addressing structural analyses of violence against women to developing new forms of masculinity. Linder and Johnson (2015) found that many feminists working with men in violence prevention programmes regarded many of the men as operating through a framework of "enlightened sexism".[7] They perpetuated sexism through both their own behaviour and their failure to challenge the sexist practices of other men.

The presence of men in mixed-gender activism leads women to be very careful about what they say. Women report that they modify their speech and behaviour so that men would not get upset. This reflects the gendered expectation that women should care about men's feelings and avoid upsetting them. Phyllis Frank (cited in Messner et al., 2015) sees women's praise of men as part of the process of women's socialization into supporting men and making them feel good. Women are often strongly sanctioned if they do not support and affirm men.

When men get involved in feminist campaigns, they often dominate in meetings. Linder and Johnson (2015) refer to "micro-aggressions" as the form of men's dominating and abusive behaviours, where they talk over women in meetings, assume a sense of superiority in relation to strategies and campaigns and use their male privilege to further their views. Such concerns expressed by women activists include the following: interrupting women when they are talking, dominating discussions and taking up the majority of time in meetings, presuming to have more expertise and knowledge than they do, receiving more praise than women activists, gaining greater status and money for the work that they do and in some instances, sexually objectifying women colleagues (Macomber, 2014). These concerns need to be addressed if the potential harms of aspiring allies are to be mitigated in mixed-sex organizations.

Further, women are sometimes challenged about why they want women-only spaces when men are interested in being involved (Castelino, 2012). In the work of engaging men, it is important to support the continuation of women-only campaigns and organizations in challenging men's violence.

Lacking historical understanding of violence against women and men's complicity in it

Many men who become involved in violence prevention do not do their "homework" and often do not know anything about the history of the women's movement responses to violence against women and have little knowledge about the structural causes of men's violence (Macomber, 2014).

It is necessary for dominant groups to educate themselves about their own privilege and power (Macomber, 2014; Pease, 2022; Tamasese et al., 1998). Men need to understand their role in the reproduction of gender inequality and their shared responsibility for the continuation of the structural gender relations and the patriarchal culture which supports men's violence against women (Pease, 2015). Such an understanding is essential if men are to become allies to women and to implement principles and practices that ensure their accountability to women's services.

The meaning of being an ally and being accountable

Margaret (2010) raises the question whether it is possible to proclaim yourself as an ally, as opposed to being defined as such by those you are in solidarity with. The Women of Color Caucus (cited in Messner et al., 2015) advise men that their ally badge runs out at the end of the day and that they have to give it back and strive to earn it again each day. However, even with aspiring allies, there are differing motivations and orientations.

Edwards (2006) differentiates between aspiring allies for self-interest, for altruism and for social justice. Aspiring allies for self-interest see themselves primarily as protectors of women, especially the women they have personal relationships with. Aspiring allies for altruism see themselves primarily as heroes and rescuers who are endeavouring to assuage their guilt for the privilege they have, whereas aspiring allies for social justice understand their privilege and complicity in the reproduction of oppression and work towards gender equality. Aspiring male allies should strive for the latter form of alliance with women.

Profeminst allies have much to learn from the failings of white allies in anti-racist practice. Indigenous Action Media (2014) highlight some of the key issues in their critique of what they called "the ally industrial complex", whereby self-proclaimed allies have developed careers out of their allyship work and have turned allyship into an identity that is disconnected from mutuality and solidarity with oppressed people. McKenzie (2015) similarly talks about "ally theatre", whereby "allies" perform their allyship on social media and other public spaces where they have an audience for their performance of activism.

Obstacles to men becoming allies

There are important challenges to identity construction facing members of privileged groups who become involved in solidarity campaigns. Whereas for oppressed groups, reconstituting one's identity involves a positive affirmation of who they are, for those in privileged groups, it means creating what can be experienced as a negative identity. Such a process involves a critical interrogation of the moral superiority embedded in privileged identities.

It is not uncommon for men who speak out against men's violence to be referred to as gender traitors. Rather than being experienced as a criticism, however, this could be embraced by male allies as a positive identity. Creating a traitorous identity (Bailey, 1998; Pease, 2022) is a way in which men can challenge patriarchal manhood. Male gender traitors are those that refuse to reproduce their privilege and who challenge the world views that dominant groups are expected to adhere to.

The contested nature of accountability

As noted in the introduction, one of the premises of accountability in campaigns against oppression is that groups who have been oppressed are in the best position to understand injustice because they are more able to understand the realities of oppression (Tamasese et al., 1998). This is why they should be leaders in campaigns to address that oppression to ensure ally actions match the needs and desires of a marginalized population (Cohen, 2002).

While the concept of accountability is much talked about in the movement against men's violence against women, it is a much misunderstood concept. Accountability is a complicated and contested process. Lack of clarity about the meaning of accountability, and lack of agreement about the importance of it, generates tensions between men's anti-violence organizations and women's services (Funk, 2008; Goldrick-Jones, 2002; Macomber, 2014).

Being accountable to women and being guided by the leadership of women entails seeking feedback from women, hearing what they have to say and being receptive to their comments (Macomber, 2014). One way to frame accountability is to ask the questions: Who benefits from men's work and who is potentially harmed by men's work?

Forms of accountability

Barone (2007) distinguishes between three different kinds of accountability. Symbolic accountability is where men let women know what they are doing and seek women's feedback. Practical accountability is where men develop relationships with individual feminist women in their lives through ongoing conversations and alliances around particular projects. This involves making agreements with particular women about their aims and intentions and making a commitment to follow through on specific undertakings. Structural accountability entails organizational relationships between the men's programmes and women's services. One form of structural accountability would be for men's organizations to incorporate a women's advisory group or a women's caucus into the structure of their organization. This would ensure that they are connected to the intended beneficiaries of their work. Ideally, all three forms of accountability should be developed.

It is important that profeminist organizations make their commitment to accountability to women's services explicit on their external websites and materials. They should acknowledge the contribution and leadership of women in challenging men's violence. They should also encourage local groups who are developing anti-violence projects to develop dialogue with women's groups in their communities (Bojin, 2012).

It is also important for organizations engaging men to develop processes within their workplaces to address male privilege and power (Macomber, 2014). Work on undoing privilege and advancing gender equality in public-sector organizations is relevant here (Flood & Pease, 2005). Naming and critically interrogating men's privilege in the context of the social divisions between men provides a valuable framework for work towards gender equality within anti-violence organizations. Such an analysis provides a basis for designing training programmes for men. These programmes should include content that examines how men's gender interests are socially constructed and psychically embedded, critique the routine accomplishment and reproduction of privilege and identify and encourage gender egalitarian orientations, identities and relations in the context of the inequalities among men (Flood & Pease, 2005).

Educating for accountability

Adopting processes of accountability requires education. The International Rescue Committee (2013, p. 14) has developed a curriculum for educating men about accountability processes. For them, accountability "is an active process where men listen to the needs of women and recognise when they act in a harmful manner, even unintentionally". They differentiate between personal accountability, where facilitators are required to monitor their attitudes, beliefs and practice, and relational accountability, where facilitators are expected to challenge power differences between men and women.

Macomber (2014) has five recommendations for engaging men as allies in anti-violence work that should form part of any curriculum on accountability: require newcomers to receive training and education work before stepping into key activist roles; cap men's speaking fees; link men's organizations to women's organizations and groups; institutionalize a process to address issues of privilege internally; and reconceptualize accountability to include an emphasis on building gender equity.

Political dilemmas about accountability

While the importance of men's accountability to women is generally accepted within feminist-informed violence prevention by men, there are nevertheless a number of political dilemmas.

Engaging with many feminisms

The women's services sector is informed by a diversity of feminist perspectives. Which feminisms should men be accountable to? (Burrell & Flood, 2019). If feminists have different views and approaches on an issue and men ask particular feminists for direction and advice, does that add to the conflict between women? Alternatively, if men choose to stay out of the disagreement between feminists, does that mean they have overstated their own influence on the discussion?

Murhpy (2013) says that it is not men's responsibility to decide whether feminists are taking the correct course of action or not. However, when profeminist men take any action, they are siding with particular feminist advocates and positions (Burrell & Flood, 2019). There is a tension between men having views about particular feminist perspectives and having input into what feminism should be prioritizing. It is understandable that feminist women will not appreciate men suggesting in some way that they are not doing feminism the right way. The language of "mansplaining" (Solnit, 2014) is used to refer to men's propensity to see themselves as experts.

Stoltenberg (1990) argues that it is appropriate for profeminist men to choose between different feminist perspectives on issues such as prostitution and pornography. If men believe that women's support of particular policies is oppressive to other women, then it is argued that they have to choose between different feminist views. Stoltenberg says that men should use their own political and moral compass to decide between different feminisms. The difficulty, he says, is how men can do this without claiming some form of moral authority or marginalizing women's voices. We also need to be aware that men may be more likely to choose strands of feminism, such as liberal feminism, which are less challenging for men than, for example, radical feminism which men may be more confronted by.

Men should not expect women to come up with the right answers to their questions and they should be able to challenge feminist women's views in certain situations (Goldrick-Jones, 2002). We should see accountability in terms of men's relationship to the women's movement as a whole, acknowledging its diversity, rather than to individual women (Messner et al., 2015). This means trying to distinguish between listening to the voices of individual women and particular women's groups with endeavouring to understand the collective voice of what feminist women are saying (Cohen, 2002). Men need to read widely, hear the diversity of views, engage with the complexities of the debates, understand the implications and potential harms and benefits of their actions and then make an informed, respectful and strategic choice about how to act and what to say in relation to an issue.

Engaging with social divisions between men

Allies who are most visible in publicly recognized violence prevention organizations are straight white able-bodied middle-class men and gay, immigrant, Aboriginal, disabled and working-class men are not as represented in violence prevention, at least in the West (Murdolo & Quiazon, 2016; Peretz, 2017).[8] How to engage working-class men and men from culturally diverse backgrounds continues to be a challenge to violence against women prevention organizations in the West. Accountability must address these social divisions between men, as well as between men and women. This raises the issue of white men's accountability to men of colour and economically privileged men's accountability to economically poor men as well as to women from those diverse communities.

Funk (2008) discusses the importance of working intersectionally when we practise accountability, both in terms of developing relationships with men across class and race differences and also acting as allies to women across class and race, as well as gender. If men are engaged in addressing violence against women in immigrant or Aboriginal communities, it means that they should be accountable to immigrant or Aboriginal feminists, as should men who are engaged in addressing violence against women more generally because their work impacts these diverse communities as well. Multiple forms of social injustice call for multiple forms of accountability (Murdolo & Quiazon, 2016).

Taking moral responsibility for actions

There is a tension between men's accountability to women and individual men's moral responsibility to decide for themselves how to act. Stoltenberg (2013) raises the concern that if accountability is applied too extremely, men have no moral involvement in decisions themselves. Men need to have a moral compass and to develop a sense of what is right and wrong and what is just and unjust. Marx (1997) argues that men need to be accountable to themselves and develop the capacity for reflectiveness about their own behaviour and the behaviour of other men. His concern is that men's accountability to feminists absolves men of moral responsibility and puts that responsibility on women.

However, women are better "experts" on gender inequalities and men's violence against women than men. Feminists are entitled to know what campaigns are being planned and should have the opportunity to comment on them. Also, men need to do more than rely upon their moral compass because it does not necessarily address their political responsibility to ensure that women's needs are being met. Accountability does not have to mean that men are just passive in response to women's permission. It is also important to ensure that any model of accountability does not impose unreasonable or excessive demands upon women.

Engaging with identity issues for men

Men's role as allies is a developmental process in which men are likely to make mistakes and missteps along the way (Edwards, 2006; Linder & Johnson, 2015). However, in acknowledging the learning journey of allies, it is important not to marginalize the experiences of those who continue to be hurt by the mistakes of allies. Women should not have to wait until men's learning process is over before they can expect to be free of sexism and abuse from men. While male allies will make mistakes, they should not use the notion of being on a learning journey to diminish their accountability or to excuse their mistakes.

Armato (2013) expresses concern about the prioritizing of reshaping men's identities at the expense of challenging gender inequality and other forms of oppression. Men's motives for getting involved in solidarity struggles with women should always be scrutinized. Funk (2008) talks about the importance of clarifying why men are involved in anti-violence work, what it means to them and how doing the work has impacted on them.

Strategies for men in promoting accountability

As men are at different stages of development when it comes to understanding patriarchy and men's violence against women, the practices involved in enacting the strategies for promoting accountability in single-sex and mixed-sex organizations require knowledge, skills and personal reflexivity. They are presented as a starting point for readings, exercises, presentations and discussions.

Learning about your own privilege as a man

A number of writers on accountability talk about the importance of men being reflective and cognizant about their male privilege (Macomber, 2014; Pease, 2022; Schacht & Ewing, 1997). Schacht and Ewing (1997) make the point that while violence against women is a structural issue, it is not only structural and that men need to work on changing their lives as part of the struggle against patriarchy.

The more that men are reflective about their own privileged positioning, and take action to challenge it, the more likely that they can be effective allies (Curry-Stevens, 2004). Bojin (2012) argues that men's capacity to interrogate their own privilege is fundamental for developing effective alliances with feminist women. It has been noted by many feminist activists, that aspiring allies are cognizant of their privilege and also have an understanding of the history of women's activism against men's violence (Macomber, 2012). Such men were less likely to present themselves as experts and were more willing to take a secondary role in support of women's work.

Acknowledging what men have learnt from women

It is important when men talk about their work in challenging men's violence that they acknowledge their debt to feminism and to women who have been working in this area for many years (Messner et al., 2015). Almost everything that I have learnt about feminist understandings of gender, I have learnt from women. It is important for male allies to recognize that we are a "Johnny come lately" to men's violence prevention and that we have much to learn from women.

This means that men need to adopt a position of moral humility and learn to see themselves as women see them. Men need to find ways in which they can learn to hear the experiences of women and allow themselves to feel in their hearts the pain and suffering of others (Pease, 2022).

Engaging in dialogue

Groups to promote dialogue between members of privileged groups and those who are marginalized have been promoted by some commentators (Curry-Stevens, 2004). Dialogue between men and women seems to be an essential element of effective alliances. However, we need to know more about how to promote the conditions upon which dialogues can best be developed and to understand how inequalities in power and privilege between men and women create barriers to effective communication (Singh, 2001). Men need to demonstrate an understanding that their knowledge and perception of the world is socially situated and only partial if they are going to avoid oppressive practices in their encounters. Men need also to problematize their own dominant position (Pease, 2022).

Developing trust

The issue of men's accountability to women is connected to trust (Goldrick-Jones, 2002). Many women are understandably suspicious and cautious of men who express solidarity with them. Because they have had bad experiences with men in the past, they are not going to offer unconditional support to men. Trust between men and women in violence prevention work has to be achieved; it is not given (Pease, 2008). Men have to earn their trust by building up a track record and by walking the walk. Women often complain about the energy and resources they expend in educating men. However, when trusting relationships are established, women are more likely to be committed to working with men (Barone, 2007).

Engaging in alliances

Temporary alliances between men and women are an important strategy for developing accountability. Bystydzienski and Schacht (2001) emphasize the importance of creating shared spaces that can assist participants to engage in alliances without domination. In effective coalitions, men are likely to feel threatened some of the time. If they do not, it is unlikely that they are emotionally committed. Alliances between men and women are specific sites where oppressive relations are likely to be enacted. When illuminated and challenged, they become microcosms of the larger struggle against men's dominance (Pease, 2022).

Acknowledging when you make mistakes

One key issue is how men respond when they receive critical feedback from women about their practice. Women often report men becoming defensive in response to feedback, whereas men should learn to receive such feedback as constructive criticism.[9] Linder and Johnson (2015) refer to feedback from women as a gift to men because it provides an opportunity for the capacity for men to learn.

Often when men are challenged by women about their sexism, they say that it was not their intent to cause harm. Their apologies, if they offer them at all, are framed in terms of being sorry if the person chose to take offense. This lets them off the hook and validates their experiences over those they have offended. Stoltenberg (2013) offers advice to men when their actions have aggrieved feminist women: hear what you did from the person that you did it to; acknowledge that you know what you did; apologize without qualification and without rationalization; make amends. When men do slip up, it is important for them to acknowledge their missteps without defensiveness.

Holding other men accountable to women

A critical step towards accountability is for men to hold other men accountable to women, rather than relying on women to call men out when they are being sexist. Challenging other men's sexism is often difficult for men because it undermines male solidarity upon which men's relationships often are based. It is easier for men to walk the walk with women in relation to gender equality than to do so with other men. It is often men's reluctance to challenge other men that leads women to mistrust male allies (Linder & Johnson, 2015; Macomber, 2014). When men do challenge other men, they break the bonds that hold men to patriarchal manhood. However, class and race differences between men complicate this practice. When white middle-class straight men challenge other men, they need to be cognizant of their own positioning with class, race and sexuality hierarchies and well as the positioning of the men they are criticizing.

Conclusion

Men's involvement in anti-violence organizations against men's power and privilege will always be fraught. Their work as allies in violence prevention will elicit contradictory responses from women (Messner et al., 2015). They will be both scrutinized and criticized, on the one hand, and praised and rewarded on the other hand. This seems to be an inevitable contradiction of men working as aspiring allies with women. It is understandable that there will always be some level of scrutiny of allies about their level of commitment to challenging their privileges. Any strategy involving men will contain contradictions and tensions between the aim of challenging patriarchal power and at the same time reproducing it. However, engaging with the principles and practices of accountability offer a way forward for men and women who are committed to working for a gender-equal and violence-free world.

Acknowledgements

Some sections of this chapter are based on the report, *Men as Allies in Preventing Violence Against Women: Principles and Practices for Promoting Accountability*, commissioned by White Ribbon Australia in 2017.

Notes

1 In my reference to men throughout this chapter, I am referring to cisgendered men whose gender identity aligns with the sex they were assigned at birth.
2 I use the language of "aspiring allies" to describe men's involvement in violence prevention to indicate that it is a process of being involved in ongoing personal and political development in alliance with feminists, in preference to other languages such as male-led campaigns, partners in violence prevention, coalition partners, active bystanders, male champions and male allies.
3 It should be noted here that throughout this chapter, I use the language of profeminism to articulate men's support for a feminist perspective. I argue that men should not call themselves feminists both because feminism is grounded in women's experiences of patriarchy and because I believe that this increases the dangers of appropriating women's work. This linguistic distinction of course does also not address whether the men who espouse profeminist politics walk the walk in their daily lives.
4 By traditional masculinity, I am referring to the Western concept of manhood that emphasizes stoicism, aggression, competitiveness and dominance.
5 The work on men's engagement with feminism and violence prevention is usually premised upon biologically distinct men and women who constitute a gender binary. We now know that this distinction does not work for many people. This raises the question of what men's aspiring allyship means for trans, non-binary and intersex people. I favour moving away from the gender binary (see Pease, 2022), but my focus in this chapter is on cisgendered men and their practices because they are the perpetrators and perpetuators of most violence.
6 The White Ribbon campaign is a global movement of men against men's violence against women. It was founded by men in Canada in 1991 in response to a massacre of 14 women students by a man at the Ecole Polytechnique in Montreal. See Pease (2019) for an outline of my involvement in the White Ribbon Campaign in Australia and my criticism of it as a violence prevention strategy engaging men.
7 "Enlightened sexism" is term Armato (2013) uses to refer to the attitudes and practices of men which appear to be egalitarian but which actually reproduce men's privilege.
8 Working-class and culturally diverse men are more likely to be involved in violence prevention in their own communities, and this work is not as widely recognized. See Ratele, Malherbe, Cornell and Suffla in this volume.
9 This defensiveness is similar to white people's responses when challenged about their racism and their white privilege. See, for example, DiAngelo (2018).

References

Armato, M. (2013). Wolves in sheep's clothing: Men's enlightened sexism and hegemonic masculinity in academia. *Women's Studies: An Inter-Disciplinary Journal*, *42*, 578–598. doi: 10.1080/00497878.2013.794055

Atherton-Zeman, B. (2009). Minimizing the Damage: Male Accountability in Stopping Men's Violence Against Women. The Voice. Spring. https://xyonline.net/sites/xyonline.net/files/Atherton-Zeman%2C%20Minimizing%20the%20Damage%20–%20Male%20Accountability%2009.pdf

Ayvazian, A. (1995). Interrupting the cycle of oppression: The role of allies as agents of change. *Fellowship*, 7–10.

Bailey, A. (1998). Locating traitorous identities: Toward a view of privilege-cognizant white Character. *Hypatia*, *13*(3), 27–42. www.jstor.org/stable/3810697

Barone, R. (2007). Men and Feminism: Structural, Symbolic and Practical Accountability. Joint Meeting Practice Brief Standing Committee for Men, Colorado State University.

Bojin, K. (2012). *"All of Our Work is Political": Men's Experiences in Pro-feminist Organizing.* Master of Arts, Ontario Institute for Studies in Education, University of Toronto.

Borshuk, C. (2004). An interpretive investigation into the motivation of outgroup activism. *Qualitative Report, 9*, 300–319. doi: 10.46743/2160-3715/2004.1930

Burrell, S., & Flood, M. (2019). Which feminism? Dilemmas in profeminist men's praxis to end violence against women. *Global Social Welfare, 6*, 231–244. doi: 10.1007/s40609-018-00136-x

Bystydzienski, J., & Schacht, S. (2001). Introduction. In J. Bystydzienski & S. Schacht (Eds.), *Forging Radical Alliances Across Difference: Coalition Politics for the New Millennium* (pp. 1–17). Lanham: Rowman and Littlefield.

Castelino, T. (2012). A feminist audit of men's engagement in the elimination of violence against women. *Paper presented at the No to Violence Conference*, Melbourne, Not to Violence, November.

Cohen, J. (2002). The Politics of Accountability in Movements for Social Justice. National Organisation of Men Against Sexism: https://nomas.org/the-politics-of-accountability/

Curry-Stevens, A. (2004). Pedagogy for the privileged: Building civic virtues in political leaders. *Unpublished paper, Transforming Learning Centre*, Portland State University.

DeKeseredy, W., & Schwartz, M. (2013). *Male Peer Support and Violence against Women*. New England: Northeastern University Press.

Diangelo, R. (2018). *White Fragility: Why It's so Hard for White People to Talk About Racism*. Boston, MA: Beacon Press.

Edwards, K. (2006). Aspiring social justice ally development: A conceptual model. *NASPA Journal, 43*(4), 39–60. doi: 10.2202/1949-6605.1722

Flood, M., & Pease, B. (2005). Undoing men's privilege and advancing gender equality in public sector institutions. *Policy and Society, 24*(4), 119–138. doi: 10.1016/S1449-4035(05)70123-5

Funk, R. (2008). Men's work: Men's voices and actions against sexism and violence. *Journal of Prevention and Intervention in the Community, 36*(1–2), 155–171. doi: 10.1080/10852350802022456

Goldrick-Jones, A. (2002). *Men Who Believe in Feminism*. Westport, CT: Praeger.

Indigenous Action Media (2014). Accomplices, Not Allies: Abolishing the Ally Industrial Complex. Retrieved from www.indigenousaction.org/accomplices-not-allies-abolishing-the-ally-industrial-complex/

International Rescue Committee (2013). *Preventing Violence against Women and Girls: Engaging Men Through Accountable Practice*. New York: International Rescue Committee.

Kimmel, M. (2000). *The Gendered Society*. New York: Oxford University Press.

Linder, C., & Johnson, R. (2015). Exploring the complexities of men as allies in feminist movements. *Journal of Critical thought and Praxis, 4*(1), 1–29.

Macomber, K. (2012). *Men as Allies: Mobilizing Men to End Violence against Women*. PhD thesis, Sociology, Raleigh, NC.

Macomber, K. (2014). Integrating Men as Allies in Anti-violence Work: Accountability and Beyond. XY: Men, Masculinities and Gender Politics: https://xyonline.net/content/integrating-men-allies-anti-violence-work-accountability-and-beyond

Marchese, E. (2008). No women allowed: Exclusion and accountability in men's anti-rape groups. *Journal of International Women's Studies, 9*(2), 59–76.

Margaret, J. (2010, August). Working as Allies. Winston Churchill Fellowship Report. https://groundwork.org.nz/wp-content/uploads/2020/04/jen-margaret-winston-churchill-report-2010.pdf

Marx, G. (1997). Profem Electronic Discussion List, April.

McKenzie, M. (2015). How to Tell the Difference between Real Solidarity and "Ally" Theatre'. Retrieved from http//www.blackgirldangerous.com/2015/11/ally-theatre/

Messner, M. Greenberg, M., & Peretz, T. (2015). *Some Men: Feminist Allies and the Movement to End Violence against Women*. New York: Oxford University Press.

Murdolo, A., & Quiazon, R. (2016). *Key Issues in Working with Men from Immigrant and Refugee Communities in Preventing Violence against Women* (White Ribbon Research Series). North Sydney: White Ribbon Australia.

Murhpy, M. (2013). The Trouble with Male Allies. Retrieved 10 September, from Feminist Current. https://www.feministcurrent.com/2013/09/10/the-trouble-with-male-allies/

Myers, D. (2008). Ally identity: The politically gay. In J. Reger, J. Myers & R. Einwehner (Eds.), *Identity Work in Social Movements* (pp. 167–187). Minneapolis: University of Minnesota Press.

Pease, B. (2008). Engaging men in men's violence prevention: Exploring the tensions, dilemmas and possibilities. In *Australian Domestic and Family Violence Clearinghouse* (Issues Paper 17). Sydney: University of New South Wales.

Pease, B. (2014). Reconstructing masculinity or ending manhood?: Transforming masculine subjectivities for gender equality. In A. Carabi & J. Armengol (Eds.), *Alternative Masculinities for a Changing World* (pp. 17–34). New York: Palgrave Macmillan.

Pease, B. (2015). Disengaging men from patriarchy: Rethinking the "man question" in masculinity studies. In M. Flood & M. Howson (Eds.), *Engaging Men in Building Gender Equality* (pp. 55–70). Newcastle upon Tyne: Cambridge Scholars Publishing.

Pease, B. (2017). *Men as Allies in Preventing Men's Violence Against Women: Principles and Practices for Promoting Accountability*. Sydney: White Ribbon Australia.

Pease, B. (2019). *Facing Patriarchy: From a Violent Gender Order to a Culture of Peace*. London: Zed.

Pease, B. (2022). *Undoing Privilege: Unearned Advantage and Systemic Injustice in an Unequal World*, 2nd edition. London: Bloomsbury.

Peretz, T. (2017). An intersectional analysis of men's pathways to antiviolence activism. *Gender and Society*, *31*(4), 562–548. doi: 10.1177/0891243217717

Piccigallo, J., Lilley, T., & Miller, S. (2012). "It's cool to care about sexual violence": Men's experiences with sexual assault prevention. *Men and Masculinities*, *15*(5), 507–525. doi: 10.1177/1097184X12458590

Salter, M. (2016). Real men do hit women. *Meanjin*, 1–12.

Schacht, S., & Ewing, D. (1997). The many paths of feminism: Can men travel any of them? *Journal of Gender Studies*, *6*(2), 159–177. doi: 10.1080/09589236.1997.9960679

Singh, B. (2001). Dialogue across cultural and ethnic differences. *Educational Studies*, *27*(3), 341–355. doi: 10.1080/03055690120076600

Solnit, R. (2014). *Men Explain Things to Me and Other Essays*. Chicago: Haymarket Books.

Stoltenberg, J. (1989). *Refusing To Be a Man*. New York: Meridian.

Stoltenberg, J. (1990). Frequently Asked Questions about 'A Principle of Accountability for profeminist Men's Activism against Pornography and Prostitution' (Unpublished paper). https://xyonline.net/sites/xyonline.net/files/2018-04/Men%20Against%20Porn%2C%20Principle%20of%20Accountability.pdf

Stoltenberg, J. (2013, September 9). John Stoltenberg on Manhood, Male Supremacy, and Men as Feminist Allies. Feminist Current: https://www.feministcurrent.com/2013/09/09/john-stoltenberg-on-manhood-male-supremacy-and-men-as-feminist-allies/

Tamasese, K. Waldergrave, C., Tuhaka, F., & Campbell, W. (1998). Furthering conversation about partnerships of accountability: Talking about issues of leadership, ethics and care. *Dulwich Centre Journal*, *4*, 51–64.

28

MEN AND MASCULINITIES IN ANIMAL ADVOCACY ORGANIZATIONS AND ORGANIZING

From men's domination and masculinized strategies towards an ethics of care and intersectional activism

Kadri Aavik

Introduction

This chapter examines men and masculinities in the context of contemporary animal advocacy organizations and organizing.[1] Questions of how we relate to the more-than-human world have become increasingly pertinent in the Anthropocene, where the human species is radically and destructively altering the Earth's ecosystems and climate (Steffen et al., 2015; IPCC, 2021; Ripple et al., 2020). The most typical relationship humans have with other animals is through consuming them. Raising animals for human food occurs in industrial settings on a massive scale. The number of non-human animals killed annually for food amounts to around 75 billion (Chemnitz & Becheva, 2021).[2] Violence towards factory-farmed animals is standard practice: they are consistently deprived of adequate space, air and light; their new-borns are removed from them; and pain is inflicted on them routinely, through practices such as debeaking and tail-docking (The Humane League, 2021). The systematic and extensive breeding and genetic manipulation of farmed non-human animals have rendered them disabled (Taylor, 2017), implying debilitating and chronic health conditions.

Animal farming for human food is a key driver of climate change (Goodland & Anhang, 2009; Steinfeld et al., 2006), having doubled over the past 20 years (Chemnitz & Becheva, 2021), at a time when countries are failing to meet international climate targets (United Nations, 2021). It is also an increasing public health concern (Landers et al., 2012; World Health Organisation, 2017; Brown, 2004; Chemnitz & Becheva, 2021; Bouvard et al., 2015; Micha et al., 2017). Intensive animal farming disproportionality affects vulnerable groups and communities (Eisnitz, 2006; Sebastian, 2018; Jenkins, 2018), particularly in the Global South (Parks & Roberts, 2006; Roy, 2018) – those least responsible for causing

DOI: 10.4324/9781003193579-32

climate change. Thus, consuming other animals is an intersectional issue of social and ecological justice. Because other animals are part of society and advocating for them addresses issues beyond animal ethics, the animal advocacy movement[3] (AAM) could be considered a social justice movement.[4]

Gender plays an important role in both the exploitation of non-human animals and advocating for their interests. Previous research has highlighted the central role of gender in shaping human–animal relations, patterns of food consumption and climate sustainability (e.g. Modlinska et al., 2020; Inness, 2001; Counihan & Kaplan, 2003). While women and other genders also consume non-human animals, there are several reasons why men's food practices and masculinities in relation to other animals should be critically examined. The practices of privileged Western white men, as well as masculine values, expressed in "industrial breadwinner masculinities" (Hultman & Pulé, 2018)[5], have led to human-induced climate change (Moore, 2017) which threatens human and non-human life on a planetary scale. A masculinized technocratic rationality (see Winter & Robert, 1980) continues to be used to justify the mistreatment of human and non-human others, exemplified by the organization of factory farming. The animal–industrial complex (Noske, 1989; Twine, 2012)[6] is overwhelmingly operated by elite men. Men, in particular, white, Western, middle class, remain the key drivers of climate change, for example, as owners and managers of extractive industries (Hultman & Pulé, 2018) and governments and transnational organizations such as the EU which regulate these industries. For instance, the world's largest factory farms are owned by Western white men (The National Provisioner, 2018). The overall ecological footprint of men is on average much higher than women's (Räty & Carlsson-Kanyama, 2010; Rippin et al., 2021), including their footprint from food, as men consume more meat, globally (Nakagawa & Hart, 2019; Prättälä et al., 2007).

Strong links exist between eating animals and constructions of Western masculinities: eating meat remains culturally coded as a masculine practice and consuming animals is a powerful norm for men through which to do masculinity (Ruby & Heine, 2011; Thomas, 2016; Szabo, 2019). Especially privileged men in Western countries are in a favourable position and could be expected to make more sustainable and ethical food choices, as they have more resources than less privileged groups to do so, and can promote more ethical human–animal relations through the institutions they dominate.

This chapter looks at men and masculinities both in formal AAM organizations and beyond organizational structures. As an example of the latter type of organizing, I examine men's veganism.[7] I explore how masculinities – for example, masculinized values and strategies – manifest themselves in the AAM and the implications of these for meeting the AAM's goals and for building a more inclusive movement. While foregrounding gender, I consider how its intersections with other categories, such as race and class shape the movement's exclusions. I end the chapter by arguing for the importance of intersectional activism and building alliances with other progressive social movements. While advocating for other animals has historically occurred and continues to take place across the world, this chapter mainly focuses on the AAM in Western contexts, largely due to lack of research on the AAM elsewhere.[8] In this chapter, I use the term "organization" in a broader sense, referring to not only physical and formal AAM organizations (local, international, transnational) but also the entire AAM, encompassing variously positioned and affiliated individuals, groups and networks organizing in diverse ways for other animals both offline and online.[9]

Gendered dimensions of animal advocacy organizing

The origins of the AAM in the West, widely regarded as a new social movement,[10] are typically traced to the animal protection movement in nineteenth-century England, termed as first-wave era of the AAM (roughly up to the civil rights period), followed by second- and third-wave activisms, beginning in the mid-twentieth century and in the 2000s,[11] respectively (Wrenn, 2019). Each wave is characterized by a focus on specific issues and tactics, shaped by the social and historical contexts in which they unfolded.

Gender has always shaped animal advocacy organizing. Women – typically white, middle- and upper-class – have been disproportionately represented among the movement's activists in the West since its inception (Wrenn, 2019, p. 62; also see Gaarder, 2011). Already in the nineteenth century, several prominent suffragettes and other women were leading figures in campaigns against animal cruelty (Wrenn, 2019, p. 34), for example, anti-vivisection activism. Historical associations of madness and hysteria with women stemming from norms of masculinity have led to animal advocates being pathologized for caring about non-human animals by the medical establishment and in cultural constructions more broadly (Gruen & Probyn-Rapsey, 2018; see also Beers, 2006). Animal advocacy organizing on the whole continues to be perceived as a feminized activity (Wrenn, 2019, p. 201; Gaarder, 2011), due to its associations with feminized emotions, compassion and plant-based diets (Wrenn, 2016c, p. 150). This has implications for the movement's legitimacy, ability to acquire funding and reach its goals, as well as for men's involvement and masculinities in the AAM.

Existing research on gender in animal advocacy organizations and organizing has tended to focus on women. Men and masculinities have received less attention. In the following sections, I examine how men's activities and masculinities shape animal advocacy organizing and organizations.

Men's involvement and masculinities in animal advocacy organizing

AAM's composition, structure and division of work

Animal advocacy organizations, akin to others in the non-profit sector, exhibit gendered and other hierarchies (for an overview of gendered organizations, see Hearn & Collinson, 2018), for example, gendered divisions of labour and assigning different value to the work of different genders. The movement in the West consists primarily of educated, white, middle-class women (Wrenn, 2019, p. 199; Wrenn, 2016c). While their work has been central to the AAM, white privileged men typically enjoy greater visibility and dominate the higher ranks of the movement (Wrenn, 2019, pp. 62–66; Kemmerer, 2018, 2023), in particular, as leaders of larger and more prominent AAM organizations in North America (Gaarder, 2011; Kemmerer, 2018). As typical in organizations generally, women are disproportionately found in care and administrative roles and perform other types of supportive work which remains less valued and visible (Wrenn, 2019, p. 201). The belief of many activists that men's greater involvement would boost the movement's legitimacy leads them to promote men to leadership positions (Wrenn, 2016c, p. 150), a strategy that retains men's privilege in the AAM. Male privilege and organizational structures modelled according to masculine values have been linked to sexism in the movement (Kemmerer, 2023).

The aforementioned insights apply primarily to the AAM in North America, particularly in the United States. In other contexts, where the AAM has a shorter history and there has been a lack of other progressive movements to pave the way, such as in post-socialist Europe, where civil society activism in general remains undervalued, animal advocacy organizing is typically even more marginalized and highly feminized (see Aavik, 2019). In these settings, where animal advocacy organizing tends to include only a few paid positions and is done largely on a voluntary basis, men's participation in the movement is low, including in its leadership, as evidence from Estonia suggests (Aavik, 2019).

A number of scholars have critically examined the AAM in the West from critical race and whiteness, Indigenous and decolonial perspectives (Harper, 2010; Polish, 2016; Ko&Ko, 2017; Wrenn, 2019; Robinson, 2013), pointing to the privileged position of most animal activists in the social hierarchy and noting the scarcity of less privileged people, for example, activists of colour in the movement. Such omissions in the AAM are not just simple issues of diversity in participation but concern the movement's core conceptual commitments and strategies, ultimately inhibiting efforts to diversify the movement, including its theoretical foundations. The construction of, and indeed change in, masculinities has an important role to play here, as will be explored in the next section.

Tactics, strategies and factions

Beyond the structure and division of labour in the AAM, the movement's conceptual basis and approaches to animal activism are significantly shaped by masculinity, as several feminist scholars have critically noted (Gruen, 1993; Wrenn, 2019; Donovan, 1990). The dominant narrative that is typically produced about the movement (also to itself) features a few elite white Western men as "founding fathers", akin to retrospective canon-making about many fields – an inevitably selective process shaped by gender (see Connell, 1997 on masculinity and the construction of the sociological canon). As feminist scholars have argued, elevating the intellectual ideas of a few prominent men has produced a masculine epistemology and rationality of the movement (Wrenn, 2016b, pp. 105, 114).

Two key men typically regarded as the intellectual founders of the movement are philosophers Peter Singer and Tom Regan whose thought continues to shape the strategies of significant parts of AAM. A number of feminist scholars who have critically engaged with their work have pointed out that both Singer (1975) and Regan (1983) explicitly sought to disentangle emotions and advocating for other animals, appealing for a "rational" approach to animal activism (for a critique of this, see Gruen & Probyn-Rapsey, 2018; Donovan, 1990; Wrenn, 2019). As Wrenn (2019, p. 77) notes, the continued influence of the ideas of these elite men in AAM means that to this day, "affective frameworks for addressing speciesism were (and still are) heavily stigmatized in the highly rationalized movement culture". Ecofeminist scholars have provided extensive critique of these reason-based arguments, pointing out how the neglect of an ethics of care and emotions in how we relate to non-human animals stems from and reproduces a masculinized rationality, dismissing important ways in which we could engage with and advocate for other animals (Adams & Donovan, 1995; Gaard, 2002; Donovan & Adams, 2007; Gruen, 1993; Gruen, 2015).

One of the most significant divisions and sources of ideological conflict within the AAM concerns the main goal of animal advocacy organizing – whether we should entirely end the use of other animals for human purposes or continue to permit this, as long as attention is paid to their welfare. Broadly, the contemporary AAM is divided into two ideological factions based on this disagreement – abolitionism and welfarism, respectively (see Wrenn, 2019, p. 18). Hegemonic ideals of masculinity and privileged men's practices shape both factions. The welfarist side typically draws on the utilitarian philosophy[12] pursued by Singer and his followers, arguing that actions that bring the most happiness or well-being to the greatest number of non-human animals should be chosen over others (see Singer, 1980). Utilitarianism forms the conceptual basis of effective altruism, an increasingly popular social movement organization strategy, "using evidence and reason to figure out how to benefit others as much as possible, and taking action on that basis" (MacAskill, 2017, p. 1). Effective altruism has become a key strategy used by the welfarist segments of the AAM and by far the most funding that the AAM receives goes to such types of organizations. From feminist perspectives, this approach has been critiqued as "business-like, data-driven [and] outcome-oriented" and "[h]ierarchical in its decision-making structures and patterned after patriarchal social relations" (Herro & Obeng-Odoom, forthcoming). In the context of animal advocacy, such utilitarian tactics lead to the "quantification of suffering", drawing from "a rationalist, calculative mode of moral reasoning" (Donovan, 1990, p. 358). For example, such positions typically lead to prioritizing certain types of animal advocacy (such as helping factory-farmed animals due to their sheer numbers) while deeming others less "effective" and thus not worth pursuing, such as animal sanctuary work which involves a small number of non-human individuals, but foregrounds close relationships of care, modelled according to feminist ethics, and thus has great potential to model and rethink human–animal relations (see Leth-Espensen, forthcoming; see also Adams et al., 2023 for a critique of effective altruism in animal advocacy from feminist, critical race and other critical perspectives).

As typical in other social movements, welfarist AAM organizations tend to be more professionalized, corporatized and bureaucratized, and increasingly focused on obtaining donations. This has involved toning down more "radical" messages to appeal to a broader public and to potential donors, reflecting the increasingly market-oriented nature of many segments of the AAM (Wrenn, 2019, p. 21). Typically, effective altruist strategies exclude intersectional activism (Wrenn, 2019; Aavik, 2019), as it appears more "rational" (e.g. easier, more profitable) to focus on a single issue. Such masculinized tactics cannot only be associated with men in the AAM, as many organizations led by women have also embraced such strategies.

The welfarist faction includes one of the largest and highly feminized sectors of AAM – companion animal advocacy. Men's participation in this type of activism is exceptional. Their involvement in such advocacy, however, does not necessarily emasculate them, as might be expected, but on the contrary, might boost their masculine capital, celebrity status and income,[13] as examples from cat advocacy in North America attest (see Joki, f.c.).

In sharp ideological disagreement with the welfarist faction, abolitionist groups are typically smaller, less professionalized and more grassroots, and many feature white men as key activists and leaders (Wrenn, 2019, p. 192). Such groups are typically more open to embracing intersectional approaches to activism, that is, seeing animal abuse as entangled with intra-human injustices. Yet, while claiming to endorse intersectional activism, this does not always translate to practice (Wrenn, 2019, p. 192) and ultimately, strategies shaped by privileged white male perspectives often prevail. A notable example of this is the US legal scholar and prominent animal activist, often regarded as a key figure of abolitionist animal advocacy organizing, Gary Francione, who campaigns for intersectional activism but has also been accused of white and other forms of privilege, for example, by not showing enough contextual sensitivity towards less privileged humans for whom adopting veganism might be difficult (Wrenn, 2019, p. 192; see also Francione, 2021).

The abolitionist faction includes organizations such as the Animal Liberation Front, known for their "radical" tactics, such as hunt sabotages, freeing animals from factory farms, intercepting illegal fishing vessels, undercover investigations, destruction of property of animal abusers and other similar kinds of direct action which can lead to legal issues. These highly visible activities are associated with masculinities (Kemmerer, 2018, p. 266) and men's practices, with strong links to male heroism (Frisk, 2019). In many Western countries, a typical "radical" abolitionist animal activist is an educated white middle-class man. Such men tend to be overrepresented among those convicted and serving prison sentences for animal activism. This is one of the rare examples where the judicial system is disproportionately harsh towards white privileged men, due to the controversial nature of animal rights in mainstream society and recent laws in several Western countries restricting several kinds of animal activism to protect the interests of animal enterprises. This includes classifying several kinds of animal activism as terrorism in some countries.[14] A notable example of this is the Stop Huntingdon Animal Cruelty (SHAC) campaign against Huntington Life Sciences, the largest animal testing laboratory in Europe. The campaign, which operated in the United Kingdom and the United States between 1999 and 2014, ended with key activists, most of whom were privileged white men, convicted as domestic terrorists (in the United States) and imprisoned for non-violent protest which resulted in lowering the economic value of the company (see Gazzola, 2015; Potter, 2011). Such legislation has the effect of suppressing animal activism and making many forms of activism more difficult and riskier, leaving such action more available for the most privileged, such as educated middle-class white men who have the resources to navigate the legal system.

Several feminist, critical race and critical animal studies scholars have critiqued white, middle-class and male privilege of the animal advocacy movement and its dominant tactics. For example, they have addressed the common assertion by many white animal and vegan activists in the West that the movement should only be focused on non-human animals and not concern itself with issues of race and/or gender. This privileged position dismisses the fact that racialized people and groups continue to be animalized[15] and that constructions of race, gender and species are intertwined (Ko&Ko, 2017; Deckha, 2012; Harper, 2010, 2011, 2012; Polish, 2016). This has material implications for the ability of less privileged people, for instance, racialized individuals to participate in the AAM. For example, in societies where racism runs deep, such as the United States, given the still disproportionately high incarceration rates of Black men (Carson, 2020), it is likely that Black men involved in more "radical" animal activism would face extremely harsh prison sentences.

A notable example of a masculinized strategy in AAM (typically in the professionalized welfarist faction) is the use and sexualization of women's bodies (in particular, young, white and thin) in naked protest as a tactic by some major AAM organizations, notably by People for the Ethical Treatment of Animals (PETA) (for a critique of this from a gender perspective, see Wrenn, 2016a, 2019). This strategy is deemed by organizations using it as "effective" and intended to appeal to audiences of heterosexual men. Critics have termed this strategy "social movement prostitution" (Wrenn, 2016a) and "the pornification of veganism" (Wrenn, 2016b, p. 102; see also Wrenn, 2013). Wrenn (2016a) associates this tactic with the increasing corporatization and neoliberalization of animal advocacy activism seeking fundraising, despite lack of evidence of the effectiveness of such tactics (2016b, p. 100). At the same time, gender stereotypes are sometimes used to market veganism to men, asserting that veganism boosts men's sexual performance and that the consumption of animal products is emasculating (Wrenn, 2019, pp. 201–202). A notable example of this is the popular US film Game Changers (Psihoyos, 2018). Such tactics illustrate how the movement (or at least some segments of it) "exploits racism, sexism, mental health stigma, fat stigma, and disability stigma in its bid to promote nonhuman interests in a competitive political arena" (Wrenn, 2019, p. 195).

Finally, in a similar way to how the feminist movement consists of activist and academic strands, interlinked with civil society animal advocacy activism are its academic counterparts, notably, vegan ecofeminism (e.g. Adams, 1990) and a relatively recent field of academic inquiry known as critical animal studies (CAS) (e.g. Taylor & Twine, 2014). Many academics in CAS position themselves as scholar-activists. CAS draws significant theoretical inspiration from ecofeminist scholarship and is committed to intersectionality, aiming to challenge speciesism alongside oppressions in human society (sexism, racism, etc.). It is typical of men in CAS to position themselves as profeminist, challenging gendered power relations, hegemonic masculinity and embracing intersectional justice in the movement and in their academic work (see Nocella II et al., p. xxii; Francione, 2009), although not all work in CAS lives up to these ideals.

Men, masculinities and animal advocacy organizing through veganism

Contemporary animal-based food production systems have been critiqued from various perspectives beyond animal ethics, highlighting their social implications. The rationality behind industrialized food production and consumption is aptly captured by the idea of "McDonaldization of society" (Ritzer, 1993). Drawing on Max Weber's ideas on bureaucracy founded on scientific rationality, within the mechanistic paradigm, the concept describes contemporary societies and social processes as increasingly organized according to five principles: efficiency, calculability, predictability, standardization and control, exemplified by the operation of the ubiquitous fast-food chain. The notion of McDonaldization has been applied to industrial food production in agricultural systems (Currey, 2011) and to the mass production of animal products for human consumption (Wilkie, 2017). The logic of McDonaldization resonates with the ideal of hegemonic masculinity, also in organizational contexts. Work organizations running according to these principles tend to be highly masculinized.

Critical race, Indigenous and decolonial scholars have argued that industrial animal farming and animal-based diets are a form of corporate neocolonial imperial power – imposing animal-based diets on racialized people constitutes a form of colonial violence, termed dietary colonialism (Chu, 2019, p. 189). Western diets high in meat are naturalized as the most appropriate diet for humans, "thus reinforcing a particular, historically white Western model of the 'human'" (Twine, 2014, p. xx) – a category shaped by the lives and practices of privileged white men and cultural ideals of hegemonic masculinity. In this context, racism, colonialism, capitalism, classism, speciesism and male supremacy intersect, as non-human animals and racialized low-income groups, in particular women, are disproportionately affected by food injustice and factory farming (Bower et al., 2014; Mirabelli et al., 2006; Roy, 2018).

Veganism[16] – the practice of contesting human use of other animals, particularly as sources of food – could be considered one way of moving towards more sustainable human–animal relations, mitigating the climate crisis and contributing to social justice goals. Veganism can also be thought of as resistance to the masculinized rationality and neocolonial implications of meat-producing processes. Established evidence of the multiple harmful effects of eating animals has prompted a number of prominent international health, sustainability and animal advocacy organizations to call for a reduction in or elimination of animal-based foods from human diets (e.g. Willett et al., 2019; Whitmee et al., 2015; Wiseman, 2008). Compared to other diets, the vegan diet has the smallest ecological footprint (Chai et al., 2019). Plant-based diets have been deemed by the world's leading nutrition organizations as appropriate for humans (British Dietetic Association, 2017; Melina et al., 2016). Thus, transition to plant-based diets constitutes a promising path to more ethical human–animal relations, planetary and human health.

Existing studies on the links between men, masculinities, eating non-human animals and veganism (e.g. Potts & Parry, 2010; Rothgerber, 2013; Sumpter, 2015; Greenebaum & Dexter, 2017; Mycek, 2018; Aavik, 2021; Aavik & Velgan, 2021) indicate that cultural constructions of masculinity are key to understanding reasons why men consume animals. Studying men's veganism and its relationship to ideals of masculinity helps to understand changing masculinities and men's roles in activism. Men's relationship to the environment and to non-human others is likely to change in the context of climate change, potentially challenging existing ideals of hegemonic masculinity. Some recent research provides evidence of men's declining attachment to meat consumption, along with critical attitudes towards cultural associations of meat with masculinity (De Backer et al., 2020). Amid the current environmental crisis and humanity's unsustainable ways of life, along with more flexibility in gender practices, veganism practised by men no longer poses a threat to their masculinity, as earlier research has suggested (e.g. Rothgerber, 2013). This applies particularly to privileged men, who may even benefit from veganism to reinforce their privileged position (Aavik, 2021, 2023). My previous research involving privileged vegan men in Finland and Estonia has demonstrated that transitioning to veganism, men started to increasingly practise care towards (non-human) others and the self (Aavik, 2021, 2023; Aavik & Velgan, 2021), offering possibilities for the emergence of more ecological (Hultman & Pulé, 2018) and caring masculinities (Elliott, 2016).

Veganism practised by men could be examined through the lens of activism, and seen as a form of everyday activism (Mansbridge, 2013).[17] Through their vegan praxis, men act as role models to other men, challenging damaging health behaviours and eating patterns associated with masculinity, for example, by sharing vegan health and nutrition advice with other men in everyday social interactions (Aavik & Velgan, 2021). This is easier for privileged vegan men whose social position facilitates communicating such knowledge to others (Aavik & Velgan, 2021; Aavik, 2023). In such a way, vegan men can act as change agents on a micro-level (Mansbridge, 2013, p. 1). Through such microactivism, men can help transform broader cultural ideals of masculinity with regard to human–animal relations.

Conclusions: towards intersectional activism and organizing

This chapter has explored the role of men and masculinities in contemporary animal advocacy organizing and how these shape the movement's strategies and outcomes. It has been noted that in the nineteenth and early twentieth centuries activism for non-human animals was interlinked with other social causes, such as poverty and women's suffrage and as such, was more intersectional than much contemporary non-human animal activism (Wrenn, 2019, p. 65).[18] For both dominant factions in the AAM – the professionalized welfare organizations and abolitionist ones – intersectional activism and collaboration with other movements has proved difficult (Wrenn, 2019, p. 195), due to their ideological positions and tactics, linked with masculinities, as this chapter has explored.

Scholars studying the animal advocacy movement and its tactics argue for the importance of developing intersectional and feminist approaches to activism (Wrenn, 2016b; Wrenn,

2019; Pellow & Brehm, 2015; Herro & Obeng-Odoom, forthcoming; Aavik, 2018). As alternatives to masculinized strategies such as effective altruism, activist tactics drawing on feminist ethics of care have been proposed, foregrounding "contextuality, relationality and gender-equitable structures of care" (Herro & Obeng-Odoom, forthcoming). To challenge animal exploitation, it would be beneficial for animal advocates to form intersectional alliances (Hancock, 2011, p. 119) with other movements and activists around issues of common interest. For instance, it would be in the interests of both vegans and feminists to challenge the ideal of hegemonic masculinity, which is partly constructed around dominating, hunting and eating animals and arguably associating femininity with animals and nature (Aavik, 2019).

While the dominant and more visible segments of the AAM in the West tend to feature the problems described in this chapter, alternative kinds of organizations and activisms exist, which challenge the strategies outlined earlier and aspire towards intersectional organizing. Some examples of such organizing include animal advocates collaborating with the LGBT+ movement, however such collaboration tends to be fleeting and unsystematic (Wrenn, 2019, p. 205; Aavik, 2018). Curiously, to this day, there is relatively little collaboration between animal advocacy and climate/environmental movements. Barriers to such collaboration include activists' fears about losing supporters, particularly in more conservative societies, as well as wanting to remain focused on their messaging, reflecting masculinized effective altruist approaches (Aavik, 2018).

Direct collaboration between movements is not always possible or practical, however, activists can display solidarity with each other's causes in alternative ways, for example, by cultivating awareness of various (invisibilized) injustices in their field of activism and making sure not to reproduce existing hierarchies. It is important to recognize the similar structural and systemic roots of various oppressions. Ecofeminist, decolonial, critical race and whiteness scholars have highlighted how white Western bourgeois masculinity has been set as a normative standard and rendered superior over all other human beings as well as over non-human animals (Harper, 2010; Polish, 2016; Ko & Ko, 2017; Chu, 2019). This ideology manifests itself through masculinized, racist, speciesist, neocolonial, capitalist and neoliberal social institutions and structures which exploit various marginalized human and non-human beings.

To challenge these systems, we need to move away from masculinized mechanistic paradigms, towards ecological justice (Baxter, 2004) which integrates environmental, animal and social justice into one holistic framework. Intersectional approaches have the potential to enhance the AAM's capacity to advocate for other animals, as well as challenge hierarchies, masculinized values, strategies and men's leadership within animal advocacy organizing and organizations. Men play a significant role in this context. As an important step, developing a greater self-reflexivity about their own privilege (see Pease, this volume) and an increased sensitivity towards the values and interests of marginalized groups and beings would be essential.

Notes

1 In this chapter, I understand the animal advocacy movement as "a collective effort to advance the interests of nonhuman species on the grounds that these animals are inherently worthy of equal consideration, not as human resources, but as persons in their own right" (Wrenn, 2019, p. 35). I consider the vegan movement as part of the AAM, as these are interlinked and overlap.

2 This figure only includes land animals.

3 I use the term "animal advocacy movement" (AAM) over other terms (e.g. "animal rights", "animal liberation") that describe the movement of people advocating for non-human animals, to cover a diverse range of perspectives and forms of activism, "not all of which can be grounded in a rights-based approach" (Bourke, 2009, p. 131).

4 According to Sorenson (2010, p. 16), the AAM shares "fundamental elements of other progressive social movements: a sense of compassion and fairness, a focus on power relations and a critique of domination, inequality and hierarchy, along with efforts to alleviate conditions of exploitation".

5 Industrial/breadwinner masculinities refer to "a category of men who have long been (and still are) enmeshed with industrial-scale extractive processes and services reliant on energy-intensive, profit-consolidating, ecologically destructive and fossil fuel-dependent processes that have been historically created and maintained through colonisation, engineering and technology, neoclassical economic theories and under-challenged social practices" (Hultman & Pulé, 2018, p. 42).

6 The animal–industrial complex is "a partly opaque and multiple set of networks and relationships between the corporate (agricultural) sector, governments, and public and private science" (Twine, 2012, p. 23).

7 I focus on veganism, as opposed to meat reduction or vegetarianism, because the former fully rejects human use of animals and thus constitutes a more radical challenge to current exploitative human–animal relations and animal-based food systems.

8 In the transnational context, this reflects the hegemony of Western AAMs whose agendas and activities tend to be more visible and imitated in other parts of the world. Some non-Western religions such as Hinduism, Buddhism and Jainism, practiced by millions of men, promote compassion and non-violence towards all living beings and therefore, vegetarian or fully plant-based eating. Although these religions are not considered part of the AAM, their practitioners challenge perceived essentialist links between men, masculinities and meat consumption.

9 For an overview of complexities pertaining to defining an "organization", see Hearn & Collinson, 2018.

10 For a discussion on new social movements, including critique of New social movement theory, see Buechler, 2013.

11 For an overview of the history of the AAM, see Wrenn, 2019; Nocella II et al., 2013; Beers, 2006.

12 For an ecofeminist critique of utilitarianism, see Donovan & Adams, 2007; Donovan, 1990.

13 Joki (forthcoming) discusses how a US-based audio engineer Mike Bridavsky became an online celebrity for caring for a now deceased disabled cat LiL BUB and how his performance of a caring heterosexual masculinity along with his whiteness boosted his masculine capital, earning him the status of an eligible bachelor in some online cat communities.

14 Since the early 1990s, "AG-Gag" laws have been passed in many countries, criminalizing undercover investigations of animal abuse (including photos and videos) in animal facilities, such as farms, slaughterhouses and laboratories, preventing the public from accessing information about the treatment of non-human animals in these facilities (see Shea, 2014; Wrock, 2016). These laws and subsequent convictions raise broader legal and philosophical questions about what constitutes legally protected speech and its social implications (see Potter, 2011, Gazzola, 2015, Lazare, 2020; Shea, 2014). These laws are an example of how governments, as part of the animal–industrial complex, protect the interests of the animal industry. The Animal Enterprise Terrorism Act was adopted in the United States in 2006 which classifies as terrorism "interfering" with the operations of animal enterprises – a vague wording which can be used to easily prosecute animal activists, even for non-violent protest. For instance, if as a result of animal activists' activities, stock value of the company falls or the sales of their animal products declines, this could be interpreted by courts as damage done to the enterprise and therefore criminalized (for an overview, see Potter, 2011; Gazzola, 2015). In the United Kingdom, the Serious Organised Crime and Police Act of 2005 introduced new offences for various "animal rights crimes".

15 Deemed closer to non-human animals in the "Great chain of being", a racist, sexist and speciesist hierarchy; and regarded as more animal-like than Western white able-bodied men in particular, who are placed at the top of the hierarchy.

16 A bulk of existing literature has used the terms "veganism" and "plant-based diets" interchangeably. One of the most often used definitions of veganism is the one provided by The Vegan Society: "Veganism is a philosophy and way of living which seeks to exclude – as far as is possible and practicable – all forms of exploitation of, and cruelty to, animals for food, clothing or any other purpose" (The

Vegan Society, n.d.). Plant-based eating is a key manifestation of veganism, although people might follow a plant-based diet for reasons other than animal ethics.

17 Everyday activism has been defined as "talk and action in everyday life that is not consciously co-ordinated with the actions of others but is (1) to some degree caused (inspired, encouraged) by a social movement and (2) consciously intended to change others' ideas or behavior in directions advocated by the movement" (Mansbridge, 2013, p. 1).

18 Although it relied on and reproduced class and race biases and inequalities (Wrenn, 2019, pp. 196–197).

References

Aavik, K. (2018). The animal advocacy movement in the Baltic states: Links to other social justice issues and possibilities for intersectional activism. *Journal of Baltic Studies, 49*(4), 509 – 527. doi: 10.1080/01629778.2018.1473263

Aavik, K. (2019). The rise of veganism in post-socialist Europe: Making sense of emergent vegan practices and identities in Estonia. In L. Wright (Ed.), *Through a Vegan Studies Lens: Textual Ethics and Lived Activism* (pp. 151 – 170). Reno, NV: University of Nevada Press.

Aavik, K. (2021). Vegan men: Towards greater care for (non)human others, Earth and self. In P. Pulé, & M. Hultman (Eds.), *Men, Masculinities, and Earth: Contending with the (m)Anthropocene* (pp. 329–350). London: Palgrave Macmillan. doi: 10.1007/978-3-030-54486-7_15

Aavik, K. (2023). *Contesting Anthropocentric Masculinities Through Veganism: Lived Experiences of Vegan Men.* Cham, Switzerland: Palgrave Macmillan.

Aavik, K., & Velgan, M. (2021). Vegan men's food and health practices: A recipe for a more health-conscious masculinity? *American Journal of Men's Health, 5*(15), 1–14. doi: 10.1177/15579883211044323

Adams. C. (1990). *The Sexual Politics of Meat: A Feminist-Vegetarian Critical Theory.* New York: Continuum.

Adams, C., & Donovan, J. (Eds). (1995). *Animals & Women: Feminist Theoretical Explorations.* Durham, NC: Duke University Press.

Adams, C. J., Crary, A., & Gruen, L. (Eds.). (2023). *The Good it Promises, the Harm it Does: Critical Essays on Effective Altruism.* Oxford: Oxford University Press.

Baxter, B. (2004). *A Theory of Ecological Justice.* Abingdon: Routledge.

Beers, D. (2006). *For the Prevention of Cruelty: The History and Legacy of Animal Rights Activism in the United States.* Athens: Swallow Press.

Bourke, D. (2009). The use and misuse of 'rights talk' by the animal rights movement. In P. Sankoff & S. White (Eds.), *Animal Law in Australasia: A New Dialogue* (pp. 128–150). Sydney: Federation Press.

Bouvard, V., Loomis, D., Guyton, K. Z., Grosse, Y., El Ghissassi, F., Benbrahim-Tallaa, L., Guha, N., Mattock, H., & Straif, K. (2015). Carcinogenicity of consumption of red and processed meat. *The Lancet Oncology, 16*(16), 1599–1600. doi: 10.1016/S1470-2045(15)00444-1

Bower, K. M., Thorpe, R. J. Jr., Rohde, C., & Gaskin, D. J. (2014). The intersection of neighborhood racial segregation, poverty, and urbanicity and its impact on food store availability in the United States. *Preventive Medicine, 58*, 33–39. doi: 10.1016/j.ypmed.2013.10.010

British Dietetic Association (2017). British Dietetic Association Confirms Well-planned Vegan Diets Can Support Healthy Living in People of All Ages. British Dietetic Association (BDA): https://www.bda.uk.com/resource/british-dietetic-association-confirms-well-planned-vegan-diets-can-support-healthy-living-in-people-of-all-ages.html

Brown, C. (2004). Emerging zoonoses and pathogens of public health significance – an overview. *Revue scientifique et technique-office international des epizooties, 23*(2), 435–442. doi: 10.20506/rst.23.2.1495

Buechler, S. M. (2013). New social movements and New Social Movement theory. In D. A. Snow, D. della Porta, B. Klandermans & D. McAdam (Eds.), *The Wiley-Blackwell Encyclopedia of Social and Political Movements.* Oxford: Blackwell Publishing.

Carson, E. A. (2020). Prisoners in 2018. U.S. Department of Justice. Retrieved from https://bjs.ojp.gov/content/pub/pdf/p18.pdf

Chai, B. C., van der Voort, J. R., Grofelnik, K., Eliasdottir, H. G., Klöss, I., & Perez-Cueto, F. J. (2019). Which diet has the least environmental impact on our planet? A systematic review of vegan, vegetarian and omnivorous diets. *Sustainability, 11*(15), 4110. doi: 10.3390/su11154110

Chemnitz, C., & Becheva, S. (Eds.). (2021). *Meat Atlas: Facts and Figures about the Animals We Eat.* Berlin: Heinrich Böll Foundation.

Chu, S. (2019). Nonviolence through veganism: An antiracist postcolonial strategy for healing, agency and respect. In L. Wright (Ed.), *Through a Vegan Studies Lens: Textual Ethics and Lived Activism* (pp. 180 – 201). Reno, NV: University of Nevada Press.

Connell, R. W. (1997). Why is classical theory classical? *American Journal of Sociology, 102*(6), 1511 – 1557. doi: 10.1086/231125

Counihan, C. M., & Kaplan, S. L. (2003). *Food and Gender: Identity and Power.* Oxon & New York: Routledge.

Currey, A. D. (2011). The evolution of industrial food production: Mcdonaldization and population health. *Scientia et Humanitas, 1*, 121 – 135.

De Backer, C., Erreygers, S., De Cort, C., Vandermoere, F., Dhoest, A., Vrinten, J., & Van Bauwel, S. (2020). Meat and masculinities: Can differences in masculinity predict meat consumption, intentions to reduce meat and attitudes towards vegetarians? *Appetite, 147*, 104559. doi: 10.1016/j.appet.2019.104559

Deckha, M. (2012). Toward a postcolonial, posthumanist feminist theory: Centralizing race and culture in feminist work on nonhuman animals. *Hypatia, 27*(3), 527–545.

Donovan, J. (1990). Animal rights and feminist theory. *Signs: Journal of Women in Culture and Society, 15*(2), 350 – 375.

Donovan, J., & Adams, C. (Eds). (2007). *The Feminist Care Tradition in Animal Ethics.* New York: Columbia University Press.

Eisnitz, G. A. (2006). *Slaughterhouse: The Shocking Story of Greed, Neglect, and Inhumane Treatment Inside the US Meat Industry.* Amherst, NY: Prometheus Books.

Elliott, K. (2016). Caring masculinities: Theorizing an emerging concept. *Men and Masculinities, 19*(3), 240–259. doi: 10.1177/1097184X15576203

Francione, G. (2009). Sexism and Misogyny in the Movement. Retrieved from www.abolitionistapproach.com/sexism-and-misogyny-in-the-movement/

Francione, G. (2021). Woke Animal Rights Means no Animal Rights. Retrieved from https://garyfrancione.medium.com/woke-animal-rights-means-no-animal-rights-bf1e420e0404

Frisk, K. (2019). What makes a hero? Theorising the social structuring of heroism. *Sociology, 53*(1), 87–103. doi: 10.1177/0038038518764568

Gaard, G. (2002). Vegetarian ecofeminism. *Frontiers: A Journal of Women Studies, 23*(3), 117–146.

Gaarder, E. (2011). *Women and the Animal Rights Movement.* Rutgers University Press.

Gazzola, L. (2015). Bad things happened: Metaphorical fingerprints, constellations of evidence, and "Guilt *For* Association". *Vermont Law Review, 40*, 813–920.

Goodland, R., & Anhang, J. (2009, November/December). Livestock and Climate Change: What If the Key Actors in Climate Change are Cows, Pigs, and Chicken? World Watch. https://awellfedworld.org/wp-content/uploads/Livestock-Climate-Change-Anhang-Goodland.pdf

Greenebaum J., & Dexter, B. (2017). Vegan men and hybrid masculinity. *Journal of Gender Studies, 27*(6), 637–648. doi: 10.1080/09589236.2017.1287064

Gruen, L. (1993). Dismantling oppression: An analysis of the connection between women and animals. In G. Gaard (Ed.), *Ecofeminism: Women, Animals, Nature* (pp. 60–90). Philadelphia, PA: Temple University Press.

Gruen, L. (2015). *Entangled Empathy.* New York: Lantern Books.

Gruen, L., & Probyn-Rapsey, F. (2018). Distillations. In L. Gruen & F. Probyn-Rapsey (Eds.), *Animaladies: Gender, Animals, and Madness* (pp. 1–8). New York: Bloomsbury Academic.

Hancock, A.-M. (2011). *Solidarity Politics for Millennials: A Guide to Ending the Oppression Olympics.* New York: Palgrave Macmillan.

Harper, A. B. (2010). Race as a "feeble matter" in veganism: Interrogating whiteness, geopolitical privilege, and consumption philosophy of 'cruelty-free' products. *Journal for Critical Animal Studies, 8*(3), 5–27.

Harper, A. B. (2011). Vegans of color, racialized embodiment, and problematics of the 'Exotic.' In A. Alkon & J. Agyeman (Eds.), *Cultivating Food Justice: Race, Class, and Sustainability* (pp. 221–238). Cambridge, MA: MIT Press.

Harper, A. B. (2012). Going beyond the normative white 'post-racial' vegan epistemology. In P. Williams-Forson & C. Counihan (Eds.), *Taking Food Public* (pp. 155–174). New York: Routledge.

Hearn, J., & Collinson, D. (2018). Men, masculinities and gendered organizations. In R. Aldag & S. Nkomo (Eds.), *Oxford Research Encyclopedia of Business and Management*. New York: Oxford University Press.

Herro, A., & Obeng-Odoom F. (forthcoming). Philanthropy and the feminist ethics of care: Prospects and problems. In R. Mirabella, A. Eikenberry & T. Coule (Eds.), *The Handbook of Critical Perspectives on Nonprofit Organizing and Voluntary Action: Concepts, Applications and Future Directions*. Edward Elgar: Cheltenham.

Hultman, M., & Pulé, P. M. (2018). *Ecological Masculinities: Theoretical Foundations and Practical Guidance*. London: Routledge.

Inness, S. A. (Ed.). (2001). *Cooking Lessons: The Politics of Gender and Food*. Lanham: Rowman & Littlefield.

IPCC (2021). *Climate Change 2021: The Physical Science Basis. Contribution of Working Group I to the Sixth Assessment Report of the Intergovernmental Panel on Climate Change* [Masson-Delmotte, V., P. Zhai, A. Pirani, S. L. Connors, C. Péan, S. Berger, N. Caud, Y. Chen, L. Goldfarb, M. I. Gomis, M. Huang, K. Leitzell, E. Lonnoy, J. B. R. Matthews, T. K. Maycock, T. Waterfield, O. Yelekçi, R. Yu & B. Zhou (eds.)]. Cambridge: Cambridge University Press.

Jenkins, R. (2018). The other ghosts in our machine: Meat processing and slaughterhouse workers in the United States of America. In A. Linzey & C. Linzey (Eds.), *Ethical Vegetarianism and Veganism* (pp. 232–244). London: Routledge.

Joki, M. M. (forthcoming). Negotiating disability in celebrity cat Lil BUB's eating videos. In K. Aavik, K. Irni & M. M. Joki (Eds.), *Feminist Animal and Multispecies Studies: Critical Perspectives on Food and Eating* (pp. xx–xx). Leiden: Brill Critical Animal Studies Series.

Kemmerer, L. (2018). Evidence of sexism and male privilege in the animal liberation/rights movement. *Between the Species*, *21*(1), 12.

Kemmerer, L. (2023). *Oppressive Liberation: Sexism in Animal Activism*. Cham: Springer Nature.

Ko, A., & Ko, S. (2017). *Aphro-ism. Essays on Pop Culture, Feminism, and Black Veganism from Two Sisters*. New York: Lantern Books.

Landers, T., Landers, T. F., Wittum, T. E., & Larson, E. L. (2012). A review of antibiotic use in food animals: Perspective, policy, and potential. *Public Health Reports*, *127*(1), 4–22. doi: 10.1177/003335491212700103

Lazare, J. (2020). Ag-gag Laws, animal rights activism, and the constitution: What is protected speech? *Alberta Law Review*, *58*, 83–106.

Leth-Espensen, M. (forthcoming). Care in a time of anthropogenic problems: Experiences from sanctuary-making in rural Denmark. In K. Aavik, K. Irni & M. M. Joki (Eds.), *Feminist Animal and Multispecies Studies: Critical Perspectives on Food and Eating* (pp. xx–xx). Leiden: Brill Critical Animal Studies Series.

MacAskill, W. (2017). Effective altruism: Introduction. *Essays in Philosophy*, *18*(1), eP1580; 1–5. doi: 10.7710/1526-0569.1580

Mansbridge, J. (2013). Everyday activism. In D. Snow, D. della Porta, B. Klandermans & D. McAdam (Eds.), *The Wiley-Blackwell Encyclopedia of Social and Political Movements* (pp. 1–2). Oxford: Blackwell Publishing.

Melina, V., Winston, C., & Levin, S. (2016). Position of the academy of nutrition and dietetics: Vegetarian diets. *Journal of Academy of Nutrition and Dietetics*, *116*(12), 1970–1980. doi: 10.1016/j.jand.2016.09.025

Micha, R., Micha, R., Peñalvo, J. L., Cudhea, F., Imamura, F., Rehm, C. D., & Mozaffarian, D. (2017). Association between dietary factors and mortality from heart disease, stroke, and type 2 diabetes in the United States. *The Journal of the American Medical Association*, *317*(9), 912–924. doi: 10.1001/jama.2017.0947

Mirabelli, M., Wing, S., Marshall, S., & Wilcosky, T. (2006). Race, poverty, and potential exposure of middle-school students to air emissions from confined swine feeding operations. *Environmental Health Perspectives*, *114*(4), 591–596. 10.1289/ehp.8586

Modlinska, K., Adamczyk, D., Maison, D., & Pisula, W. (2020). Gender differences in attitudes to vegans/vegetarians and their food preferences, and their implications for promoting sustainable dietary patterns: A systematic review. *Sustainability*, *12*(16), 6292. doi: 10.3390/su12166292

Moore, J. W. (2017). The Capitalocene, Part I: On the nature and origins of our ecological crisis. *The Journal of Peasant Studies*, *44*(3), 594–630.

Mycek, M., K. (2018). Meatless meals and masculinity: How veg* men explain their plant-based diets, *Food and Foodways*, *26*(3), 223–245. doi: 10.1080/07409710.2017.1420355

Nakagawa, S., & Hart, C. (2019). Where's the beef? How masculinity exacerbates gender disparities in health behaviors. *Socius*, *5*. doi: 10.1177/2378023119831801.

Nocella II, A., Sorenson, J., Socha, K., Matsuoka, A. (2013). Introduction: The emergence of Critical Animal Studies: The rise of intersectional animal liberation. In A. Nocella, A. II, J. Sorenson & K. Socha (Eds.), *Defining Critical Animal Studies: An Intersectional Social Justice Approach for Liberation* (pp. xix–xxxvi). New York: Peter Lang.

Noske, B. (1989). *Humans and Other Animals*. London: Pluto Press.

Parks, B. C., & Roberts, J. T. (2006). Globalization, vulnerability to climate change, and perceived injustice. *Society & Natural Resources*, *19*(4), 337–355. doi: 10.1080/08941920500519255

Pellow, D. N., & Brehm, H. N. (2015). From the new ecological paradigm to total liberation: The emergence of a social movement frame. *The Sociological Quarterly*, *56*(1), 185–212.

Polish, J. (2016). Decolonizing veganism: On resisting vegan whiteness and racism. In J. Castriano & R. R. Simonsen (Eds.), *Critical Perspectives on Veganism* (pp. 373–391). Cham: Palgrave Macmillan.

Potter, W. (2011). *Green is the New Red: An Insider's Account of a Social Movement under Siege*. San Francisco, CA: City Lights.

Potts, A., & Parry, J. (2010). Vegan sexuality: Challenging heteronormative masculinity through meat-free sex, *Feminism & Psychology*, *20*(1), 53–72. doi: 10.1177/0959353509351181

Prättälä, R., Paalanen, L., Grinberga, D., Helasoja, V., Kasmel, A., & Petkeviciene, J. (2007). Gender differences in the consumption of meat, fruit and vegetables are similar in Finland and the Baltic countries. *European Journal of Public Health*, *17*(5), 520–525. doi: 10.1093/eurpub/ckl265

Psihoyos, L. (2018). The Game Changers [Documentary Film].

Räty, R., & Carlsson-Kanyama, A. (2010). Energy consumption by gender in some European countries. *Energy Policy*, *38*(1), 646–649. doi: 10.1016/j.enpol.2009.08.010

Regan, T. (1983), *The Case for Animal Rights*. Berkeley, CA: University of California Press.

Rippin, H. L., Cade, J. E., Berrang-Ford, L., Benton, T. G., Hancock, N., & Greenwood, D. C. (2021). Variations in greenhouse gas emissions of individual diets: Associations between the greenhouse gas emissions and nutrient intake in the United Kingdom. *PLoS One*, *16*(11), e0259418.

Ripple, W., Wolf, C., Newsome, T. Barnard, B., Moomaw, W., et al. (2020). *World Scientists' Warning of a Climate Emergency*. Oxford: Oxford University Press.

Ritzer, G. (1993). *The McDonaldization of Society*. Newbury Park, CA: Sage.

Robinson, M. (2013). Veganism and Mi'kmaq legends. *The Canadian Journal of Native Studies*, *33*(1), 189–196.

Rothgerber, H. (2013). Real Men Don't Eat (Vegetable) Quiche: Masculinity and the justification of meat consumption, *Psychology of Men & Masculinity*, *14*(4), 363–375. doi: 10.1037/a0030379

Roy, S. S. (2018). *Linking Gender to Climate Change Impacts in the Global South*. New York: Springer.

Ruby, M. B., & Heine, S. J. (2011). Meat, morals, and masculinity. *Appetite*, *56*, 447–450. doi: 10.1016/j.appet.2011.01.018

Sebastian, M. (2018). Deadly efficiency: The impact of capitalist production on the "meat" industry, slaughterhouse workers, and nonhuman animals. In D. Nibert (Ed.), *Animal Oppression and Capitalism. Volume 1: The Oppression of Nonhuman Animals as Sources of Food* (pp. 167–183). Santa Barbara, CA: Praeger.

Shea, M. (2014). Punishing animal rights activists for animal abuse: Rapid reporting and the new wave of ag-gag laws. *Columbia Journal of Law and Social Problems*, *48*, 337.

Singer, P. (1975). *Animal Liberation*. New York: Avon Books.

Singer, P. (1980). Utilitarianism and vegetarianism. *Philosophy & Public Affairs*, 325–337.

Steffen, W., Richardson, K., Rockström, J., et al. (2015). Planetary boundaries: Guiding human development on a changing planet. *Science*, *347*(6223), 1259855. doi: 10.1126/science.1259855

Steinfeld, H., Gerber, P., Wassenaar, T. D., Castel, V., Rosales, M., Rosales, M., & de Haan, C. (2006). *Livestock's Long Shadow: Environmental Issues and Options* [Report]. Rome: Food and Agriculture Organisation.

Sumpter, K. (2015). Masculinity and meat consumption: An analysis through the theoretical lens of hegemonic masculinity and alternative masculinity theories. *Sociology Compass*, *9*(2), 104–114. doi: 10.1111/soc4.12241

Szabo, M. (2019). Masculinities, food and cooking. In L. Gottzen, U. Mellström & T. Shefer (Eds.), *Routledge International Handbook of Masculinity Studies* (pp. 404–413). London: Routledge.
Taylor, N., & Twine, R. (Eds.). (2014). *The Rise of Critical Animal Studies: From the Margins to the Centre.* London: Routledge.
Taylor, S. (2017). *Beasts of Burden: Animal and Disability Liberation.* New York: The New Press.
The Humane League (2021). How are Factory Farms Cruel to Animals? Retrieved from https://thehumaneleague.org/article/factory-farming-animal-cruelty
The National Provisioner (2021). The 2018 top 100 Meat & Poultry Processors. Retrieved from www.provisioneronline.com/2018-top-100-meat-and-poultry-processors
The Vegan Society (n.d.). Definition of Veganism. Retrieved from www.vegansociety.com/go-vegan/definition-veganism.
Thomas, M. A. (2016). Are vegans the same as vegetarians? The effect of diet on perceptions of masculinity. *Appetite, 97*, 79–86. doi: 10.1016/j.appet.2015.11.021
Twine, R. (2012). Revealing the 'animal-industrial' complex – A concept and method for Critical Animal Studies. *Journal for Critical Animal Studies, 10*(1), 12–39.
Twine, R. (2014). Ecofeminism and veganism: Revisiting the question of universalism. In C. Adams & L. Gruen (Eds.), *Ecofeminism: Feminist Intersections with Other Animals and the Earth* (pp. 191–207). London: Bloomsbury Press.
United Nations (2021). "Climate Commitments not on Track to Meet Paris Agreement Goals" as NDC Synthesis Report is Published. Retrieved from https://unfccc.int/news/climate-commitments-not-on-track-to-meet-paris-agreement-goals-as-ndc-synthesis-report-is-published.
Whitmee, S., Haines, A., Beyrer, C., Boltz, F., Capon, A. G., de Souza, F., Dias, B., Ezeh, A., Frumkin, H., Gong, P., Head, P., Horton, R., Mace, G. M., Marten, R., Myers, S. S., Nishtar, S., Osofsky, S. A., Pattanayak, S. K., Pongsiri, M. J., & Romanelli, C. (2015). Safeguarding human health in the Anthropocene epoch: Report of The Rockefeller Foundation-Lancet Commission on planetary health. *The Lancet, 386*(10007), 1973–2028. doi: 10.1016/S0140-6736(15)60901-1
Willett, W., Rockström, J., Loken, B., Springmann, M., Lang, T., Vermeulen, S., et al. (2019). Food in the Anthropocene: The EAT–Lancet Commission on healthy diets from sustainable food systems. *The Lancet, 393*(10170), 447–492. doi: 10.1016/S0140-6736(18)31788-4
Wiseman, M. (2008). The second World Cancer Research Fund/American Institute for Cancer Research expert report. Food, nutrition, physical activity, and the prevention of cancer: A global perspective. *Proceedings of the Nutrition Society, 67*(3), 253–256. doi: 10.1017/S002966510800712X
Wilkie, R. (2017). Animals as sentient commodities. In *The Oxford Handbook of Animal Studies* (pp. 279–301). Oxford: Oxford University Press.
Winter, M. F., & Robert, E. R. (1980). Male dominance, late capitalism, and the growth of instrumental reason. *Berkeley Journal of Sociology, 24/25*, 249–280.
World Health Organisation (2017). Antimicrobial Resistance in the Food Chain. Retrieved from www.who.int/foodsafety/areas_work/antimicrobial-resistance/amrfoodchain/en/
Wrenn, C. (2013). The role of professionalization regarding female exploitation in the Nonhuman Animal rights movement. *Journal of Gender Studies, 24*(2), 131.
Wrenn, C. L. (2016a). Social movement prostitution: A case study in nonhuman animal rights activism and vegan pimping. *Griffith Journal of Law & Human Dignity, 4*(2), 87–99.
Wrenn, C. L. (2016b). *A Rational Approach to Animal Rights: Extensions in Abolitionist Theory.* London: Palgrave Macmillan.
Wrenn, C. L. (2016c). An analysis of diversity in nonhuman animal rights media. *Journal of Agricultural and Environmental Ethics, 29*(2), 143–165.
Wrenn, C. L. (2019). *Piecemeal Protest: Animal Rights in the Age of Nonprofits.* Ann Arbor, MI: University of Michigan Press.
Wrock, R. K. (2016). Ignorance is bliss: Self-regulation and Ag-gag laws in the American meat industry. *Contemporary Justice Review, 19*(2), 267–279. doi: 10.1080/10282580.2016.1168256

29

TRACING THE SUPERHEROES OF OUR TIME

Contemporary and emergent masculinities in tech entrepreneurship

Ulf Mellström, Dag Balkmar and Anne-Charlott Callerstig

Introduction

In this chapter, we provide an overview of masculinity in relation to technology, entrepreneurship, and organizations connected to technology entrepreneurship. In doing so, we address how masculinity as an underlying gendered configuration of technology entrepreneurship, and particularly Big Tech, has been and can be conceptualized in masculinity studies, and how this kind of masculinity has taken centre stage as a dominant form of masculinity in global business masculinities (Connell & Wood, 2005), social media representations and films (Mendick et al., 2021).

In masculinity studies, tech entrepreneurship has received surprisingly little attention, although the connection between technology and masculinity is a research field in its own right. Briefly, the connection between technology and masculinity has been shown to be part of a masculine cultural script in many different contexts and connects closely to definitions of what is masculine and what is not (cf. Balkmar, 2012; Balkmar & Mellström, 2018; Mellström, 2002, 2003, 2004, 2009; Ottemo, 2020; Wajcman, 2004). In parallel with this, there is a generic and presumed notion of masculinity underpinning entrepreneurial stereotypes (Giazitzoglu & Down, 2017). Masculinity within an entrepreneurial discourse has been extensively researched (cf. Ahl, 2004, 2006; Ahl & Marlow, 2012; Bruni et al., 2004). The stereotypical image of the entrepreneur is an enactment of masculinity with typified attributes reflecting aggressive, competitive individuality and risk-taking (Ogbor, 2002; Calás et al., 2009).

We want to combine the elements of entrepreneurial and technology masculinities in order to address their importance for organizational forms and ideals. We also incorporate intersectional perspectives as far as they are applicable to the literature we review. We will also hint at the larger socio-cultural implications of the technoentrepreneurial masculinities that we outline. We want to emphasize in particular that the figuration of a hegemonic geek masculinity that we propose here needs to be contextualized within a wider frame of other gendered and racial inequalities in the tech industry (see, for instance, Benjamin, 2019; Twine, 2022).

DOI: 10.4324/9781003193579-33

In the following, we provide an overview of (a) technology and masculinity, and (b) entrepreneurship and masculinity, with the aim of building on these elements to (c) construct the contours of contemporary and emergent tech entrepreneur masculinities.

Technology and masculinity

The field of technology and masculinity studies emerged in the 1970s and has grown out of a conglomeration of different academic areas, including feminist science and technology studies, critical studies of men and masculinities, gender and technology, labour process theory, theories of patriarchy, and, more recently, queer and affect theory, posthumanism and new materialism. It is always complicated to draw up a clear lineage, but many of the early works constituting the field emanated in particular from feminist science and technology studies on the one hand and masculinity studies with a focus on technology on the other (Ottemo, 2020). Empirical and theoretical analyses of the combination of the two overarching concepts, technology and masculinity, have often tended to emphasize one of the two, leaving the other unproblematized, undertheorized or, worse, essentialized.

As several scholars have pointed out (Grint & Woolgar, 1995; Lagesen, 2008; Landström, 2006; Ottemo, 2020), achieving an analytical symmetry between the co-constructivist approach and the intersectional quality of how these quantities co-constitute each other has proved difficult. This is even more the case if we also pay attention to how they interact with different forms of organizations. The struggle to combine technology, masculinity, and organizational analysis could be said to be one of the characteristics of the field. This analytical triad has provided an interesting scholarly dynamic that has kept the field in relatively good health by comparison and has been applied to various theoretical strands since the late 1970s. Another characteristic feature of this interdisciplinary subfield is the analytical nexus of how passion, love of technology and embodiment are closely connected to power and masculine subjectivity.

These analytical challenges and themes can be observed, for instance, in the classic work of Cynthia Cockburn in her influential books *Brothers: Male Dominance and Technological Change* (1983) and *Machinery of Dominance: Women, Men and Technical Know-How* (1985) and then *Gender and Technology in the Making* (Cockburn & Ormrod, 1993) (with Susan Ormrod). Working within a Marxist tradition, Cockburn showed how technology, as part of exploitative labour relations and labour processes, organized gendered relations in both the workplace and the home. Cockburn extended her Marxist analysis by employing a feminist lens to show how women were excluded via gendered dualisms of productive and reproductive labour. Such dualisms typically occur where ("hard") masculinity is associated with skilled, heavy, dangerous and dirty machine processes, while femininity (and "soft" masculinity) is linked to unskilled, light, less dangerous and clean machinery within organizations (Hearn & Parkin, 1995, p. 86; Faulkner, 2001; Wajcman, 2004). What Cockburn also achieved in her groundbreaking work was to demonstrate how the material and the physical are part of gendered labour relations and not least "a subjective sense of self . . . including men's acquired bodily competence and technical mastery" (Cockburn, 2009, pp. 270–271).

The analytical themes outlined earlier are also mirrored in Sally Hacker's classic *Pleasure, Power, and Technology: Some Tales of Gender, Engineering, and the Cooperative Workplace* (1989), but Hacker also adds eroticism as a constitutive dimension of the embodied relation between technology, masculinity and organizational forms. In her investigation of the military roots of engineering and domination, Hacker argues not only that eroticism, domination and the subordination of women in the development of technology are a key aspect of hierarchical institutions like the military but also that eroticism is at the core of why engineering work is exhilarating and attractive. Several other scholars have followed in Hacker's footsteps, looking into the importance of passion, love, eroticism, sexuality and gender in technological work, occupations and organizations.

Thus, in many of these early studies, embodiment, passion, technology and masculinity have been analysed as key aspects of what constitutes gender relations and how power operates in ways that privilege men and masculinity in science and engineering organizations (Cockburn & Ormrod, 1993; Faulkner, 2001; Mellström, 1995, 2002; Wajcman, 2004). We see that masculinity and technology are tightly interlinked, both in practice and symbolically, and that the relations between masculinity and technology are key for understanding the (re-)production of gender hierarchies (Balkmar, 2012). However, gender has often been understood as a taken-for-granted, stable, heterosexual relation, while technology and organizational forms are open to interpretive flexibility.

Understanding the so-called woman problem, meaning the exclusion of women from science and engineering (Lagesen, 2008) was the central objective of the formative period of gender and technology studies, and gender categories were often left unproblematized. The analysis of gender segregation – as well as how passion, desire, love and eroticism are enacted – was framed within a binary heterosexual paradigm. As queer theory made its way into gender studies in general from the mid-1990s, it also affected how gender and sexuality were conceptualized in technology and masculinity studies. Following this critique, several authors came to account for passion, sexuality and love of technology with a more explicit focus on a binary understanding of these issues (Stepulevage, 1997; Landström, 2006; Vigdor, 2011). Mellström (2004, p. 379) made this explicit when he described how men "attribute their machinery with the qualities they want to see in their partner as a form of a heterosexual relationship". Mellström (2003), Schyfter (2009), Balkmar (2012) and Ottemo (2015), for instance, in their respective ethnographies of car and motorcycle mechanics, motorcycle riders, car modifiers and computer-science students, have portrayed the compulsory heterosexuality that underpins gender and technology studies in general, and technology and masculinity studies in particular. The connection between masculinity, desire, passion, embodiment and sexuality are, as Ottemo (2020, p. 345) points out, something that is an almost universal finding in studies of technology and masculinity, whether it is analysed within a non-binary, queer or binary heterosexual framework.

Of special interest in the context of this chapter, in relation to the themes discussed so far, and among the wide range of technomasculinities, are geek masculinities. Several scholars have been paying close attention to this kind of masculinity as it has undergone an interesting, rapid and fluctuating transformation since the 1980s (Turkle, 1984; Kendall, 1999; Wajcman, 1991; Bell, 2013; Mendick et al., 2021). It is a form of masculinity that cuts across the classic boundaries of the mechanic and the engineer (Wajcman, 1991, 2004), body and mind, immanence, and transcendence, as well as being closely connected to the dominant and formative social technologies of our time. As Ottemo points out (2020, p. 344), geek masculinity is a fruitful analytical lens that illustrates not only the co-construction of the technology and masculinity thesis but also the historical embeddedness and contingency of masculinity within the world of technology and technological organizations.

Geek masculinity also connects to the varying status and power dimensions of computers and digital technologies since the 1960s. During the introduction of computers in the 1960s and 1970s, programming was a female-coded occupation, and consequently had low status and pay. The cyberfeminism of the 1990s (cf. Plant, 1997; Stone, 1992) shared a common techno-optimism, which even proclaimed that finally gender would become irrelevant, and the female-bounded bodily entrapment would become a phenomenon of the past because computers are sex- and colour-blind (Corneliussen, 2012; Ottemo, 2020). This optimism soon disappeared as we moved into the new millennium, although the cultural embeddedness of gender and technology relations in non-Western contexts partly pointed in such a direction because computers and digital technologies were documented as being more "female friendly" and having a different symbolic gendering in South and Southeast Asia (Lagesen, 2008; Mellström, 2009; Gupta, 2015). However, in a Western context, the masculinization of digital technologies became even more strongly emphasized with the explosion of social media technologies during the 2000s and 2010s.

The geek has a special place in this gendered genealogy as this masculine configuration has transformed from the image of a young boy with pimply skin and thick Coca-Cola-bottomed glasses to the emergence of the brash entrepreneurial tech hero of the 2000s and 2010s. We will reconnect to this important form of masculinity in section three.

As we move into the new theoretical landscapes of the new millennium, with the rise of matter and materiality in posthumanism, new materialism, and theories of affect, we are also witnessing how the analytical nexus previously described is taking on new configurations. For instance, in his work, Steve Garlick (2019) has come to reconfigure masculinity:

> as a technology of embodiment that limits and channels the potentials of men's bodies through the invention of habitual ways of being that aim to dispel ontological insecurity through achieving and maintaining control over nature.
>
> *(Garlick, 2019, p. 394)*

Garlick is pioneering a posthumanist understanding of masculinity, which also broadens the analytical platform, including an onto-epistemological understanding of open-ended materialities of ecology, technology and corporeality in relation to masculinity. The current theoretical moves of feminist posthumanism and environmental humanities, towards a postanthropocentric world with the aim of de-centring the (hu)man subject (Alaimo, 2016), are now also appearing in masculinity studies (Pulé & Hultman, 2021; Mellström & Pease, 2022). It is interesting to note that many of the current posthumanist insights, such as that the (hu)man subject is and has always been deeply integrated with and constituted by ecology, technology and materiality in various forms of dependencies and embodiments, were foreshadowed in technology and masculinity studies. Although not swathed in the contemporary theoretical lingo, studies of technology and masculinity have constantly announced the affective, prosthetic and embodied dimensions of masculinity (cf. Balkmar, 2012; Balkmar & Mellström, 2018, 2019; Cockburn, 1983, 1985; Gray, 1993, 2000, 2003; Schyfter, 2009; Mellström, 2002, 2003, 2004, 2016), and pointed out how these dimensions cut to the core of gendered power, dualisms, segregation and – not least – the ontological politics and history of masculinity. The distributed agency and relational ontologies of the human/non-human, organic/nonorganic, etc. are thus addressing binaries that are more far-reaching than just men and women in the world of technology and technological organizations.

In sum, it is interesting to observe how the current themes in technology and masculinity studies connect back to the pioneering work of Cockburn and others, with not only dominance and control but also passion and embodiment, emerging as important themes. The early work in technology and masculinity studies, where men's domination of women and technology was a way of dominating and controlling nature, resonates strongly with contemporary questions and concerns about how technology is co-constructed with new forms of hegemonic and dominant masculinities that are shaping the future of technological work and organizations. The masculinity of tech entrepreneurship is key to understanding such forms, as is its embeddedness within tech organizations.

Tech entrepreneurial masculinity within organizations

In discussing the role of tech entrepreneurial masculinity within organizations, we recognize the multiple meanings of organizations and the myriad ways to study them invested in contemporary understandings. Hearn (2019, p. 34) highlights how these understandings are affected by changes in contemporary forms of organizing work, work organizations and the organization of organizations, characterized by change and fluidity. He notes that "[o] rganizations are no longer about a fixed structure at a certain time, in a certain place, but modes of organizing across time and place" (Hearn, 2019, p. 34). The interdependency of organizations and the changes in the organization of work are important fundamentals of emerging organizational identities and masculinities within organizations (Acker, 1992). Just as organizations and technology are "not just structured by gender but pervaded and constituted by and through gender" (Hearn & Husu, 2013, p. 104), so are tech organizations.

Masculinity is constitutive of the gender regimes within tech organizations (Mellström, 1995; Acker, 2006). Lohan and Faulkner (2004, p. 319) describe how technology, science and engineering are "widely acknowledged as power motifs of hegemonic masculinity" and, as such, are important for gender formations in relation to occupations, organizational symbols and norms. Gendered norms are present in all parts of organizational life; "in [its] processes, practices, images and ideologies, and distribution of power" (Acker, 1992, p. 567). These include both formal and informal gendered divisions of labour and authority within organizations, patterns of interactions, organizational symbols, images and artefacts. Gendered norms and ideals are thus determinants of the development of a gendered self within organizations. This is to be understood as an identity underpinned by gendered assumptions and ascriptions to which members of organizations adhere and which legitimize power disparities within the organization (Acker, 1992). Adding to the idea of a gendered self, we use the figure of the entrepreneurial self to refer to the normative demands and social and institutional arrangements under neoliberal conditions (Bröckling, 2016).

The ambition to define what the essence of entrepreneurship is – who does entrepreneurship and how – something that has preoccupied research on entrepreneurship in the past and still does so now (Eriksson, 2021). The literature on entrepreneurship is broad and draws upon several disciplines, research traditions and perspectives: economics, management and business administration, sociology, psychology, cultural anthropology, marketing, finance and geography (Carlsson et al., 2013, p. 914), including innovation, technology and entrepreneurship. Normative mainstream entrepreneurship research has either ignored female entrepreneurs and ethnic minority entrepreneurs or represented them as "exotic 'other' entrepreneurs" (Tedmanson & Essers, 2015, p. 388).

Historically, the figure of the entrepreneur links back to the Spanish "conquistadores" and the "frontiersmen" of the West, someone who conquers new markets, forges new empires overseas and generates start-ups for new market activities, often framed as typical entrepreneurial activities (Bruni et al., 2004, p. 58). Like the frontiersman, the entrepreneur could be ascribed an important role in a country's structural development and geographical growth

(Eriksson, 2021). With the advent of capitalism and a market economy during the 1800s, economic growth became ever more central. Schumpeter defined the entrepreneur as "The Great Man", someone who was assumed to conquer resistance and difficulties as he engaged his entrepreneurial abilities to create economic growth, often within large business organizations (Schumpeter, 1934, in Eriksson, 2021).

Since the 1990s, *gender in entrepreneurship* has developed as a field focusing on how gender influences women's entrepreneurship, emphasizing how entrepreneurial discourse is rooted in masculinity and thus privileges men and masculinity as the norm (Marlow & Martinez Dy, 2018, p. 3; Ahl, 2006; Bruni et al., 2004). Focusing on women's entrepreneurial activities has been a way of analysing, theorizing and critiquing the assumption that entrepreneurship is primarily about men (Ahl, 2006; Ahl & Marlow, 2012; Bruni et al., 2004; Lewis, 2006; McAdam, 2013; Marlow & Martinez Dy, 2018). White, male, middle-class entrepreneurs have been framed as fitting into a "cultural hegemony and sense of normalness", that is, the taken-for-granted norm of entrepreneurship (Giazitzoglu, 2014, in Giazitzoglu & Down, 2017, p. 40), against which women entrepreneurs have been situated as "other" in entrepreneurial discourse (Marlow & Martinez Dy, 2018, p. 5). In their critical analysis of the gender agenda in entrepreneurship research, Marlow and Martinez Dy (2018, p. 9) suggest that more research is needed on gender as an entrepreneurial resource; that intersectionality, along with queer and decolonial theory, should be incorporated into entrepreneurial research and making masculinities visible:

> Given that the entrepreneurial discourse is premised on hegemonic forms of masculinity, diverse and discrete articulations of masculinity and how they are performed and reproduced by male entrepreneurial actors demands greater consideration.
>
> *(Marlow & Martinez Dy, 2018, p. 9)*

In addition, there are very few studies on sexual orientation and business entrepreneurship among gay men and lesbian women (Bruni et al., 2004; Galloway, 2012; Marlow et al., 2018).

Studies that have explored entrepreneurial men and masculinities position hegemonic masculinity – a form of masculinity that is socially dominant and idealized (Connell, 1995; Ahl & Marlow, 2012; Bruni et al., 2004; Jernberg et al., 2020) – as a recurring concept and analytical framework. Giazitzoglu and Down (2017, pp. 43, 44) critique this assumption in the literature, which suggests that there is "a standard, accepted hegemonic masculine identity" with which enterprising agents comply, or fail to comply, through their performances. When entrepreneurship is theorized as a form of hegemonic masculinity, this often means that emphasis is put on its dominant forms and its dependence on marginalized and subordinated masculinities related to non-normative sexuality, race and ethnicity (Giazitzoglu & Down, 2017). Often, the dominant hegemonic form of entrepreneurial masculinity has been associated with white, heterosexual men doing entrepreneurship in conflictual, competitive forms, featuring strong associations with organizational leadership and management (Bruni et al., 2004, p. 60).

Takeyama's (2010) ethnographic study of entrepreneurial male subjects in Japan's host clubs presents quite a contrasting image of entrepreneurial masculinity. This study is about young male "hosts" who dream of upward mobility and fast earnings, performing an entrepreneurial masculinity that differs substantially from the conventional hegemonic masculinity of Japan, the Salaryman. Hosting means taking advantage of new business possibilities by the commodification of physical, emotional and sexual labour, as a way of commodifying the self at the nexus of neoliberalism and post-industrial Japan (Takeyama, 2010, p. 240).

In their ethnographic account of how ten enterprising men perform and negotiate entrepreneurial masculinity in a semi-rural pub, Giazitzoglu and Down (2017, p. 53) emphasize entrepreneurial masculinity as being "in part, altruistic in intent". They contrast their findings with existing research, which they feel presents entrepreneurial masculinity more in the vein of aggression, individualism and competitiveness (pp. 43–44). With this account, they emphasize the importance of context – stressing that entrepreneurial masculinities can be performed in different ways in different contexts by different sorts of enterprising men (Giazitzoglu & Down, 2017, p. 53).

Dominant and emerging masculinities in tech entrepreneurship

Summing up our argument thus far, the tech entrepreneur builds on historically determined elements of the masculine hero, who is powerful as an imaginary figure, and a solid model for how entrepreneurship is constructed, embodied and lived. Building on the forms of masculinity outlined earlier, we observe and forecast how these forms are and will be key components in the existing and emergent figuration of the tech entrepreneur as a new form of hegemonic masculinity. These foundational pillars of what Schumpeter (1934) outlined almost 90 years ago as the masculine, risk-taking and unconventional hero have now been brought into the 2020s and upgraded with the cherished sociotechnical qualities and discourses of a neoliberal hypermasculinity, propelled and in part created, by the social media technologies of our time.

During the first two decades of the twenty-first century, we have come to witness how the entrepreneurs of big tech companies – like Tesla's Elon Musk and Facebook's Mark Zuckerberg – have become heroic global entrepreneurs with huge influence, combining the image of a nerdy geek masculinity with that of entrepreneurial superheroes (Ottemo, 2020; Mendick et al., 2021). This is also what Pulé and Hultman (2021) refer to as a form of eco-modern masculinity.

Elements of contemporary tech entrepreneurs are also making their way into popular culture in films like Adam McKay's satirical comedy *Don't Look Up* (McKay, 2021). This movie addresses how difficult it can be for humanity to deal with the existential threats caused by climate change. In the context of this chapter, the onto-epistemological edge of the film is worthy of comment. In the movie, we meet Peter Isherwell, tech billionaire and CEO of the tech/media/space company BASH. Isherwell performs a gentle and soft-spoken masculinity that assures us he is in complete control of everything he does. He releases new smartphones with a similar cult of personality as that of Steve Jobs, while incorporating elements from Mark Zuckerberg's Facebook algorithms to foresee (and control) people's lives. As Crow (2021) puts it in the article "Don't look up: Who are the characters based on?", Isherwell's CEO not only looks like Jobs and draws on Zuckerberg but also combines them with elements from tech guru and SpaceX chief engineer Elon Musk. Isherwell's gentle, yet competitive and risk-taking, enactment of masculinity, in combination with his capacity to influence decision-making at the presidential level, makes the film a nail-biting example of the long-lived masculine belief that it is possible to fix existential threats – no matter how great they are – with engineering and technology (while also generating jobs and billions of dollars for the tech companies' shareholders) (cf. Buck et al., 2014; Fleming, 2017).

Clearly, the tech entrepreneurship of Elon Musk, upon which the film partly draws, feeds into the themes we are discussing here, joining together a deep-rooted belief in the technological fix with masculinity, hyper-individualism and heroism in his tech entrepreneurialism. Noticeably, Musk's entrepreneurship is not only about tech itself but also about disruptive innovations and achieving more sustainable transport futures. Musk is presented in popular media as a "revolutionary private space entrepreneur".[1] His ambition to establish a colony on Mars positions him as an upgraded frontiersman – not in the context of the Wild West but in outer space. His "private" space programme further establishes him as a heroic frontiersman, someone who can use his own private financial muscle when NASA cannot. Clearly, this form of upgraded digital frontier masculinity is spectacular and high risk on many levels – financially, and perhaps even for the survival of humanity as we know it.

A source of inspiration has been Mendick et al. (2021), who make a parallel reading to ours in their study of the cinematic representations of Mark Zuckerberg in *The Social Network* and Tony Stark in *Iron Man*. They argue that the geek entrepreneur is a new hegemonic masculine formation who is currently superseding the more traditional macho formations embodied by John Wayne and his contemporaries, or the global business masculinity theorized by Connell and Messerschmidt (2005). In their view, geek entrepreneurs build on elements of tech genius, the suffering of geekiness, disruption and the innovation of entrepreneurialism. The classic image of geek masculinity in tech companies, and in particular start-ups, has moved from marginal to mainstream and has emerged as a dominant form of masculinity in the 2020s (Mendick et al., 2021).

We also observe how a new form of hegemonic masculinity, including the heroic and passionate elements of entrepreneurship, is reproduced in the genre of entrepreneurial autobiography. Garmann and Sørensen's (2016, p. 229) study of Richard Branson's autobiography, *Losing My Virginity*, focuses on the logics of desire it generates. More particularly, applying the philosopher Slavoj Žižek's concepts of fantasy and desire, they argue that Branson's book produces a fantasy figure of the heroic entrepreneur, a figure that says something about the construction of the entrepreneur and entrepreneurship. Known for both extreme sports (flying hot air balloons in the attempt to break world records, for example) and major business conquests (turning a student magazine into a global enterprise), Branson's drive to overcome challenges is a key theme in the book. In Johnsen and Sørensen's view, the logic of Branson's narrative "is constituted by the desire for transgression (overcoming oneself) and the desire for authenticity (becoming oneself)" (Johnsen & Sørensen, 2017, pp. 232–233).

Thematically related research in business studies has focused closely on start-up entrepreneurship and how the identity of a start-up entrepreneur is constructed at tech conferences – emphasizing the meanings of emotions and affect in the construction of masculine entrepreneurship. Katila et al. (2019) argue that the socio-material practices of the technology conference *Slush* link masculinity and entrepreneurship to "comprise rock star, vital entrepreneur, and buddy in start-up ecosystem" (Katila et al., 2019, p. 382). Their conclusion is that entrepreneurship is being interlinked with heroism, whiteness and able-bodiedness in ways that exclude women, non-whites, people with disabilities, and the not so young (Katila et al., 2019).

In one of our projects, *Overcoming the Entrepreneurial Ecosystem Gender Divide: A Cross-Cultural Perspective* (GENRE), we asked Swedish tech entrepreneurs (5 men, 10 women) for their views and opinions on the term entrepreneur, including thoughts about the tech entrepreneur and related images and representations. While most informants took the opportunity to discuss their views on how to counter stereotypical representations, entrepreneur and start-up founder Johnny (pseudonym) emphasized its contradictory nature: he talked about tech superstars such as "Elon Musk, Bill Gates, and Peter Thiel and these types of people" being "well-spoken and charming and friendly" on the one hand, but on the other also "very aggressive, and they don't follow the rules and the laws of society either". Johnny's way of portraying tech superstars as well-behaved rebels means that they fit both the classic image of a geek with a specific tech interest and knowledge, and also the hegemonic entrepreneurial form of masculinity as "individualistic, ruthless, aggressive and competitive" (Giazitzoglu & Down, 2017, p. 44). Bearing Mendick et al. (2021) in mind, the geek entrepreneur seems to represent a new hegemonic masculine configuration that extends beyond more traditional forms of masculinity. In doing so, this configuration suggests a combination of several stereotypically masculine entrepreneurial forms, while also incorporating contemporary aspects of a hyperindividualized masculinity that combines the skills of networking with being a social media persona constantly performing the required script of passion, engagement and unconventional heroism out of the box. The profiled masculine geek entrepreneurs are further embedded in a stratified system of racial inequalities, where "The uneven and unequal distribution of women, Asians, Asian Indians, Blacks, and Latinx across occupational categories is a stark expression of an occupational caste system" (Twine, 2022, p. 65). In her ethnography of opportunities and inequalities in Silicon Valley, Twine has shown how racism, sexism, classism and casteism privileges Whites and Asians behind the veil of meritocracy. In the emerging field of Black critical technology studies (Noble, 2018; Benjamin, 2019; Twine, 2022), racial and gendered inequalities are highlighted within a wider frame of racial capitalism.

Conclusion

In this chapter, we have outlined the contours of a contemporary and emergent gendered figuration of the tech entrepreneur, and we have done so by combining elements of tech masculinity and tech entrepreneurship. The tech entrepreneur builds upon historically masculine-coded elements, such as those of the hero, who is powerful as an imaginary figure, and still a solid model for how entrepreneurship is constructed and imagined. Using this figure, building on previous research as well as our own, we want to establish a gendered figuration for further investigation – including the key elements it builds upon – as well as connecting that figuration to the wider analytical frame of gendered and racial inequalities in the tech industry.

We suggest that, by contrasting contemporary and emergent forms of tech masculinities, a focus on tech entrepreneur masculinity emerges that brings together two streams of gender research: technology and masculinity, and entrepreneurship and masculinity. From studies of technology and masculinity, we bring insights into how passion, commitment and love of technology are constitutive components for performing a powerful gendered and entrepreneurial self in various kinds of organizations. The core of this gendered figuration is a masculine persona that embodies the necessary performative and affective qualities of successful tech entrepreneurship. These qualities are, and have historically been, associated with a deep-rooted connection between technology and masculinity. This connection has defined what is masculine and what is not in various entrepreneurial and organizational contexts. Not least is the deep rootedness of this connection, which is literally embodied through the physicality of various work practices, as Cockburn (1983, 1985), for example, showed in her work. Such embodied work practices have also been the source of control and domination within tech organizations, working through gendered dualisms that form patterns of segregation.

Linking these insights with emerging fields such as Black critical technology studies, where gendered segregation is intersectionally paired with racial inequalities, would pave the way for a wider analytical focus on technoentrepreneurial masculinities.

From studies of entrepreneurship and masculinity, we bring a gendered configuration of heroism, risk-taking, hyper-individuality and "conquistadorism". In the neoliberal "zeitgeist" of our time, this form of entrepreneurial masculinity is more celebrated and wealthier than ever before. It is the rampant masculine superhero, often embodied in heroic narratives such as those associated with White men, and increasingly Asian men, such as Jeff Bezos, Satya Nadella, Elon Musk and Mark Zuckerberg. It is a figure that has taken centre stage as a dominant form of masculinity quite recently, as digital technologies have formatted and reconfigured social relations, in parallel with the global economy. As such, it is a form of masculinity that has moved from the margins of the geeky and nerdy to a position of being in control on a global scale.

There are good reasons to claim that we now see this form of Big Tech entrepreneur masculinity as a hegemonic masculinity on a scale that we have not witnessed before. If we return to Connell's (1995, p. 76) classic definition of hegemonic masculinity as "the masculinity that occupies the hegemonic position in a given pattern of gender relations", then the meaning of hegemonic has probably never been so salient or deeply rooted. As the COVID-19 crisis of the early 2020s has turbo-charged profits and stock prices, Big Tech companies and their founders and owners personify and embody a Big Tech entrepreneur masculinity that dominates and controls the global social networking market, as well as much of the global economy. The current record sales (2020–2022) of Big Tech have not only completely displaced older industries in terms of revenues, they have also made their hyper-rich founders into centibillionaires for the first time in history.[2] The personal wealth of these men overshadows most national economies of the world. Their social, economic and political influence are thus taking hegemonic masculinity to a new level.

Acknowledgements

The authors of this chapter would like to acknowledge the Gender-Net plus co-funded project "Overcoming the Entrepreneurial Ecosystem Gender Divide: A Cross-Cultural Perspective", GENRE, project ID: GNP-122, Swedish Research Council grant number: 2018–00937.

Notes

1 *Elon Musk: Revolutionary private space entrepreneur | Space*
2 *The Guardian*, Is big tech now just too big to stomach? 6 February 2022.

References

Acker, J. (1992). From sex roles to gendered institutions. *Contemporary Sociology*, *21*(5), 565–569. doi: 10.2307/2075528

Acker, J. (2006). Inequality regimes: Gender, class, and race in organizations. *Gender and Society*, *20*(4), 441–464. doi: 10.1177/0891243206289499

Ahl, H. (2004). *The Scientific Reproduction of Gender Inequality: A Discourse Analysis of Research Texts on Women's Entrepreneurship*. Stockholm: Liber.

Ahl, H. (2006). Why research on women entrepreneurs needs new directions. *Entrepreneurship Theory and Practice*, *30*(5), 595–621. doi: 10.1111/j.1540-6520.2006.00138.x

Ahl, H., & Marlow, S. (2012). Exploring the dynamics of gender, feminism and entrepreneurship: Advancing debate to escape a dead end. *Organization*, *19*(5), 543–562. doi: 10.1177/1350508412448695

Alaimo, S. (2016). *Exposed: Environmental Politics and Pleasures in Posthuman Times*. Minneapolis, MN: University of Minnesota Press.

Balkmar, D. (2012). *On Men and Cars: An Ethnographic Study of Gendered, Risky and Dangerous Relations*. PhD dissertation, Linköping University, Linköping.

Balkmar, D., & Mellström, U. (2018). Masculinity and autonomous vehicles: A Degendered or resegregated future system of automobility? *Transfers: Interdisciplinary Journal of Mobility Studies*, *8*(1), 44–63. doi: 10.3167/TRANS.2018.080105

Balkmar, D., & Mellström, U. (2019). Cyborgs and entanglements of technology, masculinity, and (automated) vehicles. *Feministische Studien*, *37*(2), 320–335. doi: 10.1515/fs-2019-0030

Bell, D. (2013). Geek myths: Technologies, masculinities, globalizations. In J. Hearn, M. Blagojević & K. Harrison (Eds.), *Rethinking Transnational Men: Beyond, between and Within Nations* (pp. 76–90). New York: Routledge.

Benjamin, R. (2019). *Race after Technology: Abolitionist Tools for the New Jim Code*. Cambridge: Polity.

Bröckling, U. (2016). *The Entrepreneurial Self: Fabricating a New Type of Subject*. Thousand Oaks, CA: SAGE.

Bruni, A., Gherardi, S., & Poggio, B. (2004). Doing gender, doing entrepreneurship: An ethnographic account of intertwined practices. *Gender, Work, and Organisation*, *11*(4), 406–429. doi: 10.1111/j.1468-0432.2004.00240.x

Buck, H. J., Gammon, A. R., & Preston, C. J. (2014). Gender and geoengineering. *Hypatia*, *29*(3), 651–701. doi: 10.1111/hypa.12083

Calás, M. B., Smircich, L., & Bourne, K. (2009). Extending the boundaries: Reframing "entrepreneurship as social change" through feminist perspectives. *Academy of Management Review*, *34*(3), 552–569. doi: 10.5465/amr.2009.40633597

Carlsson, B., Braunerhjelm, P., McKelvey, M., Olofsson, C., Persson, L., & Ylinenpää, H. (2013). The evolving domain of entrepreneurship research. *Small Business Economics*, *41*, 913–930. doi: 10.1007/s11187-013-9503-y

Cockburn, C. (1983). *Brothers: Male Dominance and Technological Change*. London: Pluto.

Cockburn, C. (1985). *Machinery of Dominance: Women, Men and Technical Know-How*. London: Pluto.

Cockburn, C. (2009). On "The machinery of dominance: Women, men, and technical know-how". *Women's Studies Quarterly*, *37*(1–2), 269–273. www.jstor.org/stable/27655158

Cockburn, C., & Ormrod, S. (1993). *Gender and Technology in the Making*. London: Sage.

Connell, R. (1995). *Masculinities*. Berkeley, CA: University of California Press.

Connell, R. W., & Messerschmidt, J. W. (2005). Hegemonic masculinity: Rethinking the concept. *Gender & Society*, *19*(6), 829–859. doi: 10.1177/0891243205278639

Connell, R. W., & Wood, J. (2005). Globalization and business masculinities. *Men and Masculinities*, *7*(4), 347–364. doi: 10.1177/1097184X03260969

Corneliussen, H. G. (2012). *Gender-Technology Relations: Exploring Stability and Change*. Basingstoke: Palgrave Macmillan.

Crow, D. (2021). Don't Look Up: Who are the Characters Based on? Retrieved 24 December, from Den of Geek: www.denofgeek.com/movies/dont-look-up-who-characters-based-on/

Eriksson, M. (2021). *The Silence(d) Voices of Entrepreneurship: A Narrative Study of Women Who Share Their Lives with a Man Who Is an Entrepreneur*. PhD dissertation, Stockholm University, Stockholm.

Faulkner, W. (2001). The technology question in feminism: A view from Feminist Technology Studies. *Women's Studies International Forum*, *24*(1), 79–95. doi: 10.1016/S0277-5395(00)00166-7

Fleming, J. (2017). Excuse us, while we fix the sky: WEIRD supermen and climate engineering. *Men and Nature: Hegemonic Masculinities and Environmental Change* (RCC Perspectives), *4*, 23–28. doi: 10.5282/rcc/7979

Galloway, L. (2012). The experiences of male gay business owners in the UK. *International Small Business Journal*, *30*(8), 890–906. doi: 10.1177/0266242610391324

Garlick, S. (2019). The return of nature: Feminism, hegemonic masculinities, and new materialisms. *Men and Masculinities*, *22*(2), 380–403. doi: 10.1177/1097184X17725128

Garmann, J. C., & Sørensen, B. M. (2016). Traversing the fantasy of the heroic entrepreneur. *International Journal of Entrepreneurial Behavior & Research*, *23*(2), 228–244. doi: 10.1108/IJEBR-01-2016-0032

Giazitzoglu, A. (2014). Qualitative upward mobility, the mass-media and 'posh' masculinity in contemporary North-East Britain: A micro sociological case-study. *Sociological Research Online*, *19*(2), 1–12. doi: 10.5153/sro.3273

Giazitzoglu, A., & Down, S. (2017). Performing entrepreneurial masculinity: An ethnographic account. *International Small Business Journal: Researching Entrepreneurship*, *35*(1), 40–60. doi: 10.1177/0266242615599244

Gray, C. H. (1993). The culture of war cyborgs: Technoscience, gender, and postmodern war. *Research in Philosophy and Technology*, *13*, 141–163. doi: 10.1177/1357034037736847939

Gray, C. H. (2000). Man plus: Enhanced cyborgs and the construction of the future masculine. *Science as Culture*, *9*(3), 277–299. doi: 10.1080/713695253

Gray, C. H. (2003). Posthuman soldiers in postmodern war. *Body & Society*, *9*(4), 215–226. doi: 10.1177/135703403773684739

Grint, K., & Woolgar, S. (1995). On some failures of nerve in constructivist and feminist analyses of technology. *Science, Technology, & Human Values*, *20*(3), 286–310. doi: 10.1177/016224399502000302

Gupta, N. (2015). Rethinking the relationship between gender and technology: A study of the Indian example. *Work, Employment and Society*, *29*(4), 661–672. doi: 10.1177/0950017014556410

Hacker, S. (1989). *Pleasure, Power and Technology: Some Tales of Gender, Engineering, and the Cooperative Workplace*. Boston, MA: Unwin Hyman.

Hearn, J. (2019). Gender, work and organization: A gender-work-organization analysis. *Gender, Work & Organization*, *26*(1), 31–39. doi: 10.1111/gwao.12331

Hearn, J., & Husu, L. (2013). Understanding gender: Some implications for science and technology. *Interdisciplinary Science Reviews*, *36*(2), 103–113. doi: 10.1179/030801811X13013181961301

Hearn, J., & Parkin, W. (1995). *'Sex' at 'Work'. The Power and Paradox of Organisation Sexuality*, 2nd edition. New York: St. Martin's Press.

Jernberg, F., Lindbäck, A., & Rooset, A. (2020). A new male entrepreneur? Media representation of male entrepreneurs before and after #metoo. *Gender in Management: An International Journal*, *35*(2), 211–224. doi: 10.1108/GM-01-2019-0004

Johnsen, C. G., & Sørensen, B. M. (2017). Traversing the fantasy of the heroic entrepreneur. *International Journal of Entrepreneurial Behavior & Research*, *23*(2), 228–244. doi: 10.1108/IJEBR-01-2016-0032

Katila, S., Laine, P. M., & Parkkari, P. (2019). Sociomateriality and affect in institutional work: Constructing the identity of start-up entrepreneurs. *Journal of Management Inquiry*, *28*(3), 381–394. doi: 10.1177/1056492617743591

Kendall, L. (1999). Nerd nation: Images of nerds in US popular culture. *International Journal of Cultural Studies*, *2*(2), 260–283. doi: 10.1177/136787799900200206

Lagesen, V. A. (2008). A cyberfeminist utopia: Perceptions of gender and computer science among Malaysian women computer science students. *Science, Technology & Human Values*, *33*(1), 5–27. doi: 10.1177/0162243907306192

Landström, C. (2006). Queering feminist technology studies. *Feminist Theory*, *8*(1), 7–26. doi: 10.1177/1464700107074193

Lewis, P. (2006). The quest for invisibility: Female entrepreneurs and the masculine norm of entrepreneurship. *Gender, Work and Organization*, *13*(5), 453–469. doi: 10.1111/j.1468-0432.2006.00317.x

Lohan, M., & Faulkner, M. (2004). Masculinities and technologies: Some introductory remarks. *Men and Masculinities*, *6*(4), 319–329. doi: 10.1177/1097184X03260956

Marlow, S., Greene, F., & Coad, A. (2018). Advancing gendered analyses of entrepreneurship: A critical exploration of entrepreneurial activity among gay men and lesbian women. *British Journal of Management*, *29*(1), 118–135. doi: 10.1111/1467-8551.12221

Marlow, S., & Martinez Dy, A. (2018). Annual review article: Is it time to rethink the gender agenda in entrepreneurship research? *International Small Business Journal*, *36*(1), 3–22. doi: 10.1177%2F0266242617738321

McAdam, M. (2013). *Female Entrepreneurship*. London: Routledge.

McKay, A. (2021). *Don't Look Up* [Film]. Los Angeles: Hyperobject Industries, Bluegrass Films.

Mellström, U. (1995). Engineering lives, technology, time and space in a male-centred world. *Linköping Studies in Art and Science, 128.*

Mellström, U. (2002). Patriarchal machines and masculine embodiment. *Science, Technology & Human Values, 27*(4), 460–478. doi: 10.1177/016224302236177

Mellström, U. (2003). *Masculinity, Power and Technology: A Malaysian Ethnography.* Aldershot: Ashgate.

Mellström, U. (2004). Machines and masculine subjectivity: Technology as an integral part of men's life experiences. In W. Faulkner & M. Lohan (Eds.), *Special Issue: Masculinities and Technology, Men and Masculinities, 6*(4), 368–383. doi: 10.1177/1097184X03260960

Mellström, U. (2009). The intersection of gender, race and cultural boundaries, or why is computer science in Malaysia dominated by women? *Social Studies of Science, 39*(6), 885–907. www.jstor.org/stable/27793329

Mellström, U. (2016). From a hegemonic politics of masculinity to an ontological politics of intimacy and vulnerability? Ways of imagining through Karen Barad's work. *Rhizomes: Cultural Studies in Emerging Knowledge, 30.* doi: 10.20415/rhiz/030.e07

Mellström, U., & Pease, B. (Eds.). (2022). *Beyond Anthropocentric Masculinities: Posthumanism, New Materialism and the Man Question.* London: Routledge.

Mendick, H., Ottemo, A., Berge, M., & Silfver, E. (2021). Geek entrepreneurs: The social network, Iron Man and the reconfiguration of hegemonic masculinity. *Journal of Gender Studies* (published online first), *1–13.* doi: 10.1080/09589236.2021.1981836

Noble, S. U. (2018). *Algorithms of Oppression: How Search Engines Reinforce Racism.* New York: New York University Press.

Ogbor, J. (2002). Mythicizing and reification in entrepreneurial discourse: Ideology-critique of entrepreneurial studies. *Journal of Management Studies, 37*(5), 605–635. doi: 10.1111/1467-6486.00196

Ottemo, A. (2015). *Kön, kropp, begär och teknik: passion och instrumentalitet på två tekniska högskoleprogram.* Disseration, Göteborgs universitet, Göteborg.

Ottemo, A. (2020). The coproduction of masculinity and technology: Problems and prospects. In L. Gottzén, U. Mellström & T. Shefer (Eds.), *Routledge International Handbook of Masculinity Studies* (pp. 341–351). London and New York: Routledge. doi: 10.4324/9781315165165

Plant, S. (1997). *Zeroes + Ones: Digital Women + The New Technoculture*, 1st edition. New York: Doubleday.

Pulé, M. P., & Hultman, M. (Eds.). (2021). *Men, Masculinities, and Earth: Contending with the (m) Anthropocene.* Cham: Palgrave Macmillan.

Schumpeter, J. A. (1934). *The Theory of Economic Development: An Inquiry into Profits, Capital, Credit, Interest, and the Business Cycle.* Cambridge, MA: Harvard University Press.

Schyfter, P. (2009). *Entangled Ontologies: A Sociophilosophical Analysis of Technological Artefacts, Subjects, and Bodies.* PhD dissertation, University of Edinburgh, Edinburgh.

Stepulevage, L. (1997). Sexuality and computing: Transparent relations. In G. Griffin & S. Andermahr (Eds.), *Straight Studies Modified: Lesbian Interventions in the Academy* (pp. 197–211). London: Cassell.

Stone, S. (1992). "The empire" strikes back: A posttranssexual manifesto. *Camera Obscura, 10*(29), 150–176.

Takeyama, K. (2010). Intimacy for sale: Masculinity, entrepreneurship, and commodity self in Japan's neoliberal situation. *Japanese Studies, 30*(2), 231–246. doi: 10.1080/10371397.2010.497579

Tedmanson, D., & Essers, C. (2015). Entrepreneurship and diversity. In R. Bendl, I. Bleijenbergh, E. Henttonen & A. J. Mills (Eds.), *The Oxford Handbook of Diversity in Organizations* (pp. 389–407). Oxford University Press. doi: 10.1093/oxfordhb/9780199679805.013.28

Turkle, S. (1984). *The Second Self: Computers and the Human Spirit.* London: Granada.

Twine, F. W. (2022). *Geek Girls: Inequality and Opportunity in Silicon Valley.* New York: New York University Press.

Vigdor, L. (2011). A techno-passion that is not one: Rethinking marginality, exclusion, and difference. *International Journal of Gender, Science and Technology, 3*(1), 4–32. https://genderandset.open.ac.uk/index.php/genderandset/article/view/112

Wajcman, J. (1991). *Feminism Confronts Technology.* Cambridge, UK: Polity Press.

Wajcman, J. (2004). *Technofeminism.* London: Polity Press.

30

MEN AND COVID-19

Pandemics and organizing in the "new normal"

Stephen Burrell and Sandy Ruxton

Introduction

Since the COVID-19 pandemic began in December 2019, there are few aspects of society which have not been touched by it. In the process, it has shone a spotlight on entrenched social inequalities, and responses to the pandemic have frequently aggravated these further. This certainly appears to be the case regarding gender. As with other pandemics, COVID-19 has interacted with the gender order in innumerable ways, and often its effects have been compounded by unequal gender relations and their influence on people's responses. This has played out within many different organizations and forms of organizing. This chapter focuses on three such domains: work, governmentality and social movements. It explores how, in each of these key sites, men and masculinities have been impacted by, and in turn influenced, the pandemic. It also considers the implications for future organizing, as the fallout of COVID-19 continues to shape our world in the years to come.

COVID-19 has caused untold death and suffering to human populations across the planet. At the time of writing, over 6.5 million people are recorded as having died from it (WHO, 2022). It has brought about ill health for many more, with "long-COVID" having deleterious and little-understood long-term effects. These health impacts are gendered. For instance, long-COVID appears to affect women more (Global Health 50/50, 2022). Global Health 50/50 (2022) estimates that 13 men die from COVID-19 for every ten women, and for every ten female ICU admissions, there are 17 male admissions – although many agencies do not break down such data by sex.

A mixture of biological and social factors are likely to be playing a role here. For example, men tend to have weaker immune systems than women and are more likely to possess underlying health conditions which increase the impact of COVID-19 (White, 2020). This is at least partly influenced by gender norms which mean men engage in more "risky" behaviours such as smoking, drinking and meat-eating. However, not all men are equally vulnerable; those from working-class and minoritized backgrounds have fared much worse. Gender is relational, and we cannot consider men and masculinities in isolation. Women have been affected particularly badly by many aspects of COVID-19, as has often been the case in previous pandemics, including its economic damage, the mental health impacts of increased stress

 DOI: 10.4324/9781003193579-34

and anxiety, and the exacerbation of domestic abuse for victim-survivors trapped at home (Azcona et al., 2020).

Work

COVID-19 has had tumultuous consequences for the global economy and for organizations where people work. In many cases, coronavirus prevention measures led to physical workplaces closing for months, triggering global economic recession. A number of countries in the Global North implemented "furlough" schemes where governments paid proportions of wages for millions of workers who could no longer go to work, such as in retail and hospitality. Some people, especially in white-collar jobs (including academia), were able to continue teleworking from home. However, for many others, especially working-class people, this was not an option, either because their job was defined as "essential" or because it was simply not possible to do remotely. At the forefront of the pandemic was the healthcare sector, where workers desperately struggled to save lives in the face of a deadly and little-understood virus, and under-resourced healthcare systems buckled under the pressure of major influxes of people needing urgent care.

Healthcare is a sector where women are disproportionately represented, making up 70% of its workforce internationally (Boniol et al., 2019). Women have therefore played a particularly central role in responding to COVID-19. This was true of many other crucial occupations too, including social work, pharmacies, supermarkets and education. This often placed women at particular risk of contracting COVID-19 at work, and in many contexts healthcare workers had to protest for basic safety provisions such as personal protective equipment (PPE). Indeed, it has been argued that one reason why pandemics tend to be remembered relatively little within human history (such as the 1918 Flu Pandemic, which is estimated to have killed up to 50 million people) is due to the major role women play in them, compared to events such as wars which may be of greater interest to androcentric historians (Onion, 2019). It is notable that there also appears to be a rush to move on from and "forget" COVID-19 in some quarters.

Nonetheless, COVID-19 does appear to have brought about greater social recognition of the importance of care work. Symbolic displays of gratitude have been made in numerous ways, such as people coming to their doorsteps every week to "clap for carers". Yet this appreciation has not necessarily extended to greater *material* valuing of care work, such as increased investment or pay. Indeed, Chatzidakis and Littler (2022) note that the pandemic has led to an upsurge in "carewashing", as corporations seek to commodify and claim care as part of efforts to market themselves as socially responsible.

In many settings, mutual aid groups were set up during lockdowns to support local residents. These have been instrumental in reviving notions of community and solidarity, and could point to shifts in how support is organized, independent of underfunded and bureaucratic state institutions. These structures seem to be enduring to some degree; not just through actions such as delivering food and hygiene products or dog walking but also in terms of self-organizing, community connection and information sharing. Numerous people engaged more in care work too, such as supporting family members, friends and neighbours if they were unwell or having to self-isolate.

Particularly significant in this regard was the impact of schools being closed (physically, at least), and subsequently, having to self-isolate because they or their classmates had contracted COVID-19. This greatly increased the caregiving and "home-schooling" load for parents, which in turn made maintaining paid work highly challenging. This and simply spending more time at home led to many fathers becoming more actively involved in childcare and housework than they had been previously. In UN Women (2020) surveys in 47 countries, 56% of women and 51% of men said their time spent on unpaid care work had increased since the pandemic began. Another UN Women (2020) survey in 16 countries found that for men with children, the amount of time spent on childcare per week increased by 3.5 hours (for women, it increased even more, by 5.2 hours).

Many men have described this as an unexpected positive side effect of the pandemic, that it has allowed them to spend more time with their families. This could have long-term ramifications for constructions of masculinity in some contexts; when men engage more in childcare, they tend to enjoy it and want to continue to be actively involved (Barker et al., 2021). However, this has not been possible for all families, where working from home has not been an option. And for lots of people, spending large amounts of time in close quarters with family members, during a highly stressful public health crisis, created additional relationship challenges. Many victims of domestic abuse became more isolated, and perpetrators may have sought to increase the control they had lost in other parts of their lives. Research suggests gender-based violence is often exacerbated during pandemics (Wenham & Davies, 2020).

While men's involvement in caregiving increased, it typically rose even more for women, connected to wider patterns in which women continue to do the bulk of care work while also being active in the labour market. This meant that coronavirus prevention measures such as school closures affected them in particular. As a result, many women had to leave jobs, reduce hours or be furloughed – and in some cases were forced to do so by their employers (Women and Equalities Committee, 2021). It is estimated that for every man, 1.8 women lost their jobs due to COVID-19 globally, which could also be influenced by female-dominated service sector jobs often being worse affected by lockdowns (Madgavkar et al., 2020).

There are concerns that these unequal impacts could reinforce patriarchal divisions of labour in the longer term. For many women, their position in the labour market has been weakened, and it will be harder for them to "catch-up". For instance, in academia it appears that men were on average able to be more research productive during the pandemic (such as writing more journal articles), helping them to advance further in their careers (Ribarovska, 2021).

One potentially positive development during COVID-19 has been shifts in workplace organizing, where there has been pressure on employers to do more to recognize staff caring responsibilities, and place greater priority on employee well-being and life outside of work. The pandemic forced many employers to become more flexible, and the growth of teleworking potentially makes it easier to juggle caregiving (though it can also increase demands on working parents, especially mothers). However, as many workplaces move at least partially in person again, men may be able to spend more time in the office and reap the career benefits of this, such as stronger networks.

Another issue COVID-19 has both highlighted and exacerbated is the crisis facing the care sector in many countries. Childcare and social care are typically highly under-resourced, with predominantly female staff poorly paid, and many services are under threat, with facilities such as nurseries often losing income after having to close for several months (Women and Equalities Committee, 2021). Yet as with previous economic crises, male-dominated industries such as construction and manufacturing have often been prioritized in COVID-19 recovery plans, leading to calls for increased investment in "social infrastructure" which has been so vital to the pandemic response (De Henau & Himmelweit, 2021). In the meantime, lacking high-quality, affordable childcare will hinder women's participation in the labour market. This demonstrates the need for organizations to build on the increased caregiving among men during the pandemic, and encourage and facilitate active fatherhood among employees. This could include implementing generous paternity and parental leave policies, helping men to work more flexibly, and shifting towards more sustainable work patterns, as well as ensuring childcare facilities are available.

Yet it is not only sectors such as care and education which have been a crucial part of the pandemic response. There are other relatively hidden areas of work, some of which carried out predominantly by men, which have also been providing "essential services" during COVID-19. These include emergency services, food production and distribution, communications, transportation, waste management, local government, utilities, construction, and funeral services. A number of these occupations may be perceived as traditionally "masculine", but it is interesting to consider whether some of this vital work could also be reconceptualized as engaging in care for others. However, Wojnicka (2022) warns against interpreting caring practices associated with "protective" expressions of manhood as challenging hegemonic masculinity, when in many ways they reaffirm it.

Many of these jobs have involved significant infection risk due to being in close contact with colleagues and the public. They are occupations predominantly undertaken by working-class people, with people of colour often over-represented, which is one reason why mortality rates have been higher among these groups (Baker et al., 2020). This underscores why an intersectional understanding of men's health and pandemics is so important; some men faced much greater risk from COVID-19 at work than others. There have been numerous reports – especially in low-paid, casualized occupations – of employers paying scant regard to coronavirus safety measures, and workers unable to afford to take time off if they contract COVID-19, especially where statutory sick pay is minimal (Carlsten et al., 2021).

This highlights the complex implications of COVID-19 for men in the workplace. For some, the pandemic may have transformed their relationship with work. For others, exploitative working conditions have worsened, and many have died after contracting COVID-19 at work. This demonstrates the importance of strengthening workplace health and safety. More men die from workplace accidents than women, primarily because of the kinds of jobs they are more likely to do (Stergiou-Kita et al., 2015). One factor to consider here is how some men may express a lack of concern for their well-being at work, in order to meet entrenched masculine norms around being strong, stoic and fearless.

Governmentality

COVID-19 has illustrated the contemporary relevance of Michel Foucault's (2009) theory of governmentality, in which organizations of power discipline, shape and govern human behaviour, and legitimize that power through discourses of rationality. He also devised the concept of biopower, to describe how authority is exerted over human bodies and populations through biopolitics, which are the measures utilized to regulate and administer control over human life (Foucault, 2010). The governance of disease is a major way in which states and other organizations have been able to maintain this kind of control, and COVID-19 provides manifold illustrations of this, perhaps more so than previous pandemics. Populations have to some extent willingly yielded personal freedoms (e.g. lockdowns) and permitted new levels of state surveillance and control (e.g. "track and trace" applications), including over their own bodies (e.g. regular COVID-19 testing and vaccinations). These measures enabled countless lives to be saved – the freedom to live, in healthy and safe conditions, is perhaps the most important freedom of all. However, it remains important to consider the ramifications of the pandemic for different aspects of biopower.

Colombo (2021) argues that two different forms of governmentality have dominated public and political discourses about COVID-19: biomedical and economic. These claims to truth and legitimizations of state actions were based either on the defence of biological life or on protecting economic interests. However, Colombo argues that lacking from these polarized debates was a "social" perspective which prioritized dignity and human rights, and a holistic approach to well-being, as the compass for intervention.

These different forms of governmentality have been influenced by gender in multiple ways. For instance, emphasizing public health needs was at times presented as being "weak" and "feminine". However, both dominant discourses could be perceived as being masculinized. This is not least because men have dominated decision-making in COVID-19 responses. An analysis of 115 COVID-19 government taskforces in 87 countries found only 3.5% had gender parity in their membership, while 85.2% had majority male membership (Van Daalen et al., 2020). This is of little surprise when we consider how male-dominated global politics and the upper echelons of science and medicine continue to be.

This has no doubt played a role in issues disproportionately affecting women being neglected by policymakers during this and previous pandemics (Wenham & Davies, 2021). It was often only belatedly realized that the home is not a safe space for everyone, and that domestic abuse survivors might need to breach lockdown rules for their own safety. The pandemic has underscored the gender data gap, with sex differences (such as impacts on menstruation) under-explored in vaccine research (Vassallo et al., 2021), and the needs of pregnant women frequently being an afterthought. Amid discussion about cases where the Oxford/AstraZeneca vaccine may have contributed to blood clots, it was pointed out that this is a more common but rarely discussed side effect of the contraceptive pill for women (though highly unusual in both cases). The failure to take into account the gender dynamics of pandemics has also had detrimental impacts on men themselves (Morgan et al., 2021). For instance, the fact that mothers were often forced to attend appointments and give birth alone meant many fathers missed out on this significant experience, and there have been few efforts to address how men have been particularly severely affected by the virus.

The wide range of social issues exposed by the pandemic were often obscured by a false (masculine) dichotomy which assumed policymakers had to prioritize either science *or* the economy in response to it. There is evidence that governments which placed a greater focus on the well-being of citizens – which entails a range of factors, not just protection from disease – often actually had better economic outcomes too (Coscieme et al., 2020). The two are clearly interlinked, and more proactive and strategic steps to prevent COVID-19 sometimes meant economies could re-open sooner too.

There have been suggestions that countries with women leaders were more likely to adopt this kind of approach and deal more effectively with the crisis, and there is some evidence to support this (Coscieme et al., 2020). National responses to a pandemic are too complex to be reducible to the identities of politicians, and there remain so few female political leaders that it is too small a sample to generalize from. But perhaps this does still tell us something about the nature of governmentality in a particular social context. For instance, research suggests that societies with higher numbers of women in power are likely to have higher levels of democracy and equality more broadly, and a stronger social contract (Tremblay, 2007).

Either way, the need for more diversity in political organizing is clear. Yet it is also important to avoid essentialist stereotypes about women in positions of power, as if they will inherently be more caring, nurturing and empathetic; that these are the only skills they possess; and that men are incapable of enacting such skills. Having a female leader does not inevitably mean a government will respond effectively to a public health crisis, especially if the regime is at the head of remains highly patriarchal in nature.

Indeed, one factor noticeable during the pandemic has been the influence of masculinism on biopolitics and governmentality. Some (typically male) political leaders and their governments spoke in dismissive, nonchalant terms about COVID-19, as if it posed little concern to them or their nations; that they were "tough enough" not to be threatened by something supposedly akin to a cold or flu, and should carry on as normal (Ruxton & Burrell, 2020). The administrations of Donald Trump, Jared Bolsonaro and Boris Johnson offer examples of this. From such leaders, we have seen wholesale denial and a lack of accountability for government failure, incompetence and cronyism – such as the inability to provide healthcare workers with PPE, or the neglect of care homes which in many countries saw strikingly high mortality rates. Yet there has also been a rush to claim credit when some measures, such as vaccine rollouts, appeared to be working.

Clearly then, this isn't simply an issue of rhetoric. Underneath masculinist discourses has often been flippancy towards public health measures, a neoliberal prioritization of "business as usual", and a libertarian emphasis on personal freedoms (and individual responsibility) as opposed to collective welfare. It is therefore perhaps unsurprising that many of the countries which have had the highest COVID-19 mortality rates also had governments vocally espousing such masculinist logics. Biopower at times appears to have been expressed in a willingness to sacrifice some of the most voiceless and powerless people, such as people with disabilities and elderly people, who do not fit into idealized masculine notions of strength.

The masculinization of disease governmentality was also identifiable more broadly. For instance, when politicians constructed militarized discourses about waging a "war" against COVID-19, which may have helped to legitimize the deaths of healthcare workers as if they were "soldiers" on the "frontline", "sacrificing" themselves for the nation. Some governments have used the pandemic as an opportunity to bolster state control, militarism and authoritarian rule, and clamp down on protest and freedom of expression. Masculinized institutions such as the police and army have sometimes been used to aggressively enforce restrictions, and working-class and minoritized communities have often been disproportionately policed (Amnesty International, 2020). In some countries, marginalized groups such as LGBTQ+ communities and migrants have been subjected to hate crimes after being scapegoated for the spread of COVID-19.

The United Nations Secretary-General called for a global ceasefire so that all efforts could be directed towards COVID-19, yet conflicts have continued in several settings, including Afghanistan, Yemen and Syria. This points to a masculinist prioritization of war and dominance over human well-being, even amid a gargantuan public health crisis. We have seen the invasion of Ukraine by the Russian Federation, orchestrated by an authoritarian "strong-man" regime led by Vladimir Putin, causing mass death and suffering on top of the thousands of people who have already died from COVID-19 in the region.

It is predominantly young working-class men sent to kill other men in military forces. For example, many of the Russian soldiers appear to be conscripts and male university students are not conscripted, while Ukraine restricted men aged 18–60 from leaving the country (Wojnicka et al., 2022). However, most victims of the war have been Ukrainian civilians of all genders and ages. This has created a massive influx of refugees, who are primarily women, children and older people. The war risks exacerbating the spread of COVID-19 and other infectious diseases with millions of people on the move (often in confined spaces) and has had deleterious impacts on the ability of badly damaged healthcare services to treat the virus, with oxygen supplies running low, for example (Roberts, 2022). Before the war, Ukraine already had one of the lowest COVID-19 vaccination rates in Europe at 36% (WHO, 2022).

Rather than such events simply representing unfortunate timing, it seems likely that in some cases state actors are actively *exploiting* the chaos, confusion and pacification created by COVID-19 to extend the reach of their power. This form of governmentality exemplifies what Naomi Klein (2007) describes as the "shock doctrine", in which organizations of power utilize public disorientation in the wake of disasters or crises (such as a pandemic) to engage in "shock therapy" as a way of enhancing dominance, such as intensifying state controls or pushing through neoliberal economic policies to increase corporate profits. It is notable that in Russia COVID-19 was used as justification for Putin to amend the constitution to allow him to rule until 2036 to avoid "upheaval", and to crack down on protests in the name of "public safety" (Hutcheson & McAllister, 2021).

This underscores Foucault's (2010) insights that while public health policies and programmes and the organizations administering them play a vital role, they should not simply be viewed as benign. Science and medicine have historically often acted as agents of patriarchal state power, exercising control over the bodies of women and minoritized groups in particular, so the notion that they should be trusted blindly in times of crisis warrants questioning. Indeed, many scientists would themselves encourage critical discussion about their work – openness and transparency are fundamental principles of academic discovery – and one notable dynamic of the pandemic has been increased public engagement with public health, science and epidemiology. However, perhaps there has also been neglect among decision-makers of insights from *social* science – often perceived as feminized and troublesome – in terms of the varying outcomes of their policies on different populations.

There have been highly contested biopolitical debates about the extent to which governments and organizations should be able to mandate citizens and employees to be vaccinated against COVID-19, with countries such as Austria making this compulsory for all adults. There are concerns in locales such as China that state surveillance measures introduced on public health grounds have normalized new levels of intrusion on people's privacy and human rights.

However, in many countries simply obtaining sufficient vaccines in the first place has been impossible. The pandemic has laid bare the extent of global inequities, in terms of the varying capacity of governments to invest in disease prevention tools such as vaccines, testing and therapies. Within biomedical governmentality, we have seen vaccine nationalism, with wealthier governments and pharmaceutical organizations racing to acquire COVID-19 vaccines and keeping most for themselves, or profiting from selling them to others. Most vaccinated people are therefore in Global North countries rich enough to produce or buy them (although there are some examples which buck this trend, such as Cuba successfully developing their own vaccines and having one of the highest vaccination rates in the world). There have been attempts to achieve more democratic distribution, for example, through the COVID-19 Vaccines Global Access (COVAX) scheme, and the Oxford/AstraZeneca vaccine was made available at cost price, but huge disparities remain. This is despite the fact that infectious diseases have no regard for national borders, and allowing the virus to spread in some parts of the world will inevitably enable it to spread more widely as new, vaccine-resistant variants are able to develop. One key lesson of COVID-19 is the interdependency of human life; we are only protected from disease if *everyone* is.

It seems likely that masculinities are playing a role in this problem. Governmentalities of COVID-19 have frequently been marked by national divisiveness rather than cooperation. We have seen masculinist ideals such as individualism, self-sufficiency and competitiveness shape politics on the global stage. The UK's departure from the European Union – and subsequent tensions around the distribution of the Oxford/AstraZeneca vaccine – is one example of this, as was Donald Trump's withdrawal of the United States funding from the World Health Organization (subsequently reversed by Joe Biden). Russia's war on Ukraine is surely another cause and consequence of weakening international cooperation.

Masculinities have also influenced responses to COVID-19 at a more individual level. Research during this and previous pandemics suggests that men are, on average, less likely to engage in virus prevention measures (e.g. social distancing, handwashing) than women (Levant et al., 2022; Ruxton & Burrell, 2020). One study of responses to the 2009/10 H1N1 pandemic in Australia and Scotland found men were more likely to adopt an individualized approach where they viewed themselves as "at risk" but not "a risk" to others (Davis et al., 2015). There has been attention towards men being less likely to wear face masks during COVID-19, and this issue has become politicized in some contexts, with removing masks equated with masculine notions of individual freedom. Globally, roughly equal numbers of women and men appear to be getting vaccinated, but there are sizable gaps in some countries, with fewer men getting vaccinated in the United Kingdom and the United States, for example (Global Health 50/50, 2022).

Of course, these are generalizations – many men have taken the pandemic and public health guidance seriously, and have faced the loss of loved ones or the chastening experience of ill health from COVID-19. But it seems likely that dominant ideas and expectations around masculinity, such as being invulnerable and self-reliant, may have deterred some men from expressing concerns about the virus. There are lessons here for public health about finding ways to encourage men to take up services such as vaccinations, including making them easily available (e.g. opening beyond working hours), taking them to where men are likely to be, and modelling protective behaviours among leaders. Yet there has been a dearth of gender-sensitive campaigns along these lines within the governmentalities of COVID-19, let alone efforts to question some of the ideas about masculinity which can detrimentally affect men's own well-being as well as that of others in times of crisis.

Social movements

One factor impacting vaccine take-up has been "anti-vax" movements. Vaccine hesitancy has long been an obstacle for public health agencies, and during the pandemic it has formed one aspect of scepticism and misinformation about COVID-19. This has included denying or downplaying the existence or threat of the virus, and misinformation and conspiracy theories about its origins, prevention, diagnosis and treatment. In some countries, these ideas have gained significant ground and been espoused by mainstream political figures and parties. Large groups have taken part in anti-lockdown protests (although these were typically a small minority compared to the numbers expressing care and concern about the virus and the welfare of others).

One common thread is that men seem to be over-represented in (though not the sole purveyors of) COVID-19 denialism. There are connections here with groups fomenting resistance to forms of progressive social change, such as climate change deniers, QAnon followers, the Manosphere and the far right. Sometimes the masculinist nature of such groups is made explicit; for example, "Alpha Men Assemble" in the United Kingdom engage in militarized training and seek to "wage war" on government in opposition to COVID-19 measures (Coleman & Sardarizadeh, 2022). If dominant masculine expectations discourage men from acknowledging their own vulnerabilities and suggest they are separate from and above nature, then it may be easier to deny the existence of a zoonotic virus which imperils human life – and the status quo – than re-evaluating one's self-perceptions. COVID-19 may be perceived as a threat to masculine identities which cherish individualism and personal freedom, based on notions that it is "weak" to need help from others (or to provide it). Alienated young men harbouring a sense of "aggrieved entitlement" may be particularly vulnerable to this kind of biopolitics (Burns, 2017). However, it's important to note that the biopolitics of COVID-19 denial and misinformation has also been propagated by men with significant power and influence in the "post-truth" era, such as former US President Donald Trump.

The influence of virtual spaces such as the Manosphere, vocalizing backlash against feminism and other progressive forces, is likely to have increased during COVID-19, with many of us spending much more time isolated at home online (Adams, 2021). Reactionary groups such as the far-right often seek to exploit crises and the sense of anxiety and hopelessness they generate to antagonize divisions and recruit people to their cause, utilizing simplistic explanations blaming marginalized "Others" such as women or immigrants and advocating a return to a glorious mythical past with re-entrenched social hierarchies (Greig, 2019).

This demonstrates the vital importance of engaging with men and boys about gender equality, encouraging them to develop critical thinking around social expectations of masculinity and equipping them with skills to avoid being easily seduced by harmful groups and ideologies. However, the pandemic has also provided new obstacles to organizations undertaking this work.

Lockdowns meant that in some cases, work with men and boys had to be stopped (Burrell & Ruxton, 2020). Organizations often adapted quickly and moved their work online, but this can be far from ideal for conversations which require rapport, openness and sensitivity, especially given inequalities in digital access. Gender-equality work is frequently struggling for resources, and COVID-19's economic fallout has meant this has been exacerbated in many contexts as income streams have dried up and organizations were not always able to continue funded work (Burrell & Ruxton, 2020). Work with men and boys was rarely prioritized as "essential work" by decision-makers during the pandemic, despite the issues it addresses (e.g. violence prevention, health and well-being, fatherhood) becoming even more urgent. Issues of gender and other forms of inequality often fall off the agenda during times of crisis, perceived to be not sufficiently urgent, even though they are usually compounded by (and themselves compound) such crises (Smith, 2019).

However, we have also seen movements for social justice coming to the fore during the pandemic. Black Lives Matter protests erupted in several countries in the summer of 2020, after footage of the murder of George Floyd by police officers in Minneapolis was streamed across the world. The COP26 summit in November 2021 saw environmental movements converge on Glasgow and march across the globe for climate justice. Russia's invasion of Ukraine may have been influenced partly by fear of rising movements for civil rights and democracy in former Soviet Republics including Ukraine, Belarus and Kazakhstan.

Notable in the United Kingdom was the outpouring of grief and anger after the kidnap, rape and murder of a young woman, Sarah Everard, by a serving police officer while she was walking home in London in March 2021. This and other high-profile killings of women in public spaces has led to a spike in public consciousness about men's violence against women and widespread calls for change. These have focused more than ever on the role of men in both the problem and the solution. There has been increasingly vocal outrage against violence towards women during the pandemic in other countries too, building on the impact of the #MeToo movement in many contexts (Westmarland et al., 2021).

COVID-19 made it harder to ignore these injustices. For many people, lockdowns meant more time on the internet and watching television, and it was difficult not to notice the horrifying footage of George Floyd's death, or to avoid the harrowing developments in the case of Sarah Everard. It has also brought more people to breaking point, unable to tolerate growing disparities in society and the constancy of horrors such as men's violence against women. People were left asking themselves what kind of world they wanted to live in after the pandemic, and for many, the status quo was unendurable. In her influential piece, "The pandemic is a portal", Roy (2020) wrote "Nothing could be worse than a return to normality". Previous pandemics do sometimes seem to have led to progressive social change. For instance, Spinney (2017) notes that the 1918 flu contributed to the development of welfare states in several countries. However, this is far from inevitable. The simultaneous growth of backlash demonstrates the dynamics of movement and counter-movement, and the ongoing struggle over what post-COVID societies will look like – with the governmentality of the state frequently claiming a need for "national unity" and "stability" as a guise for returning to the status quo.

The rise of different forms of movement organizing has also illustrated the interconnecting nature of calls for social justice in the COVID-19 era. While they have arisen from specific cases of inequality, they have also shown that these issues cannot be isolated from one another. For example, that racial and gendered injustices are closely intertwined, with some people – especially white, heterosexual, cisgender, able-bodied, middle- and upper-class men – able to navigate public space more freely than others. This has demonstrated that intersectionality is not an optional add-on; all men and boys are constantly entangled in complex, mutually reinforcing systems of power, and while gender is a central component, it cannot be separated from these other dynamics. It has also underlined the importance of practicing what we preach when it comes to *all* aspects of social justice; we cannot hope to understand the issues facing men if we are in fact only studying white, middle-class men.

One factor impossible to ignore in this regard is the climate crisis. Environmental movements such as School Strike for Climate and Extinction Rebellion have grown in influence in their demands for radical action to tackle global heating. They have developed novel forms of organizing, often led by women and youth and bringing into question dominant modes of masculinity, espousing non-violent, horizontal, democratic approaches and devising imaginative methods of protest and disruption (Togami & Staggenborg, 2022). Environmental activism and caring for nature have taken increasingly varied forms beyond street protest alone, especially during the pandemic. For instance, Extinction Rebellion's "Money Rebellion" not only involved breaking windows of major banks but also much larger groups of activists moving their accounts and investments. Citizens' assemblies are increasingly being promoted as an alternative way of doing politics in the face of inaction from political leaders focused on short-term election-winning goals. The calls of environmentalists have been spurred on by COVID-19, a zoonotic virus highlighting the fundamental flaws of exploitative human relationships with nature and non-human animals, which increase the likelihood of more future pandemics. Crucially, COVID-19 also demonstrates that dramatic social transformations are possible when external forces demand it.

Lockdowns have led many people to re-evaluate the way they live their lives, as the pace of life slowed down, travel and consumption reduced, and spending time in green spaces was one of the few things people were allowed to do. This is perhaps particularly significant for men, who tend to have bigger carbon footprints and express less concern about climate change than women (Carlsson Kanyama et al., 2021). Global heating brings into question whether many aspects of the current social order – including dominant constructions of masculinity – are sustainable. By forcing us to reflect on our relationships with the natural world and shift them in more caring, interconnected directions, climate change could have transformative consequences for masculinities, which may have been accelerated by COVID-19. However, there are also challenging questions about how to engage more men, from all sections of society, in seriously addressing the climate crisis.

Conclusion

The COVID-19 crisis has thrown up many new questions and possibilities regarding gender and forms of organizing. Men and masculinities have played a significant role in shaping the pandemic, especially given their hold on power within many different types of organizations; from governments, to science and medicine, to corporations, to anti-vaccination groups. Indeed, while a number of social movements have gained increasing resonance in their calls for change during the pandemic, there has also been inaction, ignorance, backlash and state repression. Black Lives Matter protesters were often met with aggressive pushback from masculinized and militarized police forces. The voices of climate justice activists and Indigenous communities went largely unheard within key meetings at COP26, which often appeared to condone "business as usual". Feminist demands for social change to stop men's violence against women have led to strong words but few deeds from policymakers. Powerful men and masculinized institutions are leading us towards yet more war, causing untold devastation to humanity and life on earth, when we should be focusing our energies on protecting rather than destroying the environment. The "new normal" imagined during the pandemic does not appear so different to the social inequality and injustice which preceded it, and in many contexts, this is being worsened further amid a cost of living emergency following in COVID-19's wake. Previous crises, such as the financial crash of 2008–2009, have also brought hope of great change followed by lengthy periods of austerity, deepening inequality and increased authoritarianism.

However, is it possible that many articulations of patriarchal backlash in fact express increasingly desperate efforts by those in power to preserve an old and crumbling social order, in the face of tides of change moving in the opposite direction from them? COVID-19 has illuminated the fundamental importance of mutual support, community interdependence and care to the survival of humanity. It has exposed how unliveable the status quo is for so many people – and for the planet we live on. This appears to have had transformative impacts among at least some men, who may now be more involved in caring for others and for themselves, more aware of the impacts of violence and abuse, and re-evaluating the way they live their lives and their place in the world. The post-COVID future currently remains unwritten. But it is clear that men have a vital part to play if it is going to be more equal, peaceful and just.

References

Adams, W. J. (2021). The augmentation of digital violence during COVID-19: Incel culture, Anon-IB, and ideological extremism. *Papers in Arts and Humanities, 1*(2), 18–30. doi: 10.52885/pah.v1i2.66

Amnesty International (2020). *COVID-19 Crackdowns: Police Abuse and the Global Pandemic.* London: Amnesty International.

Azcona, G., Bhatt, A., Davies, S. E., Harman, S., Smith, J., & Wenham, C. (2020). *Spotlight on Gender, COVID-19 and the SDGs: Will the Pandemic Derail Hard-won Progress on Gender Equality?* New York, NY: UN Women.

Baker, M. G., Peckham, T. K., & Seixas, N. S. (2020). Estimating the burden of United States workers exposed to infection or disease: A key factor in containing risk of COVID-19 infection. *PLoS One, 15*(4), e0232452. doi: 10.1371/journal.pone.0232452

Barker, G., Garg, A., Heilman, B., van der Gaag, N., & Mehaffey, R. (2021). *State of the World's Fathers: Structural Solutions to Achieve Equality in Care Work.* Washington, DC: Promundo-US.

Boniol, M., McIsaac, M., Xu, L., Wuliji, T., Diallo, K., & Campbell, J. (2019). *Gender Equity in the Health Workforce: Analysis of 104 countries.* Geneva: WHO.

Burns, J. (2017). Biopolitics, toxic masculinities, disavowed histories, and youth radicalization. *Peace Review, 29*(2), 176–183. doi: 10.1080/10402659.2017.1308723

Burrell, S. R., & Ruxton, S. (2020). *The Impact of the Covid-19 Crisis on Work with Men and Boys in Europe.* Durham: Durham University.

Carlsson Kanyama, A., Nässén, J., & Benders, R. (2021). Shifting expenditure on food, holidays, and furnishings could lower greenhouse gas emissions by almost 40%. *Journal of Industrial Ecology, 25*(6), 1602–1616. doi: 10.1111/jiec.13176

Carlsten, C., Gulati, M., Hines, S., Rose, C., Scott, K., Tarlo, S. M., Torén, K., Sood, A., & de la Hoz, R. E. (2021). COVID-19 as an occupational disease. *American Journal of Industrial Medicine, 64*(4), 227–237. doi: 10.1002/ajim.23222

Chatzidakis, A., & Littler, J. (2022). An anatomy of carewashing: Corporate branding and the commodification of care during COVID-19. *International Journal of Cultural Studies, 25*(3–4), 268–286. doi: 10.1177/13678779211065474

Coleman, A., & Sardarizadeh, S. (2022). Anti-vax Protests: 'Sovereign Citizens' Fight UK COVID Vaccine Rollout. Retrieved 17 March 2022, from BBC News: www.bbc.co.uk/news/59870550

Colombo, E. (2021). Human rights-inspired governmentality: COVID-19 through a human dignity perspective. *Critical Sociology, 47*(4–5), 571–581. doi: 10.1177/0896920520971846

Coscieme, L., Fioramonti, L., Mortensen, L. F., Pickett, K. E., Kubiszewski, I., Lovins, H., Mcglade, J., Ragnarsdóttir, K. V., Roberts, D., Costanza, R., & De Vogli, R. (2020). Women in power: Female leadership and public health outcomes during the COVID-19 pandemic. *MedRxiv.* doi: 10.1101/2020.07.13.20152397

Davis, M. D., Stephenson, N., Lohm, D., Waller, E., & Flowers, P. (2015). Beyond resistance: Social factors in the general public response to pandemic influenza. *BMC Public Health, 15*(1), 1–9. doi: 10.1186/s12889-015-1756-8

De Henau, J., & Himmelweit, S. (2021). A care-led recovery from COVID-19: Investing in high-quality care to stimulate and rebalance the economy. *Feminist Economics, 27*(1–2), 453–469. doi: 10.1080/13545701.2020.1845390

Foucault, M. (2009). *Security, Territory, Population: Lectures at the Collège de France, 1977–78.* Basingstoke: Palgrave Macmillan.

Foucault, M. (2010). *The Birth of Biopolitics: Lectures at the Collège de France, 1978–79.* Basingstoke: Palgrave Macmillan.

Global Health 50/50 (2022). COVID-19 Sex-disaggregated Data Tracker. Retrieved 7 March 2022, from UCL Centre for Gender and Global Health: https://globalhealth5050.org/covid19/

Greig, A. (2019). *Masculinities and the Far-right: Implications for Oxfam's Work on Gender Justice.* Boston, MA: Oxfam America.

Hutcheson, D. S., & McAllister, I. (2021). Consolidating the Putin regime: The 2020 referendum on Russia's Constitutional Amendments. *Russian Politics, 6*(3), 355–376. doi: 10.30965/24518921-00603004

Klein, N. (2007). *The Shock Doctrine: The Rise of Disaster Capitalism*. London: Penguin.

Levant, R. F., McDermott, R. C., Pryor, S., & Barinas, J. (2022). Masculinity and compliance with Centers for Disease Control and Prevention recommended health practices during the COVID-19 pandemic. *Health Psychology*, *41*(2), 94–103. doi: 10.1037/hea0001119

Madgavkar, A., White, O., Krishnan, M., Mahajan, D., & Azcue, X. (2020). COVID-19 and Gender Equality: Countering the Regressive Effects. Retrieved 1 March 2022, from McKinsey Global Institute: www.mckinsey.com/featured-insights/future-of-work/covid-19-and-gender-equality-countering-the-regressive-effects

Morgan, R., Baker, P., Griffith, D. M., Klein, S. L., Logie, C. H., Mwiine, A. A., Scheim, A. I., Shapiro, J. R., Smith, J., Wenham, C., & White, A. (2021). Beyond a zero-sum game: How does the impact of COVID-19 vary by gender? *Frontiers in Sociology*, *6*, 650729. doi: 10.3389/fsoc.2021.650729

Onion, R. (2019). Did We Forget to Memorialize Spanish Flu because Women Were the Heroes? Retrieved 3 March 2022, from Slate: https://slate.com/technology/2019/02/spanish-flu-women-nurses-heroism.html

Ribarovska, A. K., Hutchinson, M. R., Pittman, Q. J., Pariante, C., & Spencer, S. J. (2021). Gender inequality in publishing during the COVID-19 pandemic. *Brain Behavior and Immunity*, *91*, 1–3. doi: 10.1016/j.bbi.2020.11.022

Roberts, L. (2022). Surge of HIV, tuberculosis and COVID feared amid war in Ukraine. *Nature*, *603*(7902), 557–558. doi: 10.1038/d41586-022-00748-6

Roy, A. (2020). The Pandemic is a Portal. Retrieved 29 March 2022, from Financial Times: www.ft.com/content/10d8f5e8-74eb-11ea-95fe-fcd274e920ca

Ruxton, S., & Burrell, S. R. (2020). *Masculinities and COVID-19: Making the Connections*. Washington, DC: Promundo-US.

Smith, J. (2019). Overcoming the "tyranny of the urgent": Integrating gender into disease outbreak preparedness and response. *Gender and Development*, *27*(2), 355–369. doi: 10.1080/13552074.2019.1615288

Spinney, L. (2017). *Pale Rider: The Spanish Flu of 1918 and How it Changed the World*. London: Cape.

Stergiou-Kita, M., Mansfield, E., Bezo, R., Colantonio, A., Garritano, E., Lafrance, M., Lewko, J., Mantis, S., Moody, J., Power, N., & Theberge, N. (2015). Danger zone: Men, masculinity and occupational health and safety in high-risk occupations. *Safety Science*, *80*, 213–220. doi: 10.1016/j.ssci.2015.07.029

Togami, C., & Staggenborg, S. (2022). Gender and environmental movements. In M. Grasso & M. Giugni (Eds.), *The Routledge Handbook of Environmental Movements* (pp. 419–433). Abingdon: Routledge.

Tremblay, M. (2007). Democracy, representation, and women: A comparative analysis. *Democratization*, *14*(4), 533–553. doi: 10.1080/13510340701398261

UN Women (2020). Whose Time to Care? Unpaid Care and Domestic Work during COVID-19. Retrieved 10 March 2022, from UN Women Count Data Hub: https://data.unwomen.org/publications/whose-time-care-unpaid-care-and-domestic-work-during-covid-19

Van Daalen, K. R., Bajnoczki, C., Chowdhury, M., Dada, S., Khorsand, P., Socha, A., Lal, A., Jung, L., Alqodmani, L., Torres, I., & Ouedraogo, S. (2020). Symptoms of a broken system: The gender gaps in COVID-19 decision-making. *BMJ Global Health*, *5*(10), e003549. doi: 10.1136/bmjgh-2020-003549

Vassallo, A., Shajahan, S., Harris, K., Hallam, L., Hockham, C., Womersley, K., Woodward, M., & Sheel, M. (2021). Sex and gender in COVID-19 vaccine research: Substantial evidence gaps remain. *Frontiers in Global Women's Health*, *2*, 761511. doi: 10.3389/fgwh.2021.761511

Wenham, C., & Davies, S. E. (2021). WHO runs the world–(not) girls: Gender neglect during global health emergencies. *International Feminist Journal of Politics*, *24*(3), 415–438. doi: 10.1080/14616742.2021.1921601

Westmarland, N., Almqvist, A. L., Egeberg Holmgren, L., Ruxton, S., Burrell, S. R., & Delgado Valbuena, C. (2021). *Men's Activism to End Violence against Women: Voices from Spain, Sweden and the UK*. Bristol: Policy Press.

White, A. (2020). Men and COVID-19: The aftermath. *Postgraduate Medicine*, *132*(suppl. 4), 18–27. doi: 10.1080/00325481.2020.1823760

Wojnicka, K. (2022). What's masculinity got to do with it? The COVID-19 pandemic, men and care. *European Journal of Women's Studies*, *29*(suppl. 1), 27S–42S. doi: 10.1177/13505068221076322

Wojnicka, K., Mellström, U., & de Boise, S. (2022). On war, hegemony and (political) masculinities. *NORMA: International Journal for Masculinity Studies, 17*(2), 83–87. doi: 10.1080/18902138.2022.2069856

Women and Equalities Committee (2021). *Unequal Impact? Coronavirus and the Gendered Economic Impact* (Fifth Report of Session 2019–21, HC 385). London: House of Commons.

World Health Organization (2022). WHO Coronavirus (COVID-19) Dashboard. Retrieved 30 March 2022, from https://covid19.who.int

INDEX

Note: Page numbers in *italics* indicate a figure on the corresponding page.

FSC
www.fsc.org
MIX
Papier | Fördert gute Waldnutzung
FSC® C083411

Kolibri 360 GmbH
Ferdinand-Jühlke-Straße 7
99095 Erfurt, Deutschland
produktsicherheit@kolibri360.de